Frommer's®

South Korea

3rd Edition

by Cecilia Hae-Jin Lee

WILEY

John Wiley & Sons, Inc.

Published by:

JOHN WILEY & SONS, INC.

Copyright © 2012 John Wiley & Sons Ltd, The Atrium, Southern Gate, Chichester,
West Sussex PO19 8SQ, UK
Telephone (+44) 1243 779777
Email (for orders and customer service enquiries): cs-books@wiley.co.uk. Visit our Home Page on www.
wiley.com

Publisher: Kelly Regan
Production Manager: Daniel Mersey
Editor: Mark Henshall
Project Editor: Hannah Clement
Cartography: Andrew Murphy
Photo Editor: Cherie Cincilla, Richard H. Fox, Jill Emeny
Front cover photo: Seoraksan National Park, Ulsan © Masterfile
Back Cover photo: Colorful Paper lanterns, Gyeongsangnam-do © Michele Burgess/Alamy Images

British Library Cataloguing in Publication Data
A catalogue record for this book is available from the British Library
ISBN 978-1-118-28755-2 (pbk), ISBN 978-1-118-33363-1 (ebk), ISBN 978-1-118-33136-1 (ebk),
ISBN 978-1-118-33475-1 (ebk)

Typeset by Wiley Indianapolis Composition Services

Printed and bound in the United States of America

5 4 3 2 1

CONTENTS

10 GANGWON-DO 326

11 JEJU-DO (JEJU ISLAND) 368

12 PLANNING YOUR TRIP TO SOUTH KOREA 402

13 USEFUL TERMS & PHRASES 423

LIST OF MAPS

ABOUT THE AUTHOR

Cecilia Hae-Jin Lee was born in Seoul and is the author of several popular books including, *Quick & Easy Mexican Cooking, Quick & Easy Korean Cooking, Eating Korean: From Barbeque to Kimchi, Recipes from My Home,* and *Frommer's Day by Day Seoul.* She is also a conceptual and installation artist, a designer, an illustrator and a photographer. Her first and third language is Korean.

ACKNOWLEDGMENTS

Special thanks to Jumi-imo for her invaluable knowledge, her wit and her companionship (may she win her fight against cancer); Yeong-gyu imo for letting me take her car around the country once again; my tireless Great Aunt for feeding me; my Uncle Mangyu and the rest of the family for letting me crash at their place; and to Daniel Grey for help with restaurants in Seoul. To Kelly Regan, Mark Henshall, Scott Totman and the rest of the Frommer's staff for whipping the manuscript into shape; and to my husband Tim Maloney for putting up with a crazy, and sometimes crazed, wife.

HOW TO CONTACT US

In researching this book, we discovered many wonderful places—hotels, restaurants, shops, and more. We're sure you'll find others. Please tell us about them, so we can share the information with your fellow travelers in upcoming editions. If you were disappointed with a recommendation, we'd love to know that, too. Please write to:

Frommer's South Korea, 3rd Edition
John Wiley & Sons, Inc. • 111 River St. • Hoboken, NJ 07030-5774

ADVISORY & DISCLAIMER

FROMMER'S STAR RATINGS, ICONS & ABBREVIATIONS

Every hotel, restaurant, and attraction listing in this guide has been ranked for quality, value, service, amenities, and special features using a **star-rating system.** In country, state, and regional guides, we also rate towns and regions to help you narrow down your choices and budget your time accordingly. Hotels and restaurants are rated on a scale of zero (recommended) to three stars (exceptional). Attractions, shopping, nightlife, towns, and regions are rated according to the following scale: zero stars (recommended), one star (highly recommended), two stars (very highly recommended), and three stars (must-see).

In addition to the star-rating system, we also use **seven feature icons** that point you to the great deals, in-the-know advice, and unique experiences that separate travelers from tourists. Throughout the book, look for:

special finds—those places only insiders know about

fun facts—details that make travelers more informed and their trips more fun

kids—best bets for kids and advice for the whole family

special moments—those experiences that memories are made of

overrated—places or experiences not worth your time or money

insider tips—great ways to save time and money

great values—where to get the best deals

The following abbreviations are used for credit cards:

AE American Express	DISC Discover	V Visa
DC Diners Club	MC MasterCard	

TRAVEL RESOURCES AT FROMMERS.COM

Frommer's travel resources don't end with this guide. Frommer's website, **www.frommers.com,** has travel information on more than 4,000 destinations. We update features regularly, giving you access to the most current trip-planning information and the best airfare, lodging, and car-rental bargains. You can also listen to podcasts, connect with other Frommers.com members through our active-reader forums, share your travel photos, read blogs from guidebook editors and fellow travelers, and much more.

THE BEST OF SOUTH KOREA

We've compiled the best of the best of South Korea and we hope you'll agree. See its rugged mountain ranges slope down to pristine beaches, and experience its bustling, cosmopolitan cities surrounded by farmland. From temple stays and lotus gardens by the Han River to hiking in Seoraksan national park, the bamboo forests of Damyang and the volcanic landscape of Jeju-do, this is a land of beautiful landscapes, rife with traces of its thousands of years of history. Seoul is a celebration; an exciting metropolis that is just the beginning of your journey.

CITIES & TOWNS   Seoul is a city to be explored all on its own with its efficient subway system that takes you everywhere from **Apgujeong** to **Changdeokgung**. Take the high-speed KTX train to **Gyeongju** to experience South Korea's historic sites, or visit the beaches of **Busan.** Smaller towns hold the greatest rewards, such as the gorgeous islands viewed from the cable car atop **Tongyeong** and the neatly lined shrubs of green tea growing on soft hillsides in **Boseong.**

THE COUNTRYSIDE   South Korea is best explored when the cherry blossoms bloom in full force in the spring or when the fall (autumn) foliage lights up the landscape with fiery color, especially in **Seoraksan**. The country's mountainous terrain is best seen with comfortable shoes and a rental car. Deeper beauty can be found in quieter temples like **Hyang-ilam** or the unusual Buddha statues in **Unjusa** in Jeolla-do.

EATING & DRINKING   Each region of the country has its own specialty, based on the season and what's grown nearby. Beach towns specialize in *hwae* (raw fish) and other seafood, such as shellfish hand-caught by women divers in **Jeju-do. Gangwon-do** is known for its potatoes, **Jinju** for its *bibimbap* (mixed rice bowl) and **Danyang** for its garlic. Grill meat on your table, slurp chewy cold *naengmyeon* (buckwheat noodles) in the summer or just enjoy some spicy *boong-uh bbang* (goldfish cookies) from a street vendor.

THE COAST   Being a peninsula, South Korea has incredibly dramatic coasts. **Busan** has wide sandy beaches, like **Haeundae,** while Gangwon-do's rocky coasts cascade down to dramatic waves. Tiny islands stretch out as far as the eye can see off the southern coasts of **Jeolla-do** and **Gyeongsang-do,** including the dinosaur nesting grounds at **Goseong.** **Jeju-do** has unforgettable coasts, created when volcanic lava cooled quickly in the surrounding sea.

THE most unforgettable TRAVEL EXPERIENCES

o **Staying Overnight in a Buddhist Temple:** Many temples in South Korea offer temple stays, where you can enjoy meditation and perhaps a bit of inner peace. Wake up early to the sound of prayers, and cleanse your mind, body, and spirit with a bath and a meal of mountain vegetables. One of the best temples to do a temple stay at is **Hwaeomsa** in Jeollanam-do. See p. 224.

o **Hiking Seoraksan in the Fall (Autumn) Foliage:** Seoraksan is South Korea's most famous national park and you'll see why when you visit during the fall (autumn). Its rocky cliffs peek out from atop the clouds, while its bubbling waters cascade down steep waterfalls. Between its many mountains lie quiet valleys that are blanketed by snow in the winter and flowering trees in the spring. See p. 332.

o **Haggling with a Vendor in an Open Market:** South Korea's markets are bustling centers that can be found along winding alleyways and crowded streets. You haven't truly experienced South Korea until you've elbowed your way through and convinced a vendor to drop the price on something by at least a couple of won. Even if that souvenir is already dirt-cheap, it's fun to get caught up in the excitement of bargaining. The most famous is **Namdaemun Shijang** in Seoul. See p. 96.

o **Being Naked in Front of Hundreds of Strangers:** Okay, so nudity isn't the real attraction. That would be the traditional bathhouses (or even better, the water parks featuring hot springs) scattered throughout South Korea. Don't leave the country without relaxing in a hot sauna with a bunch of old ladies (or old men) or getting a water massage at one of South Korea's many spas.

o **Taking a Boat to One of the Many Small Coastal Islands:** South Korea's southern coast is littered with tiny islands, many of which can be seen on a day cruise. One of the best routes is to take a 4-hour ride from **Tongyeong,** which includes **Somaeumul-do** and other islands in the **Hallyeo Haesang National Marine Park.** See p. 285.

o **Seeing a Traditional Performance:** Whether you're in Seoul or hanging out in a rural village seemingly in the middle of nowhere, there is probably a festival going on nearby. Try to catch a performance of *pansori* (Korea's wailing blues), a mask dance, or just the hallowed sound of the bamboo *daegeum* (flute).

o **Visiting the DMZ:** The Demilitarized Zone is probably one of the least aptly named places on the planet. A result of the last vestiges of animosity between Soviet Russia and the U.S., Korea has been the only divided country in the world since the Berlin Wall fell. See p. 122.

THE best CITY EXPERIENCES

o **Seeing the City Lights Twinkling Below from Namsan (Seoul):** The bright white N Seoul Tower perched on top of Namsan gives you the best view of the city. Enjoy an overpriced meal from the revolving restaurant on top or add a key lock to the thousands already left by lovers along the viewing platform. See p. 88.

o **Taking a Night Cruise along the Han River (Seoul):** The lights of the city's sky-scrapers and bridges reflect on the waters of the Han-gahng. Catch a ferry from a dock in Yeouido to see the city from a different perspective. See p. 92.

o **Browsing Contemporary Art in Samcheongdong (Seoul):** What used to be an undeveloped neighborhood has grown into a hipper cousin to Insadong, the tradi-tional arts district. Take a stroll along the main street to browse tiny boutiques and galleries selling the latest from Seoul's creatives. See p. 99.

o **Enjoying an Al Fresco Cup of Joe (Coffee) on Gwangalli Beach (Busan):** The Suyeong district of Gwangalli beach becomes a no-car area on weekends as cafes bring out their outdoor tables. Summer evenings are the best for enjoying live music too, after sundown. See p. 308.

o **Shopping in a Multi-level Department Store (throughout South Korea):** Enter through the glass doors first thing in the morning and you'll be greeted by bows from the department store employees lined up to serve you. Shinsegae, Hyundae, Lotte, Galleria, and the like all have floors and floors of fashion, usually sand-wiched between a basement food court and sit-down restaurants on the top floors.

THE best FOOD & DRINK EXPERIENCES

o **Cooking Your Own Meat on a Tabletop Grill:** For the full Korean dining experi-ence you really must try *galbi* (beef short ribs), *ssamgyupssal* (sliced pork belly), or *dak galbi* (spicy chicken) that you've cooked yourself on a grill at your table.

o **Noshing from Namdaemun Market's Many Street Vendors (Seoul):** You haven't really experienced the charm of an outdoor market until you've had a bite to eat from the street vendors in this *shijang* (market). Fuel up for your next round of shopping with a fresh flatcake hot off the griddle or *hoddeok* (sweet pancake filled with sugar, cinnamon and other delights). See p. 67.

o **Picking Your Catch at Jagalchi Market (Busan):** There's a certain power to decid-ing which fish is going to get sliced up for your hwae meal. Luckily you just point and the work is done for you. It doesn't get any fresher than that. See p. 322.

o **Drinking Homemade Rice Wine in a Remote Village:** If you get a chance to travel to one of South Korea's small villages, stop under one of the thatched-roof joints to enjoy a gourd full of the milky rice wine, *makgeolli,* and some good old-fash-ioned, home-style food.

o **Stopping for Seaside Dining on the Rocks at Yongmeoli Haean (Jeju-do):** The women of Jeju-do set up impromptu "restaurants" preparing fresh shellfish and other goodies from the sea, right on the rocky coast of Yongmeoli Haean. See p. 385.

o **Enjoying a Cup of Tea while Overlooking the City's Shoppers (Insadong):** Seoul's Insadong district is chock-full of traditional tea shops. Opt for one on the second floor and watch the world pass by on the streets below, while sipping a fragrant brew from a hand-crafted teacup. See p. 74.

o **Scaring off Vampires with Garlic in Danyang (Chungcheongbuk-do):** In a country known for its garlicky cooking, you have to be a serious garlic-growing region to be known for it. Danyang is the place and one of the best restaurants in the area to enjoy garlic cooked dozens of ways is **Jangdali Shikdang.** See p. 179.

THE best WAY TO SEE SOUTH KOREA LIKE A LOCAL

o **Shopping for Herbs and Other Unidentifiable Dried Goods from Hwagae Jang-teo (Hadong, Gyeongsangnam-do):** Local farmers bring their dried wares and other items to sell in this famous market. Local wild green tea, dried herbs, seasonal fruits, and a variety of other goods are sold here in an open market. See p. 284.

o **Belting Your Heart Out at a Noraebang (Karaoke):** Koreans love to sing and that fact is borne out with the many *noraebang* ("singing" rooms) that can be found even in the smallest of towns throughout the country. Take a group of friends and enjoy a night of karaoke in a private room.

o **Sweating Your Troubles Away in a Jjimjilbang (Korean Spa):** Before Koreans had baths in every home, they visited the local bathhouse at least once a week. Even now, South Koreans love to go to jjimjilbang to sit in saunas, get a massage, or just take a nap. Those on an extreme budget can even spend the night in one, although the giant, public rooms with hard wooden floors are anything but comfortable.

o **Hiking the Baekdu-daegan (or at Least Part of It):** The Baekdu-daegan is the mountain range that is considered the "spine" of the Korean Peninsula. Although it's not possible to traverse the entire line (now that the DMZ cuts off the trail that starts in Baekdusan in North Korea), it's still possible to traverse this spiritually important mountain starting from **Seoraksan** (p. 326) and making your way down to **Jirisan** (p. 223). Although it would take months to actually walk the 1400-km (870-mile) trail, it's still possible to visit the various ranges and feel the energy of the mountains.

o **Having Noodles, Fried Chicken, or Dumplings Delivered:** South Koreans enjoy having everything from *yangnyeom dak* (seasoned fried chicken) to *jjajangmyeon* (black-bean noodles) delivered to their homes. In the summer, you can even have them deliver food to your particular umbrella in crowded **Haeundae Beach** or even while you're having a romantic stroll along the Hang-gang. Even the McDonalds in the country will bring your *bulgogi* hamburger combo right to your door.

THE best FAMILY EXPERIENCES

o **Comparing Dinosaur Footprints to Yours at the Nesting Grounds in Goseong (Gyeongsangnam-do):** This coastal site was the former nesting ground for a variety of dinosaurs. See the imprinted footprints and fossilized eggs during low-tide as the waves splash onto the rocks. See p. 289.

o **Trying Your Hand at a Traditional Game at the Korean Folk Village in Suwon (Gyeonggi-do):** The restored folk village in Suwon, the **Hanguk Minsokchon,** is a great way to see how Koreans used to live. Visit on a weekend or holiday to try your hand at some archery, wooden seesaws, or other old-fashioned games. See p. 111.

o **Spending the Day at Everland (Gyeonggi-do):** One of the largest and best amusement parks in South Korea, there are plenty of rides and amusements for the whole family. They have a small zoo with white tigers and monkeys, a white-water rafting ride, and a variety of festivals that change with the seasons. In the summer visit the water park next door, **Caribbean Bay.** See p. 110.

o **Splashing Around in the Seorak Waterpia:** While the kids splash around in the water park, the adults can take a relaxing soak in the mineral hot springs. After enough water fun, the whole family can enjoy a bit of ice cream. See p. 331.

o **Visiting the Lying Stone Buddhas in Unjusa (Hwasun, Jeollanam-do):** This temple is not only is easy to reach (no giant mountains to climb), but also houses the most fascinating array of Buddhist statuary in the country. See p. 225.

THE best HISTORIC EXPERIENCES

o **Touring the Huwon (Rear Garden) in Changdeokgung (Seoul):** If you want to see how Korean royalty used to live, this palace is a prime example. Its famed Huwon ("Rear Garden") alone is worth the visit. See p. 80.

o **Seeing the Annual Memorial Ceremony for Dead Joseon Kings in Jongmyo (Seoul):** There's a reason this *myo* (royal shrine) is a World Heritage site—it's the most important one in the country and is home to the longest traditional wooden building left in Korea. Try to time your visit for the spectacular annual memorial ceremony for the kings of Korea's longest running dynasty (usually the first Sunday in May). See p. 84.

o **Visiting the Prehistoric Dolmen on Ganghwa-do (Gyeonggi-do):** This island off the coast of Incheon is home to about 80 dolmen (prehistoric rock tombs), dating back thousands of years. See p. 127.

o **Listening to the Song of Two Lovers in Gwanghallu-won (Namwon, Jeollabuk-do):** Home of the legend of Chunhyang (a traditional love story about a nobleman's son who falls in love with a courtesan's daughter), this garden is not only a mecca for lovers, but the spot where pansori made its debut. Try to visit between April and October and catch the free performances at noon. See p. 191.

o **Walking along the Stone Fortress in Suwon (Gyeongg-do):** The best restored fortress in the country, the Suwon Hwaseong's impressive wall has historic gates and towers climbing a slope in the middle of the now-modern city. See p. 112.

o **Writing a Poem in Dosan Seowon (Andong, Gyeongsangbuk-do):** Established in 1574, this Confucian academy is a nice place for quiet reflection and to soak in the mountain scenery. Take off your shoes and climb onto the wooden platform to see if inspiration comes. See p. 254.

THE best OUTDOOR EXPERIENCES

o **Biking the Historic Sites in Gyeongju (Gyeongsangbuk-do):** The city of Gyeongju is like one giant museum and the sites can be visited easily on two wheels. The roads between **Bulguksa, Seokguram, Anapji Pond,** and the rest are nicely laid out for cyclists. The city can be seen in its entirety in 4 to 5 days. See p. 232.

o **Paragliding Anywhere in South Korea:** With literally hundreds of peaks throughout the country, South Korea is the perfect country from which to paraglide. Those who want an expansive space can launch from one of the many parasitic volcanoes in **Jeju-do** (see p. 393). From Seoul, the closest location from which to launch is **Yangpyeong** (see p. 133).

o **Hiking the Many Challenging Courses in Jirisan (Jeollabuk-do/Gyeongsangnam-do):** Of all the mountainous national parks in South Korea, Jirisan is the most favored amongs serious climbers. Choose from its many peaks and gorgeous scenery, best viewed in the fall. See p. 223.

o **Snow Skiing at High 1 Ski Resort in Jeongseon (Gangwon-do):** The country's most environmentally friendly ski resort also has the best courses for skiiers of all levels, but it's especially favored by advanced skiiers. See p. 365.

o **Walking the Easy Trails in Cheongnyangsan (Gyeongsangbuk-do):** Located a stone's throw from Andong, Cheongyangsan Provincial Park was best known as the place where high priests and scholars lived. Its easy trails make it simple for the less fit of us to still enjoy the fresh air. See p. 263.

o **Waterskiing in Cheongpyeong (Gyeonggi-do):** Fight the sweltering summer heat with a bit of wet fun, just an hour outside of Seoul. Although the weather will be a bit chillier, waterskiing in the fall is nice in order to enjoy the scenery. See p. 136.

o **Stopping to Smell the Flowers at the Korea National Arboretum (Gyeonggi-do):** Located in Gwangneum forest, you have to make reservations at least 5 days in advance to see this well-preserved arboretum. It's well worth the trouble to see the 15 different forest areas within this garden and research center. See p. 132.

THE best FREE & DIRT CHEAP EXPERIENCES

o **Strolling between the Lotus Flowers at Dumulmeoli (Gyeonggi-do):** Where two waters flow into the Han River is a beautiful lotus garden and a nice walking path where you can enjoy the blooming lotuses in the heat of summer. Park under the bridge for free. See p. 133.

o **Enjoying the Full Moon from Dalmaji Gogae near Haeundae Beach (Busan):** A narrow path between Haeundae and Songjeong beaches leads to a small hill where you can see both the moon and the ocean from inside Haewoljeong, a tiny pavilion built there in honor of two folk lovers, who got married there during Daeboreum (the "Great Full Moon") in December. See p. 294.

o **Feeling the Ocean Breezes from Sinseondae (Geoje-do, Gyeongsangnam-do):** Although several Korean TV and film drama productions left their sets and buildings here, they still didn't ruin the views of the surrounding ocean and rocky coast on this southern island off the coast of Gyeongsangnam-do. Best to visit in the spring when the yellow rapeseed flowers light up the hillside. See p. 289.

o **Driving the Coastal Road, Hunhwa-ro, in Gagneung (Gangwon-do):** Visit Gyeongpodae beach, then take a leisurely drive on the coastal route before enjoying a cup of joe on Café Street in Gagneung. See p. 341.

o **Seeing the View of the Seonam Village in Yeongwol (Gangwon-do):** Locals say that the view of this small village on the water is like looking at a miniaturized version of the entire Korean Peninsula. See it from Seogang Observatory or walk down into the village itself for a bit of small town flavor.

THE best TEMPLE EXPERIENCES

o **Catching the Sunrise at Hyangilam (Suncheon, Jeollabuk-do):** Perched on a precarious mountainside, this former hermitage is now a temple complex. Wake up early to climb up its steep steps and catch the sunrise over the ocean. You'll also miss the bus-loads of tourists, who usually arrive in the late afternoon. See p. 214.

o **Climbing up to see the Bodhisattva of Compassion at Bori-am (Namhae, Gyeongsangnam-do):** One of the three main holy sites in the country, believers come to this hermitage to pray to the Bodhisattva of Compassion. If you're pure of heart, your wishes will be granted. Even if you're not, you'll be treated to a spectacular view. See p. 286.

o **Listening to the Sound of the Drums at Sundown in Haeinsa (Hapcheon, Gyeongsang-do):** Home of the famous Tripitaka Koreana (Buddhist scripture handcarved on hundreds of wooden blocks), this famed temple (and UNESCO World Heritage site) sits in a deep forest. Try to go in the late afternoon to see the tripitaka (through locked slats), but stay past sunset to hear the sound of the gong echoing through the valleys. See p. 281.

o **Hiking the Rocky Trail to Cheongnyangsan (Gyeongsangbuk-do):** Although the temple complex itself is not the most impressive in the country, it's strategically located on the side of the Cheongnyangsan. The scenic walk to the temple culminates as you turn the corner to see the temple greeting you from its mountain perch. See p. 263.

o **Eating Feast Noodles at Naksansa (Gangwon-do):** Although this expansive temple was largely destroyed by a fire in 2008, a bright new temple has been constructed in its place. The cliffside **Hongryeon-am** hermitage is included in its grounds, so visit during lunchtime and be treated to a humble bowl of *janchi gooksu* (feast noodles). See p. 336.

THE best FESTIVALS & CELEBRATIONS

o **The Day the Buddha Came (aka Buddha's Birthday; throughout the country):** During what is sometimes referred to as the "Festival of Lanterns," every temple in the country gets lit up like a Christmas tree in celebration of the birth of the Enlightened One.

o **Baekje Cultural Festival (Buyeo or Gongju):** Every October, this historical event celebrates the great Baekje kings with over 100 traditional performances and events throughout the area. See p. 151.

o **Boryeong Mud Festival (Daecheon, Chungcheongnam-do):** Held on the muddy beaches of Daecheon every July, this is basically organized mud play. Supposedly good for your skin, too, the dirty activities include mud wrestling, mud slides, and making mud soap. Mud pies are optional. See p. 161.

o **Busan International Film Festival (BIFF, Busan):** The largest and most renowned of Korea's film festivals, it is a wonderful showcase for current films from throughout Asia. Usually held some time in October. See p. 323.

- **Andong Mask Dance Festival (Andong, Gyeongsangnam-do):** Although the highlight of the festival is the Korean *talchum* (mask dance), performers from other countries show off their masked splendor as well. See p. 252.

- **Gangneung Danoje Festival (Gangneung, Gangwon-do):** Celebrating the traditional "Dano" (the fifth day of the fifth month of the Lunar year), it is one of the few places where you can see traditional shamanistic rituals. It usually happens some time in June. See p. 25.

SOUTH KOREA IN DEPTH

The history of the Korean Peninsula spans more than 5,000 strife-filled years. That's ironic for a place that has been called the "Land of the Morning Calm." But because of its strategic location, the peninsula suffered a seemingly endless series of invasions by China and Manchuria from the north and Japan from the east. In fact, the last war, the Korean War, never actually ended—rather, it was halted by a ceasefire in 1953. That solidified a historic split, with a communist dictatorship ruling the North and a more democratic regime ruling the South. The Demilitarized Zone (DMZ), the area that marks the boundary between the two Koreas, is a painful reminder of the country's war-torn past.

While North Korea has suffered poverty and famine, South Korea has made incredible strides in the past few decades in its race toward modernization. South Korea, a country roughly the size of Great Britain, is the 15th-largest economy in the world. The city of Seoul, with its towering high-rises and modern infrastructure, is a testament to the innovative spirit of the Korean people.

SOUTH KOREA TODAY

Touted as one of the most wired (or shall we say, "wireless?") countries in the world, it's no surprise to see everyone from toddlers to grandpas texting with their smartphones on the subway. These technological advancements have not only made South Korea more prominent on the world map, but its electronics, cars, and even textiles have spread worldwide. This export of Korean goods even includes cultural phenomena, like the rise in popularity of Korean TV dramas, films, and KPop around the world.

With the opening up of the world market to Korean goods, South Korea, in return, has imported much from other countries, especially from the West. This can most easily be seen in the American fast-food chains that dot the urban landscape. However, this also means that Korea's global cuisine has come a long way. In a country where even a hamburger was hard to come by, you can now find crispy Neopolitan pizza fresh from wood-burning stoves, schwarma vendors on the street, and even get a croissant that tastes almost like it's come out of a Parisienne boulangerie.

Although the global economic downturn has affected South Korea, too, you would not be able to tell with all of the new road projects and construction going on in the country. Still, traces of tough economic times can be seen in empty storefronts and high-end restaurants with fewer occupied tables.

Unpredictable weather in South Korea and other parts of the country has driven up food prices, although it's difficult to tell the domestic problems, since prices remain generally stable due to the influx of cheap crops from China.

The price of gas remains high (averaging around ₩1950 per liter) so travel costs have increased. Still, public transportation remains affordable throughout South Korea.

As the country moved by leaps and bounds toward the technological age, some of the traditions and traces of its past were overtaken. However, in the past few years, the government has taken steps to try and preserve the architectural and natural resources that remain. Outside the large cities, you can still see older folk farming in the fields, making *kimchi* (a spiced dish) in the fall, and picking fruit by hand on the hillsides, they just happen to do it now on paved roads, mobile phones in hand.

THE MAKING OF SOUTH KOREA

Prehistory

Before humans settled on the Korean Peninsula, dinosaurs left fossils and other evidence. You can still see their footprints and fossilized eggs on the shores of **Goseong** (p. 289). The first human beings on the peninsula can be traced as far back as the Paleolithic period (about 500,000 years ago). Researchers believe that Neanderthals lived here until Paleo-Asiatic people moved in around 40,000 B.C. Very little is known about the Paleo-Asiatics, but the tools and other relics they left behind suggest that they were hunter-gatherers who also fished. It is very likely that these early inhabitants of the Korean Peninsula moved to what is now Japan about 20,000 years ago, when the Korea Strait was narrower and easier to cross.

Archaeological remains suggest that nomadic Neolithic tribes migrated from central and northeast Asia (mostly Mongolia, China's Manchu region, and southeast Siberia) to the Korean coastline around 8,000 B.C. These are the ancestors of modern Koreans, and they are responsible for the earliest versions of Korean culture and language (the Tungusic branch of the Ural-Altaic language group). Traces of these Neolithic and older cultures can be seen in the *goindol* (dolmen/megalithic stone tombs) scattered throughout the land. In fact, the largest concentration of dolmen in the world is found on the Korean Peninsula. The easiest to access from Seoul is in **Ganghwa-do** (p. 127), but more can be seen around **Gochang** (p. 194) and **Hwa-sun** (p. 195).

In around 3,000 B.C. a larger wave of immigrants from the same areas brought more developed pottery and better tools. These new arrivals contributed to the founding of small villages of pit dwellings. With the domestication of animals and the development of farming, these tribes ventured farther inland and became increasingly less nomadic. Clans developed around the start of the Bronze Age.

However, Korean history is generally considered to start with the birth of King Dang-gun in 2333 B.C. Legend has it that Dang-gun was born of a son of Heaven and a woman from one of the bear-totem tribes (shamanism was predominant in ancient Korean religions). He established the GoJoseon (Old Joseon) Kingdom, which literally translates to the "Land of the Morning Calm." This walled kingdom was located near present-day Pyongyang, the capital of North Korea.

The Three Kingdoms

By the first century B.C., three dominant kingdoms had emerged on the peninsula and part of what is now Manchuria. The first and largest was **Goguryeo** (37 B.C.–A.D. 688), in the northern part of the peninsula, encompassing part of Manchuria and what is now North Korea. It served as a buffer against aggression from China. **Baekje** (18 B.C.–A.D. 660) developed in the southwestern part of the peninsula and **Shilla** (57 B.C.–A.D. 935) in the southeastern section. This time is known as the Three Kingdoms period, even though a fourth, smaller kingdom, **Gaya** (A.D. 42–532), existed between Shilla and Baekje in the southern part of the peninsula.

Traces of Baekje history can be seen in its old capitals, the now small towns of **Gongju** (p. 151), and, especially, **Buyeo** (p. 157).

Goguryeo was the first to adopt Buddhism in A.D. 372. The Baekje Kingdom followed in 384. Shilla was later and did not adopt the religion until 528. The three kingdoms had similar cultures and infrastructures, based on Confucian and Buddhist hierarchical structures with the king at the top. Legal systems were created, and Goguryeo annexed Buyeo while Shilla took over Gaya. The kingdoms became refined aristocratic societies and began competing with each other in development of Buddhist–Confucian power and an eye toward territorial expansion.

Unified Shilla

The Shilla Kingdom developed a Hwarang ("Flower of Youth") corps, a voluntary military organization for young men, in the 600s. This popular movement helped build up Shilla's military strength. The kingdom was also looking outward, learning from its neighboring kingdoms and building amicable relations with the Tang Dynasty in China.

In the meantime, Goguryeo was in fierce battle with Tang China and the Sui emperor, with heavy casualties on both sides. Tang China eventually turned to Shilla for help. The Shilla–Tang forces were able to defeat Goguryeo and its ally Baekje, but Tang wasn't about to let Shilla have control of the land. Chinese officials took the Baekje king and his family to Tang and appointed a military governor to rule Baekje territory. Goguryeo's king and hundreds of thousands of prisoners were also taken to China. Shilla launched a counterattack against China and retook all of Baekje. In 674 China invaded Shilla, but the kingdom was able to defend itself, forcing the Tang army out of Pyongyang. Still, the Chinese forces were able to hold onto part of the Goguryeo kingdom, which is now Manchuria.

The Shilla Kingdom officially unified the peninsula in 668. Despite some turbulence, the **Unified Shilla** period (668–935) maintained close ties to China and its culture. Many Shilla monks traveled there to study Buddhism and bring back their cultural learnings. During this cultural flowering, there were new technological innovations, including the world's oldest astronomical observatory which was constructed in **Gyeongju** (p. 231), the Shilla capital. The town of Gyeongju is like one large outdoor museum, preserving the history of Shilla in its temples, shrines, and grassy royal tombs.

Goryeo Dynasty

At the end of the 9th century, the Shilla Kingdom had grown weak and local lords began fighting for control. It was a period of civil war and rebellion. In 918, Wang Geon, the lord of Songak (present-day **Gaesong**), defeated the other warring lords and established the **Goryeo Dynasty** (918–1392). Goryeo, a shortened version of the former Goguryeo kingdom, is where the name Korea came from.

New laws were created based on Chinese law as well as Buddhist and Confucian beliefs. During a period of relative peace, culture flourished under the Goryeo aristocracy. Goryeo celadon pottery was developed (see **Celadon Museum,** p. 224); the *Tripitaka Koreana,* a set of more than 81,000 wood blocks used to print the Buddhist canon, was created (see **Haeinsa,** p. 281); and the first movable metal type was invented. As the official religion, Buddhism flourished under Goryeo rule—new temples were built, wonderful paintings were commissioned, and various manuscripts were created.

Unfortunately, peace didn't last long. Although Goryeo was able to thwart attacks early on, in the 12th century it suffered internal conflicts, with civilian and military leaders fighting for control. In the 13th century, the peninsula was invaded several times by the Mongolians; traces of their invasion can be seen in the distinct type of horses on **Jeju-do** (p. 368). Luckily for Goryeo, Mongol power declined rapidly from the middle of the 14th century on, giving the kingdom some respite, though it did not quell the conflicts brewing internally. At the same time, Japanese pirates started becoming more sophisticated in their military tactics. General Yi Seong-gye was sent to fight both these pirates and the Mongols, and his victories helped him consolidate power. He forced the Goryeo king to abdicate and named himself King Taejo ("Great Progenitor"), the first emperor of the Joseon Dynasty.

Joseon Dynasty

When the **Joseon Dynasty** (1392–1910) was founded, King Taejo created a Confucian form of government that promoted loyalty to the country and respect for parents and ancestors, and in 1394 he moved the capital to what is now **Seoul** (p. 40), where many of the **palaces** (p. 79) and the **Jongmyo**, the family's royal shrine, still stand. His family, the Yis, ruled what was to become one of the world's longest-running monarchies.

Again, Korea flourished both artistically and culturally, and major advances in science, technology, literature, and the arts were made. One of the most celebrated emperors of the time was King Sejong the Great, who took the throne in 1418. He gathered a team of scholars to create Korea's first written language, Hangeul.

From 1592 to 1598, Korea was attacked relentlessly by Japanese aggressors during what is called the **Imjin Waeran** and is sometimes referred to as the Hideyoshi Invasions. Successive attacks by its eastern neighbor and Qing China from the north led to the country's increasingly harsh isolationist policy. By the time Admiral Yi Sun-shin (see **Yeosu,** p. 212) and his fleet of iron-clad "turtle" ships had fended off the Japanese for good, Korea had shut itself off completely from the rest of the world. It became known as the Hermit Kingdom, and it managed to remain relatively untouched by outsiders until the 1800s.

Floating Turtles

Korea's most famous naval commander, Admiral Yi Sun-shin, led the navy against Japanese invasion during the wars of 1592 to 1598. Legend has it that the admiral, who was killed during a skirmish in 1598 at the age of 43, never lost a single one of the 23 battles he commanded. But he may be most famous for his use of turtle ships, boats armored with thick wood planking, iron shields, and spikes that the Korean navy used to inflict heavy damage on invading Japanese ships. Capable of ramming other ships without sustaining damage, these turtle ships are considered one of the triumphs of Korean ingenuity.

Japanese Occupation

In the 19th century, Korea again became the focus of its imperialist neighbors, China, Russia, and Japan. By 1910, Japan, which had been exerting more and more control over Korea's destiny, officially annexed the country, bringing an end to the Joseon Dynasty. The Japanese tried to quash Korean culture, not allowing people to speak their own language, and attempted to obliterate Korean history.

When King Gojong, the last of the Joseon rulers, died, anti-Japanese rallies took place throughout the country. Most notably on March 1, 1919, a declaration of independence was read in Seoul as an estimated two million people took part in rallies. The protests were violently suppressed, and thousands of Koreans were killed or imprisoned (see **Seodaemun Prison,** p. 86). But independence-minded Koreans were not deterred, and anti-Japanese rallies continued until a student uprising in November of 1929 led to increased military rule. Freedom of expression and freedom of the press were severely curbed by Japanese rule.

A Korean government in exile was set up in Shanghai and it coordinated the struggle against Japan. On December 9, 1941, after the attack on Pearl Harbor, the exiled Korean government declared war on Japan. On August 15, 1945, Japan surrendered to the Allied forces, ending 35 years of Japanese occupation. Ten days later Korea became one of the earliest victims of the Cold War: It was divided in half, with the United States taking control of surrendering Japanese soldiers south of the 38th Parallel, while the Soviet Union took control of the areas north. The division was meant to be temporary, until the U.S., U.K., U.S.S.R., and China could come to an agreed-upon trusteeship of the country.

The Korean War

A conference was convened in Moscow in December 1945 to discuss the future of Korea. A 5-year trusteeship was discussed and the Soviet–American commission met a few times in Seoul, just as the chill of the Cold War began to set in. In 1947, the United Nations called for the election of a unity government, but the North Korean regime, dominated by the Soviet Union, refused to participate, and the two countries were formally established in 1948.

But on June 25, 1950, North Korea, aided by the communist People's Republic of China and the Soviet Union, invaded the South. The South resisted with help from United Nations troops, most of whom were American. Fighting raged for 3 years, causing much damage and destruction. The war has never officially ended, but the fighting stopped with the signing of a ceasefire on July 27, 1953, creating the Demilitarized Zone (**DMZ,** see p. 122).

Recent History

The Republic of Korea officially became a country on August 15, 1948. Its history after the Korean War has been marked by turbulent governments. The country has undergone five major constitutional changes, along with decades of authoritarian governments and military rule. Although an electoral college was created in the 1970s, South Korea did not hold its first democratic and fair presidential election until 1987. Despite its violent past, South Korea grew by leaps and bounds, especially in the decades from the 1960s to the 1990s. It is now the 4th-largest economy in Asia and the 15th-largest in the world. It is also one of the most wired countries in the world.

The president is the head of state of the Republic of Korea and is elected by direct popular vote for a 5-year term (with no possibility for re-election). As South Korea's first president, Rhee Syngman took power in 1954 with an anticommunist platform, but his administration collapsed in the face of a student antigovernment movement, the 4.19 (April 19th) Revolution, in 1960. In 1963, Park Chung-hee was elected president, and he ruled with military might until he was assassinated by his own men in 1979 (Im Sang-Soo's film, *The President's Last Bang,* is an excellent satire of the assassination). In 1980, Chun Doo-hwan came to power and continued his predecessor's authoritarian rule until a massive 1987 protest demanding democracy. At that point, Roh Tae-woo came to power, the country hosted the 1988 Olympics, and it joined the United Nations in 1991. Kim Young-sam became the country's first nonmilitary president in 1993 and saw the International Monetary Fund (IMF) collapse during his presidency. In 1997, Kim Dae-jung was elected and made efforts toward reviving the economy, and he hosted the FIFA World Cup in 2002. The 16th president of South Korea, Roh Moo-hyun, was elected in 2003 and committed suicide in May 2009, when he was embroiled in a bribery scandal.

After one of the lowest voter turnouts in history, Lee Myung-bak of the conservative Grand National Party was elected president in 2007. The largely unpopular President Lee was the former CEO of Hyundai and served as the mayor of Seoul. Lee's term runs from 2008 to February of 2013.

With the surprise death of Kim Jong-Il in 2011, there is uncertainty as Kim Jong-eun has taken helm as the Supreme Leader of North Korea. South Koreans are somewhat used to this opaqueness from their neighbor and everyday life is largely unaffected by changes in the north.

ART & ARCHITECTURE

Arts
CERAMICS

The earliest form of art found on the Korean Peninsula is pottery. Pottery shards from the Neolithic era are prevalent. By the time of the Three Kingdoms, ceramics were in common use in everyday life. But it was during the Unified Shilla period that the pottery began taking on interesting shapes and decorative patterns.

In the Goryeo period, a ceramics culture evolved, with the creation of *cheongja* (celadon) pottery. In the Joseon era, the white ceramics of *baekja* and *buncheongsagi* were developed. Unusually, Joseon ceramics were simpler in design than those from the Goryeo period. Of course, the tradition of Korean ceramics continues today and can be seen throughout the country, especially in **Icheon** (p. 116), where you can see Korea's potters solidify their clay creations in traditional firewood kilns.

PAINTING

The earliest known Korean paintings are murals found on the walls of tombs from the Three Kingdoms period (although painted baskets were found in the area of the ancient Lelang kingdom around 108 B.C.). The ones from Goguryeo were more dynamic and rhythmic, while those of Baekje were refined and elegant. Those from Shilla were meticulous. Unfortunately, only one example survived from the Unified Shilla period.

During the Goryeo period, painting flourished with the heavy influence of Buddhism, as shown in murals in temples and religious scroll paintings. No examples of secular paintings remain from this time, but writings talk about them and Koreans often traveled to China to buy paintings.

The rise of Confucianism during the Joseon period had a profound effect on Buddhist painting, and it has not enjoyed such artistic prominence since the Goryeo period. Paintings during this time were influenced by works of Chinese scholar-artists. The 17th century saw less of an effect of China on Korea, due to successive invasions from the Japanese and Manchus, and it was during the 18th century that Korean painting finally came to its own. Examples of this are the development of the *chingyoung sansu* ("real landscape") style and depictions of everyday life.

During the Japanese occupation, Korean painting suffered, but the introduction of modern Western painting styles influenced Korean artists. After World War II, an interest in both Western and traditional styles grew rapidly and today both continue to flourish.

SCULPTURE

The oldest known sculptures in Korea are some rock carvings on a riverside cliff, Ban-gudae, in Gyeongsangbuk-do. Smaller sculptures were made of bronze, earthenware, and clay during the Bronze Age. The art form, however, did not gain prominence until the introduction of Buddhism during the Three Kingdoms period. Buddhist images and pagodas became the main forms for sculptors during this time. Buddhas from Goguryeo had long faces on mostly shaven heads and were characteristic of the more rough style of the kingdom. Baekje Buddhas had more human features and stately but relaxed bodies with more volume beneath the robe. Early Shilla sculptures showed influences of Sui and Tang China, with round faces and realistically depicted robes.

Buddhist sculpture continued to be popular during the Goryeo period. A large number of pagodas and Buddhas were created with more Korean facial features, but stiffer bodies. Of course, Buddhist sculpture suffered during the Joseon period and declined even more under Japanese rule, when Korean sculptors began just imitating Western styles. Modern Korean sculpture came into its own in the 1960s, and contemporary Korean sculpture continues to develop today.

Architecture

Several architectural remains from Neolithic culture exist on the peninsula. Dolmens, primitive tombs of important people from ancient times, are found all over the southern areas of Korea. Other ancient structures of interest are the royal tombs from the Baekje and Shilla eras. One interesting thing of note is that evidence of *ondol*, the uniquely Korean system of under-floor heating, can be found in primitive ruins.

In general, historical Korean architecture can be divided into two broad styles—one used for palaces and temples and the other for houses of common people.

The natural environment was always an important element of Korean architecture and when choosing a site for building, Koreans gave it careful consideration. An ideal site had appropriate views of the mountains and water and aligned with traditional principles of geomancy.

The ideal *hanok* (traditional house), for instance, is built with the mountains to the back and a river in the front. The homes were built with ondol underneath for the cold winters and a wide *daecheong* (front porch) for keeping the house cool during the hot summers. In the colder, northern areas, homes were built in a closed square to retain better heat, while homes in the central region were generally L-shaped for better airflow. Houses in the southern region were built in an open I-shape for even more airflow.

Traditional homes of upper-class people, or *yangban*, took into consideration Confucian ideas, separating living quarters by the age and gender of the occupants. Males older than 7 slept in the *sarangchae* (the study and drawing room for the men), while women and children (and sometimes married couples) slept in the *anchae*, which was a place in the inner part of the home to restrict the movement of women. The servants slept in the *haengnang* and the ancestors were honored in the *sadang*. The buildings had tiled roofs and were often called *giwajib*. The entire complex was housed within stone walls with a large main gate/front door, *daemun*. Although not homes, per se, examples of *yangban* architecture can be seen in *seowon*, Confucian academies, such as **Dosan Seowon** (p. 254).

Lower-class homes had a much simpler structure of a large main room, a kitchen, and a porch. The houses were simple, with thatched roofs made of straw or bark. Examples of these can be seen in the Korean folk village of **Suwon** (p. 109) or **Andong** (p. 252).

SOUTH KOREA IN POP CULTURE

Books

Although classic texts and popular English-language literature are often translated into Korean, the reverse is not true. Very few Korean books are translated into English. However, the newer generations of Korean immigrants, foreign-born Koreans, and non-Koreans are writing interesting books about the culture.

Non-fiction books on Korea include the following: ***20th Century Korean Art*** (2005) by Youngna Kim is a solid introduction to contemporary works by current artists. ***Korean Folk Art and Craft*** (1993) by Edward B. Adams, although a bit dated, is an excellent guide to understanding Korea's folk objects. ***Korea's Place in the Sun: A Modern History*** (2005, updated edition) by Bruce Cumings is an excellent overview of the history of the peninsula. ***Korea Style*** (2006) by Marcia Iwatate and Kim Unsoo is perhaps the only book in English about Korean architectural and interior design, highlighting 22 homes in the country. **Eating Korean: From Barbeque to Kimchi, Recipes from My Kitchen** (2005) is a friendly guide to Korean cuisine. Written by the author of this guide, it includes personal stories and over 100 recipes. **Quick and Easy Korean Cooking** (2009), also written by this book's author, introduces Korean flavors into your home kitchen.

There are some good Korean fictional works translated into English, available on limited release: **Between Heaven and Earth** (1996/2002) was the winner of the Yi Sang Literature Prize in 1996. It's a story about a transient relationship between a man on his way to a funeral and a woman he meets on the way. **The Wings** (2004) by Yi Sang is a collection of three semiautobiographical short stories on life, love, and death. **The Rain Spell** (1973/2002) by Yun Heung-gil is a touching and sad story about the Korean War. **House of Idols** (1960/1961/1966/2003) by Cho In-hoon is about two soldiers in Seoul after the Korean War. It includes "End of the Road," a story about a prostitute set around a U.S. military base. **The Land of the Banished** (2001) by Cho Chong-rae is about a peasant family during the Korean War. It depicts the class struggle and describes the People's Army. **It's Hard to Say: Buddhist Stories Told by Seon Master Daehaeng** (2005) is an illustrated introduction to Seon (Zen) teachings, with fun stories for adults and children. **Meeting Mr Kim: Or How I Went to Korea and Learned to Love Kimchi** (2008) is the story of how an English writer, Jennifer Barclay, traveled around South Korea for three months, often well off the beaten track, with a tent and backpack, meeting people as she went and discovering a unique culture she had previously known nothing about. In spite of having arrived in Korea with a rock band, her journey becomes something of a spiritual one as she learns about Buddhist temples. It's an accessible and sometimes funny introduction to the country, offers inspiration on places to visit beyond the city of Seoul, and illustrates what a welcoming country it really can be.

Films

Since the late '90s, South Korean films have been gaining international recognition and winning prizes at festivals worldwide. Though not comprehensive by any means, the following is a list of films we've found notable in the past decade or so.

Hahaha (2010) won Hong Sang-soo a prize at Cannes for his usual narrative tricks of showing the same events told from different perspectives. His 2005 **Tale of Cinema** and his 2008 **Night and Day** are also standouts in his repertoire.

Actresses (2009) is a star-studded "documentary" of a supposed Vogue Korea photo shoot of the country's lead actresses on New Year's eve. The director, Lee Je-yong plays with the documentary form while letting the sharp wit of the actresses themselves shine through the loosely structured script.

Treeless Mountain (2008) is an unsentimental story of a girl (age 6) who must take care of her younger sister after their mother leaves them with an aunt to search for their father. This story of childhood resilience was written and directed by one of South Korea's few women directors, So Yong Kim.

Secret Sunshine (**Miryang**; 2007) is Lee Chang-dong's film about a woman trying to start a new life in a small town, Miryang (hence the name). The performance by Jeon Do-yeon won her the best actress prize at Cannes, but her co-star, Song Kang-ho, also does an excellent job of portraying a certain type of universal, small-town Korean man.

The President's Last Bang (2005), directed by Im Sang-soo, is a controversial political satire dramatizing the last days of President Park Chung-hee. His military dictatorship ended in 1979 with his assassination by his own men. The Korean title translates literally to *"Those People at That Time."*

Oasis (2002), an award-winning film by Lee Chang-dong, is about a relationship between an ex-convict and a woman with cerebral palsy. The brilliant acting by Moon So-ri garnered her the Marcello Mastroianni Award at Venice that year. Lee's *Peppermint Candy* (2000), though not a brilliant work of art, is an interesting historical drama depicting the Korean psyche, through one man's story told backward from the end of his life to his youth.

Spring in My Home Town (1998) is a slow-moving but nicely told story by director Lee Kwangmo about two 13-year-old boys in a small village during the last days of the Korean War. The film's Korean title is *"The Beautiful Season."*

Farewell, My Darling (1996), written and directed by Park Cheol-Su (director of *301/302*), is about a family mourning the death of its patriarch. It is an excellent commentary on the contradictions and commingling of Confucius traditions and modern life in Korea.

TV

The wildly popular television drama **Winter Sonata** (the second half of the show *Endless Love*) was one of the shows responsible for the "Korean wave" (or Hallyu) that swept through the rest of Asia in the early 2000s and popularized Korean TV shows worldwide.

There are literally hundreds of dramas to choose from, so it's difficult to recommend titles. The most popular ones from the past few years have been *My Girl, Secret Garden, 49 Days, Iris, Full House, City Hunter,* and *Heartstrings.* Also, historic dramas, like **Deep-rooted Tree** (based on the novel of the same name, dramatizing the story of King Sejong and the creation of the Korean written language) and **Queen Seon-deok** (written by the screenwriter of *Jewel in the Palace*, telling the story of the first female ruler of the Shilla Kingdom), although fictionalized, are an entertaining way to learn more about Korea's colorful history. You can even visit some of the sets built specifically for productions. We've included details of these throughout the book.

YesAsia (www.yesasia.com) is an excellent online source for Korean dramas with English subtitles.

Music

You may have heard of the KPop, made popular by **Rain** or even heard KPop groups in some clubs overseas. Of these, female vocalist **Boa** is one of the few who have been able to make a crossover album in English. Still, Korean pop singers and performers rise and fall so quickly it's hard to keep track. Kpopmusic.com, allkpop.com, and kpopseven.com are good sources for checking out the latest hits and bands.

Despite the temporary nature of today's pop music in South Korea, the country's musical roots go back centuries, back to its shamanistic roots. Korea's traditional music grew from some outside influences (for example, Buddhism), but had its own origins. Special court music and ensembles were performed for royalty and aristocrats. Although it dates back to the beginning of the Joseon Dynasty, it's very rare to be able to catch a court music performance these days, aside from special events put on by the National Center for Korean Traditional Performing Arts.

At the other end of the spectrum were the folk musicians, who traveled from town to town putting on impromptu concerts for commoners. The villagers would throw the roving musician a few coins or feed them in return for the entertainment.

Pungmul is a type of folk music tradition that grew from shamanistic rituals and Korea's agricultural society. A pungmul performance is led by drumming, but includes wind instruments as well as dancers. Because it's a kinetic, colorful performance, a recording of pungmul music rarely does it justice. However, *samul nori,* which also has its roots in *nog-ak* (farmer's music), makes use of four of the drums found in pungmul. Each drum represents various elements of weather—rain, wind, clouds, and thunder. It's a good entry into Korean traditional music, especially for those who like percussion. They have occasional performances at a variety of places around the country, including the **Korean Folk Village** in **Suwon** (see p. 111).

Pansori is one of the most famous types of traditional performance. Sometimes called the Korean "blues" (not because of the style but more because of the sadness in the music), pansori is a long, drawn-out performance by one singer and one accompanying drummer. The lyricist tells a narrative song, inviting audience participation and joke telling along the way.

Sanjo (which translates literally as "scattered melodies") is one of the most advanced forms of Korean music. It describes a solo performance on a traditional instrument in which the performer begins slowly, but builds up to a faster, more spontaneous tempo, adding improvisations and showing off his or her skills with each successive movement. In an entirely instrumental performance, the rhythms shift as the performance progresses. There are *sanjo* for *piri* (bamboo oboe), *daegeum* (bamboo flute), *haegeum* (two-string bowed instrument), *ajaeng* (bowed zither), *geomungo* (six-stringed zither), and the *gayageum* (12-stringed zither).

A modern gayageum master was **Hwang Byungki** (www.bkhwang.com), who played both traditional and original compositions on the Korean zither. His album *The Labyrinth* (2003) contains some of the most experimental of his works, while *Spring Snow* (2001) is a more meditative and minimal interpretation.

A celebrated performer of the daegeum is **Yi Saeng-gang** (www.leesaengkang.com). His album *Daegeum Sori* (2007) is an excellent introduction to the sounds of the bamboo flute, but his *Sound of Memory Vol. 2* is a more haunting study of the bamboo instrument.

EATING & DRINKING

Korean cuisine encompasses foods from the land and the sea. You can enjoy a simple bowl of noodles, a 21-dish royal dinner, or anything in between. From a humble vegetarian meal at a Buddhist temple to elaborate banquets in Seoul's most expensive restaurants, South Korea has something for even the pickiest of eaters.

Koreans enjoy dishes with bold flavors, such as chili peppers and garlic, but usually traditional royal cuisine and temple food is not spicy. Each town in the country is famous for a certain dish, a regional specialty, seafood, or a particular fruit or vegetable that is grown in the area.

What Is Kimchi?

Kimchi is a spicy dish, the most popular of which is made from fermented cabbage, and it is a source of national pride for South Koreans. When hungry, any Korean would swear that a bowl of rice and some kimchi are all that's needed to complete a meal. The most popular type is the traditional version made from napa cabbages, called *baechu kimchi*. Not only is kimchi eaten as a side dish, it is also used as an ingredient in other dishes. For instance, there is *kimchi bokkeum bap* (fried rice with kimchi), *kimchi*

jjigae (a hot pot of kimchi, meat, tofu, and vegetables), *kimchi mandu* (kimchi dumplings), *kimchi buchingae* (kimchi flatcakes), *kimchi ramen* (kimchi with noodles)—the list is endless. Koreans love their kimchi so much that many homes even have separate, specially calibrated refrigerators designated just to keep kimchi fresh. When taking a photo, Koreans say "kimchi" instead of saying "cheese." If you like spicy, salty food, be adventurous and try some kimchi. You'll have over 167 varieties to choose from!

The Korean Table

A Korean meal is usually made with balance in mind—hot and cool, spicy and mild, yin and yang. At the core of every meal is *bap* (rice), unless the meal is noodle- or porridge-based. Koreans don't distinguish between breakfast, lunch, or dinner, so it's not unusual to eat rice three times a day.

In addition to individual bowls of rice, you may get a single serving of soup. Hot pots (*jjigae* or *jungol*), which are thicker and saltier, are set in the middle of the table for everyone to share. Because beverages are rarely served during a traditional Korean meal, there should always be a soup or water kimchi (see box below) to wash the food down (although as a foreigner you'll almost always be offered filtered or bottled water with your meal).

Speaking of kimchi, there will usually be at least one type on the table. Often there are two or three kinds, depending on the season. Served in small dishes, kimchi helps add an extra kick to whatever else is on the menu. Like the rest of the food, kimchi is laid out in the middle of the table for everyone to share.

Mit banchan—a variety of smaller side dishes, anything from pickled seafood to seasonal vegetables—rounds out the regular meal. In traditional culture, the table settings varied depending on the occasion (whether the meal was for everyday eating, for special occasions, or for guests) as well as the number of *banchan* (side dishes) on the table. The settings were determined by the number of side dishes, which could vary in number—3, 5, 7, 9, or 12. As with all Korean food, the royal table was different from the commoner's.

There are no real "courses" per se in Korean meals. Generally, all the food is laid out on the table at the same time and eaten in whatever order you wish. If you order *galbi* (ribs) or other meat you cook yourself on a tabletop grill, your rice will arrive last so that you don't fill yourself up too fast. When you have *hwae* (raw fish), you will be brought a starter, the fresh fish (quite often the fish is netted for you fresh from a tank), and then a *mae-un-tahng* (spicy hot pot) made from whatever is left of your fish. Also, there is no such thing as dessert in Korean tradition; however, an afterdinner drink of hot tea or coffee is generally served with whatever fruit is in season.

Korean meals were traditionally served on low tables with family members sitting on floor cushions. Some restaurants still adhere to this older custom, but others offer regular Western-style dining tables. Although certain traditions have gone by the wayside, mealtime etiquette still applies, especially for formal meals.

For starters, you should always wait for the eldest to eat his or her first bite, unless you are the guest of honor—if you are, then everyone will be waiting for you to take your first bite before digging in. Koreans usually eat their rice with a spoon, not with chopsticks. Unlike in other Asian countries, rice bowls and soup bowls are not picked up from the table. Completely taboo at the dining table is blowing your nose, chewing with your mouth open, and talking with your mouth full. Leaving chopsticks sticking straight out of a bowl (done only during *jesa,* a ritual for paying respect to one's ancestors), mixing rice and soup, and overeating are also considered inappropriate. During informal meals, however, these rules are often broken.

For a list of popular menu items in Korean and English, see p. 429.

WHEN TO GO

South Korea has four distinct seasons, and the best times to visit are in the spring and fall, since summers are hot and humid and winters are dry and cold—though the mountainous terrain makes for great snow sports. More detailed weather information is given below, but a far bigger factor in your planning should be avoiding major Korean holidays. Domestic tourists take to the roads in the tens of thousands, crowding all forms of transportation, filling hotels, and making it difficult to visit popular attractions. By contrast, Seoul empties out and traffic is almost nonexistent. For the latest news and more detail check out the Korea Tourism Organization (KTO) at http://english.visitkorea.or.kr.

SWEET goldfish & SILKWORM CASINGS: STREET FOOD

Wandering around the streets of South Korea, you can eat your fill without setting foot in a restaurant. You can choose from a wide variety of venues and dishes—everything from little old ladies roasting chestnuts on the street corners (only in the winter) to *pojang macha* (covered tents), where you can get a beer or *soju* (rice or sweet potato "vodka"), too. Typical fare includes the following:

○ *Dduk bokgi*—seasoned rice cake sticks that are spicy, a little sweet, and a lot tasty

○ *Boong-uh bbang*—goldfish "cookies" filled with sweet red-bean paste (also available round with a flower print or in other shapes)

○ *Ho-ddeok*—flat, fried dough rounds filled with sugar

○ *Soondeh*—Korean blood sausage

○ *Gimbap*—rice and other things rolled in seaweed (also available in miniversions)

○ *Yut*—hard taffy usually made from pumpkin (may be rough on your fillings!)

○ *Bbundaegi*—boiled silkworm casings, a toasty treat for the adventurous

○ *Sola*—tiny conch shells

Peak Travel Times

Seol (Lunar New Year)   Although January 1 is also celebrated in South Korea, Seol (also known as Seollal) is a bigger holiday. It can be difficult for tourists to figure out when the Lunar New Year will fall, as Westerners rely on a solar calendar. The solar calendar equivalents of the Lunar New Year for the next few years are February 10, 2013; January 31, 2014; February 19, 2015; February 8, 2016. Most Koreans get 3 days off during the holiday and use that time to travel to their hometown. Others take the opportunity to go on ski holidays or travel abroad. Bus and train tickets go on sale 3 months beforehand and people line up for hours in order to get their passage out of town. Driving is a bad option, since the normal 5- to 6-hour drive from Seoul to Busan, for example, can take up to 14 hours due to ridiculous traffic.

Children's Day   Though not necessarily in prime travel season, May 5 is the day South Koreans celebrate their little ones. Parents dress up their kids and take them to amusement parks, zoos, theaters—pretty much anywhere children love to go. If you want to avoid big crowds, stay away from kiddie hot spots on this day.

Summer Holidays   It's not as insanely busy as the Lunar New Year or Chuseok (see below), but when the kids go on summer break, many families head out of Seoul to take a trip to the beaches or the mountains. Korean children have only about 6 weeks of summer break, usually from mid-July to late August, but university students keep trains and buses busy throughout the season. Be sure to book rooms in popular destinations (such as **Busan's beaches,** which get super-crowded June–Aug) well in advance.

Chuseok (Harvest Moon Festival)   Another traditional holiday as important as Lunar New Year, Chuseok (sometimes spelled Chusok) is celebrated on the 15th day of the eighth lunar month, usually sometime in mid- to late September. Solar equivalents for the next few years are September 19, 2013; September 8, 2014; September 27, 2015; and September 15, 2016. The days before and after are considered legal holidays in South Korea. Once again, Korean families mobilize to visit their hometowns and pay respect to their ancestors. Tickets for travel usually sell out 3 months in advance and roads and hotels are packed.

Weather

South Korea's climate can be described as temperate, with four distinct seasons. The weather is heavily influenced by the oceans that surround the Korean Peninsula and by its proximity to the rest of Asia to the north. Winters and summers are long and punctuated by short but enjoyable springs and autumns.

Winter begins in November as cold air moves south from Siberia and Manchuria. By December and January, average temperatures drop below 32°F (0°C) over the whole country, with the notable exception of **Jeju-do** and some coastal areas. In Seoul, winter temperatures usually drop to 18°F (–8°C) and have been known to fall to –11°F (–24°C).

Spring starts by the end of March, when warm air begins to move north off the Pacific Ocean. Temperatures usually average 51°F (11°C), and rainfall is unpredictable. By the end of May, summer brings a period of warmth and humidity with heavy rainfall that starts in July and lasts until the end of September. Summer temperatures average 77°F (25°C), but often approach 86°F (30°C) in July and August. It's not the heat that's the challenge; it's the humidity. South Korea gets about 125cm (49 in.) of rain annually, 60% of which falls during the summer months. In general, the southern and western regions see more rain, with **Jeju-do** having the highest average rainfall per year. The summer is also typhoon season in South Korea. Although most typhoons lose their strength by the time they make it to the peninsula, some cause flooding, structural damage, and, in extreme cases, even death.

By late September, the cool, dry winds from Siberia change the weather again. Temperatures fall to about 59°F (15°C) and skies generally remain clear and crisp, with very little rainfall. Koreans consider autumn the best season, marked by the most important national holiday, **Chuseok,** when people visit their ancestral homes and give thanks for the harvest. Trees throughout the country exchange their summer greens for fall (autumn) colors and Koreans flock to the mountains in droves to see nature's show.

Average Daily Temperatures (°F/°C) & Monthly Rainfall (in/cm)

		JAN	FEB	MAR	APR	MAY	JUNE	JULY	AUG	SEPT	OCT	NOV	DEC
Seoul	Highs	36/2	40/4	50/10	65/18	73/23	81/27	84/29	86/30	79/26	68/20	54/12	40/4
	Lows	23/–5	27/–3	36/2	46/8	55/13	65/18	72/22	72/22	63/17	50/10	39/4	28/–2
	Rainfall	0.68/1.7	0.85/2.2	1.3/3.3	2.1/5.4	3.1/7.9	4.6/11.6	10.7/27.2	11.8/30	4/10.3	1.5/3.7	1.6/4.1	0.6/1.5
Busan	Highs	46/8	50/10	55/13	64/18	72/22	75/24	81/27	84/29	79/26	72/22	61/16	50/10
	Lows	32/0	34/1	41/5	50/10	57/14	65/18	72/22	73/23	68/20	57/14	46/8	36/2
	Rainfall	1.2/3	1.5/3.7	2.5/6.3	3.8/9.7	4.6/11.8	6.2/15.7	8.3/21	7.8/19.8	4.6/11.6	1.6/4	1.3/3.3	0.7/1.9
Jeju	Highs	46/8	48/9	54/12	63/17	70/21	77/25	84/29	86/30	79/26	70/21	61/16	52/11
	Lows	39/4	39/4	43/6	52/11	59/15	66/19	74/23	75/24	68/20	59/15	51/10	43/6
	Rainfall	1.9/4.8	1.8/4.6	2.9/7.4	2.5/6.4	3.5/8.9	5/12.7	7/17.7	8.1/21	5.5/14	1.6/4.1	2.1/5.3	1.3/3.4

PUBLIC HOLIDAYS

South Koreans celebrate both holidays from the traditional lunar calendar (see above) and holidays adopted from the Western calendar. National public holidays are **New Year's Day** (celebrated Jan 1 and 2), **Lunar New Year's Day** (usually in Jan or Feb, and the 2 days following it—see "Peak Travel Times," above, for exact dates), **Independence Movement Day** (Mar 1), **Arbor Day** (Apr 5), **Children's Day** (May 5), **Buddha's Birthday/Feast of the Lanterns** (the eighth day of the fourth lunar month, usually in Apr or May), **Memorial Day** (June 5), **Constitution Day** (July 17), **Liberation Day** (Aug 15), **Foundation Day** (Oct 3), **Harvest Moon Festival** (14th–16th days of the eighth lunar month—see "Peak Travel Times," above, for exact dates), and **Christmas Day** (Dec 25).

Calendar of Events

South Korea's traditional festivals follow the lunar calendar, but modern festivals follow the solar/Gregorian calendar. For conversion to solar calendar dates, visit www.mandarintools.com/calconv_old.html or www.chinesefortunecalendar.com/CLunarCal1.htm.

With festivals for everything from fireflies and pine mushrooms to swimming in icy-cold water, Koreans will most likely be celebrating something when you visit. Regional festivals are a great way to get a sense of just how varied Korean culture is while experiencing traditional costumes, performances, and music.

For an exhaustive list of events beyond those listed here, check http://events.frommers.com, where you'll find a searchable, up-to-the-minute roster of what's happening in cities all over the world.

JANUARY

Seol (Lunar New Year) is still one of the biggest holidays of the year. Koreans get up early, put on their best clothes (usually the traditional *hanbok*), and bow to their elders. Families celebrate with feasts of *dduk guk* (rice-cake soup) or *mandu guk* (dumpling soup), and the palaces in Seoul host special events. See "Peak Travel Times," above, for dates.

Hwacheon Mountain Trout Festival (✆ 033/441-7575) is a charming festival celebrating the mountain trout (the "Queen of the Valleys"). Thousands of people descend upon this small town in Gangwon-do (see chapter 10) to catch this fish and enjoy a variety of winter sports. Through most of January.

FEBRUARY

Inje Ice Fishing Festival (✆ 033/460-2082) occurs every winter, when Soyang Lake freezes over and hundreds of people flock to this mountain village in the inner Seoraksan area (p. 326). Not only will you be able to ice fish, but you also can play ice soccer (football), go sledding, watch a dog sled competition, and enjoy a meal of freshly caught smelt. Late January through mid-February.

MARCH

Jeongwol Daeboreum Fire Festival celebrates the first full moon of the lunar year. The celebrations involve both livestock—there are duck and pig races—and nods to the island's history. The festival arose from the island's ancient practice of burning grazing fields, which served the dual purpose of razing the land for new crops and getting rid of pests. Don't miss the spectacular fireworks show. February or March on the 15th day of the first lunar month.

Gyeongju Traditional Drink & Rice Cake Festival (✆ 054/748-7721 or 2; www.fgf.or.kr) is held at Hwangseong Park in Gyeongju (p. 231) every March or April (dates vary wildly, so be sure to check ahead of time) and is the perfect place to sample everything from rice cakes to rice wine. You can also try your hand at pounding rice into cakes the old-fashioned way (with a wooden mallet), see traditional folk performers, and enjoy the market-like atmosphere.

APRIL

Gwangalli Eobang Festival (✆ 051/610-4062, ext. 4) celebrates the arrival of spring and was founded in 2001, when three smaller festivals were combined. The festivities are kicked off when hundreds of Busan residents parade in masks and costumes. The costumes are a mix of old and new, and represent a traditional play called "Suyeong Yaryu," which originated from Suyeong-gu (an area in central Busan) and which mocks the *yangban* (noble class). Other events include the local custom of praying for the safe return of fishermen (with a big catch, of course). At night, you can enjoy the fireworks and the lights of the Jindu-eoha, where fishing boats are lit to re-enact traditional torchlight fishing. Early April.

Jeonju International Film Festival (www.jiff.or.kr) is held in (where else?) Jeonju (see chapter 8). You won't catch many blockbusters here—the festival is more focused on short independent films—but you may discover a new star on the rise. Late April to early May.

Hi Seoul Festival (✆ 02/3290-7150; www.hiseoulfest.org) highlights the history and culture of South Korea's capital. Most of this festival's events, including everything from classical music to rock music concerts, happen in the downtown area. Don't miss the spectacular lighted boat parade in the evenings in Yeoui-do. Lasts about a week, usually in early May.

Icheon Ceramic Festival (✆ 031/644-2944, ext. 4) Want to experience the history and craftsmanship of Korean pottery? Then head to Icheon (see chapter 6) for this festival, where you can even buy handmade ceramics from the artists themselves. Late April.

MAY

Boseong Green Tea (Da Hyang) Festival (✆ 061/852-1330; www.boseong.go.kr) is held in South Korea's most important tea-producing region. Enjoy Jeollanam-do (see chapter 7) and taste some of the finest *nok-cha* (green tea) in the world, fresh from the plantation. You can also try foods made with green tea, try a tea facial, and participate in traditional tea ceremonies. Early May, in odd-numbered years (2013, 2015, and so on).

Lotus Lantern Festival (☏ 02/2011-1744, ext. 7; www.llf.or.kr) coincides with Buddha's Birthday (also known as "The Day the Buddha Came"), and it is not to be missed. Hundreds of thousands of people parade along the Han River with lanterns. The opening ceremony for the parade starts at Dongdaemun Stadium. Other events happen in temples throughout the country in mid-May.

Gangneung Danoje Festival (http://english. visitkorea.or.kr/enu/SI/SI_EN_3_2_1.jsp? cid=293063) celebrates Dano (the fifth day of the fifth month of the lunar year) with brewing of sacred wine. Although there are month-long events, the main festivities happen in the 3 to 4 days surrounding Dano. Highlights include the Gwanno mask drama—a pantomime combining Korea's ancient shamanistic beliefs with traditional dance and mask play that was performed and handed down by government servants during the Joseon Dynasty—and daily shamanistic rituals. The festivities have been deemed an important, intangible cultural property by UNESCO. Late May through June in Gangwon-do.

JUNE

Muju Firefly Festival (☏ 063/322-1330; festival@firefly.or.kr) honors the local ecosystem. This is the only place in South Korea where fireflies are found, and the people of Muju use the insect's annual appearance as an excuse to celebrate. The festival also includes taekwondo demonstrations, since Muju is the site of the World Taekwondo Park. Early June in Jeollabuk-do (p. 194).

JULY

Boryeong Mud Festival (☏ 011/438-4865; www.mudfestival.or.kr) is all about rolling around in the mud. Supposedly very good for your skin, mud from this region is used in cosmetics and massages. Great fun for kids, events include mud wrestling, mud slides, and making mud soap. For one week in mid-July in Chungcheongnam-do (see chapter 6).

AUGUST

Busan International Rock Festival (www. rockfestival.co.kr) turns Dadaepo Beach into an open-air concert venue. This free festival attracts over 150,000 fans to see musicians from South Korea and all over the world. Early August.

Muan White Lotus Festival (http://tour. muan.go.kr) is held at Asia's largest field of the rare white lotus. Other than walking through the gardens, you can take a boat ride to see the blooms up close, enjoy contemporary and traditional performances, and eat a variety of foods made from lotuses. Try the lotus ice cream and the lotus noodles. Mid-August in Muan-geun in Jeollanam-do (p. 222).

SEPTEMBER

Chuseok (Harvest Festival) is another important traditional holiday and is held on the 15th day of the eighth lunar month. Also called Korean Thanksgiving, this holiday celebrates the bountiful harvest and hopes for another good year to come. Although most Koreans will be traveling to their ancestral homes, festivities are held at the palaces and at the National Folk Museum in Seoul. See "Peak Travel Times" to see dates for the next few years. Usually sometime in September.

OCTOBER

Busan International Film Festival (BIFF; www.biff.kr) is one of the largest showcases for new films in Asia. The festival attracts over 200 films from dozens of different countries (with an emphasis on Asian films, of course). Usually happens in mid-October.

Jagalchi Festival (☏ 051/243-9363; www. ijagalchi.co.kr) is South Korea's largest seafood festival. Celebrating the sea, traditional fishing rituals are performed and you can enjoy raw fish and discounts on pretty much everything that's sold at the Jagalchi Market (p. 322). Mid-October in Busan.

Icheon Rice Cultural Festival (📞 031/644-4121; www.ricefestival.or.kr) celebrates the agriculture (particularly rice) from the plains of Icheon, which once grew the rice served to royalty. Held at Icheon Seolbong Park; stop in at a neighborhood restaurant for rice and vegetables in a *dolsotbap* (hot stone pot). Late October.

NOVEMBER

Gwangju World Kimchi Culture Festival (📞 062/613-3641 or 2; http://kimchi.gwangju.go.kr) highlights this 5,000-year-old Korean food tradition. Taste the variety of the region's kimchi (the most popular type being made from fermented napa cabbage), or make some of your own. Mid-November.

NATURAL WORLD

Located on the southern half of the Korean Peninsula, South Korea is surrounded mostly by ocean—nearly 1,500 miles (2,413 km) of coastline—spanning the Yellow Sea to the west, the East China Sea to the south, and the East Sea (Sea of Japan) to the east. South Korea is separated from North Korea by the DMZ, the world's most heavily guarded border, which runs about 148 miles (238 km), just north of the 38th parallel. Although the country's land mass is not large (only about 38,623 sq miles, 100,032 sq km), the country is crisscrossed by a number of mountain ranges, leaving just a small percentage of the land available for farming. The highest mountain in South Korea is Hallasan, which is on the country's largest island, Jeju-do, located to the southwest of the peninsula.

The country has 9 provinces. Gangwon-do, located in the northeast, borders the DMZ and is the most mountainous. Gyeonggi-do surrounds Seoul and also borders the DMZ. Chungcheongnam-do is located to the south of Gyeonggi-do. Its neighbor, Chungcheongbuk-do is the only land-locked province in the country. To the east of Chungcheongbuk-do lies Gyeongsangbuk-do, which includes the historic towns of Andong and Gyeongju. To the south is Gyeongsangnam-do, which includes the city of Busan and several islands. Jeollanam-do to the west is also a coast-heavy province with nearly 2,000 islands off its coast, the majority of which are uninhabited. Its neighbor, Jeollabuk-do includes Jeonju and more mountainous regions. Jeju-do is South Korea's ninth province.

RESPONSIBLE TRAVEL

Although South Korea is not particularly eco-friendly, the nation has been making more effort toward green living. Cities now have recycling (city dwellers are required to sort their waste) and buses with reduced emissions.

National and municipal governments have launched several efforts to make South Korea more environmentally conscious. Programs like the preservation of wetlands in places like **Upon-eup, Junam,** and **Suncheon-man** (p. 215) provide sanctuary for migrating birds as well as maintaining natural environments friendly to other wildlife. Unfortunately, the more they create awareness of certain areas, the more people come to visit, making it not so friendly for the birds and other animals there.

The good thing about South Korea is the country's extensive **national park** system (http://english.knps.or.kr). The government-run organization maintains the scenic mountains and the fragile environments of its islands and coastal locations as well.

In Seoul, Gyeongju, and other cities, the government has launched a bicycle program, building more trails and providing a standardized bike-rental scheme. See the "By Bicycle" section under "Getting Around," in the planning chapter (p. 408).

Another form of eco-tourism the Koreans are trying out is hands-on experiences and tours of organic farms throughout the country. We've highlighted some options in the following regional chapters.

Although South Korea has no organized dolphin or whale-watching opportunities, 41 different species of these marine mammals can be found off the coasts of the peninsula. For information about the ethics of swimming with dolphins and other outdoor activities, visit the **Whale and Dolphin Conservation Society** (www.wdcs.org) and **Tread Lightly** (www.treadlightly.org).

In addition to the resources for South Korea listed above, see www.frommers.com/planning for more tips on responsible travel.

TOURS

Since South Korea is still a mystery to most travelers, there aren't that many specialized tours offered. However, some do show off specific areas of the country's cultural kaleidoscope.

Aju Incentive Tours (www.ajutours.co.kr) has a 6-day culinary tour of Seoul, which includes a cooking class, an opportunity to sample temple fare, and a cultural performance. They also offer a 4-day Oriental health tour exploring different aspects of traditional medicine, including a sauna, foot massages, and a visit to the traditional herbal market. Their other tours highlight different aspects of South Korea's arts and culture or explore the country's historical religions; they also offer ski tours, and even a bird-watching tour. Although bird-watching is a relatively new hobby in the country, **Birds Korea** (**www.birdskorea.org**) offers guided tours to see migrating fowl and birds unique to the region.

The **KTO** (✆ **02/729-9497,** ext. 499, or the 24-hr. travel info hot line ✆ **1330;** http://english.tour2korea.com) will help you arrange seasonal and themed tours to specialized regions in the country.

Tours from South Korea into North Korea are closed for the moment (after an unfortunate incident in which a South Korean housewife was shot and killed by a North Korean soldier). The closest you can get is to the **Panmunjeom** at the DMZ, which you can access via a day tour from Seoul. Plan your trip at least 3 days in advance. See chapter 4 for detailed information on various trip options.

Many of the major cities in South Korea also offer city tours. You can tour Seoul, Busan, Gyeongju, Daegu, Daejeon, Incheon, Suwon, Gongju, and Ulsan by bus. See each of these city's specific sections or chapters for additional information.

Academic Trips & Language Classes

Many major universities in Seoul (as well as a few in Busan, Daejeon, Busan, and other cities) offer semester- or quarter-long language programs for learning the basics of Korean. The most popular programs are, of course, during the summer months, but classes are available year-round. **Ewha Women's University** (✆ **02/3277-3683;** http://ile.ewha.ac.kr) has 10-week and intensive 3-week courses. **Yonsei University** (✆ **02/2123-3464;** www.yskli.com) has a popular summer language program. **Seoul National University** (✆ **02/880-8570;** http://lei.snu.ac.kr/site/en/klec/main/main.jsp) provides a 5-week summer program, but has classes year-round.

(Goryeo) University (© 02/3290-2971 or 2972; http://klcc.korea.ac.kr/mainList.action?langDiv=2) has quarterly language programs.

Sogang University (© 02/705-8088; http://klec.sogang.ac.kr/root/index.jnp?lang=english) offers a "master class," a 6-week workshop where well-known Korean artists, filmmakers, writers, or musicians provide insight from their experiences in their particular field of expertise. You can also enroll in their regular 10-week language courses year-round.

Adventure & Wellness Trips

Adventure Korea (© 018/242-5536; www.adventurekorea.com) offers a variety of active tours around the country, based on the season. Choose from active trips, such as snowboarding in Pyeongchang, ice fishing for trout in Hwacheon, or rockclimbing Songnisan. You can also have them customize a tour for you, if you can round up 19 of your friends. **Adventure Travelers** (© 630/915-5618 from U.S.; www.adventure-travelers.com) offers specialty tours of South Korea, including a week of taekwondo training, a 2-week trip with hands-on ceramics, and trips focusing on watersports or skiing. One of the best tours from an Australian operator is by **The Imaginative Traveller** (© 1300-135-088; www.imaginative-traveller.com), which provides a 15-day "adventure" tour that hits the major destinations as well as Seoraksan and the caves in Samcheok.

Food & Wine Trips

Unfortunately, no tour company offers regular culinary tours in South Korea. However, special tour packages are offered from time to time, usually in conjunction with a special event. In Seoul, **O'ngo Food Communications** (© 02/3446-1607; www.ongofood.com) offers the best tours, including their "Korea Taste Tour," a 2.5-hour walking survey that includes tastings from street stalls and restaurants, starting at ₩57,000 per person. They also have regular cooking classes Monday–Friday at 10am and 2pm (also on Saturday, by request), which start at ₩65,000 per person and include a visit to a traditional market.

Traditional food classes are offered at the **Institute of Traditional Korean Food** at the **Tteok Museum** (© 02/741-5447; www.kfr.or.kr/eng/index.htm). For ₩70,000, you can choose two dishes to cook from a list of traditional recipes. They require a minimum of two people and reservations at least a week in advance. There are no programs on Sunday.

Volunteer & Working Trips

Habitat for Humanity (© 02/2267-3702, ext. 402; http://www.habitat.or.kr/eng_new/index.asp) has special volunteer trips to help build homes for poor South Koreans, from May through early November. No special skills are required, just a willingness to learn and roll up your sleeves. Check their website for volunteer trips and opportunities.

CADIP (the Canadian Alliance for Development Initiatives and Projects; www.cadip.org) has several volunteer opportunities working with schoolchildren in areas like Muju, Jangheung, Namwon, or Samcheok. Most of their programs cost Canadian $590 (about US$470) plus an additional US$260 (approximately) for the hosting organization, but this covers shared accommodations and three meals daily. Visit their website for details and to apply.

United Planet (℃ 800/292-2316 in the U.S.; www.unitedplanet.org) offers 6-month and 1-year volunteer programs that start in January and August. The program starts at US$6,065 per person, and includes training, food, lodging, monthly stipends, and emergency medical insurance. Airfare, vaccinations, visa costs, and travel to the pre-departure training site are not included.

Special-Interest Trips

If you've found yourself engrossed in the latest Korean drama offering, tissue in hand, yelling at the screen, you may want to tear yourself away to see some of the locations in person. **Happy Mize** (℃ 070/8627-8080; www.happymize.com) offers a 5-day/4-night tour, which costs ₩1,630 per person for two people, or ₩830 per person if 21+ people are on the tour. The price includes transportation, hotel, all admission fees, meals, and an English-speaking guide.

Grace Travel (℃ 02/332-8946; http://english.triptokorea.com) has a variety of tours including a pottery tour of Icheon, which includes the Leeum Samsung Museum. The tour from Seoul starts at 9am and costs ₩138,000 per person (minimum 3 people) or ₩10,000 more for two people. They also have a 2-day tour to Cheonghakdong that includes lessons in traditional Korean etiquette, a guided tour to Buyeo and Gongju, and a ski-tour that includes a dip in the hot springs in Yeongpyeong.

Escorted General-Interest Tours

Escorted tours are structured group tours, with a group leader. The price usually is all-inclusive, although some of the tours listed here do not include airfare to and from South Korea.

If you're interested in rail travel, **KoRail Tourism Development** (℃ 02/2084-7744; www.korailtravel.com) offers rail-based tours including one to Jeongseon, that includes a ride on the rail bikes (2- or 4-person vehicles that you peddle on the train tracks) and the "Korean Wave Express" that rolls out every Saturday and Sunday from Seoul.

All4uKorea (http://ggmland.com/tour/indexenglish.html) is a group of tour operators based out of Seoul that offer customized tours with private drivers. You can also contact them about designing your own tour. **Root Travel Ltd.** (℃ 02/542-8606; www.roottravel.co.kr), also based out of Seoul, provides 2- to 16-day general tours spanning Seoul to the rest of South Korea.

Sky Tour (℃ 02/711-0204; www.traveltokorea.co.kr) has a variety of tours including a 7-day "best of" tour that includes Seoul, Yongjin, Gyeongju, Busan, and Jeju that starts at US$1,200 per person. **Tour East Holidays** (℃ 416/929-6688 from Canada; www.toureastholidays.com), a Toronto-based company, offers a brief South Korea tour that hits the three major cities. **R&C Hawaii Tours** (℃ 808/942-3388; www.rchawaii.com) offers both escorted and non-escorted packages. **A.T. Seasons & Vacations Travel** (℃ 91-11-22794796; www.visitsasia.com), based in New Delhi, offers 4- to 7-day general tours of South Korea, starting from Incheon airport. The **KTO (http://english.visitkorea.or.kr)** also provides tours that are coming up and a list of travel agencies in your home country that can arrange escorted tours to fit your needs.

For more information on escorted general-interest tours, including questions to ask before booking your trip, see www.frommers.com/planning.

Walking Tours

The Seoul government offers several walking tours of the city free of charge. See p. 91 for more info.

SUGGESTED ITINERARIES IN SOUTH KOREA

Seoul, Busan, Gyeongju, and even Jeju-do are well traveled, and most tour companies to South Korea will cover those areas. But South Korea is an exciting place to explore on your own, so we've provided a few itineraries, most of which don't stray too far from the major cities, to help you plan your trip.

Bear in mind that although South Korea is small in land mass, the hilly terrain and lack of major roads increase travel time between locations and attractions. Although you can rent a car, it may not be the most economical option, unless you're planning to go well off the beaten track. The best ways to get around are by rail and by bus.

Trains in South Korea are cheap, reliable, and a comfortable way to travel. High-speed **KTX trains** will help you save time. Consider buying a KTX pass before you arrive, as it will save you money, too (see the "Getting Around" section in chapter 12).

In general, trains will take you only to stations in major cities, but not to many temples and other remote locations. Luckily, the **bus system** is quite efficient and all towns have at least one bus that goes to even the most remote locations. Infrequent bus routes require a bit of pre-planning on your part. A combination of train and bus travel will probably be your best bet for far-flung areas.

SOUTH KOREA IN 1 WEEK

Although a week may seem like a long time, you'll just barely scratch the surface of the country in 7 days. Still, you'll be able to experience the hustle and bustle of the capital city, explore ancient palaces and other historic sites, and enjoy South Korea's endlessly fascinating culture.

Day 1: Arrive in Seoul

Arrive at Incheon Airport and check into your hotel. Have dinner and see a show at **Korea House** ★★ (p. 103) or grab a quick bite and take a stroll on **Samcheongdong-gil** (p. 40) to see the traditional houses converted to galleries and cafes. If you get a chance, soak in a bath or sweat away your fatigue in a sauna at your hotel or at one of Seoul's many bathhouses.

Jongmyo (Royal Tombs) The oldest Confucian royal shrines left in the world are housed in the Jeongjeon in Seoul. Originally built in 1395 (during the reign of King Taejo), the Jeongjeon had seven rooms and was one of the longest buildings in Asia at that time. More and more rooms were added until there were a total of 19 shrine rooms—one to house memorial tablets for each of the Joseon kings. After it was destroyed by invading Japanese forces during the Imjin Waeran (1592–98; p. 247), a new complex was built in 1601. Each of the rooms is simple in design, as is standard for Confucian shrines. The best time to visit is during the annual memorial ceremonies usually held on the first Sunday in May.

Changdeokgung The best preserved of Seoul's palaces, it dates to the 15th century. The Biwon, or Secret Garden, is an elaborate flora-lover's dream, located behind the main palace in the back of the complex, and is a must-see. Be sure to reserve the separate tour to see the gardens, complete with English-speaking guides.

Haeinsa and the Tripitaka Koreana This lovely temple on the slopes of Gayasan houses the Tripitaka Koreana, the world's most complete collection of Buddhist scriptures. Engraved in Hanja (Chinese script) on over 80,000 wooden blocks, the birch-wood blocks date from 1237 to 1248. The temple is located in Gyeongsang-do and can be easily accessed from Busan or Ulsan.

Seokguram and Bulguksa The Seokguram grotto is part of the Bulguksa temple complex in Tohamsan, just outside of downtown Gyeongju. Built in the 8th century, this Buddha statue and its surrounding bodhisattvas and *arhats* (Buddhist saints) are impressive in their domed grotto.

Gyeongju The entire city of Gyeongju, the former capital of the Shilla Kingdom, is a historic site. It includes temples, palace ruins, royal tombs, pagodas, Buddhist art, and the world's oldest celestial observatory.

Hwaseong This large 18th-century military fortress once surrounded the city of Suwon. Built to protect the tomb of King Chongjo's father, it still sits majestically overlooking the now-modern city.

Gochang, Hwasun, and Ganghwa Dolmen Sites The hundreds of dolmens (stone tomb markers) found at the prehistoric burial grounds near Gochang, Hwasun, and Ganghwa are the largest concentrations of such dolmens in the world.

Jeju-do and Lava Tubes On the volcanic island of Jeju, there are a number of natural lava tubes originating from the Geomunoreum volcano. Also part of the natural heritage designation is Seongsan Ilchulbong, a peak formed by a volcanic eruption about 100,000 years ago.

Day 2: Explore Seoul

Tour **Changdeokgung Palace** ★★★ (p. 79)—reserve a guided tour in advance. English tours are held Tuesday to Sunday at 11:30am and 2:30pm. Then take a walk around the city's cultural street, **Insadong** ★★★ (p. 70), where you may want to stop for a cup of Korean tea or lunch of traditional temple cuisine (always vegetarian, and usually made with seasonal ingredients) at **Sanchon** ★★★ (p. 70). Then, squeeze your way between crowded stalls at **Namdaemun Market** (p. 96). Enjoy a quiet dinner or, if you want a livelier

South Korea in 1 or 2 Weeks

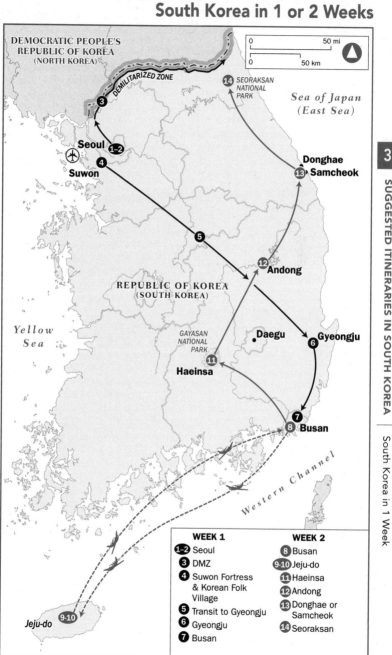

WEEK 1
- **1-2** Seoul
- **3** DMZ
- **4** Suwon Fortress & Korean Folk Village
- **5** Transit to Gyeongju
- **6** Gyeongju
- **7** Busan

WEEK 2
- **8** Busan
- **9-10** Jeju-do
- **11** Haeinsa
- **12** Andong
- **13** Donghae or Samcheok
- **14** Seoraksan

night out, take a dinner cruise on the **Han River** (p. 92). If you can't sleep, head for late-night (or early-morning) shopping action at **Dongdaemun Market ★★★** (p. 95).

Day 3: Take a Tour of the DMZ ★★★

Allow a whole day to take an organized tour to **Panmunjeom,** also known as the Demilitarized Zone (p. 122). If you're not too exhausted upon your return, head to the top of Namsan and the **N Seoul Tower** (p. 88) to admire the view of the city lights.

Day 4: Suwon Fortress ★★★ & Korean Folk Village ★

Take a subway to Suwon and get a ticket to the **Korean Folk Village** (p. 111) at the tourist information booth. Free shuttles run every hour on the half-hour. Explore the village and linger over a lunch of traditional food like *janchi gooksu* (feast noodles, a simple somen noodle soup with broth and a bit of seasoning), *nokdu buchingae* (flatcakes made from ground mung beans), *naengmyeon* (buckwheat noodles in a chilled beef broth), and *makgeolli* (a milky, unrefined, traditional rice wine), served as you sit at outdoor tables. Take a free shuttle back and catch a bus to the **Suwon Hwaseong** (p. 112). Stretch your legs and work off lunch with a nice walk around the stone fortress. Enjoy a dinner of the famous Suwon *galbi* (marinated short ribs) and then head back to Seoul for a good night's rest.

Day 5: Transit to Gyeongju

Allow half a day to travel to Gyeongju (going by either train or bus takes 4½ hr.). Explore some of downtown's historic sites, such as **Tumuli Park ★★★** (p. 236), where the Shilla kings are buried, and **Cheomseongdae Observatory** (p. 236). If you get a chance, try one of the Gyeongju's sweet bread snacks such as *hwangnambbang* (bread filled with a sweet red-bean filling).

Day 6: Explore Gyeongju

If you explored the downtown area the previous evening, pick up something for lunch and take the Gyeongju City Tour Bus to explore points farther out (which are difficult to see individually), including **Seokguram Grotto ★★★** (p. 237), where a stone Buddha sits serenely inside a man-made granite cave, and **Bulguksa Temple ★★★** (p. 236). Take an evening train or bus to Busan.

Day 7: A Brief Visit of Busan

Finish your whirlwind trip with a morning walk on one of Busan's sandy beaches, an exploration of **Jagalchi Market ★★★** (p. 322) and a lunch of *hwae* (raw fish) fresh from the water. Catch a high-speed KTX train back to Seoul for your flight back home.

SOUTH KOREA IN 2 WEEKS: CULTURE & NATURAL BEAUTY

Since you'll already have explored Seoul and Busan, South Korea's two major cities, an extra week will allow you to spend some time getting a better sense of the beautiful countryside and historic sites that South Korea has to offer.

Days 1–7

Follow the "South Korea in 1 Week" itinerary outlined above.

Day 8: Extra Time in Busan

A week's extension allows you to spend an extra day in Busan, exploring the city's charms and enjoying its nightlife. Visit the dragon temple, **Yonggungsa** ★★ (p. 311), with its rocky cliffs overlooking the sea, or the ancient temple, **Beomeosa** ★★ (p. 311). For a bit of relaxation, try the hot springs at **Heosimcheong Spa** ★★★ (p. 315). Enjoy dinner overlooking the bridge from one of the cafes on **Gwangalli Beach** ★★ (p. 316) or take a nighttime stroll on the boardwalk in **Haeundae** ★★ (p. 317).

Days 9 & 10: Korea's Volcanic Island

Catch a morning flight to **Jeju-do** ★★★ (see chapter 11). If possible, pick up a rental car at the airport. Otherwise, take a bus to your hotel and check in before heading over to the **Jungmun Resort Complex** (p. 383). Explore the area, including the **Yeomiji Botanical Garden** (p. 383) and **Jusangjeolli Cliffs** (p. 385). Visit the **Jeju Folk Village** ★★ (p. 388), check out **Manjang Cave,** and either enjoy the scenery around **Seongsan Ilchulbong** ★★★ (p. 387) or hike part of South Korea's highest peak, **Hallasan** (p. 382).

Day 11: Back to the Mainland & Tranquil Haeinsa ★★★

Take a flight back to Busan or Daegu. Grab a quick lunch before catching a bus to South Korea's most celebrated temple, **Haeinsa** ★★★ (p. 281), in Gayasan. Do an overnight temple stay here (p. 282) or overnight in Daegu.

Day 12: Traditional Aristocratic Culture

Take a bus or train to Andong and explore the **Hahoe Folk Village** ★★★ (p. 256) and the **Mask Museum** ★ (p. 256). If you don't mind roughing it a bit, overnight in a *hanok* (traditional house) inside the folk village and enjoy an old-fashioned Korean meal (p. 257).

Days 13 & 14: South Korea's Scenic Beauty

Take a bus to **Donghae** (p. 357) or **Samcheok** (p. 359) and spend the afternoon exploring the beaches and the caves there. Spend the night nearby and the next day take a bus to **Seoraksan** ★★★ (p. 326). Spend the day hiking the various trails, exploring the natural beauty of the area and its many waterfalls and valleys. Take a bus back to Seoul to catch your flight home.

SOUTH KOREA WITH KIDS: A 1-WEEK TOUR

Although traveling with children can be a challenge, South Korea can be truly rewarding fun for the whole family. Koreans take their children everywhere and at most attractions those 5 and under get in free. You'll only get a small glimpse of what the country has to offer in such a short time, but the little ones will have something to look forward to when they return.

Day 1: Arrive in Seoul

Arrive at Seoul's Incheon Airport and take a limousine bus to your hotel. Depending on what time your flight gets in, head on down to **Namdaemun Market** (p. 96) and browse the live seafood stalls or the alley for stationery and toys.

Day 2: Discover Seoul

Hop on the city's efficient subway system (kids 5 and under ride free) and head over to **Gyeongbokgung** ★★ (p. 81). If you time it right, you can see the changing of the royal guards, which is entertaining for both kids and adults. Nearby is the **National Museum of Korea** ★★★ (p. 85), which has a children's museum inside with hands-on exhibits.

Day 3: A Taste of Korea's Past

Take the subway to **Suwon** (p. 109) and visit the **Korean Folk Village** ★ (p. 111), where the children can participate in the many folk games from the past that are played here. Lunch in the village and then take a bus to the **Suwon Hwaseong** ★★★ (p. 112), where you can ride the dragon train around the fortress wall. Have dinner at one of Suwon's galbi restaurants, where you can cook meat on your own tabletop grill.

Day 4: A Day of Play

Head over to one of the Seoul-area amusement parks: **Lotte World** (p. 90), **Everland** (p. 110), or the **Seoul Grand Park** (p. 134). Spend the day riding the rides and enjoying the other amusements.

Day 5: Fun Away from the Big City

Take a morning train or bus to **Gangneung** (p. 340) and spend the afternoon on one of its many beaches or exploring the seaside town. Take a break for a hands-on art adventure at **Haslla Art World** (p. 343), where you can create your own masterpieces and explore the gardens.

Day 6: A Day of Water Fun

After your first 5 days, you're probably exhausted and, if you're visiting in the summer, pretty hot. So take a bus up to **Seorak Waterpia** (Seorak Water Park) ★ (p. 331) at the Hanhwa Resort and spend the day soaking your aches away while the kids enjoy the water slides and other splashy fun.

Day 7: A Last Bit of Nature Before Heading Home

Spend the morning hiking one of the easier trails in **Seoraksan** ★★★ (p. 326) and catch a bus back to Seoul. If you have a long wait for your flight check out the Incheon Airport's Traditional Culture Experience (on the third floor, next to gate 40), where kids can make traditional fans and other Korean handicrafts. The staff speak English, and entry is free daily from 7am to 10pm.

SOUTH KOREA'S SACRED SITES IN 11 DAYS

Since Buddhism was first introduced on the peninsula over 1,600 years ago, hundreds of thousands of temples have been built. Although the rise of Neo-Confucianism

South Korea with Kids

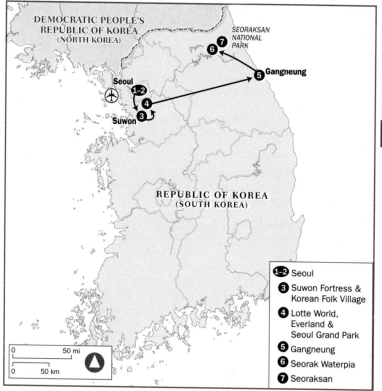

Map legend:

- **1-2** Seoul
- **3** Suwon Fortress & Korean Folk Village
- **4** Lotte World, Everland & Seoul Grand Park
- **5** Gangneung
- **6** Seorak Waterpia
- **7** Seoraksan

during the Joseon Dynasty (1392–1910) threatened to drive the religion out, Buddhism survived. There are now over 11,000 temples (many of them small) located throughout South Korea. Many are hidden retreats perched on the slopes of mountains, overlooking craggy cliffs, or simply sitting pretty next to running streams. This tour will allow you to get a good overview of some of the very best.

Day 1: Arrive in Seoul

Arrive at Incheon Airport and take the limousine bus into the city. Take the afternoon or evening to get acclimated to the city by enjoying a simple meal or a cup of tea at a traditional tea shop in **Insadong** (p. 70).

Day 2: A Bit of Peace in the City

Enjoy a tour of **Gyeongbokgung** ★★ (p. 81), **Changdeokgung** ★★★ (p. 79), and **Biwon (Secret Garden)** ★★★ (p. 80). Have a lunch of vegetarian temple cuisine at **Sanchon** ★★★ (p. 70). Stroll around the Insadong area and visit a temple in the city, such as **Hwagyesa** (p. 87) or **Bongeunsa** (p. 86).

Day 3: Arrive at a Mountain Temple

Take a bus to **Donghae** (p. 357) and have lunch at one of the many restaurants there. Overnight at **Samhwasa** (p. 358) as part of the temple stay, which includes a tea ceremony, tour of the temple, traditional vegetarian fare, and other programs such as Zen meditation or a refreshing walk in the predawn hours.

Day 4: Spend the Day in Nature

Take a bus into **Seoraksan** ★★★ (p. 326) and explore the natural beauty of the area. Visit **Sinheungsa** ★ (p. 331), one of the oldest Zen meditation temples in the world, and **Naksansa** ★★★ (p. 336) to see how a temple recovers after a fire. Overnight in Seoraksan, and enjoy a sauna or a soak at a public bath.

Day 5: The Historic Center

Catch a bus to **Gyeongju** (p. 231) and explore **Bulguksa** ★★★ (p. 236) and the **Seokguram Grotto** ★★★ (p. 237), one of Asia's nicest Buddhist shrines. Overnight in Gyeongju.

Day 6: Explore Korea's Buddhist Heritage

If you want to explore some hidden Buddhist treasures nestled in mountain ranges and valleys, take a bus or taxi to **Namsan** (p. 239). Be sure to pack a lunch and bring plenty to drink because you'll spend at least 4 to 5 hours hiking. You'll be rewarded with over 100 temples or temple ruins, and dozens of stone pagodas and Buddha statues. Take a bus or train to Busan to overnight there.

Day 7: Bustling Busan

Wake up early to catch the sunrise at **Yonggungsa** ★★ (p. 311), with its rocky cliffs overlooking the sea. Then head over to ancient **Beomeosa** (p. 311) and enjoy its lovely surroundings. Enjoy a seafood dinner in **Haeundae** (p. 317) or **Gwangalli Beach** (p. 316).

Day 8: Haeinsa ★★★

Catch a bus to Korea's most celebrated temple, **Haeinsa** ★★★ (p. 281) in Gayasan to see the Tripitaka Koreana, Buddhist scripture carved on thousands of wooden blocks. Do a temple stay there or overnight in **Jirisan** (p. 223).

Day 9: Visit One of South Korea's Holiest Mountains

Take in the early-morning fog and low clouds encircling the mountains. Visit one of Jirisan's many temples, such as **Hwaeomsa** ★★★ (p. 224) and **Songgwangsa** ★★★ (p. 215), one of the three Buddhist "jewels" in South Korea. If you have a chance, stop by the **Boseong Tea Plantation** for picturesque landscapes and some green tea to cleanse your mind and body.

Day 10: Seaside Views of Bori-am ★★★

Buses run infrequently here, so plan accordingly. Head to **Namhae** (p. 285) and hike up to **Bori-am** ★★★ (p. 286), one of South Korea's three major holy sites. Overnight in Namhae or nearby Tongyeong.

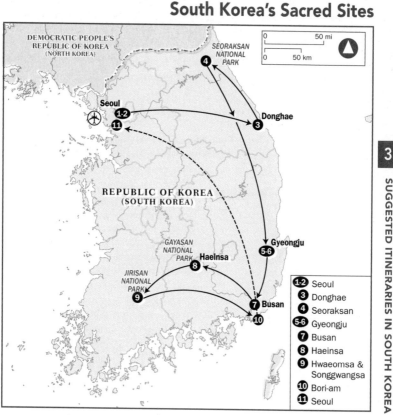

Day 11: Seoul Again

Take a bus back to Seoul and enjoy the afternoon exploring the markets, or stop by **Jogyesa** (p. 87), picking up some Buddhist souvenirs at a shop nearby before heading to the airport.

SEOUL

The charm of Seoul lies in its contradictions and surprises. This capital city, over 500 years old, still maintains its stately palaces, such as those in Jongno, under the shadows of towering skyscrapers. Rub elbows with Seoul's 10 million residents (a quarter of South Korea's population) in the city's modern underground on your way to hip galleries in Samcheongdong, funky cafes, traditional markets at Namdaemun Shijang, and Buddhist temples.

4

THINGS TO DO   The palaces in **Jongno** are a must-see to understand South Korea's history, but the galleries and *hanok* (traditional house) in **Samcheongdong** also give insight into the culture. Being jostled by little old ladies is part of the fun while you haggle your way through **Namdaemun Shijang.** End the day on top of **Namsan** for a nighttime view of the city.

SHOPPING   Luxury brands fill the tree-lined streets of **Shinsadong** and **Apgujeong** and the young love the cute shops in **Myeongdong.** The bargains, however, can be found in the traditional markets. Immersing yourself into the maelstrom as you haggle your way through **Namdaemun Shijang** is a must for any shopper. Shop for souvenirs in **Insadong** or ceramics from a **Samcheongdong** boutique.

RESTAURANTS & DINING   World-class gourmet restaurants line **Apgujeong** and **Gangnam's** fashionable streets, while **Itaewon** sports an international flair, ranging from French bistros to New York-style delis. Choose the freshest fish fare from a tank in **Noryangjin Shijang** or grab a flatcake from a street stall in **Gwangjang Shijang.** Or rest your tired feet with traditional tea at a converted hanok in **Samcheongdong** or **Insadong.** Whatever your tastes, you won't leave Seoul hungry.

ENTERTAINMENT & NIGHTLIFE   Seoulites work hard and play even harder. Friendships and even business deals are solidified in the city's *hofs* (German-style beer gardens) and *makgeolli* (the Korean milky rice wine) bars. Clubbers head to **Hongdae** night spots or sit for a quiet brew in one of the many cafes there. Young urbanites sip from glasses in an **Apgujeong** wine bar or get some late-night shopping done in **Myeongdong.**

ORIENTATION
Getting There & Away
BY PLANE

Seoul is served by two airports, but the majority of international passengers arrive at **Incheon International Airport** (ICN; ✆ **1577-2600;** www.airport.kr/eng). Located 52km (32 miles) west of Seoul, it is the world's third-largest passenger terminal and one of the best airports, winning awards every year. Arrivals are on the first floor, where you will find global ATMs, foreign currency exchanges (daily 6am–10pm), the **Incheon Tourist Information Center** (℃ 032/743-0011; daily 7am–10pm), the **Korea Tourism Organization Information Center** (KTO; ℃ **1330;** 7am–10pm), and the **Hotel Information Center** (℃ **032/743-2570;** 9am–10pm), a private company that offers some discounts to mid-range and high-end hotels. The second floor has a few domestic flights to and from Jeju-do and Busan, as well as an **Internet cafe lounge** (℃ **032/743-7427**). There are a handful of free computers on the bottom level, with a 30-minute maximum usage if there is a wait, but there is free Wi-Fi throughout if you have your own device.

Airport limousine buses are the best way to get into town. They run every 10 to 30 minutes, starting daily around 5:30am until 10pm. A trip to downtown Seoul takes about 90 minutes (longer during high-traffic times). **Limousine buses** cost around ₩10,000, while **KAL deluxe limousine buses** cost around ₩15,000 and stop at 20 of the major hotels in Seoul. Regular taxis charge around ₩40,000 to ₩60,000 to go downtown, while deluxe taxis (they're black) charge ₩63,000 to ₩90,000. Taxi fares can be considerably more during high-traffic times. After midnight, regular taxi fares increase by 20% (deluxe taxi fares stay the same). Your taxi driver will make you pay the ₩7,500 toll charge for the expressway, as well.

The **Airport Railroad (AREX)** connects Incheon to Seoul Station. From there you can connect to other parts of the city's subway. If you have heavy luggage, a taxi or a limousine bus may be your best bet, since the subway's staircases (and Seoul Station's numerous escalators) can make travel a bit awkward.

The older **Gimpo International Airport** (GMP; ℃ **02/2660-2483;** www.airport.co.kr/doc/gimpo_eng) handles all domestic flights except for a few to and from Haneda (Tokyo) and Osaka, Japan, and a flight to and from Shanghai from a separate international terminal. It is located south of the Han River in western Seoul. Arrivals are on the first floor, where you'll find a **Tourist Information Booth** (℃ **02/3707-9465;** daily 9am–9pm). *Tip:* This booth offers free Internet access. The second floor is for check-ins and the third floor is for departures. You'll find all the restaurants, duty-free shops, banks, lost luggage, and a medical center on the fourth floor. There's a pharmacy on the third floor.

The easiest way to get downtown from Gimpo is via subway—take line 5 (₩1,100 to City Hall). Taxis to city hall (18km/11 miles) are considerably more expensive, around ₩25,000 for regular taxis and ₩35,000 for deluxe taxis. Limousine buses run anywhere from ₩4,500 to ₩12,000, depending on your destination.

BY TRAIN

Seoul is the center of an extensive rail system operated by the **Korean National Railroad** (KORAIL, ℃ **1544-7788;** http://info.korail.com/2007/eng/eng_index.jsp). KORAIL operates the **KTX (Korea Train Express)** bullet train. There are two lines with stops in major cities. The Gyeongbu line goes to Busan (Seoul to Busan tickets are ₩50,600–₩74,600) in under 3 hours via Daejeon and the Honam line, which travels through west Daejeon, and ends at Gwangju (₩37,500–₩52,500 from Seoul's Yongsan Station) or Mokpo (₩43,300–₩60,600 from Seoul). Tickets are available online, at most travel agents in Seoul, or at ticket counters and automatic ticket machines at the station. You should book ahead, especially if you plan on traveling during holidays, such as the Lunar New Year (usually early Feb) or Chuseok, Korean Thanksgiving (usually sometime in Sept). See "Peak Travel Times," in chapter 2, for exact dates.

Seoul

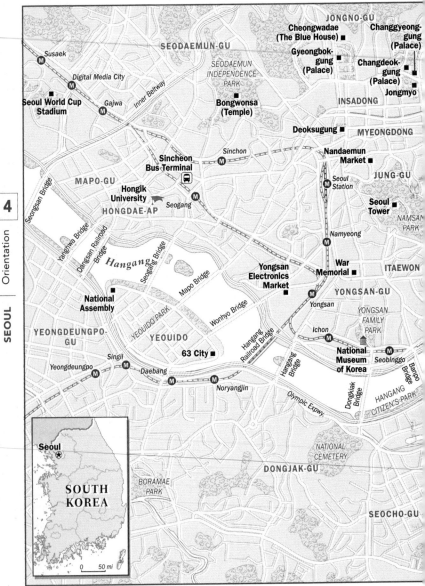

JONGNO-GU

Cheongwadae
(The Blue House) ■

Changgyeong-
gung
(Palace)

Gyeongbok-
gung
(Palace) ■

Changdeok-
gung
(Palace) ■

SEODAEMUN-GU

Susaek Ⓜ

Digital Media City Ⓜ

Jongmyo

SEODAEMUN
INDEPENDENCE
PARK

INSADONG

Seoul World Cup
Stadium ■

Gajwa Ⓜ

Inner Beltway

Bongwonsa
(Temple) ■

Deoksugung ■

MYEONGDONG

Sinchon

Nandaemun
Market ■

JUNG-GU

Sincheon
Bus Terminal 🚌

Seoul
Station Ⓜ

Seoul
Tower ■

Seongsan Bridge

MAPO-GU

Hongik
University ✈

Ⓜ

Yanghwa Bridge

HONGDAE-AP

Seogang

Ⓜ

NAMSAN
PARK

Namyeong Ⓜ

Dangsan Railroad
Bridge

Seogang Bridge

War
Memorial ■

ITAEWON

Hangang

Yongsan
Electronics
Market ■

YONGSAN-GU

Mapo Bridge

Yongsan Ⓜ

YONGSAN
FAMILY
PARK

National
Assembly ■

YEOUIDO PARK

Wonhyo Bridge

Ichon Ⓜ

YEONGDEUNGPO-
GU

YEOUIDO

National
Museum
of Korea ■

Seobinggo Ⓜ

Bampo Bridge

Singil Ⓜ

63 City ■

Hangang
Railroad Bridge

Hangang
Bridge

HANGANG
CITIZEN'S PARK

Yeongdeungpo Ⓜ

Daebang Ⓜ

Dongkiak
Bridge

Noryangjin Ⓜ

Olympic Expwy.

NATIONAL
CEMETERY

DONGJAK-GU

Seoul ★

SOUTH
KOREA

BORAMAE
PARK

SEOCHO-GU

0   50 mi

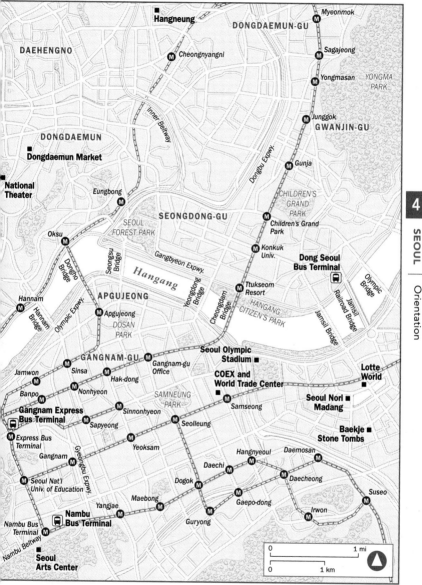

Hangneung ■

DONGDAEMUN-GU

DAEHENGNO

Ⓜ Myeonmok

Ⓜ Cheongnyangni

Ⓜ Sagajeong

Ⓜ Yongmasan

YONGMA
PARK

Inner Beltway

Ⓜ Junggok

GWANJIN-GU

DONGDAEMUN

Dongdaemun Market ■

National
Theater

Eungbong Ⓜ

Dongbu Expwy.

Ⓜ Gunja

CHILDREN'S
GRAND
PARK

SEONGDONG-GU

SEOUL
FOREST PARK

Ⓜ Children's Grand
Park

Oksu Ⓜ

Dongho Bridge

Seongsu Bridge

Gangbyeon Expwy.

Ⓜ Konkuk
Univ.

Dong Seoul
Bus Terminal 🚌

Olympic Bridge

Hangang

Yeongdong Bridge

Cheongdam Bridge

Ⓜ Ttukseom
Resort

Jamsil Railroad Bridge

Jamsil Bridge

Hannam Ⓜ

Olympic Expwy.

Hannam Bridge

APGUJEONG

Ⓜ Apgujeong

DOSAN
PARK

HANGANG
CITIZEN'S PARK

Seoul Olympic
Stadium ■

GANGNAM-GU Ⓜ

Jamwon Ⓜ

Ⓜ Sinsa

Gangnam-gu
Office

Hak-dong

COEX and
World Trade Center ■

Lotte
World ■

Banpo Ⓜ

Ⓜ Nonhyeon

SAMNEUNG
PARK

Seoul Nori ■
Madang

Gangnam Express
Bus Terminal 🚌

Ⓜ Sinnonhyeon

Samseong Ⓜ

Ⓜ Sapyeong

Ⓜ Seolleung

Baekje ■
Stone Tombs

Ⓜ Express Bus
Terminal

Gyeongbu Expwy.

Yeoksam Ⓜ

Gangnam

Hangnyeoul Ⓜ

Daemosan Ⓜ

Ⓜ Seoul Nat'l
Univ. of Education

Daechi Ⓜ

Ⓜ Daecheong

Yangjae

Maebong Ⓜ

Dogok Ⓜ

Suseo Ⓜ

Nambu Bus
Terminal Ⓜ

Nambu Beltway

Nambu
Bus Terminal 🚌

Guryong

Gaepo-dong Ⓜ

Irwon Ⓜ

Seoul
Arts Center

0   1 mi
0   1 km

4

SEOUL | Orientation

Visitors can buy a voucher for a **KR Pass** (www.korail.com/krpass.jsp) online or from travel agents in their home country and exchange these vouchers in Seoul for passes for unlimited travel on the railways (for KTX, Saemauel, and Mugunghwa trains). The passes are not available for purchase in South Korea. Once you arrive, you'll need to exchange the voucher in Seoul for the actual pass. The KR Passes are good for rides during consecutive days in increments of 1 (₩58,200), 3 (₩84,600), 5 (₩127,000), 7 (₩160,400), and 10 (₩185,100) days. A Saver Pass can be purchased for two to five people traveling together at a 10% discount. Those 13 to 24 in age can get a Youth Pass for 20% less. Children 4 to 12 pay 50% of the adult price, while those 4 and under travel free. Purchase your KR Pass on the **Korean Railroad** website (www.korail.com/krpass.jsp), from **STA Travel** (U.S. ☏ **800/777-0112** or 02/733-9494 in Seoul; www.statravelgroup.com) or **U.S .Travel** (www.koreatour.us) in Los Angeles (☏ **213/383-5511**), New York (☏ **212/643-2005**) or Hong Kong (☏ **852/2152-3133**). The actual pass can be picked up at the Railroad Information Center in Incheon (☏ **032/741-7788**), at Seoul Station (☏ **02/3149-2530**) or at Busan Station (☏ **051/440-2506**). In Seoul, STA Pass vouchers can be exchanged for train tickets at **Kises Tour,** located in the YMCA Building, 5th Floor, Jongno 2-ga. Take subway line 1 to Jonggak, exit 3 (Mon–Fri 9am–6pm; Sat 9am–3pm).

Seoul Station (☏ **1544-7788** or 3149-2530) is the most central of the country's train stations. Most railroad routes start here, except for the Jung-ang and Gyeongc-hun lines. From here, you can catch a train to Busan and Gyeongju on the Gyeongbu line. Seoul Station can be accessed via subway lines 1 or 2 (exits 2 or 13).

Yongsan Station (☏ **02/3780-5408**) is a popular station for catching the KTX train to other cities. Trains along the Honam line depart from here. To get there, take subway line 1 to Yongsan Station or line 4 to Sinyongsan Station (exit 4).

Cheongnyangni Station (☏ **02/3299-7152**) has trains that take you to Gyeongju and other places in Gyeongsangbuk-do and cities in Gangwon-do. Popular destinations from here include Gangneung (on the eastern coast) and Andong, a town well-known for its traditional village. Take subway line 1 to Cheongnyangni Station (exit 4).

For trains that run along the Gyeongchun line (a scenic route that travels along the Han River), get tickets at **Seongbuk Station** (☏ **02/3299-7194**). This station is popular, especially for weekenders wanting to get away to Chuncheon, Cheongpy-eong, Gapyeong, or Gangchon. Take subway line 1 to Seongbuk Station (exit 1).

BY BUS

You can take a bus from Seoul to and from any region and any city in South Korea. Express buses to every major bus station in the country originate from either the Seoul Express Bus Terminal or the Central City Terminal next door. To get to smaller towns, you can change buses or take a direct bus from one of Seoul's smaller bus stations. Contact the **Korean Express Bus Lines Association** (☏ **02/538-6469** or 1588-6900, 24 hr.; www.kobus.co.kr/web/eng) for schedules and other info.

Express buses to the Gyeongnam area (Gyubu line), Chungcheong area (Guma line), and Gangwon-do (Yeongdong line) start from the **Seoul Express Bus Termi-nal,** 19-4 Banpo-dong, Seocho-gu (☏ **02/535-4151;** www.exterminal.co.kr). Buses on the Honam line that go to Jeolla-do to the south and the Namhaeseon (southern coastal line) start from the **Central City Terminal,** 19-4 Banpo-dong, Seocho-gu (☏ **02/6282-0114;** www.centralcityseoul.co.kr/shopguide/sub_facilities_terminal. php), which is located right next door. Both bus terminals can be accessed by subway. Take line 3 or 7 (line 3 is easier) to the Express Bus Terminal Station and take the underground passage that leads to the bus terminals.

Buses from the **DongSeoul Bus Terminal,** 546-1 Gui-dong, Gwangjin-gu (© **02/446-8000;** www.ti21.co.kr), go primarily north and east from Seoul. You can catch a bus to Andong, Gangneung, Sokcho, and Wonju from here. Also, buses from this terminal take the scenic (but longer) route to Seoraksan National Park. You can get to the DongSeoul Bus Terminal by taking subway line 2 to Gangbyeon (exit 4).

The **Nambu Bus Terminal,** 1446-1 Seocho-dong, Seocho-gu (© **02/521-8550;** www.nambuterminal.co.kr), services mostly the southern region. Popular destinations from this station include Osan, Pyongtaek, and Songnisan National Park. You can get to the Nambu Bus Terminal by taking subway line 3 to the Nambu Bus Terminal Station (exit 5).

Buses from the **Sangbong Bus Terminal,** 83-1 Sangbong-dong, Jungnang-gu (© **02/435-2122** ext. 8; http://tm.jamycar.co.kr), go generally east and north. You can get to Chuncheon and Sokcho from this station. You can get to the Sangbong Bus Terminal by taking subway line 7 to the Sangbong (exit 2). Walk straight for about 5 minutes and the bus terminal will be on your right, across from the E-Mart.

Visitor Information

The **Korea Tourism Organization (KTO),** B1, KTO Building (T2 Tower), 40, Cheongyecheonno, Jung-gu, Seoul 100-180 (© **02/7299-600;** http://english.visit korea.or.kr; daily 9am–8pm), publishes a variety of free brochures and maps, and provides transportation, hotel reservations, and other traveler's assistance. You can also call © **1330,** the 24-hour **Korea Travel Phone,** for assistance in English. Dial Seoul's area code (02) for info about the city from elsewhere in the country.

The KTO has several tourist information locations throughout Seoul. There are two at **Incheon Airport,** between gates 12–13 and gates 1–2 on the arrival floor (© **032/743-2600,** ext. 3; daily 7am–10pm), which are the easiest places to pick up free maps and other information about the city in English. The headquarters' office (address listed above) also offers free Internet access and a travel agency desk (Mon–Fri 9am–6pm). There are other locations at **Seoul City Hall,** 2nd Floor, Main Hall, Taepyeong-no 1(il)-ga (daily 9am–9pm); **Dongdaemun,** near the construction site of the future Dongdaemun design plaza (daily 9am–5pm); **Myeongdong,** in front of the Metro Midopa building, Namdaemun-no 2(i)-ga (daily 9am–5pm); **Insadong,** Gwanhun-dong, 155-20, Jongno-gu (daily 10am–10pm); and **Itaewon,** on the basement level of Itaewon subway station (line 6), Itaewon-dong, Yongsan-gu (daily 9am–9pm).

City Layout

Your first impression of Seoul may be that it is a sprawling city of hundreds of high-rise apartments and modern buildings with the occasional historic building randomly thrown in. Once you get to know the city, you'll see that it's a patchwork of distinct neighborhoods, each with its own flavor and character. The primary landmark is the **Han-gahng** (Han River), which runs east to west through the city.

Small streets in Seoul rarely have names or signs indicating what they're called, but larger streets have signs in both Korean and English. Buildings are not always numbered and, when they are, the numbers may not make logical sense (since they were numbered by when they were built, not by physical order). Addresses don't give street names either, so it's nearly impossible to find a location by address alone. The easiest way to find a place is to start from a subway station or a major landmark and make your way from there. Luckily, the subway system is widespread and efficient, and announcements and signs are in English. Of course, residents are usually willing to help with directions, even if they don't speak English.

Neighborhoods in Brief

Seoul is made up of districts, neighborhoods, and areas, and it can be difficult to get a sense of where things are. To make matters more complicated, neighborhoods may overlap districts, or be broken down into multiple areas, each with its own name. Use the maps provided here, including the subway map on the back inside cover, and major landmarks to orient yourself.

Jongno At the center of the city, Jongno (not to be confused with the Jongno-gu district) is the oldest part of downtown Seoul. Here you will find the Gwanghwamun (the large gate) and Namsan (South Mountain), easily recognizable by the massive tower at its peak.

Insadong This area, nestled within Jongno-gu, used to be the home of royalty and *yangban* (aristocratic) families, but that was during the Joseon Dynasty (1392–1910). Insadong is now filled with art galleries and traditional handicraft shops, dotted between souvenir shops. Duck into an alley off the main drag to enjoy a traditional Korean meal or take a peaceful break alongside artists and monks in one of Insadong's many tea shops.

Samcheong-dong Located up the hill from Insadong, this area is the city's contemporary art center as galleries have migrated here from Insadong. Many art centers have their own cafes or restaurants, so you can enjoy a quick bite while admiring the paintings or ceramics in a renovated hanok. Nearby is the **Bukchon Hanok Maeul**, a neighborhood of traditional homes overlooking the city below.

Myeongdong The major shopping district for clothing and accessories in Seoul, Myeongdong has more midpriced and higher-priced items in its boutique shops than the two open markets of Namdaemun and Dongdaemun. Most of the action happens after dark.

Namdaemun The largest traditional market in all of Korea, Namdaemun *shijang* (market) has vendors selling clothing, local products, and pretty much everything but the kitchen sink. Many of the small shops sell their wares directly from their own factories, so you can get both retail and wholesale prices.

Dongdaemun The area around the future design plaza is home to one of the major marketplaces in South Korea, the Dongdaemun shijang. There are towering fashion malls next to small stands selling both retail and wholesale items that open at night and get really busy during the wee hours of the morning.

Itaewon Itaewon is the foreigners' district, which grew up around the American military base in Seoul. Once a shady red-light district, it has been cleaned up, and many excellent international restaurants have sprung up here. You can still find painted ladies walking down certain streets at night, but during the day it's a shopper's paradise. You'll find a vast selection of clothing, shoes, luggage, and leather goods, mostly made in South Korea.

Sinchon/Idae-ap (Ewha University area)/ Hongdae-ap (Hong-ik University area) These neighborhoods surround Yonsei, Sogang, Hong-ik, and Ewha universities. The area near the entrance to the Ewha Women's University is great for shopping for women's clothes and accessories (that is, if you're a size 6 or smaller—Korean sizes run very small). The area in front of Hong-ik University (Hongdae-ap) is known for its hopping nightlife and cafe culture. Indeed, all of Seoul's university neighborhoods are bustling with cafes, restaurants, bars, and plenty of shopping for college students and everyone else.

Daehangno When Seoul National University moved from this area in 1975, Marronnier Park was created on what had been the university's campus. Surrounded by other colleges, the park became a cultural and arts center for students. There are outdoor performances and dozens of small theaters, mostly running Korean productions.

Gangnam This modern and affluent area, which means "south of the river," has wider streets than you'll find elsewhere in Seoul and a variety of high-end restaurants. Home of the COEX Mall, Gangnam sports luxury stores and therefore attracts a younger crowd than the open markets found in other parts of the city.

Apgujeong Known as the "Beverly Hills of Seoul," this neighborhood (which is part of the Gangnam district) attracts those who have money and want to spend it on looking beautiful. The area offers world-class aestheticians

and plastic surgeons, as well as upscale restaurants with prices to match. International luxury stores like Gucci and Versace all have stores here.

Jamsil The Jamsil area is home to South Korea's largest indoor amusement park, Lotte World, and the Seoul Sports Complex. The area also houses the early tombs from the Baekje era (18 B.C.–A.D. 660). You'll also find the country's largest wholesale market for agricultural and marine products here, Garak-dong Shijang.

GETTING AROUND

BY SUBWAY Seoul is covered by an extensive and modern subway system, the **Seoul Metro** (www.smrt.co.kr/main/index/index002.jsp). The system is fast, clean, safe, and cheap, and runs frequently. But the best things about the Metro are that it can take you anywhere and everywhere you'll want to go in Seoul, and the maps and recordings are in English.

There are two important things to remember about the subway. The first is to avoid rush hours (weekdays from about 8–9am and 6–7pm) if you can help it, unless you enjoy being packed in like a sardine next to dozens of strangers. The second is that the trains stop running around midnight (which is also when taxi fares go up about 20%–50%), so it's best to plan your late-night travel in advance. Trains start running again at 5:30am.

Although you can buy single fares, it is much more convenient (and cheaper) to buy a pass—it will save you the hassle and time of having to wait in line to buy your ticket. The minimum fare is ₩1,150 or ₩1,050 with a **T-money card** (http://eng.t-money.co.kr) or **Seoul City Pass+** (http://www.seoulcitypass.com). *Note:* Remember to hold on to your ticket or card, as you'll need it to exit the station, as well.

You can buy or recharge a **T-money card** or a **Seoul City Pass+** (www.seoulcity-pass.com), which functions like a T-money card for tourists, at subway stations, at kiosks near bus stops, and at convenience stores displaying the T-money logo. The cards can be used on buses, subways, and some taxis, and allow free or discounted transfers on buses and subways. Just touch the card to the sensor both when you enter and when you exit a station or bus. The prepaid card has a base fee of ₩3,000 and, once purchased, can be loaded in amounts ranging from ₩1,000 to ₩90,000 from an automated travel card recharging machine, located at every subway station, or from 24-hour convenience stores (e.g. GS25, Family Mart, Buy the Way, or Mini-Stop). You can use the card for purchases at these same convenience stores, where you also can get a refund for any unused amount at the end of your visit.

The Seoul City Pass+ card can also be used at Kyobo Bookstore, Lotte World, Daemyung Resort, select vending machines, self-serve lockers, KTL public phones, some internet cafes, and a few taxis (the ones that have the card reader). It also provides discounts to some theaters, museums, and restaurants.

SEOUL CITY tour BUS

This double-decker tour bus, run by the city of Seoul, is an economical and efficient way to see the city's major tourist destinations. The main downtown tour starts in front of the Donghwa DFS in Gwanghwamun (subway line 5, exit 6 of Gwanghwamun), but you can jump on at any of the 27 stops. The buses leave daily, every 30 minutes from 9am to 7pm, with a full tour taking 2 hours. Tour guides speak English and Japanese, and can get by in a few other languages. They also provide headsets with information available in five languages. Just look for the red, white, and blue Seoul City Tour Bus signs in front of any of the 27 locales. A 1-day pass costs ₩10,000 for adults, ₩8,000 for children, and you can purchase tickets at the Gwanghwamun counter or on the bus itself. The Cheonggye/Palace Tour stops at 13 locations and costs ₩2,000 more per adult. The night courses are rather boring surveys of the Han River's bridges. **Note:** Buses do not run on Mondays, unless the Monday is a national holiday. ℂ **02/777-6090;** http://en.seoulcitybus.com.

When you leave the city, any unused amount on the card, up to ₩20,000 (minus the ₩3,000 card fee), can be refunded at any subway ticket office. See the Metro map on the inside back cover.

If you're in Seoul for a brief time, the **Seoul City Pass** (www.seoulcitypass.com) may be a better option for you. You can board any bus or subway 20 times within a 24-hour period (ending at midnight), including unlimited on/off privileges on the Seoul City Tour Bus (the double-decker tour buses run by the city; see box above). The pass does not include the red buses bound for Incheon or Gyeonggi-do. One-day passes cost ₩15,000, 2-day ₩25,000, and 3-day ₩35,000. Just touch your card to the sensor when you get on or off the bus, or enter or leave the subway. The passes are good until midnight each day. **Note:** The Seoul City Tour Bus does not run on Mondays.

Subway system maps are available on all trains and above each station's ticket window, but carrying a small map with you is more convenient (there's one on the back of this book). Neighborhood maps inside the stations can help you decide which of the many exits to take. The stations are generally clean and have restrooms (some may be the old "squat" style, but look for a stall with a toilet, since there usually is at least one in each bathroom). **Tip:** Public restrooms are sometimes lacking in toilet paper, so always carry a pack of tissues with you.

BY TAXI You can flag down a taxi almost anywhere in Seoul. There are two types of taxis, and both are generally clean and safe. All taxis are metered with fares determined by distance and time. On the way to Incheon Airport, passengers have to pay the road toll on top of the meter charge. Sharing a cab with strangers is supposedly illegal, but people often do it during rush hour and after midnight, when subways and buses stop running. Tipping is not necessary, but most passengers round up and let the driver keep the change.

Regular (Ilban) Taxis are usually silver, blue, or white and have a light-up "taxi" sign on top. The base fare is usually around ₩2,400 and goes up every 2km (11/4 miles), going up ₩100 every 144m (1/10 mile) or 41 seconds. Most drivers don't speak English, so it's best to have your destination written down in English (since most

Koreans learn written English in school), or, even better, in Korean. Fares for regular taxis increase 20% from midnight to 4am.

Deluxe (Mobeum) Taxis, which are black, cost almost twice as much as the regular taxis, but can be convenient for many reasons. The drivers are trained to serve foreigners and can speak basic English. Especially useful for business travelers, deluxe taxis have a free phone service, take credit cards, and will offer a receipt.

BY BUS Unlike the streamlined subway system, **Seoul's buses** (✆ 02/414-5005) can be complicated and confusing for visitors. The good news, though, is that with over 400 bus routes in the city, the buses can take you pretty much anywhere you want to go. A few buses have major destinations written in English on the outside and have audio announcing each major stop in Korean (an occasional English announcement will be made at subway stations or major tourist destinations). However, smaller stops won't have English-language announcements, the maps aren't in English, and the majority of bus drivers do not speak English. You can look up bus routes here http://bus.congnamul.com/SeoulRouteWebApp/view_english/map.jsp.

There are three types of buses and they run on the same schedule as the subways, daily from 5:30am to around midnight (a few routes go as late as 2am). Bus passes can be purchased at newsstands near bus stops in increments of ₩5,000, ₩10,000, or ₩20,000. However, it's best to use your T-money card or Seoul City Pass+. Just touch your card to the screen when you enter (at the front door) and don't forget to touch your card when you exit the bus (through the back door).

Express buses (usually red) although slightly more expensive, are usually faster and more comfortable than regular buses, since seats are available. There are fewer stops and they provide air-conditioning (a bonus in the summer), but only travel longer distances. The fare starts at ₩1,100 and can be paid with tokens, cash, bus passes, or a T-money card.

Ilban (regular) buses (blue) have more stops, but are cheaper than express buses. The fare is ₩1,000 (cheaper for students and children) and can be paid with a token, cash, a bus pass, or a T-money card. Route maps are in English on a few bus stops but not on the buses themselves.

Maeul **("village") buses** (green) shuttle people short distances in a neighborhood. The green buses cost ₩1,000 and travel only within a district. They usually take exact change only, tokens, bus passes, and T-money cards.

Tip: Whichever bus you take, you can get a free transfer with your T-money or City Pass+ card if you take a different bus (or transfer from bus to subway) within 30 minutes from when you get off. Just remember to touch your card to the screen before exiting the bus to get the discount.

BY CAR Driving around Seoul can be a hair-raising experience and is not recommended. However, you can rent a car starting at around ₩70,000 per day, cheaper for multiple days. You have to be at least 21 years old and have an International Driving Permit (IDP), which you can get in your home country before you leave. In the U.S. there are only two authorized organizations that provide IDPs—the **American Automobile Association** (www.aaa.com) and **American Automotive Touring Alliance** (✆ 800/622-7070). The best place to rent a car is at Incheon Airport. Check prices at South Korea's largest car-rental company, **KT Kumho** (✆ 02/155-1230;** www.ktkumhorent.com), or **AJ Rent-a-car** (www.ajrentacar.co.kr). Be sure to be aware of surrounding traffic and be sure not to drive in the blue lanes (usually on the left), which are reserved for buses only, 24 hours a day. Watch your speed limit on expressways, since there are hidden cameras waiting to catch you and administer stiff fines.

A safer option is to rent both a car and a driver, which costs about ₩75,000 for 3 hours and ₩142,000 for 10 hours. Your hotel concierge should be able to help you. Some high-end hotels also have their own limousine services.

ON FOOT Seoul is virtually impossible to explore by walking alone; however, certain neighborhoods are best enjoyed on foot and some degree of walking will be necessary to explore the city. Be careful when crossing streets, since Seoul drivers don't always stop for pedestrians or at red lights. Use pedestrian walkways and underpasses where available. Traffic turning right at lights does not give way to pedestrians, nor does any other traffic unless forced to do so by large groups of people bunching up to cross the road.

[FastFACTS] SEOUL

American Express

American Express in South Korea is run by Lotte card. They have a card center on the 12th floor of the Lotte Department store in Myeongdong. You can get a cash advance of up to US$500 per month with your card and passport. Euljiro 1(il)-ga (line 2). ℂ **02/759-7620~2;** http://www.americanexpress.com/korea/.

Banks, Foreign Exchange & ATMs

ATM machines in airports, train stations, bus terminals, subways, post offices, and department stores are the most foreigner-friendly. Of the major banks, Citibank ATMs are the most accessible for non-Koreans. Some ATMs are available 24/7, but many operate from 8am to midnight on weekdays and nonholidays. Most machines have a daily withdrawal limit of up to ₩700,000, but can be as low as ₩100,000 per day.

At banks in Seoul, you take a numbered ticket and wait until your number is called. If you want to exchange traveler's checks, make sure you have your passport. Banking hours in Seoul are from 9:30am to 4:30pm weekdays. Most bank employees speak some English.

Business Hours

Government offices: 9am to 6pm weekdays (Nov–Feb, offices close at 5pm), 9am to 1pm Saturday. Major department stores: Daily from 10:30am to 7:30pm including Sunday. Smaller shops: Hours vary, but usually are about the same as those for department stores. Many government-run museums and attractions close Mondays.

Currency Exchange

You can exchange money at any currency exchange booth, high-end hotels, and most banks in the city. Many exchange desks are in banks such as **Shinhan Bank** (main office: 120 Taepyeong-gro 2-ga, Jung-gu), off exit 8 at City Hall, line 2), **Hana Bank, Citibank,** and **Korea Exchange Bank.** Some licensed money changers in Itaewon and downtown

Seoul keep longer hours than banks. There are also many places at Incheon International Airport, including the first (arrival) floor near the east and west greater halls, and on the third (departure) floor. Hard currency, such as U.S. dollars or British pounds, is easier to exchange than traveler's checks. Exchanging currency from Asian countries other than Japan and China is difficult, so make sure to change your money back to dollars or pounds if you're arriving in South Korea from elsewhere in Asia. **Tip:** Hold onto your receipt, as it will help you secure a better deal when changing your money back before heading home.

Doctors & Dentists

Most doctors and dentists speak some English, but for medical issues it's always best to find one who is fairly fluent. You'll find English-speaking dentists at the **College of Dentistry at Yonsei University,** 134 Shinchon-dong, Seodaemun-gu, Seoul 120-752

(☎ **1599-1004**); **Kwangh-wamun Ye Dental Clinic,** 2nd Floor, Seoul Finance Center, 84 Taepyeong-no 1(il)-ga, Jung-gu (☎ **02/318-3633;** www.yefriend. com); **Asan Medical Center,** 388-1 Pungnap 2-dong, Songpa-gu (☎ **1688-7575;** www.amc.seoul.kr); or **Seoul National University School of Dentistry,** 62-1 Chang-gyeonggung-ro, Jongno-gu (☎ **02/2072-3114;** www. snudh.org/eng/). You can also visit dentists at international clinics, but they'll be more expensive. For English-speaking doctors, inquire at your hotel (higher-end places often have them on call) or see "Hospitals," below. *Note:* Korean doctors have a tendency to give you the worst case scenario first, so be sure to ask questions and take an active role in your treatment, at the risk of offending the doctor.

Embassies & Consulates The following embassies are in Seoul: **U.S.,** 32 Sejong-no, Jongno-gu, Seoul 110-710 (☎ **02/397-4114;** http://seoul.us embassy.gov); **U.K.,** 19-gil 24, Jung-gu, Seoul, 100-120 (☎ **02/3210-5500;** http:// ukinkorea.fco.gov.uk/en; take the subway to City Hall, exit 3 or 12; open Mon–Fri 9:30am–noon for fee-paying services, 2–4:30pm for general inquiries); **Canadian,** 21, Jeong-dong, Jung-gu, Seoul, 100-662 (☎ **02/3783-6000;** www.canadainternational. gc.ca/korea-coree; take the subway line 1 to City Hall, exit 1; open Mon–Fri

8–11:45am and 12:45–4:30pm); and **Australian,** 19th Floor, Kyobo Building, 1 Jongno 1-ga, Jongno-gu, Seoul (☎ **02/2003-0100;** www.southkorea.embassy. gov.au; open Mon–Fri 9am–12:30pm and 1:30–4:30pm). Various services have different operating hours.

Emergencies Dial ☎ **112** for the police. Dial ☎ **119** for the fire department and medical emergencies, also ☎ **1339** for medical emergencies (operators can understand basic English, but you should find someone who can translate for you in Korean for more complicated situations). Hotel staff can also arrange for a doctor or ambulance.

Hospitals International clinics charge more than regular hospitals, but you'll be sure to find a doctor who speaks English and many who received their training abroad. The following is a list of hospitals with international clinics: **Samsung Medical Center,** Ilwon-dong, Gangnam-gu, Seoul 135-710 (☎ **1599-3114;** http://english. samsunghospital.com); **Sinchon Severance,** 134 Sinchon-dong, Seodaemun-gu, Seoul (☎ **1599-1004**); **Asan Medical Center,** 388-1 Pungnap 2-dong, Songpa-gu (☎ **1688-7575;** www. amc.seoul.kr); **Hannam-dong International Medical Center,** Hannam Building, 5F, 737-37, Han-nam-dong, Yongsan-gu (☎ **02/790-0857**); **Seoul Foreign Medical Center**

(☎ **02/796-1871**); **Yeouido Catholic Medical Center,** Yeouido-dong 62, Yeong-deungpo-gu (☎ **1661-7575;** www.cmcsungmo. or.kr); **CHA General Hospital,** 650-9 Yeoksam-dong, Gangnam-gu, 135-081 (☎ **02/3468-3000**); **Soonchunhyang Hospital,** 657, Hannam-dong, Yongsan-gu (☎ **02/709-9114**); and **Seoul National University Hospital,** 28 Yeonggyeong-dong, Jongno-gu (☎ **02/709-9114;** www.snuh.org/ english/). The **Ewha Womans University Medical Center** (☎ **02/2650-5890;** http://eng.eumc.ac.kr; 911-1 Mok-dong, Yang-cheon-gu) specializes in health care for women.

Internet Access Internet service is offered in public places such as airports, train stations, post offices, and bus terminals, as well as at cafes like Starbucks and Coffee Bean, in Seoul. Internet cafes and PC *bahngs* (which means "rooms") are easy to find throughout the city. These rooms are filled with computer terminals where you can rent an Internet-connected PC. Many PC bahngs are open 24 hours and are located on higher floors of buildings, where rents are cheaper. To find one, just head for a commercial area and look up.

Although Seoul leads the world in Wi-Fi connectivity, the city's hot spots aren't always traveler-friendly. Since the majority of Wi-Fi hot spots are owned by previously government-controlled Korea Telecom (KT), it's best to get a prepaid Wi-Fi card, available at the KT Plaza at Incheon Airport (in the middle of the second floor; daily 7am–8pm). Prepaid cards come in ₩3,000 and ₩12,000 denominations and expire after a few months. The former is good for 60 minutes of access within a 24-hour period, while the latter allows unlimited access. Most hotels and love motels (p. 410) offer free high-speed Internet access.

Lost & Found The police lost and found number is ☏ **02/2299-1282;** the train station lost and found is ☏ **02/755-7108;** the Incheon Airport lost and found is ☏ **032/741-3114.**

Maps & Books The **Korea Tourism Organization** (KTO), B1, KTO Building (T2 Tower), 40, Cheongyecheonno, Jung-gu, Seoul 100-180 (☏ **02/729-9497** ext. 499; http://english.tour2korea.com; daily 9am–8pm), publishes a variety of free brochures and maps, as well as providing transportation reservations and other travelers' assistance. They have tourist information booths in most major tourist areas throughout the city, including

Namdaemun, Dongdaemun, Insadong, Myeongdong, and **Itaewon.**

The best selection of English-language books in Seoul can be found at the Bandi & Luni's bookstores or at one of the Kyobo Mungo bookstores (see the "Shopping" section for more info). Unfortunately, there are no maps in English that show the streets of Seoul (Korean addresses don't include street names anyway), and the ones available for purchase aren't very detailed. Your best bet is to pick up a free map from one of the KTO locations.

Pharmacies Simple Western remedies are easy to find at large box stores (e.g. E-Mart). There are no 24-hour pharmacies in the city, but you can generally find pharmacies in any given neighborhood. Most display a large cross symbol, but all of them have the Korean word for medicine (약) on their windows.

Police Dial ☏ **112** for the police. There are also police stations and booths throughout the city, clearly marked in English.

Post Office There are numerous post offices across the city, including the

central one in Myeongdong. There is also one at the southeastern corner of the Gwanghwamun intersection and one in Itaewon, near the end of the main street. They're open Monday to Friday 9am to 6pm (until 5pm Nov–Feb), with a few locations open Saturday 9am to 1pm. There are also several **Federal Express** (☏ **080/023-8000;** www.fedex.com/kr_english) locations throughout the city, including one at Incheon Airport, in the COEX Mall, near Namdaemun Shijang, and one near Seoul Station.

Visitor Information For tourist information in English anywhere in the city, just dial ☏ **1330** and someone will help you. If you have a problem with your hotel, or anything else for that matter, you can also call the **Tourist Complaint Center** (☏ **02/735-0101**).

Weather For daily weather forecasts, check www.weather.com, or tune your TV to KBS at 8:30am, noon, or 9pm. Although the news will be in Korean, it's easy to figure out the weather from the icons.

WHERE TO STAY

A wide range of places to stay is available in Seoul, with everything from very inexpensive guesthouses and love motels to high-class luxury hotels.

When you're booking a room, make sure to specify that you want a Western-style room if you prefer to sleep in a bed. Korean-style ondol rooms have thick blankets (yo) for you to use to sleep on the floor. The floors are usually heated during cold weather, so make sure not to leave any electronics or anything plastic on the floor.

Outside of high-end hotels, most accommodations require that you take off your shoes in the room's foyer, so you may want to bring slippers. Bathrooms usually don't

Navigating a Korean Bathhouse

When you first enter a bathhouse, take off your shoes. Either the staff will give you a key or you can take one out of one of the shoe lockers. Usually a number will be assigned to you on your receipt. Then go to your respective gender locker rooms, where you'll find a locker with the same number as your shoe locker (your key will work on that locker as well). Be sure to wear your key around your ankle or wrist so you don't lose it. You should then take off everything (including jewelry and watches, so consider leaving yours at your hotel) and head for the shower facilities. Koreans start going to public baths when they are very young, so no one cares about walking around naked in the locker rooms, and you shouldn't feel self-conscious either. The odds of running into someone you know are pretty low.

Everyone is expected to wash completely before going into the communal hot bath, and you'll be provided with shampoo and shower gel (along with clean towels, brushes and combs, lotion, hair dryers, and even hair spray) if you've forgotten yours. After a good soaking, most Koreans scrub themselves raw with a scratchy towel that feels like sandpaper. You can also try one of the dry or wet saunas as some places have both, or cool down in the cold bath. There is no time limit—even when you're soaked, scrubbed, and thoroughly relaxed—so linger as long as you'd like. If you visit a water park or swimming pool, all of the above applies, except you'll change into your swimsuit before going out to the public pool or water areas, and you'll wash both before and after you go in the water.

have shower curtains and are designed so that the water flows into a drain on the floor. Most places don't have cheaper rates for singles (many places have only double or twin rooms anyway), so if you want to save money, travel with a friend.

Love motels (p. 410) can be found all over the city, but if you're looking for one near downtown, there is a good grouping of them near Dongdaemun. They all range from ₩40,000 to ₩50,000 per room. If you're really on a tight budget and don't mind sleeping in a large room with a bunch of strangers, you can stay in a *jjimjilbang* ("steam room" bathhouse) for about ₩10,000 a night.

Whether you stay in one of over a dozen world-class hotels or a hanok, you'll most likely be treated to Korean-style hospitality and friendly service.

Jongno
VERY EXPENSIVE

Lotte Hotel ★★★   Centrally located, the Lotte Hotel is one of the city's largest hotels. Originally built in 1973, the second of the hotel's two towers was added later and connected by a tri-level mall. Rooms are spacious with separate showers and tubs and heated toilets. Unfortunately, surcharges seem to be added on for everything from use of the fitness center to Internet access. On the plus side, the efficient and outgoing English-speaking staff are available 24 hours a day. Ask for a junior suite in the main building if you want a view of the Cheongwadae.

1, Sogong-dong, Jung-gu. www.lottehotel.com. ✆ **02/759-7311,** or 310/540-7010 or 201/944-1117 in the U.S. Fax 02/752-3758. 1,479 units. ₩240,000 and up standard room in the old tower; ₩320,000 and up standard room in the new tower; ₩30,000 for an additional guest + 10%VAT and 10% service charge. AE, DC, MC, V. Subway line 1 City Hall or line 2 Euljiro 1(il)-ga, exit 7 or 8. KAL Limousine bus from airport stop 4B or 11A. **Amenities:** 9 restaurants; 3 bars; cafe; lounge; pool;

Central Seoul Hotels & Restaurants

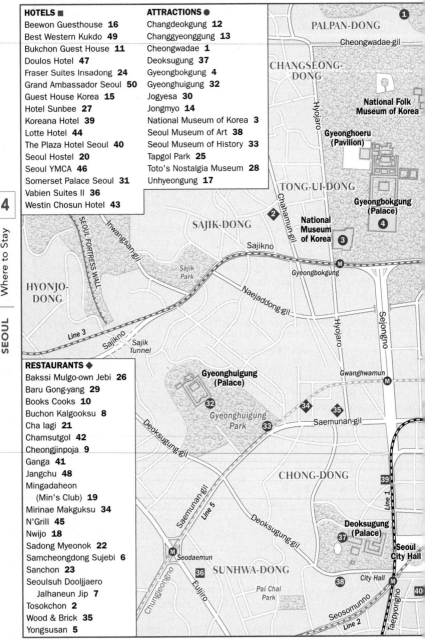

HOTELS ■

Beewon Guesthouse **16**
Best Western Kukdo **49**
Bukchon Guest House **11**
Doulos Hotel **47**
Fraser Suites Insadong **24**
Grand Ambassador Seoul **50**
Guest House Korea **15**
Hotel Sunbee **27**
Koreana Hotel **39**
Lotte Hotel **44**
The Plaza Hotel Seoul **40**
Seoul Hostel **20**
Seoul YMCA **46**
Somerset Palace Seoul **31**
Vabien Suites II **36**
Westin Chosun Hotel **43**

ATTRACTIONS ●

Changdeokgung **12**
Changgyeonggung **13**
Cheongwadae **1**
Deoksugung **37**
Gyeongbokgung **4**
Gyeonghuigung **32**
Jogyesa **30**
Jongmyo **14**
National Museum of Korea **3**
Seoul Museum of Art **38**
Seoul Museum of History **33**
Tapgol Park **25**
Toto's Nostalgia Museum **28**
Unhyeongung **17**

RESTAURANTS ◆

Bakssi Mulgo-own Jebi **26**
Baru Gong-yang **29**
Books Cooks **10**
Buchon Kalgooksu **8**
Cha Iagi **21**
Chamsutgol **42**
Cheongjinpoja **9**
Ganga **41**
Jangchu **48**
Mingadaheon
   (Min's Club) **19**
Mirinae Makguksu **34**
N'Grill **45**
Nwijo **18**
Sadong Myeonok **22**
Samcheongdong Sujebi **6**
Sanchon **23**
Seoulsuh Dooljjaero
   Jalhaneun Jip **7**
Tosokchon **2**
Wood & Brick **35**
Yongsusan **5**

4

SEOUL | Where to Stay

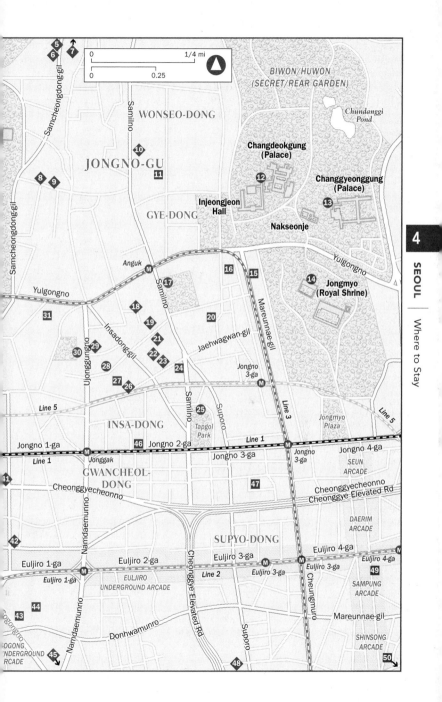

golf course; fitness center; sauna; concierge; deli; duty free shop; art gallery, Internet. *In room:* A/C, TV, minibar, hair dryer, safe, bathrobe, Internet (charge).

The Plaza Hotel Seoul ★★   Located right across the street from city hall and the financial district, this boutique business hotel has great facilities, including a wonderful fitness center and pool. The rooms are pleasant and tastefully decorated, but the beds are a bit on the hard side. Rooms on higher floors cost more, but you get a great view of the city. The hotel's restaurants and bar are nice, though a bit over-priced—some of them were just being renovated at press time, so prices may go up even more. Even the in-room minibar is good only for those on an expense account (if your boss won't balk at a ₩10,000 Coke). You'll get fabulous service with very attentive and professional staff.

23, Taepyeong-no 2-ga, Jung-gu. www.hoteltheplaza.com. ✆ **02/771-2200.** Fax 02/755-8897. 400 units. ₩340,000 for deluxe room. 10% VAT and 10% service charge not included. AE, DC, MC, V. **Amenities:** Restaurants, lounge, cafe; pool; golf range; fitness center; spa; sauna; aerobics studio; business center; bakery; flower shop; gift shop. *In room:* A/C, satellite TV, minibar, hair dryer, safe deposit box, bath robes, slippers, free Wi-Fi.

Westin Chosun Hotel ★★★   One of the best hotels in the city, this Seoul classic was built in 1914, but has been renovated since. It's conveniently located in the financial district, with easy subway access. The rooms are a bit small for the price, but very efficient and high-tech, with high-speed Internet access. Beds are quite comfortable and there are even antiallergenic carpets or wood floors, should you need. Don't forget to leave your shoes by the door before you go to sleep and they'll be waiting for you the next morning, newly shined. The English-speaking concierge and staff are incredibly friendly and helpful. Spa and gym facilities are modern, and if you've forgotten to pack your workout clothes, you can pick up complimentary attire in the locker room. You'll pay extra for higher floors (it's a 20-story building), but it's worth the splurge if you want a view.

87, Sogong-dong, Jung-gu. www.starwoodhotels.com. ✆ **02/771-0500.** Fax 02/752-1443. 465 units. ₩280,000 standard room; ₩780,000 and up suite. 11% VAT and 10% service charge not included. AE, DC, MC, V. **Amenities:** 6 restaurants; bar; cafe; pool; health club; sauna; babysitting; concierge; business center; room service; in-room massage; dry cleaning and laundry service; smoke-free rooms; currency exchange; jogging path; billiards; hair and nail salon; barber shop; safe deposit box. *In room:* A/C, TV, minibar, coffee and tea maker, hair dryer, bathrobe, slippers, Internet (for a fee).

EXPENSIVE

Grand Ambassador Seoul   A popular hotel in a central location, the facilities and rooms are modern and clean. The rooms aren't luxurious or particularly spacious, but the beds are regularly updated, the furnishings are tasteful if simple, and the amenities are up-to-date and well kept. The eager-to-please English-speaking staff are knowledgeable and helpful. Added bonus: It's close to Namsan, and within walking distance of Itaewon and Namdaemun market. *Note:* The KAL Limousine bus 6702 from Incheon Airport stops at the hotel (catch the bus at exit 4B or 11A).

186-54, Jangchung-dong 2-ga, Jung-gu. http://grand.ambatel.com. ✆ **02/270-3111.** Fax 02/2272-0773. 412 units. ₩181,000+ standard room. AE, DC, MC, V. **Amenities:** 3 restaurants; bar; cafe; pool; health club; Jacuzzi; sauna; concierge; business center; babysitting; deli; barber shop; flower shop; custom tailor. *In room:* A/C, satellite TV, minibar, hair dryer, electric teapot, iron and board, Wi-Fi.

Koreana Hotel ★   A pleasant hotel with an equally pleasant staff, this 14-story building is centrally located—it's within walking distance of Cheonggyecheon,

Deoksugung, and city hall. Although the building is starting to show its age, rooms are spacious enough, with comfortable beds. The work desk is a bit small, but they do provide in-room Internet access (for a fee). Beds are a bit hard, but comfortable. The hotel's 8th floor sauna is available for men only, unfortunately.

6-1, Taepyeong-no 1-ga, Jung-gu. www.koreanahotel.com. © **02/2171-7000.** Fax 02/730-9025. 344 units. ₩172,000 standard room; ₩600,000 suite. AE, DC, MC, V. **Amenities:** 4 restaurants; bar; cafe; health club; sauna (male only); barber; gift shop; Internet. *In room:* A/C, TV, minibar, hair dryer, electric teapot, Internet.

Somerset Palace Seoul ★★★   This well-located residence hotel (it's about 3 min. on foot to the Anguk subway station and walking distance to the U.S. Embassy, Insadong, and the Kyobo bookstore) has all the amenities of a small apartment. More like staying in a condo than a hotel, the rooms come complete with efficiency washer and dryer, which is super-convenient if you're planning a long stay (they require a 7-night minimum stay). Staff are friendly, but don't have the extensive knowledge you would get from a dedicated concierge. Bedrooms are a decent size, with TVs there and in the living room area. There is also a kitchen and dining area and good-size bathrooms, especially for the price. Rooms are nicely decorated and kept well cleaned (housekeeping is off Sun).

85, Susong-dong, Jongno-gu. www.somerset.com. © **02/6730-8888.** Fax 02/6730-8080. 465 units. ₩252,000 studio; ₩288,000 1 bedroom; ₩486,000 2 bedroom. 10% VAT not included. AE, DC, MC, V. **Amenities:** 2 restaurants; lounge; cafe; pool; health club; Jacuzzi; sauna; children's center; babysitting; laundry and dry cleaning service; 24-hour convenience store. *In room:* A/C, TV/DVD, full kitchen, hair dryer, washer/dryer, MP3 docking station, Internet.

MODERATE

Best Western Kukdo ★★   Book a west-facing high floor if you want a view from this 21-story hotel located in the middle of downtown Seoul. Convenient for public transportation, the modern amenities and relatively spacious rooms make this hotel a solid choice for exploring the central area. Although the on-site restaurant doesn't offer much variety, plenty of eateries are within walking distance and the subway is only a minute away.

310, Euljiro 4(sa)-ga, Jung-gu. http://hotelkukdo.com. © **02/6466-1234.** 295 units. ₩180,000 +10% VAT standard room. AE, DC, MC, V. Subway line 2, Euljiro 4-ga, exit 10 or limousine bus 6015 from Incheon Airport, exit 5B/12A. **Amenities:** 1 restaurant/bar; fitness center; business center. *In room:* A/C, satellite TV, minibar, fridge, coffee maker, hair dryer, safe, Wi-Fi.

Vabien Suites II ★★★ 🏠   You have your choice of six types of units, ranging from studios to two bedrooms at this all-suite hotel. Great for travelers staying more than just a couple of days, accommodations are spacious, with contemporary furnishings and hardwood floors. Bathrooms are a bit small, with showers only, but are clean with modern fixtures. The in-room washer/dryers are a plus and the kitchen is great for those on a budget. English-speaking staff are professional and quite helpful. Linens are changed every other day.

25-10, Euljiro 1(il)-ga, Jung-gu. http://www.vabiensuite.com/KOR. © **02/2076-9000.** Fax 02/752-1443. 286 units. ₩180,000 standard room. 10% VAT not included. Discounts generally available. AE, DC, MC, V. **Amenities:** 2 restaurants; bar; cafe; health club; sauna; concierge; babysitting. *In room:* A/C, satellite TV, kitchenette, hair dryer, Internet.

INEXPENSIVE

Guest House Korea   One of the cheapest places you can sleep in Seoul, this guesthouse has dormitory-style rooms with shared bathrooms and private lockers, or inexpensive single and double rooms with private bathrooms. Facilities are fairly clean, but tired. Still, it's hard to beat the price.

155-1, Kwonnong-dong, Jongno-gu. www.guesthouseinkorea.com. © **02/3675-2205.** Fax 02/764-3032. ₩18,000 25 dorm-room beds; ₩30,000 single; ₩40,000 double. MC, V. **Amenities:** TV lounge; Wi-Fi. *In room:* A/C, private rooms get TV and fridge.

Seoul YMCA You can't get any more basic than these rooms. The narrow beds are pretty hard, although the rooms are clean and serviceable. Still, you can get more comfortable accommodations in a love motel. But if you'd rather stick with something familiar, this is not a bad place to spend a few nights. The front desk and guest rooms are all located on the eighth floor.

9, Jongno 2(i)-ga, Jongno-gu. www.ymca.or.kr/en/. © **02/730-9391.** Fax 02/732-2067. 30 units. ₩55,000 single; ₩70,000 double; ₩110,000 triple. 10% VAT not included. AE, MC, V. **Amenities:** TV lounge; free use of computers and Internet access; free Wi-Fi. *In room:* A/C, private locker, shower only, private rooms get TV and minifridge.

Myeongdong/Namsan Area

VERY EXPENSIVE

The Shilla Seoul ★★★ Located on the slopes of Namsan, this 16-story hotel is übercontemporary, with minimalist decor. The location is a bit inconvenient if you want to be in the middle of it all, but it's great for those looking for a quieter place to stay. Rooms are spacious and comfortable, with goose-down comforters on the beds. There are excellent fitness and spa facilities, and the staff are incredibly polite and professional, almost to a fault. Complimentary workout clothes are available in the fitness room lockers. They'll even let you borrow a mobile phone for free, but you'll have to pay for the minutes.

202, Jangchung-dong 2-ga, Jung-gu. www.shilla.net. © **02/2233-31305.** Fax 02/752-1443. 507 units. ₩420,000 standard room; ₩500,000 and up deluxe room. Discounts are generally available. 11% VAT and 10% service charge not included. AE, DC, MC, V. **Amenities:** 4 restaurants; bar; indoor/outdoor pool; indoor golf course; health club; spa; Jacuzzi; sauna; bakery; jogging course. *In room:* A/C, satellite TV, minibar, refrigerator, hair dryer, safe deposit box, Internet.

EXPENSIVE

Grand Hyatt ★★ Perched on top of Namsan, ask for a city view when booking. The rooms make the best use of the limited space. Beds are the usual hard, Korean-style ones, and bathrooms are also on the small side, although they're quite efficiently designed. Fitness facilities and sauna are state-of-the-art and the restaurants offer great service and good food, though both come at a premium. The staff speak excellent English and are very polite.

747-7, Hannam 2-dong, Yongsan-gu. http://seoul.grand.hyatt.com. © **02/797-1234,** or 800/633-7313 in the U.S. or Canada. Fax 02/798-6953. 601 units. ₩256,000 standard rooms; ₩506,000 suite. 10% VAT and 10% service charge not included. AE, DC, MC, V. **Amenities:** 8 restaurants; cafe; pool; tennis court; health club; spa; sauna; room service; babysitting; deli; Wi-Fi. *In room:* A/C, TV, minibar, hair dryer, ceiling fan, Internet.

Millennium Seoul Hilton ★★ Conveniently located at the foot of Namsan, it's within walking distance of Namdaemun Market, but also close to a park and some green areas. Although the building is a bit dated, the rooms and facilities are still upscale. Beds are firm but comfortable, and the rooms are well maintained and tastefully decorated. Bathrooms are a good size, especially given the fight for space in the city. Staff are pleasant, relaxed, and helpful.

Myeongdong

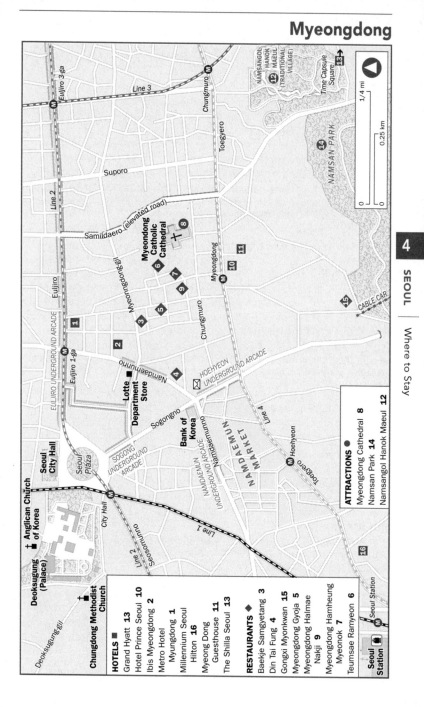

SEOUL | Where to Stay

4

ATTRACTIONS ●
Myeongdong Cathedral **8**
Namsan Park **14**
Namsangol Hanok Maeul **12**

HOTELS ■
Grand Hyatt **13**
Hotel Prince Seoul **10**
Ibis Myeongdong **2**
Metro Hotel
  Myungdong **1**
Millennium Seoul
  Hilton **16**
Myeong Dong
  Guesthouse **11**
The Shilla Seoul **13**

RESTAURANTS ◆
Baekje Samgyetang **3**
Din Tai Fung **4**
Gongxi Myonkwan **15**
Myeongdong Gyoja **5**
Myeongdong Halmae
  Nakji **9**
Myeongdong Hamheung
  Myeonok **7**
Teumsae Ramyeon **6**

395, Namdaemun-no 5-ga, Jung-gu. www.hilton.com/en_US/hi/hotel/SELHITW-Millennium-Seoul-Hilton-hotel/index.do. **683**. ℂ **02/753-7788,** or 800/774-1500 in the U.S. or Canada. Fax 02/754-25103. 683 units. ₩195,000 standard room; ₩290,000 and up executive room. 10% VAT and 10% service charge not included. AE, DC, MC, V. **Amenities:** 6 restaurants; bar; cafe; lounge; pool; health club; babysitting. In room: A/C, TV, minibar, hair dryer, Internet.

MODERATE

Hotel Prince Seoul ★★   With a nice location in the middle of exciting Myeong-dong, this is a solid hotel for those on a budget. The beds are softer than those you'd find in most hotels in South Korea, and rooms are tidy, though not spacious by Western standards; bathrooms are state-of-the-art. Overall, it's a good value for the central location and modern amenities. Although it's in the middle of the city, noise isn't much of a problem. Hotel staff don't speak much English, but do their best to be helpful.

1-1 Namsan-dong 2-ga, Jung-gu. www.hotelprinceseoul.co.kr. ℂ **02/752-711.** Fax 02/752-7118. 87 units. ₩130,000 and up single or double; ₩240,000 suite. 10% VAT and 10% service charge not included. AE, DC, MC, V. **Amenities:** Restaurant/cafe; lounge; Internet. In room: A/C, TV, fridge, hair dryer, Internet.

Ibis Myeongdong ★★★ 🔥   Set in a fantastic location near the shopping district of Myeongdong, this hotel is an exceptional value for the price. The rooms are contemporary and comfortable. The decor is simple, with firm beds, and there is good water pressure in the showers. All rooms are on higher floors, so noise isn't a problem and you still get a view of the action below. The staff are wonderful, but not all of them speak great English. The only peculiar thing is that the lobby is on the 19th floor, but it's a minor inconvenience.

59-5 Myeongdong 1-ga, Jung-gu. www.accorhotels.com. ℂ**02/6361-8888.** Fax 02/6361-8050. 280 units. ₩158,000 and up standard room; ₩200,000 and up junior suite. AE, DC, MC, V. **Amenities:** Restaurant; health club; sauna; smoke-free rooms. In room: A/C, TV, hair dryer, Internet.

Metro Hotel Myungdong ★★ 📱   The rooms are comfortable and a decent size, especially given the price and location. Decor is standard beige, but not tacky. Book online for a discount. Free Wi-Fi is an added bonus.

99-33 Euljiro 2(i)-ga, Jung-gu.   http://metrohotel.co.kr. ℂ   **02/757-1112.** Fax 02/757-4411. 75 units. ₩105,000 single, ₩130,000 double. AE, MC, V. **Amenities:** Restaurant; bar; cafe; karaoke. In room: A/C, TV, minibar, Wi-Fi.

INEXPENSIVE

Myeong Dong Guesthouse   Though rooms are pretty basic and spare, this guesthouse is conveniently located and good for those who are looking to save money. They have both Western-style rooms with beds and Korean-style ondol rooms, which are a tad smaller. The bathrooms are tiny, but facilities are well kept by the Parks, an amiable older couple who own the place. Mr. Park speaks good English and is eager to make recommendations.

17 Namsan-dong 3-ga, Jung-gu. www.mdguesthouse.com. ℂ**02/755-5437.** Fax 02/755-5438. 45 units. ₩35,000 single; ₩40000–₩50,000 double. MC, V. **Amenities:** Lounge; shared kitchen; free use of computer w/Internet access. In room: TV.

Insadong

EXPENSIVE

Fraser Suites Insadong ★★★ ☺ 🔥   This all-suite hotel is conveniently located in the old yangban neighborhood of Insadong. Fantastic for families or for long stays, you can choose from one-, two-, three-, or four-bedroom suites, all of

which come with kitchens, living rooms, dining rooms, and a small study area. There are no dishwashers in the rooms, but the housekeeping staff does the dirty dishes. The complimentary breakfast is serviceable, there are plenty of good restaurants within walking distance. The kids will appreciate the playroom and the free DVD rentals from the front desk. There's high-speed Internet service and a golf driving range on the roof.

272 Nakwon-dong, Jongno-gu. http://seoul.frasershospitality.com. © **02/6262-8282.** Fax 02/ 6262-8889. 213 units. ₩200,000 and up 1 bedroom; ₩220,000–₩270,000 and up 2 or more bed-rooms. AE, MC, V. **Amenities:** Restaurant; bar; cafe; pool; golf driving range; children's center; concierge; babysitting. *In room:* A/C, TV/DVD/VCD, kitchen, iron, safe, washer/dryer, Internet.

MODERATE

Doulos Hotel ★★   Although the rooms are a bit small, they are serviceable and kept clean at this hotel hidden down a small alley near Insadong. Rooms have hardwood floors with dark wood, clean-line furnishings. English-speaking staff are warm and friendly and go out of their way to be helpful. Although complimentary breakfast is offered, go to experience a coffee and a pastry at one of the many bakeries or cafes nearby.

112 Gwangsu-dong, Jung-gu. http://douloshotel.com. © **02/2266-2244.** Fax 02/2266-8267. 44 units. ₩100,000 standard room; ₩120,000 deluxe room. Complimentary breakfast. 10% VAT not included. MC, V. **Amenities:** meeting room. *In room:* A/C, TV, hair dryer.

Hotel Sunbee ★★★ ✦   One of the best midpriced options in the city, this hotel is great for the price and the central location. Rooms are spotless and well decorated, with hardwood floors and marble bathrooms. Many of them come with a computer and free Internet access, so ask for one when you check in. The bathroom is spacious, but as in many hotels in its class, there's no shower curtain.

198-11 Gwanhun-dong, Jung-gu. www.hotelsunbee.com. © **02/730-3451.** Fax 02/737-8857. 42 units. ₩100,000–₩140,000 standard room. MC, V. *In room:* A/C, TV, fridge, hair dryer, Internet.

INEXPENSIVE

Beewon Guesthouse ★   Another good bet for the budget traveler, the Beewon has serviceable rooms both with beds and ondol-style. They have good shared facili-ties and offer single, double, and dorm-style rooms for those on a serious budget. The convenient location and friendly staff make up for the small space and shared quarters.

28-2 Unni-dong, Jongno-gu. www.beewonguesthouse.com. © **02/765-0670.** 8 units. ₩19,000 dorm-room bed; ₩38,000 single; ₩50,000 double. MC, V. **Amenities:** TV lounge; shared kitchen; Internet. *In room:* A/C.

Bukchon Guest House ★★   If you want to experience life in a hanok, you can choose a room from one of the 3 available at the accommodations in Bukchon. These are homestays in a traditional house (updated with electricity, A/C, and free Wi-Fi). If you don't mind sleeping on a *yo* (thick blanket) on the floor, you'll get to experience old-fashioned architecture and Korean-style hospitality. Bathrooms are shared, unless you pay extra for a private room.

72 Gye-dong, Jongno-gu. www.bukchon72.com. © **010/6711-6717.** Fax 02/743-8531. 13 units. ₩40,000 single; ₩60,000 double; ₩100,000 triple; rates go up ₩10,000 on weekends. MC, V. **Amenities:** TV lounge; shared kitchen; laundry. *In room:* A/C, hairdryer, Wi-Fi.

Seoul Hostel ★   One of the best budget accommodations in the area, this hostel offers simple but very well-maintained rooms. Centrally located and close to the subway, the rooms are spare but clean and you can't beat the price.

53 Ikseon-dong, Jongno-gu. www.seoulhostel.net. © **02/3673-3671.** Fax 02/3673-3677. 30 units. ₩45,000 single; ₩60,000 double. MC, V. **Amenities:** TV lounge; shared kitchen; laundry; Wi-Fi. *In room:* A/C, TV, minifridge, hair dryer.

Sinchon, Hongdae & Idae-Ap

EXPENSIVE

Hotel Seokyo   A standard business hotel with no frills, it's convenient to the Hongdae area. Although its facilities are starting to show wear and tear, they do keep them clean. Rooms are nothing to write home about with hard beds. But it's one of the few hotels in the area and useful for those who want easy access to the airport.

54-5, Seokyo-dong, Mapo-gu. www.hotelseokyo.co.kr. © **02/330-7777.** 115 units. ₩220,000–₩290,000 standard room. AE, DC, MC, V. **Amenities:** Restaurant/coffee shop; sauna. *In room:* A/C, TV, minibar, fridge, hair dryer, Internet.

Sheratong Seoul D-Cube City ★★   Towering 15 floors above the D-Cube City mall (great for eating and shopping), this modern property has relatively spacious rooms with comfortable beds, sauna showers, and nice city views. The polite and helpful staff will make your stay even better.

662 Gyeongin-no (360-51 Sindorim-dong), Guro-gu. www.starwoodhotels.com. © **02/2211-2000.** 269 units. ₩245,000 and up standard room; ₩435,000 and up suite. AE, MC, V. **Amenities:** Restaurant; bar; cafe; indoor pool; fitness center; spa; business center; laundry; meeting room; safe deposit box. *In room:* A/C, satellite TV w/Blu-ray DVD, hair dryer, Wi-Fi.

INEXPENSIVE

Kim's Guest House ★   This cozy little guesthouse has both dormitory-style beds and private single, twin/double, or triple rooms. Definitely not fancy digs, but the owner makes you feel so welcome that you'll feel like family. They supply free breakfast (toast and coffee) and provide discounts for longer stays.

443-16, Hapjeong-dong, Mapo-gu. www.kimsguesthouse.com. © **02/337-9894.** 12 units. ₩20,000 dorm-room bed; ₩42,000 single; ₩48,000 double; ₩72,000 triple. MC, V; 4% processing fee added to credit card payments. **Amenities:** TV lounge; shared kitchen; shared bathrooms; Wi-Fi. *In room:* A/C.

Stay Korea Guest House ★★   The friendly owners here speak English, Japanese, and even French. In this converted apartment, there are dormitory-style rooms in addition to single and twin rooms, making it ideal for solo travelers. They offer free toast and coffee for breakfast and free use of their washing machine. The only minor drawback is they accept no credit cards—not a major problem since rates are so cheap.

66-4, Yeonnam-dong, Mapo-gu. www.staykorea.co.kr. © **02/336-9026** or 010/2767-0727. 6 units. ₩19,000 dorm-room bed; ₩35,000 single; ₩50,000 double. No credit cards. **Amenities:** TV lounge w/DVD; shared kitchen; shared bathrooms; Internet. *In room:* A/C.

Itaewon

EXPENSIVE

IP Boutique Hotel ★★   Look for the Mondrian-looking building on Itaewon's main drag. Young, hip, and urban, rooms come with HDTVs, Wi-Fi, and iPod docking stations. Pop art, glass, and mirrors finish the decor.

737-32 Hannam-dong, Yongsan-gu. © **02/3702-8000.** Fax 02/3702-8099. www.ipboutiquehotel. com. 133 units. ₩200,000 double; ₩375,000 suite. AE, MC, V. **Amenities:** Restaurant, cafe; business center; laundry. *In room:* A/C, TV, hair dryer, safe, Internet.

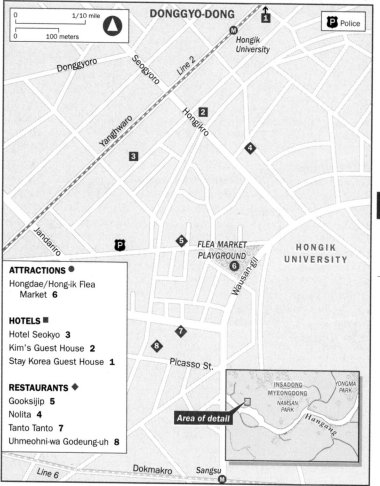

ATTRACTIONS ●
Hongdae/Hong-ik Flea
  Market **6**

HOTELS ■
Hotel Seokyo **3**
Kim's Guest House **2**
Stay Korea Guest House **1**

RESTAURANTS ◆
Gooksijip **5**
Nolita **4**
Tanto Tanto **7**
Uhmeohni-wa Godeung-uh **8**

4

SEOUL | Where to Stay

MODERATE

Hamilton Hotel   The best thing going for this hotel is its strategic location in the middle of Itaewon. The public areas have been renovated to update this old standard, while the rooms are still a bit dated and small. The beds are almost militaristic in their firmness (no down comforters here!). The staff speak English well, which is not a surprise given the hotel's location.

119-25 Itaewon-dong, Yongsan-gu. www.hamilton.co.kr. *©* **02/794-0171.** Fax 02/795-0457. 166 units. ₩99,000 and up single; ₩132,000 and up double. 10% VAT and 10% service charge not included. AE, DC, MC, V. **Amenities:** 4 restaurants; cafe; pool; sauna; room service. *In room:* A/C, TV, hair dryer, Internet.

Gangnam

VERY EXPENSIVE

Imperial Palace ★★   Convenient for those conducting business in the area, the furnishings are a bit over-the-top and ornate, but the staff will make you feel like royalty. Ask for one of their renovated rooms, although their older rooms are still well-maintained. Beds are on the firm side, but the rooms are relatively spacious, given the Gangnam location.

248-7 Nonhyun-dong, Gangnam-gu. http://www.imperialpalace.co.kr/eng/company/ip_overview. asp. ⓒ **02/5555-5656.** Fax 02/559-7990. 430 units. ₩320,000 and up standard room; ₩420,000 and up suite. 10% VAT and 10% service charge not included. AE, DC, MC, V. **Amenities:** 4 restaurants; bars; cafe; indoor/outdoor pools; golf driving range; fitness club; concierge; business center; bakery; karaoke; lobby lounge; meeting rooms; art gallery; custom tailor; photo studio; jewelry shop. *In room:* A/C, TV, minibar, coffee/tea maker, hair dryer, iron, safe, bathrobe, Wi-Fi (fee).

EXPENSIVE

Grand InterContinental Seoul ★★★   A top-notch hotel, it's located right next to the COEX Mall and the World Trade Center. Don't judge a hotel by its exterior, since the interior is much nicer than you would expect. The lobby, the rooms, and the facilities are all spacious and impeccably clean. The friendly staff speak excellent English and provide wonderful service. Rooms are contemporary without feeling too impersonal—they're tastefully done in dark wood. The beds are a bit on the firm side, but here they're a notch above, comfort-wise. Bathrooms are spacious—again, a rarity in South Korea. The restaurants are overpriced, even for a hotel of this caliber, but offer good Western and Korean fare.

159-8 Samseong-dong, Gangnam-gu. http://www.ichotelsgroup.com/intercontinental/en/gb/ locations/seoul-grand. ⓒ **02/5555-5656,** or 888/424-6835 in the U.S. Fax 02/559-7990. 535 units. ₩216,800 and up standard room; ₩306,000 and up suite. 10% VAT not included. AE, DC, MC, V. **Amenities:** 6 restaurants; lounge bar; pool; golf driving range; health club; sauna; concierge; room service. *In room:* A/C, TV, minibar, coffee/tea maker, hair dryer, iron, safe, bathrobe, Internet.

Park Hyatt Seoul ★★★   An elegant, well-designed hotel, the 24-story Park Hyatt has nice facilities. Also convenient to the COEX Mall, it has all of the modern amenities you would expect from a hotel of its class. Beds are comfortable, and the lovely floor-to-ceiling windows come with room-darkening shades. The bathrooms are superb, with granite counters and extravagantly deep tubs for soaking away the day's stresses. If you're sensitive to noise, you may want to request a room facing away from the main street, since not all rooms have great soundproof windows. The English-speaking staff are notably efficient. If you happen to be there on the 3rd Wednesday of each month, the executive chef offers a cooking class for ₩90,000, but you must reserve a space in advance.

995-14 Daechi 3-dong, Gangnam-gu. http://seoul.park.hyatt.com. ⓒ **02/2016-1234.** Fax 02/ 2016-1200. 185 units. ₩340,000 standard room; ₩420,000 and up suite. 11% VAT and 10% service charge not included. AE, DC, MC, V. **Amenities:** 3 restaurants; lounge bar; cafe; pool; health club; spa; sauna; 24-hr concierge; safe; Wi-Fi. *In room:* A/C, satellite TV/DVD, minibar, coffee maker/ electric kettle, hair dryer, Internet (fee).

Other Neighborhoods

Sheraton Grande Walkerhill Hotel ★★   Overlooking the Han River and situated on the hills surrounded by woodlands, this hotel feels very far away from the commotion and excitement of Seoul. That's because you are indeed far away, which is a problem if you want convenient access to downtown areas. But if you want to get away from the noise of the city, then this is the hotel for you. The lobby is spacious, the facilities are top-notch, and the English-speaking staff are warm and welcoming. The rooms, though not lavish, are decorated with contemporary style. The restaurants are a bit pricey, but the menus are creative. There is no direct subway access, but the hotel provides free shuttles to two nearby subway stops; otherwise, you'll have to take a taxi.

San 21 Gwangjang-dong, Gwangjin-gu. www.sheratonwalkerhill.co.kr. ✆ **02/455-5000.** Fax 02/452-6867. 597 units. ₩350,000 standard room; ₩640,000 suite. 10% VAT and 10% service charge not included. AE, DC, MC, V. **Amenities:** 13 restaurants and bars; cafe; pool; tennis court; health club; sauna; room service. *In room:* A/C, satellite TV, minibar, coffee/tea maker, hair dryer, in-room safe, 110/120V outlets available, newspaper, bathrobe, high-speed Internet access.

W Seoul Walkerhill ★★   Located away from the downtown area in Achasan like its sister, the Sheraton Grande, it's great for people who want to get away from it all but still be near a major metropolis. Characteristic of their youthful spirit, the "Wonderful" rooms and some of their suites have round beds, round chairs, and even a round bathtub, while other themed rooms have the usual angular varieties. Beds are comfortable with great sheets in spacious rooms. Bathrooms have rain-type shower heads and separate tubs. The staff are professional and helpful.

21 Gwangjang-dong, Gwangjin-gu. www.wseoul.com. ✆ **02/465-2222.** Fax 02/450-4989. 253 units. ₩285,750–₩505,000 standard room; ₩1,400,000 suite. 11% VAT and 10% service charge not included. AE, DC, MC, V. Pets welcome. **Amenities:** 6 restaurants; bar; cafe; pool; driving range; tennis court; health club; spa; sauna; concierge. *In room:* A/C, TV w/DVD, minibar, hair dryer, iron, safe, Internet (fee).

EXPENSIVE

JW Marriott ★★★   This 35-story contemporary hotel, connected to the COEX Mall and the subway, caters to the area's business travelers. Rooms are efficient and relatively spacious with nice furnishings. Beds are comfortable with foam pillows and down comforters. Bathrooms are high-tech with seat warmers and a separate tub and shower. Fitness center and sports facilities are top-notch, with a large pool that's good for laps. The English-speaking staff are accommodating and helpful.

19-3 Banpo-dong, Seocho-gu. www.marriott.com/hotels/travel/seljw-jw-marriott-hotel-seoul. ✆ **02/6282-6262,** or 888/236-2427 in the U.S. or Canada. Fax 02/6282-6263. 497 units. ₩259,000 standard room; ₩324,000 suite. 10% VAT and 10% service charge not included. AE, DC, MC, V. **Amenities:** 8 restaurants; bar; lounge; cafe; pool; health club; spa; sauna; concierge; babysitting; deli and bakery; Wi-Fi. *In room:* A/C, TV, minibar, hair dryer, Internet (fee).

MODERATE

Ohmok-gyo Co-op Residence ★★ 🍴   Located about 5 minutes from Yeouido, these accommodations are good for those staying 2 weeks or longer. From studios to two-bedroom units, all have kitchens, dining areas, and a desk. It's like renting your own apartment in the city; units are relatively spacious with efficient and modern bathrooms. Prices are very reasonable and staff are very responsive if you have any problems. They have locations in other areas, including Sincheon and Euljiro.

43-14 Yangpyung-dong 2-ga, Yeongdeungpo-gu. http://rent.co-op.co.kr/rent_coop/eng/body06-2.htm. ✆ **02/2164-0200.** 740 units. ₩80,000 and up studio. AE, DC, MC, V. Parking. **Amenities:** Restaurant; cafe; lounge; health club; business center; laundry. *In room:* A/C, TV, kitchenette, fridge, safe, hair dryer, Internet.

WHERE TO EAT

Seoul has more eateries per square mile than most large cities in the world, and there is a great deal of turnover. All manner of Korean food from the affordable to the incredibly expensive can be had. However, if you're looking for familiar Western-style dishes and menus in English, you'll have a harder time finding suitable options. That said, if you head over to Itaewon or the restaurants in some of the upscale hotels, you can get delicious world-class Western-style cuisine. It's also getting easier to find a juicy hamburger or just a good old-fashioned steak. Vegetarians will find an increasing array of options as dining has become a healthier affair in South Korea.

American chains like Pizza Hut, Starbucks, and Krispy Kreme have popped up all over the city, but don't expect the menus you find at home. You'll get a pizza, but it'll arrive with pickles and peppers, and the pasta may have squid in it. You'll also pay more to make up for the fact that many Western-style ingredients have to be imported. If you want an authentic experience and don't want to spend all your cash, you can stick with purely Korean dishes and still have a different experience at every meal. *Tip:* Most of the higher-end, non-Korean restaurants charge an additional 10% VAT on your meal, while most Korean restaurants price their items with the VAT included.

The only thing that may take getting used to is the fact that Koreans don't distinguish between breakfast, lunch, and dinner. So, it's rice, rice, and more rice all day with little besides noodles to break up the monotony. You'll be hard-pressed to find good ham and eggs first thing in the morning, and free breakfasts are a rare find, even in luxury hotels. You will find bakeries on practically every corner, but don't expect the bread and pastries to taste the way they do at home. That's not to say they taste bad, but while Korean-style bakeries may describe themselves as "French" on their signs, their goods don't offer the same flavors you'd find in Paris.

Food trends here come and go. Seoul is the origin of the Pinkberry/Red Mango yogurt craze, after all. The good news is that there's great food in every neighborhood, and for all you night owls, plenty of 24-hour places where you can get something yummy into the wee hours (some of whom deliver). Wherever you decide to eat, don't forget you don't have to tip. In traditional Korean joints, there's no tipping at all and some of the newer restaurants just take the liberty of adding the service charge (and the VAT) to your bill.

Jongno

VERY EXPENSIVE

N'Grill WESTERN   Located at the top of the N Seoul Tower on Namsan, this pricey but lovely rotating restaurant is best known for its view of Seoul (make sure to go on a clear day). It's a romantic place to enjoy an overpriced steak dinner while enjoying the city lights as the place spins 360 degrees every 120 minutes. Set courses include your choice of entree (steak, fish, or lobster), an appetizer, dessert, soup, and a beverage. At this popular place for anniversaries and birthday celebrations, be sure to book a reservation well in advance. The accommodating staff here speak English well.

100-177 Hoehyun-dong 1-ga, Jung-gu. ⓒ 02/3455-9297 or 9298. www.nseoultower.co.kr. Reservations required. Set-course meals ₩75,000–₩110,000. 10% VAT not included. AE, MC, V. Daily 11am–11pm. Subway line 3 or 4 to Chungmuro (exit 2), then take yellow bus 2 or 5 to the N Seoul Tower. Or from Itaewon (line 6, exit 4), take yellow bus 3.

EXPENSIVE

Chamsutgol ★★★ 🍴 KOREAN BEEF   In a city where galbi restaurants span multiple levels, it's difficult to decide which one is the best. But once you've tasted

Affordable Korean food is everywhere in Seoul, and *pojang machas* (tent-covered super-casual eating joints) are pretty ubiquitous. At practically every bus stop and subway station, you'll find an *ajumma* (middle-aged woman) stirring up a spicy red swamp of ddeokbokgi or frying something on a stick. Some of the tastiest options are *hoddeok* (pan-fried dough cakes stuffed with brown sugar and spices), *gimbap* (rice rolled in sheets of seaweed with a variety of different fillings), and *beung-uh bbang* (goldfish-shaped "cookies" filled with red bean).

The best places to find good street food are near Namdaemun or Dongdaemun markets, in front of tique shops in Myeongdong, and Insadong's main drag. If you're not such an adventurous eater but are still budget-conscious, head on over to the basement floors of any of the multi-story department stores found all over the city. There you'll find plenty of items on display where you can just point and buy what you want. Some places have Korean "fast-food" courts where you can get a meal for about ₩7,000. You place your order at the counters, but pay at the cash registers. They'll call your number when your order is ready.

4

SEOUL | **Where to Eat**

the galbi at this place, this may fast become one of your favorites (though it's not much in the atmosphere department). Just like most other Korean places, they bring you the raw meat to cook on your tabletop grill, but here they provide real *sutbul* (wood charcoal), which adds a smoky flavor. One of the signature dishes here is the *galbitahng* (stewed beef ribs), but you'd better arrive early because they make only 40 orders of it per day. Their *naengmyeon* (cold buckwheat noodles) and *dolsot bibimbap* (stone pot mixed rice) are also excellent.

19 Mugyo-dong (2nd floor of the Chaeyuk Hwaegwan Building), Jung-gu. © **02/774-2100.** Entrees ₩9,000–₩41,000. MC, V. Daily 11:30am–10pm. Closed Lunar New Year and Chuseok. Subway line 1 to City Hall (exit 4).

Ganga INDIAN   Located on the second basement floor of the Seoul Finance Center building, Ganga serves wonderful garlic nan, fragrant tandoori dishes, and curries that will make you forget you're not in Mumbai.

84 Taepyeong-no 1-ga, Jongno-gu (level B2). © **02/3783-0610.** Reservations recommended. Entrees ₩15,000–₩55,000. AE, DC, MC, V. Daily 11:30am–3pm and 5:30–10pm. Closed Lunar New Year and Chuseok. Subway line 1 to City Hall (exit 4) and walk 2 blocks, or line 5 to Gwanghwamun (exit 5) and walk 1 block.

Wood & Brick ★★ ITALIAN   Just like the name says, this two-story restaurant is made of wood and brick, and you'll find fantastic pastas and simple European fare. Capriccio appetizers, sandwiches (try the boccadillo!), and soups are also excellent. Weekday lunch hours are usually bustling with staff from nearby foreign embassies. There is also a fantastic bakery here. This original location is just across the street from the Brunei embassy in the Gwanghwamun area. A second location is across the street from Jaedong Elementary School.

170-2 Dangju-dong, Jongno-gu. © **02/735-1151.** Daily 11am-10pm. Main location at 5-2 Jae-dong, Jongno-gu, © **02/747-1592.** www.woodnbrick.co.kr. Reservations not necessary. Entrees ₩14,000–₩63,000. MC, V. Daily noon–10pm, closed Chuseok and Lunar New Year. Subway line 5 to Gwanghwamun (exit 7). 2nd location: subway line 3 to Anguk.

ODERATE

Jangchu ★★ KOREAN SEAFOOD   For almost 3 decades this place has been serving up their famous *jang-uh gui* (grilled eel) to a clamoring clientele. The spicy eel is done with special spices (including cinnamon) and you probably haven't tasted anything quite like it. You won't find much in the way of decor here—the dining room is efficient, though more than a bit boring. Not that the diners (who all seem to work in the area) seem to mind. Look for the squat brick building with a large white sign. Although the sign is only in Korean, you can't miss the picture of a cartoon eel wearing a chef's hat.

Behind the Chungmuro Geukdong Building; 58-8 Chungmuro 3(sam)-ga, Jongno. ℂ **02/2274-8992.** No reservations. Entrees ₩15,000–₩45,000. MC, V. Tues–Sat 11:30am–10pm. Subway line 3 or 4 to Chungmuro (exit 5), turn right at the Geukdong building, and turn left at the 2nd street; Jangchu is on your right.

Tosokchon ★★ KOREAN   You can't miss this old-fashioned building near Gyeongbokgung. Famous for their *samgyetang* (soup of whole chicken stuffed with rice, ginseng, dates, and more), Tosokchon is usually super-crowded during mealtimes, but the restaurant is large enough that you won't have to wait long. They also serve an outstanding *jeongigui tongdak* (whole roasted chicken) and tasty *pajeon* (green onion flatcakes), if you're not in the mood for a hot bowl of healthy goodness.

85-1 Chebu-dong, Jongno-gu. ℂ **02/737-7444.** No reservations. Entrees ₩15,000–₩35,000. No credit cards. Daily 10am–10pm. Subway line 3 to Gyeongbokgung (exit 2), walk up the street until you get to the GS25 convenience store and turn left.

INEXPENSIVE

If you're looking for the perfect meal on a sticky, hot summer day, nothing beats a cold bowl of naengmyeon, a dish that originated in North Korea. The best place in town to get it is in **Naengmyeon Alley** in the Ojang-dong neighborhood. Take Seoul subway line 2 to Euljiro 4(sa)-ga (exit 8), walk toward Jung Ward office, turn left, and you'll find the alley across from Mukjeong Park. Most of the restaurants in the area serve *mul naengmyeon* (cold buckwheat noodles in beef broth) or *bibim naengmyeon* (spicy mixed buckwheat noodles) for about ₩8,000 a bowl. One good place is **Ojangdong Hamheung Naengmyeon** (90-10 Ojang-dong, Jung-gu; ℂ 02/2267-9500), whose interior is cafeteria-style at best, but they do have good broth. The name out in front isn't in English, but look for the large blue sign with white lettering.

Mirinae Makguksu ★ KOREAN   Although the name of the restaurant says noodles, this spot also serves a good and affordable *ssambap* (rice with lettuce and other leaves for wrapping) and the excellent house specialty *makguksu* (mixed somen noodles). The noodles are fresh and served in generous portions, as they should be at any good Korean noodle joint. And while the food is great, the setting will leave something to be desired—people come here to eat, not linger.

11-2 Jung-dong, Mapo-gu. ℂ **02/779-2756.** No reservations. Entrees ₩6,000–₩15,000. MC, V. Tues–Sat 11am–1am. Subway line 5 to Gwanghwamun (exit 8).

Myeongdong & Namdaemun

MODERATE

Baekje Samgyetang ★★★ KOREAN CHICKEN   A great place to get samgyetang, the stuffed chicken soup that's eaten during the hottest days of summer (though it's lovely in the winter as well). The chefs here use only young spring chickens, which have the tenderest meat. This oh-so-healthy meal is best enjoyed with some *insamju* (ginseng wine). So sit down on one of the floor cushions, pull yourself up to one of the shiny wooden tables, and prepare to sweat the summer heat (or warm the winter blues) away with the hot broth.

50-11 Myeongdong 2-ga, Jung-gu. ☎ **02/776-3267.** No reservations. Entrees ₩12,000. No credit cards. Daily 9am–10pm. Subway line 4 to Myeongdong (exit 2); walk 5 or 6 blocks and it's on your left, across the street from the Lotte Department Store.

Din Tai Fung ★ CHINESE   More upscale than some of their outlets elsewhere (there are now 25 branches in eight countries), the one here still draws a crowd. In this small, streamlined spot, done up with dark wood furnishings and red Chinese-style accents, you'll find a full menu of dumplings, soup, noodles, and rice dishes. But the absolutely-do-not-miss-it dish is the juicy pork dumplings. The chefs also make good *xiaolongbao* (small steamed pork dumplings) as a nod to Korean cuisine. Look for the red sign with white *Hanja* (Chinese characters) and the huge photo of dumplings on the side.

104, Myeongdong 2-ga. ☎ **02/771-2778.** No reservations. Entrees ₩5,000–₩16,000. AE, MC, V. Daily 11am–10:30pm. Subway line 2 to Euljiro 1(il)-ga (exit 6) or line 4 to Myeongdong (exit 5). Located at the end of Myeongdong, about a block from the Lotte Department Store).

Myeongdong Halmae Nakji ★★ KOREAN SEAFOOD   In a neighborhood where restaurants come and go faster than a teenager can change her outfits, it's amazing that this place has been here for over 50 years. As the name suggests, the *halmuhni* (grandma) specializes in *nakji* (squid) and she doesn't skimp on the spice. Be forewarned: This is the kind of spicy that sneaks up on you, and your mouth will be on fire by the end. It's a casual neighborhood restaurant, with Korean-style floor tables and not much in the way of decor.

31-7 Myeongdong 2-ga, Jung-gu. ☎ **02/757-3353.** No reservations. Entrees ₩7,000–₩35,000. No credit cards. Daily 11am–10pm. Subway line 2 to Euljiro 1(il)-ga (exit 6).

INEXPENSIVE

Gongxi Myonkwan ☺ CHINESE   A new addition to the Chinese dumpling scene, this import offers less expensive *xiaolongbao* (steamed bun) than other restaurants. If you want dumplings and *jjajangmyeon* (Korean-Chinese noodles with black-bean sauce), this is the place. They even have a special jjajangmyeon set menu for kids for only ₩4,500.

In Myeongdong, next to the Chinese embassy. ☎ **02/778-8863.** No reservations. Entrees ₩4,000–₩16,000. No credit cards. Daily 11am–1am. Subway line 2 to Euljiro 1(il)-ga (exit 6) or line 4 to Myeongdong (exit 5).

Myeongdong Gyoja ★★★ KOREAN   If you want Korean-style *mandu* (dumplings) or *kal guksu* (handmade "knife" noodles), this is the place for you. For over 3 decades, this spot has been making chicken stock from bones boiled for 6 hours. The chefs here also make lovely bowls of *bibim guksu* (spicy mixed noodles) and *kohng guksu* (noodles in cold soybean soup), all at a bargain. The deep red and white sign is only in Korean, but you can't miss the mouthwatering photos of dumplings decorating the outside of this casual restaurant.

25-2 Myeongdong 2(i)-ga, Jung-gu. ☎ **02/776-5348.** www.mdkj.co.kr. No reservations. Everything on the menu ₩8,000. MC, V. Daily 10:30am–9:30pm. Closed Chuseok and Lunar New Year. Subway line 4 to Myeongdong (exit 8). Two locations in Myeongdong (the easiest to find is up the street from Shinhan Bank).

Myeongdong Hamheung Myeonok ★★★ 🎁 KOREAN   This is yet another Seoul spot where the food outperforms the decor. It's a great place for a casual meal, but not a great place to take someone you're hoping to impress. Still, for over 35 years, the owners have been making their famous naengmyeon. The noodles here are made with sweet potato and the broth is made from boiled oxtails. The excellent hwae naengmyeon is eye-wateringly spicy.

26-1 Myeongdong 2-ga, Jung-gu. ⓒ **02/776-8430.** No reservations. Entrees ₩6,000 to ₩17,500. No credit cards. Daily 9:30am–10pm. Closed Lunar New Year and Chuseok. Subway line 4 to Myeongdong (exit 5).

Teumsae Ramyeon ★ KOREAN   Hidden in a small alley is this run-down original that has spawned a line of instant noodles and chain stores throughout South Korea. This hole in the wall has been serving excellent food to regulars for over 20 years (many of whom have left behind notes on the walls and ceilings). Specialties are the *ppalgaeddeok lamyun* (really spicy ramen with rice cake) and the *ggoma gimbap* (mini seaweed rice rolls) Ask for a less spicy ramen, if you can't handle the heat.

4-1-beonji, 2nd floor, Myeongdong 2(i)-ga, Jung-gu. ⓒ **02/756-5477.** No reservations. Entrees ₩1,000–₩4,000. No credit cards. Mon–Sat 10am–9:30pm; Sun 11am–8:30pm. Subway line 4 to Myeongdong (exit 10).

Insadong

Insadong is a good area to get a traditional Korean meal. Many of the restaurants are down small alleys, tucked away from the main drag. There are also traditional tea shops and great coffeehouses (although they actually let a Starbucks open up here, they insisted that the sign be in Korean), where you'll pay as much for the ambience as the beverage.

EXPENSIVE

Baru Gong-yang ★★★ 🎁 KOREAN VEGETARIAN   Korean temple food can be bland and boring, but you'll be pleasantly surprised at the inventive and gorgeous dishes served at this temple restaurant. Located across the street from Jogyesa on the fifth floor of the temple stay building, find your inner peace as you enjoy the multiple courses of beautifully delicious food.

71 beonji Gyeongji-dong, Jongno-gu. ⓒ **02/733-2081.** www.baru.or.kr. Reservations required. Set menus ₩25,000–₩53,000. 10% VAT not included. MC, V. Mon–Fri 10am–8pm. Subway line 3 to Anguk (exit 6).

Mingadaheon (Min's Club) ★★ FUSION   The extensive wine list and modern interior is a surprise in this converted hanok in the middle of Insadong. The portions are small, but the food inventive. The Korean-influenced European menu is subtle, but changes seasonally.

66-7 Gyeongun-dong, Jongno-gu. ⓒ **02/723-2966.** Reservations recommended. Entrees ₩20,000 and up; set menus ₩60,000–₩80,000. MC, V. Daily noon–10:30pm. Subway line 3 to Anguk (exit 5).

Sanchon ★ KOREAN VEGETARIAN   Sanchon serves their variation of traditional temple fare in the charming courtyard of a hanok. A dozen different vegetarian, seasonal *banchan* (side dishes) come with your meal. Dine on the early side if you want to avoid the expensive seating for the traditional folk music and dance performance. The dining room is cozy, with traditional wooden tables, exposed wood beams, and traditional Korean paintings lining the walls. There is also a second location in Goyang-gu with a more varied, slightly less expensive menu.

Stop by Sanchon's cookie shop, **Sanchon Saramdeul,** on Insadong's main drag. They have a nice array of traditional Korean "cookies." Although some of them can be a bit pricey, most are relatively inexpensive at ₩5,000 to ₩6,000 a bag.

14 Gwanhun-dong, Jongno-gu (in the alleyway about 3 blocks past Insadong crossroads). ✆ **02/735-0312** or 735-1900. Goyang location ✆ **031/969-9865.** www.sanchon.com. Reservations recommended. Set lunch ₩22,000; set dinner ₩39,600. AE, DC, MC, V. Daily 9am–2am; performances at 8:15 and 9pm nightly. Closed Lunar New Year and Chuseok. Subway line 3 to Anguk.

MODERATE

Bakssi Mulgo-own Jebi ★★ KOREAN With its exposed wood interior, it has a distinctly "country" feel. Even the name is folksy—it's taken from a Korean folk tale and means "the swallow that brought the gourd seed." You'll find good wholesome food here; definitely try the *hang-ali sujebi* (dough flake soup in a stone bowl). If you're just looking for a light meal or snack, try the *insam dongdongju* (ginseng rice wine) with the *haemul pajeon* (seafood and green onion flatcake).

In the alley across from the Woori Bank. ✆ **02/723-3200.** No reservations. Entrees ₩7,000–₩18,000. MC, V. Daily 9am–2am. Subway line 3 to Anguk.

Nwijo ★★ KOREAN TEMPLE CUISINE Wild vegetables never had it so good as being prepared in a dish at this inventive hanok restaurant. The name means "god of the silkworm" and the owner takes his seasonal ingredients seriously. Mountain herbs, pickled roots, local meats, and a variety of fresh greens will make their way to your table after they pass the hands of the talented chef.

84-13 Gwanhun-dong, Jongno-gu. ✆ **02/730-9311.** www.nwijo.com. Reservations not required. Set menu ₩18,000–₩88,000. MC, V. Daily 11am–10pm. Subway line 3 to Anguk (exit 6).

Cha Iagi ★ KOREAN Don't be fooled by the name, which means "tea story." Cha Iagi is actually known for its delicious *nokcha daenamu tongbap* (rice and green tea steamed in bamboo). The *ssambap jeongshik* (traditional meal with lettuce and other leaves for wrapping) isn't bad either. Come early or late since it's super-popular during lunchtime.

29-11 Gwanhun-dong, Jongno-gu. ✆ **02/735-8552.** No reservations. Entrees ₩7,000–₩12,000. No credit cards. Daily noon–10pm. Subway line 3 to Anguk.

INEXPENSIVE

Sadong Myeonok ★★★ 🏮 KOREAN DUMPLINGS Although this well-known favorite is tucked away in a small alley (near the Sudo Pharmacy), you can't miss an ajumma or two making mandu in the window. Especially on chilly evenings, people line up for the restaurant's famous *mandu guk* (dumpling soup) with dumplings the size of fists, but the *bibimbap* (mixed rice bowl) is really good, too. If it's cold outside, try the *beosut jeongol* (spicy mushroom hot pot), which is big enough to warm up both you and a friend.

Insadong 5-gil, Jongno-gu. ✆ **02/735-7393.** No reservations. Entrees ₩5,000–₩25,000. No credit cards. Daily 11am–10:30pm. Subway line 3 to Anguk.

Samcheong-Dong

Restaurants serve up contemporary fusion food in remodeled hanok alongside boutique shops and galleries. To get to the main drag, take subway line 3 to Gyeongbokgung (exit 5). Walk around to the other side of the palace. Then walk across the street to the main road, turn left, and walk about 400m (1,300 ft.) until you get to the three-way intersection, where you'll turn right. This is where the main road for Samcheong-dong starts.

Insadong Street Food

If you get hungry while browsing the ceramics and paper wares on Insadong street, there are plenty of places to grab a quick bite from one of the many street vendors here, while barely breaking your stride. An unusual sweet snack is *kkultarae* (sometimes called dragon's or king's beard), sold from an open cart. They look like fine white strands of silk wrapped into balls, but are in fact edible threads made from honey, pine nuts, chestnuts, peanuts, and cornstarch. My favorites are the peanut and almond. The cart is open daily 10am to 9pm. Farther down on the same side of the street, you'll find another cart,

Sambodang Hoddeok, selling little dough cakes made with glutinous rice and stuffed with black sugar and peanuts. Delicious at only ₩1,000 each, once you've tried them, you'll know why there's such a long line. They're here most days from 10am to 8:30pm (closed the first and third Mon of each month). You'll also find men in traditional clothing selling *yut* (Korean hard "taffy" made from pumpkin), various rice cakes, and Korean cookies. On hot days, you may find the vendor selling *shikhae slushee,* an icy version of the traditional sweet fermented rice beverage, for ₩2,000 to ₩3,000.

You can also get here by walking across the street and up the hill from Insadong. Or just grab a taxi and ask the driver to take you to Samcheong-dong.

VERY EXPENSIVE

Yongsusan ★★ KOREAN   This restaurant features traditional Korean food served in a contemporary setting. The house specialty is Korean "court" food, just like the royals used to eat. With elegant service and fantastic food made with quality ingredients that don't compromise on flavor, this is a great spot for dinner. There are several locations throughout Seoul, including in Seocho-gu, Taepyeong-no, and Cheongdam.

118-3 Samcheong-dong, Jongno-gu. *©* **02/596-5599.** www.yongsusan.com. Reservations recommended. Set lunch menu ₩25,000–₩48,000; set dinner menu ₩38,000–₩128,000; a la carte dinner entrees ₩28,000–₩45,000. AE, DC, MC, V. Daily noon–3pm and 6–10pm. Subway line 3 to Anguk, up the hill from Gyeongbokgung.

MODERATE

Books Cooks ★★ CAFE   Located in Bukchon in a converted hanok, this teahouse is perfect for foodies looking for a quiet drink. Their afternoon tea (from 2 to 5pm) is a delicious way to spend a couple of hours browsing through their expansive cookbook library, while delicious aromas waft from the marvelously open kitchen.

177-4 Gahoe-dong, Jongno-gu. *©* **02/743-4003.** Reservations necessary for meals. Scone and set tea ₩12,000, other prices vary. MC, V. Daily 10am–10pm. Subway line 3 to Anguk (exit 2), a 10-min. walk up toward Bukchon hanok maeul, on the righthand side.

INEXPENSIVE

Buchon Kalgooksu ★★ KOREAN NOODLES   A great place in the area to get kal gooksu and mandu, they have good soup stock (made from boiling the bones seemingly forever), and even the small kimchi and side dishes that come with it are tasty.

84 Sogyeok-dong, Jongno-gu. *©* **02/739-6339.** No reservations. Entrees ₩6,000. No credit cards. Daily 11am–9:30pm. Closed holidays. Subway line 3 to Anguk (exit 1), a 15-min. walk on Samcheong-dong main road.

Cheongjinpoja ★ 🍴 KOREAN DUMPLINGS   If you're looking for a cheap, quick meal or snack of dumplings, you're in luck, since that's all they serve here. They won't win any interior design awards, but their steamed, fried, or boiled dumplings, filled with meat, vegetables, or seafood, will keep you satisfied.

127 Sogyeok-dong, Jongno-gu. 🕐 **02/739-6086.** No reservations. Dumplings ₩4,000–₩5,000. No credit cards. Tues–Sun 10am–10pm. Closed holidays. Subway line 3 to Anguk (exit 1), a 10-min. walk on Samcheong-dong main road.

Samcheongdong Sujebi ★★ KOREAN   This is the restaurant that started the area's reputation as a place for good food. The sujebi served here is so good that people line up to get a bowlful. The dough is made by hand and floated in an anchovy-based soup with potatoes, clams, carrots, zucchini, and onions. They also make fantastic, homemade *nokdu jeon* (mung bean flatcake).

102 Samcheong-dong, Jongno-gu. 🕐 **02/735-2965.** No reservations. Entrees ₩7,000–₩15,000. No credit cards. Daily 11:30am–9pm. Subway line 3 to Anguk (exit 1).

Seoulsuh Dooljjaero Jalhaneun Jip ★★ 🍴 KOREAN   The name of this place is a mouthful in either language (it means the "second best house in Seoul") and it's almost bigger than its small space can handle. Since 1976, it has served only traditional teas and *danpatjook* (sweet red-bean porridge), good for a light meal or snack. Wash it all down with a cup of chilled *soojeong-gwa* (ginger-cinnamon tea).

28-21 Samcheong-dong, Jongno-gu. 🕐 **02/734-5302.** No reservations. Danpatjook ₩5,500; traditional teas ₩4,000–₩5,500. No credit cards. Daily 11am–10pm. Closed holidays. Subway line 3 to Gyeongbokgung (exit 5).

Hongdae-Ap, Sincheon & Idae-Ap

MODERATE

Nolita ★ ☺ ITALIAN   The name is short for "north of Little Italy" and the place serves a wide variety of dishes from there—pastas to thin pizzas and more. Its cozy interior and hearty dishes make for an enjoyable dinner. There's another location in Gangnam (take exit 7 from the subway and it's on the basement floor on your right-hand side) and in Myeongdong (on the second floor across from the Myeongdong department store).

On the 2nd and 3rd floor of the building behind Eunha beauty salon. 🕐 **02/312-4443.** No reservations. Entrees ₩10,000–₩15,000. MC, V. Daily 11am–10:30pm. Subway line 4 to Ewha Women's University (exit 4), and walk toward the main gate of Ewha U.

Tanto Tanto ☺ ITALIAN   I wouldn't recommend a salad here (they are a bit on the boring side), but the pastas are wide in variety and hearty fare. The most popular menu item is the spaghetti with cream tomato sauce that's a bit rich but still tasty. The fun interior and menu cater to the college-age crowd in the area.

407-27 Seogyo-dong, Mapo-gu. 🕐 **02/336-6992.** No reservations. Entrees ₩5,500–₩22,000. MC, V. Tues–Sun 11:30am–10:30pm. Subway line 6 to Sangsu (exit 1).

Uhmeohni-wa Godeung-uh ★★ 🍴 KOREAN TRADITIONAL   The name, "Mother and Mackerel," should tell you everything about this cozy joint tucked away at the end of an alley. The owner serves up tasty Korean fare the way someone's mom might, and the *godeung-uh jeongshik* (mackerel meal) is not to be missed. In the summer, the college kids line up for the kohng guksu.

Although I've included details on cafes and tea shops under the "Seoul Entertainment & Nightlife" section, I thought I'd mention them here. There are so many wonderful traditional tea shops in Insadong and Samcheong-dong that it's really hard to choose. One of my favorites is the hard-to-find **Cha Massi-neun Ddeul** ★★★, 35-169 beonji Samcheong-dong (② 02/722-7006), hidden on the hillside (follow the signs to the Silk Rd. or Tibet museums). In a traditional house with floor-to-ceiling glass walls, the interior is a small courtyard garden, while the surrounding tables

look out over the city. Teas range from ₩6,000 to ₩10,000 and they bring you your own thermos full of hot water to keep refilling your teapot. Hours are daily 11am to 10:30pm. Another lovely teahouse is the **Jeontong Dawon** ★★ (② 02/730-6305), located inside the Gyeongjin Art Gallery in Insadong, open daily 10am to 9pm. In this hanok setting, you'll be surrounded by a spacious garden while you enjoy a *yuja cha* (citron tea) or one of their other traditional beverages. So sip and enjoy the relaxing atmosphere while your stress melts away.

407-19 Seogyo-dong, Mapo-gu. ② **02/337-0704.** No reservations. Entrees ₩8,000–₩19,000. No credit cards. Mon–Sat noon–9:30pm; Sun 1–10pm. Closed 1st and 3rd Mon of the month. Subway line 6 to Sangsu (exit 1).

INEXPENSIVE

Gooksijip ★ 🍴 KOREAN   If you're looking for a quick-and-dirty noodle meal, this is the place. The noodles are perfect for those on a budget, while not compromising on flavor. Unfortunately, neither the menu nor the sign is in English, but you can just point and ask for any of the dishes that look good. Items include *kohng namul bap* (mixed rice with bean sprouts), mandu guk, and bibim naengmyeon.

358-38 Seogyo-dong, Mapo-gu. ② **02/336-5235.** No reservations. Entrees ₩3,500–₩4,500. No credit cards. Mon–Fri 11am–8:30pm; Sat–Sun 11am–10:30pm. Subway line 2 to Hong-ik University (exit 6).

Itaewon

Itaewon is one of the best places in the city to find authentic international fare. Most of the good restaurants are found in the alley behind the Hamilton Hotel.

EXPENSIVE

OKitchen ★★★ 🍴 FUSION   A former New York restaurateur and his artist/food stylist wife run a teaching kitchen and inventive restaurant in a quiet alley in Itaewon. It's worth the splurge for one of their set menus to see what the culinary students have been cooking up that week. If you're lucky, you may get a little something from chef Susumu's garden or get to finish with a taste of their gorgonzola ice cream. Freshly baked bread and a solid wine list round out the ever-changing menu.

116-6 Itaewon-dong. ② **02/797-6420.** www.ofoodart.com. Reservations recommended. Entrees ₩19,000 and up, lunch set ₩25,000–₩40,000, dinner set ₩55,000–₩70,000. AE, MC, V. Subway line 6 to Itaewon (exit 1).

MODERATE

Gecko's Garden ★★ EUROPEAN ECLECTIC   A garden oasis in the middle of the city, Gecko's eclectic menu borrows from all over Europe. It's a great place for a relaxing lunch, a group dinner, or even just a glass of wine while sitting at one of the outdoor bistro tables in the courtyard or rooftop garden. There are pastas, steaks, paella, and even tiramisu on offer. The Sunday barbecues are great fun.

116-6 Itaewon-dong. ⓒ **02/790-0540.** www.geckosterrace.com. Reservations not necessary. Entrees ₩15,000–₩34,000. 10% VAT and 5% service charge not included. AE, MC, V. Subway line 6 to Itaewon (exit 1).

Le Saint Ex ★★★ FRENCH One of the few genuine French bistros in Seoul, it has a warm, cozy space inside. The menu changes every Tuesday and Friday, but expect the usual bistro items, like chicken with *pommes frites*, onion soup, or mussels, done in an honest, unpretentious way. As you'd expect, they have a decent wine list and a good selection of desserts that they tempt you with on display.

119-28 Itaewon-dong, Yongsan-gu. ⓒ**02/795-2465.** Reservations not necessary. Lunch set menu ₩16,000; dinner for 2 plus drinks ₩80,000–₩100,000. AE, MC, V. Daily noon–3pm and 6pm–midnight (last order 9:30pm); brunch menu on weekends. Subway line 6 to Itaewon (exit 1).

Ruby Edwards' Tartine Café & Bakery ★ BAKERY If you're looking for a good old-fashioned tart or some crusty European bread, follow your nose to this tiny bakery cafe tucked in a side alley. Their specialty is pie (cream pies, on weekends), but you can also get cheesecake or a nice cup of hot chocolate. Don't get comfortable, though, since table space is tight and the clock is ticking on your 1-hour limit. However, if you want a nice sit-down brunch, their new joint across the street will do you just fine.

119-15 Itaewon-dong, Yongsan-gu. ⓒ**02/3785-3400.** www.tartine.co.kr. Advance reservations for whole pies. Beverages ₩4,200–₩8,500; cookies ₩2,700, pie slices ₩7,500. MC, V. Daily 10am–10:30pm. Subway line 6 to Itaewon (exit 1), turn right into the 2nd alley, and it's on your righthand side.

Santorini GREEK If you're craving souvlakia or tzatziki, this is one of the few places in the country where you can get it. The owner and the chef are Greek, so you know you'll get good food and strong Greek coffee to end the meal. While a bit over-priced, it's a nice change from the regular kimchi and rice, and the outdoor seating on the second-floor balcony is fun when the weather is nice.

119-10 Beonji, Itaewon 1-dong (2nd floor). ⓒ **02/790-3474** or 3475. Reservations not necessary. Entrees ₩18,000–₩35,000. MC, V. Tues–Sun noon–10pm. Subway line 6 to Itaewon (exit 1).

Suji's ★★ AMERICAN The restaurant's name (after the owner, Suji Park) belies the American dishes served at this second-floor joint at the end of Itaewon's main street. Popular for weekend brunch, it's their home-cured pastrami and corn beef sandwiches that bring back the regulars. Save room for one of their warm, but yummy cheesecakes. They also have a location at the Hyundai Department Store in Gangnam.

2F, 34-16 Itaewon-dong, Yongsan-gu. ⓒ**02/797-3698.** www.sujis.net. Reservations not necessary. Entrees ₩11,000–₩21,000. AE, MC, V. Mon–Fri 11am–11pm, Sat 9am–11pm, Sun 9am–10pm. Subway line 6 to Noksapyeong (exit 3).

INEXPENSIVE

Shigol Bapsang TRADITIONAL KOREAN Decorated like an old country home, Shigol Bapsang (which means "country table") is known for the generous number of banchan that come out with the meals. The larger the group, the more side dishes you'll get to sample, so it's best to come with more people. Still, even as a meal for two it's quite a deal.

Hannam-dong, Yongsan-gu. ⓒ **02/795-9019.** No reservations. Set menu ₩7,000. No credit cards. Daily 24 hr. Subway line 6 to Itaewon (exit 2), a 15-min. walk, just past the Itaewon Hotel.

Smokey Saloon ★★ ☺ BURGERS   Reminiscent of a good neighborhood joint found in New York City, this old standard serves up some of the best burgers in Seoul. There's not much ambience, and the place has only six tables (two outside). Still, there is a whole list of burgers, like the Cowboy or the Big Islander, though you can't go wrong with the Classic. Other locations include Yeoksam, Seoul Station, Apgujeong, and on the first floor of the Ramada near City Hall.

123-5 Itaewon-dong, Yongsan-gu (in the alley behind the Hamilton Hotel). ☎ **02/795-9019.** www.smokeysaloon.kr. No reservations. Entrees ₩5,500. V. Daily 11:30am–9:30pm. Subway line 6 to Itaewon (exit 2).

Gangnam
VERY EXPENSIVE
Table 34 ★★★ EUROPEAN   This contemporary European restaurant, on the 34th floor of the Grand Intercontinental Parnas, serves up French-style cuisine with a modern flair. Let the sommelier navigate you through the largest wine cellar in Seoul. Worth a splurge for the view and the food, the executive chef has done his time in enough Michelin restaurants to earn his stars.

521 Teheran-no (159-8 Samseong-dong) Gangnam-gu. ☎ **02/559-7631.** http://www.ichotels group.com. Reservations recommended. Entrees ₩45,000–₩122,000.10% VAT and 10% service charge not included. AE, MC, V. Daily noon–10pm. Subway line 2 to Samseong, right next to the COEX mall.

EXPENSIVE
Gorilla in the Kitchen ★ FUSION   One of the better celebrity-owned restaurants, Bae Yong-joon's upscale joint is all about healthy cooking. There's no butter in the kitchen and salt is kept at a minimum. Good for you doesn't mean bad tasting, however. The chicken and garlic linguine, for example, is a tasty and healthy lunch, even with a Very Berry smoothie on the side.

650 Sinsa-dong, Gangnam-gu. ☎ **02/3442-1688.** www.gorillakitchen.co.kr/english/english01. asp. Reservations recommended. Menu items ₩17,000 and up; smoothies ₩10,000. AE, DC, MC, V. Daily 11am–11:30pm. Subway line 3 to Apgujeong (exit 3), then take a taxi to Dosan Park; when facing the front gate of the park, go right.

Gran Gusto ★★ ITALIAN   A creative Italian menu served in an elegantly furnished, understated dining area with wooden floors and contemporary accents—what's not to love? Pastas are well prepared, especially the seafood pastas (such as the anchovy or mackerel and leek pastas), although some of the tomato-based sauces can be a bit pedestrian. Servers are attentive and polite. Your best value bet is to go for the weekday lunch set menu, which includes choices from several courses—prices go up considerably on weekends and for dinner. The upstairs wine bar is open until 2am.

962-11 beonji, Daechi 3-dong, Gangnam-gu. ☎ **02/556-3960.** Reservations recommended. Weekday lunch set menus ₩20,000 and up; dinner and weekend set menus ₩35,000 and up; entrees ₩16,000 and up. 10% VAT not included. AE, DC, MC, V. Daily noon–10pm. Subway line 3 to Daechi (exit 3) or line 2 to Samseong (exit 3).

MODERATE
Todamgol ★★★ KOREAN   Just because the place is owned by actress Kim Hye-Jeong doesn't mean that the food just looks good. On the contrary, this popular restaurant serves excellent traditional Korean in generous portions. There is a nicely prepared *hanjeongshik* (Korean traditional meal) with a good array of side dishes. The *yeolmu bibimbap* (mixed rice dish with ponytail radish) and other wholesome favorites

When visiting bakeries in South Korea (like most Asian countries), remember that looks can be deceiving. That gorgeous chocolate cake beckoning from the display case may have the consistency of a dried sponge. Or those delectable-looking baguettes arrayed so nicely in the basket generally lack the fabulous crispy crust and the chewy inside you'd expect. Many of the Korean-style patisseries will have delicious-looking confections; they just might not taste as good as they look.

That doesn't mean that there aren't any great bakeries in town. If you want a genuine baguette, stop by **Wood &**

Brick in Gwanghwamun or Jae-dong (p. 67). For a fantastic *pain au chocolat* or croissant, go to **Eric Kayser ★★★** (𝄞 **02/789-5987**) at the **63 Building** (p. 90) or **Paul ★★** (𝄞 **02/2070-3000;** daily 7am–10pm) at the Marriott Executive Apartments on Yeouido (subway line 5 to Yeouido, exit 2). For overall baked goods visit the bakery in the **Grand Hyatt Hotel,** 747-7 Hannam 2-dong, Yongsan-gu (𝄞 **02/799-8167**). Of the Korean chains, **Paris Croissant** (𝄞 **02/594-4227**), especially the location across from the subway station in Gangnam, is your best option.

are also very tasty. There are two other locations, one in Cheongdam-dong and the other in Twicheon-dong, Gwangju-si, Gyeonggi-do.

236-6 Nonhyeon-dong, Gangnam-gu. 𝄞 **02/548-5121** or 548-5131. Entrees ₩9,000–₩23,000. AE, DC, MC, V. Daily 11:30am–10pm. Subway to Hakdong (exit 1) at Gyeongbok 4-way and go toward Seodaemun.

Apgujeong
EXPENSIVE
Samwon Garden ★★ KOREAN BARBECUE   Owned by the parents of pro golfer Grace (Ji-Eun) Park, this restaurant has been serving up galbi and *bulgogi* (sliced rib-eye) for over 30 years. One of the largest spaces in the city, the rustic setting and the open dining area add to the experience. Although this may not be the best or cheapest galbi joint, it's all about the ambience. It's a great place for first-timers to try Korean barbecue, where you cook your meat on the tabletop. Outdoor tables are perfect for an evening drink in the summertime. There is another location in Daechi-dong.

623-5 Sinsa-dong, Gangnam-gu. 𝄞 **02/548-3030.** www.samwongarden.com. No reservations. Entrees ₩25,000–₩52,000. AE, MC, V. Daily noon–10pm. Subway line 3 to Apgujeong (exit 2) or Sinsa (exit 1). It's easiest to take a taxi to Dosan Park from there.

MODERATE
Mealtop ★★ KOREAN DESSERT   A popular sweet treat in the sweltering summer months is *pot bingsu* (shaved iced red-bean dessert), and this place makes one of the best. Worthy of a splurge, their version has just the right combination of ice, bean, milk, and fruit, with just a couple of rice cakes to add that extra chewy texture.

429 Apgujeong-dong, Gangnam-gu (5th floor of the Hyundai department store). 𝄞 **02/547-6800.** No reservations. Pot bingsu ₩67,000. No credit cards. Daily 10:30am–9pm. Subway line 3 to Apgujeong (exit 6).

Slow Food ★ FUSION   For a leisurely lunch, sit at one of the outdoor tables here and watch the world go by. The menu features a mix of Korean and Western dishes—you can get fried rice or a sandwich. The ddeokbokgi are delightful, and the crab avocado sandwich is fantastic. They also have coffee and wine, if you just fancy a drink. Slow Food is located in front of the main entrance to Dosan Park, which makes for a nice stroll afterward.

631-34 Sinsa-dong, Gangnam-gu. © **02/515-8255.** Reservations not necessary. ₩12,000–₩15,000. MC, V. Daily 11am–10pm. Subway line 3 to Apgujeong (exit 2) or Sinsadong (exit 1). Then, take a taxi, or walk to Dosan Park.

Zen Hideaway ★ THAI FUSION One of the prettiest places to share a romantic meal, the Italian-influenced Thai dishes taste even better when enjoyed in candlelight. With all the live plants and running water, you might not even mind the extra dent in your wallet.

645-18 Sinsa-dong, Gangnam-gu. © **02/541-1461.** Entrees ₩16,000 to ₩40,000. MC, V. Daily 11:30am–2am. Subway line 3 to Sinsadong (exit 1).

INEXPENSIVE

Gustimo ★★ ☺ GELATO The first to introduce gelato to Seoul, it has been wildly popular ever since. Freshly made flavors are piled high in glass display cases, taunting you with their wonderful colors. They have standard flavors, but why not try one of the distinctly Korean flavors like ginseng, sweet potato, or red bean. Located at the basement level of the Galleria department store in Apgujeong.

494 Apgujeong-donga-dong, Gangnam-gu. © **02/3445-9475.** www.gusttimo.com. No reservations. Drinks and ice cream ₩3,500 and up. No credit cards. Daily 10:30am–10pm. Subway line 3 to Apgujeong (exit 1), and then a 20-min. walk.

Sawolae Bolibap ★★ KOREAN What used to be a humble dish has become popular as a "well-being" meal at this Apgujeong restaurant. The *bolibap* (barley rice) is served with a nice array of *namul* (vegetables) and small banchan that complement it well. There is also a lovely *gamja jeon* (potato flatcake) on offer. The interior has nice dark wood and contemporary decor, but the prices are still affordable.

610-5 Gujeong building, Sinsa-dong, Gangnam-gu. © **02/540-5292.** No reservations. Entrees ₩7,000 and up. MC, V. Daily 11:30am–10pm. Closed Lunar New Year and Chuseok. Subway line 3 to Apgujeong (exit 2), walk a bit, and you'll see the restaurant's sign on your left.

Other Places to Eat

MODERATE

Honadon ★★★ 🍴🍷 KOREAN BBQ Seeing a guy standing out front cooking ribs over a mesquite fire is a good sign that you're in for some real Korean barbecue. They par-cook the ribs outside and then bring the baby racks upstairs to your table to finish cooking. Specializing in black pig flown in from Jeju-do, their menu also includes beef ribs and naengmyeon. One small order is enough to feed two to three people, so bring friends and big appetites. Ask them for some special garlic and they'll bring garlic slices suspended in oil in an aluminum foil bowl that gets nicely caramelized over the flames.

337-2 Chang 5-dong, Dobong-gu. © **02/900-9800.** Reservations not required. Noodle dishes ₩7,000; meat ₩12,000–₩54,000. MC, V. Daily 11am–11pm. Plenty of parking. Subway line 4 to Suyu, then take a taxi from there.

Mitaniya ★★ JAPANESE Located in the "Little Tokyo" area of Seoul, Ichon, this nondescript joint serves authentic Japanese pub options in the basement of the Samik shopping mall. They don't take reservations and it can get quite crowded, but the fresh udon and tempura are worth the wait. They have a handful of locations in

Seoul, including in Apgujeong (on the fifth floor of the Hyundai department store) and in Gangnam (on the second floor of the Samsung Tower Palace arcade). The Ichon location is convenient when visiting the National Museum.

Samiksang-ga (basement floor), Ichon, Yongsan-gu. ℂ **02/797-4060.** No reservations. Menu items ₩5,000–₩35,000. MC, V. Daily 11:30am–10:30pm, closed the 1st and 3rd Monday of each month. Subway line 4 to Ichon (exit 4). Walk to the main road and turn left. The restaurant is down a narrow staircase on the right side, across the street from the school.

Tombola ★ ☺ ITALIAN   For just plain good pizzas and pastas, this spot is an excellent choice. It's a cozy place with brick walls and a warm atmosphere. The pastas are rich but not overbearing, and the pizzas are made with lovely Italian-style thin crusts, but plenty of cheese.

106-8 Banpo-dong, Seocho-gu. ℂ02/593-4660. Reservations recommended. Entrees ₩13,500–₩45,000. MC, V. Daily noon–2:30pm and 3:30–10:30pm. Subway line 3 or 7 to Express Bus Terminal (exit 6). Turn onto the alley next to the Paris Croissant and go straight for about 100m.

EXPLORING SEOUL

Seoul has an unusual amalgam of both traditional and modern attractions crowded into the city. It's best to plan your visit around an area, head there via subway, and then explore the neighborhood on foot.

Note: Street names aren't widely used in Seoul (or most of South Korea for that matter). Some major streets may have street signs, but buildings are numbered by when they were built, not location. More commonly, people will give you directions starting from a famous landmark or a store in the area. When traveling by taxi, it's best to know the *gu* (district) and the *dong* (ward) where you're headed.

Palaces

Because Seoul has been the capital of Korea for centuries, it's natural that it would have the country's most elaborate palaces and historic buildings. An important part of Korea's intricate history, these palaces tell stories of fallen kings and centuries-old dynasties, and hold more mysteries within their walls than we can ever know.

Changdeokgung ★★★ PALACE   This palace was built in 1405, the fifth year of the reign of Joseon King Taejong, as a separate palace adjacent to the main one, Gyeongbokgung. Located to its east, it is also known as Donggwol (the east palace), while the Gyeongbokgung is the north palace. Changdeokgung was also burned down the same time the main palace was in 1592, during the Japanese invasion. Reconstructed in 1609 to 1611, it served as the seat of royal power for 300 years until Gyeongbokgung was rebuilt at the end of the Joseon Dynasty. Left in disrepair afterward, the palace was renovated in 1907 and used again by King Sunjong, the country's last king. Although he lost his crown in 1910, Sunjong continued to live here until his death in 1926. His widow, Queen Yun, kept the palace as her home until she died in 1966. The last royal prince died here in 1970 and the last royal family member lived in the palace until her death in 1989.

The palace grounds are divided into administrative areas, residential quarters, and the rear garden. The existing administrative section includes Donghwamun (the front gate and the oldest existing palace structure), Injeongjeon (the throne hall), and Seonjeongjeon (the administrative hall). The residential area includes Huijeondang (the king's bed chamber), the Daejojeon (the queen's bed chamber), the royal kitchen, the infirmary, and other annex buildings.

Designated a UNESCO World Heritage site in 1997, Changdeokgung's rear garden was a resting area for the royals since the time of King Taejong. Sometimes called Huwon, Bukwon, and Geumwon, it was named **Biwon ★★★** (or "Secret Garden") by King Kojong. Some of the trees in the garden are now over 300 years old and represent the height of Korean garden design and landscaping techniques.

2-71 Waryong-dong, Jongno-gu. Ⓒ **02/762-8262.** http://eng.cdg.go.kr. Tours ₩3,000; ₩5,000 for the Huwon tour. Open 9am–6:30pm Tues–Sat (Apr–Oct), until 5:30pm Mar & Nov, until 5pm (Dec–Feb). English-language tours 10:30am and 2:20pm; for the garden 11:30am and 2:30pm. Tours last 80 min., while the Huwon tour lasts 2 hrs. Subway to line 3 to Anguk (exit 3) or line 1, 3, or 5 to Jongno 3(sam)-ga (exit 7).

Changgyeonggung PALACE   Located east of Changdeokgung, Changgyeonggung was a summer palace. Built in 1104 and called Sunganggung, the palace was given its present name in the 1390s, when the first Joseon King lived here while waiting for Gyeongbokgung to be built. Destroyed in 1592, it was reconstructed in 1616, with the majority of the buildings rebuilt in the 1830s after a terrible fire. During the Japanese occupation, a modern red building was built in the grounds and it was turned into a zoo and botanical garden. The zoo was removed, though the botanical garden remains, and the palace was completely restored from 1983 to 1986.

Unlike the other palaces in the city (which all have north–south orientations), Changgyeonggung has an east–west orientation, as was customary during the Goryeo Dynasty. The houses face south, but the office of the king, the Myeongjeongjeon, faces east. Because the ancestral shrines of the royal family are located in the south, the gate couldn't face south, according to Confucian customs. The largest building in the complex is Tongmyeongjeon, which was built as the queen's quarters. The pond, Chundangji, located in the north of the complex, was constructed during the Japanese occupation—before that, much of the land now underwater had been a rice field that the king tended.

From spring to autumn, various events (tea ceremonies, reenactments for the king's birthday, marriage ceremonies) are held at the palace on select weekend days.

2-1 Waryong-dong, Jongno-gu. Ⓒ **02/762-4868 x4.** http://jikimi.cha.go.kr/english. Admission ₩1,000 adults, ₩500 youth, free to seniors 65 and over and kids 6 and under. Tues–Sun, Apr–Oct 9am–6:30pm; Nov & Mar 9am–5:30pm; Dec–Feb 9am–5pm (last ticket sales 1 hr. before closing). Closed Mon. English tours 11am and 4pm. Subway line 4 to Hyehwa (exit 4). Walk 10 min. past Seoul National University Hospital.

Deoksugung ★ PALACE   The smallest of the city's palaces, Deoksugung is located at the corner of one of downtown Seoul's busiest intersections. Deoksugung ("Palace of Virtuous Longevity") originally belonged to Wolsandaegun, the older brother of Joseon King Seongjong, but later became a proper palace when Gwanghaegun (Prince Gwanghae) took the throne in 1608. The east wing was for the king and the west wing was reserved for the queen. In 1900, Jeonggwanheon was the first Western-influenced building to be added to the palace grounds. The red-and-gray brick structure features massive columns, ornate balconies, and a green tile roof. King Gojong, who reigned from 1863 to 1907, enjoyed having coffee and spending his free time there. The back of the building had a secret passageway, which still exists, to the Russian Emissary. The other Western-style building is Seokjojeon, which was designed by a British firm in 1905, when the Japanese occupied Korea. It was completed in 1910 and became a Japanese art gallery after King Gojong's death in 1919. After Korean independence from Japan, a joint commission of Americans and Russians held meetings there in 1946 in an attempt to reunite North and South Korea.

The east wing of Seokjojeon now serves as a gallery for Palace Treasure exhibitions, and the west wing is part of the National Modern Arts Center. Don't miss the changing of the guards in front of the main gates at 11am, 2pm, and 3:30pm daily.

5-1 Jeong-dong, Jung-gu. ℂ **02/771-9951.** www.deoksugung.go.kr. Admission ₩1,000 adults, ₩500 youth, free to seniors 65 and over and kids 6 and under. Admission includes general entry to art museum. Tues–Sun 9am–9pm (last entry 8pm); closed Mon. Subway to City Hall, line 1 (exit 2) or line 2 (exit 12).

Gyeongbokgung ★★ PALACE   Of the five grand palaces built during the Joseon Dynasty, this was the largest and most important one. Two years after King Taejo took power in 1394, he ordered the construction of this palace. It is said to have had 500 buildings when it was first built and it served as the home of Joseon kings for the next 200 years. During the Japanese Invasion (1592–98), the palace was burned, not by the invaders, but by disgruntled palace workers who wanted to destroy records of their employment as servants. The palace was later restored in 1865 under the leadership of Heungseon Daewongun during the reign of King Gojong. Using the original foundation stones, over 300 structures were completed by 1872, but at a great cost to the Korean people. Sadly, King Gojong used the palace for only 23 years after its reconstruction—he fled to Russia when his wife, Queen Min (p. 84), was murdered on the palace grounds. A year later the king moved into Deoksugung.

During the Japanese colonial period, all but 10 structures were demolished and only a fraction of its structures remain, including Gyeonghoeru Pavilion (which is on the ₩10,000 note), Geunjeongjeon (the imperial throne room), and Hyangwonjeong Pond. Free English tours are available in front of **Hongremun** (the entrance gate) at 9:30am, noon, 1:30pm, and 3pm.

The **National Palace Museum** is located south of the Heungnyemun (gate), and the **National Folk Museum** ★★ (ℂ 02/3704-3114) is located on the east side, within Hyangwonjeong. Entry to the palace includes admission to the museums as well. The National Folk Museum is well worth a visit, especially if you want an insight into Korean culture and the daily lives of Koreans throughout the country's long and turbulent history. The National Palace Museum is filled with relics collected from archaeological digs at Gyeongbokgung, Changdeokgung, Changgyeonggung, and Jongmyo. Focusing on the Joseon Dynasty (1392–1910), it's the perfect place to learn about Confucianism (once Korea's main religion) and ancestral rites that were passed on through the royal line. The displays give insight into the lives of Joseon royalty and palace architecture as well.

1 Sejong-no, Jongno-gu. ℂ **02/3700-3900.** www.royalpalace.go.kr/html/eng/main/main.jsp. Admission ₩3,000 adults, ₩1,500 youth, free to seniors 65 and over and kids 6 and under. Sun–Mon, Mar—Oct 9am–6pm; Nov–Feb 9am–5pm; closed Tues. Last entry 1 hr. before closing. English tours daily 11am, 1:30pm, and 3:30pm, last about 1 hr. Subway to Gyeongbokgung, line 3 (exit 5) or to Gwanghwamun, line 5 (exit 2). It's a 5-min. walk from either exit.

Gyeonghuigung ★ PALACE   Constructed in 1616, this was the fifth palace built in the city and one of the best royal grounds for a nice stroll—the name means "Palace of the Shining Bliss." The palace was designed following the incline of the surrounding hillside and even had an arched bridge that used to connect it to Deoksugung. The complex used to house over 100 buildings, but most of them were destroyed and the site was reduced by half when the Japanese built Gyeongseong Middle School during the colonization period. A major restoration project was started in 1988 and the palace was reopened to the public in 2002.

THE JOSEON dynasty

Lasting a whopping 518 years, the Joseon Dynasty was by far Korea's longest-lived monarchy. Founded in 1392 by King Taejo, Joseon supplanted the once powerful Goryeo Dynasty (918–1392) that brought Buddhism to prominence on the peninsula. But the Goryeo had spent most of the 13th century fighting invading Mongols, and the Joseon Dynasty seemed to bring peace to the region. Relations with neighboring China improved, and Korea's borders were extended to their current position (if you include North Korea).

But the Joseon Dynasty had problems of its own. By the mid-1400s, Confucianism—which includes a strict social hierarchy, with the king at the pinnacle and royalty just below—had taken the place of Buddhism, and many peasants and farmers saw their rights evaporate. Commoners felt the *yangban*—an educated, aristocratic class that often served as artists, teachers, and government advisors—took advantage of their positions, grabbing land and charging high rents to tenant farmers. Confucianism stresses the importance of education, and the Joseon leaders did build schools. In the 1500s, peasants began a series of revolts against excessive taxes and unfair social conditions.

Still, the Joseon Dynasty managed to survive—in part because the country was forced to contend with invasions from Japan and China. By the time peace treaties were in place with both, in the mid-1600s, Korea had turned inward and become known as the Hermit Kingdom. By the late 1800s, however, corruption and inefficiency had led to a severe weakening of the Joseon's ruling structure, and instability in the rest of Asia left Korea vulnerable to outside influence. Indeed, Japan forced Korea to become its protectorate in 1905. And when Japan formally annexed the country in 1910, they forced King Sukjong, the last of the Joseon leaders, to step down.

The **Seoul Metropolitan Museum of Art** (http://seoulmoa.org/global/eindex. jsp) and the **Seoul Museum of History** ★ ☺ (www.museum.seoul.kr/eng/eh_ main.jsp) now occupy parts of the original site. The Seoul Metropolitan Museum of Art has exhibits of contemporary South Korean artists, including painters, potters, sculptors, and photographers. The Seoul Historical Museum exhibits artifacts and documents chronicling the history of Seoul from the Stone Age to today. Walking over the miniature model of the city is the best part of the museum.

An experiential taekwondo program is held on the grounds three times daily and a taekwondo performance is held at 2pm Wednesday through Saturday.

1 beonji, Sinmun-no 2-ga, Jongno-gu. ✆ **02/724-0121.** Free admission. Tues–Fri 9am–6pm, Sat–Sun 10am–6pm. Closed Mon and Jan 1. Subway line 7 to Gwanghwamun (exit 7) and walk straight. Alternatively, take line 5 to Seodaemun (exit 4). Walk straight to the Naeil newspaper office, turn right, and then walk 10 min.

Unhyeongung PALACE   The childhood home of King Gojong (26th king of the Joseon Dynasty), Unhyeongung is smaller and architecturally different from other palaces. It is a representative home for noblemen during that period. Under the orders of the Queen Mother Jo, the small residence was renovated into a palace with four gates. Gojong's father and regent, Heungseon Daewongun, continued to live at the palace even after his son became king. Like the other palaces in the city, Unhyeongung was damaged during the Japanese colonization period and the Korean War, so it is a much smaller version of its former glorious self. The small row of rooms on the right is the Sujiksa, the quarters for the servants and guards. A bit to the left is the Norakdang hall, used for welcoming guests and for holding important events such as birthday parties and wedding ceremonies. In fact, a re-creation of the 1866 wedding of King Gojong and Queen Myeongseong is held here Saturdays from late April to late October from 1 to 3pm. Korean classical music and performances are held on Sundays from April to October at 4pm. Entrance to the palace is free starting from 1 hour before performances are held.

114-10 Unni-dong, Jongno-gu. ✆ **02/766-9090.** www.unhyeongung.or.kr/index_eng.php. Admission ₩700 adults, ₩300 youth, free to seniors 65 and over and kids 6 and under. Tues–Sun 9am–6pm Nov–Mar, until 7pm Apr–Oct. Subway line 3 to Anguk (exit 4) or line 5 to Jongno 3(sam)-ga (exit 5).

Historical Sites

Cheongwadae (The Blue House) ★ GOVERNMENT BUILDING   Known
for the azure color of its tiled roof, Cheongwadae serves as the office of the President of South Korea. Blue tiles were reserved for kings and still denote a place of authority. The presidential mansion is to the side of the main building; next door is the Yeong-bingwan, which serves as the guesthouse for visiting dignitaries. Onsite are Chun-chugwan (the Spring and Autumn Pavilion), Nokjiwon (Green Grass), Mugunghwa (Rose of Sharon) Valley, and the Seven Palaces from the Joseon Dynasty. Although the complex itself is tightly guarded, the Nokjiwon and Mugunghwa Valley areas are open to the public. A nice walk in the area starts at the east gate of Gyeongbokgung, goes past the Blue House, and continues to Samcheongdong Park.

1 Sejong-no, Jung-gu. ✆ **02/771-9952.** www.president.go.kr. Free admission, but tour reservations are required. Hour-long guided tours Tues–Fri 10am, 11am, 2pm, and 3pm (also 4th Sat of the month) at the Gyeongbokgung parking lot. Reservations can be made online (at least 2 weeks in advance) or by e-mail (tour@president.go.kr) Closed Sun, Mon, and national holidays. Subway to Gyeongbokgung, line 3 (exit 5), and then walk 10 min.

Ihwajang HISTORIC HOME   This was the home of the first president of the
Republic of Korea (South Korea's official name as of 1948), Lee Seung-man (or Rhee Syngman or Yi Seungman—no one seems to agree on a proper spelling), and his wife. President Lee was the country's controversial leader from August 1948 to April 1960. After he relinquished his office (in the wake of popular protests that followed a disputed election), he stayed here before leaving to live in exile in America. The home's architecture shows how Korean traditional homes changed under Japanese colonialization. On display are everyday household objects, clippings of historical articles, his humble clothing, and general depictions of his frugal lifestyle.

1-2 Ihwa-dong, Jongno-gu. ✆ **02/762-3171.** Free admission, but reservations required. Daily 10am–5pm. Subway line 4 to Hyehwa (exit 2); walk toward Korea National Open University and turn left at the SNU Elementary School of College Education; keep walking until you get to the crossroads and head toward Podowon Garden restaurant. Follow the road leading uphill—Ihwajang is at the end.

Jeoldusan Martyrs' Shrine & Museum MUSEUM   Thousands of Roman
Catholic believers were tortured and brutally killed here during the Byeonin Persecution in 1866 (p. 165). This shrine was built to commemorate the 100-year anniversary of that tragedy. A museum and memorial were added in 1967 and the park was created in 1972. Showing a little-known dark side of Korean history, there are displays of torture methods and memorial sculptures surrounding the main shrine.

96-1 Hapjeong-dong, Mapo-gu. ✆ **02/3142-4434** (Korean only). www.jeoldusan.or.kr. Admission not set but on a donation basis. Tues–Sun, Apr–Nov 10am–noon and 1–5pm; Dec–Mar until

The Last Empress

Queen Min (1851–95), aka Myeong-seong Hwang-hu or Empress Myeong-seong, was the first official wife of Joseon King Gojong. Alternatively remembered as a jealous queen or a national heroine, there is still controversy over her role in history. What is known for sure is that she had considerable political power and was aiming to increase diplomatic ties with Russia after the Sino–Japanese War of 1894–95. Not bad for a girl who was orphaned at the age of 8 and who went from being a member of an impoverished branch of the royal family to being queen. But since the war between China (which lost) and Japan was fought in large part over which country would have more influence over Korea, Min was taking a risk. She hoped the Russians would help keep the Japanese out of Korea.

Unfortunately, Min's risk didn't pay off. Recognizing that Min's power threatened their plans to annex Korea, the Japanese hired a group of assassins who broke into Gyeongbokgung during the early-morning hours of October 18, 1895, and stabbed three different women they thought might be the queen. Once they had confirmed that one of the three was indeed Queen Min, they took her corpse into the forest and burned it. The assassins were then given safe passage to Japan and found not guilty in a Hiroshima court, which cited lack of evidence as the reason for its verdict. By 1905, Japan was in control of Korea.

4:30pm; closed Mon and holidays. Subway line 2 or 6 to Hapjeong (exit 7) and walk 10 min., following the signs.

Jongmyo (Royal Shrine) ★★ MONUMENT   A place of worship for the kings of the Joseon Dynasty, this royal shrine was built by King Yi Seong-gye, the first in that royal line, in 1394. At this designated UNESCO World Heritage site, the annual ceremony held in honor of the dead monarchs is considered the oldest complete ceremony in the world. It is usually performed here on the first Sunday of May.

The buildings in Jongmyo include Jeongjeon (the main hall), Yeongnyeongjeon (the Hall of Eternal Peace), and other auxiliary facilities. Jeongjeon, with its attached cloister, was the longest building in Asia when it was built. Today, it contains the memorial tablets of 19 Joseon kings and 30 Joseon queens in 19 spirit chambers.

There are three paths in front of the main gate, each with a special meaning. The middle one was for the dead kings, the east road for the reigning king, and the west road for the reigning prince. The road in the middle goes to Jeongjeon, where the annual ceremony mentioned above is held. The other roads lead to Jeongsacheon. After preparing the body and mind, the king and prince go to Jeongsacheon, where a traditional meal is prepared for them. The music performed in the ceremony has been handed down for over 500 years.

155 Jongno 1(il)-ga, Jongno-gu. ⓒ **02/765-0195.** http://jikimi.cha.go.kr/english/world_heritage/Jongmyo.jsp. Admission ₩1,000 adults, ₩500 youth, free to seniors 65 and over and kids 6 and under. Mar–Oct Mon and Wed–Fri 9am–5pm, Sat–Sun and holidays 9am–7pm; Nov–Feb Mon and Wed–Fri 9am–4:30pm, Sat–Sun and holidays 9am–6pm. English guided tours daily 10am, noon, 2pm, and 4pm. Subway line 1, 3, or 5 to Jongno 3-ga (exit 8 or 11).

Namsangol Hanok Maeul (Traditional Village) ★ HISTORIC SITE   The traditional houses in this maeul were moved here from various other locations in the city. Now completely restored, they show how people (from peasants to royalty) used to live during the Joseon Dynasty. On spring and autumn weekends, traditional marriage ceremonies are staged at Bak Yeong-hyo's residence, usually around noon or 1pm.

84-1 Pil-dong 2-ga, Jung-gu. © **02/2264-4412.** http://hanokmaeul.seoul.go.kr. Free admission. Wed–Mon 9am–7pm Apr–Oct, until 8pm Nov–Mar. Closed Tues; if Tues is a holiday, then closed the following day. Subway line 3 or 4 to Chungmuro (exit 3 or 4).

Samneung (Three Tombs) Park MONUMENT   This quiet retreat in the middle of Gangnam is the final resting place for King Seongjong, the ninth king of the Joseon Dynasty, his wife, Queen Jeonghyeon, and King Jungjong, the second son of Seongjong. The tombs are the green mounds typical of royals of the era. Although they were defaced during the Japanese invasion in 1592, they were later restored. Now they serve as a little oasis as the small forested area shields the tombs from the hustle and bustle of the surrounding city.

135-4 Samseong 2-dong, Gangnam-gu. Admission ₩1,000 adults, ₩500 youth. Tues–Sun 9am–6pm Mar–Oct, 9am–5pm Nov–Feb. Closed Mon and holidays. Subway line 2 to Seolleung (exit 8); walk down the alley next to Hana Bank.

Museums

Leeum, Samsung Museum of Art ★★★ MUSEUM   The theme of this museum is the past, present, and future of art and design. With this in mind, the first building was designed by Swiss architect Mario Botta, exhibiting Buddhist art, Korean ceramics, paintings, and calligraphy. Start on the top floor and work your way down.

The second building, designed by French architect Jean Nouvel, exhibits contemporary art from Korean artists dating from 1910 to the present, as well as art from other countries dating from 1945. Its permanent collection includes works by such luminaries as Bacon, Rothko, Beuys, Warhol, Hurst, Barney, and Albers.

The third building, which serves as the Child Education and Culture Center, was designed by Dutch architect Rem Koolhaas.

English-speaking docents (tour guides) are available for tours at 3pm on Saturdays and Sundays, but make reservations 2 to 3 days in advance. Tours take about 90 minutes.

747-18 Hannam-dong, Yongsan-gu. © **02/2014-6900.** http://leeum.samsungfoundation.org/eng/main.asp. Admission ₩10,000 adults, ₩6,000 youth. Admission for special exhibitions varies, but discount tickets for permanent and special exhibitions are available. Tues–Sun 10:30am–6pm; last tickets sold 1 hr. before closing. Subway to Hangangjin (exit 1). Bus no. 11 or 0014 to Hangangjin. Walk toward Itaewon, then turn right at the 1st alley, and walk up the hill about 5 min.

National Museum of Korea ★★ ☺ MUSEUM   Included in the collections are Buddhist sculptures, metal works, and ceramics, located on the third-floor Fine Arts Gallery. Art from Indonesia, central Asia, Japan, and China along with Nangnang remains are in the Asian Arts gallery on the same floor. The second floor houses calligraphy, paintings, and wooden crafts and donations from private collections. The first floor has relics dating from Paleolithic to the Three Kingdoms and Unified Shilla periods (see chapter 2) in the Archeological Gallery. Also on this floor are maps, prints, and important documents in the Historic Gallery.

Tip: Free English-language tours of the main museum are offered daily at 10:30am and 2:30pm. Meet in front of the information desk for the 1-hour tour. Audio guides are available for ₩1,000 and digital PDA guides are available for ₩3,000, though you must reserve a rental online at least a day before your visit.

135 Seobinggo-lo, Yongsan-gu. © **02/2077-9047.** www.museum.go.kr/eng. Admission free, except for special exhibits. Tues and Thurs–Fri 9am–6pm; Wed and Sat until 9pm; Sun and holidays

until 7pm; last entry 1 hr. before closing. Closed Mon and Jan 1. Subway line 4 to Ichon (exit 2), walk straight toward Yongsan Family Park. Bus no. 0018 or 502.

Seodaemun Prison History Museum MUSEUM   This prison-turned-museum was built at the end of the Joseon Dynasty and used as a place to torture and kill Korean patriots during the Japanese occupation. Koreans have a flair for melodrama and it shows in the displays, which are complete with fake blood, pained screams, and objects of various torture methods. It is an interesting way to learn about Korea's sometimes painful past.

101 Hyeonjeo-dong, Seodaemun-gu.Ⓒ **02/360-8500.** www.sscmc.or.kr. Admission ₩1,500 adults, ₩1,000 teens, ₩500 children. Tues–Sun 9:30am–6pm Mar–Oct, until 5pm Nov–Feb. English docents available Sundays at 1pm and 2pm or by reservation 1 wk in advance. Closed Mon, Jan 1, Lunar New Year, Chuseok. Subway line 3 to Dongnimmun (exit 5). Bus no. 471, 701, 702, 703, 704, 720, 752, 7019, 7021, 7023, 7025, 7712, 7737, 9701, 9703, 9705, 9709, 9710, 9711, or 9712.

Seoul Museum of Art ★★ ART MUSEUM   Housed in the former Korean Supreme Court building, the interior space is great for contemporary exhibitions, and temporary installations include works by artists from South Korea, Asia, and beyond. Recent shows have included a portrait exchange between Korean and Australian artists, a show on Hyperrealism, and an exhibit on contemporary textbooks. The permanent collection includes Korean and Western paintings, sculptures, prints, calligraphic works, photography, and media art. They have galleries in Gyeonghuigung and in NamSeoul, as well.

37, Seosomun-dong, Jung-gu.Ⓒ **02/771-9952.** http://seoulmoa.org. Free admission, but prices vary for special exhibits. Tues–Fri 10am–8pm year-round, Sat–Sun and holidays, Mar–Oct 10am–7pm; Sat–Sun and holidays, Nov–Feb 10am–6pm; last entry 1 hr. before closing. Closed Jan 1. SeMA Gyeonghuigung daily 10am–6pm; SeMA NamSeoul Tues–Fri 10am–8pm, Sat–Sun and holidays 10am–6pm. Closed Mon and Jan 1. Subway line 1 to City Hall (exit 1), or line 2 (exit 11 or 12) and walk toward City Hall.

Seoul Museum of History ☺ MUSEUM   This museum gives an overview of Seoul from prehistoric times through today. It houses a permanent collection, rotating special shows, and a gallery dedicated to relics donated by the city's residents.

2-1 Sinmun-no 2-ga, Jongno-gu. Ⓒ **02/724-0274.** www.museum.seoul.kr/eng/eh_main.jsp. Admission free. Tues–Fri 9am–9pm, year-round, Sat–Sun and holidays (Mar–Oct) 9am–7pm; Sat–Sun and holidays (Nov–Feb) 9am–6pm; last entry 1 hr. before closing. Closed Mon, Jan 1, and days declared by the mayor. Subway line 57 to Gwanghwamun (exit 7) and walk straight.

Toto's Nostalgia Museum ★★ ☺ 👔 MUSEUM   This odd museum has objects from everyday life dating from the '60s and '70s. Displays include old Korean textbooks, report cards, junk-food packages, records, telephones, toys, and figurines. Although small, this collection shows a bit of modern South Korean culture with simple items from the not-so-distant past.

169-22 Gwanhun-dong, Jongno-gu.Ⓒ **02/725-1756.** Admission ₩1,000. Daily 10am–9pm. Subway line 3 to Anguk (exit 6) or line 1 to Jongno 3(sam)-ga (exit 6). Bus no. 162, 606, 1020, or 8000. On Insadong-gil, across the street from Ssamziegil, on the 2nd floor.

Other Sights in Seoul
TEMPLES & CHURCHES

Bongeunsa ★★ TEMPLE   Located north of the COEX Mall near the World Trade Center, this temple was founded in much quieter times—A.D. 794, during the Shilla period. One of the Seon (Zen) centers during the Joseon Dynasty, it was originally called Gyeongseongsa (which means "seeing true nature"). It fell into decline during the Goryeo Dynasty, but was renovated and given its present name in 1498. The oldest building still standing was built in 1856 and houses the 150-year-old wooden blocks of the Avatamsaka Sutra (called the "Flower Garland" or "Flower Adornment" Sutra), as well as other sutras (Buddhist scriptures). At 4:10am and 6:40pm daily, the monks play the four percussion instruments to awaken the four heavenly beings of the earth, sky, water, and underground. The best time to visit is during the early-morning percussion ceremony to hear the echoes of the gongs before the city awakens. You can also do an overnight temple stay (for ₩50,000–₩80,000) or just take a 2-hour tour of the grounds. If you're visiting in the fall, don't miss the Jeongdaebulsa ceremony held on the ninth day of the ninth lunar month, when the monks carry scriptures on their heads and recite the Beopseongge (Buddhist rites).

73, Samseong-dong, Gangnam-gu. ✆ **02/511-6070.** www.bongeun.org. Free admission. Daily usually 4am–9pm. Subway line 2 to Samseong (exit 6), walk 100m (328 ft.) toward ASEM Tower, then turn left, and walk through the Bongeunsa trail (10 min.), or line 7 to Cheongdam (exit 2), walk 150m (492 ft.) toward Gyeonggi High School, and turn right. Bus no. 361, 680, 2225, 2411, 2413, 3411, 3415, 4411, or 4428.

Bongwonsa TEMPLE   Located northeast of Yonsei University on Ahnsan, Bongwonsa is the head temple of the Korean Taego Order. Originally founded in 889 by the monk Doseon, it was moved to its current location in 1749. The original main hall was one of the most elaborate wooden sanctums of the Joseon Dynasty and it was built without any nails. However, it and other parts of the temple were destroyed during the Korean War. The main hall was rebuilt in 1966, but later moved to another part of the city. While the new hall of 3,000 Buddhas was being built in 1991, the main hall was rebuilt in 1994. Although the temple buildings aren't that impressive, the 16 Arhat statues and the judgment hall, which features murals of the judges of the underworld, are worth a gander. The best time to visit is in the summer when the Seoul Lotus Flower Culture Festival is going on, or on June 6 when they have a special ceremony for world peace and the reunification of the two Koreas.

San 1 beonji, Bongwon-dong, Seodaemun-gu. ✆**02/392-3007** (Korean only). http://bongwonsa. or.kr. Free admission. Subway line 2 to Sinchon (exit 4), or line 3 to Dongnimmun (exit 4). From either subway exit, take village bus no. 7024 to the temple (the last stop).

Hwagyesa TEMPLE   Located north of downtown Seoul, Hwagyesa sits at the foot of the Samgaksan. Part of the Chogye Order of Korean Buddhism, it has been home to a long line of Zen masters. The temple is also home to the **Seoul International Zen Center** (✆ 02/900-4326), where you can do a temple stay and experience Buddhist rituals and meditations.

487 beonji, Suyu-1-dong, Gangbuk-gu. ✆**02/902-2663.** www.hwagyesa.org or http://seoulzen. org. Free admission. Daily 9am–6pm. Subway line 4 to Suyu (exit 3), then take bus no. 2 or exit 8 and take bus no. 1165. Alternatively, take bus no. 104, 109, or 144 to Hwagyesa. Or take bus no. 151, 152, 410, or 1165 and get off in front of Hansin University, then walk up the small road toward the mountains.

Jogyesa TEMPLE   Jogyesa is at the center of Seon (Zen) Buddhism in Korea. Although the temple itself was founded in 1910, some of the trees in front of the main building date back almost 500 years. The main building, called the Daeungjeon, was constructed in 1938 and still retains its brilliant colors. Not the most stately or the most beautiful temple in South Korea, Jogyesa's main strength is its convenient location.

The temple offers a variety of programs that teach visitors about Buddhist life (for ₩10,000). They require that at least six people be signed up for each program, so you'll need to make a reservation at least a week in advance. English interpreters are available.

Around the temple, there are many shops that specialize in Buddhist items, such as prayer beads, wooden gongs, and incense. It's worth a browse in the stores—perhaps a small Buddha will make his way into your luggage.

45, Gyeongji-dong, Jongno-gu. ℭ 02/732-2183. www.jogyesa.org. Free admission. Temple site daily 24 hr.; Daeungjeon and Geungnakjeon daily 4am–9pm. Subway line 1 to Jonggak (exit 2), then 10-min. walk; line 3 to Anguk (exit 6), cross road in front of Dongduk Gallery and 10-min. walk to path to temple on the right; line 5 to Gwanghwamun (exit 2), to temple path between YTN parking tower and Hana Bank.

Myeongdong Cathedral ★ CATHEDRAL   The main Catholic church in the country, the Gothic structure is a bit of a surprise in the middle of Seoul. Construction on the building was started in 1892 and finished in 1898, on the spot where the first Catholics gathered in 1784. In this structure of brick with stained glass, the basement floor houses the remains of the Korean Catholic martyrs (p. 165). Masses are held daily, check with them for English-language services.

1-8 Myeongdong 2-ga, Jung-gu. ℭ 02/774-1784. www.mdsd.or.kr. Free admission. Daily 7am–9pm; closed to all but worshipers during services, which are held weekdays at 6:30am, 10am, 6pm, and 7pm (no 7pm service on Mon), and weekends 7am, 9am, 10am, 11am, noon, 4pm, 5pm, 6pm, 7pm, and 9pm. Subway line 2 to Euljiro 1(il)-ga (exit 5), or line 4 to Myeongdong (exit 8). Either way, it's a 10-min. walk.

PARKS & GARDENS

Han-gahng (Han River) Parks ★★★ PARK   The Han River has been an important part of Korea for centuries. For the citizens of modern Seoul, it serves as a place for leisure. The Han River Parks encompass nearly the entire shoreline on both sides. They are popular places to bike, rollerblade, jog, walk, or just sit by the water and talk with friends, especially on hot summer evenings. **Water taxis** costing around ₩1,588–₩3,960, stop at 11 locations between Yeouido and Jamsil from 10am to 8pm (commuter taxis run 7–8:30am and 6:30–8pm).

Tip: If you get hungry, you can flag down any one of the messengers delivering Korean "fast food" along the river. It takes only about half an hour for them to return with some hot jjajangmyeon noodles, mandu, or spicy fried chicken.

Free admission. Daily 24 hr. To get to the Gangdong-gu section, take subway line 5 or 8 to Cheonho (exit 1) and walk over the Cheonho Daegyo (bridge). To get to the Songpa-gu section, take subway line 2 or 8 to Jamsil (exit 5) or subway line 2 to Sincheon (exit 6). To get to the Banpo bridge, take subway line 3, 7, or 9 to the Express Bus Terminal (exit 8) and follow the signs. Or take bus no. 143, 401, or 406. Bus no. 8401 goes between the Express Bus Terminal and Noksapyeong with a stop in the middle of the Banpo Daegyo.

Namsan Park ★★ ☺ PARK   Although not terribly elevated, Namsan (South Mountain) is home to the **N Seoul Tower** (ℭ 02/3455-9277), where you can get great views of the city (at least on days when there's no smog or yellow dust from China). Best to come on a clear night, when the lights are twinkling below. The best view is from the rotating restaurant on the top floor, **N'Grill** (p. 66), but you'll have to pay a premium price for dinners there. Slightly less expensive, but still offering a view, is the **Hancook**☺ restaurant, which has set menus (lunch is ₩30,000; dinner is ₩42,000) and a buffet bar. Those on a budget can opt for the bakery, cafe, or food court on the lower floors. If you're not up for a meal, you can just go to the tower's observation floor and take in the view. You'll even get a peep at the panorama from the "sky" restrooms with their floor-to-ceiling windows. If you plan ahead, you can bring a padlock to add to the millions of locks attached to the surrounding fences by young lovers.

You can take the long stairway up Namsan (at least a 30-min. hike), take a yellow bus (with a short walk to the tower), a free shuttle ride (runs once an hour from in front of the Hotel Prince in Myeongdong) or opt for a cable car ride. No cars are allowed on top.

100-177 Hoehyun-dong 1-ga, Jung-gu. ℂ **02/753-2563** (Korean only). Free admission to the park; N Seoul Tower's observation platform ₩8,000 adults 19–65, ₩6,000 ages 14–18 and 66 and over, ₩4,000 kids 5–13; cable car ₩7,500 round-trip or ₩6,000 one-way for ages 14 and over, ₩5,000 round-trip or ₩3,500 one-way for kids 7–13. Cable car daily 10am–11pm; observation platform 9am–1am. Subway line 3 or 4 to Chungmuro (exit 2), then take yellow bus no. 2.

Seoul Forest ★★ ☺ PARK

What used to be a hunting ground for kings, a horse racetrack, a water purification plant, and a golf course, has now become an urban green space encompassing five parks, including an art park, wetlands, and part of the Han River park. The citizens of Seoul planted 48,000 trees here between 2003 and 2005 and the fruits of their labor are now maturing. The kids will especially like the woodland playground and the insect garden.

685 Seongsu 1(il)-ga, Seongdong-gu. ℂ **02/462-0253.** http://parks.seoul.go.kr/eng. Free admission. 24 hr. Bike rentals ₩3,000 per hour. Subway line 2 to Tteukseom (exit 8). Bus no. 2014, 2412, 2413, or 2224. Or for the back gate, bus no. 141, 145, 148, or 410.

Seoul Olympic Park ★ PARK

An expansive park built for the 1988 Olympics, it is filled with paths that wind in and out of an art park containing more than 200 outdoor sculptures. It's the perfect place for biking, in-line skating, or just strolling. The **Olympic Museum** commemorates the 1988 games and gives a bit of overall Olympics history. Tennis courts, a gymnasium, and other facilities are open for regular use. The indoor **Olympic pool** is also open to the public Monday to Friday from noon to 9pm.

88 Bangi-dong, Songpa-gu. ℂ **02/410-1357.** www.olympicpark.co.kr. Free admission to the park. Admission to the museum is ₩3,000 adults, ₩2,000 teens, ₩1,500 children. Park daily 5:30am–10:30pm; museum Tues–Sun 10am–5:30pm (when a holiday falls on a Mon, then closed the following day). Subway line 8 to Mongchontoseong (exit 1) or line 5 to Olympic Park.

Tapgol (Pagoda) Park ♨ PARK

Located on the former site of the Joseon Dynasty-era Weongaksa (Weongak Temple), Tapgol is the first modern park to be built in the city. The site still contains the Wongaksaji Sipcheongseoktap (a 10-level stone tower from the temple), Weongaksabi, and a statue of Son Byeong-hee. The park is where the Korean independence movement of 1919 started, but it has become a haven for Seoul's senior citizens. You'll see old men passing the time or playing *baduk* (a popular Korean game), while aged prostitutes try to tempt them with their carnal wares and energy drinks.

38-1, Jongno 2-ga, Jongno-gu. Free admission. Daily 6am–sunset. Subway line 1 or 3 to Jongno 3-ga (exit 1) and walk 5 min. toward Jonggak.

Yangjae Citizens' Forest ☺ PARK

Over 106,000 trees were planted here when this park was built for the 1986 Asian Games and the 1988 Olympics. Other than nice walking paths and plenty of greenery, there are tennis, volleyball, and basketball courts; a children's playground; and even a path where you can stimulate your *ki* (chi) energy by walking barefoot on prepared stones. (Don't worry, there's a foot bath nearby.) There is also a memorial hall for Yun Bong-gil, a famed activist during the Japanese Imperial period (1910–1945).

236, Yangjae-dong, Seocho-gu. Free admission. 24 hr. Subway line 3 to Yangjae (exit 7). From there you can take a walk to the forest, or take a bus headed toward Seongnam and get off at "Shiminae Soop." Bus no. 08, 20, 3200, 6405, or 8201.

AMUSEMENT PARKS & ZOOS

There are plenty of amusement parks both large and small in Seoul. The smaller ones may be a bit cheesy, especially by Western standards, with just a few carnival rides and games. But the larger parks are giant crowd pleasers with world-class roller coasters and high prices to boot. Information for **Everland, Seoul Land,** and **Seoul Grand Park** are in the Gyeonggi-do chapter, but the ones below are in the metropolitan area proper.

Children's Grand Park ★ ☺PARK   It would take more than a day to take in all the sights at this giant park and amusement facility, designed especially for children. The facilities include an amusement park (iLand), a zoo, pony rides, and a Marine Animal House, that exhibits seals and polar bears. There are also botanical gardens, a water play area, an ecological pond, and a "shoeless park," where you can experience a variety of different textures with the bottom of your feet. The outdoor swimming pool is open in the summer. You may want to pack a picnic lunch, since food choices in the park are limited to Korean fast food and snack offerings.

540 Cheonggyecheon-lo, Neung-dong, Songdong-gu. ☎02/450-9311. www.childrenpark.or.kr or www.sisul.or.kr/global/eng/park/park03.jsp. Free admission to park, but various facilities have different admission fees. Daily 5am–10pm (some amusements close earlier); zoo daily 10am–5pm. Subway line 5 to Achasan (exit 4) or line 7 to Children's Grand Park (exit 1). Bus no. 3216, 4212, 2221, 3215, 130, 303, 9301, or 9403.

Lotte World ☺THEME PARK   The Disneyland of Seoul (complete with the requisite "Magic Castle"), Lotte World has a variety of rides (the main attractions), an ice-skating rink, a swimming pool, and a folk museum. Be forewarned: The biggest crowds come on Friday and Saturday night, when you may have to wait in line up to 2 hours just to get on a ride. If you plan on spending a day here, it may be more economical to get a passport ticket, which gives you access to all facilities except for the carnival games, which require fees per play. Alternatively, you can visit after 4pm and get discounted admission.

40-1, Jamsil-dong, Songpa-gu. ☎02/411-2000 or 411-4000. www.lotteworld.com/Global_eng/Main.asp. Regular admission ₩25,000 adults, ₩22,000 teens and seniors 65 and over, ₩19,000 children; passport ₩40,000 adults, ₩35,000 teens and seniors, ₩31,000 children; After 4 passport ₩31,000 adults, ₩27,000 teens and seniors, ₩23,000 children. Mon–Thurs 9:30am–10pm, Fri–Sat until 11pm. Subway line 2 or 8 to Jamsil (exit 4).

OTHER LOCATIONS OF INTEREST

63 (Yooksam) Building ICON   Actually only 60 stories tall (3 of its stories are underground), what once used to be the tallest building in the city has now been dwarfed by the 69-story Mokdong Hyperion in Yangcheon and the 73-story Tower Palace in Gangnam. But its exterior still glows an impressive gold, especially at sunset, and its top-floor Sky Deck still provides a great view. Its official name is 63 City, but everyone just calls it the Yooksam Building. The tower includes an aquarium, an IMAX theater (in three languages), a wax museum, the **Eric Kayser bakery ★★★**, and a variety of restaurants. The ones on the higher floors (56–59) offer the best views, but you'll pay premium prices for the food. If you're watching your budget, head down to the food court on the first-floor basement level.

1-8 Myeongdong 2-ga, Jung-gu. ☎02/789-6363. www.63city.co.kr. Daily 10am–10pm (last entry 9:30pm). Admission to the observation deck ₩7,000 adults, ₩6,500 teens or seniors 65 and over,

₩5,500 children. Fees to other attractions vary. Subway line 1 to Daebang (exit 6) and catch free shuttle about 40m (131 ft.) from the exit toward Yeouido; line 5 to Yeouinaru (exit 1) and catch free shuttle in front of the Sambu Apts., or to Yeouido (exit 5) and catch free shuttle at St. Mary's Hospital platform. Bus no. 62, 261 362, 5534, 5633, 7611, or 9409.

Cheonggyecheon WALKING TRAIL   What used to be a small stream that flowed through the downtown area was hidden beneath a truck bypass for decades. In 2003, the mayor of the city decided to restore the stream and give the city some much-needed natural space—the bypass was removed, walking paths were opened, and 22 bridges were built. Night or day, it's a nice place to take a stroll, as Seoul's skyscrapers loom on either side of you.

The city offers two different walking tours of Cheonggyecheon three times a day. The free tours take about 2 to 3 hours and you need to make a reservation at least 5 days in advance.

Bus tours of Cheonggyecheon are also offered, departing from in front of Gwanghwamun Tourist Info Center (subway line 5 to Gwanghwamun, exit 6). The tour takes up to 2 hours (depending on traffic) and departs at 10am, noon, 2pm, 4pm, and 7pm. Call the Gwanghwamun Tourist Info Center to make reservations. There are no tours on Mondays.

Starts near the Donga Ilbo Building and the Seoul Finance Center in Sejong-no, Jongno-gu. ℂ **02/3707-9453** (Seoul City Tours) daily 9am–6pm or 02/735-8688 for the Gwanghwamun Tourist Info Center daily 9am–10pm. Free admission, but bus tours cost ₩5,000 adults, ₩3,000 youth. Daily 24 hr. Subway line 1 to City Hall, Jonggak, Jongno 3-ga, Jongno 5-ga, Dongdaemun, or Sinseol-dong; line 2 to Euljiro 1-ga, Euljiro 3-ga, Euljiro 4-ga, Sindang, or Sangwangsibni; line 3 to Jongno 3-ga; line 4 to Dongdaemun History & Culture Park; or line 5 to Gwanghwamun.

World Cup Stadium & Parks ENTERTAINMENT COMPLEX   Since World Cup matches don't happen every day, part of the stadium was turned into a retail complex with a 10-screen cineplex (the **CGV Sangam 10**). The field area isn't open, but you can tour the stadium any day of the week. The surrounding area has been turned into a bunch of different parks including Nanjicheon Park, Noeul Park, and Peace Park, with places to walk and, even better, for inline skating. The best of these is the **Haneul ("Sky") Park ★★**, which is a reclaimed landfill that has been converted into a 192,000-sq.-m (2,067-sq.-ft.) ecological site.

515 Seongsan-dong, Mapo-gu. ℂ **02/2016-2002** or 02/2128-2000. www.seoulworldcupst.or.kr. Admission to stadium ₩1,000 ages 13 and over, ₩500 ages 12 and under or 65 and over. Free admission to parks. Facilities 10am–midnight; stadium 9am–6pm. Closed Jan 1, Lunar New Year, Chuseok. Parks daily 24 hr. Subway line 6 to World Cup Stadium (exit 1 or 2). Bus no. 271, 571, 6715, 7714, 7715, or 9711.

Tours
WALKING TOURS

The city of Seoul offers nine different walking tours that cover the major downtown attractions and palaces. These tours are led by English-speaking guides who are trained in Seoul's history and culture. Tours are free, but you'll have to pay admission to sites. To make a reservation, call the city ℂ **02/2171-2459** or email dobo@seoulwelcom.com from 9am to 6pm (closed noon–1pm). There are a number of guide courses to choose from, but most last 2 to 3 hours. You can see info about the different courses at www.visitseoul.net. Tours are not offered Lunar New Year, palace holidays, or on Chuseok.

For gourmands or just people who like to eat, **O'ngo Food Communications ★★★** (ℂ **02/3446-1607;** www.ongofood.com) offer a variety of culinary tours around the city.

The most popular is the Korean Taste Tour that takes you around different restaurants, markets, and street food stalls in Insadong. The ₩57,000 fee includes more food than you can eat.

BUS TOURS

If you're short on time but want to see the major sights, try the **Seoul City Tour Bus** (✆ **02/777-6090;** http://en.seoulcitybus.com) run by the city government. Different tours include Cheonggye/Palace tour, the downtown tour (which stops at 27 locations in a 2-hr. period), and the night tour. Buses leave Tuesday through Sunday (and Mon holidays) from the tourist info booth in Gwanghwamun (subway line 5 to Gwanghwamun, exit 6) every 30 minutes from 9am to 7pm for the downtown tour, and every hour from 9am to 6pm for the Cheonggye/Palace tour with fewer departures during Mar, Jun, Sep, and Nov. The night tour (a rather boring survey of the city's bridges) leaves at 8pm.

The night-tour ticket costs ₩5,000 adults, ₩3,000 children or twice that for the double-decker bus. A 1-day ticket (good for the city circulation tour with on-off privileges) costs ₩10,000 adults, ₩8,000 children. Tickets for the Cheonggye/Palace tour is ₩12,000 adults, ₩8,000 children. You can buy tickets on the bus (or use your T-money card). Admission to palaces and other attractions isn't included, but discounts are offered.

RECREATIONAL ACTIVITIES

Biking

It's bad enough driving in Seoul, but riding a bike on regular city streets is not just unpleasant, it's virtually suicidal. However, there are some good biking trails along the Han-gahng and in Olympic Park. The most popular trail along the river spans 37km (23 miles) from Yanghwa to Gwangnaru. It takes about 2½ to 3 hours to reach Yangcheon from Gwangnaru.

Bikes can be rented cheaply throughout the city (usually for about ₩3,000 for an hour, ₩6,000 for tandems). Rental bikes are usually well used and old, but sturdy. The most convenient rental places are at Ichon (subway lines 1 or 4, exit 4) toward the Turtle Boat and Yeouinaru (line 5, exit 2) toward the underpass to Yeouido Park.

Taking a Han River Tour

Although boat tours run all day from Yeouido's Ferry Terminal, the most romantic is the last one of the evening. There are two excursion cruises available from the tiny island on the Han-gahng. The circular line goes to Yanghwa, turns east at Dongjak Bridge, and returns to Yeouido. Round-trip ferries are also available from Jamsil and Ttukseom. Boats run every hour during popular summer months (July–Aug) and every 1½ to 2 hours in the spring and fall (the river sometimes freezes in the winter, making boat tours impossible). The live concert or dinner cruises depart around 7:30pm, the magic show cruise leaves around 6:20pm and another live concert ferry leaves at 8:40pm, though times can vary, so call ahead. Live concert cruises ₩15,000 adults, ₩7,500 children; dinner buffet cruises ₩60,000 adults, ₩35,000 children. No reservations are taken, so come early, especially during the popular summer months. For additional info, call ✆ **02/3271-6900.**

Both Ichon and Yeouido parks can get pretty crowded on weekends, so Olympic Park might be a better bet.

Golf

Golfing is a popular sport in South Korea and there's no shortage of courses. There are only two within the city of Seoul, but 46 in Gyeonggi-do alone. However, the prices aren't reasonable to most visitors, and even prohibitive for most natives (costing over ₩200,000 for 18 holes and a caddy). Golf is seen as a sport for the upper crust, and that's why most Koreans travel to other countries for their golf vacations. A better option for practicing your swing is to try one of the many indoor driving ranges in the city. Almost all luxury hotels in the city offer a driving range and most of them cost ₩10,000 to ₩20,000 per hour.

Hiking

There is no shortage of hiking opportunities around Seoul. The slopes around the city offer relatively easy climbs. The hills and mountains in the vicinity get especially crowded during the pretty seasons of spring and fall. There are 37 mountains in the vicinity of Seoul with Bukhansan (Mt. Bukhan) being the highest (837m/2,746 ft.) and drawing most of the crowds.

The best day hike is a walk along part of the **Seoul Fortress** wall, that used to run along the ridges of the city's four mountains and encase the city from invaders, and is currently being restored. The best preserved part of the wall stretches from **Bugaksan** to Inwangsan. A good walk starts at **Waryong Park** (subway line 4 to Hyehwa, exit 1, then take bus 8 to the last stop) through **Seongbuk-dong** past **Sukjeongmun** (the Great North Gate, where you'll have to show your passport and get a pass) up to Bugaksan's peak and down to the sleepy neighborhood of **Buam-dong** (it's about a 20-min. walk from there to the Gyeongbokgung metro station).

A good option is the centrally located **Namsan Park** (p. 88), which has a variety of trails. Take subway line 4 to Chungmuro (exit 2) or line 3 to Dongguk University (exit 6) and take yellow bus no. 3. Get off at the National Theater, walk straight, and turn right. The trail starts on the left side of the traffic control booth.

Another easy hike is **Achasan** (Mt. Acha), which is not too steep but offers a good view of the Han River. It takes only about an hour to climb up to the top and back, but you can lengthen the hike to over 2 hours by climbing up Achasan over to Yongmasan and back. Take subway line 5 to Achasan (exit 2) and turn left at the first intersection. Keep walking until you get to the T-section and turn right. Walk for about 200m (656 ft.) more, past the temple, Hwayangsa, and you'll see the entrance to Daeseong-am, which leads to Achasan.

Nearby **Yongmasan** (Mt. Yongma) is an excellent hike with a variety of views and some fun things to see along the way, like a man-made waterfall and the remains of a small fort dating back to the Goguryeo period. Some parts of the trail can get a bit steep, so it's best to wear hiking boots. Take subway line 7 to Yongmasan (exit 2) and walk through the entrance to the Hanshin apartments. Go up the stairs next to the pavilion, past the playground and turn right. Next to the exercise facility, behind the wire fence, there are stairs that lead you up to the trails.

The most popular hike in the Gangnam area is on **Umyeonsan** (Mt. Umyeon). It will take you about an hour to hike to the mountain's main temple, Daesongsa. Plan to spend some time at the Seoul Arts Center when you reach the bottom. Take subway line 3 to the Nambu Express Bus Terminal (exit 5). Walk straight and turn right at the first intersection to the Seoul Arts Center (about a 10-min. walk). Take the overpass in front of the arts center which leads to the hiking trail.

SHOPPING

Seoul is a shopper's paradise. Some of the best deals in the city include frames for eyeglasses and sunglasses, shoes, cosmetics, accessories, and nondesigner clothes.

High-end department stores take most major credit cards and have ATMs that are foreigner-friendly. Be sure to keep your receipts so you can get your VAT back at the airport before you leave. The vendors in traditional markets only take cash, and they expect you to bargain over prices. *Tip:* When shopping in South Korea, don't step into a store first thing in the morning unless you intend to buy something (even if it's small). Superstition has it that if the first customer of the day leaves a store empty-handed, the store will have bad business all day. No need to worry—most shopkeepers in South Korea won't give you the hard sell, even if you are their first customer—but it's considered polite to wait a bit if you're just planning to browse.

Top Shopping Areas

For the fashion-conscious, **Myeongdong** is the place to be. With boutique shops and clothes galore, you can see the latest fashions geared toward the young. Unfortunately, the sizes are geared toward the petite Korean students and Japanese tourists that flock to the area. If you're lucky enough to be on the slimmer side, there are plenty of inexpensive options. There are loads of stores that specialize in accessories and shoes as well.

Another great area for young women's clothes is in **Idea-ap** (literally meaning, "in front of Ewha Women's University"), where you'll find the latest fashions and accessories. The area's **Fashion Street** starts at Ewha U's main gate and continues to Sincheon rail station. If you want something unique, get an item from one of the aspiring fashion designers who sell their experiments at affordable prices.

If you don't have the body of a fashion model, then **Itaewon** is the place for you. A popular shopping district geared toward foreigners, the stores here offer designer clothes that are manufactured in Korea but were rejected for export, at bargain-basement prices. This is one of the few places in the city where you can find inexpensive shoes to fit Western sizes. You'll also find inexpensive custom tailors and plenty of casual wear and sportswear from brand names as well. Be aware, though, that there are stalls selling brand-name knock-offs as well and it can be hard to tell the difference. The vendors are pretty blunt about the authenticity of their goods, however, and will let you know that it's not a real luxury brand. Some sellers will show you a catalog of their goods (especially knock-off handbags) and bring you to an unmarked shop to show you the items in person. Be sure to bring a friend and be careful about following strangers into dark alleys.

If you're looking for real luxury goods, head to the shops in **Apgujeong,** where Seoul's elite shop. There are three main department stores, but hordes of other boutiques and brand-name shops. The Shinsegae store is near the Express Bus Terminal and the JW Marriott Hotel. Nearby is the Gangnam underground shopping plaza at the B1 level of the bus station. The Hyundai department store is also in the area, near the Dongho Bridge. Another good place to browse is Galleria department store or Designer Club. Farther past that (toward the Cheongdam four-way) is the luxury shopping area and **Rodeo Street,** where you'll find boutiques such as Armani,

Gucci, and the like. It's a bit of a walk from the subway, but if you can afford to shop here, you can afford the short taxi ride.

On the other end of the spectrum are the bargains at **Dongdaemun** and **Namdaemun** markets. There are treasures to be found here, at the biggest traditional markets in all of South Korea, but you have to search a bit.

If you're looking for good South Korean-made souvenirs, the **Insadong** area has ceramics, paper goods, and handicrafts from both artisans and factories. For more collectible items or genuine artisan pieces, you can check out the more expensive but genuine galleries in **Samcheong-dong.**

MARKETS

Although malls and shopping centers are popular, many Seoul residents still shop in markets for the best bargains. Whether indoors or out, these markets are inexpensive, chaotic, and lots of fun. Vendors take only cash and bargaining is not only normal, but expected. The market areas tend to get crowded, so don't be offended by a bit of pushing and shoving. It's all part of the experience and one you must try if you want to get the real flavor of the city. Most of the vendors speak a little bit of English, and even if they don't, they'll bring out a calculator to show you how much things cost. Besides, why let something like language stand in the way of a good bargain?

Dongdaemun Shijang Since 1905, Dongdaemun (which means "great east gate") has been one of the major markets in the country and it spans an area larger than Namdaemun. Vendors here mostly specialize in wholesale fashion items, making it easy to dress the entire family without breaking the bank. The main street divides the market into two sections. Giant shopping malls in the first section sell wholesale and retail goods. Most are open daily from 10am to 5am the following morning. Concerts and events organized by the malls usually happen around 7 or 8pm and attract a younger crowd.

The second section is on the side, along Cheonggyecheon-no and beyond. Shops on this side of the market sell both wholesale and retail goods, but mainly sell items in bulk. The malls here open daily at 8pm and close at either 8am or 5am the next morning. The malls in this section cater to customers in their 30s and 40s. Take subway line 1 or 4 and get off at Dongdaemun History & Culture Park (exit 2 or 3).

Garak-dong Shijang (Agriculture & Marine Products Wholesale Market The largest in the country, this food market encompasses 17 buildings. Although this is largely a wholesale market, vendors will sell at retail as well. If you've never seen a wholesale agricultural market, you might be overwhelmed by the sheer quantities of food in one location. Open from 2am to 7pm daily (although the exciting auctioning and bulk wholesale transactions end at 10am and livestock sales end at 5pm), most vendors close the first and third Sundays of each month. Take subway line 8 to the Garak Market (exit 3).

Gwangjang Shijang ★ South Korea's oldest traditional market, this is a great place to get textiles, fabrics, silks, and other Korean goods. The second floor has vendors selling silks, bedsheets, satins, and more. You can also find a variety of lacquer pieces inlaid with mother-of-pearl, get a custom-made *hanbok* (Korean traditional outfit), or browse other handmade textiles. The open air food stalls is one of our favorite places to get a cheap snack. Open Monday through Sunday 7am to 7pm. Take subway line 1 to Jongno 5(o)-ga (exit 8).

Gyeongdong Shijang ★★ The country's most famous oriental medicine marketplace, Gyeongdong has over 1,000 shops selling everything from medicinal roots to dried mushrooms, all used to make hanyak. Most of the sellers grow the items themselves and sell them directly here. It's a fun place to see, smell, touch, and taste unusual things, like dried millipedes and unidentifiable barks. Open daily 8am to 6:30pm, the market is closed the first and third Sundays of the month. Take subway line 1 to Jeggi.

Hongdae/Hong-ik Flea Market ★★ Every Saturday, students and other vendors sell a variety of items at this open-air flea market at the playground in front of the main gate of Hong-ik University, South Korea's most prominent art school. You'll find handmade crafts from the art students, dolls, clothes, accessories, and a variety of knickknacks. There is an unofficial rule to not sell goods direct from a factory (like those you'd find in Namdaemun or Dongdaemun markets). Open 1 to 6pm, but check the weather before you head out, since it'll be closed when it rains or snows. Take subway line 2 to Hong-ik University (exit 6). When you exit, walk straight until you get to the 4-way, and then turn left. Keep walking to the end of that street and make a right; then go up the hill that comes on the right.

Namdaemun Shijang ★★★ The largest traditional market in the country and going strong since 1414—they say if you can't find it here, it probably doesn't exist. Centrally located in the heart of the city, the alleyways of Namdaemun (which means "great south gate") are closed to vehicle traffic so that shops and carts take over the area. Vendors sell everything from clothing to housewares, food, and accessories. Most of the shops sell directly from their own factories, so you can get both wholesale and retail prices. If you need a break from shopping, head over to one of the food alleys to grab a bite from the various vendors. There are no set hours, which vary by store, but the shijang is bustling any day of the week. Serious bargain hunters come for the night market from midnight to 4am. Take subway line 4 to Hoehyeon (exit 5).

Noryangjin Shijang ★★★ Seoul's largest and oldest fish market, the 700 plus shops are open even before the crack of dawn—at 3am, as fishermen bring in their daily catches. Due to popular demand, seafood is brought in from 15 different ports from all three of the peninsula's coasts. The marketplace is busiest in the spring months of March to May and from September to early December, but the excitement really never ends (although the crowds disperse around 2 in the afternoon). Rows of glistening fins sit next to squiggly sea creatures, all waiting to be someone's dinner. Open 3am to 9pm. Take subway line 1 to Noryangjin.

Pungmul Shijang (Seoul Folk Flea Market) ★★ Seoul's historic 5-day flea market has a permanent home, after being moved when Cheonggyecheon was built. The area has over 900 vendors selling everything from folk objects to regional clothing, to food and souvenirs. Pick up an antique statue or an unusual gift for a friend back home. Open 10am to 7pm, closed every 2nd and 4th Tues of the month. Take subway line 1 or 2 to Sinseol-dong (exit 6, 9 or 10).

DEPARTMENT STORES

Large, multilevel department stores can be found in every neighborhood in Seoul. They all have similar layouts, with the basement floor being given over to groceries and inexpensive food courts, and cosmetics and jewelry on the first floor. The middle floors are usually reserved for clothing with higher floors selling furniture, home goods, and sports supplies. The top floor or two is usually reserved for restaurants and sometimes cinemas. *Tip:* For 2 weeks each season, the stores have sales (usually in Jan, Apr, July, and Oct) at which you can get good discounts. Check each store's

Hanbang: Traditional Korean Medicine

Although stemming from traditional Chinese medicinal roots (dating back over 2000 years), Korean traditional medicinal practices have developed their own characteristics. There are four components, but all of them take a holistic approach to health and healing. The common treatment methods are *chim* (acupuncture), *hanyak* (herbal medicine), *ddeum* (moxibustion), and *buhwang* (cupping). Each can be used alone or in combination. Koreans believe that disease comes from a lack of or excess of *ki* (also called "chi" or "qi" in Chinese), which is the vital energy of life that flows through us. This problem of ki results in an imbalance of *eum* ("yin" in Chinese) and yang. The treatment is supposed to balance the two forces within a person, increase the flow of ki, and heal by creating environmental, social, and physical harmony.

A traditional Korean doctor will listen to your ailments and prescribe a combination of treatments that best suit your needs. Common hanyak items include ginseng, mushrooms, lichen, barks, seeds, and even ground deer antler.

website or call the Korea Travel Phone (© **1330**) to find out when exactly they are. Roll up your sleeves and be ready to brave the crowds.

Galleria Department Store   The Galleria stores are known as *the* fashion brand, so it's no surprise that its main store is located in Apgujeong-dong's Rodeo Street. If you want to see what the young fashionistas are buying, this is a good place to shop. Open daily 10:30am to 8pm. Take subway line 3 to Apgujeong (exit 1).

Hyundai Department Store   Since opening its store in Apgujeong-dong in 1985, Hyundai has been setting trends across the nation. If you want to see where Seoul's fashions will be heading, check out the clothes and accessories here. Open daily 10:30am to 8pm, but closed one Monday a month (varies). Take subway line 3 to Apgujeong (exit 6).

Lotte Department Store   Since it opened its first store in the late 1970s, Lotte has grown. It now has six huge stores in Seoul alone. Its flagship store is in front of the shopping district in Myeongdong. Open daily 10:30am to 8pm; they close the first and second Monday of each month. Take subway line 2 to Euljiro 1(il)-ga and the underground connects directly to the basement floor of the store.

Shinsegae Department Store   The oldest department store in the country, it started out as a Japanese store during the occupation in the 1930s and was given its current name in 1963. Although it has other locations, the one in Chungmuro/Myeongdong is the original. The reconstructed building was finished in 2005 and has 14 stories of shopping and eating fun. Open daily 10:30am to 8pm (closes one floating Monday a month). Take subway line 4 to Hoehyeon (exit 7) and the store connects directly to the underground.

MALLS & SHOPPING PLAZAS

Central City ★   When you exit the Express Bus Terminal from the metro, you'll automatically enter this megaplex. Attached is the **JW Marriott Hotel** and the **Shinsegae Department Store** (whose basement food court, incidentally is one of the best in the city). You can do your banking, have lunch, and get married without leaving the complex. Oh yes, and there's plenty of shopping options, too. Hours vary, but mostly 10:30am to 10pm daily. Take subway line 3, 7, or 9 to Express Bus Terminal.

COEX Mall In Gangnam, this mall (☏ 02/6002-0114) is home to more than dozens of stores and eating places. It also includes a 16-screen movie theater, a night-club, banks, a post office, the **Bandi & Luni's** bookstore (with one of the best selections of English-language volumes in the city), and record stores. The **COEX Aquarium ★ ☺**(☏ 02/6002-6200; admission ₩17,500 adults, ₩14,500 teens, ₩11,000 children), with thousands of underwater creatures on display, is at one end of the mall. Try to time your visit for the 1:30pm shark feeding. There's also the **Kimchi Museum** (☏ 02/6002-6456; www.kimchimuseum.co.kr), if you want to know more about the ultimate Korean dish. A favorite with teenagers, the mall is open daily from 10am to 10pm. Take subway line 2 to Samseong (exit 5 or 6). The subway connects directly to the mall.

D-Cube City ★★ Located at Sindorim, this towering complex encompasses the live/work/play philosophy with apartments, the **Sheraton Hotel,** a department store, offices, an art center, and a **Pororo Theme Park** for kids. It has plenty of clothing options (like H&M, Codes Combine, and Zara) and restaurants for your fill of fashion and food. Open daily 10:30am to 10pm. Take subway line 1 or 2 to Sindorim.

Times Square ★★ Definitely not New York City, Times Square Seoul is a mega mall that's distinctly Korean. Next to the **Courtyart by Marriott,** there are dozens of stores, a **Shinsegae Department Store,** an **E-Mart, Kyobo** bookstore, a children's theme park ("**I Like Dalki,**" www.dalkiworld.com), restaurants, shops, and a **CGV Theater** that claims to have the world's largest movie screen. Open daily 10:30am to 10pm. Take subway line 1 to Yeongdeungpo (exit 3, through the Lotte Dept. store and cross the street).

DISCOUNT MEGAMARTS

Giant discount marts can be found all over the city. You may have noticed the ubiquitous yellow box of the **E-Marts,** but other stores like **Lotte Mart, Costco, HomePlus,** and **Kim's Club** also offer similar bargains. They offer similar items (minus luxury goods) to department stores, but at discounted prices. Be prepared for crowds on weekends and weekdays evenings.

E-Mart A branch of this discount megamart is in Chang-dong. You can find groceries, household goods, clothes, and other items at discount prices. If you've forgotten your toothpaste or need a pair of slippers, this is a good store to shop. Open daily from 10am to midnight. Take subway line 1 or 4 to Chang-dong (exit 2), turn left, and walk about 5 min. (you can't miss the yellow building).

Shopping A to Z
ANTIQUES

Over 40% of South Korea's antique stores are in **Insadong,** which has been the cultural center of Seoul, if not South Korea, since the Joseon Dynasty (1392–1910). The area begins at the Anguk-dong Rotary and runs past Insadong crossroads to Tapgol Park. Antiques here tend to be more expensive than those sold elsewhere in the country, but the quality is exceptional. Prices range from inexpensive to the super-expensive (think ₩1 million and up). Be careful to shop at reputable galleries and stores when you buy antiques, because it's illegal to take items deemed national treasures out of the country.

Most of the antiques in the area tend to be ceramics, wooden containers, jewelry, and old paintings. A great store that specializes in old books, usually written in Hanja, is **Tongmungwan** (☏ 02/734-4092; 147 Gwanhun-dong, Jongno-gu; open

10:30am–5:30pm Mon–Sat), which is worth a browse even if you don't intend to buy anything. The shop (whose sign is also written in Chinese characters) was opened by the grandfather of the current owner. If you're looking for antique furniture, the friendly owners at **Gayajae** (✆ 02/733-3138; 192-46 Gwanhun-dong, Jongno-gu) have a good selection of wooden pieces, as well as stone Buddha statues. Nearby **Godosa** (✆ 02/735-4373; 192-46 Gwanhun-dong, Jongno-gu; open 10am–6pm daily) carries antique utensils, furniture, and everyday items. Another good option is **Gonghwarang** (✆ 02/735-9938; 23-2 Insadong, Jongno-gu; open 10am–6pm daily), whose owner is the president of the Korean Antique Association, so you know you're getting a genuine article.

Better than Insadong, the best place to find antiques is at the **Jang-anpyeong Antique Market ★★★**. As one of Asia's largest, over 150 vendors sell antiques (and reproductions) of furniture, paintings, calligraphy, wooden objects, ceramics, ironware, stone statues, and more. Even if you don't want an old man's pipe to take home, this market is definitely worth a browse. Although hours vary by seller, shops are generally open Monday through Saturday 10am to 8pm. Take subway line 2 to Sindap and walk past the Majang-dong intersection toward Cheonho Bridge.

ART GALLERIES & CRAFTS

Since the 1970s, galleries in **Insadong** have been selling both contemporary art by South Korean artists and collectable antiques (see above). Most galleries have exhibitions that rotate frequently, featuring either one contemporary South Korean artist or a group of recent art-school graduates. A good place to start is the **Insa Art Center** (✆ 02/736-1020; 188 Gwanhun-dong, Jongno-gu), which is a plaza complex of smaller art galleries and shops off the main drag. Also nice for browsing is the **Kyung-In Museum ★★** (✆ 02/733-4448; www.kyunginart.co.kr; 30-1 Gwanhun-dong, Jongno-gu; open 10am–6pm daily, unless they're putting up a show, and then they'll be closed on Tues; closed Jan 1, Lunar New Year, and Chuseok), which also has a small teahouse.

More upscale galleries and artisan studios line both sides of the main drag in **Samcheong-dong**, which starts from the street east of Gyeongbokgung to Samcheong Tunnel, ending at Samcheong Park. Famous galleries in the area include **Gallery Hyundai ★★** (✆ 02/734-6111; www.galleryhyundai.com; 80 Sagan-dong), **Artsonje Center ★★★** (✆ 02/733-8945; www.artsonje.org/eng; 144-2 Sokeuk-dong; open Tues-Sun 11am–7pm), and **Kukje Gallery** (✆ 02/735-8449; www.kukjegallery.com; 54 Samcheong-no; open Mon–Sat 10am–6pm, until 5pm Sun and holidays). Some of the art spaces have their own cafes and restaurants, so you can enjoy a meal and see art all in one. Even if you don't have a set itinerary in mind, the area is worth a stroll for all the galleries and other unique spaces.

A couple of small museums in the neighborhood are also worth stopping into. The **Gahoe Museum** (✆ 02/741-0466; www.gahoemuseum.org; 11-103 Gahoe-dong), located on the north of the Bukcheon Hanok village, is a privately run museum in a converted hanok with traditional folk paintings and displays of shamanistic talismans. It's open 10am to 6pm Tuesday to Sunday, and admission is ₩3,000 for ages 18 and up and ₩2,000 for children and students.

BOOKS

One of the best overall bookstores for English-language volumes is **Kyobo Mungo ★★** (✆ 02/1544-1900), located on the basement floor of the Kyobo Building (take subway line 1 to Gwanghwamun, exit 3) and in the basement level of the Kyobo Gangnam Tower (subway line 2 to Gangnam, exit 6); open daily from

10am to 9pm. Another major bookstore is **Bandi & Luni's ★★** (*©* 02/6002-6002), which stocks imported English-language books, with locations in the COEX Mall (subway line 2, Samseong, exit 6) and the basement level of the Jongno Tower (subway line 1, Jonggak, exit 2). Also a good bet is **Seoul Selection Bookshop** (*©* 02/734-9565), on the basement level of the Korean Publishers Association building. They have a wide selection of books on Korean culture. Open Monday through Saturday 9:30am to 6:30pm. Take subway line 3 to Anguk (exit 1) or line 5 to Gwanghwamun (exit 2).

The **Ulchi Book Center** (*©* 02/757- 8100), located on the subway level at Euljiro (line 2), has a good selection of bestsellers and instruction books for English-language teachers.

The **Royal Asiatic Society** has a branch in Seoul (*©* 02/763-9483; www.raskb.com; room no. 611 of the Korean Christian building). They have a solid selection of books in English about South Korea, as well as some foreign magazines. Open Monday to Friday 10am to noon and 2 to 5pm. Take subway line 1 to Jongno 5(o)-ga (exit 2). They also offer occasional tours throughout Korea.

CUSTOM TAILORS

Getting tailor-made clothes or just having a piece of clothing altered in Seoul is quick and easy. The custom tailors in **Dongdaemun Market** can alter something for you right on the spot or make shirts, suits, silk items, or dresses to your specifications. You can get a tailored suit for about ₩150,000 to ₩250,000 Unfortunately, although they are affordable, most of them don't speak a lot of English. For easier communication, try the tailors in **Itaewon** (there are dozens of them here), who are used to foreign customers. Some of the shops will even make custom-made leather items. Most of them can custom-make something for you within a couple of days (let them know when you need it) and will deliver items to your hotel.

ELECTRONIC GOODS

If you're looking for electronic goods, look no further than the **Yongsan Electronics Market ★**. A grouping of 22 buildings and thousands of small shops, they sell every electronic gadget, part, or equipment imaginable. Prices here are generally lower than those at regular stores, but they hold sales about every 3 months. Be sure to check before buying anything and ask for warranties if you're unsure about authenticity. Generally open daily 10am to 8pm, the markets are closed the first and third Sundays of each month, but the flea market happens every weekend, 9am to 7pm. Take subway line 1 to Yongsan (exit 3) or line 4 to Sinyongsan. Most eateries in the area are geared toward the vendors, but you'll find good Korean cuisine on levels 4, 5, and 6 of I'Park Mall.

JEWELRY

Wholesale and retail jewelry shops are clustered in the streets and alleyways around Jongno 3(sam)-ga to Jongno 5(o)-ga, so the area is called the **Jongno Jewelry District.** There are a wide variety of designs and items to choose from and prices are generally about 30% to 40% lower than those of other jewelry shops in the country. If you're looking for watches specifically, try Watch Alley in Yeji-dong. The back alleys in the area and in Bong-ik-dong have shops that are specifically wholesale, so they may not be willing to sell single items. Many of the stores have their own factories and production centers, so you can get items custom-made or have a designer piece copied (or you may see copies already made in some of the stores). Be sure to get an A/S warranty card and certificate of authenticity when you buy something. A bit of bargaining is possible, but since prices are already discounted, vendors won't cut the price that much. Paying with cash will always get you a better price than paying with credit cards. Take subway line 1 or 3 to Jongno 3(sam)-ga (exit 10 or 11 for the jewelry district or exit 12 for the jewelry "department store"). Open daily from 9am to 9:30pm.

SECONDHAND STORES

Koreans have a general dislike of used items, but they're trying to encourage reusing and recycling with the **Beautiful Store ★★**, 110-2 Jae-dong, Jongno-gu (𝗖 **02/736-0660;** www.beautifulstore.org; take subway line 3 to Anguk, exit 2). A bargain hunter's paradise in Insadong, it has racks filled with secondhand clothes, starting at a mere ₩3,000. Upstairs, they have art objects, books, and other items available for a reasonable price. All profits go to charitable causes, mainly Oxfam projects throughout Asia. You can even donate your nearly new items to make room in your luggage. Open 10:30am to 10pm Monday to Saturday, they have other locations in Seoul and Gyeonggi-do, including their main store in Yongdap-dong (subway line 5 to Janhanpeyong, exit 8).

SHOES

If you're looking for inexpensive tennis shoes or other footwear, check shops in **Namdaemun** and **Dongdaemun** markets. On the other hand, if you have a designer shoe fetish, walk your boots over to **Designer Shoe Alley** in Apgujeong-dong. Between the big Galleria department store and Cheongdam intersection, you'll see a street with all the luxury brands. At the Gucci store, walk up the little alley to the left and you'll find a hidden handful of South Korean designer shoe stores, with styles you won't find at home. Korean shoe sizes may be too small for you, but if you have the time, they can custom-order shoes for you and get them to you in about a week.

ENTERTAINMENT & NIGHTLIFE

Like any cosmopolitan city, Seoul comes alive when the sun goes down, and in some cases the fun just doesn't stop. Places like **Dongdaemun** have night markets that see more action during the early-morning hours than during the day. Nighttime fun can be had pretty much all over the city. Good for overall nightlife is **Myeongdong,** where you can have dinner and stop for a cup of coffee or a beer at many of the cafes and bars in the area.

Seoul's beautiful people tend to head for the most upscale and exclusive bars in **Apgujeong-dong** or nearby **Sinsadong,** where you'll find the pricey clubs, wine bars, and dancing. Also on this side of the river, **Gangnam** draws a more relaxed, younger crowd. In the evenings, pojang machas (small tented restaurants) pop up around Gangnam Station, and young professionals hit the clubs and bars after a tough day at the many IT firms in the area. Since most Korean-Americans who've relocated to Seoul live in Gangnam, it's not difficult to find Western-style clubs and bars here.

If you're not much of a drinker, or prefer a bit of culture while you imbibe, head over to the **Daehangno** area. You'll find hundreds of cafes, clubs, and bars, tucked into alleyways between little theaters and galleries. Most of the places cater to the college students in the area, so they won't be as overpriced as places south of the river.

Another area popular with students is **Sinchon,** where you'll find cute cafes (to draw the girls from Ewha University), boutiques, bars, and discos. Just a short walk beyond are the clubs and bars around **Hongdae,** which have the hippest live performances and dance floors. Make sure you're dressed to impress, or you may be denied entry to some of the clubs. If you want to hang out in a more international area,

Itaewon has cafes, clubs, and restaurants that cater to people from many nations. What used to be the seedy red-light district around the American military base has grown up to be an attractive night spot, although you can still find soldiers looking for a "meet market" and ladies of the night.

Business travelers tend to stick to the clubs and bars in Seoul's deluxe hotels. Drinks will be on the expensive side, but you'll get first-class service and get to mingle with the upper crust and South Korea's professional class. Whatever your tastes (or budget), Seoul is a city that doesn't sleep.

Performing Arts

Chongdong Theater ★★ An excellent place to see live performances of Korean traditional music, song, and dance, the Chongdong Theater was the country's first modern theater of traditional singing, instruments, and plays. Home to the Traditional Performing Arts Series, they emphasize four genres—dance, Pungmul, Sori (traditional song performance), and musical instruments. Performances happen every day (except Mon) and last about 80 minutes. English subtitles are provided. There are only 334 seats in the theater, so reservations are strongly recommended. 8-11 Jeong-dong, Jongno-gu. ✆ **02/751-1500.** www.mct.or.kr/eng/chongdong/cd_info.asp. Tickets ₩20,000 "A" seats (side and back); ₩30,000 "S" seats (middle); ₩50,000 "R" seats. MC, V. Tues–Sun 8–9:20pm Apr–Nov, 4–5:20pm Dec–Mar. The best way to get there is to take subway line 1 to City Hall (exit 1) or line 2 (exit 12) and walk 5 min. along the Deoksugung wall.

National Theater ★★ Established in 1950, the National Theater has four resident companies—the National Drama Company, the National Changgeuk Company, the National Dance Company, and the National Orchestra. Other than traditional performances, they also have international acts (the musical *Cats*, for example, played here). There is a main theater, smaller spaces for experimental performances, and an outdoor stage (with free informal performances, mostly in the summer). San 14-67, Jangchung-dong, Jung-gu. ✆ **02/2280-4114.** Fax 02/2280-4125. Foreigners need to download their booking form and either fax or e-mail to manager3@korea.kr. www.ntok.go.kr/english/index.do. Ticket prices vary by performance. AE, DC, M, V. Subway line 5 to Gwanghwamun (exit 1 or 8). Alternatively, take subway line 3 to Dongguk University (exit 6) and walk 15 min. or take yellow bus no. 2 or 5; or take exit 2 and take the shuttle bus that operates 40 and 20 min. before each performance.

Sejong Cultural Center ★★ Originally built in 1978, this is the largest arts and cultural center in the city. Remodeled in 2004, the main theater has three levels and over 3,000 seats. Each seat on the first two levels has an LCD screen for narration and information. You can see everything from chamber orchestra concerts to live rock bands, traditional Korean performances, and classical music concerts. The small chamber hall seats about 442 people. The center houses 3 art galleries and an outdoor **Garden of Art.** 81-3 Sejong-no, Jongno-gu. ✆ **1544-1887.** www.sejongpac.or.kr/eng/main/main.asp. Tickets ₩50,000–₩200,000 for major performances. MC, V. Office Mon–Sat 9am–8pm, except for holidays. Subway line 5 to Gwanghwamun (exit 1 or 8).

Seoul Arts Center ★★★ The nation's first arts complex, it houses five buildings—the Opera House, the Concert Hall, Hangaram Art Museum, the Seoul Calligraphy Art Museum, and the Arts Library/Design Museum. The center features opera performances (like *La Bohème* or *Carmen*), orchestral concerts of classical music, plays, ballets, modern and traditional dance, and imported American musicals. They also hold a variety of exhibitions of international artists, contemporary Korean artists, traditional ceramics, and the like. 700 Seocho-dong, Seocho-gu. ✆ **02/580-1300** or 1234. www.sac.or.kr/eng (there is no online booking in English). Tickets vary depending on performance or exhibition. Take subway line 3 to Nambu Terminal (exit 5) and take the free shuttle bus from there, or take green bus no. 12 or blue bus no. 4429. Shuttle buses run Tues–Sat 60, 50, 40, and 30 min. before performances, and Sun 60 and 30 min. before.

DINNER THEATER

Korea House ★★   Dining like royalty isn't cheap, but it is an enjoyable experience, especially when it's coupled with a music and dance performance. If you just want the meal, come for lunch, or skip the meal and stop in for one of two daily evening performances (only one on Sun) of *pansori* (traditional Korean "opera"), mask dances, and other music in this hanok, built during the Joseon Dynasty. Performances last an hour. On weekends, they perform traditional weddings or provide folk games for people to play. The Namsangol Hanok village is nearby and worth a gander if you have time to spare. 80-2 Pil-dong 2-ga, Jung-gu. ℂ **02/2266-9101.** www.kangkoku.or.kr/eng/index.html. Dinner and performance ₩68,000–₩150,000 depending on menu; performance only ₩50,000. AE, MC, V. Performances daily 6:30 and 8:30pm; lunch served noon–2pm. Subway line 3 or 4 to Chungmuro (exit 3) and walk toward the Pil-dong hospital.

OTHER PERFORMING ARTS VENUES

Chongdong Nanta Theater ★★★   Don't worry about not understanding the lines, because there is no dialogue. The "chefs" of this nonverbal performance dramatize Korean percussion traditions of Samulnori in a contemporary comedy as they prepare a wedding feast. Jeong-dong A&C, Jeong-dong 15-1, Jung-gu. ℂ **02/739-8288.** www.nanta.co.kr. VIP tickets ₩60,000; "S" tickets ₩50,000; "A" tickets ₩40,000. MC, V. Performances Mon–Fri 4 and 8pm; Sat 1, 4, and 8pm; Sun and holidays 3 and 6pm. Subway line 5 to Seodaemun (exit 5), walk toward the Kyunghyang daily newspaper building, walk about 50m (164 ft.), turn left at Yewon high school and walk just a bit farther to the Chongdong Nanta Theater.

Casinos

Casinos in South Korea are open only to foreigners (except for Gangwon Land), so be sure to take your passport with you. There are two **Seven Luck Casinos** in Seoul, run by a subsidiary of the Korea Tourism Organization. One is in Gangnam (take subway line 2 to Samseong, exit 5 or 6) and the other is in Gangbuk (take subway line 1 to Seoul Station, exit 8, or line 4 to Hoehyeon, exit 4). The only other casino in Seoul is inside the **Paradise Walker Hill** hotel (ℂ **02/456-2121**) in Gwangjin-gu.

Outside of organized casinos, many tourist hotels also have game rooms with slot machines.

Movie Theaters

There are dozens of movie theaters in Seoul that show the latest domestic box office hits as well as popular Hollywood films. If you do go see a movie in the theater, make sure that the movie isn't dubbed in Korean. Be aware that tickets sell out quickly, especially on Saturdays and holidays, and seats are assigned so it's best to get them early. On weekends evening shows can be sold out the day before, so plan ahead.

Some of the theaters that show international films are as follows: COEX Mall's **Megaplex Cineplex,** which has 16 screens; **Seoul Cinema** (take subway line 1, 3, or 5 to Jongno 3-ga, exit 14); **Cineplus** (subway line 3 to Apgujeong, exit 3), which has great seats and a fabulous sound system; or any one of the **CGV** theaters. The country's first art house theater showing cutting-edge films is **Dongseung Cinematheque** (subway line 4 to Hyehwa, exit 1, and walk toward the Hyehwa rotary). The nonprofit **Seoul Art Cinema** (ℂ **02/741-9782;** www.cinematheque.seoul.kr;

subway line 1, 3, or 5 to Jongno 3(sam)-ga, exit 5) shows independent, classic, and international films, with a monthly educational program with a film director. **Arthouse Momo** (www.cineart.co.kr) inside the Ewha Women's University campus complex (subway line 2 to Ewha, exit 2 or 3) is another good art house cinema with 2 screens.

The Korean Overseas Information Service also offers occasional free Korean movies with English subtitles, organized by **Seoul Selection Bookshop** (© **02/734-9565;** www.seoulselection.com). Check with them for the latest schedule and screening info.

Bars & Clubs

It can get a bit costly just walking into any drinking establishment in Seoul. Even in a casual hof, if it's frequented by South Korean patrons, they usually require that you order overpriced *anju* (drinking snacks) with your drinks. Especially pricey are "booking clubs" where singles pay "bookers" to hook them up with an available mate of the opposite sex. An unfortunate part of modern South Korean culture, these clubs are to be avoided, since neither the music nor the drinks are the attraction. Fortunately, more casual beer joints let you grab a few drinks with friends without the expensive food. You'll find there is no shortage of places to imbibe, since Koreans love to drink.

Koreans love to drink wine, but since all wine has to be imported from elsewhere, even mediocre vintages can be pricey. But the good news is that good wine and elegant places to drink it have opened up all over the city. *Tip:* Avoid the ubiquitous (and expensive) cheese platters that seem to appear on every wine bar menu. It may sound tempting, but the cheese selection is never very good and it's served with either Saltines or Ritz crackers.

One nice place is **Romanée Conti,** 6206 Samcheong-dong (© **02/722-1633**), whose sign reads WINE & PARTY. I don't know about the party part, but they do have the wine. Across the street from Samcheongdong Sujebi, they're open daily from noon to 1am. Bottles generally are in the ₩30,000 to ₩60,000 range.

You'll find business travelers (and women wanting to meet them) around the bar at **J.J. Mahoney's** (© **02/799-8601**) on the basement floor of the Grand Hyatt. Drinks are a bit on the pricey side, but you'll get solid service and live music. Mahoney's is open 6pm to 2am Sunday through Thursday, and 6pm to 3am Friday and Saturday.

College students and the 20-something crowd are usually hanging out in Hongdae-ap (the area in front of Hong-ik U). Hongdae is the area for hip-hop, punk, folk—pretty much any sort of music you're into. The live clubs are great for seeing underground bands that haven't hit the big time yet. The problem with the Hongdae scene is that it changes so much, but this is one of the few areas in the city (other than Itaewon) where you can find Western-style clubs where people actually dance.

The best time to go is the last Friday of the month, which has been dubbed **"Club Day"** (© **02/333-3910**). You pay a flat fee of ₩20,000 and get into over a dozen clubs in the area, plus one drink on the house. Although club day officially starts at 8pm, the action doesn't really begin until around 11pm. Take subway line 2 to the Hong-ik University (exit 9).

For a taste of inexpensive makgeolli, try the brown rice makgeolli at **Wolhyang ★★** (© **02/332-9202;** 335-5 Seogyo-dong, Mapo-gu; open Mon–Wed noon–4am, Thurs–Sat noon–1am). They own their own brewery and hold classes on Korea's old brew on Saturdays at noon (Subway line 2 to Hongik U., exit 4). Still, the most casual drinking joint in Hongdae is **Vinyl ★** (411-1 Seogyo-dong, Mapo-gu), where you can get fruity soju cocktails in zipper bags (complete with straws) from a take-out window.

The club with the most psychedelic design is **Space Café Oi ★★** (✆ 010/8008-0160; 364-26 Seogyo-dong, Mapo-gu), a space-age interior that makes up for its freakiness with its excellent cocktails, hookahs, and extensive menu. Mellow on weeknights, it transforms into a dance club on weekends. It's located on the third floor of the CatchLight building, across from the Adidas store.

For an international crowd, head over to Itaewon. A fun place with a tropical flair (fake palm trees and all) is **Bungalow Bar** (✆ 02/793-2344; 112-3 Itaewon 1(il)-dong, Yongsan-gu). Take off your shoes and socks at the door because the entire floor is covered in sand. A cozy place to get a tropical drink, the bar plays low-key lounge music. On Thursday nights the happening place is **Helios,** which draws a crowd more for its free drink and ladies' nights than for the music, which is the usual hip-hop fare. A classier, Euro-style joint that draws the 30-plus crowd is **3 Alley Pub** (✆ 02/749-3336; www.3alleypub.com), which has a good group of regulars who come for the congenial atmosphere and the large selection of brews. A funky place to have a drink and hear local DJs spin is **Bar Nana,** located near the French restaurant, Le St. Ex, behind the Hamilton hotel. With an eclectic interior, they have regular live bands and special events.

A mellower spot in Itaewon is the unpretentious standard, **All That Jazz ★★**, 168-17 Itaewon-dong, Yongsan-gu (✆ 02/795-5701; www.allthatjazz.kr), where the live music starts around 9pm. Take subway line 1 to Itaewon (exit 1); the club is on the second floor next to the Nike shop. Cover charge starts at ₩10,000. Arrive early, if you want to snag a table.

A great place for a craft brew and gourmet pub eats is the **Craftworks Taphouse and Bistro ★★**, 651 Itaewon 2(i)-dong, Yongsan-gu, (✆ 02/794-2537; http://craftworkstaphouse.com), about a 5-min walk from the Noksapyeong station (exit 2) toward the Grand Hyatt and the Namsan tunnel. They also have locations in Haebangchon and Gyeongnidan.

One of the best places to try different varieties of makgeolli is **H 호 Bar ★★★** in Haebangchon (Subway to Noksopyeong, exit 2), 4-18 Yongsan-dong 2-ga, Yongsan-gu (✆ 070/8950-8362; daily 6pm–2am). Their menu is a handwritten book describing the makgeollis from various regions. Start with the ₩2,000 makgeolli sampler, then choose from the many bottles that fall mostly in the ₩5,000 to ₩7,000 range. Their simple anju menu has delicious and affordable choices as well.

If you want to go where the young jet set go to play, head over to Gangnam. An excellent place to get an authentic Czech brew is **Castle Praha ★★**, 1306-6 Seocho-dong, Seocho-gu (✆ 02/596-9200; www.castlepraha.com), on the second basement level of the Pagoda Tower (subway line 2 to Gangnam, exit 6). They also have a location in Hongdae (✆ 02/334-2121; 395-19 Seogyo-dong, Mapo-gu; take subway line 2 to Hapjeong, exit 3), around the corner from the Bobo Hotel. Both locations are open noon to 2am Monday to Thursday, until 3am Friday and Saturday, and 3pm to midnight Sunday. Another place for good beer is **O'Kim's Brauhaus,** 159 Samsung-dong, Gangnam-gu (✆ 02/6002-7006), on the first floor of the COEX building (subway line 2 to Samsung). They have a brewery on the premises and make three German beers (the varieties change depending on the season) plus a Korean brew, and they have other imported bottled beers as well. Daily 11:30am to midnight.

Even more upscale are the joints in Apgujeong. An old jazz and blues standard is **Once in a Blue Moon,** 85-1 Cheongdam-dong, Gangnam-gu (✆ 02/549-5490). Music starts around 7pm on most nights and the band plays until about 12:30am (until 11:20pm Sun). A popular place in the area is **A.O.C.** (✆ 02/541-9260), which is a fancy restaurant by day, wine bar by night. They have a decent selection of wines, which are reasonably priced compared to other places in the area. Even more popular is **Grand Harue** (© **02/542-2222**) (and its little sister, **Harue,** across the alley), which started life as a French restaurant, but became more known as a drinking spot, where the Apgujeong crowds come to see and be seen. It's located near the Cheongdam intersection in the heart of the luxury-goods shopping area. Located near Dosan Park is the popular cafe/wine bar **Plastic,** which has high ceilings with blue skylights and a designer fireplace in the middle of the long, open space. The outdoor garden is also a pretty fabulous place to enjoy a glass of wine.

Gay & Lesbian Bars

Although some actors and musicians in South Korea have publicly come out, homosexuality remains largely taboo in Korean society. Same-sex couples are rarely seen in public. However, public displays of affection between friends of the same gender are common. You'll see young men holding each other's hands and girls walking with their arms linked together, but that doesn't indicate sexual preference. There is a quiet but active gay scene in Seoul, but many gay clubs keep a relatively low profile, because of the homophobia in most of society. The gay and lesbian scene can be found in **Jongno,** in the college areas of **Sincheon** and thereabouts, and especially in the area of **Itaewon** with the unfortunate nickname "Homo Hill." Lesbian clubs are more difficult to find, even for South Korean natives. But a few "Korean-style" lesbian bars can be found in the Sincheon area in **Idea-ap** (near Ewha Women's University) and Hong-ik University.

One of the oldest openly gay bars in Itaewon has become an upscale wine bar (still gay-friendly, of course) called **Bar Bliss** (© **02/749-7738**). If you take the subway to Itaewon (exit 4), walk straight and you'll see the sign GAY OR NOT; this is one of the most elegant places to get good wine in Seoul. The mood is mellow and inviting with tasteful decor. The owner, Teddy Park, speaks excellent English and offers a "blissful hour" (rather than happy hour) when drinks are two for one from 6 to 11pm. The bar closes at 3am on weekdays and 5am on weekends.

If you want to shake your booty to some electronica/dance music, head to **Del's Disco,** on the basement level of the Hamilton Hotel. Professional go-go boys in tight shorts pole dance against black walls while South Korea's fashionable gay boys dance well into the wee hours. Other gay bars in the area include the established **Queen** (which has happy hour daily 8–11pm) which is usually packed with boys dancing on Friday and Saturday nights.

For a mellower place for a cocktail, stop by **Barcode ★** (© **02/3672-0940;** subway line 1, 3, or 5 to Jongno 3(sam)-ga, exit 3 or 8), where locals (mostly in their 30s) mingle with foreigners in a simple, but classy atmosphere.

Cafes & Teahouses

Koreans love their tea and in some ways they love their coffee more. Even some of the small hole-in-the-wall restaurants will offer a free (or very cheap) machine that dispenses tiny cups of sweet instant coffee. Bad coffee aside, Western-style cafes can be found in every neighborhood. Although you'll find the American chains like Starbucks everywhere, Korean coffee shops usually have a more interesting decor, though they're higher in price (some of them tend to be rather smoky too).

For just an honest cup of coffee in Samcheongdong, try **Beans Bins,** 62-26 Samcheong-dong (© **02/736-7799**), just across the street from Samcheongdong Sujebi. Just follow your nose to the smell of roasting and brewing beans. Open daily

Sing Your Heart Out

A popular part of South Korean nightlife is the *noraebang* (singing room), where you can rent a private room with a karaoke machine so that you and your friends can belt out your favorite tunes. You choose from a menu of songs, input the numbers into the system, and take turns singing and dancing along to old American, Korean, and other Asian favorites.

You can't swing a dead cat in Seoul without hitting a noraebang. The hipper ones are in the college areas of Hongdae-ap and Daehangno. Most of them have songs in English. Some of them in more expensive areas, like Apgujeong, can get pretty steep (over ₩100,000 per hour), so be sure to ask the price before you step into a room. Most are open daily from around 5pm to 2am, and you rent rooms by the hour (₩12,000–₩20,000), depending on the place and the size of the room. They serve only sodas and beers.

from 11am to 11pm, this place sells coffee at ₩5,000. A great place to tuck yourself away in a corner with a book and a steaming mug is **To Go Coffee ★★**, 32-21 Jaedong, Jongno-gu (☎ 02/720-5001). You can get a cup for ₩4,000 and browse the selection of books or ceramics on display. They're open Monday through Saturday 7am to 11pm and Sunday 10am to 10pm. For a fresh-roasted cup made by a real-live barista, try **Bar 0101 ★★**, 124-2 Samcheong-dong (☎ 02/723-1259). Don't let the name fool you, because their specialty is coffee, with a cup of Americano starting at ₩5,500. They're open Tuesday through Sunday 10am to 1am.

Of course, there is no shortage of traditional tea shops in the area. One for animal lovers is **Shin Yeutchatjip** (☎ 02/732-5257), whose name means "new old tea house." Inside a hanok, birds, rabbits, chickens, and other animals hang out among traditional masks and kimchi pots. They have traditional floor seating in the main room and in the private rooms as well. A popular place for traditional beverages is **Juntong Chatjip** (☎ 02/723-4909), which is located across from the Insa Art Plaza. It has antique decor and instruments in a wood and *hanji* (traditional paper) interior. The outdoor courtyard is nice for warm evenings. Nearby on the second floor is the **Yeut Chatjip** (☎ 02/737-5019), which has a distinctive old-timey feel with everyday tools hanging from the warm, clay walls. You can have your choice of seating from traditional floor tables, or chunky wood tables and benches. If you had to choose only one *chatjip* (tea house) in the area, a good choice would be **Gwicheon** (☎ 02/3210-2288), a favorite among writers and poets, since it's owned by the wife of famous poet Cheon Sangbyeong. She serves high-quality teas with ingredients she grows at home. Gwicheon is open 11am to 10pm daily. If you want to get the feeling for Korea about 70 years ago, go and find **Appa Uhlyeosseul Jjeok-eh** (☎ 02/733-3126), whose name means "when Dad was young." Enter the crowded space and it's like stepping into a time warp. They have a black-and-white TV, old memorabilia, and a menu made from an old primary school board. Open daily from 11am to midnight, they're in the alley on the right side of Insa 3(sam)-gil.

Other than traditional tea shops, there are plenty of modern teahouses. One of these is **O'Sulloc Tea House ★★★**, which has several locations throughout the city. The one in Myeongdong is next to Woori Bank (near Myeongdong Cathedral) and is open daily 8am to 10pm. The one in Daehangno is huge, with a nice upstairs terrace. You can't miss it, just up the street from the Coffee Bean; it's open daily 9am

In some ways, the rest of South Korea can be considered a day trip from the big city. However, some places require overnight stays to really get the flavor of that region. The one exception is if you plan to visit the DMZ/Panmunjeom area. You pretty much have to do it in a day with an organized tour, since there are no places to spend the night, due to security concerns. See the Gyeonggi-do chapter for details. You can also make a ski trip to Gangwon-do (see chapter 10), visit the kilns in Icheon (p. 116), see the traditional village and fortress in Suwon (p. 109), or just hike the trails in any of South Korea's national parks, all while using Seoul as your base for travel.

to 10:30pm. It has a variety of food items and green tea blends, herbal infusions, and even green tea soaps for sale, in a charming atmosphere. Drinks range from ₩5,000 to ₩9,000, cakes ₩3,000 to ₩4,500.

There are dozens of fun and eclectic cafes that cater to the college kids in Hongdaeap. The **aA Café ★★★** (408-11 Seogyo-dong, Mapo-gu; ✆ 02/3143-7311; www.aadesignmuseum.com) on the second floor of the **aA Design Museum** has art, design, an outdoor patio, and great coffee in an unpretentious setting. For an excellent cup from beans roasted by Korea's 2005 Barista Champion, stop by **Coffee Lab ★★** (327-19 Seogyo-dong, Mapo-gu; ✆ 02/3143-0908; open Monday to Thursday 11am–midnight, Fri/Sat until 1am). They serve imported roasts and their own blends, like their "mad scientist," underneath a ceiling full of suspended wooden chairs (Subway line 2 to Hongik U., exit 8).

Of the unusual cafes in the area, there are a handful of cat cafes, where you can pay a flat fee (usually about ₩8,000) for a free drink and all the feline love you want. **Tom's Cat Café** and **Gio Cat** are a couple of such cafes in the area. For a cat of a different color, stop by the **Hello Kitty Café** ☺ (✆ 02/334-6570; 358-112 Seogyeo-dong, Mapo-gu; daily 11am–midnight) for a cup of decorated coffee and an overdose of pink. Dog lovers may like the **Bau House Café** for some canine love or the **Charlie Brown Café** ☺ (✆ 02/332-2600; 364-2 Seogyeo-dong, Mapo-gu) to see one of the world's most loved beagles, Snoopy.

In Myeongdong, one place to enjoy a lovely cup of tea is the **Tea Loft ★** (✆ 02/772-3996) on the 14th floor of the Lotte Department Store. Open daily from 10:30am to 9:30pm, they specialize in teas and a nice variety of *ddeok* (rice cakes). Menu items run about ₩6,000 to ₩8,000. You can enjoy a cup of coffee and get a fish pedicure at **Namu Geuneul ★★★** (✆ 02/599-1210; www.restree.net), located on the second floor above the clothing store Basic House (subway to Gangnam, exit 6). Open 10am to midnight; beverages cost ₩4,000 to ₩10,000 and you can indulge in baked goods from their "buffet," while the "doctor fish" nibble at your feet. It's ₩3,000 for 15 minutes of ticklish fun.

An unusual place to enjoy a cup of coffee and the view of the Han River is the **Hangang Jeongmang Café Rainbow ★★** (✆ 02/511-7345), located on the south side of the Hannam Bridge. Open 11am to midnight (until 11pm Nov–Feb); beverages are a reasonable ₩3,500 to ₩5,000. The cafe is easily accessible from Han River Park (you can take a water taxi to the Hannam River stop) or take bus no. 140, 142, 144, 241, 402, 407, 408, 420, 421, 470, 471, or 472 (going northbound over the bridge).

GYEONGGI-DO

L ike a giant doughnut surrounding the city of Seoul, Gyeonggi-do is the most populous of South Korea's provinces, historically rich and geographically plentiful. Hi-rise apartment towers and Korea's factories spill out into the rice paddies and dwenjang farms of the province.

Take a walk around the stone wall fortress in the capital city **Suwon** or try your hand at a traditional game at the **folk village** there. Visit the artisans firing up their outdoor kilns in **Icheon** or just take a soak in the hot springs. The **DMZ** remains a stark remnant of the Cold War and it's as close as you can get to North Korea without actually visiting that communist state. **Ganghwa-do** sits quietly to the east and holds prehistoric dolmens, signs of ancient civilizations.

Restaurants in **Icheon** serve up rice meals (*ssal bap*) from the same fields they used to grow the King's rice. Suwon's plentiful *galbi* joints fill the streets with the smoky aroma of beef cooked on tabletop grills. **Incheon's** Chinatown was the birthplace of *jjajangmyeon,* Korea's answer to China's black-bean noodles.

SUWON

Famous for its galbi (beef ribs), Suwon is home to the expansive **Korean Folk Village** and South Korea's answer to Disneyland, **Everland.** The **Suwon Hwaseong,** South Korea's best-preserved fortress, is worth a stroll around its stone terraces and towers.

Essentials

GETTING THERE The nearest **airport** is at Incheon, and there's a limousine bus from there to Suwon (in front of gate 7A, or at bus stop 3 or 12). The ride from the airport takes about 100 minutes and costs about ₩14,000. The limousine buses run daily every 20 minutes starting at 6:30am until 8:30pm. Suwon is also on the **KTX railway line** (from Seoul to Busan) and a ticket costs about ₩8,500 from Seoul. The regular train to Suwon costs ₩3,100 for a reserved seat and ₩2,600 for standing/unreserved seat.

A cheaper alternative is to take the **subway,** line 1 (the dark blue one) from Seoul. It takes about an hour from the Seoul city center and drops you off at Suwon Station (exits 2 or 4 for the tourist info center). It's a pleasant ride and costs about ₩1,500. You can also take **express bus** no. 7770 from Sadang Station, no. 3000 from Gangnam Station, or no. 900 from Guro Station. All three buses arrive at Suwon Station.

When leaving Suwon, the greatest number of options is available at the main subway/train station. Many **Korail trains** stop at Suwon on the way to several other destinations. The main subway access area is at the lower-ground-floor level, while Korail services are on the upper level. The ticket windows for regular trains are to the left of the escalators and there's a special window just for tickets to Seoul at the far left end of the windows. Station announcements are made in both English and Korean. Just remember to line up by the correct platform for your train, as passengers are allowed access to the platform only a few minutes before the train arrives.

GETTING AROUND   There is a stand for taxis right in front of the station, as well as less expensive local buses (although the stop names are only in Korean). Express buses (more expensive, but with fewer stops) will have certain tourist destinations written in English.

There is also a free shuttle bus from Suwon Station to the Korean Folk Village (Hanguk Minsokchon). You can purchase an admission ticket to the folk village at the tourist booth, to the left when you exit the station. You can board the shuttle bus near the car park. It takes about 30 to 40 minutes and brings you to the main entrance of the folk village.

VISITOR INFORMATION   There is a tourist information booth just outside of Suwon subway/train station (when you exit the main doors, go left) (✆ **031/249-5146**), one at the Korean Folk Village (✆ **031/287-1332**), and an info booth at Hwaseong Fortress (✆ **031/228-4677**). The official Suwon website is at **http://eng.suwon.ne.kr** or call ✆ **031/256-8300.**

If you prefer a quick tour of the city, board the **Suwon City Tour Bus** (✆ **031/256-8300;** www.suwoncitytour.co.kr/en/) at the Suwon Tourist Info Center for a tour of Seongjangdae, Hwaseomun, Hwaseong Temporary Palace, the Suwon Fortress, the World Cup Stadium, and the KBS Suwon Center. Tickets are ₩11,000 adults, ₩8,000 youth, ₩4,000 children under 7. The 3-hour tour runs at 10:30am and 2pm Tuesday to Sunday with longer, slightly more expensive, tours on Thursdays.

Exploring Suwon

Everland ☺ THEME PARK   On a completely different note from the traditional offerings in Suwon, Everland is the country's largest amusement park. It claims to be the fifth-most-popular amusement park in the world, and it has the massive crowds and long lines to prove it. Among the highlights are two roller coasters, a small zoo, and European World, featuring architecture and food from Europe. There are high-tech 3-D games located in an outdoor facility, although these games are not available when it's raining. **Caribbean Bay,** the water park next door, requires a separate admission fee of ₩50,000 for adults and ₩39,000 for kids during low season from January to May, going up after that (although you can get a combination discount ticket). It includes several water slides, a wave pool, tube ride, kiddy pool, and other water fun.

310 Jeondae-li, Pogok-myeon, Gyeonggi-go. ✆ **031/320-5000** or 02/759-1943. www.everland. com/MultiLanguage/english/index.html. Admission ₩38,000 adults, ₩32,000 teens, ₩29,000 children. Daily 10am–10pm (opens 9:30am on some Sun). From Seoul, take subway line 1 to Suwon Station, and then local bus no. 66. From Gangnam Bus Station take bus no. 5002, bus 5002 from Jamsil Station or bus 1113 from Gangbyeon. If driving, take Singal JC and go toward Maseong IC; then follow the signs to Everland.

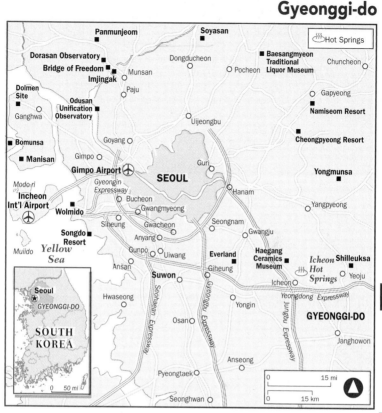

Hanguk Minsokchon (Korean Folk Village) ★★ ☺ HISTORIC SITE   More like an open-air folk museum designed to show how Koreans once lived, it's one of several such villages throughout the country. Because of its proximity to Seoul, it is the best known and most frequented, though the one in Andong (p. 252) is a more authentic example. There are over 260 traditional homes and buildings from the late Joseon period as well as folk handicrafts and artisans in costume. Try to time your visits for a performance (see below). **Note:** Performances are canceled in inclement weather. On holidays and weekends, they also hold ancestral rites and other traditional folk activities. The **Korean Folk Museum** is worth a gander, if you want to pay the extra admission, but the Haunted House can be skipped. If you visit around lunchtime, hold out until you can get to the traditional Korean food court inside the village for a larger variety of offerings.

107 Bora-dong, Giheung-gu, Yong-in-si, Gyeonggi-do 449-730. ⓒ **031/288-0000.** www.korean folk.co.kr/folk/english/about/about_intro.html. General admission ₩15,000 adults, ₩12,000 teens, ₩10,000 children; unlimited usage (including the folk museum) ₩20,000 adults, ₩17,000 teens, ₩15,000 children. Summer daily 9am–6pm; winter daily 9am–5pm; opens 30 min. later Sun and

THE RICE BOX king

Honoring ancestors is an important part of Korean culture, but King Jeongjo had particular reason to want to honor his father. His grandfather, King Yeongjo, had ruled for 52 years, but as he came to the end of his life, he became convinced that his son (Jeongjo's father), Prince Sado, was trying to overthrow him. Yeongjo had his son sealed in a rice box until he died. Young Jeongjo witnessed this tragedy, and after he ascended the throne, he had his father posthumously crowned and given the name King Jangjo. Some suggest that he built the Suwon fortress and palace structures so that he could live close to his beloved father's grave. That's why Suwon is sometimes called, "The City of Filial Piety."

holidays, last entrance 1 hour before closing. Showtimes: Farmer's music and dance 11am and 2pm; tightrope acrobatics 11:30am and 2:30pm; traditional wedding noon and 4pm at house no. 22; equestrian feats 1 and 2:30pm. Free hourly shuttle bus from the Korean Folk Village office at Suwon Station daily 11am–3pm, takes about 30 min. Bus no. 37 from Suwon Station, or no. 5001-1 from Seoul's Gangnam station. Driving from Seoul, take either the Gyeongbu or Yeongdong expressways, the Shingal-asan highway, Gyeongbu national road, or the Suwon-Yong-in national road to the Suwon toll exit and follow the signs to KOREAN FOLK VILLAGE.

Hwaseong Haeng-gung (Temporary Palace) ★ PALACE   *"Haeng-gung"* means a temporary shelter where a king rests or retires from a war, and the Hwaseong Haeng-gung is the largest of such temporary palaces in South Korea. It was built during the Joseon Dynasty. King Jeongjo stayed here at the time of his "long journey" and also used the palace as the place to celebrate his mother's 60th birthday. If you happen to visit between April and October, plan your visit for the Jangyongyeong guarding ceremony held at the front gate on Sundays at 2pm.

Jangan-gu/Gwonseon-gu/Ingye-dong, Paldal-gu, Suwon, Gyeonggi-do. http://ehs.suwon.ne.kr. ₩1,500 adults, ₩1,000 teens, ₩700 children. Tues–Sun 9am–6pm Mar–Oct, 10am–5pm Nov–Feb. Suwon Station (Seoul subway line 1, exit 6). From Jamsil station, take bus no. 1007.

Suwon Hwaseong (Suwon Fortress) ★★★ HISTORIC SITE   This impressive structure used to surround the city of Suwon; now the city surrounds it. King Jeongjo had the fortress wall built to guard the tomb of his father in 1794, during the late Joseon period. Constructed under the guidance of philosopher Jeong Yag-yong, it was Jeongjo's unsuccessful attempt at making Suwon the nation's capital. Finished in 1796, the 5.5km-long (3½-mile) wall, along with various military facilities, was severely damaged during the Korean War. Restoration work began in 1974 and was completed in 1979, with much help from records published shortly after King Jeongjo's death. It was designated a UNESCO World Heritage site in 1997. It's best to enter at the Changnyongmun (the east gate, or Dongmun), since it's easier to find from the road than the Paldalmun (the south gate), located up the road from a *shijang* (market). You can walk around the entire fortress in 2 to 3 hours or take the "Dragon train" that circles it.

There is no direct address since the fortress surrounds the old city.☏ **031/-251-4435.** http://ehs. suwon.ne.kr. Admission ₩1,000 adults, ₩700 teens, ₩500 children, but there's no designated ticket office and the fee-taking is quite lax. Dragon train ₩1,500 adults, ₩1,100 teens, ₩1,000

Suwon

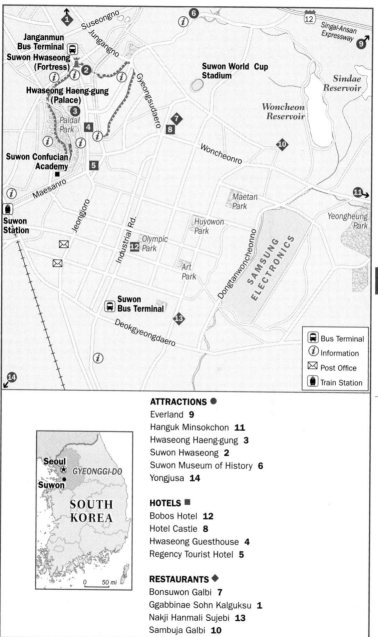

ATTRACTIONS ●
Everland **9**
Hanguk Minsokchon **11**
Hwaseong Haeng-gung **3**
Suwon Hwaseong **2**
Suwon Museum of History **6**
Yongjusa **14**

HOTELS ■
Bobos Hotel **12**
Hotel Castle **8**
Hwaseong Guesthouse **4**
Regency Tourist Hotel **5**

RESTAURANTS ◆
Bonsuwon Galbi **7**
Ggabbinae Sohn Kalguksu **1**
Nakji Hanmali Sujebi **13**
Sambuja Galbi **10**

seniors 65 and over, ₩700 children. Parking ₩2,000 for 3 hours. The wall daily 24 hr. Parking and dragon train Tues–Sun 10am–5:30pm. Bus no. 2, 7, 7-2, 8, or 13 from Suwon Station (Seoul Subway line 1); get off at Jongno 4-geoli (4-way) and walk 5 min.; bus no. 1007 or 3000 from Jongno Station.

Suwon Museum of History MUSEUM If you want to learn more about the cultural history of Suwon, this is the place to do it. The museum has a variety of relics showing the city's rich history from prehistory to present day. The building also houses the **Calligraphy Museum of Korea** and the real highlight, the personal collection of Lee Jonghak, a Suwon native, who had dedicated his life to collecting historical material related to Dokdo and Geumgangsan (a mountain range which is now part of North Korea). After his death, his family donated his collection of 20,000 items, many of which give insight into Korean culture during the time of Japanese colonialization.

443 Changryongmun-gil, Yeongtong-gu, Suwon-si (1088-10 Yiui-dong Street). http://swmuseum. suwon.ne.kr/eng/. ℂ **031/228-4150.** ₩2,000 adults, ₩1,000 teens, free for seniors over 65 and children 12 and under. Tues–Fri 9am–6pm (last admission 1 hr. before closing). Closed New Year, Chuseok, and Lunar New Year. From Suwon Station, take bus no. 24 or 46 (30-min. ride). From Suwon Station, take bus no. 60 in front of the rail freight agency and get off at the back gate of Gyeonggi Univ. Walk about 300m (984 ft.) toward the Gyeonggi provincial police office, then go toward the Suwon Foreign Language High School (about another 150m/492 ft.). From the Suwon Bus Terminal, take bus no. 3007 and get off at the back gate of Gyeonggi Univ. (and follow the directions above).

Yongjusa (Yongju Temple) TEMPLE Unlike most temples, which are usually located in fairly isolated spots in the mountains, Yongjusa can be found on the outskirts of Suwon, in Hwaseong. Built during the Shilla Dynasty (57 B.C.–A.D. 935), the original temple was destroyed during one of the many wars during the Goryeo Dynasty. But after a visit to his father's grave nearby, King Jeongjo spent the night here and had a vision of a dragon (*yong*) with a red jewel in its mouth (an image common in Buddhist art). Seeing it as an auspicious sign, he had a new temple built here in 1790 as a place to offer prayers to his father, Prince Sado. The highlights here include the dragon motifs, a massive bronze bell cast in A.D. 854 (one of only three such bells left in the country), and a mural of a tiger smoking a pipe, a prime example of the shamanistic influence on Korean Buddhism. The blocks on which the Filial Piety Sutra is carved are housed at the temple. A short walk will bring you to the royal tombs, where King Jeongjo and his parents are buried. You can also do a **temple stay** here, if you wish.

188 Songsan-dong, Hwaseong-si. ℂ **031/234-0040** (031/235-6886 for temple stay). http://eng. yongjoosa.or.kr. ₩1,500 adults, ₩1,000 teens, ₩700 seniors and kids. Daily 8 am–7pm. From Suwon Station, take bus no. 24, 46, or 46-1 (30-min. ride).

Shopping

Although Suwon itself doesn't offer a great array of traditional Korean souvenirs, you can pick up something traditional and handmade from one of the many artisans inside the Korean Folk Village. Some of them will write your name or a phrase in Korean calligraphy or *Hanja* (Chinese characters) on handmade *hanji* (traditional rice paper). The scrolls are inexpensive and lightweight, and you're directly supporting folk art.

For clothing and other items, there are some open-air market areas outside the subway/train and bus stations. The **Paldalmun Shijang** (ℂ **031/228-4675**) is located right outside the Paldal Gate of Suwon Fortress, where you can get clothes and accessories. You can also shop for blankets and traditional *hanbok* at nearby **Yeongdong Shijang** (☎ 031/251-0171)

A multistoried **Galleria Department Store** (☎ 031/229-7114) is located across from Suwon City Hall (take bus 92 or 92-1 from Suwon Station). Suwon also has several discount mega marts, like **E-Mart** (☎ 031/207-1234; take bus 88 or 82-1 north of Suwon station), **Fashion Island** (☎ 031/267-6134; close to E-Mart), or **Home Plus** (☎ 031/259-8000; take bus 777, 900 or 7770 north of Suwon station).

Where to Stay

For cheaper options, check out any number of the motels situated just around the train station and love motels (p. 410) throughout the city. As a rule, they're clean and safe, if not glamorous. Rooms usually start at ₩30,000 per night for a double on weekdays. Rates below include the 10% VAT, unless otherwise noted.

Bobos Hotel This inexpensive motel is popular with Japanese tourists. About 15 minutes from Suwon Station by taxi, the rooms are simple but relatively spacious, especially for the price. The decor is nothing special, but it's not tacky either, with off-white walls and equally off-white furnishings. Includes the usual South Korean motel amenities, as well as a few extras.

1081-14 Gwonseon-dong, Gwonseon-gu, Suwon-si, Gyeonggi-do. 48 units. ☎ **031/267-3188.** ₩40,000–₩60,000 double. No credit cards. *In room:* A/C, TV/VCR, fridge, hair dryer.

Hotel Castle Located near Suwon's World Cup Stadium, it's a bit outside of the city center, though there are some shops and restaurants within walking distance. This is one of the few "luxury" accommodations in Suwon, offering mostly Western-style rooms, though there are some Korean-style ondol suites (p. 409) available as well. Rooms have the usual Korean-style bathrooms (a drain in the floor for the shower) and the onsite sauna is only for men, unfortunately. It's not possible to book online using a foreign credit card, but you can call or e-mail them for reservations.

144-4 Uman-dong, Paldal-gu, Suwon-si, Gyeonggi-do. www.hcastle.co.kr/eng_root. ☎ **031/211-6666.** Fax 031/212-8811. 81 units. ₩190,000 double, ₩230,000 deluxe double/twin, ₩290,000 junior suite; 10% VAT and 10% service charge not included; discounts available outside of high season. AE, MC, V. Free parking. **Amenities:** 3 restaurants; lounge bar; cafe; tennis court; health club; sauna (men only); business center; bakery; barber shop. *In room:* A/C, TV, minibar, Internet.

Hwaseong Guesthouse 🛂 The best budget sleeping quarters in Suwon, this guesthouse is centrally located and good for single travelers on a budget. Although the bathrooms, TV, and kitchen facilities are communal, the free Internet and coin laundry makes this a convenient option for exploring the city.

4-beonji, Paldal-ro, Paldal-gu, Suwon-si. 48 units. http://www.hsguesthouse.com. ☎ **031/245-6226** or 010-5316-3419 (mobile). ₩15,000 bed, ₩25,000 private room, ₩30,000 private room with bathroom. No credit cards. **Amenities:** Shared kitchen; fridge; PC; Wi-Fi.

Regency Tourist Hotel More institutional than inviting, its best feature is the convenient location—within walking distance of the city center. It has both Western-style rooms and the traditional Korean ondol rooms (with heated floors). The staff's English isn't great, but they are very friendly and accommodating.

47, Gucheon-dong, Suwon-si, Gyeonggi-do 9. www.htregency.co.kr/E_index.asp. ☎ **031/246-4141.** Fax 031/243-9296. 65 units. ₩140,000 double, ₩225,000 junior suite, 10% VAT not included. AE, MC, V. **Amenities:** Restaurant; coffee lounge. *In room:* A/C, satellite TV, fridge, hair dryer, PC, Internet.

Where to Eat

Although Suwon is famous for its galbi, restaurants that specialize in other Korean cuisine will be less expensive. As in most cities, there is no shortage of places to choose from, but here are a handful of delicious options.

Bonsuwon Galbi ★★★ KOREAN BEEF   At this establishment well known for its beef dishes, you can get everything from meat you cook yourself at the table to *galbi jjim* (stewed beef ribs). As with most galbi places, you'll get a few *kimchi* on the side and your rice may come last if you're grilling, since you don't want to fill up before you've finished your meat. There's not much in the way of interior design, but people come for the food, not the environment. The menu is only in Korean.

51-20 Uman 2-dong, Paldal-gu, Suwon-si, Gyeonggi-do. ℂ **031/241-8434.** Entrees ₩33,000–₩45,000. No credit cards. Daily 11am–10pm.

Ggabbinae Sohn Kalguksu ★ ☺ KOREAN NOODLES   The menu in this informal noodle joint is quite simple: You can get *kal guksu* (hand-cut noodles) or *gongi bap* (bowl rice), served with a couple of sides of kimchi. It's great for a quick lunch or dinner, but not a place where you'd want to linger and take in the nonexistent atmosphere. The menu is only in Korean, but with the few options, it shouldn't be a problem. A child-sized bowl of noodles is only ₩3,000.

763-20, Jowon-dong, Jangan-gu, Suwon-si. ℂ **031/242-4673.** Reservations daily 11:30am–1pm; afterward it's first come, first served. ₩5,000–₩9,000. No credit cards. 11:30am–9pm.

Nakji Hanmali Sujebi (One Squid Sujebi) KOREAN SEAFOOD   As you could guess by the name, this eatery is well known for its seafood and its squid *soondae* (sausage). With Korean-style floor tables, the service is quick, the *nakji bokkeum* (stir-fried squid) is quite spicy, and the *haemul pajeon* (seafood flatcakes) are generously large. The seafood flatcakes make a nice snack or light lunch, but the spicy squid is what brings people back. A spicy seafood hot pot is nice to share with a friend on cold days. The menu is only in Korean.

On the 3rd floor of the GS Mart, Gwonseon-dong, Paldal-gu, Suwon-si. ℂ **031/215-8605.** Entrees ₩9,000–₩30,000. No credit cards. Daily noon–10pm.

Sambuja Galbi ★★ KOREAN BEEF   Serving Suwon-style galbi at this location for over 18 years, this spacious restaurant serves up beef, beef, and more beef and a plethora of *banchan* (sides) to go with it. The most expensive cuts are reserved for the *saeng galbi* (unmarinated beef ribs), but the marinated *yangnyeom galbi* is a better way of getting a taste of the regional flavor. In the summer, get a bowl of cold *naengmyeon* (buckwheat noodles) on the side to cool you down.

96-1 Woncheon-dong, Yeongtong-gu, Suwon-si, Gyeonggi-do. ℂ **031/211-8959.** Entrees ₩29,000–₩45,000. MC, V. Daily 11:30am–10pm.

ICHEON

The center of Korean ceramics for over 500 years, Icheon has about 80 pottery factories and over 300 active kilns. Spend the morning gingerly stepping over broken shards and watching Korea's "intangible cultural assets" at work in their ceramic mastery. Then, enjoy a lunch of Icheon ssal bap, and soak the afternoon away in an **oncheon** (hot spring).

THE pottery WARS

During the 15th and 16th centuries, Korean *buncheong* pottery (a grayish-colored pottery in everyday use at the time) was revered throughout Asia. So much so, in fact, that when Japan invaded Korea during the Imjin Waeran ("The Japanese Invasion in the Imjin Years"), the Japanese destroyed many kilns and kidnapped thousands of potters so that they could gain their coveted knowledge and skills. The war itself lasted for 7 years, but the rash of kidnappings happened in two waves, first in 1592 and then again from 1597 to 1598.

The arrival of Korean potters in Japan introduced certain advanced ceramic techniques, such as the kick wheel and the climbing kiln, to that country and started Japan on its way to being one of the most revered ceramic producers in the world. Rather amazingly, one of these kidnapped Korean potters, Yi Sam-Pyong, is today referred to as the "father of Japanese pottery." Indeed, most of the forcibly relocated artisans settled in Japan's Satsuma province, and their descendants continue to make pottery there using traditional techniques to this day. Korea didn't fare quite so well: With virtually all of its potters gone, buncheong pottery was nearly wiped out.

Essentials

GETTING THERE   From **Incheon International Airport,** you can take a limousine bus (from bus stop 7A) that stops at Gimpo International Airport, then the Dong Seoul Terminal, and then Icheon. Run by **Buspia** (*☏* **02/575-7710;** www.buspia. co.kr), the buses run daily from 5:10am to 10pm; the whole ride takes about 2 hours and 20 minutes and costs ₩17,000 (₩9,000 from DongSeoul). You can also get a bus bound for Icheon directly from Seoul at the **Gangnam Express Bus Terminal.** Buses start running daily at 6:30am and run every 30 minutes or so until 10pm. You can also take a bus from the **Dong Seoul (Gangbyeon) Bus Terminal** (Seoul subway line 2, Gangbyeong Station). The buses from here start daily at 6:10am and run every 15 minutes until 10:40pm. It's about an hour ride (longer on weekends with traffic) and will cost ₩3,600 for a standard bus and ₩4,200 for a deluxe bus (which has guaranteed seats and air-conditioning). If you're driving, take the Jungbu Expressway (no.35) and get off at the Icheon or Seo-Icheon toll exit.

GETTING AROUND   There is a long line of taxis waiting outside of Icheon Bus Terminal to take you around. Average cost to go to the kilns is about ₩5,000, or you may want to take one of the local buses (which will cost you about ₩1,000). Bus no. 14 will take you to Sindun-myeon, where the majority of the kilns are located.

VISITOR INFORMATION   There is a visitor center near the Seolbongho (Seolbong Lake). They speak English and you can get excellent maps in English. The city's official website is www.icheon.go.kr, but you can also get info by calling the **Tourist Information Bureau** at *☏* **031/644-6770** or by dialing the **Korea Travel Phone** (*☏* **1330**). See "Special-Interest Trips," in chapter 2, for companies that offer specialized ceramics tours from Seoul.

Exploring Icheon

Haegang Ceramics Museum MUSEUM   Run by the Haegang Institute of Koryo Celadon, this small museum displays several historical ceramic pieces as well as items by potters working today (although many of the masters are aging rapidly and fewer apprentices are learning the craft). Check to see when they'll be firing up the kilns, since that's more exciting to see than the small collection housed here. Since Korean ceramics are made at very high temperatures, there is a high attrition rate. Nowhere is that more evident than the piles of discarded shards visible on the site surrounding the kilns.

330-1 Sugwang-li, Sindun-myeon, Icheon-si. 🕐 **031/634-2266.** www.haegang.org. Admission ₩2,000 adults, ₩1,000 teens, ₩500 children. Tues–Sun 9:30am–5:30pm (last entry at 5pm). Closed Jan 1, Lunar New Year, and Chuseok. Bus: From the Icheon Bus Terminal, take the bus headed toward Sindun-myeon, Sugwang-li, to the museum (a 3- to 5-min. ride). Driving: Head to Icheon and take national road 3, following signs to museum.

Icheon Ceramic/Pottery Village ★★★ HISTORIC SITE   It's not really a "village" per se, but the kilns span the areas of Sugwang-li, Sindun-myeon, and Saeum-dong. Although people of the peninsula have been creating ceramics for thousands of years, this "village" has been a center of Korean traditional ceramics since its production of white porcelain during the Joseon Dynasty. To this day, the artisans here create celadon, whose production was started during the Goryeo Dynasty and has evolved into the ghostly green color we're familiar with today. Over 300 active ceramics studios here (about 40 of which use traditional firewood kilns) offer educational insight and hands-on classes for visitors. You can even buy the handiwork of some of Korea's "living cultural treasures."

No direct address, but studios span Sugwang-li, Sindun-myeon, and Saeum-dong in Icheon-si. 🕐 **031/635-7976** or 031/644-2280. Free admission. All kilns Mon–Sat 10am–5pm, but artisans have the weekends off. Bus: 14 (head for Sindun-myeon) from Icheon Bus Terminal runs every 10 min. and takes 5 min.

Cerapia (Icheon World Ceramics Center) MUSEUM   The site of the biennial Icheon Ceramics Festival, which is held in odd-numbered years, the center is dedicated to ceramic making in South Korea and throughout the world. It has four main exhibition halls and a large open space for festivals and special events. You can visit the museum and ceramics center, run by the World Ceramics Exposition Foundation, even when the expo is not going on. On permanent display are works by major Korean artists and international ceramists. The park in which the ceramics center is located includes **Seolbong Lake,** the **Icheon City Museum** and other attractions.

San 69-1, Gwang-go-dong, Icheon-si (inside Seolbong Park). 🕐 **031/631-6501.** www.wocef.com/eng/index.asp. Admission free, except when the ceramics biennale is being held. Tues–Sun 9am–6pm Mar–Oct, 10am–5pm Nov–Feb. Closed January 1, Chuseok and Lunar New Year. Bus: Take bus no. 1113-1 from the "jwaseok" bus stop in front of Techno Mart (near Gangbyeon Station), and get off at the Gwangju Joseon Royal Kiln Museum. From there, take a bus going toward Icheon Terminal and get off at the Icheon Fire Station. From there, it's a short walk to the center. From Seoul take a bus from either the DongSeoul Bus Terminal or the Seoul Express Bus Terminal to Icheon and grab a taxi in front of the Icheon Bus Terminal. The ride is only about 10 to 15 min. Driving: From Seoul's Jungbu Expwy., go to Seo-Icheon IC and take national road 3, and follow the signs; from Yeongdong Expwy., go toward Icheon IC, take national road 2, and follow the signs.

Jisan Forest Resort SPORTS VENUE   While not the largest ski resort in South Korea, this is definitely the closest to Seoul. You can get lift tickets for both skiing and snowboarding by time of day, starting at ₩85,000 and up. They also offer skiing in the wee hours, from midnight to 4am. Season usually runs late Dec–mid-Feb.

Outside of ski season, golfers can take advantage of their 18-hole courses, if you reserve at least a week in advance (✆ **031/330-1441** or -1442; www.jisangolf.com). Greens fees are ₩50,000 for weekdays and ₩65,000 on weekends for non-members, with additional fees for rentals and cart use.

San 28-1 Haewol-li, Majang-myeon, Icheon-si. ✆ **031/644-1200.** www.jisanresort.co.kr/eng/index.html. Bus: 12 from the Icheon Bus Terminal; free shuttle buses are available, but prior reservations must be made by calling 031/644-1390. Driving from Seoul: Gyeongbu or Jungbu expressways to the Yeongdong Expwy. to the Dukpyung TG and follow the signs to resort (40-min. drive from Gangnam).

Termeden Spa & Resort ★★★ ☺WATER PARK If you have an afternoon free, pack your swimsuit and head for this water park. If you've forgotten your suit, you can always buy one (at a markup, of course). Open year-round, this spot is most popular on weekends and in the summer, which means summer weekends are ridiculously crowded. Termeden is a "German"-type spa, hence the name, which is a Korean amalgam of "terme" ("spa" in German and Italian) and "eden" ("paradise"). It has a *bade* pool, a large wading pool with both indoor and outdoor sections where you can swim, soak, or get a water massage. You can also get massages for an additional fee, soak in an open-air spa, or scrub yourself in a Korean-style bath. During colder weather, you can also try the stone dry sauna, which feels a bit like being baked in a clay oven. The pool is co-ed, while the baths are segregated by gender.

372-7 Singal-li, Moga-myeon, Icheon-si, Gyeonggi-do. ✆031/645-2000. www.termeden.com/english/index.asp. Admission weekdays ₩28,000 adults, ₩21,000 children; weekends and holidays ₩32,000 adults, ₩24,000 children, "sunset" discounts after 4pm and kids 36 months and under are free. Bath open weekdays 8am–8pm; weekends 8am–9pm; longer hours during high season; pools open 1 hour after and close 1 hour before the baths. Bus: From Icheon Bus Terminal, take bus no. 16-1 to Maok Nonghyup Station in Singal-li. Buses are also available from the Dong Seoul Terminal at 9:20 and 10:40am daily, with returns at 4 and 5pm for ₩5,500 adult, ₩3,900 students. Call Daewon Tour at 031/645-2093 for more info. Driving: Take the Jungbu Expwy. (road 35) and get off at Seo-Icheon toll exit; turn right and then turn left at Majang Sageoli (4-way), taking state road 42. Turn right onto state road 70, turn right into the Eonong Seongji district, and follow the signs to Termeden.

Shopping

If you're shopping for Korean pottery, Icheon is the place. Most shops will pack your fragile purchases in special boxes for safe transport on the plane. If you buy from a high-end artisan, this may include a wooden box with a résumé of the potter.

Where to Stay

Most visitors don't overnight in Icheon, but you may wish to if you're heading out to places beyond. There are a large number of lower-end, midpriced motels in town, many located around the bus terminal and some in the ceramics village. No matter what they are called, they are all very similar, offering both Western-style and ondol rooms for about ₩30,000 on weekdays and ₩40,000 to ₩50,000 on weekends for doubles. The owners usually don't speak much English, but it's not difficult to get a room at the last minute (except during the ceramics festival). As with a majority of motels in Korea, you pay cash upfront. Below are a couple of higher-end accommodations where you can make reservations in advance.

EVERYTHING YOU wanted TO KNOW ABOUT KOREAN CERAMICS

Korean ceramics are famous worldwide for their sophistication and artistry. This all started during the Goryeo Dynasty, when Korean potters learned the art of celadon from Chinese artisans. This greenish pottery was created to emulate jade, which was super-popular and expensive at the time. Of course, Koreans also developed other types of ceramics, but all of them are characterized by the high heat of the kilns in which they are baked. Here are some different types.

- **Celadon (*Cheongja*)**—Characterized by its green color and crackled glaze, this type of ceramic is highly prized by collectors. Today, only a few artists create celadon in select small towns in South Korea. Of course, cheaper imitations are widely available.

- **Buncheong Ware (*Buncheong Sagi*)**—Made with a white slip painted over green pottery, this type of pottery was unique to Korea until the Pottery Wars, when the artisans were kidnapped and taken to Japan. When this form had almost completely disappeared from Korea, potters turned to white pottery.

- **Whiteware (*Baekja*)**—A process developed in 14th-century China, white pottery replaced celadon in popularity as Neo-Confucians adopted simplicity in life, as well as in their ceramics, during the Joseon Dynasty. Korean whiteware is characterized by simplicity in design with symbolic images and much of the surface left white. There are only three places in South Korea where white pottery is still made: Namjong-myeon in Bunwon-li, Geumsa-li, and Gwangju-si.

- **Brown Earthenware (*Onggi*)**—This is the simplest form of utilitarian pottery, developed from the earliest forms of pottery. This dark-brown earthenware was used as everyday cooking and storage in kitchens of rich and poor alike. Even now, you will see traditional *hahng-ali* (clay bowls used for fermenting) holding chili paste or kimchi outside of homes in the countryside.

Hotel Miranda ☺   The only truly high-end accommodation in the whole town, it's one of the largest buildings in the city. Attached to the hotel is the **Icheon Spaplus,** an oncheon (hot spring), and a water park with its own food court (30% discount for hotel guests). Both Western-style and Korean-style ondol rooms are available. Rooms range from twins to deluxe suites that include their own steam sauna booths and spa tubs. There are no single rooms, as all rooms sleep two or more. Rooms are simple and comfortable with both Western and Korean-style bathrooms. Practically the whole lobby is a ceramics store, so you can shop without even leaving your hotel, though buying from the artisans directly is best.

408-1, Anheung-dong, Icheon-si. www.mirandahotel.com.✆ **031/633-5118.** 165 units. ₩195,000 double or twin room; ₩410,000 suite. Discounts of over 50% not unusual. 10% VAT and 10% service charge not included. AE, MC, V. **Amenities:** 2 restaurants; bar; spa; sauna; business center; smoke-free rooms; bakery; karaoke lounge; bowling alley. *In room:* A/C, cable TV, minibar, fridge, hair dryer, bathrobe, Internet (for business-class rooms).

Jisan Maple Condo Convenient if you're planning to ski or golf at the Jisan Forest Resort, you can rent a Korean-style ondol room with a kitchen. As in most Korean "condos," there are separate bedrooms and living room/kitchen areas. Accommodations are clean but minimalist, with basic furnishings and no beds. Most rooms have tiny balconies. Although it's quiet most of the year, winter ski season can bring crowds and sometimes noisy families. Foreigners can only make reservations by phone, but you can also have a Korean travel agent book a room online for you. See the listing for the Jisan Forest Resort, above, for directions and additional information.

www.jisanresort.co.kr. *(C)* **031/644-1261.** Fax 031/638-5941. 66 units. ₩100,000–₩120,000 off season; ₩85,000–₩170,000, semi-high season; ₩120,000–₩195,000 high season late Dec to mid-Feb. AE, MC, V. **Amenities:** 2 restaurants; basketball court; soccer field; daycare center; outdoor stage. *In room:* A/C, kitchen, fridge, hair dryer.

Where to Eat

When in Icheon, eat the rice. That doesn't mean it'll be a boring meal, it just means that rice is the centerpiece, and it comes served with a ridiculous number of smaller banchan. Many restaurants serve the ssal bap starting at ₩10,000 per person, which is affordable and well worth the money. Several restaurants specialize in this local meal, but here are a few that merit a mention.

Hanilkwan KOREAN In business for years, this traditional Korean restaurant offers the usual ssal bap with over 15 side dishes, as well as a variety of other menu offerings. The *ingeum-nim ssal bap* (rice meal for a king) is priced economically and therefore perfect for commoners, but the galbi jjim is worth handing over the extra won. They have the usual Korean floor-level dining tables in a cozy setting. Private rooms are available for groups.

380-8 Jeungpo-dong, Icheon-si. *(C)* **031/633-1500.** Entrees ₩10,000–₩20,000. MC, V. Daily 9:30am–10pm. Take national road 3 and go toward Sindun-myeon, Sugwang-li, on the righthand side.

Icheon Ssalbapjib KOREAN RICE MEAL The name (which roughly translates to "Icheon Rice Meal House") should tell you everything about this sprawling place, which serves the traditional rice meal and cooks the rice in traditional stone pots.

591-1, Sugwang-li, Sindun-myeon, Icheon-si (at Mt. Jong-gae near Dongwon College, off national road 3). *(C)* **031/634-4813.** Entrees ₩10,000 and up. MC, V. Daily 10:30am–9pm. Closed Lunar New Year and Chuseok.

Jung Il Poom KOREAN RICE MEAL This place serves the traditional Korean meal with so many side dishes that you tire of counting. It does a brisk business, probably thanks to all the press it has got from various Korean media outlets. You can't miss the old-fashioned two-story building with mostly wood interior and the usual Korean squat tables. After you've had your fill, you can let all the food settle with a drink, which is included in the price of your meal, in one of the tea rooms.

630 Bunji, Saeum-dong, Icheon-si. *(C)* **031/631-1188.** Entrees ₩10,000–₩30,000. MC, V. Daily 11:30am–10pm. Difficult to get there by bus, it's best to take a taxi (just off of road 24).

Yeoju

Located in the southern valley of the Han River, this county, with its neighboring city of Icheon, is known as one of the centers of Korean contemporary ceramics. It is also home to the tomb of Korea's most popular emperor, the great King Sejong (Sejong Daewang), who developed the written Korean language, *Hangeul*. The tomb of King Sejong, the fourth ruler of the Joseon Dynasty, is a wonderful example of those from that era. The **Yeongneung Royal Tombs (Royal Mausoleum of King Sejong),** 83-1 Wangdae-li, Neungseo-myeon, Yeoju-gun (© 031/885-3123), is open 24 hours Tuesday through Sunday. Admission is ₩500 adults, ₩300 teens, free for children and seniors. King Sejong and his wife, Queen Soheon (Soheonwanghu), were buried together. Legend has it that, because the tombs face south, a spirit can oversee a country from this site for 10,000 years. *Note:* Watch the TV series "Deep Rooted Tree" (p. 18) for a dramatized version of King Sejong's history.

Nearby at the **Nyeongleung Royal Tombs** are buried the 17th Joseon emperor, King Hyeojong (Hyeojong-wang) and his wife, Queen Inseong (Inseong-wanghu).

Yeoju is also the **Birthplace of Empress Myeongseong,** 250-2 Neunghyeon-li, Yeoju-eup, Yeoju-gun (© 031/887-3575), the 26th ruler of the Joseon Dynasty. Her childhood home and memorial hall can be visited daily from 9am to 5pm (except Lunar New Year and Chuseok). Admission is ₩500 adults, ₩400 teens, ₩200 children.

Built along the ridgeline of Pasasan is the relatively well-preserved fortress, **Pasaseong,** San 9 Cheonseo-li, Daeshin-myeon, Yeoju-gun. The mountain's peak is at its center and some of the walls remain intact. From certain spots along the fortress walls, you can get a pretty nice view of the southern Han River. It takes about an hour to circle the fortress walls.

Worth a special trip to the area is the scenic **Shilleuksa ★★★**, 282 Cheonsong-li, Yeoju-eup, Yeoju-gun (© **031/885-2505**). Originally founded during the Shilla Dynasty, it is the only lakeside temple in South Korea. Rumor has it that famous Shilla Monk Wonhyo founded this temple during King Jinpyeong's reign (A.D. 579–632), but there are no relics or historical data supporting that myth. Although its actual founding is unknown, it became famous in 1376, during the second year of Goryeo Dynasty's King Wu's reign, when the monk Nawung came here to meditate. Flowering trees make this a beautiful site in the spring, while the yellowing ginkgo trees add to its fall (autumn) beauty. The most famous structure here is the multi-tiered stone pagoda. Admission is ₩2,200 adults, ₩1,700 teens, and ₩1,600 children. Buses to Shilleuksa run hourly from the Yeoju Bus Terminal.

While you're in town, don't miss the **Moka Buddhist Museum ★**, lho-li, Gangcheon-myeon, Yeoju-gun (© **031/885-9952**). Founded by Bak Chansu (whose pen name is Moka), the museum was created to uphold the traditions of Buddhist art and the traditional processes used in woodcrafts. An unusual combination of traditional and modern architecture, the three-floor building houses everything from paintings and calligraphy to wooden sculptures. With over 6,000 pieces in its collection, its outside sculpture garden displays some historic pagodas and Buddha statues. It's open daily from 9am to 6pm (until 5pm Nov–Mar). Admission is ₩5,000 adults, ₩4,000 teens, ₩3,000 children and seniors. Take Yeoju city bus no. 10 or 10-1 bound for Gangcheon-myeon and get off at the museum.

To reach Yeoju by bus, from Seoul's Express Bus Terminal take the bus to Yeoju-gun's Bus Terminal. Buses to Shilleuksa run every hour, but you can walk to the temple from Yeoju city center in about 30 minutes. By car, take national road 37 from Seoul and Yeoju is about 70km (43 miles) away.

PANMUNJEOM & THE DMZ ★★★

The Demilitarized Zone (or the DMZ, as it is more commonly called) is the 241km-long (150-mile) strip of land that separates North and South Korea. It has served as a buffer zone since the signing of the 1953 ceasefire agreement that ended the fighting during the Korean War (although the war itself has officially never ended). Located near the 38th parallel, it cut the peninsula roughly in half but separated the natural resources (in the north) from the breadbasket (in the south). Surrounded by barbed wire and untouched by humans for over 50 years, the area is one of the last physical remnants of the Cold War and has become an unintentional wildlife refuge, as migrating birds and other wildlife thrive here.

Inside the DMZ, near the western coast of the peninsula, is Panmunjeom, which lies outside the jurisdiction of either North or South Korea. Located 62km (39 miles) northwest of Seoul and 215km (134 miles) south of Pyongyang, this was where ceasefire talks were held during the Korean War. At the time, it was only a tiny place with four thatch-roofed houses and a couple of temporary buildings and barracks. Officially called the Joint Security Area (JSA), the name "Panmunjeom" came from the name of a store nearby (*jeom* means "small store" in Korean). Over a thousand meetings were held within a period of just over 2 years, before the armistice agreement was signed here by the U.N. forces, the North Korean army, and the Chinese army (the Republic of Korea refused to take part). *Note:* For more detailed information about the Korean War, see chapter 2.

You can visit Panmunjeom from 9am to 2:30pm Monday through Saturday by tour only. Visits by individuals to Panmunjeom are not allowed, but other areas near the DMZ can be explored independently.

Essentials

GETTING THERE   Although you can drive yourself to the DMZ (the areas on the eastern side of the peninsula are easier to explore on your own), an organized tour is your best option. Not only will you get a detailed history lesson, but you will not have to stop at the numerous checkpoints along the way. Some locations you'll want to visit don't allow individual visitors anyway. Below is a list of several recommended tours. For information on the sites described in the tour listings, see "Exploring the DMZ," below. Hopefully, these descriptions will help you decide which tour you'd like to take (although most of them will hit the same major highlights). The Panmunjeom and JSA areas are closed on Sundays, Mondays, and national holidays, so plan accordingly.

Warning: For all tours, remember that you must have your passport with you. Dress conservatively—that means no crop tops, flip-flops, faded jeans, sleeveless tops, or sheer clothing. Do not wear anything displaying communist insignia (Leave your Che Guevara T-shirt at home.). Also, photography (no lenses larger than 90mm) and video is restricted in certain areas, so be sure to ask before shooting.

TOURS   The following are some places where you can book guided tours in English. Most of the tours cost ₩130,000 or less, last most of the day or all day, and include lunch.

The **Panmunjom Tour Information Center** provides travel and tour info to Panmunjom and the DMZ. It's located in the Lotte Hotel in Seoul (on the sixth floor of the main building in Sogongdong; ℂ **02/771-5593;** www.panmunjomtour.com). Take subway line 1 to City Hall Station or line 2 to Euljiro-Ipgu Station (exit 8). The Panmunjom Tour (which includes the Mt. Odu Observatory, the Unification Bridge, and Camp Bonifas) lasts from around 8am to 8:30pm and costs ₩120,000, which includes lunch.

The **Korea Tourism Organization (KTO),** B1, KTO Building, 40, Cheongyecheonno, Jung-gu, Seoul 100-180 (ℂ **02/7299-600;** http://english.visitkorea.or.kr;

daily 9am–8pm), offers several different DMZ tours on their site (operated by different travel agencies). If you have limited time, a half-day tour run by **Sally Tour** (*C* **02/2635-1230;** www.seoulcitytourinkorea.com) may be your best option. Costing ₩46,000 (not including lunch), it runs 7am to2pm Tuesday through Sunday. It includes a tour of Imjingak Park, Bridge of Freedom, the 3rd Infiltration Tunnel, and the Dora Observatory, but does not take you to the JSA. For that you'll have to book their full day tour which costs ₩135,000 (including lunch), goes from 8am–5pm Tuesday through Saturday, and includes everything in the half-day tour, plus stops at the Panmunjeom, Camp Bonifas, and the JSA.

The **USO** also offers a Panmunjeom/DMZ Tour (with a markedly American perspective), which costs a little less than other tours, but is not as comprehensive. They ask that you reserve your place at least 7 days in advance. Call or e-mail them for available tour dates (*C* **02/724-7781;** www.uso.org/korea).

Grace Travel (*C* **02/332-8946;** http://english.triptokorea.com/english/portal.php) also offers Panmunjeom tours from Seoul. Their morning tour goes from 8am to 2:30pm and covers Imjingak Park, the Bridge of Freedom, the DMZ Theater and Exhibition Hall, the Third Infiltration Tunnel, Mt. Dora Observatory and Station, and a ginseng center or amethyst factory. The half-day tour costs ₩46,000 (lunch not included) while their full day tour (which goes until 6pm), including lunch and the 2nd Infiltration tunnel, costs ₩85,000. They'll pick you up from your hotel but drop you off at Itaewon. They also have several tours to Pyeongyang and other accessible parts of North Korea. Be sure to book at least 20 days in advance in order to get an entry visa. *Note:* Korean-born foreigners are not allowed to visit North Korea.

Please see the Gangwon-do chapter for additional locations you can visit along the DMZ (like the Fourth Infiltration Tunnel, near Yang-gu).

Exploring the DMZ

Imjingak PARK   Located 7km (4⅓ miles) from the Military Demarcation Line, Imjingak is a park and a monument, and includes a three-story building housing photos, documents, and anticommunist relics from North Korea. It was built in 1972, as a consolation for North Koreans living in the South who were unable to return to their homes. It is a testament to the hopes of many Koreans that unification may be possible someday. It is surrounded by several war memorials, including **Unification Park** and the North Korea Center. Across from Imjingak is **Mangbaedan,** where North Koreans who live in South Korea come on New Year's Day and Chuseok to perform ancestral rites while facing their hometowns. Behind Mangbaedan is the **Bridge of Freedom,** which the South Koreans who fled the North during the war crossed when returning to their homeland. Imjingak is one of the few places in the DMZ that tourists can visit without having to go through security checkpoints. Admission includes tour of Dorasan Observatory, Dorasan Station, and the Third Infiltration Tunnel (below).

1325-1 Majeong-li, Munsan-eup, Paju-si, Gyeonggi-do. *C* **031/953-4744.** Tues–Sun 9:20am–3pm in order of arrival. Closed national holidays. Admission (including monorail ride) ₩11,700 ages 19 and over, ₩8,700 ages 18 and under; on foot ₩8,200 ages 19 and over, ₩6,200 ages 18 and under. Subway: Take the Gyeongui line to Munsan Station Imjingak Station (runs every hour), then take a train to Imjingang Station (hourly 10am-3pm), and then walk about 600m (⅓ mile). Bus: From the Munsan Bus Terminal, take local bus no. 94 (runs every 30 min.).

Dorasan (Mt. Dora) Observatory OBSERVATION POINT   You can get a glimpse of North Korea through the built-in binoculars/telescopes on the observation platform here. On a clear day, you'll see North Korean soldiers, the outskirts of the city of Gaesong, some farms, and Geumgangsan (Diamond Mountain). Admission is included in the entry price for the Third Tunnel (see listing below).

Dorasan Station TOUR The last station on the Gyeongui line, Mt. Dora Station was restored in the hope of reconnecting the rail service from Pyeongyang to Seoul. It is located 205km (127 miles) from Pyeongyang and 56km (35 miles) from Seoul. It is hoped that the station will be a hub of trade between South Korea and North Korea, China, and Russia. To ride a train to the station, you must get off at the Imjin River Station and get permission, but the station is included in tours of the Third Tunnel (see listing below).

Odusan (Mt. Odu) Tong-il Unification Observatory HISTORIC SITE Opened to the public in September 1992 on Odusan (Mt. Odu), it offers views of some of the area's most beautiful scenery, where the Han River meets the Imjin River flowing down from North Korea. Not your traditional "observatory" for looking at celestial beauties, this five-story building (four aboveground and one under) has an observation platform, from which you can see Geumgangsan (Diamond Mountain) in North Korea's Gaesong and as far as the 63 Building in Seoul. The North Korea and Unification Rooms offer displays of photographs, maps, and a video of the history of the two Koreas.

88 Seongdong-li, Tanhyeon-myeon, Paju-si. ✆ **031/945-3171** or 945-2390. www.jmd.co.kr. Apr–Sept daily 9am–6pm; Mar and Oct–Nov daily 9am–5:30pm; Dec–Feb daily 9am–5pm. Admission ₩3,000 ages 19 and over, ₩1,600 students, ₩1,000 seniors and those age 6 and under. Parking ₩2,000 for a compact car, ₩3,000 for a midsize car. From Geumchon station, take bus no. 2 or 3 bound for Seongdong-li; get off at Tongil Dongsan parking lot. Or take Seoul subway line 3 to Daehwa Station (exit 5); walk to the bus station at the back and take bus no. 200 to the observatory. Driving: Take the Jayu road (no. 23) and follow the signs. There are free shuttles from Tongil Dongsan parking lot to the observatory.

Second Infiltration Tunnel TOUR In 1974, the South Korean army discovered a major tunnel running under the southern sector of the DMZ. What came to be called the First Infiltration Tunnel was destroyed by a bomb blast (and two members of the United Nations command were killed). But soon after, the Second Infiltration Tunnel, twice as wide as the first, was discovered, in March 1975. Measuring about 2m (6½ ft.) high and over 2m (6¾ ft.) wide, it is located in the middle of the DMZ, about 13km (8 miles) north of Jorwon. It has three exits. It is actually located in Gangwon-do, but is sometimes included in tours of the DMZ and Panmunjeom—in fact, you can visit only if you're part of a tour group.

Third Infiltration Tunnel ★★ TOUR When this tunnel was discovered in October 1978, North Korea insisted that South Korea dug it to invade the north. The underground tube is 1.6km (about a mile) long, 1.95m (6⅓ ft.) high, and 2m (6½ ft.) wide. It penetrates 435m (1,427 ft.) south of the demarcation line at a point only 4km (2½ miles) south of Panmunjeom. It runs through bedrock about 73m (240 ft.) below ground. Almost identical to the Second Infiltration Tunnel, about 10,000 armed soldiers are able to move through it in an hour. Four such tunnels have been discovered, although defectors from the north say there are many more.

To enter the tunnel without a tour, you must buy a ticket at the Imjingak DMZ ticket office. The ticket includes a shuttle to the Dorasan Observatory and the Dorasan Station. Soldiers will guide you, but they only speak Korean (so it's best to arrange an English-language tour before you arrive). There is a monorail that takes you halfway into the tunnel (walking down the entrance is very steep and narrow). The tunnel may be a bit cramped for you if you are tall (although they do provide helmets) and you should avoid it if you're claustrophobic or have heart problems. No photos are allowed inside. See Imjingak listing (above) for ticket prices and additional info.

Where to Stay

The DMZ area is best visited as a day trip from Seoul. There are no places to stay for tourists in the area.

Where to Eat

Most fullday, DMZ/Panmunjeom tours include lunch, but if you decide to go there on your own, you should stop in at the **Heyri Art Valley,** 1652-beonji Bupheung-li (in Tongil Dongsan), Tanhyun-myeon, Paju-si, Gyeonggi-do (𝒞 **1588-7387;** www. heyri.net). Not only is it a great place to see artists of all genres in their living/work spaces, but there are regular performances and plenty of restaurants and cafes to soak in the culture. From Seoul, take subway line 2 to Hapjeon Station (exit 2). From there, take bus no. 2200 (which runs every 15 min., 7am–11:20pm), which is about a 50-min ride to Heyri. It's a 20-minute walk from the Unification Hill parking lot (or 8 min. by bus no. 200). The art valley is accessible 24/7, but the galleries are only open Tuesday through Sunday 10am–7pm, with cafes and restaurants holding longer hours.

The specialty dish of the north Gyeonggi region is freshwater eel, which is marinated in a sweet and spicy sauce and eaten cooked from a tabletop grill. You can order *jang-uh* (eel) from many restaurants in the area, but a couple of good places in Paju are **Imjingang Pokpo Eojang (Imjin River Waterfall Fish),** 254-4 Deokcheon-li, Papyeong-myeon, Paju-si (𝒞 **031/959-2222**), and **Jinmi Sikdang,** 370-119 Jangpa1-li, Papyeong-myeon, Paju-si (𝒞 **031/958-3321**).

INCHEON

You most likely arrived at the Incheon airport, but didn't get to enjoy the surrounding area. Incheon has the country's only official **Chinatown,** where *jjajangmyeon* (Korean-Chinese noodles with black-bean sauce) was born. Its beaches and many small islands are positively crawling with Seoulites escaping the heat on summer weekends. The amusement rides and *hwae* (raw fish) restaurants along **Yeonan Pier** bring in the crowds, but those in the know take a bus tour to see the prehistoric dolmen on **Ganghwa-do,** explore **Wolmi-do's** Culture Street, and hike the small mountains of **Muui-do** that reward their climbers with views of the surrounding sea.

Essentials

GETTING THERE From **Incheon International Airport,** you can take a limousine bus (from bus stop 2B or 9B) to Incheon city, running daily from 4:21am to 9:30pm. Regular buses from the airport run at bus stop 2A/B or 9A/B. From Seoul, the easiest way to get to Incheon is to take subway line 1, which intersects the Incheon city subway system at Bupyeong Station.

The **Incheon International Ferry Terminals** (𝒞 **032/891-2030** terminal 1, 032/761-3068 terminal 2) have ferries to and from China, including Dallan, Dandong, Yingkou, Qinghuandao, Tianjin, Yantai, Weihai, Seokdo, Qingdao, and Lianyungang.

The boats take anywhere from 12 to 25 hours to travel to/from Incheon to selected cities in China. Call the KTO Travel Service (© 02/1330) to make a reservation.

GETTING AROUND   Incheon has its own subway system that connects with Seoul's system. The ride to Incheon Station from Seoul Station takes about an hour. Its website is www.incheonmetro.co.kr/eng/index.asp.

Most ferries to the outlying islands leave from Yeonan Harbor. From here, you can take a boat to and from Baknyeongdo, Yeonpyeongdo, Deokjeokdo, Jawoldo, Ijakdo, Seungbongdo, Yeongheungdo, Muuido, and even overnight to Jeju-do. You can also take an excursion ferry that circles the area from either Yeonan Pier or Wolmido. See the section on Wolmido below for additional information and prices.

VISITOR INFORMATION   There are tourist information centers off the subway at Incheon's City Hall, in front of Incheon and Bupyeong stations, on the promenade at Wolmido, and in Sinpo-dong. At these centers you'll find helpful English-speaking staff, brochures, and good maps.

The city of Incheon (© **032-/40-2114;** http://english.visitincheon.org) offers several bus tours, including a 3-hour downtown tour that starts from Incheon Station at 10am, with subsequent tours every hour until 5pm. It costs ₩1,500 adults, ₩750 children with on-off privileges all day.

Exploring Incheon

Chinatown ⚜ HISTORIC SITE   Established by Chinese immigrants in 1884, a year after the harbor was opened, today, it is home to descendants of those immigrants. The birthplace of jjajangmyeon (a Chinese-Korean noodle dish with black-bean sauce, caramelized vegetables, and meat), most of its cultural history has now faded. Remnants of its Chinese history remain in the area's numerous eateries.

No direct address, but in Jung-gu Icheon-si (you can see the gate across the street from Incheon Station). © **031/777-1330.** www.ichinatown.or.kr (Korean only).

Coastal Wharf & Yeonan Pier MARKET   If you're interested in venturing out to any of the smaller islands off the coast of Incheon, this is the place to get your trip underway. Always bustling with travelers, the Yeonan ferry terminals offer boats to and from Baknyeong-do, Yeonpyeong-do, Deokjeok-do, Jawol-do, Ijak-do, Seungbong-do, Yeongheung-do, Muui-do, and even distant Jeju-do (via overnight boat). Nearby is the **Fish Market** where you'll see hundreds of shops selling all manner of live seafood, raw fish, and salted and dried goods from the ocean. Though the tanks are freshly filled every morning, by the end of the day you'll be hard-pressed to even see one crab still lingering about, since most of the freshly caught critters sell out the same day. Yeonan Pier is an affordable place for you to enjoy hwae.

© **032/760-7550.** Take subway line 1 to Dongincheon station, then take bus no. 12 to Yeonan Pier. You can also get a taxi from the station and it'll be about a 10min. ride.

Ganghwa-do (Ganghwa Island) ★★★ HISTORIC SITE   To make things confusing, Ganghwa-do is the name of the island, as well as the group of islands. Since the Goryeo Dynasty, Ganghwa-do has played an important role in defending the mainland (remains of fortresses and memorial sites attest to its turbulent history), but since it's connected by two bridges, it now feels more like part of the mainland.

Famous for the high-quality *insam* (ginseng) that grows here (you can buy some to take home with you at the **Insam Center**), the island is also known for its 80 dolmen (called the **Ganghwa Goindol**), prehistoric rock tombs built by Megalithic cultures in the 1st millennium B.C.. These, in conjunction with dolmen found in Gochang and Hwasun in Jeolla-do, have been designated a UNESCO World Heritage site. The largest of their kind in South Korea, the Ganghwa Goindol is located about a kilometer from Hajeom, but the rest are scattered throughout the island. Additionally, Ganghwa-do is home to **Bomunsa ★★** (Treasure Gate Temple) (© **032/933-8271**; www.bomunsa.net), one of South Korea's eight special shrines for the Bodhisattva of Compassion. Bomunsa is actually located on **Seokmo-do,** a small island located west of Ganghwa-do, reachable via bridge or ferry. Seokmo-do is a great place to enjoy the sunset over the west sea. Open daily 9am to 6pm, admission is ₩2,000 adults, ₩1,500 teens, ₩1,200 children.

Although most visitors come to see the island as a day trip from Seoul, there is enough to see here to warrant at least 2 or 3 days of exploring. There are no high-end hotels on the island, but there are a dozen smaller motels, of similar price and quality, located in the center of town.

© **032/930-3515.** http://english.ganghwa.incheon.kr. Tourist info office (at the Ganghwa Bus Terminal) Wed–Mon 9am–5pm winter, until 6pm summer. From Seoul, take subway line 2 to Sincheon Station (exit 7), and then take the Ganghwa-do bus from the Intercity Bus Terminal. The 1st bus leaves daily at 5:40am, last bus at 10pm (90-min. trip). From Ganghwa-do, you can take local buses or even passenger cruises around the area. The city of Incheon also offers two tours of Ganghwa-do that run twice a day on weekends (April–October). Starting at Incheon Station, they cost ₩10,000. Course A covers Ganghwa History Museum, the site of the Goryeo Royal Palace, Yongheunggung (a royal residence), Ganghwa Pyeonghwa Observatory, Ganghwa Dolmen, and the ginseng center. Course B covers Chojijin Fortress, Gwangseongbo Fort, Jeondeungsa, Seonwonsaji, Armiae World, and the ginseng center.

Jayu Park PARK The first Western-style park built in South Korea, Jayu ("Freedom") Park borders the older areas of the city. Located on Mt. Eungbong, this is where American General Douglas MacArthur led the Incheon Amphibious Land Operation during the Korean War. You can see the inner harbor and enjoy the city lights from the pavilion. It's best enjoyed when the cherry blossoms are in bloom in early spring.

Eungbongsan, Jung-gu, Incheon-si. © **032/760-7597** (Korean only). Free admission. About a 5-min. walk from Incheon Station.

Jeondeungsa (Jeondeung Temple) TEMPLE Situated on Jeongjoksan, like many of South Korea's temples, Jeondeungsa has been burned down and rebuilt a number of times. Located inside the Samrangseong walls, the temple was originally called Jinjongsa. The name was changed when Princess Jeonghwa gave a rare jade lamp as an offering to the Buddha during the Goryeo Dynasty, giving the temple its current name, which means "inherited lamp." Its last reconstruction in 1621 makes it a relatively old temple and it's heralded as an example of fine architecture from the Goryeo era. You'll notice, in the main Daeungjeon, a sculpture of an ugly naked woman on top of the four pillars that support the eaves of the roof. The story is that the carpenter who was building the temple fell in love with a "hostess" at a bar. He gave her all his money and she ran off with it. The carpenter fell ill, but recovered and created this sculpture as both revenge and a way to cleanse her of her sins. The Yaksajeon houses a more beautiful sculpture, a representation of the healing Buddha.

635, Onsu-li, Gilsang-myeon, Ganghwa-gun, Incheon-si. © **032/937-0125.** www.jeondeungsa.org. Admission ₩2,500 adults, ₩1,700 teens, ₩1,000 children. There is a direct bus to the temple from Seoul's Sinchon Bus Terminal.

Muui-do (Muui Island) ★★ ☺ BEACH   Located 18km (11 miles) from Incheon port, it is no longer the remote island of days past. Its name means "dress of a dancer," referring to its gorgeous scenery. Both Silmi and Hanagae beaches are wide and sandy, and the hiking trails of Horyonggoksan and Guksabong are not too steep. During low tide, you can even walk to the uninhabited **Silmi-do** (Silmi Island) from Silmi Beach.

✆ **032/751-3354** (Korean only). www.muuido.co.kr. From Incheon Station, take city bus no. 306 bound for Eulwang-li and get off at Geojampo. From there it's a 10-min. walk to the Jamjinnaru Ferry Terminal (✆ **032/751-3354**). Ferries to Muui-do run daily 7am–10pm (every 30 min. on weekdays, every 15 min. on weekends). Round-trip fares ₩2,000 ages 13 and over, ₩1,400 children 7–12, and free for children 6 and under.

Wolmi-do (Wolmi Island) ★★ ☺ MARKET   An island about 1km (⅔ mile) off the coast of Incheon, it is now connected to the mainland by a highway. There are dozens of seafood restaurants clustered together here, and it's an excellent place to get fresh hwae. The **Street of Culture** is a promenade filled with musicians, performers, and caricaturists. The island is also home to a small amusement park, **Play Hill,** and ferry cruises, both of which are great for families. Daily cruises around the island run every hour starting at 11am, with the last boat leaving at 7:30pm in the summer. They last 80 minutes and cost ₩15,000, ₩8,000 for kids 11 and under. From March on, you can also take a dinner cruise on Saturday nights for ₩43,000, ₩32,000 for children 11 and under.

✆ **032/440-2114.** From Incheon Station, take the subway to Wolmi-do or take city bus no. 2, 23, or 45 to the last stop. Taxis take 5 min. from Incheon Station.

Shopping

Like most major cities in Korea, there is no shortage of things to buy, but the best place to shop is in the traditional **Sinpo Shijang,** where you can haggle with street vendors for anything from clothing to grains and dried seaweed. The rubber walkways and archway make it a bit more comfortable to shop this old market. From the subway, take the Gyeongin line to Dongincheon Station. Also, express buses nos. 105, 113, and 206 come to Sinpo-dong. Regular city buses that stop here are nos. 2, 3, 4, 6, 10, 15, 16, 17-1, 23, 28, 41, 45, and 46.

You don't even have to venture aboveground for your shopping experience. The expansive (and confusing) underground shopping arcade expands outward like a web from Dongincheon Station to Sinpo-dong. With hundreds of stores, you can spend an hour just walking without even stopping to browse.

For a more contemporary shopping experience, both **Shinsegae** and **Lotte** department stores have branches in Incheon. Take Incheon Subway to the Incheon Terminal Station or bus 4, 6, 11, 22, 35, 41, 111, or 700 to Incheon Terminal. There are also plenty of American chain restaurants in the area, as well.

Where to Stay

Almost all the major hotels are located near the airport in Unseong-dong or Eulwang-dong, but you can find cheap motels on the side streets below Jayu Park. Business class hotels can be found on Songdo, accessible by Korea's largest bridge, the Incheon Bridge. Also, there are plenty of smaller motels on Ganghwa-do, and many near the bus station on the edge of town.

Hotel Incheon Airport ★ A convenient place to stay if you're just stopping overnight in Incheon or have an early-morning flight, as it's only 8 minutes from the airport. This modern hotel has helpful, multilingual staff.

2790-4, Airport Town Sq., Unseo-dong, Jung-gu, Incheon. www.incheon-hotel.com. © **032/752-2066.** Fax 032/746-2067. 40 units. ₩150,000 and up standard double; ₩240,000 and up suite; discounts if you book online. AE, MC, V, and foreign currencies accepted. Pets allowed. **Amenities:** Restaurant; bar; wine and coffee lounge; pool; driving range; health club; Jacuzzi; sauna; casino; karaoke; free airport transfers. *In room:* A/C, TV/VCR/DVD, fridge, minibar, hair dryer, hot and cold water dispenser, computer, Internet.

Incheon Airport Guest House ★★ Only a few minutes from the airport, this guesthouse is an affordable and convenient stay for those just passing through Incheon or having to catch an early flight. Each room is simple but clean, with bare walls and fluorescent lighting. Some rooms have their own small dining/tea table. It's the best place in the area for the price, and they'll even pick you up from the airport, if you make arrangements in advance.

2850-2 Unseo-dng, Jung-gu, Incheon. www.ghincheon.com. © **032/743-3060.** Fax 031/743-3062. 201 units. ₩40,000 single; ₩50,000 double. AE, MC, V. **Amenities:** Restaurant, bar; health club; laundry; conference room; free airport transfers; Internet. *In room:* A/C, TV, kitchen (in some rooms).

Paradise Hotel This established business-class hotel is only a few minutes from Incheon Airport and walking distance from Incheon Station. Centrally located, both the Western-style and ondol rooms are done in light colors with dark wood furniture. Ceilings are a touch on the low side, but some rooms make up for it with views of the ocean. The biggest draw is the casino, which, like all casinos in South Korea, is open to foreign guests only.

3 Hang-dong 1-ga, Jung-gu, Incheon. www.paradisehotel.co.kr. © **032/762-5181.** Fax 032/763-5281. 175 units. ₩230,000 and up double; ₩400,000 and up suite. 10% VAT and 10% service charge not included. AE, MC, V. **Amenities:** Restaurant; bar; wine and coffee lounge; driving range; health club; Jacuzzi; sauna; casino; karaoke. *In room:* A/C, TV, hair dryer, safe, electric teapot, bathrobes.

Sheraton Incheon Hotel ★★ One of the first business hotels to open on Songdo, this modern building is LEED certified and 100% non-smoking (which is rare in South Korea). The comfortable beds in the spacious rooms make for a good night's sleep, while the rain shower heads make it easier to get up for an early morning flight. *Note:* The KAL Limousine bus stops here from Incheon Airport every hour (gate 4B or 11A from the arrival level).

6-9 Songdo-dong, Yeonsu-gu, Incheon. www.starwoodhotels.com/sheraton/property/overview/index.html?propertyID=3342 © **032/835-1000.** Fax 032/835-1001. 319 units. ₩145,000 single/double; ₩295,000 suite and up.11% VAT and 10% service charge not included. AE, MC, V. **Amenities:** 4 restaurants; bar; lounge; indoor pool; health club; spa; concierge; business center; florist; beauty shop; gift shop. *In room:* A/C, cable TV, minibar, coffee maker, iron and board, electric safe, Wi-Fi (fee).

Where to Eat

Incheon has some of the freshest seafood in the metropolitan Seoul area, especially in the restaurants on Wolmi-do, all of which have ocean views, and at the Yeonan Raw Fish Plaza on Yeonan Pier, where you'll get the best deals. It's the perfect place to give hwae or spicy seafood hot pot a try. Incheon's Chinatown is where jjajangmyeon was invented. There are a handful of good, but small, Chinese restaurants there. You can also stop in at one of the trendy restaurants and cafes on Gourmet Street when shopping in Sinpo-dong, or try traditional street food at Sinpo Market.

Pyeong-yangok ★★ KOREAN   For over 50 years, Pyeong-yangok has been serving Incheon customers its famous *maeuntang* (spicy catfish hot pot). The owner has the fish delivered daily from a fish farm near Gimpo. You'll see diners slurping broth over steaming pots of bubbling red seafood, spicy and full of flavors.

503-13 Seogu, Gajeong 1-dong, Incheon (north of the Uri Department Store). ✆ **032/582-5959.** Entrees ₩15,000–₩30,000. MC, V. Daily 11am–midnight.

Suta Jjajangmyeon KOREAN/CHINESE   Handmade black-bean noodles (jjajangmyeon) are this restaurant's specialty, but they also serve other Korean-influenced Chinese dishes like *jjamppong* (noodles and seafood in a spicy hot broth) and *ggangpong saewoo* (kung pao shrimp). As in most Korean-Chinese restaurants, the decor is cheesy Chinatown, but the noodles are still worth slurping. And by all means, slurp—Koreans don't consider it rude.

32 Sunlin-dong, Jung-gu, Incheon. ✆ **032/772-3058.** Entrees ₩4,000 and up. No credit cards. Daily 9am–10pm. From Incheon Station, go toward Jayu Park, turn right at the 2nd 4-way.

Yejeon FUSION/WESTERN   Considered one of the original joints that began Wolmi-do's "cafe culture," this unlikely restaurant is in the middle of Munhwa (Culture Street). In this red-brick building, you can enjoy ocean views with your pizza or spaghetti. With the decidedly dark wood interior and old-world European feeling, you'll forget you're in South Korea—until they bring your *donkatsu* (fried pork cutlet) and pickled peppers.

98-444, Bukseong-dong 1(il)-ga, Jung-gu, Incheon (near the excursion ferry terminal on Wolmi-do). ✆ **032/772-2256.** Entrees ₩10,000–₩35,000. AE, MC, V. Daily 10:30am–2am.

THE REST OF GYEONGGI-DO

There are still more tiny towns to explore in Gyeonggi-do—royal tombs to explore in **Yeoju,** spam stew to be eaten in **Uijeongbu,** and traditional performances to see in **Andong.** For more information, check out the province's website at http://english. gg.go.kr.

Uijeongbu

Uijeongbu has many military bases and is home to foreign workers from poorer parts of Asia. This is also the town in which the fictional troops of *M*A*S*H* were stationed (although the show was shot largely in Southern California), and actual U.N. troops were stationed here during the Korean War. The U.S. armed forces brought about a new city specialty, *budae jjigae* (Spam stew, which is exactly what it sounds like), made from the canned meats available from army camps when food supplies grew scarce during the war. You can still try this American-influenced dish at **Budae Jjigae Golmok** (Spam Stew Alley) at such joints as **Boyeong Sikdang,** 214-127 Uijeongbu 1-dong (✆ **031/842-1129**), or **Euijeongbu Budaejjige Bonjeom,** 220-31 Uijeongbu 1-dong (✆ **031/846-9977**). To get to the famed alley, take the Seoul subway to Ujjeongbu Station. Once outside, walk toward the police station and the Halla apartments, and you'll see a blue arch (it's written in Korean) that marks the start of Budae Jjigae Golmok.

Unfortunately, most of the town was destroyed during the war, but there are a few cultural relics and some restored buildings around today. From the center of Seoul, it takes about 40 minutes to get to Uijeongbu by subway. There are five stops in the city off of Seoul's subway line 1. The city's official site is www.ui4u.net/site/english.

Between Uijeongbu and Pocheon is the **Gwangneung Sumeogwon (Korea National Arboretum)** ★, 51-7 Jikdong-li, Soheul-eup, Pocheon-si (𝄫 **031/540-2000;** www.kna.go.kr), a peaceful nature preserve with original trees and dense undergrowth. Because of the fragility of the landscape, you must make a reservation a week to 30 days in advance. It's worth it, especially if you're a nature lover or bird-watcher, since various fowl pass through during different seasons. Open Tuesday to Saturday 9am to 6pm April to October, until 5pm November to March, the arboretum is closed on weekends and national holidays. The last entry is 1 hour before closing. Admission is ₩1,000 adults, ₩700 teens, ₩500 children, free for seniors and kids 5 and under. Take Seoul's subway line 1 to Uijeongbu Station, then take bus no. 21 to Gwangneung-nae. It'll cost ₩1,250 and the bus leaves from Uijeongbu at 10 and 40 minutes past each hour, and at 15 and 45 minutes past each hour from the arboretum. If you're driving, it'll be ₩3,000 for parking.

Pocheon

Northeast of Uijeongbu (about a 30-min. bus ride) is Pocheon, another satellite city in Gyeonggi-do. Since the city is so close to the border, it's popular with Korean military; however, it's still largely undeveloped and can be a nice getaway from Seoul. A relaxing visit could include a stop at the *oncheon* ("hot spring") in the **Hanhwa Resort,** 454-4 Sanjeon-li, Yeongbuk-myeon, Pocheon-si (𝄫 **031/534-5500**). Hot springs open 6am to 9pm, ₩9,000 for adults and ₩5,000 for children. Another good option is the **Idong Jaeil Yuhwang Oncheon** ("Idong's First Hot Spring"), 663 Hwadae-li, Idong-myeon, Pocheon-si (𝄫 **031/536-6000**). Open 6am to 10pm; a soak costs ₩6,000 for adults and ₩4,000 for children.

After a good soak, you can fill up on the city's famous galbi and *makgeolli* (milky rice wine). So famous is the dish that there is even a "village," the **Idong Galbi Maeul**, a cluster of restaurants where the galbi is grilled over oak charcoal. A couple of good options in the area are **Idong Galbi,** 216-3 Jangam-li, Idong-myeon, Pocheon-si (𝄫 **031/531-4459**), and **Ijo Garden,** 852 Yunheon-li, Naechon-myeon, Pocheon-si (𝄫 **031/532-6466**).

Soyosan (Mt. Soyo)

Soyosan and its associated Tapdong Valley are called the "Mujugucheondong," the prettiest mountain valleys in Gyeonggi-do. A nice day trip away from the insanity of Seoul, there are steep slopes, deep valleys, several waterfalls, and a small hermitage, the **Jajae-am** (𝄫 **031/865-4045;** 1-beonji Soyosan, Sangbong-am-dong, Dongducheon-si,). Across from the Soyosan Train Station is the entrance to Tapdong Valley. Jajae-am is about a 30-minute hike up, past Wonhyo waterfall. The hermitage is said to have been founded by the famous monk Wonhyo.

It's not too difficult to get there via Dongducheon. From Seoul's Suyu-li, take bus no. 36 or 136 to Dongducheon Bus Terminal. From there, take a bus bound for Dok-goli. If you're driving, take road 3 toward Uijeongbu. Then, take local road 334 at the Dongducheon Yurim four-way (sageoli).

Yongmunsan (Mt. Yongmun)

Called the "Geumgangsan of Gyeonggi-do," Yongmunsan is well known for its rocky valleys and hiking trails. The hiking entrance begins at **Yongmunsa** ("Dragon Gate

Temple"), where you will see a huge ginkgo tree. The temple was originally built in A.D. 913, but expanded in 1392. It was burned down, like many of Korea's temples, by the Japanese in 1592, but rebuilt. It was burned down by the Japanese again in 1907. The current main hall was reconstructed in 1984 entirely by hand. The village below the temple was also rebuilt while the temple was being constructed.

Open all year, the **Yongmunsan Resort** (✆ **031/773-0088**) is popular with vacationing families in the fall. Admission is ₩1,800 adults, ₩1,200 students, ₩800 children. There are recreational facilities and campsites nearby.

At the entrance to the resort, there are numerous restaurants that serve the fabulously delicious *sanchae bibimbap* (mixed rice bowl with wild mountain greens) as well as dishes made from other local vegetables and wild mushrooms. This is also a great place to enjoy homemade rice wine after a long day of hiking.

From Seoul's Sangbong Bus Terminal, take the bus bound for Yongmun, which runs nine times daily. At the Yongmun Bus Terminal, take the nonstop bus to Yongmunsa. By subway, take the Jung-ang line and get off at Yongmun Station. Then, take the nonstop bus to Yongmunsa. By car, from Yangpyeong, take state route 6 toward Hongcheon for 14km (8⅔ miles). Then, take local road 331 for about 6km (3¾ miles).

Yangpyeong

Located east of Seoul along the Han River, at the foot of Yongmunsan, lies the county of Yangpyeong. During the warm months, a visit to **Semiwon,** Yangsu-li, Yangseo-myeon, Yangpyeong-gun (✆ **031/775-1834;** www.semiwon.or.kr), is an excellent way to see acres of waterlilies and watch the sun set over the Han River. It's open Tuesday to Sunday 9am to 6pm March to October, until 5pm November to February. Admission is ₩3,000, but get an early start since only 500 people are allowed per day. To get to the park, take bus no. 2228 toward Yangsu-li from Cheongnyangni Station (Seoul subway line 1) and get off at the last stop. You can also take bus no. 2000-1 toward Yangpyeong from Gangbyeon Station and get off at the park (the bus runs only once an hour).

Nearby is the **KOFIC Namyangju Studios,** 100 Sambong-li, Joan-myeon, Namyangju-si (✆ **031/579-0605**), a working film and TV set, open to visitors. The studios are open Tuesday to Sunday 10am to 6pm March to October, until 5pm November to February. Admission is ₩3,000 adults, ₩2,500 teens, ₩2,000 children. To get here, take bus no. 2228 from Cheongnyangni Station and get off at Yangsu-li or take bus no. 2000-1 from Gangbyeon Station and get off at Jinjung 3(sam)-geoli. From there you'll have to take a local bus or taxi to the studios (about a 5-min. ride).

A better place to enjoy the Hangahng is **Dumulmeoli** (which translates as the "head of two waters"), Yangsu-li, Yangseo-myeon, Yangpyeong-gun (✆ **031/770-2068**), where the north and south sections of the Han River meet. What used to be a quiet refuge for lovers has become a popular spot after being featured in TV dramas and films. Even on crowded weekends, it can be a nice place to walk along the water. To get here, take bus no. 2228 from Cheongnyangni Station (subway line 1) and get off at Yangsu 4(sa)-geoli. Alternatively, take bus no. 2000-1 or 2000-2 from Gangbyeon Station and get off at Yangsu 4(sa)-geoli (the first stop after crossing Yangsu Daegyo (bridge).

A nice place to stay in the area is the **Yangpyeong Hanhwa Resort ★★**, 141-5 Sinbok 3-li, Okcheon-myeon, Yangpyeong-gun (✆ **031/772-3811;** www.hanwha resort.co.kr), a Korean "condo-style" facility with over 400 rooms and plenty of recreational sports facilities for the family. There are hiking trails, a swimming pool, outdoor hot springs, and great slopes for sledding in the winter.

Myeongseonsan (Mt. Myeongseong) & Sanjeong-ho (Sanjeong Lake)

East of Uncheon in Yeongbuk-myeon is Sanjeong-ho, a beautiful lake at Myeong-seongsan (whose peaks are reflected in the lake's still waters). Myeongseongsan straddles the border between Gyeonggi-do and Gangwon-do and is covered with thick pine forests and large rock formations that look their best in the midst of the autumn foliage. Although Sanjeong is a small lake, Deungryong and Biseon waterfalls enhance the beauty of the area. It used to be a quiet mountain region, but since they built the tourist complex, with snow sledding, ice-skating rink, swimming pools, and saunas, its quiet charm has almost disappeared. A small temple, **Jainsa,** Sanjeong-li, Yeongbuk-myeon, Pocheon-si (✆ **031/532-6141**), sits at the foot of the mountain.

From Seoul's Sangbong Bus Terminal, take a bus bound for Sincheolwon and get off at Uncheon. From there, you can take a bus to Sanjeong Lake. Buses run every 15 minutes and take about 80 minutes. If you're driving, take road 43 from Suyu-li in Seoul toward Uijeongbu. Pass Pocheon-eup, and go straight toward the Manse-gyo (bridge). Make a right at the Seongdong three-way (sam-geoli), and then a left at the checkpoint three-way. Turn right at the Bunam four-way (sa-geoli) to get to the lake's parking lot.

Gwacheon

Gwacheon is one of the many small cities surrounding Seoul. Accessible by Seoul subway, south of Gangnam, it has a number of mountains and good parks.

One of the main attractions in the city is the **National Museum of Contemporary Art ★★**, 209 Gwangmyeong-gil, San 58-1 Makgye-dong (✆ **02/2188-6000;** www.moca.go.kr). The museum's design encompasses elements of old fortress walls and traditional houses, and is made to work with the surrounding landscape. Exhibits include works by both South Korean and international contemporary artists and include an outdoor sculpture garden. Take Seoul subway line 4 to Seoul Grand Park Station (exit 4) and take the museum shuttle bus. (Be sure to buy an admission ticket to the museum from the ticket machine at the subway station.) The shuttle runs every 20 minutes, 9:40am to 5pm Tuesday through Friday and until 6pm Saturday and Sunday during the high season from March to October, and daily from 9:40am to 4pm in the off season of November to February. The last bus leaves from the museum at 4:50pm off season, and 5:50pm high season. The museum is open in the high season Tuesday through Friday 9am to 6pm (until 9pm Sat–Sun and holidays), and in the off season until 5pm Tuesday through Friday (until 8pm Sat–Sun and holidays). Ticket sales end 1 hour before closing, closed Jan 1. Admission is ₩1,000 adults, ₩500 youth, free for seniors 65 and older and kids 6 and under.

Nearby is **Seoul Grand Park** ☺ (✆ **02/500-7335;** http://grandpark.seoul.go.kr). With a lake at its center, the park includes a zoo (which has a dolphin and seal show), botanical gardens with a pleasant walking trail, and an educational center for children. Admission is ₩3,000 adults, ₩2,000 teens, ₩1,000 children. Tickets for the dolphin show are ₩1,500 for adults, ₩1,000 teens, ₩500 children. The park is open daily from 9am to 7pm April to September, and until 6pm October through March. Last entrance is 1 hour before closing. Take Seoul subway line 4 to the Seoul Grand Park Station (exit 2).

In the same area is the amusement park **Seoul Land** ☺, 121 Seoul Land, Mak-gye-dong (✆ **02/509-6000;** www.seoulland.co.kr). It has 40 different rides, including roller coasters and water rides, as well as movie theaters and other amusements. They hold a tulip festival in the spring, rose festival in the summer, chrysanthemum festival in the fall, and snow light festival in the winter. Hours are 9:30am to 9pm weekdays, 9:30am to 10pm weekends and holidays. Nighttime admission starts at 5pm and the park closes at 11pm from the end of July to mid-August. Admission is ₩17,000 adults, ₩14,000 teens, ₩12,000 children. Additional fees apply for certain attractions. Take Seoul subway line 4 to the Seoul Grand Park Station (exit 2).

Also great for children is the **Gwacheon National Science Museum** ☺, 100 (Gwacheon-dong), Daegongwon, Gwangjang-gil, Gwacheon (✆ **02/3677-1500;** www.scientorium.go.kr). There's everything from a planetarium to a little area where visitors can interact with live insects. Give yourself at least a couple of hours to explore the exhibitions and the grounds. Hours are 9:30am to 5:30pm Tuesday to Sunday with the last admission 1 hour before closing (closed Chuseok and Lunar New Year). Admission is ₩4,000 adults, ₩2,000 children and seniors 65 and older, with a separate admission for the Planetarium at ₩2,000 adults, ₩1,000 children and seniors. Take Seoul subway line 4 to Seoul Grand Park Station (exit 5).

For horse-racing fans, the **Seoul Racecourse,** 685 Juam-dong, Gwacheon-si, offers races every Saturday and Sunday from 9am to 5:30pm. Admission is ₩800 and betting starts from ₩100 and can go as high as ₩100,000. Bring your passport, since you'll need it to get in. Take Seoul subway line 4 to the Seoul Racecourse Station (exit 3).

Anseong

If you have a Saturday free and you're visiting sometime between April and October, don't miss the **Anseong Namsadang Nori** ★★ ☺, 31-3 Bongsandong, Anseong-si (✆ **031/676-4601;** www.baudeogi.com), where a variety of performers take the stage all day. Namsadang was Korea's first popular performance troupe, which used to travel around markets and villages singing and dancing for the common people during the late Joseon period. The troupe usually had about 40 to 50 members, most of whom joined voluntarily, though parents sometimes brought their children to the troupe because they were too poor to feed them. The program is free to the public and includes tightrope walkers, exorcism rituals, a puppet show, dancers, drummers, musicians, and more.

While you're in Anseong, you can visit **Mahno Art Center** ☺, 34 Bokpyeong-li, Bogae-myeon, Anseon-si (✆ **031/6767-8151**). You can't miss the building, which is an upside-down house. There are hands-on programs for both children and adults. The art center has some galleries, an Italian restaurant, and a shop, and is open daily 10am to 10pm. Admission is ₩2,000 for adults, ₩1,000 for those 17 and under.

If you're in the area, stop in at the **Seoilnongwon** ★★, 389-3 Hwabong-li, Injuk-myeon, Anseong-si (✆ **031/673-3171;** www.seoilfarm.com), a farm where they make fermented soybean paste, *dwenjang,* the old-fashioned way. You'll see rows and rows of clay pots filled with the paste fermenting. They also have an on-site restaurant.

To get to Anseong, take a bus from the DongSeoul Bus Terminal. There are 25 departures daily from 6:45am to 9:10pm. The ride takes about 80 minutes and costs around ₩4,200. From the Anseong Bus Terminal, you'll have to take a taxi to the

Namsadang performance. It's about a 10-minute ride, but be sure to ask your driver to pick you up at the end of the performance, since public transportation is scarce.

Gapyeong

About an hour and a half northeast of Seoul is Gapyeong-gun (Gapyeong County), which rests on the border of Gyeonggi-do and the mountainous province of Gangwon-do. The most popular destination in the area is **Cheongpyeong-ho**, the lake created by the construction of Cheongpyeong Dam in 1944. A popular resort for water-skiing and camping, it gets crowded with Seoulites especially during the summer. Gapyeong's tourist office can be reached at © **031/580-2066** or -2067.

To get to Gapyeong by rail, take the train headed for Chuncheon from Seoul's Cheongnyangni Station and get off at Gapyeong. Buses to Gapyeong can be taken from the DongSeoul Station or Sangbong Terminal. Take a bus headed for Chuncheon and get off at Cheongpyeong Dam. The bus and train terminals are about a 5-minute walk from each other.

Fauna lovers will enjoy the nearby **Achimgoyo Sumogwon** (the "Garden of Morning Calm") ★★, San 255 Haenghyeon-li, Sangmyeon, Gapyeong-gun (© **031/584-6702** or 1544-6703; http://morningcalm.co.kr/?module=Default&action=DefaultEng) Korea's oldest private garden in the quiet of the mountains. With over 4,500 plant species, this is a nice place to see native Korean plants as well as imported flowers. Admission prices vary depending on the season: Weekends April to November ₩8,000 adults, ₩5,000 teens, ₩4,000 children, ₩1,000 less on weekdays, ₩1,000 less from December through March. Local buses from Cheongpyeong Bus Terminal run at 10:20am, 10:50am, 11:20am, 1:20pm, 2:20pm, 4pm, 4:30pm, and 6:30pm. The ride lasts about 30 minutes and costs ₩1,200. A taxi to the garden will cost about ₩12,000 to ₩15,000.

Goyang

Located northwest of Seoul, the city of Goyang has grown as housing needs in Seoul expanded to the surrounding province. A climb up Daegyangsan affords a nice view and a visit to the **Haengju Sanseong (Haengju Mountain Fortress),** San 12 Haengjunae-dong, Daegyang-gu, Goyang-si (© **031/961-2580**). This fortress, which was mostly likely built during the Baekje period, was instrumental in defending Korea against the invading Japanese army some 4 centuries ago. The **Haengju Great Victory Festival** is held here every March 14 to commemorate the event. The fortress is open 9am to 6pm March to October, 9am to 5pm November to February. To reach Daegyangsan, take Seoul subway line 3 to Hwajeong Station, then take a shuttle bus to the fortress. You can also take bus no. 88 from Seoul City Hall or bus no. 921 from Sinchon. Drivers should take road 23 and follow the signs to the fortress.

In the Ilsan district of Goyang-si sits the **Ilsan Lake Park** ★, Janghang-dong, Ilsan-gu, Goyang-si (© **031/906-4557**), the largest artificial lake in Asia. Its paths are perfect for joggers, bikers, or casual walkers. The musical fountains and cultural performances draw crowds on weekends. To get to the park, take Seoul subway line 3 Jeongbalsan Station (exit 2). The park is about a 10-minute walk. You can also take bus no. 77 or 903-1 from Sinchon.

Osan ✋

Most people have heard of this small city south of Incheon only because the U.S. Air Force has a major air base here (it's actually between Osan and Pyongtaek). There isn't much here as far as history and culture go, but the American military has fueled the growth of the main street outside the base, now called **Shinjang Shopping Mall,** a pedestrian street closed to car traffic. The area is full of souvenir shops, clothing stores, restaurants, and clubs, many run by foreign women and military wives. On weekends, the area is packed with military personnel and expats who make the trek down from Seoul to hit the wide selection of restaurants and bars that cater to Western tastes. From Osan, take bus no. 2 to Songtan for the shopping district. To get to Osan, take bus no. 300 or 301 from Suwon or catch an Osan-bound bus from Seoul's Nambu Terminal.

6

CHUNGCHEONG-DO

Nestled in South Korea's central region, the Chungcheong province includes Chungcheongbuk-do, Chungcheongnam-do, and the city of Daejeon. Since this area is just south of Seoul, it has benefited economically from its proximity. Industrial centers have grown especially around the Asanman area on the western coast. The two provinces of Chungcheong-do are actually side by side, although they are called north and south Chungcheong-do.

A major transportation thoroughfare for the capital region and the Honam (Jeolla-do) and Yeongnam (Gyeongsang-do) regions, the province's largest city, Daejeon, serves as a junction for both rail lines and highways.

Chungcheong-do specializes in dairy farming and agriculture to meet the huge demands of the capital region. The eastern part of the province, which borders Gangwon-do, is mountainous, but the western section is lower and flatter. Its major agricultural products are grains (mostly rice and barley) and a variety of vegetables, including radish, cabbage, and sweet potatoes. In fact, it has been a rice-producing area ever since the Baekje period. The mountainous parts of the province produce *sanchae* (wild greens) and mushrooms.

DAEJEON

The capital of Chungcheongnam-do, Daejeon is South Korea's industrial heart, producing everything from tires to textiles to pharmaceuticals. Only about 2 hours from Seoul by car, it is a major transportation hub and one of South Korea's main centers for science and technology, but not a major tourist destination. The Yuseong *oncheon* (hot springs) area, a mecca for Baekje royalty, is still a quiet place to get in a soak. Centrally located, it's a good place to begin your exploration of Bomunsan, Gyejoksan and other natural locations nearby.

Essentials

GETTING THERE Although it's a major transportation hub, there is no airport in Daejeon. The nearest airport is **Cheongju Airport** (CJJ), 50-1, Ipsang-li, Naesu-eup, Cheongwon-gun (✆ **043/210-6114**), about a 35-minute drive north of the city. Buses run from Daejeon's Dongbu Terminal five times a day. From the Incheon Airport, you can get a limousine bus directly to Daejeon. Catch the bus in front of gate 8. Regular buses cost ₩14,500 and the deluxe bus costs ₩23,100. The airport limousine bus stops at the Mokwon Daedeok Cultural Center, the Daejeon Government Complex, the Lotte Hotel in Yuseong, and the Dongbu Intercity Bus Terminal.

Daejeon is located at the junctions of the Gyeongbu and Honam rail lines. It has two train stations. The larger **Daejeon Station,** located in the center of town, has trains to or from Seoul or Busan. Other trains travel to Pohang, Ulsan, Jinju, Masan, or Jecheon. The smaller **Seo-Daejeon (West) Train Station** is the first stop on the Honam Line. These trains make more frequent stops and run from Seoul through Daejeon, and south to Mokpo, Gwangju, Suncheon, Jinju, and Yeosu. A **KTX** (http://info.korail.com/2007/eng/eng_index.jsp) express train from Seoul will get you to Daejeon in under an hour. From Seoul, train fares start at ₩22,900 for KTX (₩32,100 for first class), ₩15,500 for Saemaeul, and ₩10,300 for Mugunghwa trains. Fares are slightly lower for standing/unassigned tickets.

Daejeon is on the Gyeongbu and Honam expressways. To make things confusing, Daejeon has an express bus station and two intercity bus stations. The main bus station in Daejeon is the **Dongbu Intercity Bus Terminal** (℃ 042/624-4452) which has over 80 routes to mostly regional destinations, but also has buses to Gimpo and Incheon airports. It's about a 15-minute taxi ride from the train station and within walking distance to the **Daejeon Express Bus Terminal** (℃ 042/625-8792; www.kobus.co.kr/web/eng/index.jsp), which has longer-distance buses, including those to/from Seoul and Dong-Seoul—both take about 2 hours.

Daejeon

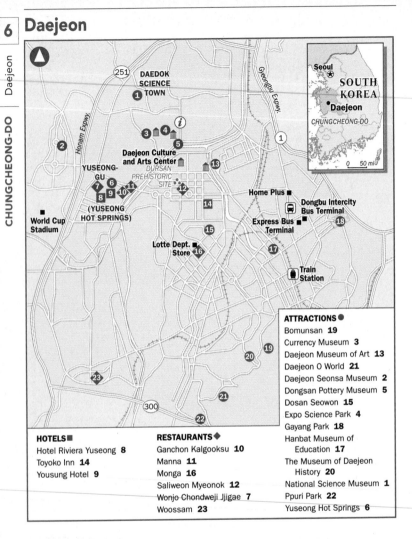

251 DAEDOK SCIENCE TOWN

Gyeongbu Expwy

Seoul
SOUTH KOREA
•Daejeon
CHUNGCHEONG-DO
0   50 mi

Honam Expwy

Daejeon Culture and Arts Center

YUSEONG-GU

DURSAN PREHISTORIC SITE

(YUSEONG HOT SPRINGS)

World Cup Stadium

Home Plus ■
Dongbu Intercity Bus Terminal

Express Bus Terminal

Lotte Dept. Store 16

Train Station

ATTRACTIONS ●
Bomunsan **19**
Currency Museum **3**
Daejeon Museum of Art **13**
Daejeon O World **21**
Daejeon Seonsa Museum **2**
Dongsan Pottery Museum **5**
Dosan Seowon **15**
Expo Science Park **4**
Gayang Park **18**
Hanbat Museum of Education **17**
The Museum of Daejeon History **20**
National Science Museum **1**
Ppuri Park **22**
Yuseong Hot Springs **6**

HOTELS■
Hotel Riviera Yuseong **8**
Toyoko Inn **14**
Yousung Hotel **9**

RESTAURANTS◆
Ganchon Kalgooksu **10**
Manna **11**
Monga **16**
Saliweon Myeonok **12**
Wonjo Chondweji Jjigae **7**
Woossam **23**

GETTING AROUND   A major subway system (with a planned five lines) is currently under construction. The first section, **subway line 1** (www.djet.co.kr), is currently running daily from 5:30am to 12:12am. The short trains run every 5 minutes during rush hour (usually around 7–9am and 5–7pm) and every 8 to 10 minutes the rest of the day. With 22 stations, the line runs northwest from Wisa-dong in Banseok through the center of the city to Daejeon University in Panam. You can connect to the Korean National rail line at Daejeon Station. The base fare is ₩1,000, ₩950 with a TrafficCard, with reduced fares for teens and children.

Daejeon has a good bus system that goes pretty much anywhere you want to go. There are three types of buses: Red, express buses that only stop at major stations; blue (regular) buses that connect the downtown areas to the outlying suburbs; and green (local) buses. Regular fares are ₩1,000 adults, ₩700 for teens, and ₩300 for children, with a reduced fare for using a TrafficCard. Up to three transfers to another bus or subway are free with a traffic card. Fares for express buses are about twice those of regular buses.

Taxis are usually waiting outside of the bus and train stations and you can just flag one down on any street. Basic taxi fares start at ₩2,300, with 20% higher fares from midnight to 6am. Look for those with "free interpretation" stickers on the windows to get free interpretation services through a mobile phone installed in the taxi.

VISITOR INFORMATION   A **tourist information center** (✆ 042/632-1770) is located in front of the main Express Bus Terminal. There is also another booth inside Daejeon Station plaza (✆ 042/221-1905). Another **tourist info center** (✆ 042/1330) can be found inside the Expo Science Park, which also has free Internet access and a souvenir shop. All are open 9am to 6pm daily.

Note: The city of Daejeon offers a bus tour that runs Tuesday through Sunday 10am to 5pm. The tours depart from Daejeon Station at 10:00am. On Tuesday, Thursday, and Saturday, the tour goes to the Daedeok Research Complex (via Expo Science Park), to the main office of Dosolcheon (Stream) and World Cup Stadium, to Ppuri (Root) Park, and to Uam Historical Park. On Wednesday, Friday, and Sunday the tour goes through Daedeok Research Complex, to the National Cemetery, to Gongsanseong (fortress), to the Tomb of King Muryeong, and to the Gongju National Museum and Donghaksa Temple. There are no tours on Sundays. Tours cost ₩3,000 adults, ₩2,000 teens and seniors over 65, and ₩1,000 for kids 6 and older. Contact either the **Tourism Department of Daejeon City Hall** (✆ 042/600-3114) or **Baekje Tours** (✆ 042/253-0005, or in Seoul 02/222-5901; http://baekjetour.com/djcity, Korean only) for reservations and additional information.

[FastFACTS] DAEJEON

Banks, Foreign Exchange & ATMs Most major banks are located in the city center. They're open 9:30am to 4:30pm Monday through Friday. For changing foreign currency, your best bets are the Foreign Exchange Bank, the Chohung Bank, and the Shinan Bank, but most banks in the city will perform the service. Major hotels also have desks that exchange foreign currency and traveler's checks.

Internet Access Most large hotels and even some lower-priced motels and youth hostels offer Internet access. If you don't have your own computer, your cheapest options are the PC *bahngs* (rooms) in town. Just look for the letters PC; most of them are found on the second or third floors above restaurants. You can also use the free computers inside the tourist information center at the Expo Science Center daily from 9am to 6pm.

Post Office The main post office (Mon–Fri 9am–5pm) is located behind Daejeon Station.

Exploring Daejeon
HISTORIC SITES
Dosan Seowon (Dosan Confucian Academy) MEMORIAL   The Dosan Confucian Academy and Shrine was built at the suggestion of scholars in 1693. In 1868, King Gojong ordered the destruction and removal of the main building. However, it was restored in 1921 and a *danso* (memorial shrine) was built. The academy honors two Confucian scholars, Gwon Shi and Gwon Deuk-gi, whose tombs are located on the hill to the west of the complex. Although the architecture is

interesting, there isn't much to see here outside of when they hold memorial services for the two scholars in the spring and fall. Do not be confused by the academy in Andong with the same name and a better location.

233, Tanbang-dong, Seo-gu, Daejeon-si. © **042/486-7771.** Free admission. Sunday-Friday 9am–5pm, Saturdays until noon.

Gayang Park ★ PARK   A forest park in the eastern part of the city, it is divided into two smaller parks—**Uam Sajeok Park** (Uam Historical Park) and **Central Square.** Uam Sajeok Park was created to honor Confucian scholar Song Shi-yeol, who was a tutor and political advisor to kings in the mid-1600s. When you walk into the front gate, you'll see **Namgangjeongsa ★★★**, a 350-year-old tile-roofed pavilion used as his study. A small stream flows below the main hall into a pond in front of the complex.

65 Gayang-dong, Dong-gu, Daejeon-si. © **042/581-3516** (city park control office) or 042/673-9286 (Uam Sajeok Park Office). Free admission. Daily 5am–9pm. Take bus no. 104, 161, 211, 223, 310, 310-1, 320, 321, or 810.

Ppuri Park PARK   A scenic park filled with flower beds and walking paths, located east of Bomunsan, Ppuri (which means "root") Gongweon is home to stone tablets carved with Korean family names and their origins—hence the "root" of the park's name.

15 Jinhyeon-dong, Gyeongju-si, Gyeongsangbuk-do. © **042/581-4445.** Free admission. Oct–Feb daily 7am–9pm; Mar–Sept daily 6am–10pm. Take bus no. 310, 310-1, 320, or 321.

MUSEUMS
Currency Museum ★ ☺ MUSEUM   Located next door to the South Korean mint, it has four permanent exhibition halls with thousands of coins and bank notes dating back through the peninsula's history—some of the coins are more than 1,000 years old. There are also displays of foreign currency, historic Korean stamps, and a printing machine.

Gwahangno, Yuseong-gu, Daejeon-si. © **042/870-1000.** Free admission. Mar–Oct daily 10am–5pm; Nov–Feb daily 10am–4pm. Located a 20-min. walk from Expo Park; go behind the Science Museum and walk along the stream.

Daejeon Museum of Art ART MUSEUM   Sometimes called the Daejeon Metropolitan Museum of Art, both Korean and foreign contemporary artists are on display in these galleries. Their permanent collection includes paintings, drawings, prints, and more from contemporary Korean artists as well as revolving exhibitions. The museum is located directly across the river from Expo Science Park and across the street from the Daejeon Government Complex.

396 Mannyeon-dong, Seo-gu, Daejeon-si. © **042/602-3200.** http://dmma.daejeon.go.kr/foreign/main.do. Admission ₩500 adults, ₩300 youth, free for seniors 65 and over and kids 6 and under, separate admission for special exhibits. Tues-Sun Mar–Oct 10am–7pm; Nov–Feb 10am–6pm, Fri until 9pm. Entrance up to 30 min. before closing. Closed Mondays, Jan 1, Lunar New Year, and Chuseok. Take city bus no. 606, 618, 911 or take the subway to Daejeon Governmental Office Station; it's a 15-min walk from there.

Dongsan Pottery Museum MUSEUM   This tiny museum provides a glimpse into the area's history and folk traditions. There are three exhibition halls—one dedicated to earthenware, the second to crockery and pottery, and the third to folklore and ceramics.

107-1, Seo-gu, Daejeon-si. ℭ**042/534-3453.** Free admission. Daily 10am–4pm. Closed on national holidays.

Hanbat Museum of Education MUSEUM   With over 6,000 items in its collection, this museum gives a solid overview of the history of Korean education. It includes social customs and folkloric items dating back to the Joseon Dynasty, rooms for scholars, and items from the Japanese occupation. The outdoor exhibit has animal statues made of stone, sun and water clocks, and a variety of school gates.

113-1 Samseong 1-dong, Dong-gu, Daejeon-si. ℭ **042/670-2200.** Free admission. Tues–Sun 9:30am–5pm. Closed Monday and national holidays. From the Express Bus or Dongbu terminals, take bus no. 102, 703, 851 or 860 and get off at Samseong intersection. The museum is right next to Samseong Elementary School.

The Museum of Daejeon History MUSEUM   True to its name, this museum was created to preserve and educate the public about the historic traditions of the Daejeon area. An active institution, it conducts ongoing research on cultural relics and historic data from prehistory to more recent folklore.

(145-3 Munhwa 1-dong) 222 Hanbat Doseogwan-gil, Jung-gu, Daejeon-si. ℭ **042/580-4359.** http://museum.daejeon.go.kr. Free admission. Mon–Sun 10am–6pm (Mar–Oct 10am–7pm). Take bus no. 115, 116, 223, 310, 310-1, or 813. Not far from the Hanbat Museum.

Daejeon Seonsa (Prehistoric) Museum MUSEUM   A recent addition to Daejeon's museum scene, the collection is anything but new, since it exhibits relics from prehistoric times found in Noeun-dong in 1997. The dioramas show how people of the regions may have lived during Neolithic and bronze ages.

(920-beonji, Jijeok-dong) 100 Noeundong-gil, Yuseong-gu, Daejeon-si. ℭ**042/826-2814.** http://museum.daejeon.go.kr. Free admission. Tues–Sun 9am–6pm, until 5pm Nov–Feb; last entry 30 min. before closing. Closed Jan 1, Lunar New Year, Chuseok. Daejeon subway to Noeun Station (exit 4), about a 7-min. walk. Alternatively, take bus no. 101, 109, 114, 116 or 121.

National Science Museum ★ ☺ MUSEUM   Permanent exhibits at this museum, located in **Expo Science Park,** include a fascinating look at Korea's geological and natural history, and a section on the history of Korean technology. At the center of the museum is the Astronomical Hall, the largest dome in the country. There is also a 242-seat space theater, similar to a planetarium, where you can see the night sky projected on the dome. Outside the hall is **Cheomseongdae,** a structure used to predict the weather during the Goryeo Dynasty. Science and nature documentaries are shown at 11am and 2pm daily, but are in Korean only, unfortunately. There isn't much in the way of English signage, but it's worth a visit for those interested in science.

32-2 Guseong-dong, Yuseong-gu, Daejeon-si. ℭ**042/601-7894** (Korean only). www.science.go.kr. Admission to the Astronomical Hall and Permanent Exhibit Hall ₩1,000 adults, ₩500 youth. Tues–Sun 9:30am–5:50pm. Closed Mondays and the day following a national holiday. From Daejeon Station, take *jwaseok* (express) bus no. 105 or 105-1, or city bus no. 180, 513, or 814, and get off at Gwahakgongweon (science park) or the front gate of the museum (a 45-min. ride). From Daejeon Express Bus Terminal, take city bus no. 113 (an hour ride).

Yeojin Gallery of Buddhist Art ★★ ART MUSEUM   The director of the museum, Lee Jin-hyung (pen name: Yeojin), is himself designated an intangible cultural asset (no. 6) by the Korean government. If you forget to make a reservation, a stroll around the sculpture garden is still worth the visit. It's a wonderful way to learn more about both modern and traditional Buddhist art.

442-1, Tamlip-dong Yuseong-gu, Daejeon-si. © **042/934-8466.** www.yeojingallery.co.kr (Korean only). Free admission, but reservations required. Tues–Sun 10am–5pm.

NATURAL SITES

Bomunsan ★ PARK   Located south of the city center, Bomunsan is a mountain park, throughout which there are ancient sites dating back to the area's Baekje past. At the entrance to the park are restaurants, accommodations, and a folk museum. The remains of a fortress, **Bomunsanseong,** are on the southern ridge of the mountain. Once you take the cable car up, there are several walking trails to explore, leading to a number of small temples, an amusement park, and a few war monuments. Above the amusement park is an observation site from which you can get a good view of the city below when the weather is clear. An even better view can be had from the pavilion, which is part of the fortress wall.

15 Jinhyeon-dong, Gyeongju-si, Gyeongsangbuk-do. © **042/581-3516.** Free admission. Cable car ₩2,000 round-trip, ₩1,500 one-way. Take regular city bus no. 111, 113, 116, 310, 310-1, 726, 813, or 888.

Daecheongho (Daecheong Lake) NATURAL ATTRACTION   This artificial lake was created with the damming of the Geumgang ("Gold" River). The reservoir provides water to the Daejeon and Cheongju areas. The clear waters reflect the nearby mountains, and the lake area is one of the most scenic in Daejeon.

Miho-dong, Daedeok-gu, Daejeon-si. © **042/930-7204** (Korean only). Free admission. Water culture exhibition room Tues–Sun 10am–5pm. From Daejeon Station, take jwaseok bus no. 701 (which runs every 10 min.) and get off at Sintanjin. From there, transfer to circular shuttle bus no. 70 (which runs every 80 min.) and get off at Daecheongdam.

OTHER POINTS OF INTEREST

Daejeon O World ☺ AMUSEMENT PARK   This amusement park encompasses a zoo (Zoo World), a garden (Flower Land), and rides (Joy Land).

70 Sajeonggongwin-ro, Jung-gu, Daejeon-si. © **042/580-4820.** www.oworld.kr/eng/index.asp. Admission to Zoo Land and Flower Land only ₩8,000 adults, ₩4,000 teens, ₩3,000 children/seniors. Admission + safari tour and movie theater tickets are ₩25,000 adults, ₩20,000 teens, ₩18,000 children/seniors. Hours vary, but most daily 9:30am–6pm, open later on weekends and summer season. Take city bus no. 311 or 314 from Daejeon Station, or bus nos. 2, 102, 501, or 701 from the Express Bus Terminal.

Expo Science Park ★ AMUSEMENT PARK   Located in northwestern Daejeon, next to **Gyeryongsan National Park,** this was the site where the Daejeon Expo was held in 1993. The area has since been renovated and transformed into a science theme park. The park includes the **National Science Museum** (see listing above) and several other science facilities, including the Daedeok Science Research Complex and displays of cultural relics from Buyeo and Gongju from the Baekje period.

3-1 Doryong-dong, Yuseong-gu, Daejeon. © **042/866-5114.** www.expopark.co.kr (Korean only). Admission and hours vary for different attractions, but the base rate is ₩7,000 adults, ₩5,000 teens, ₩4,000 children. Take bus no. 180, 185, or 513 from Daejeon Station.

Yuseong Hot Springs NATURAL ATTRACTION   A popular place for the royals during the Baekje Kingdom, this *oncheon* (hot spring) feeds water to various hotels and spas in the area. One of the best in the area is the **Yousung Spa** (© **042/820-0100**), located inside the Yousung Hotel. Open daily from 5am to 10pm, it costs ₩4,500 for adults, ₩2,200 for children. Early birds can get in before 8am for only ₩3,000.

Bongmyeong-dong, Yuseong-gu, Daejeon-si. © **042/611-2130.** Admission and hours vary by spa. Take Daejeon subway to Yuseong Oncheon Station (exit 6). From Daejeon Station, take city bus no. 110, 111, 111-1, 120, 160, 160, or 222 and get off at Yuseong oncheon (about a 40-min. ride). From the Daejeon Express Bus Terminal, take city bus no. 102, 104, or 509 and get off at oncheon 4(sa)-geoli.

GYEJOKSAN

North of Daejeon are the small ridges of Gyejoksan (Mt. Gyejok, a.k.a. "Chicken Foot" mountain), which is sometimes called "Bonghwangsan" (Phoenix Mountain). It stands 423m (1,388 ft.) high and offers a good view of Lake Daecheong. On top is **Gyejok Sanseong** (© **042/623-9909**), the largest of the fortresses left from the Baekje period. There are two hiking trails to the fortress, one that is 5.6km (3½ miles) long and takes about 2 hours and a longer 6.3km (4-mile) hike that takes about 3 hours. Most people time their hikes to catch the sunrise or sunset from the top.

Gyeryongsan National Park

Located just 50 minutes from Daejeon by bus, **Gyeryongsan (Mt. Gyeryong) National Park** (© **042/825-3003;** 777 Hakbong-li, Banpo-myeon, Gongju-si, http://english.knps.or.kr) is one of South Korea's few rugged mountain ranges located near a major city. The national park stretches from Daejeon to Gwangju, Gongju and Nonsan, and includes 15 peaks, the main one being **Cheonhwang-bong.** The park has several beautiful waterfalls and interesting rock formations—the name Gyeryong-san means "Chicken Dragon Mountain," because the granite peaks rise up like a cock's comb or like the scales on a dragon's back. The spring brings cherry blossoms along the Donghaksa mountain trail, which leads to a lush green valley in the summer. The maple trees are gorgeous in the autumn (especially on the trail that leads from Gapsa to Sanbul-bong) and the snow-capped mountains are lovely in the winter. A mountain full of stories and myths, the area has had a long history of shamanism, animism, and the supernatural. Although most of the believers are long gone, traces of those ancient beliefs still exist in the area today. From the Daejeon Bus Terminal or Yuseong Intercity Bus Terminal, take city bus no. 102 or 103 to Donghaksa. You can also take bus no. 2 bound for Gapsa, from the stop in front of the Yuseong Police Station. Running about 14 times daily, the ride takes about an hour. From the old Gongju Bus Terminal, take a bus bound for Donghaksa. Alternatively, take a city bus from Gongju to Sinwonsa. The park is open 6am to 7pm daily and admission is ₩2,000 adults, ₩1,500 teens, ₩1,000 children (off season ₩1,600 adults, ₩1,200 and ₩800 children). Parking is ₩2,000 and up. The park is closed during dry seasons (Mar 1–May 15, Nov 15–Dec 15) to protect it from forest fires.

There are *minbak* (homestay) places lining both sides of the road up to the parking lot. Once you continue up the road on foot, there are plenty of eating options lining the walkway to Donghaksa. The hiking trails begin after you pass the temple.

Donghaksa (Donghak Temple) ✋ TEMPLE   Located in the Sangbong Valley, this small temple was founded by Monk Hoeui-hwasang in A.D. 724. It was later expanded by Monk Dosungooksa during the reign of King Taejo. Home to Buddhist nuns since the Shilla period, it is now also a study center, so parts of the complex are off-limits to visitors. Because the nuns live here, some of the historic architecture has unfortunate modern updates that may be comfortable for the residents but not pleas-ant to view. This temple's best assets are the doors to the main hall, carved with cranes, bamboo, and cherry blossoms. To the right is a shrine built in 1456 for the deposed boy-king Kim Shi-seup, whose throne was usurped by his uncle. The original

💬 **Almost a Capital**

The village of Seokgyeri, on the southern side of the mountain, was selected by King Taejo, founder of the Joseon Dynasty, to be his capital in the mid-1300s. But before construction could get fully underway, the king's geomancers (those who divine spiritual wisdom from the landscape) told him it was a poor choice, and that Seoul would serve his needs better. So the king halted construction, and all that's left today are a few stones marking what might have been the capital of Korea.

shrine was destroyed—this is a modern version. Just 2km (1¼ miles) north of the temple are the twin pagodas **Nammaetap,** at the site of **Chongnyangsa** (Chongnyang Temple). They were both built during the Shilla period and modeled after the sculptural style popular in the Baekje period.

Hakbong-li, Banpo-myeon, Gongju-si, Chungcheongnam-do. © **042/825-2570.** Admission ₩2,000 adults, ₩1,000 teens, ₩500 children. Daily 6am–7pm. From Gongju take bus no. 6 to Donghaksa (should take 40 min.). From Daejeon Station or Yuseong, take bus no. 102. It'll take an hour from Daejeon and 20 min. from Yuseong.

Gapsa (Gap Temple) ★★ ☺ TEMPLE   Established in A.D. 420 by Monk Ado-hwasang, who is credited with having brought Buddhism to the Shilla Kingdom, Gapsa is said to be one of the oldest temples in the country. Although the oldest of its current buildings dates to 1604, there is much to see in this small temple complex, and the place is famous for the numerous cultural treasures it houses. When you first enter the temple site, you'll see a lecture hall with large words GYERYONG GAPSA written in blue. To the right of that hall is the Dongjonggak (where the site's copper bell, cast in A.D. 584, is housed). To the left stand the Pyochungwon and the Palsangjeon buildings. The Pyochungwon was created to honor high priests and monk warriors Yeong-Gyu, Sa-Myeong, and Seosan. The Palsangjeon is where the Palsangdo (a visual depiction of the life of Buddha) is preserved.

If you follow the road past the temple, you will find the trail to the rest of Gyeryongsan. There is a lovely little teahouse nearby and a small valley.

52 Jungjang-li, Gyeryong-myeon, Gongju-si, Chungcheongnam-do. © **042/857-8981.** www.gapsa.org (Korean only) Admission ₩2,000 adults, ₩700 teens, ₩400 children, free for kids 6 and under. Daily 8am–6pm. From Gongju, take a bus bound for Gapsa and the ride should take 30 min. From Yuseong, a direct bus (no. 2) to Gapsa takes 50 min. Parking ₩4,000 and up, depending on the size of the car.

Sinwonsa (Sinwon Temple) TEMPLE   Built by Monk Bodeokhwasang in A.D. 651, this temple has undergone several renovations since and was rumored to have been moved to its present site after it was destroyed in the Imjin Waeran. Repaired by Monk Boryeonhwasang in 1876, the last renovations were done in 1946.

Yanghwa-li, Gyeryong-myeon, Gongju-si, Chungcheongnam-do. © **042/852-4230.** Admission ₩2,000 adults, ₩1,800 teens, ₩600 children, free for kids 6 and under. Daily 8am–6pm. A short walk from Donghaksa. See directions to Donghaksa, above.

Shopping

As in all Korean cities, there is no shortage of places to shop here. Daejeon has a nice range of traditional open markets and multistoried department stores.

TRADITIONAL MARKETS

Daejeon has a bunch of small neighborhood markets, but the largest one is the central **Jung-ang Shijang,** 40, Won-dong, Dong-gu (*€* **042/256-0567**), located right near Daejeon Station. Started in 1953, the city government updated the facilities in an attempt to attract customers lost to the major discount stores (like E-Mart). A bustling market, it's open most days from 9am to 7:30pm.

Another fun open marketplace is **Indong Shijang,** 42, In-dong, Dong-gu (*€* **042/283-2029**). Started in 1919, it has been shrinking in size in the past few years. It sells mostly agricultural products from the area—mainly rice and grains. It's open 9am to 7pm Monday through Saturday.

Located in Jangdae-dong, Yuseong-gu, is the **Yuseong O-il (5-day) Market,** going strong for nearly a hundred years. Taking over a large triangular space (encompassing five or six alleys in the area), the marketplace comes alive on dates that end in 4 or 9. An open market for goods of all kinds, it's open 9am to 8pm on market days.

SPECIALTY STREETS

Tucked between small alleyways and side streets, groups of specialty shops have popped up all over Daejeon. One such area is the **Wondong Tool Street,** where (you guessed it) you can buy many kinds of tools sold by local foundries. Within walking distance from Daejeon Station, the grouping of about three dozen shops is located between Daeheung bridge and Jung bridge. Most shops are open daily from 7:30am to 6:30pm.

Of more interest to you may be **Hanbok Street** (Korean Traditional Clothing Street) ★★★ in Wondong. There are about 300 stores specializing in *hanbok* (the traditional Korean outfit), some of which have been in business since 1954. Some of the stores sell clothes for both wholesale and retail, while others specialize in just mending and modifying outfits you may have already. You can also find Korean handicrafts, blankets, and other traditional fabric products for good prices here. Shops are generally open daily from 9am to 8pm.

Although the goods sold here will mostly be too large to take home with you, it's fun to browse **Hanbat Furniture Street** in Jungri-dong. Since most of the shops here sell factory direct, you can find some good deals. Open daily 9am to 10:30pm, they're closed every third Tuesday of the month. Another area that specializes in furniture is the **Seodaejeon Furniture Street** in Jung-gu. An older area than the one in Jungri-dong, the prices are more expensive here, but products are more upscale. The stores are generally open daily from 10am to 8pm.

Another fun place to browse is the **Herbal Medicine Street** in Jung-ang-dong. Started in 1958, it is one of only three markets in South Korea that specialize in herbal medicine. About 100 shops are located in the area, peddling everything from dried roots, unidentifiable plants, and interesting specimens of who-knows-what in little jars. You can also get herbal tea, herbal rice cakes, and a variety of herbal cures for minor ailments. The shops are open Monday through Saturday 9am to 6pm.

If you're just interested in Korean *insam* (ginseng), look no further than the ginseng and herbal medicine shops in **Busa-dong** that sell the insam grown in nearby Geumsan. There are a variety of roots and medicinal plants at decent prices. Most stores are open daily 8:30am to 8:30pm, but close the first and third Sundays of the month.

DEPARTMENT STORES

Most major department stores are pretty much the same throughout South Korea, and those in Daejeon are no exception. They are huge multistory complexes with

The Root of the Matter

Ginseng (called "insam" in Korean) is probably the most famous ingredient in traditional folk medicine, both in China and in Korea. This thick, tubular root is taken for everything from the prevention of diabetes and hypertension to the strengthening of memory and digestive function, and the encouraging of longevity and sexual vigor. Those who take it (in the form of pills, powders, and teas) swear by it, and South Korea's ginseng is considered the world's finest. The root can take years to mature—even the lowest-grade ginseng spends 4 to 5 years in the ground, and some wild ginseng is over 100 years old. Not surprisingly, those roots are extremely expensive. Just remember that you're allowed to take only red ginseng (more expensive than the more common white ginseng) out of the country.

several floors of fashion sandwiched between a basement level with a grocery store and Korean fast-food joints and a top floor full of mid- to high-priced restaurants.

In the Jung-gu area, there are two major department stores. One is **Galleria Dongbaek,** 3-14, Seonhwa-dong, Jung-gu (✆ **042/221-3000**), which has parking and is open daily from 11am to 8:30pm. Take the subway to Jungang-no Station (exits 6 or 7). Avoid the store on weekends if you don't like crowds, since they usually have concerts, celebrity events, and contests then. The other department store in Jung-gu is **Say,** 1-16, Munhwa-dong, Jung-gu (✆ **042/226-1234**), which has a cultural and sports center on its top two floors and a CGV movie theater on floor 6. They're open daily 10:30am to 8pm. Take buses 111, 201, 212, 220, 222, 222-1, 230, 701, 703, 810, 828, 841, or 851.

In central Seo-gu, the popular department store is **Galleria Timeworld,** 1036, Dunsan 2-dong Seo-gu (✆ **042/480-5000**). They also have a sports center and cultural complex, as well as a beauty shop and travel agency. With nine floors, musical instruments and CDs are on the first-floor basement, with books and stationery items on the second basement floor. The larger **Lotte Department Store,** 423-1 Goejeong-dong, Seo-gu (✆ **042/601-2500**), has 12 floors, which include a cultural center, movie theater, game room, and coffee shops. They're open daily 10am to 8pm, but close two Mondays a month (the dates vary each month, so call ahead).

Where to Stay

Daejeon is not a tourist destination, so accommodations here are serviceable, but not exciting. Most hotels in the city are located in the Yuseong oncheon area and include small spas for visitors. There are some love motels in the area too, ranging from ₩30,000 to ₩40,000 for a single/double on weekdays and going up during weekends and high season. A number of economical *yeogwan* (budget motels) and smaller motels are located around the bus terminals. None of them takes reservations, and most are designed to serve late-night travelers stopping overnight before continuing to far-flung places.

EXPENSIVE

Hotel Riviera Yuseong ★   A hot springs hotel located in Yuseong, this is the best place in the area, which is still not saying much. It has spacious, but tired rooms with comfortable beds. The bathrooms have both shower and tub with a phone, should you need to make an urgent call. Built in 1988, the 13-floor building has the amenities you would expect for a hotel of its type, but Wi-Fi is only available in the lobby (free wired Internet in rooms).

444-5, Bongmyong-dong, Yuseong-gu, Daejeon-si. http://www.shinan.co.kr/yusong/eng/index_yuseong.asp. © **042/828-4001.** Fax 042/822-0071. 174 units. ₩200,000 standard single/double; ₩350,000 and up suite; 50% discount is not unusual. 10% VAT and 10% service charge not included. AE, DC, MC, V. **Amenities:** 4 restaurants; lounge; cafe; health club; spa; sauna; bakery; Wi-Fi. *In room:* A/C, TV, minibar, fridge, hair dryer, safe, Internet.

Yousung Hotel   Located in the Yuseong oncheon area, the hotel is conveniently located near to Expo Science Park and other attractions. The hot springs have been a favorite of the royal family since the Baekje Kingdom, and the hotel itself was founded in 1915. Both Western-style and Korean-style ondol rooms are available, and both have nice views of the surrounding park. Beds are comfortable though on the small side, but the rooms themselves are a bit dated. Even if you're not staying here, you can have access to their pool or visit their hot spring spa.

480, Bongmyeong-dong, Yuseong-gu, Daejeon-si. www.yousunghotel.com. © **042/820-0100.** Fax 042/822-8860. 189 units. ₩190,000 standard room; ₩330,000 and up deluxe room; ₩300,000 suite, 10% VAT and 10% service charge not included. AE, MC, V. **Amenities:** 3 restaurants; cafe; lounge; pool; health club; spa; sauna. *In room:* A/C, TV, minibar, fridge, hair dryer, Internet.

MODERATE

Toyoko Inn ★★ 🗡   One of Asia's largest business hotel chains has a location in Daejeon, near the government complex. They keep their prices low by doing without unnecessary amenities, so their lobby area is pretty spare. Still, the small but clean rooms and free breakfast make a stay here a bargain.

922, Dusansan-dong, Seo-gu, Daejeon-si. http://www.toyoko-inn.com/e_hotel/00234/index.html. © **042/545-1045.** Fax 042/545-1046. 60 units. ₩60,500 single, ₩82,500 double. MC, V. **Amenities:** Restaurant; non-smoking rooms available; free PC and Wi-Fi in lobby. *In room:* A/C, TV, fridge, electric kettle, hair dryer, safe, Internet.

Where to Eat

One of the specialties of Daejeon is *dotoli muk* (acorn jelly), a dish created when times were hard and people had to collect acorns in the mountains to feed themselves and their families. A brown-colored gelatin, dotoli muk doesn't offer much flavor but is not bad when served with *yangnyeom ganjang* (a seasoned soy sauce) on top.

Another famous dish from the region is *samgyetang*, a chicken soup made with a whole young chicken stuffed with glutinous rice, dates, garlic, and ginseng. It's a traditional dish that is supposed to be healthy for you (and was eaten to fight the heat during the three hottest days in the summer). The people of Daejeon say that theirs has a unique flavor because of the insam gathered from Geumsan. You can try this tasty dish at **Seumsung Samgyetang,** 32-14 Jung-dong, Dong-gu, Daejeon (© **042/254-3422**), who sell the soup for only ₩9,000 a bowl. They're open 10am to10pm daily.

A special favorite of the region is *seolleongtang*, a milky white soup made from boiling beef bone forever, that you season with as much green onion, chili powder, and salt as you like. It's usually served with a side of rice and *kkakdugi* (cubed daikon kimchi), and enjoyed year-round. Head to **Bonga Gamasot Seolleongtang,** 452-2

Gayang-dong, Dong-gu (☏ **042/673-8826**), where they cook the broth for 48 hours in a *gamasot* (a large traditional metal pot, heated over wood flames).

EXPENSIVE

Manna ★★ KOREAN   This spacious and upscale restaurant has four different locations in the city (I've included the addresses for a couple of locations, below). They have wonderfully friendly staff and a variety of set menus to choose from. Their specialty is *shabu shabu* (Japanese-style beef hot pot).

552-9 Bongmyeong-dong, Yuseong-gu, Daejeon-si. ☏ **042/825-2001.** www.manna.co.kr (Korean only). 2nd location at 502-1 Suik Tower Food Store, 2nd floor (☏ **042/628-9290**). Shabu shabu ₩35,500, set menus ₩60,000 per person. AE, MC, V. Daily 11am–11pm. Closed Lunar New Year and Chuseok.

MODERATE

Wonjo Chondweji Jjigae ★★ 🍴 KOREAN PORK   Known for their country pork, it's worth making your way to this alley restaurant for their pork hot pots, which are best shared with friends over some beer or soju.

281-10 Jangdae-dong, Yuseong-gu, Daejeon-si. ☏ **042/823-1131** (Korean). Entrees ₩10,000–₩38,000. MC, V. Daily 11am–10pm.

Woossam ★★ KOREAN BEEF/PORK   For a place that specializes in Korean meat dishes, this joint is surprisingly affordable. Regular tables and Korean-style floor tables are available. All have tabletop grills for your eating pleasure. Try the *wang-ggot ssamgyupssal* (thinly sliced pork belly), the *naechuleol modeum seng-gogi* (various beef cuts), or the *galbi ssal* (unmarinated rib-eye meat).

943-944 Gwanpeong-dong, Yuseong-gu, Daejeon-si. ☏ **011/403-5941** (Korean). Entrees ₩5,500–₩8,000; set menu for 2 ₩24,000. MC, V. Daily 11am–11pm.

INEXPENSIVE

Ganchon Kalgooksu KOREAN   One of the few decent places within walking distance to the motels in the Yuseong area, this family-run restaurant specializes in *kalguksu* (homemade "knife noodles") and sliced meats, which you can cook on the tabletop grill. Ask for the noodles to be mild if you can't handle the spice.

537-5 Bongmyeong-dong, Yuseong-gu, Daejeon-si. Flatcakes and noodles ₩5,000; beef and pork meals ₩10,000–₩20,000. MC, V. Daily 10am–midnight.

Monga ★★ 🍴 KOREAN   This restaurant specializes in *jokbal* (sliced pork hock) and *sujebi* (dough flake soup). It may seem like an unusual combination, but they do both quite well. And at ₩5,000 per serving, the sujebi is quite a bargain. The *nakji bokkeum* (stir-fried squid) is terrific, too. Look for the Korean letters with the name in Chinese characters on the second floor of the SK Telecom Building (just about a block from the Lotte Department Store corner).

424-1 Guijeong-dong, Seo-gu, Daejeon-si. ☏ **042/536-8870** (Korean). Entrees ₩5,000–₩33,000. MC, V. Daily 5pm–midnight.

Saliweon Myeonok KOREAN NOODLES   Known for their *naengmyeong* (cold buckwheat noodles) and their *galbi tang* (beef rib soup), their dishes come out quickly and deliciously. They also have another location on the second floor of the Suik Tower.

968 Dunsan 2(i)-dong, Seogu, Daejeon-si. ☏ **042/487-4209.** Entrees ₩7,000–₩10,000. MC, V. Daily 10am–midnight.

Entertainment & Nightlife

For a medium-sized city, Daejeon has a relatively active nightlife. The most popular areas are the Yuseong district, the Dunsan-dong area (the "new" downtown), the city's old downtown region, and Gung-dong, near Chungnam University.

A good place to get imported beers or a cocktail is **WA Bar** (© 042/222-5858, 227 Daeheung-dong, Jung-gu) located across the street from the Galleria department store. A casual place, it's popular with Daejeon's English teachers for grabbing a drink with friends after work.

Just down the street is the most popular bar for expat English teachers, **JRock.** The owner is American and all of the staff speak English. A small, smoky place, it's a great place to get tips from people who've been in Daejeon for a while. There is a small dance floor and a pool table. For a late-night beer, cocktail, or coffee, you can try the dimly lit **Aram,** 104 Dunsan-dong, Seo-gu, Daejeon-si (© 042/485-6699), located on the second floor of the Myeongseong Building, a couple of blocks from the Bennigan's. Open daily from 4:30pm to 4am, this cafe bar has unusual decorations (including a fake pond with plastic swans). You can order food until 8pm, but the beverages flow until the wee hours. Cocktails start at ₩7,000; most teas are ₩5,000.

For a more relaxed atmosphere, you might want to try the **Shisha House ★★** (© 042/825-4157, 404-5 Gung-dong), an excellent cafe and hookah lounge, down the street from the local police booth, where you can smoke cigars or grab a good, non-Korean brew 5pm to 2am Tues–Sun ('until 3am Fri/Sat).

You can also catch the latest Hollywood fare at one of the many multiplex movie theaters in town—they're hard to miss, but ask at your hotel if you have trouble finding one.

GONGJU

Once the capital of the ancient Baekje Kingdom, Gongju is now a sleepy little town situated between two major mountain ranges. Relics, tombs, and a stone fortress show off Gongju's history and nearby Gapsa and Magoksa are worth a special visit, too.

Every year in October the **Baekje Cultural Festival ★★★**, one of the best festivals in South Korea, is held either here or in Buyeo. There are about 100 events held throughout the area, including ceremonies for the four great Baekje Kings, a mask parade, folk-art events, and cultural performances.

Essentials

GETTING THERE   There are no direct buses to Gongju from the **Incheon Airport**. You'll have to take a bus to Seoul's Gangnam Express Bus Terminal and transfer to a bus there, or take a bus to Daejeon Bus Terminal and catch a bus from there. The way via Daejeon requires less walking, but will add about 1½ to 2 hours to your trip.

From **Seoul's Express Bus Terminal,** you can get a bus to Gongju (which terminates at Buyeo). Express buses run every 30 to 40 minutes and take under 2 hours. The intercity and **express bus terminals** (© 041/854-3136) are next to each other, north of the river. Express buses from Daejeon go to Gongju every 5 to 10 minutes and take under an hour. From the **East Daejeon Terminal,** there are 22 departures daily 7am to 9pm and the bus takes 70 minutes. From the **West Daejeon Terminal,** buses run about every 5 minutes, daily from 6:30am to

The Chungcheong Provinces were once part of the legendary Baekje Kingdom, which was one of the Three Kingdoms of Korea (the other two are Shilla and Goguryeo kingdoms—for more information, see p. 11). According to the *Samgook Sagi* (Chronicles of the Three Kingdoms), Baekje was founded by King Onjo in 18 B.C. as an offshoot of the Goguryeo Kingdom. That may be correct, but what is known for sure is that the kingdom didn't become a cohesive state until sometime in the 1st century. The Baekje, who were heavily influenced by China and who helped spread

Buddhism (which they adopted as their religion in 384) to this part of Korea, were by the 400s a significant trading and naval power. Unfortunately, the Shilla and Goguryeo were each eager to expand their own territory and began encroaching on the Baekje. In 660, after years of fighting, the Baekje Kingdom fell to the Shilla Kingdom, which unified the Korean Peninsula for the first time. But the influence of the Baekje—their ceramics, architecture, and spirituality—can still be felt, especially around Gongju and Buyeo.

10:30pm, and take an hour. If you take a bus from Daejeon, they'll most likely take you to the city center.

There are no direct trains that come into Gongju; you'll have to take a train to Daejeon and transfer to a bus.

GETTING AROUND   The city bus station is in the middle of town. Here you can catch local buses to most places of interest. You can also flag down a taxi from any street. Neither bus nor taxi drivers speak English, but they will help you get where you want to go, regardless.

VISITOR INFORMATION   The **Gongju Tourist Info Center,** 65-3 Geumseong-dong, Gongju-si (📞 **041/856-3151**), is at the parking lot for Gongsanseong (Gongsan Fortress) and a Cultural Heritage Information Center (📞 **041/840-2548**) at the tomb of King Muryeong.

The city offers a **free bus tour ★★** of some of the area's historic locales every Sunday from April to October. The all-day tour (it lasts 7 to 8 hours) starts at 10am from the parking lot of the Gongsang fortress. It stops at King Muryeong's Tomb, the city's national museum, the Gyeryeongsan Ceramic Art Village, and the folk museum. Call the **Gongju Tourist Info Center** (📞 **041/856-7700**) to make the required reservations.

Exploring Gongju

Gongju National Museum ★ MUSEUM   Founded in 1935, this museum focuses on bronze, silver, and wooden relics excavated from the tomb of the Baekje King Muryeong, who died in A.D. 529. The rest of the items on display were found elsewhere in the area—keep an eye out for the bronze Goddess of Mercy statue from the late 500s and the lovely jade flute.

314-020 Ungjin-dong, Gongju-si, Chungcheongnam-do. 📞 **041/850-6300.** http://gongju.museum.go.kr/html/en/index.jsp. Free admission. Tues–Fri 9am–6pm; Sat–Sun and holidays 9am–7pm (last ticket 1 hr. before closing). Closed Jan 1. From the bus stop near the Gongju Express Bus Terminal, take bus no. 8.

Gongsanseong (Gongsan Fortress) ★★ HISTORIC SITE A fortress dating from the Baekje Kingdom, it was originally made of mud but was renovated to stone in the 17th century, during the Joseon Dynasty. Originally called Unjinseong, its name was changed at that time. It affords a great view of the city and the Geumgang (Geum River). If you can visit on a Saturday from April to October (excluding July–Aug), you can see the Unjinseong guard-changing ceremony every hour from 2 to 8pm. A re-creation of the Baekje ceremony, the costumes and props are almost near replicas of the old style.

In the nearby **Gongju Fortress Park,** the **Geumgang International Arts of Nature Festival** happens annually for 50 days in August and September. There are art installations, temporary outdoor sculptures, seminars, and performances.

Geumseoru, Gongsanseong, Sanseong-dong, Gongju-si, Chungcheongnam-do. ✆ **041/856-0331** or 010/5024-2421 for English. Admission ₩1,200 adults, ₩800 teens, ₩600 children. Nov–Feb daily 7am–5pm; Mar–Oct daily 7am–6pm. From Gongju, take a city bus to Gongsanseong or walk 10 min. from downtown. Free parking.

Gyeryongsan Natural History Museum ☺ MUSEUM The largest natural history museum in the country, this place exhibits more than 300,000 domestic and foreign animals (stuffed, of course), plants, minerals, fossils, mummies, and jewels. When you enter the lobby and spot the life-size dinosaur skeleton, you'll know you're in for a treat.

511-1 Hakbong-li, Banpo-myeon, Gongju-si, Chungcheongnam-do. ✆ **042/824-4055.** http://krnamu.or.kr/eng/index.html. Admission ₩9,000 adults, ₩7,000 seniors 65 and over, ₩6,000 youth. Apr–Oct daily 10am–8pm; Nov–Mar Tues–Sun 10am–6pm. Take bus no. 107 from Daejeon.

King Muryeong's Tomb & Songsan-li Burial Mounds ★ HISTORIC SITE Although most tombs from the Baekje Kingdom were pillaged over the centuries, including six of the seven found here, King Muryeong's tomb miraculously escaped vandals and thieves and was discovered by accident in 1971, while pipes were being installed to prevent the already excavated tombs from flooding. Thankfully the government took precautions, and archaeologists discovered a treasure-trove of Baekje wares in the stone chambers. Today, most of the excavated relics, which include some exquisite examples of Baekje artisans' simple yet stunning gold, silver, and stonework, are now in the Gongju National Museum collection or in the Seoul National Museum. Still, the tombs—which appear from the outside to look like plain grassy mounds—are interesting in their own right, although visitors are no longer allowed inside.

Geumseong-dong, Gongju-si, Chungcheongnam-do. ✆ **041/856-0331.** Admission ₩1,000 adults, ₩500 youth, free for kids 6 and under. Daily 7am–6pm. Closed Lunar New Year and Chuseok. From Gongju Bus Terminal, take local bus no. 1, 25, or 25-1.

Magoksa (Magok Temple) ★★★ TEMPLE Founded by Monk Jajangyulsa in A.D. 640, this lovely temple offers an excellent example of local Buddhist architecture—happily, it was not damaged during any of the wars in the Joseon period. The complex is divided by a stream (in a yin-yang shape), and connected by a stone bridge. In the courtyard is a slim stone **Ocheong Pagoda,** which dates from the Goryeo Dynasty. With its bronze crown, it was influenced by the Lama Buddhist Sect of Tibet and is one of only three such structures left in the world. In the hall behind the pagoda, you'll find an altar dedicated to Vairocana, the Buddha of Infinite Light—the paint is faded, but still visible. This is an excellent place to do a temple stay.

567, Unam-li, Sagok-myeon, Gongju-si, Chungcheongnam-do. ☎ **041/841-6221.** www.magoksa. or.kr (Korean only). Admission ₩2,000 adults, ₩1,500 teens, ₩1,000 children, free to seniors 65 and over and kids 6 and under. Mar–Oct daily 8:30am–6pm; Nov–Feb daily 9am–5pm. From the Gongju Bus Terminal, take city bus no. 7 to the last stop, which should take about 40 min. (buses run daily 6am–8:30pm). It's a 20-min. taxi ride from the terminal. Parking ₩2,000–₩4,000, depending on size of vehicle.

Seokjangni Museum ★ ☺ MUSEUM   The only museum dedicated solely to Korea's prehistory, the museum is located near the Stone Age site of Seokjangni (hence the name). Excavated between 1964 and 1992, the site has yielded proof that human beings have been living on the Korean Peninsula for 700,000 years. In addition to replicas of Stone Age dwellings and tools, there are hands-on exhibits for visitors to experience life back then.

99 Jangam-li, Janggi-myeon, Gongju-si, Chungcheongnam-do. ☎ **042/840-2491.** www.sjn museum.go.kr. Admission ₩1,500 adults, ₩1,000 teens, ₩700 children. Tues–Sun 9am–6pm (last ticket sold 30 min. before closing). Closed other days designated by the mayor. From the Gongju Crosstown Bus Terminal, take local bus no. 15 (which runs every 40 min.) and get off at Jangam-li LPG gas station.

Seonggoksa (Seonggok Temple) ★★ TEMPLE   The construction for this temple began in 1983 and didn't finish until 1995. While the structures aren't architectural wonders, the draw is the hundreds of thousands of statues of the Buddhas and bodhisattvas that surround a giant bronze Buddha, who sits on a lotus base and is quite impressive, if not a bit garish, at 12m (39 ft.) tall. Behind them are 333,333 small Buddha statues, which are backlit at night. If you think the bronze statue is impressive, keep going down the hill and you'll see a taller copper Buddha statue and, just a bit farther around, an even taller Jijang Bosal (the Boddhisattva of Transition, the ruler of the underworld).

Bangmun-li, Useong-myeon, Gongju-si, Chungcheongnam-do. ☎ 042/853-3355. www.seonggoksa. or.kr (Korean only). Admission ₩4,000 adults, ₩3,000 teens, ₩2,000 children, free for kids 6 and under. Nov–Feb daily 7am–5pm; Mar–Oct daily 7am–6pm. From Gongju, take the bus bound for Magoksa and get off at Seonggoksa. A taxi from downtown Gongju should take 15 min.

Where to Stay

Although there are no upscale hotels in Gongju, there are some midpriced and economical sleeping options. A cute place to stay just outside of Magoksa is **Awoollim Pension ★★**, 452-3 Gugye-li, Ugu-eup, Gongju-si (**www.awoollimpension.com** (Korean only); ☎ **041/841-9963**). A wooden cabin-like building with mountain views, the Awoollim has a decor that is a bit girly, but done with care. Pensions are like a combination of a bed-and-breakfast (minus the breakfast, but including a kitchenette) and Korean-style condos. The Awoollim Pension has only six rooms, so it's best to reserve in advance. Their site is only in Korean (and the staff's English isn't great), but e-mail them for information at awlks@naver.com. Doubles start at ₩110,000 to ₩140,000 on weekdays off season, going up to between ₩125,000 and ₩140,000 on popular summer weekends.

To experience the traditional Korean lifestyle, you can stay at the **Gongju Hanok ★**, 337 Eungjin-dong, Gongju-si (☎ **041/840-2763**). The ondol-style rooms have been modernized with TVs, minifridges, and private baths. Rooms that sleep 3 to 8 start at ₩120,000.

One of the better places in town is the **Geumgang Hotel,** 595-8, Singwan-dong, Gongju-si (☎ **041/852-1071**). Rooms go for about ₩50,000 to ₩70,000.

Although not fancy by any means, the rooms are comfortable, relatively spacious, and have beds.

Where to Eat

Gongju is famous for its agricultural products, like their *sagwa* (apples), *bahm* (chestnuts), and *ddalgi* (strawberries), which can be found in their open markets, like the largest and most popular, **Sanseong Shijang.** Otherwise, Gongju has a good variety of locally owned Korean restaurants and not too many Western options.

In front of Gongsanseong is a place to get great *bibimbap* (a mixed rice bowl), **Ochae Bibimbap (𝓒 041/856-0757).** They serve their bibimbap with a variety of seasonal vegetables, some banchan, and *dwenjang* (fermented soybean paste) instead of the usual *gochujang* (chili paste), and it costs only ₩6,000. Also near Gongsanseong is **Saeihak Garden (𝓒 041/854-2030),** well known by locals for their *ddalo gookbap* (a meal of rice and soup, made with beef). They make their soup with beef bones and simmer them for 2 days to extract all the flavor from them. The meal comes with a nice array of banchan and kimchi and costs only ₩6,000, but their meat dishes are a bit more.

For a seriously old-style Korean flavor, go to **Naegohyang Mookjip,** 297 Gongap-li, Banpo-myeon, Gongju-si (𝓒 041/857-4884), whose name translates to "My Hometown *Mook* House." Mook is a Korean savory jelly, and the kind that is locally popular is made from acorns (*dotoli mook*). In a traditional building that's at least 200 years old, they serve up the acorn jelly or *soon dubu* (handmade tofu) in the traditional way. They're located not far from Donghaksa.

THE REST OF CHUNGCHEONGNAM-DO

Located in the west central part of the country, Chungcheongnam-do (South Chungcheong Province) was the center of the ancient Baekje Kingdom. Gongju (above) and Buyeo (discussed below) have the most treasures from that lost civilization, but traces of its history are scattered about the region. Despite its strong ties to Baekje, the region's history dates farther back into the Paleolithic age.

Included in its boundaries is **Gyeoryongsan National Park** and **Taean Marine National Park,** which has some of the best swimming beaches in the country. The provincial capital is Daejeon, which has its own governing body as a "special city." Called Chungnam for short, the province includes the cities of Asan, Boryeong, Cheonan, Gongju, Nonsan, Seosan, and Gyeryong.

In this mainly agricultural province, most of the people here are tied to the land and maintain long-held traditional values. The low plains grow much of the food for the capital region, and its western coasts, though not the best for fishing, are used for salt production. Small islands are located off the coast—the largest being **Anmyeon-do,** which is connected to the Taean Peninsula by bridge.

Essentials

GETTING THERE   The province has no airports, but you can get there by car, bus, or train.

The KTX from Seoul takes 35 to 40 minutes to the Cheonan-Asan station. The **Gyeongbu line** skirts around the eastern edge of the province, connecting from

Seoul to Cheonan, Jochiwon through Daejeon, continuing down to Busan, via Gimcheon and Daegu. The older **Junghang line** connects to the Gyeongbu line at Cheonan and continues west and south through the province, ending at Janghang. Part of the **Honam line** starts from Daejeon going though Dugye and continuing down through Jeolla-do, ending in Mokpo. If taking a train into the area, it's best to stop at Daejeon or Cheonan and transfer to a bus to outlying areas.

You can even get to **Cheonan** from Seoul's subway (line 1), but it takes 1½ to 2½ hours to get here. The train or bus trip is faster, but the subway is cheaper. The most frequent travelers on the subway train are usually older folks, who get to ride the subway for free. Weekends can be standing room only, so it's best to choose alternative transporation instead of this slow ride.

Buses to **Buyeo** leave only from Seoul's Nambu Terminal, once an hour daily from 6:30am to 7:20pm. Costing ₩12,200, the trip takes about 2½ hours. Nonstop buses to **Cheonan** run every 10 to 15 minutes from Seoul's Express Bus Terminal daily from 6am to 9:20pm, costing between ₩4,800 and ₩7,100 with a travel time of about an hour. From Seoul's Nambu Terminal, buses run to Cheonan about every half-hour, daily from 6:40am to 7:40pm, costing ₩5,200 for 80 minutes of travel time.

Buses to **Taean** go from Seoul's Nambu Terminal every 30 to 50 minutes daily from 6:40am to 8pm, a ride of 2 hours and 20 minutes. Buses also run from the DongSeoul Bus Terminal, only three times daily from 7:40am to 5pm. Although it's only ₩500 less, it takes almost twice as long.

Buses to **Geumsan** only go from Seoul's Express Bus Terminal every 40 minutes, daily from 7am to 6:40pm. Fares run at ₩9,400 to ₩13,700 with about 2 hours and 40 minutes of travel time. Buses also go to **Yeongi** from this terminal every hour daily from 6:30am to 8:30pm, costing between ₩5,900 and ₩8,700 for a 1-hour-and-40-minute ride.

Nonstop buses to **Hongseong** only go from Seoul's Nambu Terminal 18 times a day from 6:40am to 7:30pm. The 2-hour ride costs about ₩9,100. Also from the Nambu Terminal, express buses run to **Nonsan** 10 times daily from 6:50am to 6pm, costing ₩10,200 for a 3-hour trip. Buses to **Seocheon** run only twice a day from the Nambu Terminal at 7am and 4:40pm, costing ₩14,600 and taking almost 4½ hours. Buses run from this terminal 13 times daily to **Yesan,** 7am to 7:05pm, costing ₩7,100 for about 2 hours and 20 minutes of travel time.

From the **Seongnam Intercity Bus Terminal,** buses run on an irregular schedule (about every hour), daily from 6:20am to 7:15pm. The 1-hour ride costs about ₩4,600. Buses to Geumsan run daily only at noon, costing ₩11,200 and taking about 3 hours. Buses to Asan run about every hour, daily from 7:50am to 6:50pm, costing ₩6,000 for a 90-minute ride. Buses to **Iksan** run daily at 7:30am, 8:40am, 9:30am, 10:30am, noon, 1pm, 2pm, 4pm, and 5:50pm. Costing about ₩11,000, the travel takes about 3 hours. Buses to **Gimje** leave daily at around the same time, but cost ₩13,000 and travel time is an additional 30 minutes. Buses to **Busan** take about 4 hours and run daily at 7:30am, 8:40am, 10:30am, noon, 2pm, and 4pm, costing ₩14,000.

The **Seohaean Expressway** (road 15) runs from Seoul down the western coast outside of Boryeong and continuing down Mokpo in Jeollanam-do. The **Gyeongbu Expressway** (road 1) cuts through Daejeon and continues down to Daegu and Busan in Gyeongsang-do. When roads 17, 25, and 30 are completed in Cheonan, it will be faster to get through parts of the province with Gongju serving as the intersection for these new expressways.

The only ferry port in the province is at **Boryeong** (℃ **041/930-5000**), which has domestic service to nearby islands Anmyeon-do, Oeyeon-do, Godae-do, Nok-do, Sapsi-do, Wonsan-do, Janggo-do, Ho-do, and Hyoja-do. To get to the ferry terminal from either the Daecheon Train Station or Bus Terminal, take any bus heading for Sinheuk-dong or Daecheon Beach. Get off at the last stop (about a 20- to 30-min. ride). Taxis should take about 15 minutes.

GETTING AROUND   There are local buses available that can take you to most tourist attractions. In such a rural area, though, many of the buses don't have numbers and will just have their destinations written in Korean. Most small-town bus stops are right in front of local grocery or convenience stores. So ask the owner which bus to take. *Tip:* Buses don't always stop at bus stops, so be sure to raise your hand to flag down the driver.

Taxis are available outside of intercity bus and train stations, or can be flagged down on the street, if you can find them. Taxi drivers in the region generally don't speak English, so be sure you can say the name of your destination or have it written in Korean for them to read.

VISITOR INFORMATION   The province's main **Tourist Information Center,** 57 Dongnam-gu, Cheonan-si, Chungcheongnam-do (℃ **041/521-2038;** http://tour. chungnam.net/ctnt/engl/index.jsp), is located next to Cheonan Station. It's open all year round daily from 9am to 6pm, and there are maps and brochures for the region and some English-speaking staff.

In Buyeo you can find the **Buyeo Tourist Information Center,** 112-1 725 Dongnam-li, Buyeo-eup, Buyeo-gun (℃ **041/832-0101**), at the entrance to Buso-sanseong. There are also a couple of tourist info booths in front of the Buyeo National Museum and inside Jeongnimsaji.

In Asan, the **Tourist Information Center,** 69-10 Oncheon-dong, Asan-si (℃ **041/1644-2468**), is located in front of Onyang Oncheon Station. The **Boryeong Tourist Information Center,** 321-2 Daecheon-dong, Boryeong-si (℃ **041/932-2023**), is in front of Daecheon Station.

Buyeo

Buyeo is both a town and a county, and it was the capital of the Baekje Kingdom from A.D. 538 until its defeat by the Shilla in 660. Though today Buyeo is surrounded by farms, during its short reign it was a center of culture and art, and the town is proud of its heritage. Indeed, some of the sidewalks here are paved with tiles meant to replicate those used in neighboring royal tombs.

The mascot of this small city, which is nestled alongside the Geumgang (Geum River), is "Geumdongi," a cartoon version of a famous gilt-bronze incense burner from the Baekje Kingdom. It's just one example of the way history pervades this place. For more information, the county's official site is http://www.buyeo.go.kr/eng/html/main.html.

GETTING HERE   Buses from Seoul's Nambu Terminal (Seoul subway line 3, exit 5) depart about once an hour and costs about ₩12,500. The ride takes about 2 hours and 20 minutes.

EXPLORING BUYEO

Buyeo National Museum ★★★ MUSEUM   Built to reflect the architectural styles prevalent during the Baekje period, the museum has many interesting artifacts from the ancient kingdom, many of them excavated from the royal tombs in Neung-san-li. One of the most impressive items on display is the Geumdongi, a gilded bronze incense burner recovered from one of the tombs. The base of this unique piece is a rising dragon and it's topped by a phoenix—it is the item that is most emblematic of the height of Baekje skill and craftsmanship. They also have relics that date from prehistory to the Joseon period, including a gilt bronze sitting Buddha, prehistoric pottery, and musical instruments. All are displayed in three exhibit halls and an outdoor exhibit space, where a variety of stones from the area are displayed.

San 16-1 Dongnam-li, Buyeo, Chungcheongnam-do. ℓ **041/833-8562.** http://buyeo.museum. go.kr. Admission free. Tues–Sun 9am–6pm (last tickets sold at 5pm). Closed Jan 1. 15-min. walk from Buyeo Bus Station.

Gwanchoksa (Gwanchok Temple) ★★ MUSEUM   Located southwest of Buyeo, near Nonsan, this temple has one of the country's most unusual Buddha statues. Dating from the Goryeo period, the **Eunjin Mireuk** (the Maitreya Buddha of Eunjin) has a small body, a large head, and a flat mortarboard-like hat on top of its headpiece with wind chimes hanging from its four corners. Standing at 18m (59 ft.), it's the largest Buddha statue dating that far back.

254, Gwanchok-li, Eunjin-myeon, Nonsan-si, Chungcheongnam-do. ℓ **041/736-5700.** Admission ₩1,500 adults, ₩800 youth. Daily 7am–6pm. From Nonsan Bus Terminal, take a bus bound for Gayagok and get off at Gwanchoksa. It should be a 10-min. taxi ride. Parking ₩1,500–₩3,000 depending on vehicle size.

Jeongnimsaji (Site of Jeongnim Temple) TEMPLE   Excavated relics show that the temple site dates back to the Baekje Kingdom (not a surprise given its location). But its name dates from a tile found near the remains of a sitting Buddha statue, which reads, TAEPYEONG THE EIGHTH YEAR MUJIN JEONGNIMSA DAE JANG DANG CHO, which falls during the reign of King Hyeonjong of the Goryeo Dynasty, or around A.D. 1028. After a 5-year excavation, locations and arrangements of buildings and ponds were confirmed and now the site shows where they were. To prevent further deterioration of the remaining Buddha statue, a structure has been built around it. Besides the Buddha, only a five-tier granite pagoda and a lotus pond remain of the original temple complex. A Baekje museum is also on this site.

36 Jeongnimsaji-gil, Buyeo-eup, Buyeo-gun, Chungcheongnam-do. ℓ **041/832-2721.** www. jeongnimsaji.or.kr. Admission ₩1,000 adults, ₩500 youth. Oct–Mar daily 10am–5pm; Apr–Sept daily 9am–7pm. Located in the center of town, the temple site is a 10-min. walk from Buyeo Inter-city Bus Terminal.

Tumuli (Baekje Royal Tombs) of Neungsan-li ★ HISTORIC SITE   There are seven tombs grouped together in Neungsan-li, which is located on the way to Nonsan from Buyeo. Thought to have been the tombs of kings or royal family members from the Baekje Kingdom, they are smaller in scale than the Shilla tombs found in Gyeongju. One central tomb is similar in structure to King Muryeong's grave in Songsan-li, and they are decorated with directional animals/gods and astronomical symbols. Most of the excavated artifacts (those that were left after burglars got there first) are now in the collection of the Buyeo National Museum.

The Legend of the White Horse

The Baengma (White Horse) River runs past Buyeo, and in A.D. 660 the Shilla and Tang troops had to cross it in order to make their final assault on the Baekje stronghold at Busosan. Legend has it that every time the Tang general, Su Dingfang, attempted to cross the river, a thick fog would form. The general was convinced that King Mu, the Baekje leader, had transformed himself into a dragon so that he could protect his people. So General Su cut off the head of a white horse and, using it as bait, went fishing for the dragon. It worked—he caught the dragon and was able to invade, and defeat, the Baekje Kingdom.

254 Dongnam-li, Buyeo-eup, Buyeo-gun, Chungcheongnam-do. ℂ **041/830-2114** (Korean only). Admission ₩1,500 adults, ₩900 teens, ₩700 children. Mar–Oct daily 8am–6pm; Nov–Feb daily 8am–5pm. From the Buyeo Bus Station, take a bus going to Nonsan and get off at the Tumuli in Neungsan-li.

BUSOSAN (MT. BUSO)

This hill overlooking Buyeo is the site of the Baekje Kingdom's last fortress—and the site where the kingdom fell to the Shilla armies, which had joined forces with Tang Dynasty troops from China.

Busosanseong (Busosan Fortress) ★ HISTORIC SITE A mud fortress on top of Busosan, it was the primary Baekje defense against the Shilla for 123 years, starting in 538. It was reconstructed in 605 and today only a few foundations and earthworks remain. Historians believe that the Baekje royalty used the fortress as a park during times of peace.

San 1, Gwanbuk-li, Buyeo-eup, Buyeo-gun, Chungcheongnam-do. ℂ **041/830-2527.** Admission (includes entry to Goransa and Nakhwa-am) ₩2,000 adults, ₩1,100 teens, ₩1,000 children, free for seniors 65 and over and kids 6 and under. Mar–Oct daily 7am–7pm; Nov–Feb daily 8am–5pm. It's a 10-min. walk to the old gate of Busosan from Buyeo Intercity Bus Terminal.

Goransa (Goran Temple) TEMPLE This small temple, located below Nakhwa-am, was limited in size by its rocky location. The temple's name comes from *gorancho*, a medicinal herb that grows nearby. But more famous than the structure is the nearby spring water. Legend has it that a cup of this water will make a person 3 years younger. There is a local tale that an old man became a baby after drinking too much of this water. If you get a chance, take a ferry ride along the river for a scenic view of the area.

Busosan, around Gugyo-li, Gwanbuk-li, and Ssangbuk-li, Buyeo-eup, Buyeo-gun, Chungcheongnam-do. No phone. Admission (includes entry to Busosanseong and Nakhwa-am) ₩2,000 adults, ₩1,100 teens, ₩1,000 children, free for seniors 65 and over and kids 6 and under. Mar–Oct daily 7am–7pm; Nov–Feb daily 8am–5pm. It's a 10-min. walk to the old gate to Busosan from Buyeo Intercity Bus Terminal.

Nakhwa-am ★★ HISTORIC SITE The "Rock of the Falling Flowers" is located at the top of the summit overlooking the Baengma River. You can get a nice view from the **Baekhwajeong** pavilion. According to old legend, 3,000 women from the Baekje royal court jumped to their deaths into the river below. It was said that they chose an honorable death rather than dying at the hands of the enemy (the Shilla–Tang alliance).

About 2km (1¼ miles) to the east is another site of Baekje graves at Neunganggol. Excavated from 1995 to 1996, these tombs with their tunnel-like stone rooms helped solve some of the mysteries of Baekje burials. Although there isn't much to see here, there are single graves, double tombs, and a grave for children.

15 Neungsan-li, Buyeo-eup, Buyeo-gun, Chungcheongnam-do. No phone. Admission (includes entry to Busosanseong and Goransa) ₩2,000 adults, ₩1,100 teens, ₩1,000 children, free for seniors 65 and over and kids 6 and under. Mar–Oct daily 7am–7pm; Nov–Feb daily 8am–5pm. It's a 10-min. walk to the old gate to Busosan from Buyeo Intercity Bus Terminal.

WHERE TO STAY

There are no upscale accommodations in Buyeo, but there are a number of motels and yeogwan available in town. One of your best options is the **Baekje Tourist Hotel,** 433 Ssangbuk-li, Buyeo-eup, Buyeo-gun, Chungcheongnam-do (www.bchotel.co.kr, Korean only; ✆ 041/835-0870). Simple but comfortable, the location has a restaurant that serves Korean cuisine and Korean versions of Western food, as well as a cafe. The rooms have A/C, satellite cable, and a hair dryer. Standard rooms go for ₩68,000–₩120,000.

Totally on the other end of the economic scale is the **Samjung Buyeo Youth Hostel,** 105-1 Gugeyo-li, Buyeo-eup, Buyeo-gun, Chungcheongnam-do (www.buyeoyh.com; ✆ 041/835-3101). Though it's mostly for groups of traveling school-children, adults can get a bed for ₩27,000 if you're a member.

WHERE TO EAT

Buyeo isn't known for any specific dishes, but there are some solid places here that serve good traditional Korean food. The most popular place in town is the **Gudulae Dolssambap,** 96-3 Gua-li, Buyeo-eup, Buyeo-gun, Chungcheongnam-do (✆ 041/836-9259 or 041/835-0463). The place offers a delicious *dolssambap* (stone pot rice served with lettuce and other leaves for wrapping), and it comes with a gener-ous number of banchan and *suyuk* (cold, sliced pork), which makes the price higher. They give you a raw egg for you to pop into your rice so that it can cook in the hot stone pot and the rice gets nice and crispy on the bottom. The *dolssam jeongshik* (traditional rice meal in a stone pot) is still a bargain at ₩10,000. Unfortunately, the sign is only in Korean, so look for an orange sign with black lettering outlined thinly in white.

If you want a *maeuntahng* (spicy seafood hot pot), the best place in the area is **Baengmagang Shikdang** (✆ 041/835-2752), which is right across from the Baek-jaedaegyo (bridge). They also have a pretty tasty grilled eel, fresh from the river (hence the name of the restaurant). Most dishes fall in the ₩10,000 to ₩20,000 range.

If you just want a good Korean spread, go to the **Gaeseong Shikdang** (✆ 041/834-3999), where the resident *halmuhni* (grandma) has been making *han jeongshik* (traditional Korean meals) for over 45 years. The country-style han jeong-shik will set you back only ₩10,000, but you can splurge and get one of the beef or pork dishes for ₩25,000. This unassuming restaurant is located on the main drag if you're going toward Guncheong, across the street from Jeongnimsa.

Geumsan

Geumsan is a small country town in the hills just south of Daejeon. Well known for its insam, this little town is responsible for about 70% of Korea's ginseng production. If you happen to be visiting in the fall, don't miss the annual **Geumsan Insam**

Festival, which includes traditional folk performances, ginseng cooking contests, and all things ginseng.

Buses from Seoul's Express Bus Terminal go to Geumsan about every 1½ to 2 hours, daily from 6:30am to 6:30pm. Bus fares range from the regular ₩11,200 to ₩16,800 for a fancier bus.

You can also make a stop in Daejeon and transfer to a Geumsan-bound bus from there. You can take buses or trains to Daejeon from Seoul or any number of major cities (see the Daejeon section earlier for fares and details). Buses from Daejeon run about every 30 minutes to Geumsan.

To get to the **Geumsan Ginseng and Medicinal Herb Market,** just walk about 5 minutes from the Geumsan Bus Terminal (follow the signs on the main drag). The best time to come is when the ginseng has been freshly harvested in the fall. The marketplace consists of a large alleyway lined with shops selling the root as well as a variety of other medicinal herbs. The **Susam Center** (which sells the root fresh), the Ginseng Agricultural Cooperative, and the Ginseng Shopping Center are all located in the area. Try the *insam makgeolli* (milky rice wine made with ginseng) or deep-fried ginseng for only ₩1,000 a piece from one of the street vendors here. You might not want to buy any dry roots to arouse the suspicions of Customs officers, but you can get a bag of red ginseng candy as a souvenir.

If you're in the area for more than a day, you might want to try a hike in **Daedunsan Provincial Park,** which is reachable via local bus from Geumsan. Although the peaks aren't very high, the hike will still give you a workout and you'll be rewarded with spectacular views of the craggy rocks and the valley below. The easiest way to the top is by taking the cable car, ₩8,000 round-trip, ₩5,000 one-way. About a 10-minute walk from the cable car station is the best part of the mountains, the **Geumgang Gureum (Cloud Bridge),** a suspension bridge built across a crevasse 81m (266 ft.) high. Another 10-minute walk from the bridge brings you to a metal staircase that leads to the top and a wonderful view. Entrance to the park is free, but parking is ₩1,000 to ₩2,000 per car. Express buses from Daejeon run 6 times a day and take about 40 minutes. Buses from Jeonju run 5 times a day and take about an hour.

Geumsan is a small village with no large hotels, but there are a handful of older motels in the downtown area. One economical option is the **Hwanggeumjang Motel,** 429 Jungdo-li, Geumsan-eup, Geumsan-gun, Chungcheongnam-do (© **041/ 753-2828**). Although the owners only speak Korean, they're friendly and will give you a standard room for about ₩30,000 on weeknights. The hotel is about a 5-minute walk from the bus station.

Boryeong & Daecheon

A small seaside village on the coast of Chungcheongnam-do, Boryeong is known for its beaches. Its most famous beach, **Daecheon Beach,** is the site of the annual **Boryeong Mud Festival ★★★** (© **041/930-3820** or -3822; www.mudfestival. or.kr), which is hugely popular with foreigners living in South Korea and happens every year in July. The mud from the area's beaches is sold throughout the country for its healthful and cosmetic properties. A bunch of small rural islands lie off its coast in the Yellow Sea, some of which can be reached by ferry from Daecheon Port.

Boryeong is on the **Jung-ang rail line,** which connects to Seoul via the Gyeongbu Line. From Seoul, take a train to Yeongdeungpo Station and transfer to a train to Daecheon Station.

The **Seohaean Expressway** (15) connects Boryeong, Seoul, Jeolla-do, and nearby coastal towns. Trains and buses run more frequently from Seoul (with travel time doubled on the roads) during high season from early July to late August. From the **DongSeoul Bus Terminal,** take a bus headed for Daecheon. Buses run daily from 6:40am to 5:50pm, taking about 3 hours. From Seoul's Express Bus Terminal, buses headed for Daecheon run daily from 6am to 9:50pm, taking about 2 hours and 20 minutes.

Other than the tourist info booth (𝒞 **041/932-2023;** http://ubtour.go.kr/lang/en/index.jsp) in front of Daecheon Station, there is a **tourist information center** (𝒞 **041/933-7051**) inside the Mud House in Daecheon Beach, open 9am to 6pm daily.

The best beach on the west coast is **Daecheon Beach,** located about 12km (7½ miles) west of Boryeong. The shallow beach and warm waters make this an ideal beach for swimming. If you come during the popular summer months, you'll think that most of South Korea had pretty much the same idea that you did. The mud from this beach is supposed to have astringent qualities and benefits the skin, yielding mud packs, mud soaps, and other beauty products. The southern end of the beach is usually quieter, with private homes. This is in stark contrast to the rest of the beach's noise and tourist attractions. At this veritable playground for Koreans, there are plenty of bars, nightclubs, *noraebang* (karaoke rooms), billiard rooms, cafes, and hwae restaurants.

If you want to experience a mud bath, the **Boryeong Mud House** (𝒞 **041/931-4021;** 2022 Shinheuk-dong, Boryeong-si; open Tues-Sun) offers a mud bath, sauna, and "aroma spa" for only ₩5,000. Massages and mud packs cost extra and you can get a number of mud products (including mud shampoo) to take home with you.

South of Boryeong is the small **Muchangpo Beach,** the first beach opened to the public on the west coast (in 1928). Although it's not very populous or favored by tourists, if you time your visit right you can see the "Moses Miracle" parting of the sea, on a smaller scale but similar to Jin-do, where the waters off the island also part at certain times. In the middle and end of each lunar month, the water recedes and reveals the mud and rock below. There you can join the locals in catching baby octopus, sea cucumbers, and various shellfish that normally live underwater. From Daecheon, the city bus takes about 40 minutes.

There are plenty of places to sleep in the Daecheon Beach area. If you don't mind sleeping on the floor, there are dozens of minbak. Doubles are ₩30,000 on off-season weekdays, ₩50,000 on weekends. They charge an extra ₩5,000 per person for up to four. High season, rooms go up to ₩80,000, with an additional ₩10,000 for each extra person. Motel prices are just a bit higher during high season (comparable in low season), but you'll have a firm bed to sleep on.

The **Ocean of Fantasy Motel,** 945-15 Sinheuk-dong, Boryeong-si (www.oceanoffantasy.com; 𝒞 **041/931-1111**), is a good option if you want a small kitchen. Don't let the name fool you. It's not a love motel but rather good for families (sleeping four, six, or eight). There are motel, condo, or pension-style rooms, all with kitchenettes (the condo rooms have the smallest ones). Their bathrooms are a bit small with only a shower head and no tub, but they're clean and functional. Ask for a room with a balcony on an upper floor to get the best ocean views. Motel-style rooms are the cheapest with off-season weekdays starting at ₩40,000 to ₩50,000.

Unless you absolutely have to stay overnight, Daecheon Beach is best as a day trip from elsewhere, especially during the summer months.

If you visit Boryeong in the winter, you can enjoy the **Cheonbuk Oyster Festival** (*©* **041/641-9031**), which happens usually in early December. Apparently, the geographic climate of the area and, of course, their much-touted mud, help create the best climate for tasty oysters. In the winter, the little devils are grilled over open flames, making their shells pop open and baking the soft meat inside. They are savory, slightly salty, and chewy. You can try the grilled oysters with some local soju, or have some of the other dishes like raw *gul* (oysters), pork ribs cooked with oysters, *gul bap* (rice mixed with oysters), and *gul jeon* (oyster flatcakes).

If you're feeling more adventurous, another local seafood delicacy is small pen shells. Boryeong accounts for 60% of domestic production for this shellfish and winter is the peak season. Locals eat their *myeok gook* (seaweed soup) and *jook* (porridge) with these little shellfish. Another type of seafood that is best in the winter is the *ganjaemi,* a fish that looks like a small stingray but tastes very similar to skate. Ganjaemi are the most tender in the winter, before their bones get harder and flesh thickens when the water warms. Since it's so soft, locals eat the fish raw, dipped in a seasoned gochujang, or cooked in a maeuntahng.

Taean Marine National Park

Taean Marine National Park (*©* **041/672-9737**) stretches from Taean Peninsula (South Korea's westernmost stretch of land) down to the southern end of Anmyeon-do. It includes 327 sq. km (about 126 sq. miles) of land and sea. Within its boundaries are about 130 islands, many of which are just tiny specks and totally uninhabitable. Designated in 1978, it includes 30 sandy and very swimmable beaches, including what's considered to be South Korea's third most beautiful, **Mallipo.** Mallipo Beach, the largest in Taean, is located on the western end. This broad sandy beach's former beauty is now marred by the dozens of *hwae jib* (raw fish restaurants), motels, and shops that butt right up to the sand. About a 30-minute walk from here is **Cheollipo Beach,** a smaller, more run-down version of Mallipo, with a couple of minbak and a small fishing harbor. You can take a bus to Taean from Seoul's Nambu Terminal every 40 minutes from 6:40am to 8pm, which takes about 2 hours and 20 minutes.

In between these two beaches is **Cheollipo Arboretum** (*©* **042/672-9982;** www.chollipo.org), a scenic location built by an American expat, Carl Ferris Miller. Since its opening in 1966, he has collected over 6,500 species of both native and other plants, which grow in the seven different habitats within its boundaries. Once accessible only to scholars and scientists, the arboretum is now open to the public for an admission fee of ₩7,000 adults, ₩5,000 seniors, ₩4,000 teens, ₩3,000 kids; an extra ₩1,000 on weekends. It's open Thursday to Tuesday 8am to 5:30pm April through October, closing at 5pm from November to March; closed Lunar New Year, Chuseok, and Christmas. It is now run by the founder's son. Buses to the arboretum run 8 times daily from the Taen Bus Terminal and take about 35 minutes.

Other popular beaches in the area include **Sinduri Beach,** located farther north, and **Hagampo,** which is even father up from there. Other than the beaches, recreational fishing is popular off the shores, for fish, crab, lobster, and oyster.

Trains from Seoul to Hongseong run every hour daily, starting from 5:20am until 8:40pm, with a travel time of about 3 hours. The bus station is located right across the street from the train station. Express buses from Seoul's Nambu Terminal go to Taean every 10 to 49 minutes from 6:40am to 10pm, taking about 2 hours and 30 minutes. Less frequent are buses from the DongSeoul Bus Terminal to Taean.

Running only three times daily, they take about 3 hours. From Taean, regular and express buses to Mallipo run every 20 min.

You can also get a long-distance bus directly to Taean from Incheon Airport (bus stop 9D), which runs every 60 to 90 minutes from 7am to 7:40pm, costing ₩14,500 to ₩21,700.

ISLANDS

Anmyeon-do ★★   The sixth-largest island in the country is located about 30km (19 miles) from Taean. Originally a waterway created to help transport ships during the Joseon era, it became an artificially made island. A bridge built in 1970 connects it to Nammyeon on the peninsula. There are 16 beaches on the island's coast as well as a plethora of pine trees (called *anmyeonsong* that only grow here) near the beaches and in **Anmyeon-do National Forest,** located in the center of the island. The island is one of the best places in the country to watch the sunset, and Kkotji Beach is the best on the island, because of its cute bridge and rock formations.

There is a small seafood marketplace, **Baeksajang ★★★** 🛍, just up the road from Kkotji Beach, where you can choose fish, crustaceans, or shellfish from a variety of bubbling tanks. They'll cook your fresh catch, slice it raw, or fire up the tabletop grill so you can cook it yourself. I recommend getting fresh shrimp, which you can cook on a bed of sea salt over hot coals.

Gonam-myeon, Anmyeon-eup, Taean-gun, Chungcheongnam-do. ☎ **041/670-2612.** www. anmyondo.com (Korean only). Free admission. Daily 24 hr. From Taean Intercity Bus Terminal, take a bus to Anmyeon-eup, which runs every 30 min. daily 7am–9pm. It takes 40 min. You can also take a direct bus from Seoul's Nambu Bus Terminal. Buses run daily 6:40am–4pm with a travel time of 3 hr.

Sapsi-do   This small island (whose name translates to "Arrow Island," because of its shape) used to be a little-known secret with relatively unspoiled beaches and clean water. Now, however, so many South Koreans on trips have discovered it that practically every household here offers minbak. Outside of the summer season, though, it is still a quiet retreat. Its three main beaches are **Geomeolneomeo, Jinneomeo,** and **Bamseom Beach,** the least developed of the three

Take a ferry bound for the island from Daecheon Harbor. To get to the harbor, take a bus from Daecheon Station (buses run about every 15 min.).

Seosan

Located on the end of the Taean Peninsula, Seosan is a quiet little fishing town with some interesting historical remains. The most famous is the **Seosanmaae Samjong Bulsang** (the "Seosan Buddha Triad"; ☎ **041/660-2538**), located in the hills east of town in Yonghyeon-li, Unsan-myeon. Created during the Baekje era, this bas relief carved on the face of stone cliffs depicts a smiling central Buddha figure with a bodhisattva to the right and a meditating Maitreya to the left. The mountain where these figures are located, **Unsan,** served as the main thoroughfare of the Taean Peninsula and the major passageway from Buyeo to boats heading to China during the Baekje period. This is a prime example of the cultural influence of China at that time. About a kilometer up the road, you'll chance upon **Bowonsaji,** a former temple site. From the Seosan Bus Terminal, take a bus headed for Unsan, which runs every 10 to 15 minutes and takes about 30 to 40 minutes.

The most important temple in the area is **Gaeshimsa,** Shinchang-li, Unsan-myeon, Seosan (☎ **041/688-2256**), located in the northern part of Deoksan Provincial Park. Founded by Monk Hyegam in A.D. 651, it was rebuilt by Monk Cheonueung.

It was burned down in the 1470s and rebuilt again a decade later. The temple is especially nice during the spring when the valley comes alive with cherry blossoms. From the Seosan Bus Terminal, take a bus bound for Gaeshimsa and it's quite a bit of a walk from there.

About 12km (7½ miles) southeast of the town is **Haemi,** home of the former **Haemi Fortress,** 16, Eumnae-li, Haemi-myeon, Seosan-si, Chungcheongnam-do (© **041/660-2540**). Built in 1421, it was originally built as a prison for captured Japanese invaders. From 1414 to 1651, Haemi served as a center and occasional training spot for the military. In 1866, about 1,000 Catholics were executed here for their beliefs during the Byeonin Persecution. There is a monument for those martyrs near the west gate. The south gate (Nammun) is still in its original form, while the west (Seomun) and east (Dongmun) were renovated in 1974.

An older but similar fortress lies in **Hongseong,** which is located about midway between Boryeong and Seosan. The **Hongseong Simgeumseong** was originally made of mud, but later reconstructed in stone. Located behind city hall, the fortress was largely destroyed in an earthquake during the 1970s, but parts of it were rebuilt in 1982. There isn't much left—a restored magistrate's office (from the Joseon Dynasty), a pavilion, and a front gate—but it's still a pleasant walk around its perimeter. A train service is provided from Cheonan and Yongsan Station in Seoul (the ride takes about 2 hr.). Buses run from Seoul's Gangnam Station, Cheonan, and Daejeon.

Cheonan

Cheonan is the second-largest city in Chungcheongnam-do. Cheonan and its neighboring city Asan share a station on the KTX train line and a train from Seoul takes only about half an hour. It is located on the **Gyeongbu rail line** and it is where the **Jung-ang rail line** branches off, making its way down the province's west side. There is a **tourist information center** (© **041/551-2011;** daily 9am–6pm) at the KTX station, where you can get maps, but the staff here speak limited English.

From Incheon Airport, buses to Cheonan can be found at bus stop 9D. Buses run about every 2½ hours from 6:30am to 7:20pm daily and cost about ₩17,700.

A few kilometers from the center of town is **Taejosan Park,** on whose mountain sits one of the largest seated bronze Buddhas in all of Asia, inside the temple **Gakwonsa ★★** (© **041/561-3545;** www.gakwonsa.or.kr). The 15m-high (49-ft.) statue weighs 60 tons and took 2 years to make (1975–77). It was built in the hope of unifying the two Koreas. You will have to walk up 203 stairs (the number represents merit and virtue in the Buddhist religion) to reach it, but you'll be rewarded with a nice view of the city below. Buses run to Gakwonsa regularly from downtown Cheonan.

The city is most famous to Koreans for being the birthplace of Korean independence heroine Yu Gwan-Soon, a 17-year-old student who rallied against the repressive Japanese Occupation and was killed for participating in a student uprising in 1919. **Independence Hall,** 230 Namhwa-li, Mokcheon-eup, Cheonan-si (© **041/560-0014;** www.i815.or.kr/html/en/), was built here to memorialize Korea's fight for independence from the Japanese who controlled Korea's fate from the 1870s to 1945. The largest museum in the country, it is even more nationalistic than other Korean museums, which are busting with national pride already. Admission is free, but parking is ₩2,000 to ₩3,000. The museum is open Tuesday through Sunday 9:30am to 6pm March through October, and until 5pm November to February, with last admissions an hour before closing (open Mon on national holidays). Local bus nos. 320, 350, 352, 380, 381, 382, 390, 400, 410, and 420 go to the museum (the 400-series buses are "seated" buses).

If you're looking for a place to sleep, just cross the street from the bus terminal and walk straight for 1 block and turn right. There you'll find a handful of motels, including **Joatel,** 455-8 Sinbu-dong, Cheonan-si (☎ **041/622-7942**), which opened in 2004. There are PCs, Internet access, and good bathtubs and showers with rooms going for ₩40,000 to ₩60,000, with an additional charge of ₩10,000 on weekends. The only unusual thing is that they won't give you a key, but the owners speak enough English and there's always someone there to let you in.

A more upscale option is the **Cheonan Metro Tourist Hotel,** 57-9, Daeheung-dong, Cheonan-si (☎ **041/622-8211**), an 11-story hotel conveniently located within walking distance of Cheonan Station. Local bus nos. 100, 230, 330, 420, and 900 also stop at the hotel. Their on-site restaurant is affordable and convenient but nothing to write home about. There are standard rooms for ₩150,000 and suites starting at ₩260,000.

One of Cheonan's most famous foods is *hodo gwaja* (walnut cookies), a round, walnut-shaped dough mixed with crushed walnuts and sweet red bean in the middle. Walnuts were first brought to Korea by local Monk Yu Cheongsin, who brought a young tree from China. Since then, **Gwangdeoksa** has been the largest walnut-producing site in the country. The original walnut tree, which is over 400 years old, still grows at the temple today. All the bakeries in town sell these fun and inexpensive treats. One place near the train station is **Cheonandang** (☎ **041/555-5111**).

Another delicacy of the region is the *Byeongcheon soondae,* a special kind of Korean blood sausage created here about 50 years ago. Because a pork and ham factory was created in Byeongcheon-myeon, the people used the ox blood and vegetables instead of the usual kimchi and *japchae* (sweet potato noodles) inside the sausages. The result was a richer sausage that became popular with locals and visitors alike. If you head over to Byeongcheon-li, you'll find a bunch of *soondae* restaurants located here. The oldest one is **Cheonghwajib** (☎ **041/564-1558**), which sells a bowl of *soondae gook* (sausage stew) for ₩6,000 and a plate of soondae for ₩10,000, which is large enough to share with a friend.

Asan

Asan is located about an hour's drive south of Seoul off the Seoul–Busan Expressway. A small town, it's a popular honeymoon spot for native Koreans because of the **Onyang Hot Springs,** which Asan has incorporated into its town. It shares a KTX station, the **Cheonan-Asan Station,** with its neighbor, and the train ride from Seoul takes just about 30 minutes. The city's website is **www.asan.go.kr**.

The most famous historical site is **Hyeonchungsa** (☎ **041/539-4600**; www.hcs. go.kr), a shrine built in honor of General Yi Sun-Shin of Turtle Ship fame. Hours are Wednesday to Monday 9am to 6pm (until 5pm Nov–Feb), the last entry is 1 hour before closing. Admission is ₩500 for adults, ₩300 for youth, free for children 5 and under and seniors 65 and over. From either the Cheonan Bus Terminal or the train station, take bus no. 900, 910, 920, or any bus heading for Hyeonchungsa. Buses run frequently and it's about an hour's ride. From the Onyang Bus Terminal, take bus no. 900, 910, 920, or any bus headed for the shrine. The ride takes about 15 to 20 minutes.

More fun and relaxing is the **Asan Spavis ★★ ☺** (☎ **041/539-2000**; 288-6 Sinsu-li, Ombung-myeon, Asan-si; www.spavis.co.kr), a popular spa and water park located in the Geumho Resort complex. It has a huge wave pool that can fit up to 1,000 people. The spa is open on weekdays 8am to 10pm, from 7am to 11pm on weekends or holidays; the "bade" pool opens from 9am to 7pm weekdays and 8am to 8pm weekends. The oncheon pool is open 10am to 6pm weekdays, 9am to 7pm weekends; and the water park opens 10am to 6pm daily. The oncheon plus spa (which gives you access to the bade pool and everything else) is ₩29,000 for adults, ₩22,000 for kids on weekdays, and ₩43,000 for adults, ₩30,000 for children on weekends and holidays. Entrance to just the oncheon is 50% less. From the Onyang Bus Terminal, cross the street and take bus no. 512 or 980 to Asan Oncheon. The buses run every hour and it's about a 30-minute ride. (A taxi from there will cost about ₩10,000.) From the Cheonan Bus Terminal, take bus no. 980 to Asan Oncheon. The buses run every hour and take about 45 minutes.

Deoksungsan

Located in Yesan County, the Deoksung mountain ranges are known for their unusual shapes, which locals say look like people or ferocious beasts. The nice thing about Deoksungsan is that it's beautiful but has gentle slopes, which makes for good hiking for even the less fit. An excellent hiking course starts from Sudeoksa up to the mountain's peak and then around past Jeonghyesa and back to Sudeoksa. For those looking for a place to sleep and a nice soak after a day of hiking, the **Resom Spa Castle** (© 041/330-8000; 361, Sadong-li, Deosan-myeon, Yesan-gun; www.m-castle.co.kr), which uses water from the 600-year-old Duksan oncheon, is located conveniently nearby.

Sudeoksa (© 041/337-6565; 20-beonji, Sacheon-li, Deoksin-myeon, Yesan-gun, www.sudeoksa.com), the head temple of the Jogye Order of Korean Buddhism, is located on the southern slopes. It was one of the few temples not destroyed during the Imjin Waeran (1592–98). Its main hall is one of South Korea's oldest wooden buildings, having been built in 1308 during the Goryeo Dynasty. They offer temple stays here that center around meditation.

Entrance to Deoksungsan is ₩2,000 adults, ₩1,500 teens, ₩1,000 for children.

CHEONGJU

The capital of Chungcheongbuk-do, Cheongju (not to be confused with Chungju) is located on the western side of the province in the center of the Korean Peninsula.

During the Unified Shilla period, Cheongju (whose name was Seowongyeong back then) served as a secondary capital. A transportation, industrial, and educational center for the region, the city has grown a bit lopsided with expansion mostly on the west side of town. Cheongju's downtown area still remains a bustling and popular place to eat, shop, and play. One of the city's most unusual relics is an iron flagpole, the **Yongdusaji Cheoldanggan** located at the former Yongdusa site. This flagpole dates back to A.D. 962, during the Goryeo Dynasty, and now stands outside the Cheongju Department Store.

From 1999, the city has hosted the **Cheongju International Craft Biennale** (© 043/277-2501; www.okcj.org) every 2 years, in odd-numbered years.

Essentials

GETTING THERE The **Cheongju International Airport** (CHN), San 5-1, Ipsang-li, Naesu-eup, Cheongwon-gun, Chungcheongbuk-do (© 043/210-6114;

http://cheongju.airport.co.kr), has limited flights. There are flights three times a week to and from Shanghai, a couple of flights to and from Shenyang, and irregular flights to and from Taipei and Kaoshung. There are 5 flights to/from Jeju-do run by **Korean Airlines** (☎ **043/213-2107**) and **Asiana Airlines** (☎ **043/214-6416**). There are no flights to or from Seoul or other domestic airports. Buses to downtown Cheongju run 25 times daily, costing ₩1,100. Other buses that run much less frequently go to Chungju, Cheonan, and Daejeon. From **Incheon Airport,** you can catch a bus to Cheongju in front of bus stop 9D. Buses run irregularly (every 20–60 min.) daily from 6:30am to 10:40pm and cost about ₩18,700 with a travel time of about 3 hours.

Cheongju's train station is located about 20 minutes west of the city and is not very convenient. Only about 10 trains pass through the city daily terminating at Daejeon and Jecheon. There is one train that goes from Seoul to Cheongju on the way to Andong. If you want to catch a train to destinations on the Gyeongbu line, it's best to take a bus to Jochiwon Station and get a train there instead of transferring between rail lines.

Express buses from Seoul cost about ₩12,000. Buses from the **DongSeoul Station** run every 15 to 20 minutes, daily from 6am to 9pm, taking about 100 minutes. From Seoul's **Sanbong Bus Terminal,** there are seven buses a day from 6:10am to 8:10pm, with a running time of about 90 minutes. There are buses from Busan every 80 minutes, daily from 7am to 6pm, which take over 4 hours. Express buses are available only from Seoul, Busan, Daegu, and Gwangju. More frequent intercity buses go to most major towns nearby, including Buyeo, Gongju, Daejeon, Jeonju, Chungju, and Suwon.

GETTING AROUND Cheongju has an extensive and efficient bus system, and it's the cheapest way to get around. However, drivers don't speak English and the stops are written only in Korean. If you know how to say where you're going in Korean (or have it written down—ask for help at your hotel), you can ask the driver to let you know when your stop is.

Taxis are inexpensive and usually waiting in front of all bus and train stations. You can also flag down a taxi from any street. Most taxi drivers don't speak English either, but if you have an address or the name of a destination, they'll get you there in no time.

VISITOR INFORMATION The **tourist information center,** 1449 Gagyeong-dong, Heungdeok-gu, Cheongju-si (☎ **043/233-8431**; daily 9am–6pm; http://english.cjcity.net/main/english), is next to the Cheongju Bus Terminal.

[Fast FACTS] CHEONGJU

Banks, Foreign Exchange & ATMs There are plenty of banks in the downtown area of Cheongju, along the pedestrian street near Jung-ang Park. They're open Monday to Friday 9:30am to 4:30pm. Major hotels will exchange foreign currency and traveler's checks at their currency exchange desks.

Internet Access Most large hotels, lower-priced motels, and youth hostels offer Internet access. If you don't have your own computer, ask for an Internet room when you check in. Your other option is the PC bahngs in town. Just look for the letters PC; most of them are found on the second or third floors above restaurants. There are some that can be easily found in the **Chungbuk University** (Chungdae) area. The tourist info center outside the intercity bus terminal also offers free Internet access.

Post Office There are a number of post offices (Mon–Fri 9am–5pm) in town, but the most convenient one is in Sajing-no in the heart of the city.

Exploring Cheongju

Cheongju Early Printing Museum ★ MUSEUM The oldest metal printed book in the world was the "Jikji" by Monk Baekun Hwasang from the temple Heungdeoksa in 1377, created 78 years before the Gutenberg Bible. Although the actual book is in the National Library of France (well, the 38 pages left), this museum shows the evolution of printing in Korea with models of the printing process from wooden type to movable metal printing developed during the Goryeo Dynasty. Although it's a small museum, the displays are well done, with good English signage.

San 81, Myeongwang-dong, Sangdang-gu, Cheongju-si, Chungcheongbuk-do. ℂ **043/200-4511.** www.jikjiworld.net. Admission free. Mar–Oct Tues–Sun 9am–6pm; Nov–Feb Tues–Sun 9am–5pm (last ticket sales 1 hr. before closing). Closed Mondays, Jan 1, Lunar New Year, and Chuseok. From the Express Bus Terminal, take local bus no. 720, 728, 731, or 734. From downtown, take bus no. 691, 692, or 693.

Cheongju National Museum ★★ 🏛 MUSEUM In the first section of the museum, you can see treasures from the Guseok, Sinseok, and Cheongdong periods. In the second gallery you'll find various artifacts from the homes and tombs of the Samhan and Samgook periods. In the Unified Shilla–Goryeo (918–1392) gallery, clay pottery, metalwares, and gold artifacts are on display. In the fourth room, you can see the treasures from the Joseon period (1392–1910). The children's exhibit lets kids (and adults) experience the culture of Korea's past firsthand.

87 Myeongam, Sangdang, Cheongju-si, Chungcheongbuk-do. ℂ **043/229-6300.** http://cheongju.museum.go.kr/coding/eng/eng_main.htm. Admission free. Tues–Fri 9am–6pm; Sat–Sun and holidays 9am–7pm. Closed Mondays and Jan 1. From the bus terminals, take bus no. 230, 231, 232, or 233, and get off at the museum stop (takes 30 min.).

Sangdang Sanseong (Mountain Fortress) ★★ HISTORIC SITE A large-scale stone fortress on the slopes of Uamsan, there is no record of when it was actually built (although there are some mentions of it in writings from the Three Kingdoms period). The present structure is the one rebuilt by King Sukjong in 1716, after its restoration in 1596 from damage during the Japanese invasion. There are now three main gates, east, west, and south; two plain gates; three turrets; and three waterways. A small village inside the fortress walls includes some cozy, informal restaurants.

Sanseong-dong, Sangdang-gu, Cheongju-si, Chungcheongbuk-do. ℂ **043/200-2227.** Mar–Oct daily 9am–6pm; Nov–Feb daily 9am–5pm (last admission an hour before closing). Take bus no. 862 from Cheongju stadium or take a taxi from downtown Cheongju (about a 20-minute ride)

Yonghwasa (Yonghwa Temple) ★ TEMPLE In 1901, seven stone Buddhas, each representing the Buddha of the Future, were found in a swamp northwest of Cheongju. Legend has it that seven Buddhas appeared to King Gojong's consort in a dream and asked her to build them a house; she sent workers to find and remove them from the swamp. The Yonghwasa was built and the seven statues were enshrined in the Mireuk Bojeon Hall ("the hall to conserve the Buddha image"). Actually, the seven statues are five Buddhas and two bodhisattvas, but who wants to mess with a legend? The largest has a swastika on his chest, but don't be alarmed—before the symbol was co-opted by the Nazis, it was an ancient symbol of luck. When it appears on Buddhas, it is meant to symbolize the radiation in all directions of the Buddha's power.

The temple sits over the levee from the stream, north of the city's main bridge, and is walking distance from downtown.

216-1, Sajik-dong, Heungdeok-gu, Cheongju-si, Chungcheongbuk-do. © **043/274-2159.** http://yonghwasa.com (Korean only). Free admission. Daily 24 hr., but best to visit 9am–6pm in order not to disturb the monks.

Cheongnamdae ★★ HISTORIC HOME This former presidential villa is located in a hidden area surrounded by mountains near Daecheong Dam. Closed to the public for over 20 years, it was opened to visitors by former president Roh in 2003. It's a peaceful place to take a walk along the expansive trails, look for wild cranes, or see how former presidents spent their leisure time.

San 26-1 Sindae-li, Munui-myeon, Cheongwon-gun, Chungcheongbuk-do. © **043/220-6412.** http://chnam.cb21.net. Admission ₩5,000 adults, ₩4,000 youth, ₩3,000 children and seniors. Tues–Sun 9am–6pm (closes at 5pm Dec–Jan), last tickets and bus 1½ hr. before closing. Closed Jan 1, Lunar New Year, and Chuseok. Take bus no. 311 to Munui at the Cheongju Express Bus Terminal (the bus runs every 30 min. and takes about 50 min.). Individual visitors must get tickets at the ticket office (located in front of the Munui-myeon Police Station), then board a bus to get to Cheongnam-dae (which takes about 20 min. and costs ₩2,400 adults, ₩2,000 teens and children).

Shopping

Cheongju has a pedestrian shopping street (Seong-an-gil) in the *shinae* (downtown) area, as well as the covered *shijang* (market) which draws crowds all week long. There are clothing shops, restaurants, and cafes. It's a great place to shop, browse, or just people-watch.

The **Cheongju Department Store,** 1-2 Nammun-no, 2-ga, Sangdang-gu, is a popular large store with several floors of clothes and household items.

If you're looking for a shopping megaplex, head over to **Dream Plus,** 1416-3 Gagyung-dong, Heungeok-gu, located next door to the Lotte mart, near the bus terminal. It has many levels of boutiques and tiny shops, and a 24-hour spa and sauna, the **Spa-ville** ★★, on the third floor. The food court on the sixth floor is a good place to get tasty, cheap meals, and you can head up to the eighth floor if you want to catch the latest Hollywood flick.

Where to Stay

You'll find the best motels and inexpensive yeogwan grouped together around the express and intercity bus terminals. Some of the higher-quality ones look like fake European castles. Of course, there are plenty of clean and economical love motels in the city as well.

Newvera Tourist Hotel ★ This friendly tourist-class hotel is just down the street from the bus terminals. The beds are comfortable with good rooms for the price. Some rooms have a bit of mismatched furniture, but they're clean. Tubs are a bit small and there's not a shower curtain (as in many of Korea's hotels). Staff are generally friendly and speak a little English.

1027 Gagyeong-dong, Heungdeok-gu, Cheongju-si, Chungcheongbuk-do. www.newvera.co.kr (Korean only). © **043/235-8181.** Fax 043/235-8180. 35 units. ₩96,000 standard room; ₩180,000 and up suite. AE, MC, V. **Amenities:** Restaurant/cafe. *In room:* A/C, TV, hair dryer.

Ramada Cheongju ★ This 21-story hotel is one of the most upscale in the city. There are the usual modern amenities, including a nice fitness center and a pretty decent restaurant. Rooms have reasonably comfortable beds and either city or mountain views. They charge a bit extra for a corner room, but not higher floors—ask for one if you want a better view. Staff speak perfectly good English and are very polite.

500-3 Yulyang-dong, Sangdang-gu, Cheongju-si, Chungcheongbuk-do. www.ramada.com. *℃* **043/290-1000.** Fax 043/290-1010. 328 units. ₩150,000 and up standard room; ₩300,000 and up suite. 10% VAT not included. AE, MC, V. **Amenities:** 4 restaurants; bar; cafe; pool; health club; putting green; babysitting; smoke-free rooms; deli. *In room:* A/C, TV, minibar, hair dryer, Internet.

Shil Motel ★★ ✦ Remodeled in 2007, this motel is a bargain, especially for the location. It's near the park downtown in the *mokja golmok* (Let's Eat Alley), so there is no shortage of places to eat within walking distance.

1680 Yeongam-dong, Sangdang-gu, Cheongju-si, Chungcheongbuk-do. *℃* **043/296-5210.** 28 units. ₩35,000 and up standard room. *In room:* A/C, TV, Internet.

Where to Eat

Bongchang-i Haemul Kalgooksu ★ 🏠 KOREAN NOODLES If you want a hot bowl of kalgooksu, this place is known by locals to make a mean bowl of the *haemul* (mixed seafood) variety. It's the perfect spot for a hearty meal that'll fill you up and won't break the bank. They also have good *mandu* (dumplings).

765-3 Sadang-gu, Yongy-am-dong, Cheongju-si. *℃* **043/298-8895** (Korean). Entrees ₩5,000 and up. No credit cards. Daily 11am–9pm. Closed Lunar New Year and Chuseok.

Dotoli Maeul ★★★ 🏠 KOREAN The name means "acorn village," which evokes a sort of traditional, country feeling. This place does inexpensive and unpretentious overall Korean food so well that you'll be hard-pressed to find a seat during lunch and dinner times. Go early or late, and be sure to try the very tasty sujebi.

103-14 Yeong-un-dong, Cheongju-si, Chungcheongbuk-do. *℃* **043/254-3330** (Korean). Entrees ₩5,000 and up. No credit cards. Daily 11am–8pm. Closed Lunar New Year and Chuseok.

Gilseong-i-baeksuk ★★ KOREAN The restaurant's specialties are *baeksuk* (fish boiled in plain water) and *nooloongji* (burned rice). I know they don't sound great, but the fish is tender and fresh and the nooloongji is toasty and delicious. They also make a delicious samgyetang. It's a bit pricier than some other spots in town, but the food is well worth the cost. Despite the fact that there's a second location in town, the building is ridiculously large, but you'll understand why once you see how crowded it is inside.

407 Yeongjeong-dong, Sangdang-gu, Cheongju-si, Chungcheongbuk-do. *℃* **043/296-2965** (Korean). Entrees ₩26,000 and up. MC, V. Daily 10am–10pm.

Entertainment & Nightlife

There are plenty of places to have a drink in the city and several foreigner-friendly bars. As in other South Korea's cities, most of the action happens in the area near the universities. One of the most popular bars in the *Chungdae jungmun* (Chungbuk University's main gate) area is **Pearl Jam,** located on the second floor on Gungmuli-gil. The owner's English isn't great, but most of the staff speak it pretty well. The bar has all-you-can-drink specials on Friday and Saturday nights (which is cheaper for women than for men). Open from around 6pm to the wee hours, they often have live music on weekends. Its sister bar, **The Attic,** located a couple of doors down from Pearl Jam, on the third floor, has a small dance floor and a pool table and has more of an intimate club feeling.

THE REST OF CHUNGCHEONGBUK-DO

The only landlocked province in the whole country, Chungcheongbuk-do (North Chungcheong Province, called "Chungbuk," for short) is the center and heart of Korea. Known as a good agricultural region, the province's main products are ginseng and tobacco. One of the oldest temples in the country, **Beopjusa** is located here in the **Songnisan National Park.** The land consists of mostly mountainous regions, with Charyeongsan to the north and Sobaeksan to the east, which separate it from Gyeongsangbuk-do. Chungcheongbuk-do includes the cities of Cheongju (its capital, discussed earlier), Chungju, and Jecheon. Nine counties fall within its boundaries, which are Boeun-gun, Cheongwon-gun, Danyang-gun, Eumseong-gun, Goesan-gun, Jeungpyeong-gun, Jincheon-gun, Okcheon-gun, and Yeongdong-gun.

Essentials

GETTING THERE   The province has only one commercial airport in Cheongju, which has a few flights to and from Jeju-do and a couple of cities in China. The **Gyeongbu rail line** crosses the southern portion of the province with main stations only at Okcheon and Yeongdong. The **Jung-ang rail line** crosses the northeastern corner of the province, passing through Jechon and Danyang. The **Chungbuk rail line** connects cities in the province from Jecheon to Jochiwon, passing through Cheongju and Chungju.

The **Gyeongbu Expressway** (road 1) cuts through the southwestern part of the province. The **Jungbu Expressway** (road 35) connects Cheongju to Seoul and parts north and goes down to intersect the Gyeungbu Expressway. The **Jungbu Naeryuk Expressway** (road 45) goes down the middle of the province through Chungju and Suanbo. In the eastern part of the province, the **Jung-ang Expressway** (road 55) connects Jecheon and Danyang to points north and south of the province.

GETTING AROUND   A network of smaller highways and country roads connects major cities and towns to remote villages and country areas. Renting a car is the easiest way to get around, especially to remote parts of the region. Traveling by bus is the cheapest, though not the fastest nor most convenient, way to get around the province, since many of the buses aren't numbered and schedules are erratic. The drivers generally don't speak English, but if you know the name of your destination in Korean, they'll let you know where to get off.

VISITOR INFORMATION   The province's main **tourist information center,** 1440 Gagyeong-dong, Heungdeok-gu, Cheongju-si, Chungcheongbuk-do (✆ **043/ 233-8431**), is located next to the Cheongju Bus Terminal. Open all year daily from 9am to 6pm, there are maps and brochures for the region. The official site is http://www.cbtour.net/index_eng.jsp.

Songnisan National Park ★★★

In the center of the Sobaek mountains, **Songnisan National Park** (✆ **043/543-6522;** http://english.knps.or.kr/Knp/Songnisan) lies on the border between Chungcheongbuk-do and Gyeongsangbuk-do. Due to its numerous trails, the park attracts hikers all year, with its southern portion being the most crowded. Its most popular attraction is the temple, **Beopjusa** (see below). Most people enter the park in the

Beopjusa area in Boeun-gun, but you can enter the park from the Hwabuk area, if you want to avoid the crowds. Although the Hwabuk section of Songnisan has fewer famous locations and relics, its valleys are more beautiful with larger waterfalls. Admission to the park from the Beopjusa area is ₩3,000 adults, ₩1,400 teens, ₩800 children. From the Hwabuk/Ssanggok area, admission is ₩1,600 adults, ₩600 teens, ₩300 children. The park is open daily 5am to 5pm November through February, until 7pm March through October.

From the Boeun Intercity Bus Terminal, take a bus to Songnisan. Buses run every 30 to 40 minutes, daily from 6:30am to 8:10pm, and the ride takes about 20 minutes. There are also buses from Seoul's Nambu Terminal to Songnisan three times daily and from the DongSeoul Bus Terminal 12 times a day. Both buses take about 3 hours and 30 minutes. Buses from Cheongju run 26 times daily, 6:40am to 8:40pm, taking 90 minutes. There are also direct buses from Dong Daejeon, Daegu, and Busan.

About a kilometer below Beopjusa is the Songnisan tourist village where you can find restaurants, teahouses, souvenir shops, and drinking establishments. The one first-class hotel is the rather aged **Lake Hills Hotel** (☎ **043/542-5281**). The lower-class hotels or the handful of motels in the area are better, more economical choices. The village also has a small post office, a police station, and the park's main office.

The area is usually most crowded during the popular fall (autumn) months when crowds of visitors come up to see the gorgeous scenery and buy giant bags of dried mountain vegetables gathered from the slopes. The rest of the year, you can expect it to be quieter, although it never loses its "tourist" feeling. There are also a few yeogwan and smaller restaurants near the entrance to Osong Falls. Try the trout, which are caught fresh from the valley near the falls.

Beopjusa (Beopju Temple) ★★★ TEMPLE   The site of a giant bronze Buddha statue, this temple was originally built in A.D. 553. The buildings on-site have been destroyed and rebuilt many times throughout its sordid history, but now it houses the country's only remaining five-story wooden pagoda, the **Daeungbojeon.** When you enter the park, follow the yellow dirt road to the Orisup Trail. Pass the trail and go through a grove of pine trees and you will come to the temple's main gate. The **Seokryeongji (Lotus Flower Pond)** is most beautiful when the flowers are in bloom in the fall (autumn). The complex also holds the **Ssangsajasekdeung (Twin Lion Stone Lantern)** and the **Maaeyeorae Uisang,** the Maayerae Sitting Buddha carved into a rock. But, of course, what everyone is here to see is the 33m-tall (108-ft.) bronze standing Buddha, which was built here in 1990.

209 Sanae-li, Naesongni-myeon, Boeun-gun, Chungcheongbuk-do. ☎ **043/543-3615** (Korean only). Admission ₩3,000 adults, ₩1,400 teens, ₩800 children. Daily 5am–5pm Nov–Feb, until 7pm Mar–Oct. From the Boeun Intercity Bus Terminal, take a bus to Songnisan. Buses run every 30–40 min., and the ride takes 20 min. Daily 6:30am–8:10pm. From Songnisan Bus Terminal, it's a 20-min. walk to Beopjusa. There are also buses from Seoul's Nambu Terminal to Songnisan 3 times daily and from the DongSeoul Bus Terminal 12 times a day. Both buses take 3½ hr. Buses from Cheongju run 26 times daily 6:40am–8:40pm, taking 1½ hours. There are also direct buses from Dong Daejeon, Daegu, and Busan.

HIKING TRAILS

Past the temple complex, hiking trails continue up the various peaks of the park. The trail that leads up to the **Munjangdae** peak is a relatively easy one and by far the most popular in the park. The entire hike, which offers some fantastic views, should take about 5 hours round-trip on foot. If you want a little variety on the hike back, take the trail down to Shinseondae and then down past the Geumgang hut. That will lengthen your trip another 2 hours. If you want to start early in the morning, take the trail up to Munjangdae and follow the ridge trail to Chonhwangbong, coming back past Sanghwanam and Sanggoam. This itinerary will take about 10 hours, so plan ahead and bring plenty of water.

North of Beopjusa is the middle section of the park, which is split into two sections. The largest is the narrow valley of **Hwayangdong Gugok.** A beautiful area with white rocks lining the bottom of clear streams, a small temple, **Chaeunsa,** sits overlooking the valley from its rocky perch. At the eastern end is a nature preserve.

From **Osong Falls,** on the slopes of Shinseondae, there is a shortcut to climb up to the summit of Munjangdae, which takes about 2 hours. On the way to Osong Falls from Jangamgyo (bridge), you will find an old mountain fortress, **Geyonhwon Sanseong,** if you walk about 25 minutes along the trail to the right. Originally measuring 650m (2,133 ft.) around, only parts of the fortress remain today.

The other waterfall in the area is the **Janggak Falls** that descend to a deep pond below. The waters are actually a bit dangerous and people drown here every year, so it's best not to swim in the pond (though you may be tempted in the summer heat). Nearby is the pretty Geumranjeong Pavilion sitting on a cliff covered with pine trees. About 1.5km (1 mile) up from the falls is the seven-level **Sangori Pavilion,** which was originally built during the middle of the Goryeo Dynasty. Destroyed during the Japanese colonial period, it was restored in 1977. A large temple is said to have been in the area, but there are no remains of its structure today. It takes about 5½ hours for a round-trip to the peak and back down to the waterfall.

Chungju

Chungju (not to be confused with Cheongju) is Chungcheongbuk-do's second-largest city, but with a small-town feel. Since it became an official city in the late 1950s, it has enjoyed continued industrial growth. It serves as the gateway to the Chungju Lake area, Woraksan National Park, and Suanbo Hot Springs.

Every fall (autumn) the city comes alive with the **World Martial Arts Festival** (© **043/850-6720;** www.martialarts.or.kr), usually in late September or early October. It usually overlaps the **Ureuk Cultural Festival,** which commemorates the achievements of the great Shilla musician Akseong Ureuk, who invented the *gayageum* (a Korean zither-type string instrument).

From the **DongSeoul Express Terminal,** you can board a bus to Chungju every 30 minutes daily. The 2-hour trip costs about ₩9,000. The tourist information booth (© **043/845-7829**) is located inside the bus terminal and is open daily from 9am to 6pm.

EXPLORING CHUNGJU

Traditionally serving as a border land shared by the Three Kingdoms—Baekje, Shilla, and Goguryeo—Chungju had a unique culture that was a mixture of the three, called Jungwon culture. A number of precious relics and artifacts remain from that period and are scattered throughout the city. One of those is the **Jung-angtop,** a pagoda tower which indicates the actual center of the Korean Peninsula and also serves as a monument to the victory of Jungwon during the Goguryeo Dynasty. The park around the pagoda has an exhibition hall with historic relics from the region.

In a small park near the post office is the **Jung-ang Gongwon** (central park), inside which are structures from the late Joseon era: The **Cheongnyeongheon,** which used to be the office of the city magistrate, and the **Jegeomdang,** part of the magistrate's residence. Across the stream on the north is the **Chungju Hyanggyo,** a Confucian academy, originally built in 1398 (and rebuilt in 1897).

Cheongpung Cultural Properties Complex HISTORIC SITE   When the Chungju Dam was built, historic and cultural items had to be relocated from the flooded area and many of them were moved here, on a small hill overlooking the lake. Located about a kilometer from Cheongpung, the collection includes older homes, the Hanbyeongnu and other pavilions, and the Cheongpung Confucian school.

Jongmin-dong, Chungju-si, Chungcheongbuk-do. *©* **043/641-5741.** Admission ₩3,000 adults, ₩2,000 teens, ₩1,000 children. Mar–Oct daily 9am–6pm; Nov–Feb daily 9am–6pm.

Chungju-ho (Lake Chungju) ★★★ PARK   An artificial lake created by the construction of the Chungju Dam in the mid-1980s, Chungjuho is considered the best lakeside resort in the country. There are a variety of recreational, sports, and entertainment facilities. Ferries operate in the five areas of the lake, but the most popular route is the Chungjunaru course. A ferry also runs as far as Shin Danyang and is an incredibly scenic ride. In the summer, the boats run daily every hour from 9am to 4:30pm. In the winter season, the boats run daily about every 2 hours 10am to 3pm.

Jongmin-dong, Chungju-si, Chungcheongbuk-do. *©* **043/850-5114.** www.chungjuho.com (Korean only). Free admission to the lake, but ferry prices vary in the ₩12,000 to ₩20,000 range. A city bus runs 6 times daily, late spring to early fall. Other times during the year, the bus runs about 5 times a day from 10am.

Liquorium MUSEUM   This three-story collection claims to be the world's first liquor museum. The galleries are separated into exhibitions on wine, beer, Asian liquor, and aqua vitae. There is also a display explaining various drinking cultures worldwide.

Inside Jung-angtop Park, Chungju-si, Chungcheongbuk-do. *©* **043/855-7333** (Korean only). Admission ₩6,000 ages 17 and over, ₩2,000 children 16 and under. Daily 10am–6pm. Closed Lunar New Year, Chuseok, and the day before and after Chuseok. From the Chungbu Bus Terminal take bus no. 400, 401, 403, 404, 410, 411, 412, or 413 and get off at Gageum Jung-angtop.

Tangeumdae ★★ MONUMENT   Not far from Chungjuho is this shrine on a hilltop, whose name means "the hill where the gayageum played." This is where the legendary musician Ureuk used to play his instrument during the reign of Shilla King Jinheung. A small hill, called Daemunsan, overlooks the waters of the Han River below. Outdoor concerts are held here in the summer.

San 1-1 Chilgeum-dong, Chungju-si. *©* **043/850-5831.** Admission ₩1,000. Mar–Oct daily 9am–6pm; Nov–Feb daily 9am–5pm. Hike from Chungjuho; for directions to Chungjuho, see above entry.

AROUND CHUNGJU

Sajo Ski Resort ★ SPORTS VENUE   Just under 2km (1¼ miles) from Suanbo is this relatively small ski resort. There are seven slopes of different levels, accessible by four lifts. The season runs from December to early March, depending on weather conditions. Open 9am to 12:30am, the resort offers evening and night skiing. There's a hotel, youth hostel, restaurants, supermarket, souvenir shop, and campsite in the area.

642-1 Oncheon-li, Sangmo-myeon, Chungju-si, Chungcheongbuk-do. *©* **043/846-0750** (Korean only). www.sajoresort.co.kr. Ski rentals are ₩24,000 for a full day, ₩19,000 for half-day or evening skiing. Lift tickets are ₩55,000 for a full day, ₩40,000 night skiing (6–9:30pm) with other prices depending on times; children get a discounted rate. From the Chungbu Bus Terminal, take a bus bound for Suanbo. From the Suanbo Bus Terminal, take a shuttle to the resort. Shuttles run only in the winter.

Suanbo Hot Springs ★ NATURAL ATTRACTION   About 21km (13 miles) southeast of Cheongju, this oncheon supposedly began spewing water over 30,000 years ago. It's officially mentioned on the record in 1018, during the ninth year of King Hyeongjong's reign. The water originates deep beneath the earth and has an average temperature of 127°F (53°C). Alkaline in nature, it contains such minerals as calcium, fluoride, lithium, sodium, and magnesium and is supposed to be good for your health. Now, it is a cozy spa resort with spas such as **Suanbo Hi Spa** (✆ **043/846-8898**) and the **Nakcheongtang** (✆ **043/846-2905**).

100, Oncheon-li, Sanmo-myeon, Cheongju-si, Chungcheongbuk-do. ✆ **043/845-7829** (Korean only) or call the Suanbo Tourist Interpretation Service on 043/848-4826. www.suanbo.or.kr (Korean only). Rates and times vary depending on the facilities, but generally are daily 6am–9pm, with a soak costing ₩7,000 adults, ₩3,000 children 7 and under. From the Chungju Intercity Bus Terminal, take a bus headed for Suanbo, Songgye Woraksan, or Samgwanmun and get off at the Suanbo post office. Daily buses run about every 20 min., 5:45am–9:50pm, and take about 35 min.

WHERE TO STAY

Near the bus station you will find clean and inexpensive motels (they run at about ₩35,000 per night for a single/double) and a few fancier accommodations near the train station. An older but good hotel in the city center is **Friendly Hotel ★★**, 102 Hoam-dong, Chungju-si (✆ **043/848-9900;** www.friendlyhotel.co.kr), near the Hoamji reservoir. Standard rooms start around ₩80,000, ₩240,000 for a suite.

If you want upscale sleeping quarters with hot springs to boot, book a room at one of the hotels in the Suanbo resort area. One of the better options is the **Chosun Tourist Hotel ★**, 109-2 Oncheon-li, Sangmo-myeon, Chungju-si (http://www.suanbo.co.kr/english/intro/intro.asp; ✆ **043/848-8833;** fax **043/848-8830**), with 103 rooms and standard rooms starting at ₩140,000.

WHERE TO EAT

There is a grouping of restaurants near Jung-ang Park in the downtown area. One place that does good Korean food is the **BokSeoul Shikdang ★**, 249-1 Seongnae-dong, Chungju-si (✆ **043/842-0135**), located next to the post office. Open daily from 4am to 8:30pm, they serve bibimbap or *haejang gook* (spicy seafood hot pot) for only ₩6,000 each.

A good option in the Suanbo area is **Hyundae Shikdang,** 191-1 Oncheon-li, Suanbo-myeon, Chungju-si (✆ **043/846-3363**), which has seafood, chicken, and even rabbit on their menu. You can get a mushroom hot pot for ₩13,000 or enjoy a rabbit feast for ₩40,000. For a *hanjeongshik* (Korean traditional meal), a good option is **Hyangnamu Shikdang** (✆ **043/846-2813,** 613-4, Bugok-dong, Sangluk-gu, Anshin-si), located behind the Gloria Hotel. A meal with several banchan will set you back ₩8,000 to ₩11,000. Splurge on their pheasant shabu shabu for ₩45,000 or go budget with their *haejang gook* for a mere ₩5,000.

Danyang

Located along the upper parts of the Namhan (South Han) River, **Danyang** is a resort town which sits at the foot of the Sobaeksan National Park in the county of the same name. Part of the original town was flooded with the creation of the Chungju Dam in 1986, and parts of it were reconstructed. The town is a great base for exploring the region.

THE 8 scenic WONDERS OF DANYANG (DANYANG PALGYEONG)

When Scholar Yi Hwang (1501–70) came to Danyang as a chief governor, he was so moved by the natural beauty that he designated eight scenic areas.

1. **Dodam Sambong**—This island in the Namhan (South Han) River has three peaks, which are said to represent three people involved in a love triangle: The husband, the concubine, and the wife. The story is that a man couldn't have a son with his wife, so he took on a concubine. The wife was so upset that she refused to speak to him and turned away. Locals say that the orientation of the rocks symbolizes this relationship.

2. **Seokmun**—Going upriver from the three peaks about 200m (656 ft.), you will find a stone gate shaped like the arc of a rainbow. Locals say that heavenly spirits must have sung a song when they passed by.

3. **Sainam Rock**—This large rock cliff, surrounded by old pine trees, hangs over a clear stream. On it is inscribed a poem by Confucian scholar Utak (pen name, Yeoktong). The poem reads: "Something far superior to other things / indeed matchless, cannot be cast aside. / There is nothing to be afraid of, even standing all alone. / There is nothing to worry about, in this secluded life."

4. **Haseonam**—Along the range of Doraksan are three peaks that people liken to brothers. Haseonam is the first, with a large boulder on it said to look like a reclining Buddha (so it's called "Bulam," Buddha Rock). During the Joseon Dynasty, it was given the name "Sonam," which

means "a rock where the mountain wizards strolled." And local legend has it that the gods once descended from heaven and had a banquet there.

5. **Jungseonam**—About 5km (3 miles) from Haseonam is the middle brother peak. On its slopes are the Ssang-yong Falls, where it is said that twin dragons ascended to heaven through a crevice. During the Joseon Dynasty, many *yangban* (those from the gentlemen class) would come here to make music, write poetry, and commune with nature.

6. **Sangseonam**—Sangseonam was named by Gwon Sang-ha, who was said to have built a thatched pavilion and lived here writing poetry. There are three hermitages in the nine valleys surrounded by the rocky peaks.

7. **Gudambong**—This peak gets its name, which means turtle, from the shape of its reflection in the lake below, which is said to look like a turtle swimming just below the surface of the water. Gudambong and nearby Oksunbong are both popular in the fall season when their trees change color.

8. **Oksunbong**—This peak was originally a part of Cheongpung-gun, but the story is that the female entertainer Duhyang coaxed Yi Hwang into including it in Danyang-gun. The magistrate of Cheongpung didn't agree but Yi Hwang carved DANGU DONGMUN on the rock wall, stating that it was "the gateway to Danyang." The unusually shaped boulders are surrounded by various trees.

Trains from Cheongnyangni Station depart for Danyang about 10 times daily and take about 3 hours. You can also take an express bus from the DongSeoul Terminal. Buses run 12 times a day. Intercity buses run from Jecheon to Danyang frequently.

If you're driving from Seoul, take the Yeongdong Expressway to the Manjong IC. Then, take the Jung-ang Inland Expressway and exit at Buk (North) Danyang. Follow the signs to the Maepo IC and to Danyang.

EXPLORING DANYANG

AquaWorld ★★ WATER PARK   Located inside Daemyung Resort, this indoor water park was opened in 2003. Open all year, the water park and spa are divided into two main areas. The health pool section includes various water massages. The amusement section has a water slide, baths, and a massage corner just for women. A variety of hot spring soaks include mineral water and pine and they also have a couple of different sauna options.

4-1 Sangjin-li, Danyang-eup, Danyang-gun, Chungcheongbuk-do. ☏ **043/1588-4888.** www. daemyungresort.com/asp/language/english/danyang/aquaworld.asp. AquaWorld admission on weekdays ₩33,000 ages 13 and over, ₩29,000 children; on peak weekends ₩43,000 ages 13 and over, ₩38,000 children. Admission to sauna only ₩10,000 ages 13 and over, ₩8,000 children. Sauna Sept to mid-July Mon–Fri 7am–9pm, Sat 6am–10pm, Sun 6am–9pm; end of July to Aug daily 6am–11:30pm. Pool zone Sept to mid-July Mon–Fri 10am–8:30pm, Sat 9am–9:30pm, Sun 9am–8:30pm; end of July to Aug daily 9am–11pm. From either the Danyang Bus Terminal or the train station, it's easiest to take a taxi; fare starts at ₩1,700 for the 5-min. ride. Shuttle bus from Seoul at the Asia Park (take Seoul subway to Jonghap sports center, exit 1) requires reservation (☏ **02/222-7474**); leave daily at 9:30am and return at 2pm; the ride takes 2½ hr.; one way ₩17,000 adults, ₩10,000 children.

Cheondong-donggul (Cheondong Cave) NATURAL ATTRACTION   Discovered in 1977, this cave is 300m (984 ft.) long and goes almost straight down into the ground. The inside is a lighter yellow than Gosu Cave (see below), but its pathways are quite narrow.

Danyang-eup, Danyang-gun, Chungcheongbuk-do. ☏ **043/422-2972** (Korean only). Admission ₩5,000 adults, ₩3,000 teens, ₩2,000 children. Daily, Mar–Oct 9am–5:30pm; Nov–Feb 9am–5pm. From the intercity bus terminal, take a bus toward Cheondong-donggul. Buses run every 10–15 min.

Gosu-donggul (Gosu Cave) ★★★ ☺ NATURAL ATTRACTION   A huge limestone cave, it is the most famous in the area. Discovered in the early 1970s, this 1,300m (4,265-ft.) cave is pretty impressive. After the cave was discovered, rough stone instruments were excavated from the cave's entrance, showing that this used to be a home to prehistoric people. About 120 different stalactites and stalagmites are found here and it takes anywhere from 50 to 80 minutes to traverse it.

Danyang-eup, Danyang-gun, Chungcheongbuk-do. ☏ **043/422-3072.** www.kosu.or.kr (Korean only). Admission ₩5,000 adults, ₩3,000 teens, ₩2,000 children. Mar–Oct daily 9am–5:30pm; Nov–Feb until 5pm. From the Danyang Intercity Bus Terminal, take a bus toward Gosu-donggul. Buses run every 10–15 min. It's a 5-min. taxi ride, or you can walk the distance in 15 min. Parking ₩3,200 to ₩4,000.

Guinsa (Guin Temple) ★★ TEMPLE   Squeezed into a narrow valley northeast of Danyang is this temple, the headquarters of the Cheontae sect of Buddhism (Korea's version of China's Taintai). Unlike most of the country's temples, this one is fairly new, having been founded by Monk Sangwon Wongak in 1945. Even so, the original was burned down during the Korean War, and the current building was completed in 1966, with expansions since. Although there are many buildings squeezed into this complex, the highlight is the five-story main hall, the only such building in the entire country.

132-Baekja-li, Yeongchun-myeon, Danyang-gun, Chungcheongbuk-do. ℂ **043/423-7100.** www. guinsa.org (Korean only). Free admission. Daily sunrise–sunset. From Danyang, take a bus to Guinsa (a 30-min. ride), which leaves 20 min. past each hour. There are also direct buses from the DongSeoul Terminal, via Danyang (3 hr. 40 min. ride) or a couple from Busan (a 5-hr. ride).

Nodong-donggul (Nodong Cave) ★★ NATURAL ATTRACTION   In the same area as the other two caves, but down a different road is this limestone cave, which is about 800m (2,625 ft.) long. Visitors are allowed into the first 1.4 km. It has a 300m (984-ft.) drop, and a steep incline. They've constructed an extensive system of stairs and railing making the descent possible, but this cave has fewer visitors than the other two. There are the usual stalactites and stalagmites, but also cave pearls and unusual formations. It features the largest stalagmites in Asia and some unusual species found only in vertical caves. It is said to have been created about 500 million years ago. In the middle of the slope are broken pieces of pottery left behind by those who hid here from the Japanese army during the Hideyoshi Invasion of Korea. It takes about 40 minutes to see the cave.

Nodong-li, Danyang-eup, Danyang-gun, Chungcheongbuk-do. ℂ **043/422-2251** (Korean only). Admission ₩5,000 adults, ₩3,000 teens, ₩2,000 children. Mar–Oct daily 9am–5:30pm; Nov–Feb daily 9am–5pm. From the Danyang Intercity Bus Terminal, take a bus toward Nodong-donggul. Buses run every 10–15 min.

WHERE TO STAY

Danyang isn't a huge tourist destination yet, so it means fewer crowds, but also older, less upscale accommodations. The **Danyang Tourist Hotel** 264-2 Sangjin-li, Danyang-eup, Danyang-gun (www.danyanghotel.com; ℂ **043/423-7070;** fax **043/423-4234**), which is not the most conveniently located, has nicely decorated rooms and views of the lake. Standard Western-style and ondol rooms start at ₩120,000, triples ₩140,000, and suites ₩200,000. There are several restaurants, a cafe, a night club, and a spa on-site.

Even more economical quarters can be found in Shin Danyang, between the lake's ferry pier and the bus station. A perfectly serviceable "love motel" in the area is **Opera House,** 512 Dojeon-li, Danyang-eup, Danyang-gun (ℂ **043/423-5751**). With doubles going for just ₩35,000 to ₩45,000, it's a bargain. Rooms come with the basic bed, minifridge, and TV, and also include a computer with Internet access. In downtown Danyang, just look for the ridiculously ornate, white Greco-Roman facade.

WHERE TO EAT

Danyang is known for its watermelon in the summer and its apples and garlic in the fall. Vampire hunters will love **Jangdali Shikdang ★★★** ✦, 599 Byeolgok-li, Dangyang-eup, Danyang-gun (ℂ **043/423-3960**), where they'll serve you a huge spread of garlic banchan for a mere ₩15,000 per person. Their multigrain rice takes over 15 minutes to make, but it's worth the wait since it's made to order in individual stone pots. Go along the end of the main drag until it ends, then turn left. The two-story restaurant is located next to the gas station. They're open daily 8:30am to 10pm, closed Lunar New Year and Chuseok.

A good place is **Sambongsobaek Shikdang,** 84-1 Hagui-li, Maepo-eup, Danyang-gun (ℂ **043/421-1175**). They serve *maeuntang* (spicy hot pot) with fish freshly caught from the nearby river. Open daily from 6:30am to 9pm, the restaurant offers dishes ranging from ₩7,000 to ₩12,000, and their maeuntang (meant to be shared) for ₩35,000 to ₩80,000.

Another place to get tasty fare is the **Doljib Shikdang ★★ (② 043/422-2842)**, located near the Danyang Bus Terminal. Most of their jeongshik have to be ordered for at least two people, so it's best to bring a friend. However, their prices are good and the food is made with care. Their *maneul ssam jeongshik* (traditional meal with lettuce and other wraps and garlic) is ₩10,000, ssamgyupssal ₩10,000, and *beosut jjigae* (mushroom hot pot) ₩8,000.

JEOLLA-DO

Both economically poor and rich in natural beauty, Jeolla-do is one of Korea's most fascinating regions. Located in the southwestern part of the peninsula, it is bordered on the south by the East China Sea and on the west by the Yellow Sea.

Perhaps the poorest of the country's provinces, due to the area's history of conflict with the central government (it has long been viewed—and some would say has long behaved—like Seoul's rebellious little brother), Jeolla-do has largely been left behind as the rest of South Korea has boomed. Although this is not so great for the people who live there, it is wonderful for visitors. Not only will you get to experience the country's rural past, but you'll get to see wonderful scenery not yet ruined by huge highways, high-rise apartments, and industrial complexes.

The irregular coastline, numerous tiny islands, and a vast array of tidal flatlands, make for ideal fishing and diving conditions. The southern coastline has some of the best scenic ocean views anywhere in the country. Some of South Korea's most picturesque towns are in Jeolla-do. Don't miss the seaside town of **Yeosu** and the beautiful tea plantation of **Boseong**. If time and weather permit, take a boat out to one of the many small islands that fade into the distance off the southern coast. The people from Jeolla-do take pride in their food. Ask anyone from the region and they'll say that the best food in South Korea can be found here. Historically, Jeolla-do is the ancestral home of members of the royal Yi family (of the Joseon Dynasty). Their refined cooking techniques have been handed down for centuries. Even the simplest of dishes seems to have been made with extra care.

JEONJU

Perched on the edge of the fertile Honam plains, Jeonju is the capital city of Jeollabuk-do (North Jeolla Province). Famous for its regional cuisine and historic buildings, the city has long been regarded a spiritual center of the Joseon Dynasty, since Jeonju was home to the Yi family, which produced a long line of Joseon kings. It was also the capital for the ancient Baekje Kingdom, making this a spot rich with history.

This capital city has a bit of something for everyone: Historical sites and parks, gorgeous mountain scenery, and the remains of ancient Buddhist temples in the surrounding hills. And after you've exhausted yourself exploring, you can refuel with some of the best food in South Korea.

Well known for its *hanji* (traditional rice paper), there is even a paper museum, and an annually held **Jeonju Paper Culture Festival** (✆ **063/210-8103**), which includes a fashion show of couture all made from paper. More contemporary events include the **Jeonju International Film Festival** (℗ 063/288-5433; http://eng.jiff.or.kr), a small but growing festival showcasing films from South Korea and abroad, held in the spring.

Essentials

GETTING THERE Gunsan Airport (KUV, http://www.airport.co.kr/doc/gunsan_eng) is the closest airfield to Jeonju. Only **Korean Airlines** (www.koreanair.com) and **Eastar Jet** (www.eastarjet.com) offer flights to/from Jeju-do. From Gunsan, you have to take a bus to Jeonju. The nonstop bus runs depending on flight schedules, takes about 90 minutes, and costs ₩4,500 one-way.

You can also take a train from Seoul's **Yongsan Sation**, departing daily from 5:40am to 10:45pm. Fares vary from ₩16,800 for a **Saemaeul** train, ₩2500 for a **Mugunghwa** train and ₩30,600 for a **KTX** train. Most trains take about 3 to 3½ hours (2 hours for the KTX) to get to Jeonju. From the south, you can take a northbound train from Yeosu—the first train of the day departs at 5:10am and the last train leaves at 9:30pm. Most northbound trains cost ₩9,600 to ₩21,100 and the ride lasts about 2½ hours. The train station is in the northeastern part of Jeonju. You can contact the **Korea National Railroad** (www.korail.com) for more info.

From Seoul's Express Bus Terminal, **buses** to Jeonju run every 10 min., from 5:30am to 9:30pm with fares ranging from ₩12,200 to ₩17,900. Buses also run from Seoul's Nambu Terminal every 30 min., from 6:10am to 8:30pm and from Seoul's Sangbong Terminal five times daily from 6am to 6pm. The ride lasts about 3 hours. Express buses also run to and from Sangbong, Sungnam, Busan, Ulsan, Daegu, Gwangju, Daejeon, Goyang, and Incheon. You can also take an **airport limousine bus** directly to and from Incheon Airport (at bus stops no. 9C). Buses run daily from 6:30am to 10:30pm and run every 30 to 60 min. The 4-hour ride costs ₩29,000.

GETTING AROUND Unfortunately, none of **Jeonju's city buses** stops right at the **bus terminal** (℗ 062/277-1572, 767-2 Geumam-dong, Jeonju-si), but the walk to the main road to catch a bus is quite short. The good thing is that the city bus system is widespread and efficient, even providing service to nearby towns. There are also plenty of **taxis** available to be flagged down on the street or waiting by the train or bus stations. The base fare starts at ₩1,200 and goes up based on time and distance.

VISITOR INFORMATION There is a tourist information center (℗ 063/288-0105; http://tour-eng.jeonju.go.kr/index.sko) in "Reunion Square" off Jeonju Train Station, at the Jeonju Express Bus Terminal (℗ 063/281-2739), at Gyeonggijeon (℗ 063/281-2891), and at the Jeonju Hanok Maeul (℗ 063/282-1330). They all have English speakers and are open daily 9am to 6pm. The city's official website is http://www.jeonju.go.kr/open_content/en/main_page.jsp.

Exploring Jeonju

Gyeonggijeon (Gyeongi Shrine) MONUMENT Built in 1410, this shrine houses the portrait of King Taejo, first emperor of the Joseon Dynasty, as well as successive other kings. Funerary tablets for both the king and his queen are enshrined here. Although part of the structure was destroyed during the Imjin Waeran, the building was renovated in 1614 and still stands today.

102 Pungnam-dong 3(sam)-ga, Wansan-gu, Jeonju-si. ℗ **063/287-1330.** Free admission. Mar–Oct daily 9am–6pm; Nov–Feb daily 9am–5pm. From the Jeonju Train Station take bus no. 79 or

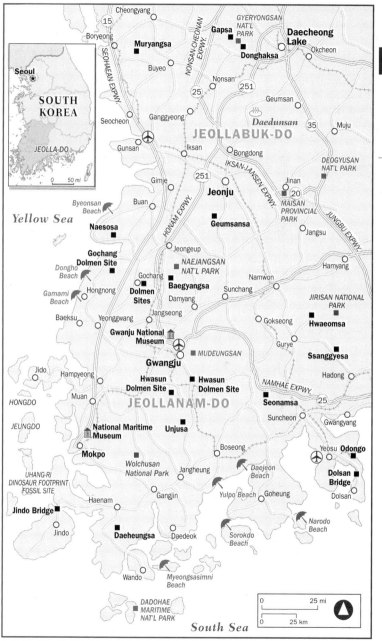

119 and get off at Jeongdong Cathedral. From the Jeonju Bus Terminal, take bus no. 70 and get off at Jeongdong Cathedral. It's about a 5-min. walk from the cathedral. It's about a 15–20 min. taxi ride from train or bus stations.

Gyeonhwon Palace Site RUINS   This is the site where King Gyeonhwon decided to build a palace about 1,300 years ago, during the Baekje Kingdom. Legend has it that he stayed here and intercepted the crops and taxes headed for Gyeongju, the capital of the Shilla Kingdom. Later, during the HuBaekje (Later Baekje) period, General Gyeonhwon (who, rather confusingly, has the same name as the king) attempted to establish a capital here, but he was ultimately defeated by the Shilla Kingdom (see chapter 2). Although the palace is no longer here, some older stones and relics remain on-site.

San 9-1, Gyo-dong, Wansan-gu, Jeonju.© **063/281-2553.** Free admission. Daily 24 hr.

Jeonju Hanok Maeul (Traditional Village) ★★ HISTORIC SITE   With over 800 traditional houses, this ancient village retains its former charm, while the rest of the city has industrialized around it. Unlike buildings in other traditional Korean villages, the roofs here have a slight curvature, adding to the place's unique beauty. For a full experience, you can spend the night in one of the traditional homes (see "Where to Stay," on p. 187, for more info).

Pungnam-dong/Gyo-dong, Wonsan-gu, Jeonju. © **063/282-1330.** http://hanok.jeonju.go.kr. From the Intercity Bus Terminal, take bus no. 211, 221, 231, 241, 251, or 291 bound for Nambu Market; get off at Jeongdong Cathedral or Jeonbuk Art Center. From the Express Bus Terminal, take bus 5-1 or 79.From the train station, take bus no. 12, 60, 79, 109, 119, 142, 508, 513, 536, 542, or 546 (25-min. ride); get off at Jeongdong Cathedral or Jeonbuk Art Center. It's about a 10-min. walk from the bus stop.

Jeonju Historical Museum MUSEUM   This modern museum's exhibits illustrate many of the rebellions and turmoil of recent Korean history, from the Donghak revolution onward. It's best to visit first thing in the morning or in the afternoon since the building is usually overrun with visiting schoolchildren from 10am to noon on weekdays.

Hyoja-dong, Wansan-gu, Jeonju (right across from the Jeonju National Museum, below). © **063/228-6485** or 6. http://jeonju.museum.go.kr (Korean). Free admission. Tues–Sun 9am–6pm (closes at 5pm in winter); last admission 30 min. before closing. Closed Jan 1.

Catholicism in Korea

Long isolated, Korea was first exposed to Christianity when envoys to Beijing brought books back home with them. In 1784, a Chinese priest arrived, and a French priest followed in 1836.

Although a small percentage of Koreans were intrigued by Catholicism and converted, the Joseon Dynasty saw the religion as a tdanger. Threatened by the fervor of these newly converted Catholics, the Confucian government cracked down hard, and there were multiple mass executions of believers. The most well known of these are the Sinyu Persecution of 1801, Gihae Persecution of 1839, Byeongo Persecution of 1846, and Byeongin Persecution of 1866. These bloody conflicts took the lives of over 800 Catholics, some of whom were canonized by Pope John Paul II in Seoul in 1984. Today, Catholicism is one of South Korea's three major religions (along with Protestantism and Buddhism), with over five million followers.

Jeonju

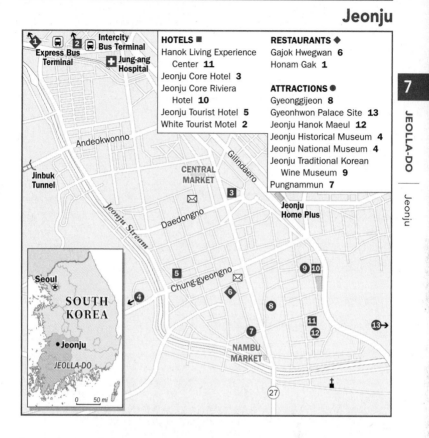

Express Bus Terminal
Intercity Bus Terminal
Jung-ang Hospital

HOTELS ■
Hanok Living Experience
  Center **11**
Jeonju Core Hotel **3**
Jeonju Core Riviera
  Hotel **10**
Jeonju Tourist Hotel **5**
White Tourist Motel **2**

RESTAURANTS ◆
Gajok Hwegwan **6**
Honam Gak **1**

ATTRACTIONS ●
Gyeonggijeon **8**
Gyeonhwon Palace Site **13**
Jeonju Hanok Maeul **12**
Jeonju Historical Museum **4**
Jeonju National Museum **4**
Jeonju Traditional Korean
  Wine Museum **9**
Pungnammun **7**

Andeokwonno

Jinbuk Tunnel

Jeonju Stream

CENTRAL MARKET

Gilindaero

Daedongno

Jeonju Home Plus

Chung-gyeongno

Seoul

SOUTH KOREA

•Jeonju

JEOLLA-DO

0   50 mi

NAMBU MARKET

(27)

7

JEOLLA-DO | Jeonju

Jeonju National Museum MUSEUM   The research and preservation center for Jeollabuk-do's rich cultural history, it is home to over 24,000 artifacts, only a fraction of which are on actual display. Although the exhibition space is small, it is a great place to see local finds from the Baekje period as well as artifacts from the lesser-known Seonsa and Mahan kingdoms. They also have a sizeable collection of Buddhist art, ceramics, and folk items from the area.

2-900, Hyoja-dong, Wansan-gu, Jeonju-si. ⓒ **063/223-5651.** http://jeonju.museum.go.kr. Admission free. Tues–Fri 9am–6pm; Sat–Sun 9am–7pm (last admission 1 hr. before closing). Closed Monday and Jan 1. Take bus no. 9, 31, 49, 61, 62, 161, 354, 378, 554, 559, 644, 684, 807, 814, 816, 817, 834, 837, 838, 839, 855, or 866, and get off at the Jeonju National Museum.

Pungnammun (South Gate) HISTORIC SITE   This impressive gate is the only surviving section of the wall that once surrounded the city. Originally built to serve as one of 4 gates in 1389, the present structure was built in 1768 and renovated in 1979. Not only is it a relic from the Joseon Dynasty, but it is also the site where the conflict between Catholicism and Confucianism was played out. The first Korean Catholic martyr was executed here in 1790 for his religious beliefs (see box below).

185

83-4 Jeon-dong, Wansan-gu, Jeonju-si. ℰ **063/221-5553** or 2114. Free admission. From the bus terminal take a bus bound for Nambu market no. 211, 221, 231, 251, 220, 229, 241, 291, 501, 502, or 700 and get off at Pungnammun. From the train station, take bus no. 118, 119, 211, 221, 231, or 241 and get off at Jeondong Cathedral.

Jeonju Traditional Korean Wine Museum MUSEUM   This may sound like a place to put on your party hat and imbibe, but it's actually a serious museum created to preserve the traditional rice wine brewing process. It harks back to a time when each household brewed its own rice wine using wood-burning stoves. On the first and third Saturdays of each month there is a traditional liquor brewing demonstration. On the second and fourth Saturdays they have tastings.

39-3 3-ga Pungnam-dong, Wansan-gu, Jeonju. ℰ **063/297-6305**. Free admission. Tues–Sun 9am–6pm. From the bus terminals, take bus no. 79-2, 88, 88-1, or 126 and get off at Jeondong Cathedral. From the train station, take bus no. 111 or 163 and get off at Jeonbuk Art Center. It's about a 10-min. walk from the bus stops.

Shopping

Jeonju is well known for its traditional crafts, especially fans and other items made from hanji (mulberry paper). Historically, Jeonju was known for making the best bamboo and paper fans in Korea, and has been home to master fan makers called

YOU SAY YOU want A REVOLUTION?

In 1894, long-suffering Korean peasants reached the end of their patience with royalty and with the *yangban* (the aristocracy) class. Tensions had long been simmering among the peasants, angry over the oppressive rule of the Joseon Dynasty, which taxed them heavily while providing little in return. Severe droughts in the early 1800s had led to crippling famines, and taxes had grown so onerous that many farmers were forced to sell their ancestral farms to wealthy landowners, who then rented it back to them at outrageous prices. In local uprisings in 1812 and 1862, farmers focused their rage on these landowners, and were brutally suppressed by government soldiers.

At the same time, an ideology called Donghak (Eastern Learning) was spreading throughout Korea's rural areas. A mix of Buddhism, Confucianism, and other elements, it was both a political and a spiritual movement. Akin in many ways to Marxism, it was centered on the premise of basic human rights—and on driving out foreign influences. The

peasant class had grown frustrated by the influence exerted over Korean politics by the Chinese and particularly the Japanese, whom they felt did not care about their needs.

Finally, in January 1894, the peasants rose up en masse in what is known as the Donghak Peasant Revolution. Their aim was to expel foreigners (specifically the Japanese) and to bring about social reforms like democracy, land redistribution, and tax reduction. At first they managed to defeat some government troops, but by March 1895 the military, with the help of Japanese soldiers, had crushed the rebellion completely.

While the revolution itself failed, it did have a lasting impact. It sparked the Sino-Japanese War (1894–95), as China and Japan struggled for dominance over the Korean Peninsula. Japan won—and promptly made Korea its pawn. Within 10 years, Japan had formally annexed Korea and would remain in control until the end of World War II.

"Seonjajang," for centuries. Cheap paper fans can be found all over the city, but for higher-end crafts, try the **Crafts Exhibition Center,** 1-65 Gyo-dong Wansan-gu, or the larger **Jeonju Masterpiece Shopping Center** (📞 063/285-0002), which sells a variety of traditional handicrafts. Both centers are open daily 10am to 7pm; the latter is closed on Mondays.

If you want to do some upscale clothes shopping, stop by the Jeonju branch of the **Lotte Department Store** (📞 063/289-2500), which has several floors of fashions and home goods sandwiched between a basement food court and restaurants and a cinema above.

If you're an early riser or late sleeper, you can browse the **Nambu Shijang (Southern Market)** (📞 063/284-1344), which is open daily from midnight to 9pm. It has been the largest market in the Honam region since 1905 and is a living history of the people of this region. Most goods sold here are agricultural in nature, but there are other items for sale. Take a bus to Paldal Road or the Nambu Shijang. Other traditional markets include the **Joong-ang Shijang (Central Market),** which is open daily from 6am to 9pm, and the **Dongbu Shijang (Eastern Market),** which has rotating items on sale depending on the day of the week (blankets, Korean traditional clothing, and rice cakes on Mon; school uniforms on Tues; produce on Wed; and so forth).

Imsil

When one thinks of South Korea, cheese is usually not the first thing that comes to mind. In Imsil, however, cheese making not only is a way of life, but has become a tourist attraction as well. Cheese was introduced to South Korea in 1959 by a Belgian missionary, who came to Jeollabuk-do to help people surviving the Korean War. The **Imsil Cheese Village** (📞 063/643-3700) was founded much later, in 2005. Originally called Zelkova Village (after the trees that line the entry), its name was changed by the village assembly. They offer 1- to 2-day programs, including the regular cheese experience. This program starts at 10:10am and lasts about 3 to 3½ hours. It includes hands-on cheese making, plus your choice of an additional program (e.g. goat milking, soap making, rice planting, etc.) and lunch. The overnight experience starts around 1:30pm with lunch, a tractor ride, cheesemaking, bike rides/strolls around the village, and more.

If you're not into cheese or want to also enjoy some of the most beautiful scenery the countryside has to offer, head to **Okjeongho ★★** (Okjeong Lake, aka Unam Lake; 📞 063/640-2641). This is a gorgeous body of water created by a dam on the Seomjin River. It's best viewed via a 2-hour drive around the water or from the top of Guksa Summit. Buses to Okjeong village run 5 times daily from 6:08am–10:15pm or take bus 976 (which runs 6:40am–9:40pm) and get off at Unam-gyo (Unam Bridge).

From **Jeonju Bus Terminal** (📞 063/281-2739), buses run every 10 minutes, from 6:05am to 10pm. The 30- to 40-minute ride costs ₩5,000. From the Dong-Seoul Bus Terminal, buses to Imsil run from 10:00am–3:20pm. The nearly 4-hour ride will cost about ₩15,000.

Imsil has a train station off the Jeolla line.

Where to Stay

As in most cities in South Korea, there is no shortage of safe, clean, inexpensive motels and their Korean equivalent, called *yeogwan*. In Jeonju, many of them can be found near the train and bus stations in town. They are very similar to each other, most take cash upfront, and they charge around ₩35,000 to ₩45,000 for a standard room. Below, I've listed more upscale options.

EXPENSIVE

Jeonju Core Riviera Hotel At this place, rooms (both Western-style and Korean-style ondol) are a bit on the small and spare side. Built in 1996, this hotel has great service and is a popular place to hold academic seminars, since it has large meeting and banquet rooms.

26-5 Poongnam-dong 3-ga, Wansan-gu, Jeonju. http://www.core-riviera.co.kr. ⓒ **063/232-7000.** 166 units. ₩132,000 and up standard room. AE, MC, V. **Amenities:** 3 restaurants; bar; cafe; health club; sauna. *In room:* A/C, TV, hair dryer.

Jeonju Core Hotel Conveniently located in downtown Jeonju, the Jeonju Core is close to Jirisan and Naejangsan. Although the hotel is more than 20 years old, the rooms are comfortable—both Western and Korean style available. Unfortunately, the sauna is open only to male guests.

627-3 Noseong-dong, Wansan-gu, Jeonju. http://corehotel.co.kr. ⓒ **063/285-1100.** Fax 063/285-5707. 111 units. ₩150,000 standard room; ₩218,000 and up suite. AE, MC, V. **Amenities:** 3 restaurants; bar; pool; cafe; health club; sauna; bakery. *In room:* A/C, TV, minibar, hair dryer.

MODERATE

Jeonju Tourist Hotel ★ The first tourist hotel to be established in the city, this place has dated facilities, but it is still clean and comfortable. Rooms are basic and spare with small windows that don't offer much of a view. Conveniently located near the train station, it is right next to Jeonju-cheon (Jeonju Stream) and Daga Park. Rates include a complimentary breakfast. ⓒ **063/280-7700.** www.jjhotel.co.kr (Korean only) 42 units. ₩60,000 single/double. MC, V. **Amenities:** 3 restaurants; bar; cafe; nightclub. *In room:* A/C, TV, hair dryer.

28 Taga-dong 3-ga, Wansan-gu, Jeonju. ⓒ **063/280-7700.** www.jjhotel.co.kr (Korean only) 42 units. ₩60,000 single/double. MC, V. **Amenities:** 3 restaurants; bar; cafe; nightclub. *In room:* A/C, TV, hair dryer.

Hanok Living Experience Center 🎁 This traditional village has over 800 houses, renovated and preserved from the Joseon Dynasty. You can experience how the traditional royal class lived firsthand by staying in one of their traditional rooms. The ondol rooms feature traditional furniture made by a master craftsman and all stays include breakfast. Don't expect high-end facilities here (you are staying in a traditional village, after all). All rooms are the basic Korean style, thick blankets laid on the floor. You leave your shoes at the door and step in between sliding wooden doors covered in paper. First- and second-class rooms have personal restrooms, but the third-class option has shared facilities. All rooms include free use of on-site bicycles.

33-4 Pungnam-dong 3-ga, Wansan-gu, Jeonju. www.jjhanok.com/english. ⓒ **063/287-6300.** 15 units. ₩110,000–₩130,000 1st-class room; ₩90,000–₩100,000 2nd-class standard room; ₩70,000 3rd-class standard room. Extra person ₩10,000. Reservations should be made at least 2 weeks in advance, with 30% deposit due 1 week before. MC, V. **Amenities:** Shared kitchen facilities; free admission to Hanok Village. *In room:* Underfloor heating, breakfast included (except on Mondays).

INEXPENSIVE

White Tourist Motel Conveniently located within walking distance to the bus stations the rooms are clean and comfortable. Both beds and ondol rooms are available. If you want a room with a computer, ask for a "PC *bahng.*"

754-4 Geumam-dong, Deokjing-gu, Jeonju. ⓒ **063/271-3992.** 35 units. ₩35,000 single or double. MC, V. **Amenities:** Karaoke bar. *In room:* A/C, TV, hair dryer.

Where to Eat

Jeonju is famous for its *bibimbap* (mixed rice bowl), which can come with up to 30 local ingredients. Virtually every traditional restaurant in town will have a version of it on their menu, so be sure to try it at least once while you're here.

EXPENSIVE

Jeollado Eumshik Iyagi ★ KOREAN Plan on spending a long time at this place, known for *hanjeongshik* (traditional formal meals), since the meal comes with a seemingly endless number of dishes. You can splurge and get the ₩60,000 to ₩100,000 *teukbyeol hanjeongshik* (special traditional meal), or opt for the more economical *hanjeongshik bibimbap* for ₩15,000. Bring a friend because these formal meals with various *banchan* (side dishes) of seasonal vegetables and seafood require at least two people to finish.

899-1 U-ah 2(i)-dong, Deokjingu, Jeonju-si. ✆ **063/244-4477.** Entrees ₩10,000–₩20,000. MC, V. Daily noon–10:30pm. Limited parking. Just a block past the Pyeong-hwadong 4-way, across from the Hyundai Apts.

MODERATE

Gabgi Hwegwan ☺KOREAN Another joint well known for bibimbap, this spot also specializes in *yook-hwae* (raw beef) and *galbi* (beef short ribs). This is one of the few places in town that offer a kid's size serving of the famous Jeonju bibimbap.

265–34 Palbok-dong 2-ga, Deokjin-gu, Jeonju. ✆ **063/212-5766.** Entrees ₩10,000–₩15,000. MC, V. Daily 9am–10pm. Plenty of parking available. Right after you cross the Yongsan Bridge (also called Jeonju Daegyo).

Gajok Hwegwan ★★ KOREAN Famous for the bibimbap, this place really knows how to do it right (it helps that they've been cooking it up since 1980). You know this is a high-volume business when you see the giant pyramid of bowls kept on hand just for their signature dish. The menu has limited English, but it's easy to order and everything comes with a generous number of banchan.

80 Jung-ang-dong 3-ga, Wansan-gu, Jeonju. ✆ **063/284-0982** or -2884. Set menu ₩10,000 to ₩15,000. MC, V. Daily 11:30am–9:30pm. Plenty of parking available. Located on the diagonal corner from the Jeonju post office (across from the Sanup Bank).

INEXPENSIVE

Honam Gak KOREAN You'll find an array of local Jeonju cuisine in this large restaurant, which was built to look like a traditional house, curved roof and all. You can try one of the tasty bibimbap dishes or splurge and get the house special meal (*Honam Gak teukseon jungchan*), which comes with more banchan that you could ever finish in a day, let alone one meal. The side dishes vary depending on the season, but you'll likely get sautéed vegetables, *kimchi* (spiced dish), flatcakes, salted seafood, *shinseollo* (a "wizard's stew"), and more.

560-5 Songchundong 2-ga, Deokjingu, Jeonju. ✆ **063/278-8150.** Entrees ₩9,000–₩25,000. MC, V. Daily 11:30am–10pm. Plenty of parking available.

NAMWON

This city is known as the "City of Love" or the "Town of Fidelity," because it served as the setting for the traditional Chunhyang-jeon, a story about a beautiful girl born into a low-class family who falls in love with the son of the town's magistrate (see the box "The Legend of Chunhyang," below). There is even a **Chunhyang Festival** (www.chunhyang.org, Korean only), every year on the eighth day of the fourth lunar month (usually late Apr or early May).

In addition to its romantic history, Namwon serves as the transportation hub for climbers visiting **Jirisan National Park** (see p. 223).

Essentials

GETTING THERE There is regular train service to **Namwon Station** (*☎* **063/633-7788**) on the Jeolla line, which connects Seoul to Yeosu. The **Sae-maeul** trains take 4 hours and cost ₩20,100 to ₩24,000. The **Mugunghwa** trains run more frequently and take an additional half-hour. Seats cost ₩13,800 to ₩17,400.

Buses are available to/from Seoul's Express Bus Terminal. They run about 17 times a day, 6am to 10:20pm. The ride lasts just under 4 hours and costs ₩9,800 to ₩15,500. You can also catch an intercity bus from Jeonju (only 45 min. away), Gwangju, Daegu, and Hwaeomsa.

GETTING AROUND Local buses will take you pretty much anywhere you want to go, but can have infrequent service. There are taxis available to be flagged down on any street or in front of train and bus stations. Taxi drivers generally don't speak English, but if you tell them where you want to go, there shouldn't be a problem. Luckily, some of the main attractions in Namwon are within walking distance.

VISITOR INFORMATION There is a small tourist information booth in front of the train station, where you can get a map and general information from the friendly staff, who speak pretty good English. You will also find a small tourist information booth at Gwanghallu-won. The **Namwon City Tourism Department** can be reached at *☎* **063/632-1771** or http://en.namwon.go.kr/en.

THE PANSORI tradition

Sometimes called Korean opera, pansori is a form of storytelling by a singer and a drummer. The *sorrikkun* (the singer, or "noisemaker") tells a story (usually a satire or a love story) while the *gosu* (drummer) beats out the rhythm and sometimes makes short sounds of encouragement (called *chuimsae*) as the story is told. Members of the audience also belt out short words or sounds as well. A full story or *madang*, with alternating speaking parts (*anili*) and singing parts (*chang*), can take hours (sometimes 4 to 5) to complete. The singer holds a fan in one hand and uses it for emphasis, to show emotion and to indicate changes of scene.

Originating during the middle of the Joseon period (1392–1910), pansori began as part of the oral tradition by traveling performers. Although performers were considered low-class by the aristocrats, by the end of the Joseon Dynasty, the yangban began to appreciate the pansori performances. Due to its oral nature (it was passed down from person to person and not written), of the original 12 *pansori madang* only 5 remain today—"Simcheong-ga," "Chunhyang-ga," "Heungbuga," "Jeokyeokga," and "Sugung-ga." In 2003, UNESCO added pansori to its list of Masterpieces of Oral and Intangible Heritage of Humanity.

Exploring Namwon

Gwanghallu-won (Gwanghallu Garden) ★★★ GARDEN The beautifully landscaped Gwanghallu-won is the site of the annual Chunhyang Festival, since this is supposedly where the legendary lovers met. The buildings inside include the historic Gwangtong Pavilion, which is now called Chunhyang Hall. The Ojak Bridge, built over a pond, is supposed to ensure a happy marriage to any couple who step on it once a year. Other than being known for the traditional love story, Namwon is also the mecca for Korean *pansori* (blues-opera-style performance). From April to October, there are free daily performances here at noon. In July and September, you can enjoy evening performances at the open-air stage of the Chunhyang Cultural Arts Hall across the stream. The gardens are especially nice at night when the buildings are under-lit and admission is free the last hour before closing.

78 Cheongeo-dong, Namwon-si. ⓒ**063/620-6182.** www.gwanghallu.or.kr (Korean only). Admission ₩2,000 adults, ₩1,800 teens, ₩1,100 children. Daily 8am–8pm, free admission the last hour. Parking ₩2,000. From the bus station, take a bus heading for Suji, Daesan, Daegangor Songdont and get off at the Jaeil Bank intersection, then walk 3 min. A taxi ride from the bus station will cost about ₩4,000.

Namwon Tourist Complex AMUSEMENT PARK This large complex rests on the foothills across the Yocheon stream from Namwon. Sleeping options, restaurants, and amusements line **Dongpyeonje Street** (the main drag). Many sculptures and other works of art are scattered throughout the area. Also inside the complex is the small but interesting **Chunhyang Theme Park** (ⓒ 063/620-6836), with old-fashioned swings, a fish pond, and a fake house that someone like Chunhyang would have lived in. On the top of the complex, you'll find **Namwon Land,** an amusement park with a Ferris wheel and usual rides.

Eohyeon-dong, Namwon-si. ⓒ **063/632-6070.** www.namwontheme.or.kr (Korean only). Free admission to the complex, but separate admission for various attractions. Admission to Chunhyang Theme Park is ₩3,000 for adults, ₩2,500 teens, ₩2,000 children. No set hours for the complex, but Namwon Land and several eating establishments open late on weekends. Chunhyang Theme Park 9am–10pm Apr–Oct (until 9pm Nov–Mar).

National Center for Korean Folk Performing Arts ★★ PERFORMING ARTS VENUE This center was created in 1992 to preserve Korean folk traditions, and it organizes performances throughout the country and internationally, in addition to publishing any related research. The collection of traditional instruments is impressive and educational. At 5pm every Saturday (4pm in winter, and other times throughout the year), they put on Korean traditional music performances. Those held here and at the **Chunhyang Cultural Arts Hall** (across the stream from the Gwanghallu-won) include folk songs by *nongak* (farmers' percussion band) and other forms of traditional music.

37-40, Eohyeon-dong, Namwon-si. ⓒ **063/620-2324.** Admission ₩2,000 adults, ₩1,500 students, ₩1,000 children. Daily 9am–5pm. There are no direct buses to the center, but the best way to get there is to take a bus to Gwanghallu and then walk 10 min.

Shilsangsa (Shilsang Temple) TEMPLE Located along the northern border of Jirisan, this temple (sometimes spelled Silsangsa) faces Cheonwangbong, the mountain's highest peak. Originally built in 828 during the Shilla Dynasty, it is the first of the Gusan Seonmun (the nine Zen Buddhist temples that started "Seon," the Korean

THE legend OF CHUNHYANG

The story of Chunhyang, *Chunhyang-ga*, is one of a handful of surviving Korean pansori, in which a performer sings a story while a drummer sets the rhythm. Korea's version of *Romeo and Juliet* is about Chunhyang, the daughter of a *gisaeng* (a female entertainer for government officials akin to a Japanese geisha), who falls in love with Mong-ryong, the son of a magistrate.

The two marry in secret, but Mong-ryong is forced to return to Seoul to finish his education. While he is away, a local magistrate tries to force Chunhyang to be his concubine. She refuses and is thrown into prison, tortured, and sentenced to death. At the last minute, Mong-ryong returns disguised as a beggar (but in fact is a secret royal inspector) and rescues her.

Zen sect). Japanese invaders burned down the complex in 1592, and it was completely burned down again during King Gojeong's reign. It was rebuilt in 1884 on a smaller scale than its former self. Its iron Buddha from the late 9th century is one of the earliest examples of its kind.

50 Ipseok-li, Sannae-myeon, Namwon-si. © **061/636-3031.** Admission ₩1,500 adults, ₩1,200 youth, ₩800 children. Summer daily 9am–6pm; winter daily 9am–5pm. From Namwon, take road 24 to Unbong, go toward Inwol, and then take local road 60 toward Sannae-myeon. Follow the signs to Silsangsa.

Shopping

Namwon is well known for its wooden crafts, and you can find some traditional folkware at the **Namwon Folkcrafts Sales Center,** 470 Uhhyeoon-dong, Namwon-si (© **063/626-5840**), or the **Namwon Lacquer Center,** 515 Josan-dong, Namwon-si (© **063/631-5725**). There are also some shops in the **Namwon Tourist Complex** and near **Gwanghallu-won,** where you can buy furniture and other wares made from local bamboo.

Where to Stay

The largest concentration of accommodations is at the **Namwon Tourist Complex,** which has hotels and lower-priced *yeogwan* (low-end motels) and *minbak* (homestays), for the more price-conscious. There are also several motels near the bus terminal. They run from about ₩35,000 to ₩45,000 for a standard room that sleeps one or two. Newer accommodations are located near the Express Bus Terminal.

A conveniently located, slightly more upscale accommodation is the **Namwon Kookmin Hotel,** 437 Shincheon-dong, Namwon-si (© **063/626-5300;** fax 063/632-3436), with rooms starting at ₩60,000 per night. Cheaper options are the **Greenpia Motel,** 277-1, Yongdamil, Juchon-myeon, Namwon-si (© **063/636-7200**), and the **Chunhyanjang,** 37-121, Oyon-dong, Namwon-si (© **063/626-0330**), with rooms starting at ₩35,000 per night.

For a casual place to lay your head and a good home-cooked meal, try the **Namwon Shikdang Minbak,** 167-1 Bukcheon-li, Unbong-eup, Namwon-si (© **063/634-0044**) in Unbong. The accommodations are basic, but they serve great roasted pork.

Where to Eat

The **Namwon Tourist Complex** has a number of reasonably priced restaurants to choose from. For late-night amusements, there are also a number of *noraebang* (private karaoke "singing" rooms) and bars in the area.

For the specialty of the region, try the restaurants around **Gwanghallu-won** (some of the best ones are between the back gate and the post office). Many of the restaurants are decorated to imitate the kind run by Wolmae (Chunhyang's mom), who was a gisaeng. A famous restaurant in the area, well known for its *chueoh* (loach, or mudfish that live in rice paddies, a type of freshwater fish that is small, flat and has mild, white meat), is **Namwon Chunhyang-gol Saejip,** 60-206 Cheongeoh-dong, Namwon-si ($\textcircled{C}$ **063/625-2443**), whose name means "new house." They do all things loach, including loach stew, loach sashimi, and deep-fried loach. Dishes range from ₩7,000 to ₩25,000.

THE REST OF JEOLLABUK-DO

The northern half of Jeolla-do, Jeollabuk-do (sometimes called "Jeonbuk") encompasses six small cities, including Jeonju and Namwon (see earlier), Iksan, Gimje, Gunsan, and Jeong-eup. Still, most of its residents live in rural areas. Due to its shallow water, there is almost no good natural harbor. Only Gunsan has a large-scale harbor and ferry terminal. Unlike Jeollanam-do to the south, Jeollabuk-do has virtually no wide, sandy beaches and very few associated islands.

Still, because of its fertile soil, the area has been the primary rice provider for the peninsula for centuries. Its red soil is also supposedly good for your health and can be found in specialized cosmetics and beauty products from the region. Although there aren't any major tourist destinations in the province, there are many national parks, historical areas, and quieter temples.

Essentials

GETTING THERE There is only one airport in the province at **Gunsan,** 385 Seonyeon-li (KUV; $\textcircled{C}$ **063/469-8345;** www.airport.co.kr/doc/gunsan_eng). Korean Airlines ($\textcircled{C}$ **1588-2001;** www.koreanair.com) offers flights to and from Jeju twice daily. There are **local city buses** to Gunsan city that run every hour. There are also two nonstop intercity buses to Jeonju and Iksan, which run twice a day. One auto-rental company, **Kumho Rent-a-Car** ($\textcircled{C}$ **063/468-8000**), has a kiosk at the airport.

It is easier to reach the region by train as the **Honam line** runs south from Daejeon and connects Iksan and Jeong-eup to Mokpo (the end of the line). The **Jeolla line** runs southeast from Iksan to Jeonju, Imsil, and Namwon before going to Suncheon and Yeosu in Jeollanam-do. The short **Gunsan line** starts from Iksan and heads west to Gunsan.

It's best to take a bus to Jeonju from Seoul, and then explore the rest of Jeollabuk-do from there.

The Honam Expressway (road 25) runs through the middle of the province. It connects Iksan and port city Gunsan to Jeonju.

GETTING AROUND Local buses will take you pretty much anywhere you want to go; the only problem is that they run pretty infrequently (about every hour or two) from select destinations. So make sure you know what time the return bus is so that you're not stuck waiting an hour for the next bus. Fares run to about ₩1,000 to ₩1,400 for local buses, so be sure to have plenty of ₩1,000 bills and coins with you (drivers usually don't give you change). Unfortunately, bus schedules aren't always posted at the bus stops (sometimes there aren't even bus stops), so ask your driver what time the return trips run and plan accordingly, especially when venturing out to less popular places.

If you want to rent a car, rent one in a city (like Seoul or at least Jeonju) because you won't find car-rental companies in remote areas (for instance, there is only one company that services Namwon).

Taxis are usually available to be flagged down in cities and major tourist attractions, but you won't find them in some of the smaller remote villages. As in most places outside of Seoul, drivers don't speak English, so be sure to have a map or know the name of your destination in Korean.

VISITOR INFORMATION   The **Jeollabuk-do Tourist Information Center** (✆ **063/281-2739**) is located in front of the Jeonju Bus Terminal (Geumam-dong, Deokjin-gu, Jeonju-si) and is open daily from 9am to 6pm. The official website for the province is http://en.jeonbuk.go.kr.

Muju & Deogyusan National Park

About 4 hours from Seoul, **Muju County** (✆ 063/321-2114; 10am–5pm, http://neweng.muju.org/index.sko?menuCd=AD01000000000) is known for its annual **Firefly Festival** in mid-June. Because the Sobaek Mountains divide the county, the beautiful **Muju Resort** (✆ 063/322-9000; for more information see "Where to Stay," later) is popular for skiing and sledding in the winter. The summer attracts golfers and hikers.

The **Deogyusan (Mt. Deogyu) National Park** (✆ 063/322-3174; http://english.knps.or.kr/Knp/Deogyusan) spans a large area of the Sobaek Mountains and includes the scenic **Gucheondong Valley,** which is worth exploring for its interesting rock formations, wonderful cliffs, and waterfalls. The town of Muju, the gateway to the valley on its Jeollabuk-do side, is not much of a destination. The city does have the **Hanpungnu Pavilion,** said to be one of the most beautiful in the province.

One of the remaining temples in the valley is the **Baengnyeongsa** (✆ 063/322-3395 Korean only) named because of a white lotus that appeared after the death of a monk who meditated here in seclusion. The most popular and scenic hiking trail takes you up from the park's entrance to Baengnyeongsa. It takes about 3 hours round-trip.

Also in the national park are **Anguksa (Anguk Temple)** and the **Jeoksangsanseong (Jeoksan Fortress),** both of which offer beautiful views from their height in the mountains.

Entrance to the national park is free. Plan to head to the Jeoksang entrance if you want to see Anguksa, and the Samgong entrance if you want to see Baengnyeongsa. To get to Baengnyeongsa from the Muju bus terminal, take a bus heading toward Gucheon-dong and get off at the last stop (buses run once an hour from 7:25am to 8:30pm and take about 45 min.).

Gochang

This small town and county of **Gochang** (http://culture.gochang.go.kr/site_english) are located southwest of Jeong-eup in the southwestern part of the province. This largely rural area is known for its hundreds of dolmen and its most famous attraction,

Prehistoric Dolmen Sites

The prehistoric burial grounds of Gochang, Hwasun, and Ganghwa contain hundreds of dolmen (stone tombs) from the first millennium B.C. Although similar stone tombs from Megalithic culture are found in other parts of the world (mainly Asia, Europe, and North Africa), nowhere else are they found in such concentration and variety. Dolmens are Megalithic-era funerary monuments consisting of large "capstones" placed on top of two other stone slabs. Like the stones of Stonehenge and Orkney in Britain and the stone circles of West Africa, South Korea's dolmen are also remnants of a Megalithic culture that thrived in the Neolithic and Bronze Ages during the 2nd and 1st millenniums B.C. The Korean dolmen appear to have arrived with the Bronze Age.

The dolmen of Gochang are said to be from the 7th to 3rd century B.C. Those in Hwasun date around 6th–5th century B.C., while the dates of the Ganghwa dolmen are yet to be determined (although archaeologists figure around 1st century B.C., based on stylistic traits.)

the **Gochang-eupseong (Gochang-eup Fortress)** ★★ (aka Moyangseong, after Gochang's name during the Baekje period, ⓒ 063/560-2710), located on the hill overlooking the village. Built in 1453, during the early Joseon Dynasty, it is surrounded by the slopes of Bandeugsan and has three gates, one each to the east, west, and north; two floodgates; and a tower. Most of the original fortress is intact and the rest has been reconstructed, so it is in fine shape these days. The **Gochang Moyang Fortress Festival** (http://gochang.go.kr/festival, Korean only) is held here on the ninth day of the ninth lunar month of the year (usually in early Oct). If you happen to be in the area then, make sure to catch it, as it is one of the few traditional festivals left of its kind.

Next to the fortress (and in walking distance from the bus station) is the **Gochang Pansori Museum** (http://www.pansorimuseum.com/eng). A private museum, it is a nice introduction to this historic and uniquely Korean way of singing. It's open Tuesday through Sunday 9am to 6pm, last tickets sold 30 minutes before closing. The museum is closed Jan 1. Admission is ₩800 for adults, ₩500 for youths 7 to 18, and free for those 65 and older and kids 6 and under.

The prehistoric cemeteries surrounding the small town of Gochang (along with those at Hwasun and Ganghwa) have been collectively declared a UNESCO World Heritage site. The thousands of *goindol* (dolmen) found in these sites form part of the remnants of a Megalithic culture found both here and in other parts of the world. There are over 2,000 (out of the 36,000 on the entire Korean Peninsula) found in the eastern mountains of Gochang-eup. The Korean word for dolmen, goindol, literally means "a rock that is propped up by other rocks." The **Gochang Dolmen Museum** (ⓒ 063/560-8666; 676 Dosan-li, Gochang-eup; www.gcdolmen.go.kr/english/2011/sboard.php?sMenu=main), which is mainly a bunch of dioramas depicting the life of the prehistoric dolmen makers, is open Tuesday through Sunday 9am to 6pm (until 5pm Nov–Feb). Admission is ₩3,000 for adults, ₩2,000 for teens, ₩1,000 for children.

Daily buses from Seoul's Express Bus Terminal go to Gochang about every 40 minutes, from 7am to 7pm. The ride takes about 3 hours and 40 minutes. Buses are also available from Jeonju (80-min. ride) every 30 minutes. Those from Gwangju run

The King of Harmless Ghosts

The Jijang Bosal, or King of the Harmless Ghosts (he's also known as Bodhisattva Ksitigarbha, as Dizang in Chinese, and as Jizo in Japanese), is a popular bodhisattva for Mahayana Buddhists. A Buddhist saint of sorts, he made a vow not to achieve "Buddhahood" until all the hells were emptied, and thus became the bodhisattva of beings in hell. He is usually depicted as a monk with a shaved head and often carries a staff to force the gates of hell open. He also carries the "wish-fulfilling jewel" to light the darkness.

every 30 minutes and take just under an hour. Buses also run from Jeong-eup every 10 minutes and take about 30 minutes to arrive in Gochang.

Seonunsan (Mt. Seonun) Provincial Park

This park is famous for its dense forest, steep peaks, and oddly shaped rocks (some are sheer-faced as if they've been sliced in half, while others are rounded and almost form figures). Although these are not the highest ranges in the country, the sheer faces of some of the rocks here make this a very popular spot for rock climbers.

The original **Seonunsa (Seonun Temple) ★★**, built in 577 during the Baekje period, was an impressive complex. It is now only a shadow of its former self (at its height, it had 89 shrines and 3,000 monks living within its confines), ever since much of it was destroyed during the second Japanese invasion in 1597. Still, the temple is renowned for its beautiful scenery during all four seasons—brilliantly blooming 500-year-old camellia trees and cherry blossoms in the spring, thick green forests hiding cool valleys in the summer, colorful foliage in the fall, and peaceful white snow blanketing the winter scenery. It also houses a Buddha statue from the early Goryeo Dynasty, which was later found to have a hidden record from the Donghak Farmers' Revolution (see p. 186) hidden in its chest. Admission to the temple is ₩2,500 adults, ₩1,500 teens, and ₩1,000 children.

While in the area, walk up a bit from Seonunsa to the **Jinheung-gul** (Jinheung cave) and the **Dosol-am** (sometimes spelled Dosoram), a hermitage set in a pine and bamboo grove. Enshrined in the hermitage is the **Jijang Bosal,** the "King of Harmless Ghosts" and the lord of the underworld, where many come to pray for help in the afterlife.

You can take a direct bus to Seonunsan from Jeong-eup Station. Buses run four times a day and the ride takes about 50 minutes. Buses are also available from Gochang, which take about 30 minutes and run about eight times a day. The park is open daily from 8am to 6pm in the summer, 9am to 5pm in the winter.

If you decide to overnight in the area, your best bet is the **Seonunsan Tourist Hotel** (© 063/561-3377). Located near the entrance to the park, it is the largest hotel in the area. Its facilities are a bit dated and show wear, but their ondol rooms are comfortable and clean, ranging from ₩60,000 to ₩100,000. Even if you decide to stay at the less expensive **Seonunsan Youth Hostel** (© 063/561-3333) or any of the private minbak in the area, you can still drop in for a soak, the sauna, or a mud massage at the Seonunsan Tourist Hotel's Cheongjutang (bath).

As for eats, the regional specialty is Puncheon eel, caught in the area streams, where freshwater meets seawater. Many restaurants specialize in this somewhat sweet-tasting fish. Most of them are located around the entrance to the park. One good joint is the **Cheongwon Garden** (🕿 **063/564-0414**), where they serve it broiled in soy sauce for about ₩22,000. You can wash it all down with some of their special (and fragrant) wild berry wine for ₩9,000.

Byeonsan Bando (Mt. Byeon Peninsula) National Park

At the only national park in South Korea to encompass both a seashore and mountains, the mountains here are surprisingly rugged for being so close to the ocean and rising up from the fertile plains. Stretching 35km (22 miles), the park is divided into two large sections—**Oebyeonsan** (outer Byeonsan), on the coast, and **Naebyeonsan** (inner Byeonsan) inland.

The main attractions at Oebyeonsan are **Byeonsan Beach** and **Chaeseokgang (Chaeseok River).** One of the few good beaches on South Korea's west coast, its fine sand and nearby pine forest attracts tourists, especially during the summer. Chaeseokgang lies on the west of the Byeonsan Peninsula, where it meets the sea and the cliffs. Those cliffs, the **Toejeokamcheong,** look like thousands of books stacked on top of each other. It's a great place to enjoy the sunset any time of year.

Seafood restaurants line the shore of Byeonsan Bando on the way to Chaeseokgang. Great scenery and a bowl of *hwaeduphap* (rice and raw fish) can be had for ₩10,000 at such places as the **Hwang-geum Hwaetjib** (🕿 **063/582-8763,** San 47, Gyeonpo-li, Byeonsan-myeon, Buan-gun). Plates of fresh *hwae* (raw fish) cost anywhere from ₩20,000 to ₩80,000 depending on the size and assortment of fish.

Naebyeonsan is especially well known for its waterfalls, gorgeous valleys, and fragrant pine woodlands. On the east side of the mountain is the diminutive **Gaeamsa (Gaeam Temple),** originally built in 676. It was expanded in 1313 and has gone through many reconstructions. Admission is free and it's open from sunrise to sunset.

The largest temple in the park is **Naesosa ★★★** (🕿 **063/583-7281,** 268 Seokpo-li, Jinseo-myeon, Buan-gun, www.naesosa.org), which was originally built in 633 during the Baekje period. It has also been through many renovations, with the latest carried out by a Zen monk in 1865. It's one of the few temples in the country with buildings left unpainted. The walk to the temple is beautiful, lined on either side with fir and pine trees (although the recorded Buddhist chanting can be a bit distracting). It's definitely worth a visit if you're in the area. Entrance to Naesosa is ₩2,000 adults, ₩800 teens, and ₩500 children. Open daily 8:30am–5:30pm winter, 8am–6pm summer.

From the Buan Bus Terminal, there are buses to Naesosa every 20 to 30 minutes from 6:30am to 8:30pm. The ride takes about 50 minutes. Buses to Buan from Seoul's Express Bus Terminal go from 6:50amto 7:30pm about once an hour, taking just under 3 hours. Buses from DongSeoul run five times daily from 7:40am to 5:40pm and take about 4 hours. Both buses cost about ₩13,700.

The easiest way to get to Byeonsan Bando National Park (http://english.knps.or.kr/Knp/Byeonsanbando/Intro/Introduction.aspx?MenuNum=1&Submenu=Npp) is to take a bus or taxi from either Jeong-eup Station or the Buan Bus Terminal. The park is open daily March through October from 8:30am to 6pm (from 9am Nov–Feb). Admission is free. If you get a chance, pick up a jar of the wonderfully aromatic wild honey from local vendors in the Naebyeonsan area, which is supposed to have medicinal value and is one of the three famous things (*sambyeon*) from the region. The other two are the wild orchids and the tall, straight fir trees.

Accommodations in the area include a number of small yeogwan and minbak with single/double rooms usually in the ₩35,000 to ₩40,000 range on weekdays and ₩40,000 to ₩50,000 on weekends. The most high-end hotel in the area is the **Byeonsan Daemyung Resort ★ ☺ ✦** (© 063/580-8800 or 1588-4888 257 Gyeoppo-li Byeonsan-myeon, Buan-gun; http://www.daemyungresort.com/asp/language/english), which also has an attached water park, **AquaWorld.** Both Korean and Western-style rooms start at ₩51,000 on off-season weekdays. In popular summer months (July–Aug), it may be easier to find a place to sleep in the nearby town, Gyeokpoham.

Daedunsan (Mt. Daedun) Provincial Park ★

Daedunsan is almost equidistant from both Jeonju and Daejeon, making it an ideal day trip from either city. Its dramatic high peak can be reached by hiking up for 2 hours or by taking the cable car (which offers beautiful views of the valley below). At the top, one trail leads you straight up to a metal staircase (go up about 10 min.) to the **Geumgang Gureumdali (Geumgang "Dream" Bridge),** a narrow suspension bridge which is 50m (164 ft.) long, 1m (3¼ ft.) wide, and about 80m (262 ft.) high. But the fun doesn't end there. After the bridge is another set of metal stairs, steeper and more precarious than the last one. Climbing up those stairs takes you to the top of the mountain, where you may be surprised to find *ajummas* selling bottles of water and candy bars, which they carry up the mountain every morning. Admission to the park is free, but the cable car costs round-trip ₩8,000 ages 14 and up, ₩5,000 kids 3 to 13.

You can take a bus from either Jeonju or Daejeon and get off at the small tourist village near the Daedunsan Tourist Hotel. There are six buses daily from Daejeon Seobu Bus Terminal to Daedunsan (about a 40-min. ride) and 5 buses from the Jeonju Bus Terminal (about an hour ride).

Maisan (Mt. Mai) Provincial Park ★★ ☺ & Jinan

The name "Maisan" means "horse ear mountain," so named because two of its peaks are said to look like the ears of a horse (especially when looking at them from Jinan).

Tapsa (Pagoda Temple) ★★★ is one of the most interesting small temples in the country. About 120 pagodas made from neatly piled stones were created here by Yi Gapyong, a hermit who lived here for 30 years. Only 80 of them exist today. You'll pass the smaller **Eunsusa** ("Silver Water" Temple) on the way up, and another temple, the **Geamdangsa** (a garishly gold temple), just below Tapsa. Near this temple, there is a trail that leads up to **Naong-am,** a grotto cave used as a sanctuary by a Shilla monk. Farther down the road is the **Isan-myo,** a shrine dedicated to Dangun and Joseon Dynasty kings Taejo and Sejong. The way up to Tapsa is steep and precarious, but it's worth the climb. You can also get to Tapsa without the arduous hike by entering via the north parking lot. The easy path gives you access to the small lake that has swan-shaped paddle boats available during summer months. Admission to the park costs ₩2,000 adults, ₩1,500 teens, ₩1,000 children.

You can take a daily local bus from Jinan, which leaves every 40 minutes to North Maisan from 7:30am to 6pm, and takes about 10 minutes. Buses to South Maisan run only five times daily from 10am to 7pm and take about 20 min. To get to Jinan, catch the 50-minute bus ride from Jeonju (buses run 7:30am to 6pm). **Jinan** (© 063/433-3313; www.jinan.go.kr/english/sub0401.jsp) itself is a charming little provincial town near the edge of a forest, well known for its *insam* (ginseng) and shiitake mushrooms.

Gangcheonsan County Park

Although national and provincial parks are popular tourist destinations, county parks are usually lesser known. That's a shame, because some of them are truly special. Jeollabuk-do has two county parks, one of which is **Gangcheonsan.** Located southeast of Naejangsan, it is just outside of the small village of Sunchang (see section below). Although this park's peaks aren't very dramatic, the big draws here are the gently curving surrounding valleys and streams that flow through them.

To the left of the park's entrance is a lake, **Gangcheon-ho,** which usually has clear, calm waters that mirror the surrounding landscape. The area is great to visit any time of year, with cherry blossoms, forsythias, and azaleas blooming in the spring; refreshingly cold waters flowing in cool valleys in the summer; maple trees aflame with color in the fall (autumn); and snow-capped mountains in the winter.

The main hiking trail runs along the stream to **Gangcheonsa (Gangcheon Temple).** Built in 887 by Monk Doseon Guksa, the temple used to be a huge complex with several associated hermitages, but it was destroyed during the Imjin Waeran in the 1590s, and again during the Korean War. It was reconstructed slowly thereafter but it never again attained its former glory. The buildings are rather unimpressive today, but the setting is still idyllic.

Just beyond the temple is a suspension bridge that was built in 1980. If you cross the bridge and follow the trail up the hillside, you'll reach a pavilion, where you'll get the best view of the valley below. From the top of the reservoir there are two steep trails that lead up to the fortress. The southern trail is steeper, while the northern one runs along the ridge.

You can catch a bus to Gangcheonsan from the **Sunchang Bus Terminal** about 12 times daily from 7am to 6:50pm (taking about 20 min.). Buses also run from Gwangju and Jeong-eup (the one from Jeong-eup stops a few kilometers below the mountain village). Many restaurants, souvenir shops, and a handful of accommodations are available in the small village outside the park's entrance. Admission is ₩2,000 for adults, ₩1,000 for youth.

Sunchang

Sunchang (the village and county) is well known for its *gochujang* (chili-pepper paste). It's so popular, in fact, that it has a museum dedicated to the fermented condiment, the **Janghada** (Jangnyu Museum), Baeksan-li, Sunchang-eup, Sunchang-gun (© **063/650-5432;** www.janghada.com). If you reserve in advance, you can make your own gochujang and take a jar home with you. Visitors can also learn how to make *shikhae* (the sweet rice drink) and *injeolmi* (a traditional rice cake dusted in toasted soy bean powder). Open Tuesday to Sunday 9am to 6pm; the last admission is an hour before closing. Admission is free, but it costs ₩24,000 for adults and ₩14,000 for children for the 40-min. experiential program. They even have sleeping quarters for those who want to spend the night in Sunchang.

Nearby, at the foot of Amisan is the **Sunchang Gochujang Minsok Maeul** (Chile Paste Folk Village) (© **063/653-0703**), a relatively new village, where several dozen artisans moved into the town's *hanok* (traditional houses) to make and sell their handmade chili paste. Visitors can visit each place and taste the gochujang and *jjangajji* (picked vegetables), made the old-fashioned way. They even have a **Sunchang Gochujang Festival** in early November. From the Sunchang bus terminal, take a bus going to either Geumgwa or Jangan Deokcheon, which runs once an hour 6:30am to 7:30pm, and get off at the Gangcheon gas station (about a 10-min. ride).

Buses from Seoul's Express Bus Terminal go to Sunchang five times daily, at 9:30am, 10:30am, 1:30pm, 2:45pm, and 4:10pm. The ride costs about ₩14,300 and takes about 3½ hours. There are buses from Incheon (via Damyang) to Sunchang twice a day, taking about 5 hours. There are also direct buses from Jeonju (every 30 min. 6:30am to 8:30pm) and from Gwangju (every 20 min. 6am to 9:30pm).

Shopping

Jeollabuk-do is known for its regional traditional crafts. The **Iri Gems and Jewelry Center** (② 063/835-8007) in Iksan is the only jewelry center in the country. Jewels are processed locally, set, and sold at the center daily, except on Tuesdays. Inside the Wanggung Jewelry Theme Park is the **Iksan Jewelry Museum** (② 063/859-4641; www.jewelmuseum.go.kr, Korean only, 575-1 Dongyong-li, Wanggung-myeon, Iksan-si), which has an impressive, and unusual, collection of rare gemstones and dinosaur fossils. They host jewelry-making classes each Saturday and Sunday, March to November, open Tuesday through Sunday 10am to 6pm. Admission to the museum is ₩3,000 adults, ₩2,000 teens, ₩1,000 children. Classes are free, but there is a ₩5,000 to ₩10,000 material fee. Also in Iksan is the **Jinan Ginseng Center** (② 063/433-0292 or 3), which is well known throughout South Korea for its high-quality insam.

As far as traditional crafts are concerned, Gosu ceramics from Gochang and woodenware from Jangsu are representative Korean handiworks that make nice souvenirs. In Gunsan, try the **Gunsan Korean Traditional Specialty Products Center** (② 063/433-3113) for shopping. If you're into musical instruments, check out the traditional drums made in Jangsu.

Where to Stay

There are plenty of places to sleep in Muju, most notably the **Muju Deogyusan Resort**, which includes the modest and economical **Gukmin Hotel,** at San 43-15 Simgok-li, Seolcheon-myeon, Muju-gun (www.mdysresort.com; ② 063/320-7000; fax 063/320-7055). As at most resorts in South Korea, the rooms will be a little overpriced, especially during high season. Singles/doubles start at ₩80,000.

In Gunsan, there are two first-class tourist hotels, the **Gunsan Riverhill Tourist Hotel** (② 063/453-0005, 428-4 Seongdeok-li, Seongsan-myeon, Gunsan-si), and the more upscale **Ritz Plaza Hotel** (② 1588-4681, 1195-49 Beonji, Namun-dong, Gunsan-si).

Although Iksan's tourist industry has not begun to boom, the most upscale accommodation in the city is the **Grand Plaza Tourist Hotel** (② 063/843-7777 or 843-1714, 329-2 Pyeonghwa-dong, Iksan-si). Other lower-price options can be found in the same area, around the Iksan Express Bus Terminal and the train station.

There are a few motels in Gochang and an economical choice is **Cheong Green Park Motel** (② 063/561-3161 or 011/9627-6072, 512-12 Chiryong-li, Heungdeok-myeon, Gochang-gun), a love motel with doubles starting at ₩35,000.

If you want to stay and have an unusual Korean spa, visit the **Jinan Red Ginseng Spa Hotel ★★** 🏨 (www.redginsengspa.kr; ✆ **1588-7597** or 063/433-0393; 744 Danyang-li, Jinan-eup, Jinan-gun) with singles/doubles starting at ₩80,000. Their spa is centered around experiencing the 5 elements and includes a red gingseng-scented communal bubble bath and a rooftop spa with fabulous views of Maisan.

Where to Eat

Other than the bibimbap, the region is famous for its hanjeongshik, which comes with two soups, 13 banchan, four or five vegetable banchan, and a salted fish.

In Muju, try the **Jeonju Hangukgwan,** 418-19 Deogyu-li, Seolcheon-myeon, Muju-gun (✆ **063/322-3162**), open daily from 7am to 11pm, or **Seommaeul,** 1357-1 Eupnae-li, Muju-eup, Muju-gun (✆ **063/322-2799**), open daily from 9am to 10pm.

In Gunsan, if you like blue crabs, try **Goongjeon Ggotgyejang,** 23 beonji, Geumseon-li, Oksan-myeon, Gunsan-si (✆ **063/466-6677** or 8), with meals ranging from ₩20,000 for a raw crab meal to ₩45,000 for a steamed crab meal. They're open daily from 10am to 10pm. **Geumgang Ggotgyejang,** 644-6 Hyeongam-dong, Gunsan-si, also does the local raw crab, but with an inexpensive meal starting at ₩5,000, or you can get a kilo (2.2 IB) of the seasoned blue crab for ₩57,000 to share with friends. If you're looking for a cheaper meal in Gunsan, **Jayu Shigan,** 742-1 Jochon-dong, Gunsan-si (✆ **063/452-7522**), whose name translates to "free time," has *kal gooksu* (hand-cut noodles) starting at ₩3,000, daily 11am to 2am (they close the second Sun of every month).

There are small restaurants at the entrances to the national and provincial parks, where local owners serve dishes from the region. Ask the *ajumma* (married women) what the specialty of the region is, or you can't go wrong ordering the *hanshik,* which is short for *hanjeongshik* (traditional Korean meal).

GWANGJU

One of the administrative centers of the Baekje Kingdom, Gwangju now looks like any other South Korean city. However, its citizens have an independent spirit, exemplified by Gwangju's importance in the country's civic and human rights movements. The last rebellion was May 18, 1980, and echoes can still be felt here today.

Known as the economic and educational center for the region, it is famous for its **Art Biennale,** held every other year in the fall. If you happen to be in the city in October, don't miss the **Kimchi Festival,** a wonderful introduction to Korea's famed pickled dish.

Surrounded by the great agricultural plains of the region, the city nestles up against Mudeungsan. The old section of town follows the path of a stream, stretching northwest and including the main business and entertainment areas. The best pedestrian street is **Jungjang-no,** where you'll find shops, restaurants, cafes, bars, and theaters. Major businesses have their offices in **Geumnan-no,** which has an arcade of shops underneath the serious businesses. East of Geumnan-no (toward Jungjang-no) is an area called **Art Street** where you'll find galleries, traditional teahouses, and art-supply stores.

Essentials

GETTING THERE The **Gwangju Airport** (KWJ, ℂ **062/940-0214;** www. airport.co.kr/doc/gwangju_eng) is located 11km (6¾ miles) west of the city center in the Gwangsan area of town. It is a domestic airport with flights 8 times a day to and from Seoul's Gimpo Airport, 10 times a day to and from Jeju-do. There is one flight daily from Shanghai (by **China Eastern Airlines**) and one flight daily from Shenyang (by **China Southern Airlines**). You can find out schedules from **Asiana Airlines** or **Korean Air,** both of which have offices in the city. Several **local buses** go from the airport into the city, daily from 5:30am to 10:30pm, costing ₩1,000. The **airport limousine bus** runs daily from 6:20am to 10:10pm and will set you back ₩1,500. There are, of course, plenty of taxis waiting outside the terminals. Deluxe taxi base fares start at ₩3,500 and regular taxi base fares start at ₩2,200. There is also an airport stop on the city's one-line subway.

There are plenty of trains to and from Gwangju, since the city has two train stations. The Songjeongni Station (ℂ **062/1544-7788**) is not too far from the airport and the Gwangju Station (ℂ **062/514-7788**) is closer to the center of town. Trains from Seoul arrive at Yongsan Station and run several times daily. KTX trains are the fastest, run most frequently, cost ₩33,000, and take 2½ to 3 hours. While the Saemaeul trains take about 4 hours, the Mugunghwa trains take about 4½ hours, costing ₩20,000 to ₩29,700.

Buses to and from **Gwangju's Express Bus Terminal** (ℂ **062/360-8114**) run much more frequently than trains. Direct buses are available from Seoul, DongSeoul, Busan, Daegu, Daejeon, Ulsan, Incheon, Suwon, Wonju, and Jeonju.

GETTING AROUND Gwangju has a small **subway** system (www.gwangjusubway. co.kr/engsubway/main.jsp), currently with only one line, which is pretty inexpensive, but doesn't go to far-flung places. A one-way trip costs ₩1,200 (or ₩1,100 with a Travel-Card) and ₩400 for children. Trains run 5:30am to midnight daily, and run at 8- to 10-minute intervals, except during rush hours, when they run every 5 to 7 minutes.

You can get a **Bitgoeul Card** (ℂ **062/226-5053 or 4**), which is good for both buses and subways, at subway stations and the Kwangju Bank. The base fee is ₩4,000 and you can recharge the card in any amount from ₩5,000 to ₩500,000. Not only does the card give you a discount on travel (a trip costs ₩1,000 for adults, ₩750 for teens and ₩350 for children), but it allows you a free transfer from subway to bus (or bus to different bus) within 30 minutes, and a free transfer from bus to subway within 1 hour.

Buses are an inexpensive and easy way to get around Gwangju. They run frequently and take you pretty much where you want to go. Bus fares in cash start at ₩1,200 adults, ₩900 for students, and ₩400 for children, and the easiest stop to find downtown is the one in front of the YMCA. For more information on bus routes, consult the tourist information center (see "Visitor Information," below).

Taxis in Gwangju are fairly inexpensive, costing about ₩15,000 to get across town. Deluxe taxis (the black ones) cost more money, of course, but the drivers tend to drive a bit slower (and safer) and they speak a bit of English.

VISITOR INFORMATION The **Gwangju Tourist Information Center** (ℂ **062/525-9370;** http://utour.gwangju.go.kr) runs several kiosks throughout the city, including inside the airport in front of the arrival gates on the first floor (ℂ **062/233-3399**), open daily 8am to 8pm. There are also tourist information centers at the train station (📞 **062/522-5147**), inside the bus station (📞 **062/365-8733**), at Songjeongni Station Plaza (📞 **062/941-6301**), and on the first floor of the YMCA (📞 **062/233-9370**). The city's website is http://eng.gjcity.net.

FAST FACTS   Near the main intersection in Gwangju are the **police station, post office,** a **bank,** and some accommodations.

Exploring Gwangju

Gwangju Art & Culture Center ★★ ART MUSEUM   The main cultural center of the city (and the region), this is one of the locations for the Gwangju Biennale (which happens during even-numbered years), a showcase of South Korean art and artists.

328-16 Unam-dong, Buk-gu, Gwangju-si. 📞 **062/608-4114.** Admission ₩1,000 adults, ₩700 teens, ₩300 children. Tues–Sun 9:30am–5pm. Closed on, and the day after, national holidays. Take bus no. 16, 18, 27, 29, 48, 51, 58, 63, 72, 83, 84, 85, or 192. 15 min. by taxi from Gwangju Station.

Gwangju National Museum ★ MUSEUM   Among the more than 1,000 items on display here are relics from the Paleolithic age through the Baekje period, pieces from Buddhist temples, and pottery from the Honam region. One of the highlights of the museum's collection is an assortment of 14th-century Chinese ceramics from a shipwreck discovered in 1975.

114 Bakmulgwan-lo, Maegok-dong, Buk-gu, Gwangju-si. 📞 **062/570-7000.** http://gwangju.museum.go.kr/eng/index.jsp. Admission free. Tues–Fri 9am–6pm; Sat until 9pm Mar–Dec, Sun and holidays 9am–7pm (ticket booth closes 1 hr. earlier). Closed Jan 1. Take bus no. 16, 19, 26, 35, 55, or 745 to the museum. The museum is on the edge of Biennale Park.

Jeungshimsa (Jeungshim Temple) ★ TEMPLE   Located in western Mudeung-san, this temple was founded by Julgam Seonsa during the Shilla Dynasty. Like many of Korea's temples, it was destroyed during the Korean War and rebuilt. On-site is the oldest structure in the area, the **Obaek-jeon,** which houses 500 Nahan statues and the 10 judges of the underworld. Just about a kilometer up from Jeungshimsa is **Yaksasa,** the only temple in the city that survived destruction during the Korean War.

56 Unlim-dong, Dong-gu, Gwangju-si. 📞 **062/226-0107.** Free admission. 24 hr. but best to visit 9am–6pm so as not to disturb the monks. Bus nos. 15, 23, 27, 52, 106, 555, 771, and 1001 go to the Jeungshimsa entrance. Parking available.

Gwangju Folk Museum MUSEUM   In the same park as the Gwangju National Museum (it's a 15-min. walk between the two) is the folk museum. Most of the important relics from the region are in the national museum, and this museum's collection is mostly geared toward dioramas, depicting lifestyle and folk traditions of the Honam region.

1004-4 Yongbong-dong, Buk-gu, Gwangju-si. 📞 **062/613-5337.** http://gjfm.gwangju.go.kr/index.do?S=S22 (Korean only). Admission ₩500 adults, ₩300 youths, ₩200 children. Tues–Sun 9:30am–5pm. Closed days after national holidays. Take the bus to the National Museum and walk from there.

May 18th National Cemetery MONUMENT   Opened in 1997, the cemetery was created to commemorate the civilian casualties from an uprising that occurred on May 18, 1980. Similar but smaller than the Tiananmen Square massacre, the Gwangju uprising was fueled by student protests demanding democracy. The official count was

259 dead, but many claim that there were hundreds more. A short walk through the memorial garden leads to the cemetery where the victims were initially buried.

34 Unjeong-dong, Buk-gu, Gwangju-si. Free admission. Mar–Oct daily 8am–7pm; Nov–Feb until 5pm. From Gwangju Express Bus Terminal, take bus no. 25-2 or 311, which takes 30 min., and runs every 40 min. Bus no. 518 also comes here. Parking available.

Mudeungsan (Mt. Mudeung) Provincial Park ★★ PARK   Overlooking Gwangju city, this beautiful mountain is an easy climb. The highest peak is Cheonwang-bong with two other lower peaks. The best views are in the Wonhyo Valley (on the north) and Yeongchu Valley (on the south). At the base of the mountain there are famous temples: **Yaksa-am, Jeungshimsa,** and **Wonhyosa.** The mountain is gorgeous all yearround, even in the white of winter. It is famous for the tea that's grown at the **Chunseol Tea Plantation,** as well as the mountain-grown watermelon that used to be a favorite gift for royalty. All of the dozen or so trails here have their own charm, but only a couple go through the forest.

Hwasun-gun, Damyang-gun, Jeollanam-do or Jisan-dong, Dong-gu, Gwangju-si. ⓒ 062/365-1187 (Korean only). Free admission. Parking ₩2,000. From Gwangju Station, take bus no. 18 to Wonhyosa or take bus no. 777 or 1187 from other parts of the city. Bus nos. 9, 15, 27, 52, 555, 771, and 1001 go to the Jeungshimsa entrance.

Wonhyosa (Wonhyo Temple) TEMPLE   Located near the entrance to the Mudeungsan Provincial Park, Wonhyosa was also founded by the famous Great Monk Wonhyo. Excavations show that the temple was built at the end of the Shilla Dynasty and renovated during the reign of Goryeo King Chungsuk (1314–39). Destroyed during the Korean War, it was rebuilt from the mid-1950s to the 1960s. Three of the main buildings were renovated in the 1980s. During the renovation some 100 relics of copper, gold, and clay were excavated; these are on exhibit at the Gwangju National Museum.

3-3, Maegok-dong, Buk-gu, Gwangju-si. ⓒ 062/266-0326 (Korean only). Free admission. 24 hr. but best to visit 9am–6pm so as not to disturb the monks. From Gwangju Station, take bus no. 18 to Wonhyosa. From the provincial office, take bus no. 777.

Shopping

Gwangju is a traditional city in the middle of an agricultural area. Specialties of the area include handmade brushes (for calligraphy and ink painting), lacquerware, and tea grown in nearby Mudeungsan.

Stop by **Art Street★★** (ⓒ 062/233-9370), which becomes the **Gaemi Shijang ("Ant" Market)** on Saturdays, a flea market where you'll find local art and antiques. Even on weekdays this three-street area is the city's cultural hub. Masters of pansori and *gayageum* (a traditional Korean "zither"), as well as master calligraphers and potters, live and work in the area. Be sure to check out the beautiful musical instruments and the calligraphic works from the region. To reach Art Street, located behind the Jung-ang Elementary School, take bus no. 11, 17, 30, 222, or 333 to the Docheong bus stop and walk about 5 minutes.

For more modern shopping, head to the nearby **Migliore** Department Store, (ⓒ **1588-9101;** www.mc12.co.kr, Korean only, 25-1 Chungjang-no1(il)-ga, Gwangju-si), which incidentally has a cinema and a great 24-hour sauna on the 11th floor. You can't miss it since it's the tallest building you'll see when you get out of the Geumnamno 4(sa)-ga subway station. You would never know that the **Geumnam-no** area had historic significance as the route the demonstrating militia took in order to protest on May 18th. It now fills up every night with young people shopping, eating, and drinking at the many restaurants and boutique shops here. For bargains, head underground to the **Geumnam Underground Shopping Center.**

Where to Stay

Of course Gwangju has a large number of accommodations to choose from, ranging from your budget quarters to high-end, tourist-class hotels. You can find inexpensive motels throughout the city, but the most convenient ones are located near the train station. There are some low-priced options also near Art Street.

EXPENSIVE

Holiday Inn Gwangju ★★   Located near the Kim Daejeong Convention Center, it's convenient for the subway and a good option for business travelers. Rooms are spacious, quiet, and clean with rain showerheads. The young, eager staff will go out of their way to be helpful.

1158 Chipyeong-dong, Seo-gu, Gwangju-si. http://holidayinngwangju.com/eng/html/main.asp. ✆ **062/610-7000.** Fax 063/610-7099. 205 units. ₩320,000 standard room; ₩490,000 and up suite. AE, MC, V. **Amenities:** Restaurants; bar; lounge; indoor pool; fitness center; sauna; business center; laundry/dry cleaning service; meeting rooms; safe. *In room:* A/C, TV, minibar, coffeemaker, hair dryer, bathrobe, free Internet.

Mudeung Park Hotel   At the base of Mudeungsan at Jisan Park, this high-end hotel has seen better days. The rooms have nice views of the mountain and comfortable beds—quite a nice combination. The staff are friendly, but speak poor English. Both ondol rooms and beds are available.

San 63-1, Jisan-dong, Dong-gu, Gwangju-si. www.hotelmudeungpark.co.kr. ✆ **062/226-0011.** Fax 063/285-5707. 110 units. ₩140,000 standard room; ₩435,000 and up suite. AE, MC, V. **Amenities:** 3 restaurants; cafe; pool; driving range; hot springs spa; sauna; night club; bowling alley; bakery. *In room:* A/C, TV, minibar, hair dryer.

Ramada Plaza Gwangju ★★   One of the few world-class hotels in Gwangju, they have both regular rooms and residential suites for those looking for a longer stay. Comfortable linens, spacious rooms, and floor-to-ceiling windows make for a good stay. Ask for a higher-floor room if you want a view. The top floor has a breakfast buffet, which turns into a bar at night.

1238 Chipyeong-dong, Seo-gu, Gwangju-si. www.ramadagwangju.com. ✆ **062/717-7000.** Fax 063/717-7700. 205 units. ₩320,000 standard room; ₩490,000 and up suite. AE, MC, V. **Amenities:** Restaurants; bar; coffee shop; fitness center; Jacuzzi; sauna; business center; massage; meeting rooms; safe. *In room:* A/C, TV, minibar, coffeemaker, hair dryer, Internet (fee).

MODERATE

Santamo Tourist Hotel ★   For the price, you'll get a relatively spacious room with clean and comfortable beds. The hotel is close to a subway station and convenient for banks and restaurants. The staff will make up in friendliness what they lack in English. Both Korean and Western-style rooms are available.

1585-2 Usan-dong, Gwangsan-gu, Gwangju-si. www.hotelsantamo.co.kr. ✆ **062/956-5000.** Fax 062/956-3000. 54 units. ₩70,000 and up single/double. AE, MC, V. **Amenities:** 2 restaurants; cafe; sauna. *In room:* A/C, TV, hair dryer.

INEXPENSIVE

Geumsujang Hotel ★   Located within walking distance from the train station, this hotel has more ondol rooms than Western beds, but usually has Western options available. Really a bargain for a hotel of its class, the rooms are clean and spacious compared to most South Korean hotels in this price range. The restaurant and amenities are excellent for the price.

559-1 Gyerim-dong, Dong-gu, Gwangju-si. © **062/525-2111.** 45 units. ₩45,000 standard room. MC, V. **Amenities:** 2 restaurants; cafe; room service. *In room:* A/C, TV, hair dryer, Internet.

Gwangsan-gu Youth Hostel ☺   If you're on a budget, you can't get any cheaper than this hostel. Good for both solo travelers and families, the hostel offers shared kitchen and laundry facilities. The location has great amenities for the price.

38-3, Songhak-dong, Gwangsan-gu, Gwangju. www.gsyouth.or.kr (Korean only). © **062/943-4378.** 49 units. ₩12,000 bed. MC, V. **Amenities:** Restaurant; pool; health club; shared kitchen; TV room.

Windmill Motel ⚑   A love motel in downtown Gwangju, you can't miss the giant windmill on the building. Ask for a "PC bahng" if you want a computer with Internet access, or pay a bit more for a deluxe room with better furnishings.

42-6 Honam-dong, Dong-gu, Gwangju. www.windmillmotel.co.kr. (Korean only) © **062/223-5333.** 37 units. ₩30,000–45,000 double. MC, V. **Amenities:** none. *In room:* A/C, cable TV, mini-fridge, hair dryer.

Where to Eat

There are a couple of neighborhoods in the city with concentrations of restaurants specializing in certain dishes. There is **Oritang (Duck Soup) Street** on Yudong Street, which is the alley next to the Hyundai Department Store. Most restaurants are open daily 9am to 10pm (a few stay open into the wee hours). A whole duck costs around ₩30,000, or ₩20,000 for a half portion. Grilled duck (seasoned with salt and sesame oil) goes for about ₩35,000.

In Jisan-dong, there is a street called **"The Street of Traditional Food"** where there are dozens of restaurants specializing in *bolibap* (barley rice). Located in the Jisan Resort near the Mudeungsanjang, the restaurants here serve bowls of barley rice with seasonal vegetables, spicy chili paste, and a spoonful of sesame oil. Supposedly health food, it's also quite tasty and will cost you only about ₩5,000 for a bowl. Many restaurants in the area are open 24 hours.

If you're into fresh seafood, look no further than **Hwae Town** at the Daein Market. Over a dozen raw-fish restaurants are lined up between the Gwangju Dongmun Bridge and the market in Gyelim-dong. The Living Fish Center is open 24 hours, but the restaurants are open daily from 10am to midnight. You can get your fill of raw fish for about ₩30,000 to ₩80,000.

For the beef lovers among us, the area in front of the Gwangsan-gu Office in Songjeong-dong is the place to go. Your nose will lead you to the collection of *ddeok galbi* joints in the alley there. Ddeok galbi, supposedly invented by a *halmuhni* (grandma) in Jeonju, is made by mincing beef rib and other beef parts, shaping it into a square like a Korean rice cake *(ddeok),* and roasting it on charcoal. An order of the delicious beef costs about ₩10,000, and all of the places on this street are excellent.

If you're tired of Korean food and don't mind splurging a bit, stop in at **Paripara-mong,** 120-2 Shinan-dong, Buk-gu, Gwangju-si (© **062/528-2251**). They specialize in high-end European cuisine. Although the food may not be "authentic," you'll get great service if you want a break from rice and noodles. Meat-course meals start at ₩38,000 and the house-special full course is ₩80,000.

DAMYANG

Located just 22km (14 miles) north of Gwangju is the center of the country's bamboo cultivation. Filled with stunning bamboo forests, Damyang-gun (Damyang County) will be one of the most scenic stops on your South Korea journey. Although plastics have replaced the everyday use of many bamboo products, the area still attracts visitors who are drawn to the quiet, simple beauty of the bamboo groves. Other than its famous bamboo products, there are many pavilions and historical places where literary works have been created in centuries past. Once you visit the area, you'll see why scholars and poets were inspired by the beauty of the surrounding mountains and the fields to write. If you're here during the spring, don't miss the **Bamboo Festival** (http://bamboofestival.co.kr/ENG/02_part/part_01.jsp).

Essentials

GETTING THERE   There is no direct train to Damyang, but you can take a train to Gwangju and take either a bus or a taxi on to Damyang. Intercity buses that run to Damyang from the **Gwangju Bus Terminal** run daily from 6am to 10:30pm, every 10 minutes.

You can take a bus directly from Seoul to Damyang daily at either 10:10am or 4:10pm. The nearly 4-hour ride costs ₩15,900 to ₩23,600. If you're driving, take the Honam Expressway (road 25 from Seoul) and follow the signs to get off at Damyang. You'll pass through the **Metasequoia Road,** a small stretch of scenic road, lined on both sides by the tall trees creating a canopy of leaves in the spring and summer and dramatic snow-covered branches in the winter.

GETTING AROUND   Local buses will take you pretty much anywhere you want to go; the only problem is that they run pretty infrequently (about every hour or two) from select destinations. So make sure you know what time the return bus is so that you're not stuck waiting an hour for the next bus.

If you're not the adventurous type and prefer to take a tour, you can catch a **bus tour** (© 061/380-3154) of Damyang at the **Gwangju Station Plaza.** The tour starts just before 9am on Saturdays and Sundays and takes 6½ hours. There are 4 different routes that alternate on different Saturdays and Sundays, costing ₩17,000 per person.

VISITOR INFORMATION   Contact the Damyang Culture and Tourism Department at © 061/380-3150 or http://eng.damyang.go.kr/eng.

Exploring Damyang

Bamboo Theme Park (Daenamugol Tema Pakeuh) ★ NATURAL ATTRACTION   The largest bamboo forest in Korea, it was designed by Shin Bokjin, a former photographer. Taking more than 30 years to create, this bamboo garden is thick with grass, which makes it especially nice to hear the rustling of the leaves when the wind passes through.

51 san, Bongseo-li, Geumseong-myeon, Damyang-gun. © **061/383-9291.** Admission ₩2,000 adults, ₩1,500 students, ₩1,000 children. Daily 9am–5pm. From the Damyang Bus Terminal,

buses leave daily at 8am, 11am, 1:10pm, and 8pm, returning from the park 20 min. after departing. By car, from the Damyang IC, take road 24 toward Sunchang, turn right after Seokyeongyo bridge, and follow the signs to the park.

Byeongpungsan (Folding Screen Mountain) HIKING TRAIL
When you see the highest point in Damyang, you'll understand immediately how it got its name—the rock outline does indeed resemble a folding screen. Two lakes atop the mountain run down to provide water to the Yeongsan River. There is a nice hiking trail that goes through Mannamjae Pass, Mumyeongbong Peak, and Daebang Lake; it is about 9km (5⅔ miles) long and takes about 4 hours to complete.

Subuk-myeon, Damyang-gun. ✆ 061/380-3150 or 4. Free admission. From the Damyang Bus Terminal, buses run here about 13 times a day. From Gwangju, take a bus to Subuk-myeon and catch a local bus to Byeongpungsan. The bus runs about every 40 min.

Chuwolsan (Mt. Chuwol) NATURAL ATTRACTION
Located on the border of Bukheong-myeon, Sunchang-gun, and Yong-myeon, Damyang-gun, this is said to be one of the most beautiful mountains in Jeollanam-do. The strange rock formations jut out between green bushes and flowering shrubs, creating a wonderful backdrop for hiking.

Wolgye-li, Yong-myeon, Damyang-gun. ✆ **061/380-2794.** Free admission. From the Damyang local bus station, buses run about 4 times a day. By car, pass the Damyang IC, going toward Damyang, and cross the Dang-eup Hyanggyo, taking national road 29 at the Yongmyeon 3-way, follow the signs to Chuwolsan. The entrance to the hiking trail is right after the Chuwolsan tunnel.

Damyang Bamboo Museum MUSEUM
This is the place to learn everything you've ever wanted to know (and some things you didn't realize you wanted to know) about bamboo. Created to promote the region's prime agricultural product, it has more than 2,500 bamboo products on display, dating from the Joseon Dynasty to modern day. With over a 500-year history, the bamboo products of the region are made by skilled craftsmen, whose art has been handed down through generations.

401-1, Cheonbyeon-li, Damyang-eup, Damyang-gun. ✆ **061/380-3114.** www.damyang.go.kr/museum/ (Korean only). Admission ₩1,000 19 and over, ₩700 teens, ₩500 ages 7–12, free for children 7 and under and seniors 65 and over. Daily 9am–6pm, last admission 30 min. before closing. From Gwangju, take the express bus going toward Damyang and get off at the Baekdong intersection. From Damyang, take local bus no. 311 or 322 and get off at the Baekdong intersection (and walk 1 min. from there). You have to catch the return bus on the main road (a 5-min. walk from the museum). It's a 15-min. walk from the bus terminal.

Jungnogwon (Bamboo Garden) NATURAL ATTRACTION
Take a walk through this natural bamboo forest for a relaxing time. Although the bamboo here has been around for centuries, they've added some cheesy things (like statues of fake pandas frolicking). The rustling of the bamboo and catching the light through the tall grasses is still a treat for the senses. Springtime is a nice time to visit, but summer is when the bamboo is at its greenest.

37-6 Hyanggyo-li, Damyang-eup, Damyang-gun. ✆ **061/380-3244.** www.juknokwon.org (Korean only). Admission ₩2,000 adults, ₩1,000 children, free for children 6 and under and seniors 65 and over. Daily 9am–7pm. Take bus no. 303 or 311 and get off at Jungnogwon, then walk about 5 min. Alternatively, take a taxi from the Damyang Bus Station—it should cost under ₩3,500.

Soswaewon (Soswae Garden) ★★★ 🏛 GARDEN
This small private garden, whose name means "clean and refreshing," was built by Yang Sanbo (1503–57) when he decided to retire into nature. One of the representative gardens of the

Joseon Dynasty, it was created in 1530. The original 10 buildings were designed so that the inhabitants could best see and hear nature around them. Only a few of them remain today. Still, it is a beautiful garden (sometimes compared to Thoreau's Walden, though much smaller in scale) and you can see how someone was inspired to write and grow old there.

123 Jigok-li, Nam-myeon, Damyang-gun. ✆ **061/382-1071.** www.soswaewon.co.kr (Korean only). Admission ₩1,000 ages 19 and over, ₩700 teens, ₩500 ages 7–12, free for children 6 and under and seniors 65 and over. Daily 9am–6pm. From Gwangju Bus Station, take local bus no. 225 (it's an hour ride and the bus runs every 40 min.). Driving from Seoul, take the Honam Expwy. (road 25) toward Damyang. From Damyang, take Hwy. 12 to local road 887 and follow the signs.

Shopping

As you'd figure, you can find all manner of bamboo products, from back scratchers to works of art created by master craftsmen. The **Traditional Bamboo Market** is held every 5 days or so (when the date ends with a 2 or 7) by the flats of the Baekchon River. The market starts around 7am and goes to midafternoon. If you miss those days, you can still find stores that sell bamboo wares any day of the week.

Where to Stay

The **Damyang Resort Spa & Hotel,** 399 Wonyeul-li, Geumseong-myeon, Damyang-gun (www.damyangresort.com; ✆ **061/380-5000;** fax 061/381-0606), is the only upscale accommodation available in the area and has standard rooms starting at ₩159,000. It is on 13 hectares (32 acres) of land and has several spas, a swimming pool, and its own arboretum and pond. If you just want to visit the **spa** (✆ **061/380-5111**) and swimming pool, it'll cost ₩10,000.

There are plenty of love motels in the area, and most of them will set you back ₩35,000 to ₩45,000 for a double. Many of them won't take reservations, but generally it isn't difficult to get a room, even during high season in the summer. You just pay cash at the front desk when you check in and leave the key at the desk when you go. Just down the road from Soswaewon is the **Lucky House,** 55 Yeoncheon-li, Nam-myeon, Damyang-gun (✆ **061/382-3312**), which has the characteristic circular beds.

If you're looking for other budget accommodations, try the **Park Village,** 119-1 Unam-li, Daeduk-myeon, Damyang-gun (✆ **061/383-7800**), which has rooms for ₩30,000 to ₩40,000 a night. Another inexpensive option is the **Best Yeogwan,** 52 Yeoncheon-li, Nam-myeon, Damyang-gun (✆ **061/383-8800**), which also has rooms for ₩35,000 a night.

Where to Eat

The specialty of the region is bamboo, of course. So, perhaps not surprisingly, you'll find dishes made with bamboo shoots, bamboo tea, and *daetong bap* (rice steamed in the hollow of bamboo stalks). Some places add other grains, chestnuts, pine nuts—you name it—to the rice, and these additions mix well with the subtle flavor infused by the bamboo. Chefs also cook chicken in a bamboo pot (the chicken is mixed with rice, jujubes, and chestnuts). Another regional specialty is *ddeok galbi*, an especially tasty beef rib dish from the area.

There are many places that serve these regional specialties, but a couple of places of note include **Songjukjeong** (located in front of the Bamboo Museum;

© 061/381-3291), which is slightly better than the **Bakmulgwan Apjip** (whose name means "house in front of the museum"; © 061/381-1990), though the latter also serves good regional specialties. One of the best joints in town is **Hyang-gyo Juknogwon** ★★★, Hyang-gyo-li, Damyang-eup (© 061/381-9596), which serves bamboo-steamed rice with a wonderful array of banchan for the usual ₩10,000.

BOSEONG & YULPO

Just as Damyang is synonymous with bamboo, mention Boseong-gun (Boseong County) to any Korean and they'll immediately think of green tea. The region reportedly produces nearly 70% of the country's tea leaves.

With beautiful scenery in any season, the best time to visit is spring, when there is a **Dahyangje Festival (The "Aroma of Tea" Festival)** in early May and when you can watch women harvesting the bright green new leaves by hand.

Yulpo is a seaside town just down the mountain from the Boseong tea fields. There you will find hot springs where you can soak in green tea baths, enjoy foods made with green tea, and stay in an inexpensive yeogwan or minbak near the ocean. Yulpo beach is best visited in July or August, when the water is at its warmest.

Essentials

GETTING THERE   There is no direct train to Boseong from Seoul, but you can take a train to Gwangju and then take a bus from the **Gwangju Intercity Bus Terminal.** Buses bound for Boseong come every 30 minutes, and the ride lasts about 90 minutes. You can also take a 5-hour ride to Suncheon, then take an hour bus ride from there. From Boseong-eup, take a bus bound for Yulpo or the Daehan Daeup (Boseong Tea Plantation; see listing below). The Yulpo-bound buses run every 30 minutes, and it's a 15-minute ride.

You can take a bus directly from Seoul's Express Bus Terminal to the **Boseong Bus Terminal.** Buses run twice a day from Seoul at 8:10am and 3:10pm (more frequently in the spring) and take just under 5 hours. Other than Seoul and Gwangju, you can also catch buses to Boseong from Suncheon, Yeosu, Busan, and Masan, which all run several times a day.

GETTING AROUND   There are local buses that run from the Boseong Bus Terminal. Most of them run on a 30- to 60-minute schedule, so plan accordingly. You can also catch taxis outside the bus terminal, or flag them down if you see them pass on the street.

VISITOR INFORMATION   The website for Boseong County (© 061/850-5224) is www.boseong.go.kr.

Exploring Boseong & Yulpo

Daehan Dawon (aka Boseong Dawon, Tea Plantation) ★★★ WALKING TRAIL   Established in 1939, this still-operating tea plantation is open to tourists year-round. The best time to come is early in the morning, so you can watch the fog lift from the lush green fields. It's easier to take the paths to the side of the fields than the steep wooden stairs that go straight up, but it's worth the climb, since the view of the fields from the top is pretty spectacular. You know these must be old fields since they've left a couple of family burial mounds undisturbed in the middle of the tea bushes.

1291, Bongsan-li, Boseong-eup, Boseong-gun. © **061/852-4540.** www.daehantea.co.kr (Korean only). Admission ₩2,000 adults, ₩1,000 youth and seniors 65 and over. Daily 9am–7pm; until 6pm in winter. From Boseong, take the local bus bound for Yulpo and get off at Daehan Dawon. The bus runs every 30 min. and it's a 15-min. ride. By car, take road 18 (past road 2) toward Yulpo and the plantation will be on your right side.

Daewonsa (Daewon Temple) TEMPLE   One of the oldest Buddhist temples in South Korea, it was originally founded during the Baekje era and rebuilt during the Shilla Dynasty. They offer a temple stay based on the theme "Let us prepare for death," which has programs on death invocations and praying before death. The road to the temple is lined with cherry trees that bloom beautifully in the spring. The temple proper is located behind the **Tibetan Museum** (© 061/852-3038), which houses a collection of over 600 pieces, brought over by Monk Hyeonjang.

On Cheonbongsan, Juksan-li, Mundeok-myeon, Boseong-gun. © **061/852-1755.** Admission ₩2,000 adults, ₩1,000 youth. Daily 10am–6pm, closes at 5pm in winter. From Boseong, take a local bus to Daewonsa. If you're driving, take road 18 to road 15 (toward Gwangju) and follow the signs to the Daewonsa.

Yulpo Haesu Nokchatahng NATURAL ATTRACTION   In Yulpo, you can visit the hot springs, where you can soak in a hot bath of seawater and green tea. Located on the seaside, down the mountain road from the tea plantations, the hot springs are small with only four pools and one sauna, but you get a view of the ocean while you soak.

Dongyul-li, 678, Hoecheon-myeon, Boseong-gun. © **061/853-4566.** Admission ₩5,000. Daily 6am–10pm. From Boseong, take the local bus bound for Yulpo and get off at the *nokchatahng* (green tea bath), and walk on the road perpendicular to the main road. The bus runs every 20 min., takes 25 min., and costs ₩1,300. From the Daehan Dawon, the bus will cost ₩850.

Shopping

Save room in your luggage for some green tea, since you can buy the products straight from the source, including *hyunmi nokcha* (green tea with toasted brown rice), the *naeng nokcha* (tea bags for making iced green tea in cold water), and *galu nokcha* (green tea powder). Other than Daehan Dawon, there are dozens of other green tea plantations in Boseong that sell their green tea products directly.

For other items, try the traditional **O-il Jang ("5-day" Markets)** in Boseong County. The **Boknae-myeon Shijang,** 152-14 Boknae-li, Boseong-gun, and the **Joseong-myeon Shijang** are open on dates that end in 3 or 8. The **Boseung-eup Shijang,** 2-1 Wonbong-li, Boseung-eup, Boseong-gun, and the **Deungryang-myeon Shijang,** 446 Yedang-li, Deukryang-myeon, are held on dates that end in 2 or 7. The **Beolgyeo-eup Shijang,** 663-2 Hwaejeong-li, Beolgyeo-eup, Boseong-gun, and the **Hwacheonmyeon Shijang** in Hwacheon-myeon are open on dates that end in 4 or 9.

Where to Stay

There aren't many places to stay in Boseong, since it is mainly an agricultural area. However, if you want to overnight in the region, you can stay at any number of min-bak or yeogwan in the seaside town of **Yulpo.** Most places are similar and usually cost ₩30,000 to ₩40,000, but prices can double during the popular summer season.

For a unique experience, you and your family can stay overnight at the **Ungchi Vacation Farm,** 1412-4 Gangsan-li, Ungchi-myeon, Boseong-gun (© 061/852-6300), a sortof government-run farm, located in the middle of a dense pine forest.

They have a huge mushroom field, freshwater shrimp, chickens, and a deer "farm" within an enclosed forest.

Where to Eat

This being the green tea region of the country, it stands to reason that you'll find many dishes featuring it as a special ingredient. These include *nokcha sujebi* (green tea dough flake soup), *nokcha naengmyeon* (cold buckwheat noodles with green tea), and *nokcha kalgooksu* (handmade noodles with green tea).

Other than the two restaurants at the Daehan Dawon, you can try regional specialties at places in Yulpo, including **Nokcha Hyangi** (the name means "the fragrance of green tea"), 321-1 Yulpo-li, Hwacheon-myeon, Boseong-gun (✆ **070/8824-9790**). Located close to the Yulpo Nokchatahng, they serve all manner of green tea dishes (even a green tea pork cutlet, *nokcha donkatsu*), which start at ₩5,000.

There are some restaurants in Boseong, too, including **Teukmi Gwan,** located in front of the Boseong Hyang-gyo, 93-13 Boseong-li, Boseong-eup, Boseong-gun (✆ **061/852-4545**). They specialize in pork and beef dishes, but you can also get regional green tea dishes, including their *nokcha naengmyeon* with bright green tea noodles, starting at ₩6,000. For a traditional hanjeongshik, **Hangil-lo** (✆ **061/852-3281,** 766-3 Boseong-li, Boseong-eup, Boseong-gun) is a solid option with meals at ₩10,000, or hwae plates starting at ₩20,000.

YEOSU & SUNCHEON

Located on the southern coast of the peninsula, Yeosu is a pretty little port city. The town, whose name means "beautiful water," is located on the western end of the Hallyeo Haesang National Park. The city includes 317 tiny islands off the coast, most of them uninhabited. A couple of those islands, **Odong-do** and **Dolsan-do,** are now connected by bridges to the mainland. Yeosu was the naval command center for Admiral Yi Sunshin, who invented the turtle ship (see p. 13). There is still a full-size replica of one of the iron-clad ships that helped defeat the Japanese navy.

Sitting pretty on the upper end of the Yeosu Peninsula, just 40 minutes from Yeosu, is Suncheon. Sometimes called the "City of Beautiful People," it is the second-largest metropolis in Jeollanam-do. Nearby is **Jogyesan Provincial Park,** which surrounds Mt. Jogye. At its base are two Seon (Zen) Buddhist temples which have been instrumental in introducing and spreading this sect in Korea.

Both cities, currently experiencing rapid expansion and industrialization, are in danger of losing some of their original charm.

Essentials

GETTING THERE   There are direct flights from Seoul's Gimpo Airport to **Yeosu Airport,** 979 Sinpung-li, Yulchon-myeon, Yeosu-si (RSU; ✆ **061/689-6300;** www.airport.co.kr/doc/yeosu_eng), which is located equidistant to Yeosu and Suncheon. Asiana Airlines and Korean Airlines offer a total of eight flights daily to and from Gimpo Airport. Korean Airlines has one flight daily to and from Jeju-do. There are both airport limousine and local buses available to Yeosu or Suncheon. Local service starts at ₩1,500.

Yeosu is the last stop on the **Jeolla line,** which starts in Iksan. There are 15 daily trains from Seoul's Yongsan station to Suncheon with just as many trains from

Suncheon to Yeosu, with the total trip taking about 6 hours. Trains run once a day to Mokpo, Iksan, and Jinju, and more frequently to Busan.

Buses from Seoul's Express Bus station to Yeosu run daily about once every hour from 6am to 11pm. Fares start at ₩30,600 and the ride lasts about 5½ hours. Daily buses from Busan run every 40 minutes and take about 3 hours. Daily buses from Gwangju run every 30 minutes and take about 2 hours. Express buses run from Daegu also, but from other cities, you'll have to take regular intercity buses, which take a bit longer.

From the **Yeosu Ferry Terminal** (© 061/663-0117), you can take boats to and from islands, including Jeju-do, Geomun-do, Geumo-do, Sa-do, Yeon-do, Oenaro-do, and Cho-do.

If you're driving, take either the Honam Expressway (road 25) or the Namhae Expressway to the Suncheon IC. To get to Yeosu from there, take national highway 17 and follow the signs to Yeosu.

GETTING AROUND Both Suncheon and Yeosu have good bus systems that will carry you around the cities, between them, and to sites on the outskirts of each. Most buses in Yeosu start from the bus terminal and run through downtown. In Suncheon, you can catch buses from (and between) both the bus terminal and the train station.

Suncheon offers a free **city tour** that starts from Suncheon Station. There are 5 different routes that vary depending on the day of the week. Unfortunately, the guides only speak Korean, but it's a convenient way to get to the bay, Naganeupseong, and nearby temples.

There is one **Yeosu city tour** (© **061/666-1201** or 061/690-2036) starting in front of Yeosu Station daily at 10:30am, returning around 6:10pm. Unfortunately, the commentary is only in Korean or Japanese, but they'll take you to the city's top spots, including Hyangiram for a mere ₩3,000 adults, ₩1,000 youth. Admission fees aren't included and you'll have to reserve a spot in advance.

VISITOR INFORMATION You can find a **tourist information center** (© **061/690-2939**) on the first floor of the Yeosu Airport. There is also one at the entrance to Odong-do (© **061/664-8978**), one at Yeosu harbor (© **061/690-7532**), and one in front of the Suncheon Train Station. The Yeosu city website is **http://yeosu.go.kr** and Suncheon's is **http://english.suncheon.go.kr.**

FAST FACTS In Yeosu, the **post office** is located on the city's main street. You will find many **banks** and businesses around the old city center. Most banks are open from 9am to 4:30pm Monday to Friday.

In Suncheon, the **post office** is just a little way down from the train station. Most **banks** can be found in the business district between the bus terminal and the central market.

Exploring Yeosu & Suncheon

Goindol (Dolmen) Park ★★ HISTORIC SITE   One of UNESCO's World Heritage sites, the park has a collection of dolmen (megalithic stone tombs) and other relics uncovered from 49 villages in Suncheon, Boseong, and Hwasun counties. They were excavated before the Juam Lake creation in 1984, when the land was submerged. The original excavated area included Paleolithic sites with a total of 140 dolmens from nine different clusters.

466 Usan-li, Songgwang-myeon, Suncheon-si. © **061/755-8363.** www.dolmenpark.com. Admission ₩700 adults, ₩350 teens, ₩300 children. Mar–Oct daily 9am–6pm; Nov–Feb daily 9am–5pm. Take bus no. 63, which takes you right in front of Dolmen Park.

Hyangilam TEMPLE   Originally a small mountain-top hermitage, Hyangilam is now a turtle-themed temple complex. There are 291 steps up to the temple, where you'll get a spectacular view of the ocean. It is said that if you make a wish watching the sunrise from here on New Year's morning, your wish will come true. Superstitions aside, the sunrise on any day is quite spectacular and arriving in time to catch it is a great way to beat the busloads of tourists who arrive in the afternoon. Don't bother waiting for the free shuttle bus (especially when they take their lunch break noon–1pm), because it's just a short ride to the foot of **Impo Village,** where you'll have to pass a gauntlet of ajumma trying to sell you *got* (mustard) kimchi. You'll have to walk the difficult part uphill anyway. There are plenty of small motels in the village below if you want to catch the sunrise in the morning.

San 7 Yullim-li, Dolsan-eup, Yeosu-si. ✆ 061/644-4742 (Korean). Admission ₩2,000 adults, ₩1,500 teens, ₩1,000 children, free for kids 6 and under. Mar–Oct and Dec–Jan daily 6am–10pm; Nov and Feb daily 6am–9pm. Parking ₩2,500. From Yeosu Station, take bus no. 111 or 113. The ride lasts just over an hour.

Naganeupseong Folk Village ★ CASTLE   In ancient feudal fashion, this folk village consists of a "castle," with about 100 families still living inside the fortress walls. It is a wonderful snapshot of how the people of the region used to live, with their thatched roofs and clay kitchens. If you happen to be here for the first full moon of the year, you'll be able to see a traditional folk celebration. The rest of the year, be sure to make your way up to the castle to take in the view of the entire village.

Dongnae-li/Seonae-li/Namnae-li, Nakan-myeon, Suncheon-si. ✆ **061/749-3347.** www.nagan.or.kr. Admission ₩2,000 adults, ₩1,500 teens, ₩1,000 children. Dec–Jan daily 9am–5pm, Feb–Apr 9am–6pm, May–Oct 8:30am–6:30pm. Closed Lunar New Year and Chuseok. Free parking. From either Suncheon Train Station or the bus terminal, take bus no. 61, 63, or 68 (takes 50 min.).

Odong-do (Odong Island) ★ WALKING TRAIL   Now connected by a bridge and a walkway, this rocky island is the perfect place for a leisurely stroll. The best time to go is right around sunset, just in time to see the island's dancing fountains, whose lights change color and water moves to piped-in music. You'll have a prime view of the city and port lights when you walk back after sundown. The island is famous for its camellias, which bloom from around mid-February to mid-March. Boat trips around the island start from the wharf. Some will cross Dolsan Bridge and Hangilam.

San 1-1, Sujeong-dong, Yeosu-si. ✆ **061/690-7303.** Admission free. Daily 6am–midnight in summer, until 11pm in winter. Lighthouse daily 9:30am–5pm. Bus nos. 2, 8, 10, 17, 18, 85-1, 101, 103, 107, and 555 all take you to the entrance. If you don't want to walk the 15 min. to the island, you can take the little train, which costs ₩500 adults, ₩400 youth, ₩300 children. Parking ₩600/hr., ₩6,000 daily maximum.

Seonamsa (Seonam Temple) ★★ TEMPLE   This beautiful temple is on the west side of Jogyesan. You'll have to walk about 1km (⅔ miles) from the mountain's entrance to reach the temple, but the walk along the valley past two arched bridges (one is Seungseon Bridge, considered South Korea's most beautiful stone bridge) is a pleasant one. If you have time, take the hiking course to the left of the temple. It takes you to **Ma-aebuli,** the 17m-tall (56-ft.) sculpture engraved on a rock.

Jukhak-li, Seungju-eup, Suncheon-si. ✆ **061/754-5247.** www.seonamtemple.com (Korean only). Admission ₩1,500 adults, ₩1,000 teens, ₩600 children, free for seniors 65 and over and kids 6 and under. Daily 4am–10pm. From either the Suncheon Train Station or the bus terminal, take bus no. 1 (which runs every 30–35 min.). The ride takes 40 min.

Songgwangsa (Songgwang Temple) ★★★ TEMPLE Also located on the west side of Jogyesan, Songgwangsa is one of the Sambosachal (three temple treasures of Buddhism) in South Korea. Songgwangsa became the Seungbo (monk) temple, since so many high monks were produced here. In 1969, the temple was reorganized as a monastic center for Mahayana Buddhism with the establishment of an international meditation center so that non-Korean monks could also study and train here. One of the most impressive treasures here is the Bisari Gusi, a rice storage container carved from a tree so large that it could hold enough rice for 4,000 monks. They have regular prayer services daily at 6:30pm (5pm in the winter), at lunch, and at dawn. About an hour's walk from the temple is a tiny hermitage called **Cheongja-am.** The best part of its site is the two 700-year-old juniper trees.

12 Sinpyeong-li, Songgwang-myeon, Suncheon-si. ℂ **061/755-0108** (Korean). www.songgwangsa. org. Admission ₩3,000 adults, ₩2,500 youth, free for children 6 and under and those over 65. Mar–Oct daily 7am–7pm; Nov–Feb daily 7am–6pm. From the Suncheon Train Station take *jwaseok* (express) bus no. 111 (the ride takes 1½ hr.).

Suncheon Drama Film Set ★★ ENTERTAINMENT COMPLEX Although this is an artificial film set (the largest in South Korea), the three villages in this open *seteuh-jang* provide a trip to South Korea's not-so-distant past. One set is a re-creation of the streets of Suncheon from the 1950s. The '60s and '70s sets are a replica of Seoul's *daldognae* ("moon neighborhood"), poor areas found in the less desirable uphill areas of the city. There's a total of about 200 houses in all, making it the largest film set in the country. If you're a fan of Korean dramas, you may recognize locations from shows like *East of Eden* and *Love and Ambition*.

22, Jorye-dong, Suncheon-si. ℂ **061/749-4003** (Korean). http://scdrama.sc.go.kr. Admission ₩3,000 adults, ₩2,000 teens, ₩1,000 children. Daily 9am–6pm. From the Suncheon bus terminal take bus no. 77, 99, or 777.

Suncheon-man (Suncheon Bay) Ecological Park PARK A wide estuary and tidal flatland, Suncheon Bay became an established natural eco-park in 2004, but has been overdeveloped in the past couple of years. Several endangered birds stop here along their migratory routes, when the place isn't overrun by noisy families fishing for crabs. The best time to see our feathered friends is in the quiet winter months, but dress warmly since the ocean breezes can be quite chilly. You can take a boat around the area for ₩6,000 adults, ₩3,000 for kids. There is a separate admission for the **Suncheon Bay Eco-Museum** which has displays largely dedicated to the endangered hooded crane.

53-1 Jangcheon-dong, Jangmyun-lo, 92 Suncheon-si. ℂ **061/749-3006.** www.suncheonbay.go.kr. Admission ₩2,000 adults, ₩1,500 teens, ₩1,000 children. Daily 9am–sunset. Parking ₩2,000. From the Suncheon train or bus stations, take bus no. 66 or 67, which run every 20 min. and take 30 min.

Shopping

Being a midsize South Korean city, Suncheon has no shortage of shopping available. Your best bet is to head over to Jung-ang-dong, to **Hwanggumno Fashion Street★★** near the medical rotary, where you'll find dozens of boutique stores lining the streets, as young people windowshop every night of the week. There is also an underground shopping center and several open-air markets, including the **Jung-ang Shijang** and the **Bukbu Shijang** in Maegok-dong. There are also the usual huge departments stores and discount marts, including **Home Plus** (in Jorye-dong; take bus no. 50, 55, 56, 58, or 59), **E-Mart** (in Doekam-dong, about 10 min. from the train station), and **Homever** (which is located about a block from the E-Mart). For higher-end fashions, try **New Core Outlet** in Jorye-dong (take city bus no. 50, 55, 58, or 59). There is also a **Toy Department Store** (Jangnan-ganm Baekhwajeom) in Jorae-dong.

Yeosu, though smaller, has some shopping options as well. In Jung-ang-dong, there is a shopping area akin to Seoul's Myeongdong, mostly for fashion and jewelry. There is an **E-Mart** right across from the bus terminal, open until midnight. For more upscale shopping, try either the **JU Department Store** in Munsu-dong or the **Lotte Marts** in either Guk-dong or Seowon-dong.

Where to Stay

There are plenty of low-budget options in Suncheon, including hostels, love motels, yeogwan, and minbak. The largest groups of inexpensive **love motels** (about ₩35,000 for a standard room) are near the train station, in Yeonhyang-do, and in the Geumdang area. Tourist-class hotels can be found in the old downtown area of Jangcheon-dong. And, of course, there are the really cheap 24-hour saunas, called *jjimjilbahng*, where you can get a bath and sleep in group quarters for ₩10,000.

City Tourist Hotel, 22-24 Namnae-dong (✆ 061/753-4000; fax 061/753-3049), with rack rates starting at ₩65,000, has a bar, cafe, bakery, and a couple of restaurants, and it offers free shuttle service to and from the airport. Conveniently located and more upscale is the **Suncheon Royal Hotel,** 35-8 Jangcheon-dong (✆ 061/741-7000; fax 061/741-7810), with rates starting at ₩90,000 for a standard room. Located just a couple of blocks from the bus station, they also offer free airport shuttle service.

If you're looking for other budget accommodations, in Yeosu there is a small cluster of **love motels** on the main street near the Expo center and the docks.

For more midrange accommodations near Odong-do, try the tourist-class **Yeosu Chambord,** 1054-1 Gonghwa-dong (✆ 061/662-6111; fax 061/662-1929), with rates starting at ₩870,000. Probably the best hotel in Yeosu is the **Yeosu Beach Tourist Hotel,** 343 Chungmu-dong (✆ 061/663-2011; fax 061/664-2114), within walking distance of the train station. Rack rates start at ₩120,000.

Where to Eat

Being a port town, it goes to figure that Yeosu is well known for its hwae. There is even a **Hwae Town,** where dozens of seafood restaurants line the streets, some of them opening as early as 5am.

Other than hwae, there are a plethora of seafood specialties in the region. You can indulge in everything from oysters to spicy eel and a variety of grilled fish. A concentration of good restaurants can be found in the Jung-ang-no area. For spicy octopus, try **Myeongshin Nakji,** 441 Gyeo-dong, Yeosu-si (✆ 061/662-7056), which has spicy sautéed octopus for ₩8,000 or (for the adventurous eater), live octopus for ₩15,000, from 10am to 10pm daily. For overall fresh seafood, there are **Baekcheon Shikdang** (✆ 061/662-3717), **Ihak Shikdang** (✆ 061/662-1661), and **Geumcheon Shikdang** (✆ 061/662-4883).

Suncheon is also well known for its seafood. There are good Korean restaurants concentrated in the Jung-ang-dong (the "old" downtown) area and some traditional restaurants in between American-style fast-food joints in Yeonhyang-dong (the "new" downtown) area. For just plain good Korean food, try **Seonamsa Saejogye Sikdang** (📞 061/751-9121). **Seomjingang Garden** (📞 061/782-3712) serves delicious local seafood.

If you happen to be in the area in mid- to late October, don't miss the **Namdo Food Festival** (📞 061/749-4456; www.namdofood.or.kr, Korean only), held at the Naganeupseong Folk Village, featuring regional foods from 22 cities across the area.

Entertainment & Nightlife

In Yeosu, there are a couple of bars in Yeoseo-dong (not too far from the bus terminal). One that is popular with expats is the cafe/restaurant/bar **Yellow Monkey,** 229-6 Yeoseo-dong (📞 061/653-6633). Another bar popular with expats is the franchise beer joint **Wa Bar** (📞 061/654-2229), just a block away with another location in Hak-dong (📞 061/682-0281). There are a number of bars, *hofs* (German-style beer bars), and noraebang in the area, as well.

The popular foreigner bar in Yeosu is in Hakdong—the **Lost Shepard Girl Freehouse ★★** (📞 010/8502-0288), where you can play darts, pool, or foozball and get Guiness on tap. Located on the north side of Turtle Park, they're open Wednesday through Saturday, until 3am on Fri/Sat.

In Suncheon, there are a couple of places popular with English speakers, including **Elvis,** 1593-4 Jorye-dong (on the second floor), and **Julianna's,** a Western restaurant/bar (where you can get burgers and chicken wings) in Yeonhyang-dong.

THE REST OF JEOLLANAM-DO

Jeollanam-do (South Jeolla Province) is in the southwestern part of the Korean Peninsula. Its name is often abbreviated Jeonnam. Other than the cities highlighted above, the region has some wonderful places to visit. The province is well known for its traditional culture, including the art of pansori, which originated here.

With its interesting coastline, nearly 2,000 islands, and mountainous national parks, there are small pockets of scenery to be discovered all along Jeollanam-do's shoreline. Inland, there are historic ceramic kilns, ancient mountain temples, and hidden valleys to be found. Of course, the region is also well known for its fresh seafood and other dishes. So be sure to savor the flavors of each area as you visit.

Essentials

GETTING THERE & AROUND The province has "international" airports at Gwangju (see p. 202) and Muan (MWX, 📞 061/455-2114; www.airport.co.kr/doc/muan_eng) and domestic airport in Yeosu (see above). Muan Airport is serviced by **Korean Airlines** (📞 061/985-2000), **Asiana Airlines** (📞 061/453-8811), and a couple of other airlines. There is an **Avis Rent-a-car** (📞 061/285-2769) desk at the airport.

The **KTX** high-speed rail offers services to Jangwong, Songjeongni, Naju, Mokpo, and Gwangju. The **Korean National Railroad (www.korail.com)** has a number of lines that run through the province and end at Mokpo, Yeosu, or Suncheon.

Buses connect Jeollanam-do to all parts of the country. Major cities are accessible from Seoul and from each other's local bus terminals. Buses bound for tourist destinations are best reached from local bus terminals in the nearest city or town.

VISITOR INFORMATION The Jeollanam-do Tourist Information Center is at 𝒸 **061/286-4052,** with the official provincial site at http://english.jeonnam.go.kr.

Mokpo

Mokpo is Jeonnam's major port city and was first opened for trade in 1897. A rail line from Seoul connected it to the capital region in 1913, after which it became a vitally important harbor, especially during the time when Japan colonized Korea. Vestiges of Japanese influence can be seen all over town, even with the overwhelming presence of celebrated Naval Admiral Yi everywhere as well.

Mokpo used to be one of the largest cities in the country before the 1970s. Since then, it has seen many of its population migrate to more industrial cities. That doesn't mean it's a quiet town, however. The city has plenty of residents and has taken great pains in the past few years to attract more visitors. The high-speed KTX train from Seoul has contributed to the tourist boom to the city.

Buses from Seoul's Express Bus Terminal come to Mokpo every 40 min. from 5:30am to midnight taking about 4 hours.

Between the train station and the ferry terminal is the old town, which is always bustling with activity. The **Mokpo Tourist Information Center** (𝒸 **061/244-0939**), 10 Hang-dong, Mokpo-si, is located at the Yeogek Terminal. It's open daily 9am to 6pm. There is also another tourist info center at Yeongsan Lake (𝒸 **061/270-8279**), 300 Jukgyo-dong, Mokpo-si.

EXPLORING MOKPO

Conveniently, many of the city's top tourist sites are in the **Gatbawi Culture District,** which is home to the Namnong Memorial Hall, National Maritime Museum, the Mokpo Natural History Museum, the Hall of Folk Culture, and the Culture and Art Center. Plan to spend about 3 hours exploring this area.

From the Mokpo Bus Terminal, take bus no. 6 or 14 and get off at Yonhae-dong Geumho Apts.; from there, transfer to bus no. 7 and get off at the Gatbawi Cultural Center. From the Mokpo Train Station, take bus no. 1 and get off at the Mokpo MBC Studio; from there, transfer to bus no. 7 and get off at the Gatbawi Cultural Center. It's a 15- to 20-min. ride from the bus terminal by taxi or car.

Culture & Art Hall PERFORMING ARTS VENUE Built in 1997, this four-story center stands overlooking the ocean. It has six exhibition halls and a theater that seats almost 700 people. They don't have any permanent displays here, but have revolving exhibits and occasional folk and international performances. The building is located in front of the **Hall of Folk Culture,** which shows traditional arts and culture.

12-1 Yongdang-dong Mokpo-si. 𝒸 **061/274-3655.** Entrance fees and hours vary. From the Express Bus Terminal, walk toward the Mokpo Science College and go left; turn left at Jeil Middle School and the museum will be on the left-hand side of the street (next to the tourist information booth).

Mokpo Natural History Museum ★★ ☺ MUSEUM This two-story building has the usual suspects you would expect in a natural history museum. There are dinosaur bones, exhibits of mammals and birds found on the peninsula, over 900,000 species of insects, various plant specimens, whale skeletons, and a small pool where visitors can observe and even touch live crawfish, snails, minnows, and other creatures from South Korea's freshwater streams.

92-8 Yonghae-dong, Mokpo-si. © **061/274-3655.** Admission ₩3,000 adults, ₩2,000 teens, ₩1,000 children 7–12, ₩500 children 5–6, free for seniors 65 and over and children 4 and under. Tues–Fri 9am–6pm; Sat–Sun and holidays 9am–7pm (until 6pm Nov–Feb); ticket sales end 1 hr. before closing. Closed Jan 1.

Namnong Memorial Hall ★ MUSEUM   This private museum was created as a memorial to Namnong Heo-Geon, who was a master of the Korean version of Namjonghwa (Chinese painting of the Southern School). The collection includes masterpieces of five generations of their family as well as about 400 works from other great painters of the Joseon period.

91 Yonghae-dong Mokpo-si. © **061/276-0313.** http://namnongmuseum.com/english.htm. Admission ₩1,000 adults, ₩500 youth, free for children 6 and under. Mar–Oct daily 9am–6pm; Nov–Dec daily 9am–5pm.

National Maritime Museum MUSEUM   Dedicated to preserving and presenting Korea's rich maritime history, the first exhibit hall displays over 3,000 excavated relics from the "Underwater Cultural Heritage of Wando" and a replica wooden ship from the Goryeo Dynasty. The second hall is the "Underwater Cultural Heritage from Shinan" exhibit and includes over 22,000 items from Chinese ships of the 14th century. The third hall shows the "Life of a Korean Fishing Village," with displays of traditional and modern fishing methods. The last hall shows models of "Korean Traditional Boats," although modern ships, like oil tankers, are also included here.

8 Yonghae-dong, Mokpo-si. © **061/270-2000.** www.seamuse.go.kr. Admission ₩600 adults, ₩300 youth, free for children 6 and under. Tues–Fri 9am–6pm; Sat–Sun and holidays 9am–7pm (until 6pm Nov–Feb).

Yudalsan (Mt. Yudal) ★ PARK   From the park atop its peak you can get a nice view of downtown Mokpo and the harbor, as well as the many small islands that dot the archipelago of Dadohae Maritime National Park. There are five pavilions, a memorial tower, a statue of Admiral Yi, and a monument to the royal dead on its slopes.

Under **Ideungbawi,** there is also an outdoor sculpture park with more than 100 sculptures by the Korean Sculpture Association. On the right side of the parking lot is Dalseong Park, which includes an orchid garden. **Dalseongsa** is located in Jukgyo-dong on the southeastern section of the mountain. A newer temple, it was built by Dae Heungsa in 1915.

The best time of year to visit is from late March to early April, when the forsythias are in bloom, painting the entire hillside with their yellow flowers.

27-1 Jukgyo-dong, Mokpo-si. © **061/272-2171** (Korean only)**.** Free admission. From the Mokpo Train Station, it's a 20-min. walk. Walk past the Kookmin Bank, and past the Cheukhudong Church up Mt. Yudal. From Mokpo Bus Terminal, take bus no. 1, 1-1, 1-2, 2, 13, 17, or 20. By car, exit the Mokpo tollgate and take the road that leads to Mokpo Port, following the signs to Yudalsan.

SHOPPING

Although you won't be packing a live fish in your luggage, it's worth taking a look at the **Mokpo Seafood Market.** Stands that sell the region's popular delicacy, fermented skate, are everywhere, but you can also find dried fish, the catch of the day, and a lot of other wiggly, shiny, wonderful things from the sea. It's open daily from 7am to 8pm.

About a 5-minute walk from Mokpo Station is **Carless Street,** where the alleyways are closed to vehicular traffic, and you can view your share of boutique shops and open stalls, selling everything from clothing to manufactured goods from the region.

For large-scale discount and department stores, Mokpo has more offerings than most other cities in Jeollanam-do. The most popular is the **E-Mart** in Okam-dong, open daily from 10am to 11pm. Nearby are **Homeplus, Lotte** (© **061/280-2500**) and **Hyundai** department stores, as well. You can get there by taking bus no. 10, 13, 20, 105, 109, 112, 119, or 300. There is also the **Formo** (short for "For Mokpo") shopping center, a megaplex with stores, amusement centers, and a large movie theater.

WHERE TO STAY

There is no shortage of cheap places to sleep in Mokpo, and most of the inexpensive motels are located between the train station and the ferry terminal. There is also a grouping of yeogwan and love motels near the bus terminal.

Your best bet, just outside of the city proper, is the **Hyundai Hotel Mokpo ★★** (http://hotel.hshi.co.kr/english/main.asp; © **061/469-5050;** 1237-6 Sampo-li, Samho-eup, Yeongam-gun), but you'll pay for the convenience of staying in one of the few places with English-speaking staff. Standard rooms start at ₩330,000, with free Wi-Fi and VAT included.

In Mokpo, the dated, but comfortable **Shinan Beach Hotel** (http://shinanbeach hotel.com; © **061/243-3399;** 440-4 Jukgyo-dong, Mokpo-si) looks down over Yudal Beach. It has both beds and ondol rooms starting at ₩99,500. It's ₩20,000 more for an ocean view. Suites start at ₩270,000. Another option is the **Shangria Beach Hotel,** 1144-7 Sangdong, Mokpo-si (© **061/285-0100;** fax 061/285-0101). An economical place is the **Baekje Tourist Hotel,** 10-13, Sangnak-dong 1-ga (© **061/242-4411**). Although its facilities are a bit dated, the staff is accommodating and the rooms are good for the price.

WHERE TO EAT

Being a seaside city, Mokpo is well known for its seafood. There is no shortage of hwae joints in town. One of the specialties of the region is *sebal nakji* (baby octopus), which is sometimes served raw or cooked in a gochujang sauce. Another specialty is *galchi jolim* (stewed hairtail fish).

The best bargain for hwae in the city is at the **Bukhang Hwae Center,** a live fish market that attracts hungry diners, who haggle for the best deals on their dinner. Hwae stands and restaurants around here have the lowest prices in town.

For restaurants and upscale cafes, head over to **Carless Street,** about a 5-minute walk from Mokpo Station. Here you can get a taste of an unusual local coffee (you'll wonder why it's so rich until you find out that they've put a raw egg yolk in it) or just grab an inexpensive bowl of noodles.

If you're tired of Korean food, head on over to the Gatbawi area in Hadang, where you'll find a handful of bistros serving Western food.

ENTERTAINMENT & NIGHTLIFE

Being a small city, Mokpo doesn't have a really hopping nightlife. There are the usual cocktail bars and clubs where you can get overpriced drinks and have to pay a premium for the *anju* (drinking snacks). The hofs are your best bet for inexpensive drinks.

One of the main attractions of Mokpo when the sun goes down is **Luminarie, "The Avenue of Light."** Located not far from the shops and restaurants of Carless Street, the street of brightly lit arches starts from in front of the Mokpo Cinema down about 500m (1,640 ft.). There are some late-night cafe and bar options on Carless

Street as well. Not to be overshadowed, Yudalsan is also brightly lit at night, almost like an amusement park.

Muan

Muan is the name of the county (*gun*) and town (*eup*) in Jeollanam-do. Best known for its **White Lotus Festival** ★★★ (✆ **061/450-5473**) in late July/early August, the **Muan Hoesan Baekryeonji (Muan White Lotus Habitat)** ★★ (✆ **061/285-1323**) is considered the largest one for the rare flower in all of Asia. Entrance to the gardens is ₩3,000 for adults, ₩2,000 for children.

The **Muan Airport** (MWX, ✆ **061/455-2114**; www.airport.co.kr/doc/muan_eng) is serviced by **Korean Airlines** (✆ **061/985-2000**), **Asiana Airlines** (✆**061/453-8811**), and a couple of other airlines. There are a few international flights to and from China and Japan. Avis (✆ **061/285-2769**) provides car-rental service. There are four limousine buses daily to and from Gwangju and Mokpo airports, costing about ₩5,000 for a 60-minute ride.

To get to Muan by train, you can catch a train bound for Mokpo from Seoul Station and get off at Illo Station. From there, take local bus no. 800 to Muan. To get to Muan via bus, take a bus from Seoul's Express Bus Terminal to Muan. There are two buses a day, 8:30am and 4:20pm, and it's about a 4-hour ride.

You can try one of the specialties of the region, pork cooked over rice straw at **Dooam Shikdang** (✆ **061/452-3775**), which is served with Muan's famous onion kimchi. For another specialty of the region, stop by **Haneul Baekryeon Brau** (✆ **061/285-8503**) for their homemade lotus beer. They also have other lotus-inspired dishes, like rice steamed in lotus leaves and donkatsu made with powdered lotus root.

Jirisan National Park

South Korea's first national park, **Jirisan** (tourist info ✆ **061/780-2224**) was established in 1967. Its highest peak, **Cheonwangbong**, is 1,915m (6,283 ft.) high, but several other peaks climb over 1,000m (3,281 ft.). Home to numerous historical sites and temples, the mountain range is surrounded by five cities/counties—**Namwon, Gurye, Hadong, Sancheong,** and **Hamyang** (the latter three are in Gyeongsang-do).

Climbing Jirisan for more than a day without a guide is not recommended, since the national park does not have many amenities and there are many precipitous cliffs. There are, however, less difficult trails for nonprofessional climbers.

The easiest trail is the **Nogodan course,** which starts from the Seongsamjae rest area. The full course takes about 3 hours.You can make a camping reservation 2 to 15 days in advance starting at 10am on their site at http://english.knps.or.kr. Access to the summit is open only four times a day (10:30am, 1pm, 2:30pm, and 4pm). Take a bus from the Gurye Bus Terminal to Seongsamjae. Buses take only 30 minutes but leave every 2 hours, so plan accordingly.

The most scenic course also starts at the Seongsamjae rest area, but takes you up to **Hwaeomsa.** You can also take a 3-hour hike up a side road from Nogodan ridge. If you prefer a shorter walk, there is a promenade near the entrance to the path to Nogodan from the temple Hwaeomsa. The promenade takes about an hour round-trip. Additional information about Hwaeomsa is in the "Temples in Jirisan" section, below.

The third, longer trail is best experienced when the leaves show off their fall (autumn) colors. The trail starts at **Jikjeon Village** and goes to Piagol, where a

JIRISAN'S 10 scenic BEAUTIES

Koreans love to make lists of nature and Jirisan is no exception. This is a list put together by the Jirisan Alpine Club and published on their mountaineering maps in 1972.

1. **Cheonwang Sunrise**—Some say that a person lucky enough to catch the sunrise on Cheonwang peak must have accumulated enough good deeds for three generations. I say you just have to wake up really early.

2. **Nogo-unhae (The Sea of Clouds from Nogodan)**—Considered an "immortal" place, the sea of clouds over the valley from the Nogodan peak is another of Jirisan's beauties.

3. **Banyabong Nakjo**—Banya peak is supposed to look like a pair of women's breasts. One of the beauties of Jirisan is to see the *nakjo* (the rays of the setting sun) reflected here.

4. **Sunset from Banyabong**—Banyabong, the second-highest peak of Jirisan, has beautiful sunsets, especially in the summer.

5. **Piagol Samhong (Autumn Foliage at Piagol)**—"Samhong" means the three reds, which can be seen in the color of the changing leaves. Joshik, a Confucian scholar during the Joseon Dynasty, said, "People who do not see the red-tinted leaves in

Piagol dare not say they know red-tinted leaves."

6. **Byeokso Myeongwol (The Bright Moon from Byeoksoryeong)**—Byeoksoryeong, which stands in the middle of Jirisan, is known for its icy blue moon that rises above the peak when the moon is full.

7. **Buli-hyeon-pok (Bulil Falls)**—Just southeast of Ssanggye Temple, this waterfall makes a wonderful sound that resonates throughout the valley.

8. **Seseok Royal Azaleas**—"Seseok" refers to the cold water that flows through the pebbles here. In the springtime (from early May to late June) the plateau is blanketed by the colorful blooms of the azaleas.

9. **Seomjincheongryu (The Clean Water of Seomjin)**—The Seomjin River that starts in the mountains is known for its beautiful clean waters, compared to blue silk that flows on the white silk of the sand on the riverbed.

10. **Chilseon-gyegok (Seven Gods Valley)**—The last wild forest left in Jirisan, the Chilseon Valley is supposed to hold enchanted purity and is a beautiful sight. According to legend, seven gods are said to live in the valley, hence the name.

Maple Tree Autumn Foliage Festival is held every year in late October or early November. You'll pass the largest temple in Jirisan, **Yeongoksa,** at the entrance to Piagol Valley. The full course to the top takes 7 hours round-trip, but you can stop midway and return if you don't have that much time. Take a bus to Piagol from Gurye to the last stop. The buses from Gurye Terminal to Piagol Valley run nine times a day at 2-hour intervals and take about 40 min.

Admission to Jirisan is free, but admission to temples varies. A bit more information about Jirisan is in the **Hadong** section of the Gyeongsang-do chapter.

TEMPLES IN JIRISAN

The following are temples on the Jeollanam-do side of Jirisan (except Silsangsa, which is detailed in the Namwon section earlier in this chapter). The temples on the Gyeongsang province are detailed in chapter 8.

Jirisan National Park

7

JEOLLA-DO | The Rest of Jeollanam-do

Hwaeomsa ★★★ TEMPLE   One of South Korea's top 10 temples, Hwaeomsa (pronounced "*Hwa*-umsa") sits on the southwestern part of Jirisan in the middle of Nogodan peak. Built during the Shilla Dynasty, the original structure was burned down during the Imjin Waeran in 1592. The temple was rebuilt during the Joseon Dynasty. In front of the main Buddha hall are a stone lantern and lion pagoda, both of which date back to A.D. 670.

12 Hwangjeon-li, Masan-myeon, Gurye-gun. ☏ **061/782-7600** (Korean). www.hwaeomsa.org (Korean only). Admission ₩3,500 adults, ₩1,800 teens, ₩1,300 children, free for seniors 65 and over and children 6 and under. Daily 7am–7:30pm. From Gwangju Bus Station, take local bus no. 225 (it's an hour ride and the bus runs every 40 min.). From the Gurye Bus Terminal, take a bus to Hwaeomsa Temple (the buses run every 20 min. from 8am-8:10pm). Then walk 15 min. to the temple.

Saseong-am ("Four Sages" Hermitage) ★★ TEMPLE   If you look at the top of Osansan, you'll see the main hall of this small hermitage perched on precarious columns, hugging the side of the mountain. It's worth a trip up the steep incline just for the dramatic scenery (they provide shuttle buses from the bottom). Originally called Osansa, it was founded during the Baekje period by Monk Wonhyo (the same guy who founded Hwaeomsa and Yeongoksa). The hermitage fell into ruin during the Joseon Dynasty, but was renovated in the 1980s. A steep, rocky stairwell leads up to the Sanshin-gak area and the entrance to the Doseon-gul (cave), where Wonhyo supposedly meditated.

186 Jukma-li, Muncheok-myeon, Gurye-gun. ☏ **061/781-4544.** Located southeast of Gurye, it's across the Seomjin River from the Nogodan area of Jirisan. Buses from Gurye to Saseong-am run only 3 times a day 6:40am–6:20pm (a 20-min. ride). A better option is to take a taxi from Gurye-gu Station, which takes about 15 min. and costs around ₩12,000.

Yeongoksa ★ TEMPLE   The largest temple in the national park, Yeongoksa lies in the Piagol valley of Jirisan. Like its neighbor Hwaeomsa, the temple has a rich history and is surrounded by picturesque scenery. The first temple built in Jirisan, it was founded by Yeongijosa in 543. Like most temples, it was destroyed during the Imjin Waeran, but was rebuilt in 1627. Unfortunately, it didn't escape the Korean War unscathed, either, so it was rebuilt in 1981.

Naedong-li, Toji-myeon, Gurye-gun. ☏ **061/782-7412** (Korean). Admission ₩1,600 adults, ₩700 teens, ₩400 children, free for children 6 and under. Mar–Oct daily 6am–8pm; Nov–Feb daily 6am–7pm. Local buses from Gurye Bus Terminal run about every hour and take an hour. Costing ₩2,300, they run daily 6:40am–7:40pm. Buses from Suncheon run twice a day and take 90 min.

Exploring Jeollanam-do

Jeollanam-do has beautiful scenery and some of the most interesting temples in the country. Many of them are outside the major cities, but they're worth a side trip.

Bulgapsa (Bulgap Temple) TEMPLE   South of the small town of Yeonggwang is a small temple at the base of Bulgapsan and said to be Korea's oldest temple. Originally built in A.D. 384, it has been rebuilt several times since. The main hall was built sometime in the 1700s and has been renovated since. The temple is known for its beautiful surroundings.

8 Moak-li, Bulgap-myeon, Yeonggwang-gun. ☏ **061/352-8097** (Korean). www.bulgapsa.org. Admission ₩2,500 adults, ₩1,500 teens, ₩1,000 children, free for children 4 and under. Daily 8am–6pm. From Gwangju city's Gwangcheon terminal, take bus no. 218 or 318 (a 1½-hr. ride).

Gangjin Celadon Museum MUSEUM   Celadon, Korea's ethereal green porcelain, has been produced in the Gangjin region for centuries and this museum is the only one dedicated to the Goryeo celadon, made here from the 9th to the 14th century. There are 188 celadon kilns in the area (about half the celadon kilns for the entire country). The museum has a couple of skillfully created pieces. Unfortunately, the signage is only in Korean upstairs, with just a few English labels downstairs. More fun is the hands-on experiential zone, where you can make mosaics from broken celadon, spin a masterpiece on a potter's wheel, or have your hand- and footprints baked in celadon.

127 Sadang-li, Daegu-myeon, Gangjin-gun. ☎ **061/430-3718** (Korean). Admission ₩2,000 adults, ₩1,500 teens, ₩1,000 children. Daily 8am–6pm. From the Gangjin Gunnae Terminal, take a local bus headed for Malyang and get off at the museum. The bus runs every 30 min. 6am–8:40pm, and the ride lasts about 30 min. There are also buses to Gangjin from Seoul, Gunsan, Gwangju, and Mokpo.

Seomjingang Train Village ★★ ☺ HIKING TRAIL   This is a re-created train station made from refurbished wood. There's also a renovated an old train to take you on a scenic, 25-minute ride (50 min. round-trip) along the Seomjin River to Gajeong Station, where you can go for a lovely hike in the woods and take the train back. For serious train enthusiasts, this place even offers an overnight in a converted **train "pension"** ★★★ ☺ (☎ 061/362-5600; www.gspension.co.kr). Rooms range from ₩70,000 to ₩180,000, depending on the size. Reservations are recommended for both the train ride and the pension stay.

770-5, Ojili, Ogok-myeon, Gokseong-gun. ☎ **061/360-8309.** www.gstrain.co.kr. Rides are ₩5,000–₩6,000 adults, ₩4,500–₩5,500 children round-trip (₩500 less one-way). Daily 9am–6pm, but trains run 9:30am, 11:30am, 1:30pm, 2:30pm, and 5:30pm. It's best to take a taxi from the Gokseong bus or terminal.

Unjusa (Unju Temple) ★★★ ☺ TEMPLE   Located in Hwasun County, south of Gwangju, no one knows the actual founder of the temple, but it is believed to have been constructed during the Shilla Dynasty. Although the temple structure itself is not very impressive, the site is renowned for its pagodas and unusual Buddha statues. Of the original 1,000 pagodas and 1,000 Buddhas, only 18 pagodas and 70 statues remain. The most interesting stone statues are located to the left of the road leading up to the temple, especially the two lying figures, the only ones in the country.

Yonggang-li/Daecho-li, Doam-myeon, Hwasun-gun. ☎ **061/374-0660** (Korean). www.unjusa.org (Korean only). Admission ₩2,500 adults, ₩1,500 teens, ₩1,000 children, free for children 4 and under. Daily 8am–6pm. From Gwangju city's Gwangcheon terminal, take bus no. 218 or 318 (a 1½-hr. ride).

DADOHAE MARITIME NATIONAL PARK

Dadohae-haesang (http://english.knps.or.kr) includes Shinan-gun, Jindo-gun, and Goheung-gun of Yeosu-si and Wan-do-gun in Jeollanam-do. When it was designated a national park in 1981, it became the largest in the country. The entire park includes 1,596 islands and small islets (many uninhabited) with gorgeous views and varying landscapes. The eight sections of the park include the southern shore of Dolsan-do and a group of small islands to the south; the southern tip of the Goseun Peninsula and Naro-do; Geomun-do, Baek-do, and their associated islands south of the Goheung Peninsula; the southern tip of Wan-do, Shinji-do, and the islands to the south; the southern part of Jin-do and islands to its south; parts of Docho-do, Bigeum-do, and Eui-do; Heuksan-do and Hong-do and islands farther west; and the remote Manjae-do.

The most popular site in the park is the temple **Hyangilam,** which sits majestically upon a cliff on the southern tip of Dolsan-do. Since the maritime park consists of islands near and far, the best way to see parts of it is by ferry. Passenger boats are available to various islands from harbors on Mokpo, Yeosu, and Wan-do. Since some of the islands are remote, plan ahead and check the weather beforehand.

ISLANDS

Bigeum-do ★★ 🏛   The quiet beauty of this island is still preserved since it's still largely undiscovered by tourists. The island is the leading producer of naturally sun-dried salt, and the salt fields are indeed a sight to behold. The island's two beaches, Hanuneom and Wonpyeong, have facilities that are open mid-July to mid-August.

Bigeum-myeon, Shinan-gun. 𝓒 061/243-2171 (Korean). From Mokpo Ferry Terminal 1, take the fast-sailing liner bound for Bigeum-do at 7:50am (the ride lasts about 50 min.). Alternatively, from Mokpo Ferry Terminal 2, take one of the ferries bound for Gasan or Sudae. They run at 7am, 1pm, and 3pm and the ride lasts 2 hr. to 2 hr. 20 min.

Bogil-do 🏛   About an hour south of Wan-do by boat lies this quiet little island, which was made popular by artist Yun Seondo, who lived here for 10 years. While the 17th-century scholar Song Siyeol was on his way to exile in Jeju-do, he was forced to dock on the island due to bad weather. He carved some of his poetry on a rock, which remains today. Although the island has some beautiful sandy beaches, it's best known for its pebble beach, **Yesong-li,** and the sound the rounded stones make as the waves lap the shore. The best time to visit is May to June or August to September. Taxis and various minbak are available on the island.

Bogil-myeon, Wan-do-gun. 𝓒 **061/553-5177** (Korean). Ferries from Haenam take 90 min. and run about 12 times in the summer, 6 times in the fall. Ferries are also available from Wan-do, Hwa-heungpo, and Nohwa-do.

Hong-do ★★★   The name Hong-do means "red island," but no one knows for sure if the name came from the island's red soil or because it seems to turn red when the sun sets over the ocean. Whatever the case, the island is an ecological wonder, because of its soil and its unusual plants. Because of its protected status, visitors are allowed to go only to villages and designated tourist areas. Hong-do is composed of about 20 small islets, but the main island (which is said to be shaped like an ant) has two villages, one in the pinched waist center and one on the northern section. The middle village is where the wharf is and several minbak are clustered around it. A sightseeing ferry around the island takes about 2½ hours. If you have the time, visit nearby **Heuksan-do,** which is about 30 minutes away by boat. Some parts of the island (like the lighthouse) are accessible only by boat. You can rent a private boat for about ₩60,000 round-trip. Ask at the ferry information booth on the wharf.

Jeollanam-do. 𝓒 **061/246-2244** (Korean). Admission ₩2,600 adults, ₩1,100 teens, ₩550 children ages 8 to 12. From Mokpo Express Ferry Terminal (𝓒 061/240-6060), take the ferry to Hong-do. Sightseeing ferries run about every 2 hr. 7am–5pm (depending on the weather). Starting at ₩15,000, the ferry lasts 2½ hr.

Jeung-do ★★★ 🏛   Since 2008, the **Tapyeong Salt Farm** and its associated **Salt Museum** have been an ecological tourist location. Residents of Jeung-do have been producing salt since the 1950s (about 15,000 tons per year), but it hasn't been open to visitors until recently. Watching the workers harvest the salt from the ocean flats is a sight to see, but visitors can participate in the salt-collecting process, including turning the water wheels and raking the salt. At the end of the experience, they'll give you a kilogram to take home with you (you can also buy their special local sea salt flavored with dry seaweed). Be sure to book your salt harvesting experience at least 3 days in advance. It costs ₩7,000 for adults, ₩6,000 for those 17 and under.

Tip: Pack a picnic lunch or dinner if you plan to visit on a Sunday, since most of the restaurants on the island will be closed as the Christian residents take the day off.

1648 Daejo-li, Jeungdo-myeon, Shinan-gun. © **061/275-0829.** www.saltmuseum.org. Thurs–Mon 9am–6pm. Closed Jan 1. Admission ₩2,000 to the museum. To get to Jeong-do, take a bus to Jido from Seoul's Express Bus Terminal. From the Jido Bus Terminal, take the shuttle bus to Saokdo's Jisingae Dock (the bus runs frequently, depending on the boat schedule, costs ₩1,500, and takes about 15 min.). The ferry to Jeung-do runs at 7am, 9am, noon, 3pm, and 5pm and takes about 30 min.

Jin-do   The third-largest island in South Korea, Jin-do includes an archipelago of about 230 smaller islands. The Jin-do itself is known for two things: Its native dogs, the *jindokgae,* and what's called the "Moses Miracle of Jin-do." Near the end of the second month of the lunar calendar to the middle of the sixth month, a "road" appears in the middle of the ocean when the water recedes for about an hour a day. You should call the Korea Travel Phone (© **1330**) to see when peak times are before you visit. There are taxis and buses available on Jin-do.

Jodo-myeon, Jin-do-gun. © **061/544-2181** (Korean only). Free admission. From Jindo-eup Bus Terminal, take a bus to Jin-do Island or Hoedong-li.

Wan-do   The largest island in Jeollanam-do, Wan-do is also the name of the county that encompasses it. The county includes 203 islands, 143 of which are uninhabited. Wan-do is famous for **Cheonghaejin,** a military complex created by Jang Bogo, a famous general from the Shilla Kingdom. The island has wonderful hiking trails and the **Wan-do Botanical Garden.** A bridge connects Wan-do to Sinchi-do.

Wan-do-gun. You can drive to Wan-do from Haenam, or take an intercity bus from Gwangju, Busan, Mokpo, Gangjin, or Yeongam. Express buses are also available from Seoul. You can also take a ferry to and from Jeju-do.

Naejangsan National Park

Declared a national park in 1971, **Naejangsan** (© **063/538-7875;** http://english. knps.or.kr/Knp/Naejangsan/#) is one of the smallest in the country. But that doesn't mean you should skip it—quite the contrary. Naejang, which means "many secrets," is beautiful, particularly in the fall, thanks to the 13 varieties of maple that grow here. Its highest peak, Shinseonbong, is relatively low, but still rugged for its height (only 763m/2,503 ft.). The valley and ridge trails aren't very strenuous, but those up the sides of the hills are very steep. That's why they've built a cable car that goes up to the peak from the entrance to Naejangsa. If you follow the valley to the left from the ticket booth, you'll see **Dodeok Falls. Geumseong Falls** is farther along the valley, if you take the path to the left.

If you pass the wooden path lined with white oaks and maples in the southern part of the park, you'll arrive at the entrance to **Baegyangsa ★★★**, 26, Yaksu-li, Bukha-myeon, Jangseong-gun. Built in 632 during the Baekje period, its name was changed by Monk Chongtosa, then again during the reign of Joseon King Sonjo. The word *baegyang* means "white sheep," based on a legend that one of the temple's monks, Hwanyangsonsa, was delivering a sermon and a white sheep came down from the mountain to listen. At the end of the ceremony, the sheep appeared again in the monk's dream and told him that he was turned into a sheep after having committed a crime in heaven. The next day, the sheep was found dead in the temple. Admission is ₩2,500 for adults, ₩1,000 for teens, ₩700 for children, free for those 65 and over and kids 6 and under. The temple is open daily March through October 9am to 6pm (until 5pm Nov–Feb). From the Gwangju Bus Terminal, buses run daily 6am to 7:50pm every hour, and the ride takes about an hour.

The other major temple in the mountains is farther away, but the scenic walk makes it worth the extra effort. When you enter the ticket booth, walk by the marketplace and shops and you'll come to a small river valley (Naejang-cheon). Walk on this trail for 30 minutes and you will come to a lotus pond with a garden house in the middle, the **Uhwajeong.** After you pass it, you'll come to a cable car—walk beyond that, through a canopy of maple trees, and you'll reach the main entrance to **Naejangsa ★★.** Originally called Yeonggeunjosa, the temple was built by Monk Yeongeun-josa in 636 during the Baekje period. It was destroyed and rebuilt many times, but it was completely destroyed during the Korean War and rebuilt in its current incarnation in the 1970s. Admission is ₩3,000 for adults, ₩1,200 for teens, ₩700 for children, free for those 65 and over and kids 6 and under. The temple is open daily from sunrise to sunset. From the Jeong-eup Bus Terminal take bus no. 171 to Naejangsan National Park. The bus runs every 20 minutes or so. A taxi from the bus terminal should take about 20 min. Admission to the park is free.

Wolchulsan National Park

Wolchulsan's granite peaks rise dramatically from the flat fields surrounding it. It has a narrow and deep valley and interesting trails. The highest peak in the area is **Cheonghwang-bong,** which climbs up 809m (2,654 ft.). To the south lies Muwisa and to the west is the quiet **Dogapsa,** a temple built by the Shilla monk Doseonguksa that was burned during the Korean War and has yet to be restored. Still, it's worth a quick visit (Dogap-li, Gunseo-myeon, Yongam-gun; ℭ 061/473-5122). The main entrance is the oldest structure still standing in the temple complex (built in 1493). The newer main hall has newly painted pillars and walls. During its repair in 1960, an ink sign was discovered, shedding light on the temple's history. It read that the temple was built by the great Monk Sinmi in the fourth year of King Seonjong. Monk Sinmi was highly trusted by King Sejo and probably received compensation from him to build the temple. During the height of its glory, 730 monks lived on-site.

About 500m (1,640 ft.) down from the top of Gujeong-bong is the **Maae Yeorae Jwasang ★★,** a stone Buddha carved in the rock there. Some say that his eyes are looking at the west sea, but to me, they look closed as if he is meditating or sleeping. The Maae Buddha is said to have been created in the year A.D. 9.

Though most people take day trips to the area, there are camping facilities available in the Cheonghwangsa area. There is also a minbak area in the Gyeongpodae district.

Just outside of the national park is **Gurim Village ★★★,** which has an ancient history (as you can see by the prehistoric relics found here). Popular because of its 4th- and 5th-century kilns, its **Yeongnam Pottery Culture Center ★★,** 354 Seogurim-li, Gunseo-myeon, Yeongnam-gun (ℭ 061/470-2566) is on the site of the original kilns where they first produced glazed pottery during the Unified Shilla period. Not only do they house artifacts which have been excavated from the area, but they also create replicas of historic works for sale. The center is open daily 9am to 6pm throughout the year; admission is ₩1,600 adults, ₩600 teens, ₩300 children.

Duryunsan Provincial Park

Located on the southernmost point on the Korean Peninsula, Duryunsan with its beautiful scenery is home to many temples and ruins. Its dense forest of subtropical plants leads up to a rocky peak, with views of the surrounding sea and nearby islands.

The most famous temple here is **Daedunsa ★★★** (✆ 061/534-5502; www. daeheungsa.co.kr, Korean only), built during the fifth year of Baekje King Jinheng's reign by Monk Ado. Situated on the northern slope of Mt. Duryun, the temple is the headquarters of the Jogye Buddhist order. There is a free shuttle that will take you up the first 2km (1¼ miles) of the mountain, if you don't want to make the full hike. The long walk through the forest to the temple entrance is supposed to be part of the meditation process of visiting. You will be rewarded with the view of 1,000 smiling Buddha statues inside the Cheonbuljeon. The temple is open daily from 9am to 6pm, and admission is ₩2,500 for adults, ₩1,500 for teens, ₩1,000 for children, free for kids 6 and under and seniors 65 and up. In a separate area to the right is **Pyochungsa,** a shrine built in 1788. It is dedicated to the warrior monk generals who fought the invading Japanese army during the Imjin Waeran. There are many trails spidering out from Daedunsa, but the most popular goes up to its associated hermitage **Bungmireuk-am,** where a majestic stone Buddha has been sculpted from the flat rock face (now housed inside a wooden hall). It's worth the 45-minute climb up for the wonderful views.

There are seven buses daily from Seoul to Haenam, starting at 7:30am with the last bus at 5:55pm. The 5½-hour ride costs ₩17,800 (₩26,500 for deluxe buses). From the **Haenam Intercity Bus Terminal** take a bus bound for Daedunsa. Buses run every 30 minutes daily, 6:50am to 7:40pm, taking about 20 min.

The **Haenam Cable Car ★★** (✆ 061/534-8992; 138-6 Gurim-li, Samseon-myeon, Haenam-gun; http://haenamcablecar.com) starts at the village and goes to the tallest peak of Duryunsan. The 10-minute ride, which affords a spectacular view of the surrounding scenery, costs ₩8,000 adults, ₩5,000 children ages 3 to 12. The cable car runs daily 8am to 6pm (until 5pm Dec–Mar).

Where to Stay

Outside the major cities and tourist areas, you can find low-cost sleeping quarters in minbak everywhere. In low season, costs range from ₩30,000 to ₩40,000, but prices can double during popular summer months. Although you can make reservations in advance for some of the upper-end resorts and condos, you'll sometimes get better rates if you just walk in, especially on weekdays and during the low season.

In the Haenam area, there are plenty of low- to midpriced motels. Some love motels like the **Sapphire Motel** (✆ 061/537-4825) and **Motel Tiffany** (✆ 061/537-0080) offer Internet access. The **Ddang-ggeut Tema Pakeuh** (✆ 061/535-1000), shaped like one of General Yi's turtle ships, is a midpriced option in the area. Double/single rooms cost ₩48,000 on weekdays.

For a taste of history, stay at the **Yuseongwan ★★**, 799 Gurim-li, Samsan-myeon, Haenam-gun (✆ 061/534-2959), which has been a yeogwan since 1914, but is located in a 400-year-old home. Room rates range from ₩35,000 to ₩130,000, depending on size. There are no televisions or refrigerators, but there are shared shower facilities and a generous, home-cooked meal for only ₩7,000 for breakfast (₩10,000 for dinner).

Most first-class hotels can be found in the Jirisan area or near beaches. One nice place is the **Jirisan Hanhwa Resort,** 32-1 Hwangjun-li, Masan-myeon, Gurye-gun (✆ **061/782-2171;** fax 061/782-3675), with rack rates starting at ₩180,000. A slightly better bargain with nicer rooms is the **Jirisan Swiss Tourist Hotel,** 427-1 Hwangjeon-li, Masan-myeon, Gurye-gun (✆ **061/783-0156** or 7; fax 061/782-1571).

Another good option is the **Wolchulsan Hot Springs Tourist Hotel,** 6-10 Haechang-li, Gunsan-myeon, Yeongam-gun (✆ **061/473-6311**), with rates from ₩96,800 for a standard, ₩193,600 for a suite.

An excellent place to stay in Jeung-do is the **El Dorado Resort ★★★**, 233-42 Ujeon-li, Jeungdo-myeon, Shinan-gun (www.eldoradoresort.co.kr; ✆ **061/260-3300**). This upscale set of "villas" is set on a small peninsula, so every one of them has an ocean view. Breakfast and use of their seawater spa and sauna are included in the room rates, which range from ₩250,000 for a double to ₩768,000 for a six-person villa.

Where to Eat

Being on the South Seas with miles of coastline, the Jeollanam-do region is well known for its fresh and varied seafood. Although outsiders make fun of their provincial ways, everyone agrees that this region's food is the best. The residents are known to be generous people by the sheer number of banchan laid out for the simplest of meals.

In the Jirisan area, try the local blue crab at **Gokseong Saesugung Garden,** 937 Hahan-li, Jukgok-myeon, Gokseong-gun (✆ 061/363-4633), on the way to Seom-jin-gahng from Namwon.

The chargrilled beef at **Gwangyang Hanguk Shikdang** is worth a special trip, 206-1 Eupnaeri, Gwangyang-eup, Gwangyang-si (✆ 061/762-9292), they serve a recipe handed down through three generations.

In Haenam, try **Haenam Jeonju Shikdang,** 140-5 Gurim-li, Samsan-myeon, Haenam-gun (✆ 061/532-7696), which serves regional specialties, including *sanchae hanjeongshik* (mountain vegetable traditional meal), for ₩60,000 for four people, but their sanchae bibimbap for ₩6,000 is a better option if you're traveling alone. If you're hankering for *haemultahng* (spicy seafood hot pot), look no further than **Haenam Yonggung Haemultang,** 18-4 Pyeongdong-li, Haenam-eup, Haenam-gun (✆ 061/535-5161), which specializes in the dish.

For wholesome food, try the oxtail soup made by the halmuhni at **Naju Nampyeong Sikdang,** 13 Geumgye-dong, Naju (✆ 061/334-4682). This milky white soup is served with only two side dishes, traditional kimchi and *ggakdugi* (daikon kimchi). **Naju Yeongsa Hong-ga,** 265-9 Yeongsan-dong, Naju (✆ 061/334-0585), is well known for their various *hong-uh* (skate) dishes. Another good restaurant is **Yeongsan Hong-uh,** 272-2 beonji, Yeongsan-dong, Naju (✆ 061/334-0305), which offers hong-uh kimchi, hong-uh noodles, and all things skate.

GYEONGSANG-DO

L ocated in the southeastern part of the peninsula, Gyeongsang-do is home to the former capital of the Shilla Dynasty,
Gyeongju, as well as South Korea's largest port, Busan (see
chapter 10).

You don't want to miss Gyeongju, the whole town is like one big open-air
museum, with its royal tombs, historic temples, and historic villages. The
largest and best-preserved traditional village in the country is in Andong,
where people are paid to continue living in the old houses. For really old
relics (as in prehistoric), make a special trip to Goseong to see the former
nesting grounds of dinosaurs and the footprints they've left on the rocky
coast. While you're in the area, take a detour to Tongyeong, one of the
most dramatically beautiful coastal towns in the country. Other points
along the southern coast are also great for ocean views, small temples
hidden in the mountains, and some of the natural beauty of South Korea.

Gyeongsang-do is famous for its salty and spicy cooking. Although the
dishes are not as refined as those from Jeolla-do or the Seoul area, the
ingredients are always fresh and seafood abounds from both the southern
and eastern coasts.

GYEONGJU

Once the capital of the Shilla Kingdom, today Gyeongju is the historical
center of South Korea. The Shilla Kingdom came into power around A.D.
57 and conquered the Baekje and Goguryeo kingdoms in 660 and 668,
respectively, ruling as the Unified Shilla Kingdom until 935, when the
Goryeo Dynasty took power. A large number of sites from that time
remain in the city today.

Located in the southeasternmost corner of the Gyeongsangbuk-do,
Gyeongju is a medium-size city by South Korean standards. It benefits
from tourism and the proximity to its industrial neighbor Ulsan to the
south. The entire city's historic areas were designated a World Heritage
site by UNESCO in 2000. Three major sites make up the Gyeongju Historic Areas: The Namsan belt, which includes the ruins of 122 temples,
53 stone statues, and 64 pagodas; the Wolseong Belt, which includes the
palace ruins of Wolseong and the Gyerim woodland; and the Tumuli Park
Belt, which includes the three groups of royal tombs. The UNESCO
designation also covers nearby Hywangnyeongsa (Hywangnyeong Temple)
and Sanseong Fortress.

Essentials

GETTING THERE   The nearest airport to Gyeongju is Ulsan Airport; Busan's **Gimhae Airport** is a bit farther away, but it offers many more flights. Intercity buses from Gimhae leave for Gyeongju Terminal daily every hour, 8:30am to 8:20pm, and cost ₩9,400. Daily buses from Ulsan Airport run four times a day (8:20am, 11:40am, 4:10pm, and 6:40pm) and cost ₩4,500—they take about an hour.

Gyeongju lies at the junction of two minor train lines run by the **Korean National Railroad** (KoRail). The Jung-ang line has one *mugunghwa* train that starts from Seoul and ends at Gyeongjuat at 10:35pm, costing ₩25,300, (it takes a little more than 5 hours). *Saemaeul* trains from Seoul run twice a day at 5:55am and 5:40pm, take 4½ hours, and cost ₩37,700. The **KTX** express train from Seoul stops at Singyeongju Station, in Geoncheon-eup south of Gyeongju's city center, and costs ₩43,400. It's about 80 minutes faster than the regular train.

You can also take an express bus from **Seoul's Express Bus Terminal** (Seoul subway line 3 or 7, exit 2), which will take about 4 hours and 20 minutes. Regular express buses run daily from 6:30am to 7pm, costing ₩17,500 to ₩26,000. The **Gyeongju Express Bus Terminal** and **Intercity Bus Terminal** are right next to each other. Buses from Seoul go to the express terminal, as well as those to and from Busan, Daegu, and Daejeon while those from Busan, Daegu, Gangneung, Uljin, and Ulsan end up at the intercity terminal.

The bus terminals and train stations are within 20 minutes' walking distance from each other.

GETTING AROUND   There are local buses available that can get you to all of the sites listed below, but if you have limited time, you may want to hire a **taxi** for a day. Taxis can always be found outside the bus and train terminals. Negotiate with your driver, but rates are usually around ₩90,000 to ₩110,000 for 6 to 8 hours. The driver likely won't speak much English, but he will know exactly where to take you, and you'll be able to hit the historic sites quickly and easily. Regular taxi fares start at ₩1,500.

If you have time to spare and want to be environmentally savvy, you can rent a **bicycle** for a day or two. There are some biking trails and biking on the regular roads is pretty safe (which is definitely not the case in major cities like Busan or Seoul). Some trails around Namsan are rather hilly, but there are paths in the flood plains, which are fairly flat. Be aware that the bike paths are side by side with walking paths and are marked in red, while the pedestrian paths are marked in green. One such trail connects the central business district with the university area (a shortcut compared to the regular road). Another links the city to the Bomun Lake Resort area. As you go farther toward Bulguksa, the road gets hillier and more degraded thanks to increased traffic from visitors. Bicycle rentals are widely available (there are almost a dozen in the downtown area alone, including a few each near the train station, the bus terminal, and Bomun Lake), and rates are pretty much the same wherever you go. Rentals cost ₩5,000 per hour or ₩10,000 to ₩15,000 per day. Be sure to bring plenty of water and lunch or snacks, since there are very few eating options off some of the bike paths.

Gyeongju is also not a bad city for walking. Most locations of interest are located close to one another, making it relatively easy to explore on foot. For those sites outside of town, it's best to take a local bus or a taxi.

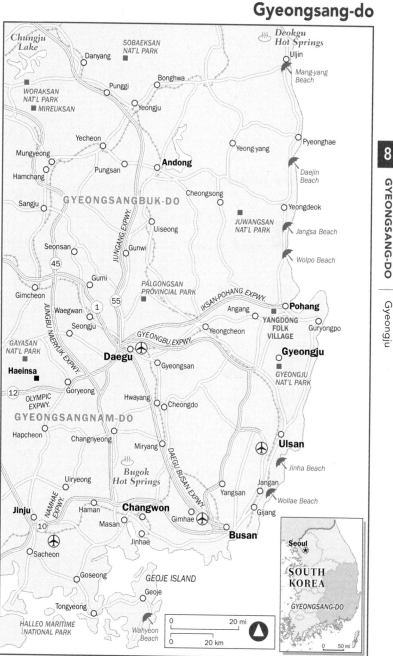

Chungju Lake

Deokgu Hot Springs

SOBAEKSAN NAT'L PARK

Danyang

Uljin

Mang-yang Beach

Bonghwa

Punggi

WORAKSAN NAT'L PARK
MIREUKSAN

Yeongju

Pyeonghae

Yecheon

Mungyeong

Yeong-yang

Daejin Beach

Hamchang

Pungsan

Andong

GYEONGSANGBUK-DO

Cheongsong

Sangju

Yeongdeok

JUWANGSAN NAT'L PARK

Jangsa Beach

Uiseong

Seonsan

Gunwi

Wolpo Beach

45

Gumi

PALGONGSAN PROVINCIAL PARK

IKSAN-POHANG EXPWY.

Gimcheon

JUNGBU NAERUK EXPWY.

Waegwan

1

55

Angang

Pohang

Seongju

GYEONGBU EXPWY.

Yeongcheon

YANGDONG FOLK VILLAGE

Guryongpo

GAYASAN NAT'L PARK

Daegu

Gyeongsan

Gyeongju

Haeinsa

12

OLYMPIC EXPWY.

Goryeong

Hwayang

Cheongdo

GYEONGJU NAT'L PARK

GYEONGSANGNAM-DO

Hapcheon

Changnyeong

Miryang

Ulsan

Jinha Beach

DAEGU BUSAN EXPWY.

Bugok Hot Springs

Uiryeong

Jangan

Wollae Beach

Jinju

NAMHAE EXPWY.

Haman

Changnwon

Yangsan

10

Masan

Gimhae

Gijang

Jinhae

Busan

Sacheon

Goseong

GEOJE ISLAND

Tongyeong

Geoje

HALLEO MARITIME NATIONAL PARK

Wahyeon Beach

0   20 mi

0   20 km

Seoul ★

SOUTH KOREA

GYEONGSANG-DO

0   50 mi

VISITOR INFORMATION Gyeongju's tourist information offices (① 054/779-6077; daily 8:30am–6pm) are located in key places throughout town. They provide both brochures and maps in English and have friendly staff who speak English well. The booths are located in front of **Gyeongju Train Station** (① 054/772-3843), in front of the **bus terminal** (① 054/772-9289), at the entrance to the **Bulguksa parking lot** (① 054/746-4747), next to the Chosun Hotel in **Bomun Lake Resort** (① 054/745-0753) and at **Shingyeongju station** (① 054/771-1336). The city's official website is www.gyeongju.go.kr/english.

Cheonma Tours (① 054/743-6001) offers three different tours of the city, two daily from 8:30am to 4pm and 10am to 6pm. Course 2 runs only on Tuesdays, Thursdays, and weekends and departs from the Bulguksa visitor's center. Courses 1 and 3 start at the city's Express Bus Terminal. Course 3 is probably your best bet for hitting the important historic sites, while course 2 hits more obscure spots. The tours cost ₩15,000, or ₩12,000 for teens, ₩10,000 for children.

[FastFACTS] GYEONGJU

Banks, Foreign Exchange & ATMs All of South Korea's major banks have branches in downtown Gyeongju's main street. All of them will change foreign currency, but the easiest ATM to use is the Korea Exchange Bank (KEB) (① **054/742-7133;** 396-12 Seong-dong-dong, Gyeongju-si) just about a block from the train station Most banks are open Monday to Friday 9:30am to 4:30pm, though ATMs stay open longer. Most major hotels will also exchange foreign currency and traveler's checks.

Internet Access Most large hotels, and even a couple of the lower-priced motels and youth hostels, offer Internet access. If you don't have your own computer, your cheapest option is the **PC bahngs** in town. Just look for the letters PC—you'll find most of these Internet "rooms" above restaurants, on the second or third floors.

Post Office The post office (open weekdays 9am–5pm) is located on the south side of Hwarang-no, about a block west of the train station.

Exploring Gyeongju

Although it is possible to see most of the major sites in a day, I recommend spending at least a night in Gyeongju so that you have time to properly explore the historic district (the entire city is pretty much one giant national treasure). Sites in the downtown area can be easily explored on foot or by bicycle in 1 day, but should you wish to see sites in Namsan nearby, you'll want to take a bus or taxi. The famous Bulguksa and the Seokguram Grotto are a bit far from the central city area as well, but easily accessible by bus or taxi. Not all of these sites have phones, so if you need additional information, call the Gyeongju Tourism Office at ① **054/779-6077.**

Anapji Pond ★ HISTORIC SITE This pond was created during the Shilla Dynasty and was within the walls of the royal palace. A 1974 excavation revealed three underwater mounds, indicating that the pond used to have artificial islands within it. At the same time, the pond draining revealed several artifacts, including gold and bronze bowls, gilt ornaments, various jewelry, door knockers, and mirrors, which are now on display in the Gyeongju National Museum. The stately but diminutive **Imhae Jeonji,** the crown prince's palace, was historically the most important building on the property and has been restored along with other structures. ***Tip:*** For

Gyeongju

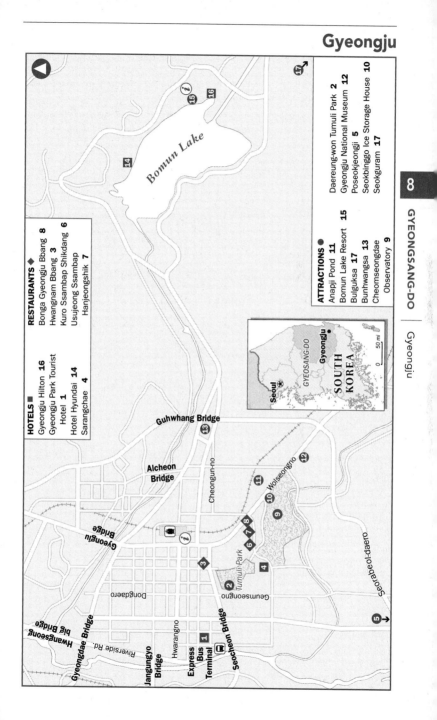

HOTELS ■

Gyeongju Hilton **16**
Gyeongju Park Tourist
Hotel **1**
Hotel Hyundai **14**
Sarangchae **4**

RESTAURANTS ◆

Bonga Gyeongju Bbang **8**
Hwangnam Bbang **3**
Kuro Ssambap Shikdang **6**
Usujeong Ssambap
Hanjeongshik **7**

ATTRACTIONS ●

Anapji Pond **11**
Bomun Lake Resort **15**
Bulguksa **17**
Bunhwangsa **13**
Cheomseongdae
Observatory **9**

Daereung-won Tumuli Park **2**
Gyeongju National Museum **12**
Poseokjeongji **5**
Seokbinggo Ice Storage House **10**
Seokguram **17**

Bomun Lake

Guhwhang Bridge

Alcheon Bridge

Cheongun-no

Wolseongno

Tumuli Park

Geumseongno

Gyeongju Bridge

Dongdaero

Hwangseong big Bridge

Gyeongdae Bridge

Jangungyo Bridge

Riverside Rd.

Hwarangno

Seocheon Bridge

Express Bus Terminal

Seorabeol-daero

SOUTH KOREA

GYEOSANG-DO

Gyeongju

Seoul

0   50 mi

8

GYEONGSANG-DO | Gyeongju

235

a romantic view of the site, visit after dark, when the buildings, pond, and surrounding forests are lit up.

26 Inwang-dong, Gyeongju-si, Gyeongsangbuk-do. ℗ **054/779-6391.** Admission ₩1,000 adults, ₩500 teens, ₩400 children. Daily 9am–10pm. Parking free. From the bus terminal or across the street from the train station, take bus no. 11, 601, 602, 603, 604, 605, 606, 607, 608, or 609 to the Gyeongju National Museum stop and walk 3 min. A 10-min. walk from Cheomseongdae.

Bulguksa (Bulguk Temple) ★★★ TEMPLE

Perhaps the most famous of South Korea's many temples (thanks to its location and its UNESCO World Heritage designation), Bulguksa was originally built in 528 during the Reign of Shilla King Kim Daeseong, who had it built in honor of his parents. Although the original wooden structures have all since been rebuilt (between 1604 and 1805, the temple was renovated no fewer than 40 times), the stone bridges, the stairways, and the pagodas are original. The most recent rebuilding and repairs were made in 1973 and the buildings do show signs of wear and tear. Still, the complex and its structures are impressive in design and are a striking testament to the skill of the architects. Try to visit the site in the early morning or late afternoon to avoid the hordes of schoolchildren who get bussed in for field trips.

15 Jinhyeon-dong, Gyeongju-si, Gyeongsangbuk-do. ℗ **054/746-9933.** www.bulguksa.or.kr. Admission ₩4,000 adults, ₩3,000 teens, ₩2,000 children, free for kids 6 and under. Nov–Feb daily 7am–5pm; Mar–Oct daily 7am–6pm. Take bus no. 10 or 11 from either the bus terminals or the train station. It's a 40-min. ride. A taxi will take 20–25 min. from downtown. Driving from Gyeongju-si, take road 7 toward Bulguksa, turn left on road 902, and follow the signs to the parking lot.

Bunhwangsa (Bunhwang Temple) TEMPLE

One of the most important temples during the Shilla Dynasty, it was established by Queen Seondeok during her reign (A.D. 632–637). A haven for artists and monks, many Buddhist paintings and sculptures were created here. Unfortunately, most of them were destroyed during the Imjin Waeran (1592–98). Although Bunhwangsa is only a shadow of its former self, it is still famous for its Mojeon Stone Pagoda, which has only three of its original nine levels still intact.

313 Guhwang-dong, Gyeongju-si, Gyeongsangbuk-do. ℗ **054/742-9922.** www.bunhwangsa.org (Korean only). Admission ₩4,000 adults, ₩3,000 teens, ₩2,000 children, free for kids 6 and under. Nov–Feb daily 8am–5pm; Mar–Oct daily 8am–6pm. Across the street from the bus terminal, take bus no. 10, 11, 15, 17, 18, or 277 (takes 15 min.). A taxi will take 20–25 min. from downtown.

Cheomseongdae Observatory HISTORIC SITE

You may be surprised to see that this, the oldest existing astronomical observatory in all of Asia, is not on the top of a mountain—it's actually on flat land. The 362 stones that make up the 27-level structure represent each day of the lunar year. Built during the reign of Shilla Queen Seondeok, it was used for observing the stars in order to forecast the weather.

Inwang-dong, Gyeongju-si, Gyeongsangbuk-do. No phone. Admission ₩500 adults, ₩300 teens, ₩200 children, free for kids 6 and under. Mar–Oct daily 9am–7pm; Nov–Feb daily 9am–6pm. It's a 3-min. walk from Tumuli Park.

Daereung-won Tumuli Park (Royal Burial Grounds) ★★ MEMORIAL

If you see only one tomb park in South Korea, this should be it. Tumuli Park contains 23 of the over 200 royal tombs found in Gyeongju. At times, the sense of history, and of secrets buried along with the royals, is almost palpable in the quiet between the large grass-covered mounds. Of the various round burial mounds only the **Cheonmachong (Heavenly Horse) Tomb** has been excavated (in 1974). The excavation of this tomb, presumed to be from the 5th century, revealed over 10,000 treasures inside, including a well-preserved ceremonial saddle piece made of painted bark stitched with leather. The tomb is named after a painting of a galloping horse—the first pre-Shilla painting found in Korea—and is open for you to see how it was constructed and how the artifacts were arranged.

6-1 Hwangnam-dong, Gyeongju-si, Gyeongsangbuk-do. No phone. Admission ₩1,500 adults, ₩700 teens, ₩600 children, free for kids 6 and under. Summer daily 9am–6pm; winter daily 9am–5pm. Bus no. 10, 11, or 70 from the bus terminal brings you to the front of Daereung-won Tumuli Park. Bus no. 42 goes to the back entrance.

Gyeongju National Museum ★ MUSEUM   Outside of Seoul, this museum has the largest collection of Shilla Dynasty relics in South Korea (and the world, for that matter). Of over 100,000 pieces in its possession, only about 3,000 artifacts are on view, but the displays are well lit and presented in four exhibit halls. Still, the explanatory text could use some punching up. Highlights include the gold crowns and other treasures excavated from nearby tombs and King Seongdeok's famous bell. Buddhist sculptures make up a majority of the stone pieces in the collection.

76 Inwang-dong, Gyeongju-si, Gyeongsangbuk-do. ⓒ 054/740-7500. http://gyeongju.museum. go.kr. Admission free. Mar Tues–Wed 9am–6pm, Thurs–Sun 9am–9pm; Apr–June Tues–Wed 9am–6pm, Thurs–Fri 9am–9pm, Sat–Sun 9am–7pm; July–Feb Tues–Sun 9am–5pm. Closed Jan 1. From the bus terminal or across the street from the train station, take bus no. 11, 601, 602, 603, 604, 605, 606, 607, 608, or 609 to the museum.

Poseokjeongji (Poseokjeong Pavilion) NATURAL ATTRACTION   Poseokjeong, which loosely translated means "where rocks are placed in the shape of an abalone," was given its name because of the shape of the rock grooves. Originally the site of a royal Shilla villa, all that remains today is a stone waterway. It was said that the Shilla kings came here with their nobles and officials. They would place their wine glasses in the water and recite a poem before their glasses floated to the top. This is also the site where Shilla King Gyeong-ae was attacked by Gyeonhwon of the Later Baekje (HuBaekje) Kingdom. It is said that Gyeong-ae killed himself rather than surrender, and thus the pavilion is the symbol of the fall of the Shilla Dynasty.

454-3 Bae-dong, Gyeongju-si, Gyeongsangbuk-do. ⓒ 054/745-8484. Admission ₩500 adults, ₩300 teens, ₩200 kids, free for children 6 and under. Mar–Oct daily 9am–6pm; Nov–Feb daily 9am–5pm. Parking ₩2,000 for small cars, ₩4,000 for large cars. Buses (505-1 and 507) run to Poseokjeong from either the train or bus station, about every 20 min. It's a 5-min. walk from the stop.

Seokbinggo Ice Storage House NATURAL ATTRACTION   This humble stone structure was a way for ancient Koreans to store ice before the invention of refrigeration, almost 1,500 years ago. The floor, walls, and ceiling are made of granite, with half of the structure underground. When you walk inside on a warm day, you'll feel the significant temperature drop.

449-1 Inwang-dong, Gyeongju-si, Gyeongsangbuk-do.No phone. Free admission. Daily 24 hr. Take bus no. 10, 11, 600, or 608 across from the train station or in front of the bus terminals.

Seokguram (Seokgul Grotto) ★★★ HISTORIC SITE   At the same time that Bulguksa was being constructed in honor of his parents, King Kim Daeseong had Seokguram built in honor of his parents from a former life (Buddhists believe in reincarnation). The grotto is an artificial stone structure made of granite, located on the eastern peak of Mt. Toham. Inside the domed main hall is one of the

Although much of Korea's ancient history is shrouded in myth (legend has it that the leaders of Korea's first three kingdoms emerged out of eggs), it is known that the Goguryeo, Baekje, and Shilla kingdoms were viable entities by the early A.D. 200s. Each had a monarchy and distinct borders; each gradually shrugged off China's influence; and each developed a system of law and had its own military. Through the late 500s, these three kingdoms ruled the Korean Peninsula, with the Goguryeo on the east coast and in Buyeo; the Baekje in the southeast; and the Shilla, which developed slightly later, controlling Gyeongju and the southwest. By the 600s, the Shilla were rapidly taking over land from both of its neighbors, and in 676 they established the first unified kingdom on the Korean Peninsula, stretching from Pyongyang in the north to the Wonsan Bay in the south.

world's finest shrines to the Buddha, surrounded by bodhisattvas and his guardians. Unfortunately, there is an added wooden entrance to the grotto, covering its original, unassuming stone facade. Still, it can't detract entirely from the place's beauty. Seokguram joined Bulguksa on UNESCO's World Heritage site list in 1995.

Tohamsan, Jinhyeon-dong 999, Gyeongju-si, Gyeongsangbuk-do. © **054/746-9933.** www.sukgulam.org. Admission ₩4,000 adults, ₩3,000 teens, ₩2,000 children, free for kids 6 and under. Nov–Jan 7am–5pm; Mar–Sep 6:30am–6pm; Feb–Mar and Oct 7am–5:30pm. Take bus no. 10 or 11 from either the bus terminals or the train station (takes 35 min.) and get off at the Bulguksa stop. A taxi will take 10 min. from the downtown area. Driving from Gyeongju-si, follow the directions to Bulguksa, above, and continue up the hilly road following the signs to Seokguram.

Around Gyeongju

Bomun Lake Resort ENTERTAINMENT COMPLEX   If you're tired of all the ancient sites, head over to this tourist complex, located about 6km (3¾ miles) east of the downtown area, for a little mindless fun. There are five super-deluxe hotels, a casino, a ferry port, Yukbu Village (a re-creation of a traditional village), the contemporary Seonjae Art Gallery, a drive-in theater, a golf course, a shopping mall, restaurants, and the amusement park Gyeongju World. From April to January, there are free traditional Korean music performances at the outdoor performance hall. You can also enjoy the hot springs or the cherry blossoms in the spring.

375 Sinpyeong-dong, Gyeongju-si, Gyeongsangbuk-do. From the intercity bus terminal, cross the street and take bus no. 10 or 18. The ride takes 20 min.

Gameunsa Temple Site TEMPLE   King Munmu, the Shilla king who unified the three kingdoms in the late 7th century, had this temple built in an attempt to drive away Japanese pirates with the power of the Buddha. Unfortunately, he died before the temple was completed, but his son finished it and had his father buried nearby in the East Sea. Only two stone pagodas remain at the site today, since the temple was not rebuilt after all its wooden structures burned down years ago.

55-1 Yongdang-li, Yangbuk-myeon, Gyeongju-si, Gyeongsangbuk-do. Free admission. Daily 24 hr. From the bus terminal, take bus no. 150 and get off at Gameunsa. The buses run about every 40 min. and take about 60 min.

Underwater Tomb of King Munmu MEMORIAL   When you walk on the beach in Bonggil-li, you will see a small islet just off the shore. This is the underwater tomb of King Munmu (A.D. 661–681), who unified the three kingdoms (see box above) and became the 30th ruler of Shilla. Before his death, the king asked to be buried in the East Sea so that he could become a dragon and protect the peninsula from Japanese invaders. There is a piece of granite at the center of the islet, where a pool of water forms. Historians still debate whether King Munmu's cremated remains are buried beneath it or if his ashes were scattered into the sea. You can't actually set foot on the islet, since it's so small and rocky, but you can see it from the beach.

Bonggil-li, Yangbuk-myeon, Gyeongju-si, Gyeongsangbuk-do. Free admission. Daily 24 hr. From the bus terminal, take bus no. 150 and get off at the underwater tomb or walk 10–15 min. from the Gameunsa site.

NAMSAN (MT. NAM)

Located south of Gyeongju, Namsan (which means "south mountain") is often called a "museum without walls," since it houses over 100 temple sites, 80 stone Buddhist statues, and 60 pagodas. It has 40 valleys and is divided into the southwestern region, which was worshiped by the people of the Shilla Kingdom, and the southeastern section, which includes the valleys of Mireukgol, Tapgol, and Bucheogol.

The best way to see Namsan is to take one of the many hiking trails, but be prepared with snacks and drinks, since it takes about 4 to 5 hours to do the entire course. The most popular trail starts in Samneung Valley, goes to Sangseonam, and past Sangsa Rock to the top of Geumobong. From there, you can stop in at Buheungsa, see the Poseokjeong Watercourse, and then return to Samneung Valley.

Shopping

The best place to find traditional Korean crafts is at the **Gyeongju Folk Craft Village** (✆ **054/746-7270**), which is located on the way to the Bomun Lake Resort from the downtown area. Within this cluster of about 45 traditional houses, artisans make pottery, woodcrafts, jewelry, embroidery, earthen burial figures, and other replicas of handicrafts from the Shilla Kingdom using traditional methods. Although some artisans keep their doors closed, many of them have open studios where you can see them work. The traditional pottery can be a bit pricey, but remember, you're getting a work of art straight from the hands of the artisan. The village is surrounded by several souvenir shops. Be sure to shop around for the best prices before opening your wallet.

For more modern shopping options, head over to the **Bomun Tourist Shopping Center,** which features souvenir shops galore, in the Bomun Lake Resort complex.

Where to Stay

All of Gyeongju's high-end hotels are located in the Bomun Lake Tourist complex. One of the best upscale accommodations is the **Hotel Hyundai ★★**, 477-2, Shinpyeong-dong, Gyeongju-si (www.hyundaihotel.com/gyeongju_en; ✆ **054/748-2233;** fax **054/748-8234**), which has standard rooms starting at ₩230,000 plus 10% VAT and a service charge. For an extra ₩20,000 you'll get a lakeview room. Also nice is the nearby **Gyeongju Hilton ★★★**, 370, Shinpyeong-dong, Gyeongju-si (www1.hilton.com/en_US/hi/hotel/KYOHITW-Gyeongju-Hilton/index.do; ✆ **054/740-1234;** fax **054/744-7799**), with rates starting at ₩150,000 for a standard room.

At the opposite end of the spectrum, the city has some youth hostels, which are located on the street on the way up from the Bulguksa parking lot to the temple itself. One of the larger ones is the **Bulguksa Youth Hostel,** 530-3 Jinhyeon-dong, Gyeongju-si (✆ **054/746-0826**). In the Bomun Lake area, there is also the

Gyeongju Bomun Youth Hostel, San 87, Songok-dong, Bomun, Gyeongju-si (🕿 054/749-5000), about a 15-minute walk from the Chosun Hotel. Most youth hostels have adult rates at ₩30,000 per person, lower for junior-high and high-school students.

For a more personal touch and family atmosphere, the *minbak* (homestay) **Sarangchae ★★★**, 238-1 Hwangnam-dong, Gyeongju-si (www.kjstay.com/content_eng/iboard.cgi; 🕿 054/773-4868), is a hanok conveniently located within walking distance of the bus stop and Tumuli Park. Rates are ₩25,000 for a single with bathroom or ₩30,000 for a double (₩5,000 per extra person), which includes a free breakfast and a shared kitchen.

Most midrange and budget accommodations are scattered throughout the city. Some of them can be found in the western area of downtown, with similar prices and facilities. One of the better ones in the downtown area is the **Gyeongju Park Tourist Hotel,** San 87, Songok-dong, Bomun, Gyeongju-si (🕿 054/742-8804), with twin rooms starting at ₩65,000 on weekdays. Prices go up slightly on weekends and a bit more during high season in the summer.

If you're on a really tight budget, you can stay in group sleeping quarters in a *jjimjilbang* (bathhouse) for about ₩8,000, which isn't recommended for light sleepers. One to check out is **Cheomseongdae Bulhanjeonmak** (191 Hadong, Gyeongju-si, Gyeongsangbuk-do; 🕿 054/777-7600), which is open 24 hours and costs ₩8,000 adults, ₩5,000 children.

Where to Eat

Unlike most towns in South Korea, Gyeongju isn't really known for any particular regional dish. The one thing invented in the city is its bread filled with sweet red beans, *Hwangnam-bbang,* named after the Hwangnam-dong area of Gyeongju where it originated. First made in 1939, the bread is available in many places in the downtown area. The **Hwangnam Bbang** bakery near Daereung-won does a brisk business. At night they have a huge staff making the *hwangnam-bbang* as fast as the people snatch them up, a bargain at only ₩500 each. Ready-made gift boxes of *boli bbang* (a chewier, less sweet bread made from rice flour and barley) can be purchased from **Bonga Gyeongju Bbang,** 802-3 Inwang-dong, Gyeongju-si (🕿 054/749-0456), which is open 8am to 10pm daily, and located on the corner down the street from Anapji Pond and Tumuli Park.

A traditional meal in Gyeongju is the *ssambap* (wrapped rice), where you'll get a table full of various *banchan* (side dishes) and greens (lettuce, perilla leaves, and steamed cabbage, among others) to wrap your rice in. You take a leaf in your hand, put a bit of rice in it, add a side dish and some seasoned *dwenjang* (fermented soybean paste), fold it up, and stuff the whole thing in your mouth. Most of the ssambap restaurants in town are clustered between the southeast corner of Tumuli Park and Wolseong Park, sometimes called **Ssambap Maeul** (Ssambap Village).

Kuro Ssambap Shikdang ★★ 🍴 KOREAN   There is only one thing on the menu and it's done exceptionally well. All of the banchan are handmade on the premises and you can taste the difference. On weekends the place is crawling with customers who've come for their ssambap with a ridiculous number of banchan laid out before them.

106-3, Hwangnam-dong, Gyeongju-si, Gyeongsangbuk-do. 🕿 **054/749-0600** (Korean only). Ssambap ₩8,000 per person with a 2-person minimum. No credit cards. Daily 11am–9pm. Closed Lunar New Year and Chuseok.

Usujeong Ssambap Hanjeongshik ★★ KOREAN There is a limited menu of a few traditional dishes at this casual spot with plastic patio chairs for alfresco dining, but no matter. The food is terrific, and the locals rave about the ssambap and the homemade *dongdongju* (an unfiltered rice wine, similar to *makgeolli*, but with bits of rice floating inside). And make sure to try the *haemul pajeon* (seafood green-onion pancake)—it's fantastic.

193-6 Ma-dong, Gyeongju-si, Gyeongsangbuk-do. ✆ **054/771-0786** (Korean). Ssambap ₩8,000. No credit cards. Daily 10am–10pm. Closed Lunar New Year and Chuseok.

DAEGU

Daegu is the capital of the Gyeongsangbuk Province. Lying at the junction of the Geumho and Nakdong rivers, the city has always served as a transportation hub for the region. The extremes in temperatures and the geographic peculiarity of the area may make the city uncomfortable at times for the residents, but it's very comfortable for apples. Christian missionaries in the early part of the 20th century grafted their imported apples to the local crabapple trees, resulting in a delicious hybrid fruit.

Daegu's economy is driven by the metal and machine industries centered here. Of more interest to visitors is the city's Oriental medicine herb market in the central area. Although it is a major city, Daegu still retains some of its small-town charms. It is also a good place to base your exploration of surrounding attractions, such as **Haeinsa** and **Gayasan National Park.**

Essentials

GETTING THERE The **Daegu International Airport** (TAE, ✆ **053/980-5290;** http://daegu.airport.co.kr), located just 2km (1¼ miles) outside of the city, serves as the central air hub for the area. International flights arrive at the Daegu airport from major Asian cities, including Beijing, Bangkok, Shanghai, Shenyang, and Qingdao. There are a couple of domestic flights a day from Seoul's Gimpo and Incheon airports, offered by Korean Airlines (KAL) and Asiana Airlines. Regular buses (nos. 401 and 718), costing ₩1,100, run daily every 6 to 12 minutes from the airport and go to most parts of the city. More upscale buses (nos. 104, 105, and 719) with guaranteed seating cost ₩1,500. If you want to take the subway, take bus no. 104 or 401 to the Ayanggyo Station to catch the subway from there. Taxis to Daegu city hall cost about ₩5,000.

There are two **train** stations in Daegu: The old station in the middle of the city, **Daegu Station,** and the newer and larger **Dongdaegu Station** to the east. The eastern train station is served by the **KTX** high-speed train. Both train stations have subway stops off line 1. Daegu is located on the Dongbu (Seoul–Busan) line. KTX trains from Seoul run daily every 20 minutes from 5:30am to 10:10pm and take about 1 hour and 40 minutes to Dongdaegu. Standard fares are ₩38,400 and first-class seats are ₩453,800. Mugunghwa trains from Seoul to Daegu station are ₩19,400 for adult standard fares, while Saemaul trains are ₩28,800 for standard adult fares. Child fares are about half price. KTX trains from Busan run daily every 20 to 30 minutes from 7:15am to 9:45pm to the Dongdaegu Station. The 1-hour train ride costs ₩10,800. Daegu is also served by the **Daegu line,** which runs east–west between Daegu and Gyeongju and connects to the Jung-ang line, which goes north from Yeongcheon.

A regular **limousine bus** service runs from Incheon airport (catch the bus from stop 10C) to Daegu via Gumi or Gimcheon. Buses run daily about every 30 to 50 minutes from 6:40am to 10:30pm. The 5-hour ride costs ₩34,100, with an increase to ₩37,500 at night.

You can also take a nonstop bus from Seoul's Express Bus Terminal or the Dong-Seoul Bus Terminal to the **Daegu Express Bus Terminal.** Buses run more frequently from Seoul's Express Bus Terminal, but they both have buses daily from 6am with buses from DongSeoul going as late as 1:30am, with regular fares at ₩16,300, ₩21,800 for deluxe buses, and ₩24,100 for the midnight fare (a bit misleading since it applies to buses that run 10pm–5am). The ride lasts about 3 hours and 40 minutes. Children's fares are half the adult prices.

Somewhat confusingly, Daegu has three different express bus terminals located right next to each other just south of the Dongdaegu Train Station, and another one, the **SeoDaegu Express Bus Terminal,** in the northwestern part of the city. Pretty much any bus going north or west of Daegu will stop at the SeoDaegu terminal, which includes buses to Seoul, Gwangju, Daejeon, Masan, Jeonju, Cheongju, Suncheon, Chuncheon, and Uijeongbu. The SeoDaegu terminal is right down the street from the Bukbu Bus Terminal and Daegu city buses.

The main Daegu Express Bus Terminal complex is more complicated. If one of the bus terminals doesn't service your destination, try the other two. The one closest to the train station runs mostly south to cities like Busan, Jinju, and Ulsan. The one across the street serves Seoul, Incheon, and areas northeast. The one next door to the east has buses to Daejeon, Gyeongju, Jeonju, Jinju, and Busan. Unfortunately, the buses are run by different companies and you'll have to know which companies go where to find out the schedules by phone. The companies are **Hanjin Express** (🕿 054/743-3701), **Hanil Express** (🕿 054/743-2956), **Kumho Express** (🕿 054/743-1101), **Dongyang Express** (🕿 054/743-3950), **Jung-ang Express** (🕿 054/743-2662), **Cheonil Express** (🕿 054/626-8001), and **Samhwa Express** (🕿 054/754-1001).

GETTING AROUND Daegu has a small **subway system** (www.dtro.or.kr/) with two lines that intersect each other at Banwoldang Station. The regular fare is ₩1,100. The subway doesn't go everywhere, but the stations are announced and clearly marked in English. If you plan on being in Daegu for more than a day, I suggest getting a **transportation card,** available at any subway station or newsstands near bus stops. The card's base cost is ₩2,000, but you can add any amount. It gives you a discount for both the subway and local buses, plus free transfers within 30 minutes of your last trip.

Buses in Daegu go pretty much anywhere you want to go. There are two types of **buses** (http://businfo.daegu.go.kr/ba/index/index.do?locale=en)—local (₩1,100) and express (₩1,6500). The first buses of the day depart daily at 5:30am and stop running by 11pm. The great thing about city buses is that they are numbered by their routes. Bus numbers have three digits, each number indicating the zone that the bus serves. For instance, bus no. 704 runs from zone 7 to zone 0, and then to zone 4. Other routes that are circular are named for the districts they serve and are numbered 1 through 3. For instance, bus no. 242 has a circular route starting at zone 2, going though zone 4, and ending back in zone 2. Bus no. 242-1 has a circular route going the opposite direction.

There are two types of **taxis** in the city: regular and deluxe. Regular taxis are usually silver with a blue or green sign on top. Deluxe taxis are black with a yellow sign on top and offer a free interpretation service (using the phone in the taxi). Although

Daegu

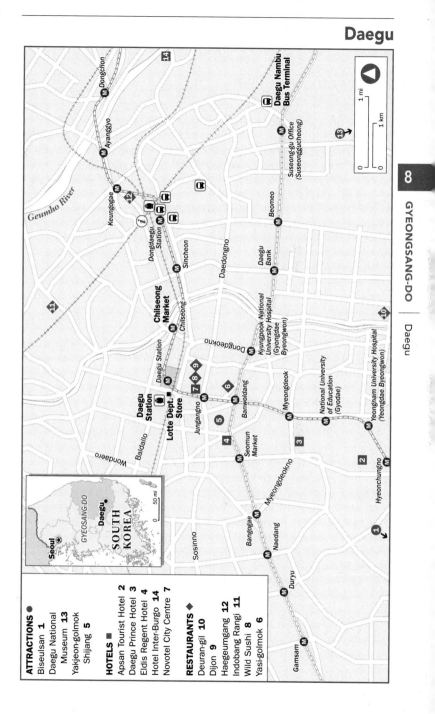

ATTRACTIONS ●
Biseulsan **1**
Daegu National
   Museum **13**
Yakjeon-golmok
Shijang **5**

HOTELS ■
Apsan Tourist Hotel **2**
Daegu Prince Hotel **3**
Eldis Regent Hotel **4**
Hotel Inter-Burgo **14**
Novotel City Centre **7**

RESTAURANTS ◆
Deuran-gil **10**
Dijon **9**
Haegeumgang **12**
Indobang Rangi **11**
Wild Sushi **8**
Yasi-golmok **6**

most taxi drivers won't know how to speak English, many taxis have a destination guide, including the names of most hotels and shopping centers in English. You can flag down a taxi anywhere on the street. Regular taxi fare starts at ₩1,500 for the first 2km (1¼ miles), while deluxe taxi fares start at ₩2,500 for the first 3km (1¾ miles).

VISITOR INFORMATION The main **Daegu Tourist Information Center** (**DTIC;** ℂ 053/627-8900; Apr–Oct 9am–8pm, Nov–Mar 9am–6pm) is located right next to the outdoor concert hall in Duryu Park. Their English-speaking staff provide reservations for train or plane tickets and offer brochures and maps in English. There are also information booths, open daily, on the first floor of the **Daegu Airport** (ℂ 053/984-1994; 7am–8pm) at **Daegu Station** (ℂ 053/660-1432; Mar–Oct 9am–7pm, Nov–Feb 9am–6pm), at **Dongdaegu Station** (ℂ 053/939-0080; Mar–Oct 8:30am–7:30pm, Nov–Feb 8:30am–7pm), in **Seomun Market** (ℂ 053/661-3266; Mar–Oct 9am–6pm, Nov–Feb 9am–5pm), at **Dongseogno Street** (ℂ 053/252-2696; 10am–7pm), at the herbal market's **Yangnyeongsi Exhibit Hall** (ℂ 053/631-3324; 9am–6pm), and at the entrance to **Palgongsan** (ℂ 053/985-0980; Mar–Oct 9am–6pm, Nov–Feb 9am–5pm). The city's official site is http://english.daegu.go.kr.

The city of Daegu offers a variety of inexpensive (only ₩4,000 adults, ₩3,000 children) bus tours. Tours leave from the DTIC in Duryu Park, DongDaegu Train Station and the bus stop in Banwonldang, in front of the Dong-A Shopping Center. Tours begin at 10am Tuesday through Sunday and are determined by demand, so call (ℂ 053/627-8900) or check ahead to make reservations (www.daegutour.or.kr).

[FastFACTS] DAEGU

Banks, Foreign Exchange & ATMs At the airport, Daegu Bank has two English-language ATMs—one on the first floor next to the money-exchange booth and another on the second floor. There is also a money-exchange booth on the second floor next to the international departures, which opens whenever the first international departures occur. Although most banks have ATMs outside their branches, most of the machines close at midnight. Some ATMs with the Cirrus or Star logos are open 24 hours and can be found in most popular public areas. The most foreigner-friendly ATMs can be found at Korea Exchange Bank (KEB) branches.

Internet Access Most large hotels and even a couple of the lower-priced motels offer Internet access. If you don't have your own computer, your cheapest option is the **PC bahngs** in town. Just look for the letters PC; most of them are found on the second or third floors above restaurants. You can also use the free computers with Internet access at the main DTIC at 588 Duryu-dong, Dalseo-gu, inside Duryu Park.

Post Office Post offices in Daegu are open weekdays March through October 9am to 6pm, November to February 8am to 5pm. On Saturdays they're open 9am to 1pm. They are closed Sundays and holidays.

Exploring In & Around Daegu

Daegu covers a larger land area than the city of Seoul, but parts of it still retain its small-town feel. Because of its location, it has some relics from the Shilla Dynasty, and it is a great jumping-off point to nearby national parks and the famed temple Haeinsa. The city's most fascinating attraction is the traditional herb market at Yakjeon-golmok.

Biseulsan (Mt. Biseul)   Although not one of the higher mountains on the peninsula, Biseulsan is nonetheless known for its scenic beauty, especially in the spring when the red azaleas are in bloom. Legend has it that 1,000 Buddhist saints have come from the surrounding area, so it's known for being a holy place. Its twin peaks, Johwabong and Gwangibong, attract thousands of climbers annually.

One of the most famous temples at Biseulsan, **Yugasa** (144 Yang-li, Okpo-myeon, Dalseong-gun; *℃* **053/614-5115;** http://yugasa.net), is hidden in the valley between the mountain ranges. Founded by the Buddhist teacher Doseonguksa in A.D. 827, this temple is known as a good place for meditation because of its quiet and serenity.

Farther up from the temple are the hermitages Sodu-am and Doseong-am. Behind the Doseong Hermitage is the Dotong Bawi (rock), on which Doseonguksa is said to have achieved nirvana.

Yuga-myeon, Dalseong-gun, Daegu. *℃* **053/614-5481.** www.dalseong.daegu.kr/bisulsan/html/main.html (Korean only). Admission ₩1,000 adults, ₩700 ages 13–18, ₩500 ages 7–12, free for seniors 65 and over and kids 6 and under. Daily 24 hr. From the Seongdangmok Station (take exit 3), cross the street and take bus no. 601 toward Wolbae; get off at the Sodaesa bus stop. Buses run irregularly, about every 1½ hr. Yugasa can also be reached by taking bus no. 66-2 (a 50-min. ride).

Daegu National Museum MUSEUM   There are three permanent exhibition halls, focusing on archaeological finds from the region, fine arts, and traditional folk life, with displays ranging from Neolithic tools to pottery and other items from the Three Kingdoms period. You'll see a variety of Buddhist statues and sculptures as well as Goryeo and Bucheon celadon porcelain. Artifacts in the museum date far back into the area's prehistory and culture. The museum also organizes activities for children, has an auditorium for special lectures and presentations, and keeps a nice outdoor garden area with flowers and herbs, where you can learn a bit about traditional herbal medicine, local plants, and edible grains.

Namseong-no, Jung-gu, Daegu. *℃* **053/768-6051.** http://daegu.museum.go.kr. Admission ₩1,000, ₩500 ages 18 and under, free to seniors 65 and over and kids 6 and under. Sun–Fri 9am–6pm; Sat and holidays 9am–7pm, closed Mondays and Jan 1. Free parking. Bus no. 100, 349, 414, 414-1, 427, or 449. Subway Manchon Station, line 2, exit 3.

Yakjeon-golmok Shijang (Yakjeon Alley Market) ★★★ MARKET   The biggest draw of Daegu is this 350-year-old market. With its origins during the Joseon Dynasty, the entire alley is lined with herbal medicine shops, acupuncturists, and all manner of traditional Oriental medicine. Even if you're not looking for a cure, it's great fun to smell the earthy scents of dried roots and peer into glass jars filled with ginseng roots and other bizarrely beautiful cures. The Wholesale Herbal Medicine Fair is held on the first floor of the nearby **Yangnyeongsi Exhibition Hall** every first and sixth day of the month. The **Yangnyeongsi Festival** ★★ is held here usually the second week in May.

Namseong-no, Jung-gu, Daegu. Free admission. Exhibition hall Mon–Sat 10am–5pm. Bus no. 104, 106, 306, 349, 401, 402, 439, 524, 535, 613, 650, 704, 730, or 909. Located across Jung-ang-no from the police stand (a 5-min. walk from the Jung-ang-no subway station). You can also walk here from the Banwoldang subway station.

PALGONGSAN (MT. PALGONG) PROVINCIAL PARK

Located just 20km (12 miles) north of Daegu, Mt. Palgong (*℃* **053/602-5900;** www.gbpalgong.go.kr) is considered one of the most spiritually important mountains in the country, primarily because of the many famous temples and associated hermitages that are located on its ridges. Koreans believe that the spiritual energy that lives in the mountain will eventually bring about the reunification of the two Koreas.

This is the nation's largest provincial park and features a ridgeline that runs in an east–west direction and forms Daegu's northern boundary. If you hike the ridgeline, you'll be treated to beautiful views of the surrounding valleys on both sides of the mountains.

Offering challenging (though not at all dangerous) climbs, the mountain's numerous and varied trails are popular with hikers year-round, but they're positively packed in the fall when the maple trees are in full flaming colors. Give yourself a day to explore the temples, the hermitages, and the various stone statues around the mountain. The shortest hike in Palgongsan starts at Donghwasa (Donghwa Temple; see p. 246), which is the most popular attraction in the park. Follow the trail to Budo-am, then Yeombur-am up to Dongbong Peak, and then you can make your way back down to the ticket booth. The path takes about 3½ to 4 hours.

A longer route takes you from Pagyesa (one of Donghwasa's auxiliary temples) through the Pagyejae pass up to Dongbong Peak. Then you can take a trail up to Inbong down to Bakhong-am, then down to Eunhaesa. This path will take you 8 to 10 hours, so it's best to start early in the morning.

A less stringent route starts from Eunhaesa. From there, you can go up to Bakhong-am, up to Inbong peak, to the Gatbawi, and down to the parking lot. This route will take about 5½ to 6 hours.

There are a variety of ways to get to Palgongsan from Daegu proper. To get to the main entrance and Donghwasa, take express bus no. 1 from either the Dongdaegu Station or across the street from the Migliore department store (it's about a 40-min. ride). To get to Pagyesa, take bus no. 401 from Hyanggyo Station. To get to Gatbawi, take bus no. 131 from the same station. Although there are plenty of restaurants and shops around, it's always best to carry at least some water with you (especially during the dog days of Daegu's summer).

Due to the influx of hikers, restaurants and sleeping quarters have sprung up in the area. The best restaurants in the area are in the popular southern side of the mountain as well as the west side near Pagyesa. There is also a good (and moderately priced) restaurant on top if you take the cable car. As for accommodations, it's probably best to spend the night in Daegu and just spend the day exploring Palgongsan.

Donghwasa (Donghwa Temple) ★★ TEMPLE Situated on the southern side of Palgongsan, this temple was built by Monk Geuk-Dal in A.D. 493. Originally called Yugasa, the temple was given its current name when it was rebuilt in 771 by Simjiwongsa. The current temple structure was built in 1732, but it has had serious renovations, additions, and landscaping in the past few decades.

During the Joseon Dynasty (1392–1910), Buddhism was heavily persecuted in Korea. Monks hid in remote mountain temples and Donghwasa is a good example of one of the hidden sanctuaries of the time.

The eastern section of the temple site is the **Geumdang-am** hermitage hall, built next to twin stone pagodas dating back to the Unified Shilla era. The road in front of the hermitage was the original entrance to Donghwasa and the original gate pillars and stone relief still remain. There are a number of other hermitage sites and many Buddhist images engraved on rocks scattered throughout the forest nearby. You will see them as you climb the hill to the newer section, the National Reunification (Tongil) Temple, which was built in the 1980s by the South Korean president, who was a Buddhist. The temple is dedicated to the peaceful reunification of the two

WAR WITH JAPAN, round ONE

From 1592 to 1598, Korea was attacked by Japanese invaders. This war is called the Imjin Waeran (translates roughly to "the war started by the Japanese in the year of imjin"), the Seven-Year War, or the Hideyoshi Invasions. There were two major invasions during that time—the first led by the legendary Japanese warrior Toyotomi Hideyoshi (1592–93) and the second from 1597 to 1598. Originally, the Japanese saw success on land and failure at sea, mostly thanks to the naval defenses led by Admiral Yi Su-shin and his turtle ships (see the "Floating Turtles" box in chapter 2). The Korean navy was able to intercept communication and supplies to the Japanese forces. Ming China intervened, trying to bring a peaceful end to the war (through both diplomatic and military means), stalling the war for 5 years, until Japan invaded

for a second time in 1597. The war ended with the naval battle at Noryang in 1598, when the Korean navy forced the retreat of the Japanese forces.

Unfortunately for Korea, this was just the first of many subsequent attacks by the Japanese, and in 1910, Japan officially annexed Korea. The indignities suffered under Japanese rule—for example, many Korean women were forced to serve as prostitutes, or "comfort women," for occupying Japanese troops—still resonate today. In 2007, Japanese premier Shinzo Abe made a statement implying that the Japanese had not forced women into sexual slavery. The resulting outcry both in Korea and around the world led to a formal apology, but tensions between Japan and Korea still run high.

Koreas. Above the complex is a giant white marble Buddha of Reunification in the ample courtyard.

35-beonji Dohak-dong, Dong-gu, Daegu. © **053/982-0101.** www.donghwasa.net (Korean only). Admission ₩2,500 adults, ₩1,500 teens, ₩1,000 children, free to kids 6 and under and seniors 65 and over. From the Dongdaegu Station, take bus no. 1 to Donghwasa (a 45-min. ride). The temple is a 10-min. walk from the bus stop. You can also take bus no. 105 from Daegu.

Eunhaesa (Temple of the Silver Sea) TEMPLE   On the east side of Palgongsan is this temple, founded by Monk Hyecheol, who was known as the Great Meditation Master, in A.D. 809. The original temple, Haeinsa (Temple of the Tranquil Sea), was burned during the Imjin Waeran in the 1590s. It was subsequently transferred to its current location, rebuilt, and given its present name. A stately temple complex, the main hall, which dates from the 16th century, has been designated a national treasure.

579 Chiil-li, Cheongtong-myeon, Yeongcheon-si. © **054/335-3318.** http://eunhae-sa.org (Korean only). Admission ₩2,000 adults, ₩1,500 teens, ₩1,000 children, free to kids 6 and under and seniors 65 and over. From the Hayang Bus Terminal, take the bus headed for Eunhaesa, which runs daily every 30–60 min. 6am–10pm. From the Yeongcheon Bus Terminal, take a bus headed for Eunhaesa. Buses run 8 times a day 6:20am–10pm.

Gatbawi (a.k.a. Gwanbong Seokjoyeoraejwasang, Stone Hat Buddha) ★ HISTORIC SITE   Considered one of the masterpieces of Buddhist sculpture, this 4m-tall (13-ft) stone Buddha with a big stone "hat" was carved in the 9th century. Since he is the Buddha of Medicine, he holds a medicine pot in his left hand. His stone headpiece represents his supreme wisdom, and the position of his hands symbolizes the expelling of evil and is typical of Buddha statues carved during that period.

Legend has it that if you pray to this Buddha, he will grant at least one of your requests. Despite the fact that seeing this statue involves a hike of several hours, you'll see a long line of people waiting to make their prayers, usually on the first of the month or when it's time for entrance exams to universities. This is also a popular place for people to come to watch the sunrise and pray for good luck on New Year's morning.

Daehan-dong, Wachon-myeon, Gyeongsan-si. ✆ **053/983-8586.** Free admission. Sunrise–sunset. Hike from Eunhaesa or Donghwasa. To get to the main entrance to Palgongsan and Donghwasa, take express bus no. 1 from either the Dongdaegu Station or across the street from the Migliore department store. Bus no. 131 (from the same station) will get you a bit closer to Gatbawi. Plan to spend several hours.

Gunwi Samjeonseokbul (Grotto Statues) ★★ HISTORIC SITE Said to have been carved in A.D. 700, these three sculptures are set within a natural grotto on the mountainside. These statues are of historic significance, since they illustrate the artistic style between the Three Kingdoms and the Unified Shilla periods. Similar to (but less refined than) the Seokguram Grotto in Gyeongju, the Buddha carved here (he's the one in the middle, flanked by two bodhisattvas) is said by many to have been the inspiration for and precursor to the one in Gyeongju, so it's often referred to as Seokguram II. The statues were rediscovered after Korea's liberation from Japan in the early part of the 20th century.

Associated with this unusual grotto is a small temple, said to have been originally built by Ado Hwasang in the mid-A.D. 400s, but the current buildings were constructed in the 1980s. The grotto is about 2km (1¼ miles) up from Daeyul village. You can get buses to Daeyul from Daegu's Bukbu Bus Terminal and then walk—admission is free and the grotto is open as long as the park is.

Yeombul-am (Chanting Rock Hermitage) HISTORIC SITE The Chanting Rock Hermitage got its name from a legend that a monk from the area heard the sounds of a chanting Buddha coming from a large boulder in the hillside. So, in 928, Yeombul-am was built next to that giant rock and Buddha images were carved in relief on its two flat sides. Along the trail toward this hermitage is a smaller one, **Budo-am,** which serves as a retreat for meditating female monks.

Above Yeombul-am are two additional Buddha carvings—the beautiful, seated Buddha of Medicine at Biro-bong (the highest peak in the mountains) and a larger, cruder Buddha at Dong-bong.

There is no additional fee, and the hermitage is open as long as the park is, but plan to spend about 90 minutes hiking uphill to get here. You can start your walk at Budo-am (see above). Take express bus no. 1 from either the Dongdaegu Station or across the street from the Migliore department store. You can also take bus no. 105 from the stop in front of the former Hanil Theater.

Shopping

Because Daegu is the region's transportation hub, it's a shopper's dream. With its textile industry and herbal markets, it's also a great place to browse without spending a single Won.

FASHION & TEXTILES

For textiles, clothing, and other related items, head over to the **DDC Textile Product Complex** ★★, 1667, Sangyeok 2-dong, Buk-gu, Daegu (✆ **053/381-3690**).

DDC, which stands for Daegu Distribution Complex, is a wholesale market, which also does regular retail business. The over 600 stores each specialize in things like fabric, yarn, blankets, clothing, and other textiles, all at great prices. Open daily from 9am to 8pm, the complex is closed on the first and third Saturdays of each month, as well as holidays. Take bus no. 305, 306, 535, 613, or 929 to get here.

For hipper, younger styles the **Yasi-golmok,** in the Samdeok-dong area downtown, has several streets of boutique shops that sell the latest fashions. The name of the street, *yasi,* means "cute foxes," referring to those who shop here. Prices are reasonable, but the wares are pretty much limited to women's clothes. Take bus no. 306, 404, or 613.

MEGASTORES

Large discount stores can be found all over Daegu. Most of them are open 10am to 11pm daily with a couple of popular locations open until midnight on Saturdays. All of them have parking available and sell everything from groceries to toothpaste.

The familiar yellow-and-black cube of **E-Mart** (© 053/605-1234) has four locations in the city—in Seongso at 1254, Igok-dong, Dalseo-gu; Manchon at 1356-5, Manchon-dong, Suseong-gu; Wolbae at 555, Daecheon-dong, Dalseo-gu; and Chilseong at 20, Chilseong-dong 2-ga, Buk-gu.

There are also a couple of **Home Plus** stores in town, one in Chilseong-dong, 378-23, Chilseong-dong 2-ga, Buk-gu (© 053/350-8000), and the other in Chilgok, 968, Dongcheon-dong, Buk-gu. They're closed for New Year, Lunar New Year, and Chuseok.

TRADITIONAL MARKETS

Other than the Yakjeon Golmok medicine market, there are large markets for all manner of agricultural and local goods throughout the city. The historic **Seomun Shijang ★★★**, 115-378, Daesin-dong, Jung-gu (© 053/256-6341), is a great place to start. One of the country's main markets since 1669, the Seomun market's current location doesn't reveal the character of its historical past, but with over 4,000 little shops, you're sure to find something of interest. Other than seafood and agricultural goods, this is one of the best places in the country to buy fabric and clothes (though remember that South Korean sizes run very small). Open daily 8am to 8pm, the market is closed on the second and fourth Sundays each month. Bus nos. 404, 504, 514, 603, 836, and 910 all stop here.

The **Nammun (South Gate) Shijang** is a similar but smaller market. The **Chilseong Shijang,** located on the east edge of downtown near the stream, has great housewares and furniture. Even smaller is the **Gyodong Shijang,** an open-air market found south of Daegu Station and east of Dongseong-no.

Where to Stay

Daegu has several Western-style hotels throughout the city. Some of them are concentrated in the downtown area, though others are scattered around other outlying areas. Low-budget *yeogwan* (small inns) and motels are concentrated near the train and bus terminals and in the downtown area. All of them are in the ₩35,000 to ₩40,000 range.

EXPENSIVE

Daegu Prince Hotel ★   Centrally located, the hotel is across the street from the Daegu tower. With both Western-style and Korean-style ondol options, the rooms are quite yellow, but tastefully decorated. Staff are friendly and accommodating, though not all of them speak great English.

1824-2, Daemyeong 2-dong, Nam-gu, Daegu. www.princehotel.co.kr. © **053/628-1001.** Fax 053/628-2833. 117 units. ₩145,000 and up standard room; ₩560,000 and up suite. 10% VAT and 10% service charge not included. AE, MC, V. **Amenities:** 4 restaurants; cafe; health club; sauna; bakery; nightclub. *In room:* A/C, TV, hair dryer, minibar, Internet.

Eldis Regent Hotel Conveniently located downtown, this first-class hotel has quiet Western-style rooms with either mountain or garden views. All rooms have soundproof windows and decent beds that are a bit on the hard side. The bathrooms, though quite small, are clean and have good water pressure.

360 Dongsan-dong, Jung-gu, Daegu. http://eldisregenthotel.com. © **053/253-7711.** Fax 053/256-0406. 54 units. ₩76,200 single; ₩101,600 double; ₩290,000 and up suite. 10% VAT and 10% service charge not included. AE, MC, V. **Amenities:** 3 restaurants; bar; lounge; cafe; health club; sauna; smoke-free rooms. *In room:* A/C, TV, minibar, hair dryer, Internet.

Hotel Inter-Burgo ★ Opened in 2001, this hotel has clean facilities and friendly, English-speaking staff. Its Spanish theme is a bit odd, but it doesn't take away from the comfort of the place. The rooms, and especially the bathrooms, are a bit on the small side, but the location, on the Geumho River in Mangu Park, more than makes up for it.

San 92-1, Manchon-dong, Susong-gu, Daegu. www.ibhotel.com. © **053/952-0088.** Fax 053/952-2008. 342 units. ₩275,000 and up standard room; ₩330,000 and up suite. AE, MC, V. **Amenities:** 4 restaurants; bar; lobby lounge; cafe; pool; putting green; health club; spa; sauna; smoke-free rooms; beer garden. *In room:* A/C, TV, minibar, fridge, hair dryer, Internet.

Novotel City Centre ★★ ☺ Convenient for the subway and the KTX station, the hotel is connected to the Doran Plaza Shopping Mall. Rooms are relatively spacious and tastefully decorated with modern furnishings and comfortable bathrooms. Suites on higher floors have free Wi-Fi, but lower floor standard rooms have hi-speed wired access. Ask for a corner room if you want more space or a higher floor for better city views. Kids stay free.

11-1 Munhwa-dong, Jung-gu, Daegu. www.novotel.com. © **053/664-1101.** Fax 053/664-1102. 203 units. ₩150,000 and up single/double; ₩220,000 and up suite. 10% VAT not included. AE, MC, V. Subway: Jungangno Station (line 1). **Amenities:** Restaurants; bar; lounge; cafe; health club; sauna; concierge; massage; dry cleaning; smoke-free rooms; gift shop; ATM; beauty salon; florist; currency exchange. *In room:* A/C, satellite TV, minibar, hair dryer, safe, Internet.

MODERATE
Apsan Tourist Hotel ★ Convenient for Apsan Park, the hotel is in the downtown area. You'll get better service from the 24-hour front desk than you will at most other hotels in this price range. The rooms are clean and spacious with comfortable beds and the usual Korean-style (in other words, tiny) bathroom.

1713-2, Daemyeong 5-dong, Nam-gu, Daegu. © **053/629-8800.** Fax 053/629-8801. 42 units. ₩96,800 and up standard room, ₩136,730 and up suite. AE, MC, V. **Amenities:** 2 restaurants; bar; cafe; nightclub. *In room:* A/C, TV, minibar, hair dryer.

INEXPENSIVE
For budget digs, try the **Sanjang Yeogwan** (© **053/622-7782**), 477-19 Duryu 3-dong, Dalseo-gu, Daegu, or the **Greenjang Yeogwan** (© **053/767-9822**), 9-1 Ureuk-li, Gachang-myeong, Dalseong-gun, Daegu. Both are no-frills joints with

reasonably priced rooms starting at ₩35,000 for one or two people. There are dozens of yeogwan and love motels throughout the city, which are similar in price and quality.

Where to Eat

The specialty in Daegu is not for the faint of heart, or of stomach, for that matter. *Makchang* is pork large intestine that is cooked on a tabletop grill, just as you would cook *galbi* (beef ribs). The small intestines are called *gobchang*. Both are served with a light *yangnyeom dwenjang* (seasoned, fermented soybean paste) and green onions.

Regional specialties aside, as in any large city there is no shortage of places to eat. Just north of the Suseong reservoir in Suseong-gu is **Deuran-gil ★★**, an area famous for its restaurants. With over 200 places in this area alone, you can choose from traditional Korean to Western fast food, or just stop in at a pub for a drink. Although it doesn't have the older charm of places in **Yasi-golmok,** you can't beat it for the variety of choice.

EXPENSIVE

Dijon ★★★ FRENCH/MEDITERRANEAN   A romantic restaurant in the downtown area, Dijon may be a little bit difficult to find, but it's worth the effort. The authentic French and Mediterranean food is outstanding, and the menu is varied with gourmet touches you won't find anywhere else outside of Seoul. Everything from the salade niçoise to the pastas are made with fresh ingredients. Don't forget to save room for dessert. The same owner owns the cozy Italian restaurant next door, **Into,** whose menu changes weekly, but it's hard to secure one of the only four tables.

21-9 Samdeok 1-ga, Jung-gu, Daegu. ℂ **053/422-2426.** Entrees ₩25,000–₩40,000. MC, V. Daily 11:30am–10:30pm, last order taken an hour before closing, closed Lunar New Year and Chuseok. In a small alley behind the Samdeok Catholic Church.

MODERATE

Haegeumgang KOREAN SEAFOOD   Specializing in hwae and other cooked delicacies from the ocean, this city favorite has been serving up dishes for over 30 years. They have a huge menu so the hardest part may be just deciding what to eat, but you can't go wrong with the simple *hwaedupbap* (raw fish rice bowl). Sit yourself down on one of the floor cushions, pull yourself up to a shiny wood table, and indulge in a veritable seafood frenzy.

345-8 Shinam 4-dong, Dong-gu, Daegu. ℂ **053/954-2323.** Entrees ₩9,000–₩50,000. MC, V. Daily 10am–11pm. Closed holidays. Take subway to Keungogae Station (exit 2).

Wild Sushi ★ JAPANESE   You can enjoy any one of the funky sushi rolls in this sleek, modern Korean sushi joint. But one of the best items on the menu is the chicken salad, which comes with a pineapple ring on top, and the udon noodles are good, too. There are plenty of pictures available so you know what you're ordering.

15-6 Samduk-dong 1-ga, Jung-gu, Daegu. ℂ **053/426-0044.** Dishes ₩4,000–₩8,000 (about ₩30,000 per person). MC, V. Daily 11am–10pm. Closed holidays. In the downtown area, down the alley to the right of the department store Gallery Zone.

INEXPENSIVE

Indobang Rangi ★ INDIAN   Perhaps the only good Indian restaurant in town, this small restaurant (on the third floor) has excellent curries and vegetarian options on the menu. The friendly manager speaks English well.

1338-5 Sangyeok 3(sam)-dong, Buk-gu, Daegu. Across the street from the Kyungpook University's north gate. © **053/956-9940.** Dishes ₩8,000–₩20,000. MC, V. Daily 11am–10pm. Closed holidays.

Entertainment & Nightlife

Your best bet for happening nightlife in the city is in the **Yasi-golmok** area, where dozens of bars, cafes, and nightclubs are concentrated. The central shopping district also has a bunch of cafes, *noraebang* (singing rooms), *hofs* (beer halls), and bars. Most of the places listed below are casual, foreigner-friendly, and have no set dress code, but Koreans usually dress up to go out after dark. The city's gay district is near the express bus terminal.

The area around Samdeok Fire Station downtown is where most foreigners living in Daegu hang out. The largest concentration of foreigner-friendly bars and clubs is on **Rodeo Street,** which runs north–south from the fire station. **9Bar,** on Rodeo Street, is a wine bar with a fun interior, good for a cozy glass before heading out to nearby clubs. A fun place for a drink is **Bus ★★** (52-1 Samdeok-dong, Jung-gu), a retrofitted bus, located near the dance club **G2.** A popular club just off the street is **Club Frog ★,** which plays a mix of hip hop, techno, and K-pop. Electronica fans head over to **Pasha ★★.** But be aware that clubs in Daegu shift popularity quite quickly. Also in the area is **Hof Alley,** which is lined with German-influenced beer bars.

The **Kyungdae** area around Kyungpook University is also a happening spot for nightlife. There are plenty of bars, nightclubs, and noraebang that cater to the college-age crowd. The area starts across the street from the university's main North gate, the *bukmun.* It's a 5-minute taxi ride from either the Dongdaegu or Keungogae stations off the subway.

In Dong (East) Daegu, there is also a handful of foreigner-friendly bars in Siji-dong. The streets just east of the Yeonho subway station (off line 2) are home to a small concentration of bars catering to the foreigners who've come here to teach English. A couple of the bars even have weekly trivia nights and open mics.

ANDONG

The largest city in the northern part of Gyeongsangbuk-dol, Andong has been known as the cultural and folk center of the region since the Shilla Dynasty. During the Joseon Dynasty, the town attracted many Confucian scholars since it had the largest number of Confucian schools in the country. Even today, there are dozens of private Confucian schools that were established during those years.

The city gained international fame when Queen Elizabeth II celebrated her 73rd birthday here in 1999. In preparation for her visit, the city government improved the roads and even expanded the highway that runs through it (road 34) to two lanes in both directions. East of the city center, the 600-year-old **Folk Village** (Hahoe Maeul) is Andong's biggest draw. Although the residents now have modern amenities (like electricity and satellite dishes), it is still a wonderful trip back in time to South Korea's not-so-distant rural past. Unlike other villages that date back to the Goryeo period, both common folk and the *yangban* (upper class) lived in the same village.

Every October, the Andong Folk Festival draws thousands of visitors to see performances, including the Andong Mask Dance Festival in the Hahoe Maeul.

Essentials

GETTING THERE   The Jung-ang rail line that connects Seoul to Busan runs through Andong. There is only one train that runs only on Saturday or Sunday from Seoul Station to Andong. The ride takes about 4 hours and costs about ₩25,000. Seoul's Cheongnyangni Station has more trains (seven daily), with trains running daily from 9am to 9pm, but the trip lasts about 5 hours. There are also trains from Busan several times a day.

There is one limousine bus to Andong (via the DongSeoul Bus Terminal) from Incheon Aiport at 12:10pm. It can be picked up at stop 10C on the first floor. The 4-hour ride costs ₩30,800.

You can also take an **express bus** from Seoul's Express Bus Terminal. However, buses from the DongSeoul Bus Terminal run more frequently, although they take longer. Buses run daily from DongSeoul from 6:20am to 6:30pm about every half-hour and cost about ₩15,700. Daily buses also run frequently from Daegu (about every 7–20 min.). You can also take a bus from Busan, Cheongsong, Daejeon, and Pohang. The **Andong Intercity Bus Terminal,** 713-6-beonji, Songhyeon-dong, Andong (℗ **1688-8228**), has both express and regular buses.

The bus terminals and train stations are on the same street within walking distance of each other in downtown Andong.

If you're driving from Daegu, take highway 14 north to the Seo-Andong (West Andong) exit. Then, take highway 34 into the city.

GETTING AROUND   There are local buses available that can take you to most places in town. For sites farther out, they run infrequently and the times are erratic.

If you have limited time, you can hire a **taxi** for a day. Taxis are always waiting outside the bus and train terminals. Negotiate with your driver, but rates are usually around ₩120,000 per day. The base fare starts at ₩1,500.

Andong is not an easy place to explore on foot. Although some sites of interest are clustered together (the Hahoe Village and the Folk Museum are within walking distance), many other attractions are difficult to reach even by bus.

Andong does offer a **city tour bus** (℗ **054/855-7179;** http://andongtour.kr, Korean only), which you have to reserve at least a day beforehand. There are two courses that start from the bus terminal, each costing ₩18,000 per person. The first one, which includes the Hahoe Maeul, runs Wednesday, Saturday, and Sunday, March through December. The other course runs only on Fridays and includes the Dosan Seowon. Both tours run from 10am to 5:30pm.

VISITOR INFORMATION   The **Gyeongsangbuk-do Tourist Information Office** (℗ **054/852-6800;** Nov–Feb daily 9am to 5pm; Mar to Oct daily 9am to 6pm) is right in front of the Andong Train Station (turn left when you exit). They have friendly English-speaking staff and great maps of Andong as well as the rest of the province. There is also a small information booth in front of the **Hahoe Maeul,** which has the same operating hours. The city's tour info website is http://en.tourandong.com.

FAST FACTS   The central city post office is located just up the street from the train and bus stations. You will find banks and other businesses in the same area. The larger, central post office is on the west side of town on the same street as the police station. You can access the Internet from a handful of PC bahngs in town, or use the free computers at the tourist information office.

Exploring Andong

Andong Folk Museum ★ MUSEUM   When the Andong Dam was created in 1976, the resulting lake would have submerged many cultural relics. Instead of leaving them to an underwater grave, the buildings and historical relics were moved to the museum's outdoor space to create a park and the **Andong Folk Village (Hahoe Maeul).** The indoor exhibits illustrate traditional Confucian culture and traditions, as well as highlighting dozens of pieces of pottery, utensils, and other objects.

784-1 Seonggok-dong, Andong-si. © **054/821-0649.** www.adfm.or.kr/english/main.asp. Admission ₩1,000 adults, ₩300 ages 7–19, free for seniors 65 and over and kids 6 and under. Daily 9am–6pm. Closed Jan 1, Lunar New Year, and Chuseok. From Andong Bus Terminal, take bus no. 3 to the museum; it runs every 20 min.

Andong Soju Museum MUSEUM   The traditional rice liquor (often compared to vodka) from Andong is so famous that it was designated a cultural asset of the province in 1987. Located on the grounds of the still-operational Andong Soju Brewery, this museum shows how soju is made. The alcohol content is 45%, but they claim that you won't have a hangover the next morning. Good luck!

280 Beonji, Susang-dong, Andong-si. © **011/390-6922.** www.andongsoju.net. Free admission. Mon–Sat 9am–5:30pm. Closed national holidays. From Andong Bus Terminal, cross the street and take bus no. 34 or 36 (from in front of the Andong Elementary School), a 15-min. ride. A taxi from the Andong Intercity Bus Terminal will take about 10 min.

Bongjeongsa (Bongjeong Temple) ★ TEMPLE   South Korea's oldest wooden structure, parts of this temple miraculously survived destruction during the Imjin Waeran (p. 12). The temple was originally built by Monk Uisang in A.D. 673. The 850-year-old structure sits in the left courtyard of the compound. The temple itself is the largest in Andong. Surrounded by ancient pine trees gnarled with age, you can compare architecture from both the Goryeo and the Joseon dynasties.

About 20 minutes on foot east of Bongjeongsa is a peaceful little hermitage, the **Yeongsang-am,** with undecorated wooden walls and humble buildings. A 20-minute walk to the west of Bongjeongsa is another hermitage, **Jijo-am,** which is dedicated to the goddess of mercy, Gwaneum. Even farther north (about a 30-min. walk) are the remains of a small temple, **Gaemoksa,** also built by Monk Uisang.

901 Taejang-li, Seohu-myeon, Andong-si. © **054/853-4181.** www.bongjeongsa.org (Korean only). Admission ₩2,000 adults, ₩1,300 teens, ₩600 ages 7–12, free for seniors 65 and over and kids 6 and under. From Andong Bus Terminal, cross the street and take bus no. 51 (from in front of the Andong Elementary School); it runs about 7 times a day and takes 30 min.

Dosan Seowon (Dosan Confucian School) ★ HISTORIC SITE   Established in 1574, this school was built in memory of Confucian scholar Yi Hwang by some of his disciples. Like other schools of this type, it was built both as a place for education and in honor of past Confucian scholars. Although its scholarly functions ceased long ago, it still serves as a ceremonial center, with commemorations held here twice a year. It has been featured on the back of the ₩1,000 bill since 1975.

680 Toegye-li, Andong-si. © **054/840-6599.** www.dosanseowon.com. Admission ₩1,500 adults, ₩700 teens, ₩600 ages 7–12, free for seniors 65 and over and kids 6 and under. Daily 9am–6pm. From Andong Bus Terminal, take bus no. 67, which runs 4 times a day and takes 30 min. Parking ₩2,000 to ₩4,000, depending on the size of vehicle.

Andong Hahoe Maeul (Andng Folk Village) ★★★ HISTORIC SITE   The residents of this 600-year-old village have maintained many aspects of their

BUDDHISM VS. neo-confucianism

When the Joseon Dynasty began in 1392, the height (or some would say the excesses) of Korean Buddhism abruptly came to an end. In addition to fundamental spiritual conflicts, the Confucians, who were high up in the Joseon government, resented how much of the nation's money was being used by Buddhists to construct elaborate statues and hold increasingly expensive rituals. They believed that Buddhism was a serious drain on the country's economy, so in the 1390s King Taejo removed Buddhist monks from his government, expelled them from the capital, and confiscated Buddhist property. The building of temples in the capital was forbidden and the number of monks and nuns who could live in monasteries, and how much land they could own, was tightly regulated. Buddhist practices were forced out of the cities, begging was made illegal, and Buddhist funerals were outlawed.

Despite strong oppression from the government, Buddhism (especially the Seon, or Zen, sect) maintained its popularity among commoners, especially women. Neo-Confucians believed that power and morality came from an ultimate spirit of the universe, one that controlled the yin and yang and the five elements (fire, water, wood, metal, and earth). Women declined in status and had to be subservient to their husbands and their eldest sons. Inheritance became exclusively through patrilineage, and marriage between people of different social classes was prohibited.

During the nearly 500 years of Joseon oppression, the number of Buddhist monasteries dropped from several hundred to a mere three dozen. One of the main reasons for Buddhism regaining the acceptance of the government was the role of guerrilla warrior monks in repelling the Japanese during the Imjin Waeran (p. 12). Although the government maintained tight control of Buddhist practice in the country, there was never again such extreme oppression.

traditional lifestyle. Although most homes now have telephones, electricity, and even satellite televisions, the old-fashioned homes and the dirt roads between them are like an open museum to a time long past. Unlike many other villages, both upper and lower classes lived together, with the higher classes living in the center of the village, and the lower-class homes farther out. While most other traditional villages in Korea have homes that face south for better sun exposure, this village's homes face toward the S-shaped river (the Nakdong-gang) that flows through it. Near the entrance is a fun collection of *changseung,* wooden statues that stood in front of traditional villages to guard them from evil spirits. The village loses its quiet charm when the streets get overrun by visitors on weekends and holidays, so it's best to come on weekdays, especially in the morning. However, be respectful of the people, who live here. The **Exorcism Mask Dance,** a shamanistic ritual meant to drive away evil spirits, is performed here every weekend, May through October, and only on Sundays March and April.

To get a bird's-eye view, cross the Nakdong River on the northwestern end of the village and there's a trail next to the pine forest that leads up to the **Buyongdae,** a 64m-high (210-ft.) cliff that affords a great view of the village, the river, and the surrounding scenery.

690 Hahoe-li, Pungcheon-myeon, Andong-si. ©054/841-2896. Admission ₩1,000 adults, ₩800 teens, ₩300 children, free for seniors 65 and over and kids 6 and under. Daily 9am–6pm. From the bus terminal, take bus no. 3, which should take about 15 min. to Hahoe Maeul. Also, you can take

Outside of the Hahoe Maeul, as well as many other traditional villages in South Korea, you'll find a collection of long wooden statues, carved with funny or scary faces. Originally called *pupsu* or *puksu*, these *changseung* were guardians for the village. Usually found in pairs on either side of the entrance to a village, the one on the left appeased the air spirits, while the one on the right appeased the earth spirits.

bus 46, whose last stop is the Hahoe Maeul. Taxis from Andong Station take about 10 min. Parking ₩2,000 for small cars, ₩4,000 for large.

Hahoe Mask Museum ★ ☺ MUSEUM   Located near the entrance to the Hahoe Folk Village, this museum displays masks from Korea and around the world. A variety of Hahoe *tal* (masks), a special type of mask used in performances in the region, are shown here along with other traditional Korean masks and 500 masks from other countries. Visitors can make their own masks from *hanji* (traditional rice paper).

287 Hahoe-li, Pungcheon-myeon, Andong-si.✆ **054/853-2288.** www.maskmuseum.com. Admission ₩2,000 adults, ₩1,000 youth, free for seniors 65 and over and kids 6 and under. Daily 9:30am–6pm. Closed Lunar New Year and Chuseok. See instructions for Hahoe Mauel (above).

Icheondong Seokbulsang/Jebiwon Seokbul (Stone Buddha) HISTORIC SITE   Almost an unofficial symbol for Andong, this beautiful Buddha statue stands on an ancient path looking over the mountains at Jebiwon, which used to be a resting place for travelers crossing to and from the Sobaek Mountains. It's a Mireuk Buddha, which is usually a standing statue, sometimes called the "Buddha of the Future," and it is carved into a piece of granite that is 12m (39 ft.) high. (During the Goryeo Dynasty, many such Buddhas were created at the entrances to mountains and villages.)

San 2, Icheon-dong, Andong-si. Free admission. Daily 24 hr. From the Andong Intercity Bus Terminal, take bus no. 54 (which runs every 40 min.); you must tell your driver to stop at the *jebiwon seokbul* (stone Buddha). For the return trip, hail the driver when the bus approaches. It's a 15-min. ride from the bus terminal.

Jirye Art Village (Artists' Colony) ★★ HISTORIC SITE   This artists' colony houses some cultural assets, like traditional houses and stone monuments, that were moved here due to the damming of the Imha area to create an artificial lake. This 350-year-old village has homes that have preserved traditions, including those still heated with wood. It's a bit out of the way, but a wonderful place to see traditional culture preserved in time. If you wish to spend the night in an old-fashioned Korean home, you can reserve a spot in advance and someone will pick you up from the bus or train station.

769 Bakgok-li, Imdong-myeon, Andong-si. ✆ **054/822-2590.** www.jirye.com. Free admission. From Andong Bus Terminal, take bus no. 11 and get off at Imdong (20 min.). Then take a taxi to the village (a 20- to 30-min. ride).

Pungsan Hanji Factory ★★ FACTORY TOUR   Hanji, paper made from mulberry bark, is one of South Korea's most beautiful traditional products. You can see how the paper is made—a painstaking process that hasn't changed much from ancient times. Even without the hands-on demonstrations, the warehouse and gift shop with all the various colors and grades of hanji for sale are worth the trip to this tiny factory.

36-1 Sosan-li, Pungsan-eup, Andong-si. © **054/858-7007** (Korean only). Free admission. Most days 10am–6pm, but call ahead. On road 916 off of road 924, not too far from the Pungsan Elementary School. Best to take a taxi from the train or bus station.

Shopping

Andong has several small traditional markets, since it serves as the trading hub for other smaller towns in the region. The **Andong Shijang** is a great place to get the regional hemp cloths and traditional wooden masks. It's open on dates ending in 2 or 7.

You can also find mask reproductions and other souvenirs at the **Hahoe Mask Museum** at the entrance to the Hahoe Folk Village. Other than its masks and soju, Andong is also famous for its rice paper, its apples, and its red peppers, whose thick skins make for really great powder and chili paste.

Where to Stay

Andong doesn't have any high-end hotels or many midrange accommodations, but there are several inexpensive motels around the train and bus stations. However, you may want to spend a night or two in a traditional house (*hanok*) and get a real flavor of life in rural South Korea. We've listed several good ones below.

The **Jirye Art Village ★★**, overlooking Imha Lake (about a 45-minute drive from Andong), is probably one of the best places to experience the way Korean nobles used to live. Rooms range from ₩50,000 to ₩120,000 with shared bathroom facilities. Ask for a lakeview room, if so desired. Meals are ₩6,000 and you should reserve them in advance when making your sleeping reservations (www.jirye.com; © **054/822-2590;** San 769 Bakgong-ri, Imdong-myeon, Andong). You can look around Andong during the day and the village chief will pick you up at 5pm in front of the bus or train station.

Also in the Imha Lake area is **Suaedang,** 470-44 Sugok-dong, Imdong-myeon (www.suaedang.co.kr, Korean only; © **054/822-6661**), with buildings from the Joseon Dynasty, which were also relocated because of the Imha Dam. It's a peaceful retreat. Rooms sleep two to four and range from ₩70,000 to ₩150,000, depending on size and location. Suaedang has traditional Korean rooms with shared bathroom facilities and you'll need to bring your own towel.

Less remote but still with traditional flair is the **Imcheonggak,** 20 Beopheung-dong (www.suaedang.co.kr, Korean only © **054/853-3455**), the birth home of Lee Sang-ryong. The ondol rooms range from ₩40,000 to ₩200,000, depending on size. During the Joseon Dynasty, a law prevented civilians from building houses with more than 100 rooms. So Mr. Lee's hanok complex had 100 rooms (only 50 of which remain today). Although the railroad ruined the view it once had, the complex maintains its traditional atmosphere.

There are also plenty of minbak available in the **Hahoe Village,** but very few of the owners speak English. If you want to do a homestay in the traditional village, call the **Korea Travel Phone** (© **1330**) and have them make a reservation for you or see if rooms are available on a walk-in basis (on weekdays, outside of summer and holidays, there should be no problem).

For more Western-style accommodations downtown, try the **Park Tourist Hotel** (© **054/853-1501;** fax 054/857-5445; 324 Unheung-dong, Andong-si). It has bland but comfortable rooms from ₩60,000 to ₩87,000. Of course, there are plenty of love motels in town as well, with doubles going for about ₩40,000 per night. The staff speak limited, but serviceable English.

Where to Eat

Andong is known for several traditional dishes. One of the local dishes is *heotjesatbap,* a "fake" version of the rice dish eaten during *jesa* (ancestor honoring) ceremonies; it is a mixed rice bowl similar to bibimbap, but was traditionally eaten with leftover food from ancestral rite ceremonies. You can find restaurants that specialize in this dish and other traditional cuisine near the Hahoe Village, Andong Dam, and near the downtown area. A well-known place that has been making heotjesatbap for 50 years is **Andong Minseok Eumshikjeom** (✆ 054/843-2100) in front of the Hahoe Maeul, where you can get the famed dish for ₩5,000. Another good place is the **Ggachi Gumeong Jib** (✆ 054/821-1056) also in front of the Andong Folk Village.

Also downtown is an area, **Jjimdak Golmok (Steamed Chicken Alley),** that specializes in another regional specialty—*jjimdak,* a spicy steamed chicken dish, usually with onions, rice cakes, sweet potatoes, and a sweet *ggochujang* (chili paste) sauce. The **Maeil Tongdak** ("Daily Steamed Chicken" ✆ 054/854-4128) is one of the better places on the street, but most of them are quite good. Pretty much all the restaurants in town price jjimdak from ₩10,000 to ₩15,000. One order usually can feed two to four people.

Andong is famous for its homegrown beef, which they claim is the best in the country, so don't miss out on having a galbi meal here. One of the best galbi places in town is **Andong Munhwa Galbi** (✆ 054/857-6608 or 857-6565), a tiny unassuming spot located just up the way from Andong Station (walk up the main road away from the station, and turn into the alley where the Muhwha Motel is located—it's a few minutes' walk down the alley). Galbi for one will set you back ₩17,000, but it comes with rice, soup, kimchi, lettuce, and other stuff you can snack on as you cook your meat on the tabletop charcoal grill in front of you. Another tasty place is **Seoul Galbi Shikdang** (✆ 054/859-6264, 136 Dongbu-dong, Andong-si), located within walking distance from Andong Station, where they've been serving Andong beef since 1969. Open 11am to 10pm, they're closed major holidays and the second Sunday of each month. Galbi dishes range from ₩5,000 to ₩25,000.

The city is also known for its salted mackerel, *shikhae,* a delicious sweet rice dessert drink, and its local soju, which tastes a little smoother and more sour than regular soju, that natives claim is the best in the country.

THE REST OF GYEONGSANGBUK-DO

Mostly surrounded by the Taebaek Mountains in the east and the Sobaek Mountains in the west, The North Gyeongsang Province is South Korea's hottest province in the summer with average temperatures hovering around 95°F (35°C).

Gyeongsangbuk-do (sometimes shortened as Gyeongbuk) was once home to the ancient Gaya culture. The province is known as the birthplace of Confucian culture and home to many Confucian academies. Indeed, Gyeongsangbuk-do is known throughout the country for its steadfast loyalty to Korea's traditional culture. Small localities have festivals based on regional agricultural crops (such as mushrooms and ginseng), and the mountains in the area, especially Juwangsan, are great for enjoying the country's scenic beauty (without running into the hordes of tourists that frequent the more popular mountains).

The province includes two national parks—Juwangsan and Gyeongju (see p. 259). It also has several other national and provincial parks within its borders.

Most of its eastern coast remains largely indented, except for Yeonghil Bay in Pohang, which has the region's best harbor. The coastal drive has unexpected scenery that varies with sandy stretches, craggy rocks, lowlands, and isolated fishing villages. It would be one of the most scenic areas of the peninsula, except for some of the barbed wire installed between marine lookouts perched on coastal viewpoints.

Despite its eastern coastline, Gyeongbuk is oriented inland, focusing mainly on the agriculture and land of the region. The only sizable island in the province is Ulleung-do, about a 3-hour boat ride away from the mainland.

Essentials

GETTING THERE   The province has only two airports, one in Daegu and the other at Pohang (KPO; ✆ **054/289-7399;** http://pohang.airport.co.kr/doc/pohang_eng), which has four flights a day from Seoul, two each from Asiana and Korean airlines. The airport offers buses only to Pohang city, so it's more convenient to fly into Daegu.

The **Gyeongbu rail line** with both high-speed KTX and regular trains runs through the province. The **Jung-ang rail line** also goes through the area, ending at Gyeongju. Connecting lines go from Gimcheon to Yeongju and Daegu to Pohang.

If you're driving, the Gyeongbu Expressway (road 1) goes through the southern part of the province, passing through Daegu and Gyeongju. The Olympic Expressway (road 12) runs southwest from Daegu. The Jung-ang Expressway (road 55) cuts through the middle of the province going through Daegu, Andong, and Yeongju.

You can also take an **express bus** from Seoul to Andong, Sangju, Gimcheon, Gumi, Daegu, Gyeongju, Pohang, Yeongju, and Yeongcheon. Intercity buses travel all over the province, but usually have infrequent schedules.

The only boats from the province leave from Pohang Ferry Terminal (✆ **054/242-5111**) and go to Ulleung-do.

GETTING AROUND   Local buses from smaller cities and towns take you to outlying areas, but some of them run infrequently to remote or less popular places, so check your return bus schedule and plan accordingly.

VISITOR INFORMATION   At the Pohang Airport, there is a **tourist information booth** (9am–7pm weekends and holidays only) on the first floor of the terminal. The Gyeongsangbuk-do website is www.gb.go.kr.

Juwangsan National Park

One of South Korea's most isolated and least visited national parks, **Juwangsan National Park ★★★**, Sangeui-li, Budong-myeon, Cheongsong-gun, Gyeongsangbuk-do (✆ **054/873-0015;** http://english.knps.or.kr), is part of the Taebaek mountain range. Mt. Juwang is known by many other names, like Seokbyeongsan, Jubangsan, and Dedunsan.

From a distance Juwangsan doesn't look like much, but you'll see its gorgeous scenery once you arrive in the middle of it. It's best known for its mountain streams, waterfalls, and the limestone peaks that jut out from green valleys. The park is divided into three areas: **Jubanggol** (Jubang Valley) at the entrance, **Jeolgocheon** in the east, and **Yaksutang** (mineral springs) in the west.

Many legends are associated with the mountains, including the story of King Juwon, the Shilla king, who supposedly lived here after handing over the Shilla Kingdom to the Goryeo Dynasty. Another legend, from which the name derived, has it that King Ju-do (the "Juwang" of the name, "wang" meaning king) of China's Tang Dynasty hid in the mountains when he was fleeing from revolutionaries after an attempted coup.

The curious-shaped peaks and rocks of Juwangsan were created by sudden volcanic activity (apparently about 70 million years ago, when dinosaurs were hanging out on the Korean Peninsula) and many years of erosion.

There are six temples and hermitages inside Juwang-an. Located just past the entrance to the park is the largest temple, **Daejeonsa ★★**, which was built in the 12th year of Shilla King Munmu (A.D. 672) and named after King Ju's son. The temple was later rebuilt in 1672 after being destroyed by war and fire. **Gwangamsa** and **Yeonhwasa** are also nestled in the mountains here, as well as the hermitages of **Juwang-am** and **Baengnyeon-am,** a hermitage of nuns dedicated to King Ju's daughter.

All trails in the park are good for day hikes. The main trail goes around Jubong-cheon in a circular route. There are four other trails, all of which can be completed in 4 to 6 hours.

The park started seeing more visitors after Kim Ki-duk used **Jusanji Lake ★★★** as the setting for his movie *Spring, Summer, Fall, Winter, and Spring.* Although the "island temple" set used in the film had to be dismantled for environmental reasons, you can still enjoy the changing seasons at this location, which is most beautiful both in the spring when the entire valley is ablaze with colorful blooms and in the fall as the autumn leaves create a gorgeous scene. The small, man-made lake (created in 1721) is located in the inner part of Juwangsan, parts of which are closed as natural preservation areas. Jusanji is closed until 2028 and Giamgyo (Giam Bridge) is closed until 2026.

The closest town is Cheongsong, which is located about 13km (8 miles) from the park's entrance. Intercity buses arrive at the **Cheongsong Intercity Bus Terminal** from Yeongcheon, Andong, Daegu, Busan, and DongSeoul. Buses from **DongSeoul Bus Terminal** run five times daily starting from 8:40am and take about 5 hours. From Cheongsong, city buses go to the park entrance daily, every 20 minutes or so, and take about 30 minutes. Admission to the park is ₩2,000 adults, ₩1,500 teens, ₩1,000 children with discounts off-season. Parking is ₩2,000 to ₩5,000, depending on the size of the car.

If you're driving from Seoul, take the Gyeongbu Expressway (road 1) to the Shingal IC and go east on the Yeongdong Expressway (road 50). Take the Manjong IC exit to the Jung-ang highway (road 55) south toward Daegu, take the Seo-Andong (West Andong) exit, and take road 34 east, following it toward Jinan-dong and turning right on road 31, heading south toward Cheongsong. Pass Cheongsong and take road 914 east to Juwangsan.

Most people visit Juwangsan as a day trip, but you can rough it at the **Sangui Campground** (www.juwangspahotel.co.kr, Korean only; ☎ **054/873-0014**) near the entrance for only ₩7,000 to ₩8,000 per night. You have to make reservations at least 5 days in advance (up to a month in advance during popular seasons). You can also stay at any number of minbak across from the bus terminal or the small motels near the park entrance or the Yaksutang district. The most upscale accommodation in the area is the third-class **Juwangsan Tourist Spa Hotel,** 69-2, Wolmake-li, Cheongsong-eup, Cheongsong-gun, Gyeongsangbuk-do (*©* **054/874-7000**), about 2km (1¼ miles) below the park entrance. They have doubles starting at ₩100,000, and discounts are not uncommon off-season. The park is open 2 hours before sunrise and closes 2 hours before sunset. Night hiking is prohibited, due to danger of forest fires.

You can sample local mountain cuisine in Cheongsong, which is famous for its *samgyetang,* a chicken soup made with a whole young chicken stuffed with glutinous rice, garlic, ginseng, dried dates, and ginger from the Yaksutang area. You can also have *sanchae bibimbap* (wild mountain vegetable mixed rice bowl) or other dishes that feature vegetables from the region or *songi* mushrooms that grow in the area's pine forests.

Sobaeksan National Park

Sobaeksan (Mt. Sobaek, *©* **054/638-6196** or 6796; http://english.knps.or.kr) is part of the Taebaek Mountains, which are called the "backbone of Korea." Historically, these mountain ranges have been tall barriers preventing travel or communication, but their rugged height proved to be ideal for many Buddhist monks, who found them to be wonderful retreats away from the material world. Many temples still remain hidden in nooks and crannies of the mountains and several national and provincial parks are part of this range.

Sobaeksan is known for its wildflowers, and their springtime blooms attract visitors from near and far.

The easiest way to get to Sobaeksan is to take a bus from downtown Yeongju or Pung-gi. You can also take an intercity bus from Danyang to Yeongju, which stops at the park's entrance. Entrance to the park is free, but separate admission fees for temples and historical sites are included in individual listings below.

There are five trails accessible from Gyeongsangbuk-do. Most are long but not too difficult. Among them, the Heuibangsa trail, which passes through the Heuibang Temple and the waterfall, is the most popular and the best one to take with children. The second most frequented is the trail from Samgari to Birobong (the Yew habitat area is closed until 2026). The most varied is the trail from Choamsa to Gukmang-bong (the trail is open, but the peak is closed until 2026). For more experienced climbers, the roughest course goes from Jungnyeong through Dosolbong to Myojeokbong.

If you want to rough it, you can choose from three campsites, one below Heuibangsa, one below Birosa, and another on the west side between Birobong and the Cheondong-donggul (Cheondong Cave).

Other than the major temples listed below, there are other points of interest in Sobaeksan. The limestone caves **Cheongdong-donggul, Gosu-donggul,** and **Nodong-donggul** and other points in that area are discussed in chapter 7 on Chungcheong-do in the Danyang section.

Birosa (Biro Temple) TEMPLE   Birosa is a temple which sits to the east, just below Birobong, the highest peak in the mountain range. Very little remains of this former Shilla temple—just a stone marker and its flagpole supports—but the area is lovely. A waterfall lies just about 1.5km (1 mile) from the temple site. The trail from Samga-li goes past the temple en route to the top of Birobong and takes about 4 hours.

Buseoksa (Buseok Temple) ★★★ TEMPLE   Hidden on the southern slope of Bonghwangsan, one of South Korea's most famed temples is a bit out of the way, but worth the trip. Constructed during King Munmu's reign in 676, the temple has been renovated several times since. A large site with gorgeous scenery, it is considered a "masculine" temple. Several national treasures are included in the temple complex, including the second-oldest wooden structure and some of the oldest murals in the country. At the entrance to the temple, you'll see 108 steps between the Cheonwang and Anyang gates. They represent redemption from agony and evil passions through 108 cycles. The Muryangsujeong (the "Hall of Eternal Life"), which houses a clay Buddha statue made during the Goryeo Dynasty, is one of the oldest wooden structures in the country. The bus will drop you off at the small enclave of shops, restaurants, and accommodations below the temple.

350-1 Bukji-li Buseok-myeon Yeongju-si, Gyeongsangbuk-do. ℂ **054/634-0747.** www.buseoksa. net (Korean only). Admission ₩3,000 adults, ₩2,000 teens, ₩1,000 children, free for seniors 65 and over and kids 6 and under. From across the Yeongju Bus Terminal, take the bus to Buseoksa. Buses run about every hour and take 50 min. Alternatively, from the Yeongju Train Station, take bus no. 2 to Nonghyeop; from there take a bus to Buseoksa from in front of the Jangchudang pharmacy. You can also take a bus from Pung-gi Station, which takes 30 min.

Choamsa (Choam Temple) TEMPLE   North of Birosa in the next valley over is Choamsa, just above the village of Sunheung, which they claim is the birthplace of Goryeo King Chungyeol. The Choamsa trail, which runs from the park entrance through the Jukgye Valley to Gukmangbong and back, takes about 6 hours and is one of the prettiest in the park.

Huibangsa (Huibang Temple) TEMPLE   The most popular valley for hiking in Sobaeksan is the Huibang Valley, where most people start their treks. When you hike along this road, you'll reach a waterfall, Huibang Pokpo, and the temple just a few minutes farther up the trail. Built during the Shilla Dynasty, it is a smaller version of its former self after its destruction during the Korean War. The trail goes up a series of stone steps and continues to the observatory on Yeonhwabong (about a 2-hr. hike).

ℂ **054/638-2400.** Admission ₩2,000 adults, ₩1,000 teens, ₩600 children, free for seniors 65 and over and kids 6 and under. From across the Yeongju Bus Terminal, take the bus to Huibangsa, which runs about 12 times a day and takes 50 min.

Yeongju

The gateway to Sobaeksan National Park, Yeongju is a pretty city surrounded by the Sobaek and Taebaek mountains. The **Naeseongcheon** (Naseong Stream) runs along the length of the town and is a popular gathering place for residents. The tourist information booths can be found at **Yeongju Station** 349-1, Hyucheon 2-dong (ℂ **054/639-6788**), **Sosu Seowon** (ℂ **054/634-3310**), **Buseoksa** (ℂ **054/638-3464**), and at **city hall** (ℂ **054/639-6062**). The city's website is http://english. yeongju.go.kr/pages/main.jsp.

The **Yeongju Intercity Bus Terminal** (ℂ **1577-5844**) is located on the northwest corner of downtown Yeongju. The local bus terminal is on the same street but on the opposite end of the downtown area.

The city has more public markets than any other of its size. The largest one is located just north of the train station. There are several smaller markets across the north section of town. The eastern market, the Gongseol Shijang, is a nice one to go to in bad weather since it's covered. The market snakes out toward the west until it connects to the main Jung-ang Shijang. Another popular market is the Yeongju

Pung-gi Insam Shijang (© **054/636-7948**), which specializes in all things ginseng and is one of the largest such markets in the country. It's located right near Pung-gi Station.

Sosuseowon (Sosu Confucian School) ★★ HISTORIC SITE The first private academy established in Korea, it was created by governor of Pung-gi County Jusaebung in memory of Yuhyeon Anhyang, one of the greatest Confucian scholars of the Goryeo Dynasty. Because of its historic significance, the *seowon* escaped destruction during the nationwide closure of private academies in 1871.

152-8 Naejuk-li, Sunheung-myeon, Yeongju-si, Gyeongsangbuk-do. © **054/634-3310.** www. seonbichon.or.kr (Korean only). Admission ₩3,000 adults, ₩2,000 teens, ₩1,000 children, free for seniors 65 and over and kids 6 and under. Jun–Aug daily 9am–6pm; Nov–Feb daily 9am–5pm, last admission 1 hr. before closing. From the Yeongju Bus Terminal, take the bus bound for Sunheung, which runs about 8 times a day and takes 30 min, and get off at Sosu Seowon. From Pung-gi Station, buses run about 15 times a day and take 15 min.

WHERE TO STAY
Most motels are concentrated just west of the Yeongju Train Station, with other accommodations scattered in the north part of town, and around the Gongseol and Jung-ang *shijangs* (open markets). A good place to sleep is the **Shilla Gukjeong Hotel,** 329-5 Hyucheon 2(i)-dong, Yeongju (© **054/634-7800**), which costs ₩30,000 for a double. A decent love motel in the area is the **Rich Hotel,** Hyucheon 2-dong, Yeongju (© **054/638-7070**). In the Buseoksa area there is the **Koreana Hotel,** Socheon-li, Puseok-myeon, Yeongju (© **054/633-4445**).

WHERE TO EAT
There is no shortage of Korean restaurants that serve locally grown vegetables in the area. If you want something other than rice, though, your pickings are pretty slim. There are a handful of American-style fast-food restaurants in downtown Yeongju-si (the likes of Domino's Pizza and Lotteria hamburgers), but you'll find more Korean joints.

The places around Buseoksa, such as **Pusoeksa Shikdang** (© **054/633-3317**) or **Myeongseong Shikdang** (© **054/633-3262**), specialize in sanchae bibimbap.

The restaurants in the Sosuseowon area specialize in traditional Korean food. A good one to try is the **Cheongdari Old House** (© **054/633-4288**), where you can get a meal with vegetables usually prepared for traditional rituals.

Cheongnyangsan Provincial Park
The majority of Mt. Cheongnyang Provincial Park (© **054/672-4994**) lies within Bonghwa County. The most famous temple in the park is **Cheongnyangsa ★★★**, 247 Bokgok-li, Myeongho-myeon, Bonghwa-gun (© **054/672-1446;** www. cheongryangsa.org, Korean only), located on the side of Yeonhwabong. Built by Buddhist monk Wonhyo in A.D. 663, this well-located temple is best viewed in the fall when the leaves show off their color. A few hundred meters below the temple is **Cheongnyang Jeongsa,** a small retreat used by scholars for study and meditation in solitude. Above that is the Kimsaeng-gul, a shallow cave named after the famous Shilla Dynasty calligrapher who is said to have practiced his writing there a thousand years ago.

Several trails start from the park's main valley road. Major trails are marked by signs, but many of the tiny trails above the temple are not. Most of the trails up to the temple are steep and difficult, but the easiest and most pleasant one is the Ipseok trail, which heads around the side of the hill near Cheongnyangsa. The trail splits into two directions, the upper trail going up to the cave while the lower trail goes to the temple.

The park is open daily sunrise to sunset, year-round, and entrance is free.

The nearest town is **Bonghwa,** from which you can take a bus bound for Bukgok and get off at the park. The bus runs four times a day and takes about 30 to 40 minutes (then it's about a 30-minute walk to Cheongyangsa). You can take a bus to Bonghwa from the DongSeoul Bus Terminal 6 times a day from 7:40am to 6:10pm. From Andong (use the bus stop in front of the Gyobo Building between the train station and the bus terminal), take bus no. 67 (runs six times a day) to Cheongnyang-san, which takes about 50 minutes.

If you have extra time in Bonghwa County, make a visit to the **Dakshil Maeul** (☎ **061/472-1524,** 171-1 Yugeok-li, Shingbuk-myeon, Yeongam-gun), a 500-year-old traditional village, where the yangban class used to live. Sometimes called Jeong-tong Han-gwa Maeul, the homes are a glimpse into how the upper crust of ancient Korea used to live.

Mungyeong Saejae Provincial Park

The Mungyeong Saejae, which overlays Joryeongsan, has always been the highest and most dangerous mountain pass in the country. Created during the reign of King Tae-jong of the Joseon Dynasty, it was used as the main way to get past these mountains until a new road was built through the Ihwaryeong Gyegok (valley). The **Mungyeong Saejae Provincial Park ★★** (☎ **054/571-0709;** http://saejae.mg21.go.kr) has three entrance gates, which were built here with castle walls after the Japanese invasions in 1592 and 1598. They were damaged, like so many other historic relics, but were restored in 1976.

To get to the first gate, **Juheul-gwan,** go 2km (1¼ miles) west of Sangcho-li and 3.5km (2¼ miles) farther along a deep gorge to the north. The second gate, **Jogok-gwan,** is located about 3km (1¾ miles) from the first gate, at the opening of a small valley. The area between Juheul-gwan and Jogok-gwan is known for its birch trees. The **Mungyeong Saejae Revolt Monument** is on the left side of the road. The third gate, **Joryeong-gwan,** is 3.5km (2¼ miles) past the second gate. If you take the small trail (following the sound of the stream) instead of taking the large road to Joryeong-gwan, you'll pass the **Yeogung Waterfall,** the **Hyeguksa** (a temple of female monks built over 1,100 years ago), and the **Royal Palace** before reaching the peak of Juheulsan, which has a fantastic view. It takes about 4 hours to get to the third gate from the first one. The three entrances collectively are called the **Mungyeong Samgwanmun (The Three Gates/Doors of Mungyeong).**

The KBS TV channel has an open-air studio inside the park, from which they shoot most of their historic dramas. It includes three palaces and many houses styled after those from the Baekje and Goryeo periods. Entrance to the KBS set is ₩2,000 adults, ₩1,000 teens, ₩500 children.

To get to the park, take the city bus bound for Mungyeong Gwanmun from the Mungyeong Intercity Bus Terminal and get off at the parking lot (about 10 min.) or take a taxi. The park is open daily from 8am to sunset (6pm in summer and 5pm in winter) and admission is free, but there is a small cost for the ecological center. Parking costs ₩2,000 to ₩4,000 depending on the size of your vehicle.

There are plenty of minbak and eating options all along the road on the entryway to the park. A cheap sleeping option is the **Ongdalsaem Hwangto Minbak** ★

(© **054/572-3555,** 345-10 Hacho-li, Mungyeong-eup, Mungyeong) that has ondol rooms starting at ₩35,000. Look for the friendly orange building on the right side of the road on the way up to the gates.

Geumosan Provincial Park

About 5km (3 miles) west of the small industrial city of Gumi is the Geumosan Provincial Park. Local legend claims that a monk was walking through here and was looking for a place to build a temple. As he was passing the mountain, he saw a crow lit with the golden rays of the setting sun, hence the name "geumo," which means "golden crow." The temple he built at the base of the mountain is now gone, but the name stuck.

As you make your way up the mountain, **Myeonggeum Waterfall** is the halfway point. It used to be called the Daehye Waterfall until 1931, when the Myeonggeum characters were etched on the cliff to the east of the falling water. To the right of the waterfall is **Doseon Cave,** where legend has it that Monk Doseon achieved enlightenment. Nearby (just below the cave) is the temple **Haeunsa,** which was originally constructed in the late Shilla period, destroyed in 1592, reconstructed in 1925, and restored in 1980.

Another hour's climb from the waterfall leads to a Buddha carved in relief on a large rock, during the Goryeo Dynasty. Nearby is the hermitage **Yaksa-am,** built to honor Monk Uisang's attainment of nirvana. Although it was reportedly built during the Shilla Dynasty, no relics have been found to support that claim.

At the entrance to the park is a small tourist village with a cluster of restaurants, a small amusement park for kids, and a few motels. Admission to the park is ₩600 for adults, ₩400 for teens, ₩200 for children, free for seniors 65 and older and kids 6 and under. The park is open daily from March to October, 9am to 6pm, closing an hour earlier November through February.

The best way to get here is to take bus no. 12 or 12-1 from Gumi; both run daily, every 10 to 15 minutes. For those who don't want to hike up the mountain, a cable car runs up the incline to the entrance to Haeunsa. The ride costs ₩4,500 round-trip, ₩3,000 one-way. It runs daily, every 15 minutes from 9am to 4:30pm.

Uljin

A traditional farming and fishing region, the county and city of Uljin have seen growth since the 1980s, thanks to its nuclear power plant. Being on the coast, it has some nice sandy beaches with fresh seafood restaurants and natural hot springs. Major attractions are all accessible by bus, which runs along the main street in town.

Uljin's most famous tourist attraction is the limestone cave, **Seongnyugul,** which got its name (meaning "the cave where the holy Buddha stayed") because it was the hiding place of an important Buddha statue during the Imjin Waeran. Although it's not the most spectacular of South Korea's caves, it may be the most famous due to the fact that it was the first one opened to tourists in 1963. The area surrounding the cave is blanketed with juniper trees, and a riverside walkway leads to the entrance. Inside, they've lit up the strange formations and columns with colored lights and given them all amusement park-like names. With a cool, humid interior, be aware that there are a couple of low points, which may be difficult if you're tall (although they do provide helmets), but they've built plenty of stairs and pathways for easy access. Short bus rides are available from Uljin. The cave is open daily from April to

October, 8am to 6pm, until 5pm November to March. Entrance costs ₩3,000 for adults, ₩2,000 for youth.

The coastal road from the town of Uljin to Bonghwa twists and turns through **Bukyeong Valley ★★**, which has some spectacular scenery in all four seasons. Be aware that if you visit the area during high season in the summer (July–Aug), you'll have to pay a small admission fee to the **Bukyeong Valley County Park.**

Hidden inside the valley at the upper part of the park is **Bulyeongsa,** the "Buddha Shadow Temple." Originally built in 651 by Uisang (its original name was Guryongsa, or "Nine Dragons Temple"), the temple casts a shadow on the lake below that resembles the shape of the Buddha (hence its new name). A well-kept temple on the hillside, it takes 30 minutes by bus from Uljin.

If you continue north, you'll come upon **Deokgu Valley,** which stretches across Buk-myeon. This valley starts a couple of kilometers from Eungbongsan to Bugu-li and its nuclear power plant. A thick forest, the most beautiful spot in the valley, is home to **Deokgu Hot Spring,** the country's only natural open-air spa. The spa was discovered by hunters about 600 years ago while they were out chasing wild boars. Unfortunately, the people who run the hot spring have ruined the view with a shiny insulated pipe that runs down the valley, bringing the hot water down to the bathhouse. It's popular in the winter as people soak in the 105°F (41°C) water while surrounded by the snowy landscape. Winter is also a great time to enjoy the local snow crabs while they are in season.

The other *oncheon* (hot spring) in the area is the **Baegam Hot Spring** in Onjeong. This was found by a monk named Baekam during the Shilla period. Here, at one of the best known oncheon in the country, the water is about 109°F (43°C) and it has a high concentration of sulfur.

After you're done with all this soaking around, be sure to stop by the **Wolsong-jeong ★**, built in 1326, during the Joseon period. The pavilion is located a few kilometers north of Pyeonghae, a small farming community, and offers great views of the surrounding mountains.

Also in the county is **Mangyang-jeong,** a pavilion originally built at the foot of Hyunjongsan in 1858. It was later moved to its current site and expanded in 1958. The name means "boundless ocean" due to the view that stretches out far into the East Sea.

Uljin's Tourism Office can be reached at ℂ **054/782-1501,** http://eng.uljin.go.kr/open_content/main_page. There is also a tourist info office at the Baegam Hot Springs (ℂ **054/789-5480**).

GETTING THERE Buses from DongSeoul Bus Terminal to the **Uljin Intercity Bus Terminal** (ℂ **054/782-2971**) run every 20 to 30 min. from 7:10am to 8:05pm and take about 4½ hours. Buses from Busan to Uljin run four times daily and take 4½ hours. You can also catch a bus from Daegu, which takes 4 hours.

WHERE TO STAY

Although not a major tourist destination yet, Uljin has a range of accommodations to fit any budget. The most upscale is the **Deokgu Spa Hotel** (ℂ **054/782-0671;** 575 Deokgu-li, Buk-myeon, Uljin-gun), which has both Western and ondol-style rooms starting at ₩120,000.

Hotel Sung Ryu Park (ℂ **054/787-3711;** 968-5 Onjeong-li, Onjeong-myeon, Uljin-gun) is a large seven-story building with an oncheon bath. They also have both Western-style and ondol rooms starting at ₩75,000.

The **Good Morning Motel** ★★ (www.gmmotel.com; ✆ **054/782-3392;** 151 Bongmyeong-li, Jukbyeon-myeon, Uljin-gun) is an affordable motel that has rooms starting at ₩60,000.

WHERE TO EAT

Being on the eastern coast of the peninsula, there is no shortage of good seafood restaurants here, but the regional specialty is *daegae* (snow crab). Because of their size and popularity, they're quite expensive—₩70,000 to ₩120,000 for a meal. You'll start with *gaejang* (raw crab seasoned with sesame oil, salt, chili powder, and so on) and finish off the meal with *daegae tahng* (a hot pot of crab and other seafood).

A good place that specializes in crab and other seafood from the area is the **Hae-dong Sanghwae Daegae Maeul** (✆ **054/781-1585;** 32-48 Beonji, Jukbyeon-li, Jukbyeon-myeon, Uljin-gun), located inside the Jukbyeon Seafood Market.

For hwae, try **Namdo Hwae Iyagi** (✆ **054/782-2090,** 125-7 Nagok-li, Buk-myeon), overlooking the beach and open daily from 8:30am to 10pm. Also, there's a cropping of seafood restaurants in the alley behind the **Uljin Shijang** (✆ **054/783-2988**), where you can see vendors hawk their catch of the day, as well as fresh songi mushrooms from nearby mountains.

Ulleung-do

Next to Jeju-do, **Ulleung-do** ★★ (✆ **054/791-2191;** www.ulleung.go.kr/English) is probably the second-most-famous island in South Korea. Like its larger cousin, it was created due to volcanic activity. But unlike Jeju-do, Ulleung-do was a result of a violent volcanic eruption, resulting in extreme cliffs and high rocks. Most places where the land meets the ocean are high cliffs, but there is a village along the coastline on the slope of **Seonginbong**, the highest point on the island. On the north side, there are a couple of basins created from a collapsed crater, the Nari Basin and the Albong Basin. Mainly a fishing village, the island may possibly be the quietest place in South Korea on a dark, off-season evening.

Sightseeing boats make regular 2- to 4-hour tours around the island, starting at Dodong Harbor. In most months the boat leaves at 9am, with a late-afternoon boat during good weather, and more frequent schedules during high tourist season in July and August. Unfortunately, the tour is only conducted in Korean.

Boats to the island leave once a day (twice a day from the end of July to Aug) from **Pohang Ferry Terminal** (✆ **054/242-5111**) or **Mukho Ferry Terminal** (✆ **033/531-5891**). From Pohang, the boat leaves at 10am with a return trip from **Ulleung Ferry Terminal** (✆ **054/791-9330**) around 3pm. From Mukho, the ferries leave at 9am and 10am and return at 5:30pm. Regular fares range from ₩49,000 to ₩64,400, with lower prices for children and teens. There is also a boat from the **Gangneung Ferry Terminal** (✆ **1544-5117**), which leaves at 8:40am, arriving at Ulleung-do at 11am and costs ₩98,000. Check weather conditions and confirm times with the Korea Travel Phone (✆ **1330**) before setting out.

There is a tourist information center when you arrive at **Dodong Harbor.** Not all of the staff are fluent in English, but they will provide you with maps and bus schedules (super-important since schedules are irregular and change often), and even make sleeping arrangements, should you wish to overnight on the island. There are bus tours of the island available from Dodong Harbor, as well. The tour takes about 4 hours and costs ₩18,000 per person. Because it's so far away from the mainland, goods on the island tend to be more expensive. If you didn't bring enough won with you, you can exchange money at the Nonghyeop Bank in Dodong-li.

EXPLORING ULLEUNG-DO

Bongnae Waterfall ★ NATURAL ATTRACTION   The only source of drinking water on the island, this trilevel fall is about 25m (82 ft.) high. When you pass the entrance, follow the trail up around a reservoir, but stop at the **Punghyeol,** a small hole in the hillside that blows a stream of constant cold air from April to September, especially nice during a summer hike up. Next to the Punghyeol is a pretty cedar forest, which is worth a stop on the way to see the falls.

© 054/791-2191 (Korean only). Admission ₩1,200 adults, ₩700 teens, ₩600 children, free for kids 6 and under. From Dodong Harbor, buses run daily 7:30am–8:10pm on an irregular schedule, but usually every 45 min.–1 hr. It takes 20 min. by taxi from the harbor.

Dodong Yaksu (Mineral Spring) Park NATURAL ATTRACTION   Many locals visit the mineral spring here to have a healthful drink early in the morning. There is a path that leads up to the western ridge for a spectacular view, but no one uses it anymore, since they can take the cable car instead (₩7,500 adults, ₩5,500 teens, and ₩3,500 children, round-trip). Also in the park is the **Dokdo Museum** built to commemorate Korea's independence and to disprove Japan's claim to the island (see below).

The park is located up the alley to the side of the island's hospital, a 15- to 20-min. walk from Dodong Harbor. Alternatively, take a bus from Dodong going to Jeodong and get off at the hospital. Park daily 24 hr.; museum daily 9am–6pm daily. Both closed Jan 1, Lunar New Year, and Chuseok.

Dokdo TOUR   Dokdo is an island on the easternmost end of South Korea, located 87km (54 miles) southeast of Ulleung-do. Dokdo encompasses two islets, Dondo and Seodo, as well as 36 small rock islets. After the Russo-Japanese War of 1905, Japan unilaterally transferred Dokdo to the Shimane Prefecture, renaming it Dakesima. The issue remains unresolved. You can take one of the two daily ferries that circle the island. Ferries run irregularly, depending on the weather, but are scheduled for 7:30am and 2:30pm.

© **053/959-0114.** http://en.dokdo.go.kr. 3- to 4-hr. ferry ride ₩41,200 to ₩45,000 round-trip.

WHERE TO STAY

There are no fancy accommodations and only four hotels on Ulleung-do. The rooms generally start at ₩50,000, but go up to ₩60,000 during high season, which is from late July to August. The fanciest place on the whole island is the **Ulleung Marina Tourist Hotel** (© **054/791-0020 or 4;** fax 054/791-0025). Rooms start at ₩86,000, but can be discounted during off season (late fall to spring).

There are dozens of yeogwan and minbak that offer traditional ondol rooms, generally concentrated around Dodong-li, but some in Jeodong-li. Most of them run to about ₩35,000 to ₩45,000 per room. Only certain rooms in the inns have private bathrooms, so be sure to request one, if you wish. Few take credit cards, so be sure to bring enough cash to cover your expenses. Minbak owners will greet you as you get off the ferry and try to get you to stay in their place. They generally charge about ₩30,000 per room, but the rates can be negotiated down off season. An excellent pension on the island is the **Chusan-ilga Pension ★★** 🍴 (www.chusanilga.com; © **054/791-7788**), with a lovely view of the surrounding sea. It may look like an old hanok on the outside, but they've added modern amenities on the inside (though they have only Korean-style ondol rooms). Doubles start at ₩90,000 in summer, ₩60,000 off season.

If you want to camp on the beach, you can do so at Naesujeon and Sarong-li, which have bathrooms and showers available in the summer. More primitive are the camping facilities at Namyang-dong and Nari-dong, but camping at Nari is free. During winter, many of the accommodations close, but you'll still be able to find a place to stay, since there will be fewer visitors.

WHERE TO EAT

The local foods of Ulleung-do include *honghapbap* (rice with mussels), *ddalgaebibap* (rice with a variety of small shellfish), *yakso bulgogi* (marinated beef from cattle raised on medicinal herbs), *ojingeuh bulgogi* (barbecued sweet-and-spicy squid), and sanchae bibimbap (mixed rice bowl with vegetables unique to the island). Many restaurants close in the winter, but you'll still be able to find enough seafood to sate your appetite. To remember your trip, you can buy some dried cuttlefish ("squid jerky") or the famous Ulleung-do *hobak yeot* (pumpkin taffy).

A place known for its honghapbap, served in a stone pot, is **Seonchang Hwae Shikdang** (☎ 054/791-1148), 135 Dodong-li, Ulleung-eup. They have ojingeuh bulgogi or ddalgae bibimbap for ₩13,000.

Also in Dodong, try the **Bobae Shikdang** (☎ 054/791-2683), where the specialty is mussels. You can get an order of honghapbap for ₩10,000. A bit more pricey, but fancier, is the honghapbap at **Haeun Shikdang** (☎ 054/791-7789) for ₩13,000. They also offer other seafood dishes, including the ojingeuh bulgogi for ₩10,000.

For a taste of the tender "medicinal cows," look no further than **Ulleung Yakso Sutbul Garden** (**Ulleung Medicinal Cow Charcoal Fire Garden;** ☎ 054/791-0990), which serves locally grown beef meals from ₩6,000 to ₩15,000. The yakso bulgogi is also tasty at **Subok Shikdang** (☎ 054/791-4440), which serves an organic version of the dish for ₩15,000.

In Nari-dong, try the flavors of the regional mountain vegetables at **Sanmaeul Shikdang** (**Mountain Village Restaurant;** ☎ 054/791-4643). Their sanchae bibimbap is ₩6,000, while their sanchae jeongshik goes for ₩10,000.

JINJU

Jinju (meaning "pearl" in Korean) is a pretty city with a pretty name. An ancient city with a long history, it was founded during the Gaya period and received its present name during the reign of Goryeo King Taejo. The city suffered through two battles during the Imjin Waeran of the 1590s—the first time Jinju was able to defend itself against the Japanese, but the second time it fell after a prolonged siege of Jinju Fortress. In 1812, Jinju was the center of an ineffectual but memorable peasant uprising, which foreshadowed a larger rebellion later on. Beginning in 1895, it was the capital of Gyeongsangnam-do until Busan outgrew it and took over in 1925.

Despite its volatile history, Jinju has been the cultural and transportation center of the area for centuries. The vibrant arts and culture scene comes alive during the annual **Gaecheon Yesulje Festival** in early October. The festival began in 1949 to commemorate the Korean victory in the Jinjuseong Battle of 1592, but has grown into the best arts festival in the country. It has been held at the Jinju Fortress every year since, except in 1950, during the Korean War, and during the military coup in 1979. Highlights include historical costume plays, classical Korean musical performances, and fireworks. It coincides with the **Jinju Namgang Lantern Festival★★★** and the **National Bullfighting Contest.** If you're in the city in the spring, don't miss the annual **Jinju Bibimbap Festival,** which highlights the city's traditional food and happens the fourth week of May.

The **Namgang (Nam River)** snakes through the city's center and determines the orientation of its buildings. The city is a convenient starting point for exploring the eastern section of Jirisan National Park.

Essentials

GETTING THERE The airport in Jinju is the **Sacheon Airport (HIN),** 1720-1, Guam-li, Sacheon-eup, Sacheon-si (✆ 055/831-9300; www.airport.co.kr/doc/sacheon_eng), about 20km (12 miles) from Jinju-si. Currently, the airport serves about three flights daily from Seoul's Gimpo Airport and one from Jeju-do by Asiana and Korean airlines. Long distance taxis can be found right in front of the terminals, while short-distance taxis are to the right on the national road. Buses from Sacheon to Jinju (about a 30- to 40-min. ride) are cheaper, only ₩3,000 for adults and ₩2,000 for children.

The **Jinju Train Station** (✆ 1544-7788) is located on the south side of the river. There is one first-class Mugunghwa train (₩29,600) from Seoul and four to and from Busan. Other trains go once a day to Suncheon, Masan, and Gwangju, with three trains daily to Mokpo.

The **Jinju Express Bus Terminal** (✆ 055/752-5167 or 8) is right near the train station. Buses from Seoul's Gangnam Express Bus Terminal leave daily every 20 to 30 minutes. The almost 4-hour trip costs ₩18,700 to ₩24,200. Daily buses leave about every 10 minutes from Busan's Seobu Terminal. Rides last about 90 minutes and cost ₩6,900. There are also frequent daily buses from Daegu, which take over 2 hours and cost ₩8,600 to ₩13,700, as well as daily buses from Gwangju, Daejeon, Suwon, and Incheon.

The **intercity bus terminal** (✆ 1688-0841) is located on the north bank of the river and has buses to/from nearby towns, including Samcheonpo, Namhae, Hadong, and Tongyeong.

GETTING AROUND There are local buses available with frequent services within the city and outlying areas. As in most small South Korean cities, the buses have postings only in Korean and the drivers generally can't speak English. Still, buses are the least expensive way to get around. Your best bet is to ask for bus information at your hotel or at the tourist information office (see below).

Taxis are available outside the airport and the bus and train terminals, but drivers generally won't know English. It's best to have your destination written in Korean so that the driver knows where you want to go. Yellow taxis are less expensive than the deluxe black taxis, which can cost up to 20% more.

Jinju is small enough to explore on foot, especially since many sites of interest are located in the vicinity of the **Jinju Fortress.** Be sure to pick up a detailed city map at the tourist information office before putting on your walking shoes.

VISITOR INFORMATION There is a **Jinju Tourist Information Office** (✆ 055/749-2485; daily 8am–6pm) right in front of the fortress's north gate, and another at the east gate (weekdays 8am–6pm). You can also find a tourist information

Jinju

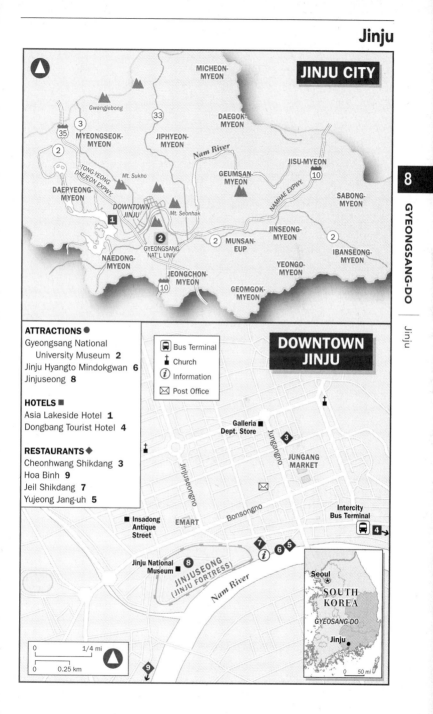

JINJU CITY

MICHEON-MYEON

Gwangjebong

DAEGOK-MYEON

(33)

(3)
(35)
MYEONGSEOK-MYEON

(2)

JIPHYEON-MYEON

Nam River

JISU-MYEON

(10)

TONG-YEONG DAEJEON EXPWY.

Mt. Sukho

GEUMSAN-MYEON

NAMHAE EXPWY.

SABONG-MYEON

DAEPYEONG-MYEON

DOWNTOWN JINJU

Mt. Seonhak

1

JINSEONG-MYEON

(2)

2

(2) MUNSAN-EUP

GYEONGSANG NAT'L UNIV.

IBANSEONG-MYEON

NAEDONG-MYEON

YEONGO-MYEON

JEONGCHON-MYEON

(10)

GEOMGOK-MYEON

ATTRACTIONS ●
Gyeongsang National
   University Museum **2**
Jinju Hyangto Mindokgwan **6**
Jinjuseong **8**

HOTELS ■
Asia Lakeside Hotel **1**
Dongbang Tourist Hotel **4**

RESTAURANTS ◆
Cheonhwang Shikdang **3**
Hoa Binh **9**
Jeil Shikdang **7**
Yujeong Jang-uh **5**

🚌 Bus Terminal
✝ Church
ⓘ Information
✉ Post Office

DOWNTOWN JINJU

Galleria ■
Dept. Store

Jungangno

JUNGANG MARKET

3

Jinjuseongno

✝

✉

Bonsongno

Intercity
Bus Terminal

🚌 4→

Insadong
Antique
Street

EMART

7 6 5

ⓘ

Jinju National
Museum 8

JINJUSEONG
(JINJU FORTRESS)

Nam River

Seoul
✪

SOUTH
KOREA

GYEOSANG-DO

Jinju ●

0   50 mi

0   1/4 mi
0   0.25 km

9
↓

8

GYEONGSANG-DO | Jinju

271

booth at Sacheon Airport (© **055/852-8490**). The website for the city is http://
english.jinju.go.kr/main.

[FastFACTS] JINJU

Banks, Foreign Exchange & ATMs There are a handful of banks in the downtown
area of Jinju, along the main street; the most convenient is the Foreign Exchange Bank
across from the intercity bus terminal (near the fortress). They're open Monday to Friday
9:30am to 4:30pm.

Internet Access Most large hotels and even a couple of the lower-priced motels offer
Internet access. If you don't have your own computer, your cheapest option is the **PC
bahngs** in town. Just look for the letters PC; most of them are found on the second or third
floors above restaurants and other businesses.

Exploring Jinju

Gyeongsang National University Museum ★ 🏛 MUSEUM   If old relics
are your thing, look no further than this research museum located on the sixth floor
of the university's main library. With over 8,000 artifacts dating back to Korea's prehistory, most of the collection is from the Gaya period. Only about 500 pieces are on
display at any given time, but it is an active archaeological museum and an interesting
glimpse into eras past.

Gyeongsang University 900, Gajwa-dong, Jinju-si, Gyeongsangnam-do. © **055/772-0600.** http://
museum.gnu.ac.kr (Korean only). Free admission. Mon–Sat 10am–6pm. Closed holidays. From the
Jinju Intercity Bus Terminal, take bus no. 26 or any local bus that goes to Samcheonpo. From the
express bus terminal, take bus no. 33. From the train station, take bus no. 17, 21, 27, 221, or 226.

Jinjuseong (Jinju Fortress/Castle) ★★ CASTLE   Although it's called a
"castle," it mainly served as a fortress, defending the Honam region from Japanese
invaders during the Imjin Waeran. One of the best reconstructed fortresses in the
country, Jinjuseong sits on the north side of the Nam-gang overlooking the city. Inside
the east gate is the famous Chokseong-nu pavilion. Other outlooks and pavilions are
along the fortress wall, with the highest one at the southwest corner. Also, inside the
walls are a memorial to Kim Shi-min, the Uigisa Shrine, Seojangdae, Bukjangdae, the
Changyeolsa shrine, and Hoguksa, most of which are closed to the public. The complex is spectacular at night when its lights are reflected in the river below.

   Inside the fortress walls is the **Jinju National Museum** (© **055/742-5951;**
http://jinju.museum.go.kr), which offers an in-depth history of the Imjin Waeran.
Hours are Tuesday to Friday 9am to 6pm, until 7pm on weekends; the museum
closes at 5pm November to February. It's closed January 1. Admission is free.

Namseong-dong, Jinju-shi, Gyeongsangnam-do. © **055/749-2480.** Admission ₩1,000 adults,
₩500 teens, ₩300 children, free for kids 6 and under. Parking ₩1,000. Daily 9am–6pm. Across
from Jinju Express Bus Terminal, take bus no. 15, 17, 21, 22, 25, 27, 37, 38, 50, or 51. Buses run daily
6am–11pm, every 5 min.; get off at National Agricultural Cooperative Federation, pass Jinju
Bridge, and walk 3 min.

Jinju Hyangto Mindokgwan (Local Folk Collection) ★★ 🏛 MUSEUM   If
you leave the fortress from the east gate, this folk museum is located just down the
street on the second floor of the Cultural Center. Once owned and operated by a
local shoemaker, Kim Changmun, the small museum has a collection of over 20,000
pieces of furniture, bowls, ornaments, and other household items. Unfortunately,

only a small fraction of the craft items are on display at any given time. If the doors are locked during business hours, ring the bell for someone to let you in.

10-4, Bonseong-dong, Jinju-si, Gyeongsangnam-do. ☎ **055/746-6828.** Admission ₩1,000 adults, ₩500 youth, free for seniors 65 and over and kids 6 and under. Tues–Wed and Fri–Sun 9am–6pm. Closed Jan 1, Lunar New Year, and Chuseok. A 10-min. walk from the Jinju Intercity Bus Terminal.

Shopping

Since Jinju opened its first silk factory in 1910, it has been the center of silk production in the country. Now the city produces the majority of the country's silk, as well as being one of the five largest silk producers in the world, exporting the fabric to Europe and the Americas. You can find the best deals on locally produced silk at the **small silk center** in front of the Jinju Fortress. The city holds an annual **Silk Festival** in October, at the same time as most of their main festivals.

If you're looking for antique paintings, crafts, and sculptures, head over to the **Insadong Antique Street,** which is located behind the General Social Welfare Center, near the fortress. There you'll find more than 20 shops carrying things like stone sculptures, ceramics, silver pieces, lacquer and inlaid boxes, and more.

The city's central market, the **Jung-ang Shijang,** is on the east side across the main road, while the principal produce market is closer to the intercity bus terminal. The underground market, located south of Jinju's central intersection, has everything from traditional medicine to beauty supplies on sale.

Where to Stay

Most of the city's love motels and inexpensive yeogwan are concentrated along the riverfront near the bus terminal. There is also a good selection of yeogwan a couple of blocks from the fortress's east gate. Rooms generally start at ₩35,000 to ₩45,000 and you shouldn't have any trouble just walking in and booking a place, except in October, when the city is crawling with festival-goers.

Asia Lakeside Hotel ★★   The only downside to the Asia Lakeside is its location. Although the setting on Jinyang Lake is beautiful, it's not convenient for downtown. But if you're okay with that, it's a great place to stay. Rooms are airy and designed to optimize natural light, and the furnishings are modern and stylish. All rooms have nice views of the man-made reservoir and balconies from which you can enjoy the surroundings. Beds are comfortable with super-soft bedding, and bathrooms are surprisingly well appointed. The hotel bar even has a pretty good wine list.

1077-1, Panmun-dong, Jinju-si, Gyeongsangnam-do. www.asiahotel.co.kr/eng/index.php.☎ **055/746-3734.** Fax 055/746-4505. 29 units. ₩120,000 and up standard double or ondol room; ₩350,000 and up suite, 10% VAT not included. AE, MC, V. **Amenities:** 2 restaurants; bar; karaoke club. *In room:* A/C, TV, minibar, fridge, hair dryer, Internet.

Dongbang Tourist Hotel ★   Located right on the river, near the intercity bus terminal, the hotel is one of the only tourist-class hotels in the city. The rooms are spacious and comfortable, though not terribly exciting (although the view of the river is lovely). The furnishings are a bit dated, but still clean and well maintained. High-speed Internet access is available in all rooms, or you can pay to use a computer in the business center. Staff speak English and are quite friendly and helpful.

803-4, Okbongnam-dong, Jinju-si, Gyeongsangnam-do. ☎ **055/743-0131.** Fax 055/742-6786. 125 units. ₩106,000 ondol room; ₩115,000 standard; ₩165,000 and up suite. 10% VAT and 10%

service charge not included. AE, MC, V. **Amenities:** 3 restaurants; bar; lounge; cafe; health club; sauna; room service; smoke-free rooms. *In room:* A/C, TV, minibar, fridge, hair dryer, Internet.

Where to Eat

Jinju is known throughout the country for its bibimbap (sometimes called *ggotbap* or "flower rice"), a mixed rice bowl with a variety of vegetables. A couple of restaurants that specialize in bibimbap are **Cheonhwang Shikdang** (*©* 055/741-2646), located near Jung-ang Shijang, just a block off the main drag, and **Jeil Shikdang** (*©* 055/741-5591), right next to the fortress and the folk museum.

Other specialties of the area include heotjesatbap, a "fake" rice meal traditionally made for the ancestral memorial table by starving scholars. Another Jinju favorite is *jang-uh gui,* grilled eel. A concentration of restaurants specializing in the fish dish is located along the waterfront near the fortress. They are all very similar to each other and charge a universal price of about ₩13,000 for an eel meal. **Yujeong Jang-uh** (*©* 055/746-9235) is one such restaurant that specializes in both freshwater and saltwater eel. The restaurant doesn't have an English sign, but just look for the ornate, traditional-looking house just west of the bridge. A meal will easily feed two, especially if you pay the extra ₩1,000 for rice.

For a totally different meal, you can have Vietnamese cuisine at the chain place **Hoa Binh,** 768-4 Pyeonggeo-dong, Jinju-si (*©* 055/747-4554), a block from the river. A bowl of *pho* (Vietnamese rice noodles) will set you back ₩8,000.

Entertainment & Nightlife

Jinju has a quiet nightlife. There are no clubs in town, but there are plenty of hof-style bars where you can grab a beer, or cafes where you can get an overpriced cup of coffee. Most of them are in the downtown area, where the streets are closed off to cars at night, with some isolated action around the universities.

TONGYEONG

Situated on the coast of Gyeongsangnam-do, Tongyeong is a gorgeous seaside city in the middle of Hallyeo National Maritime Park. It covers the southern part of the Goseong Peninsula and includes 151 islands (only 43 of which are inhabited). Gwang-do and Dosan are to the north, while the west faces Namhae.

With warm currents from the East Sea, Tongyeong has been an ideal fishing location. In addition to having warmer weather, the area is one of the rainiest in the country. Because of its seaside location, its picturesque attributes also bring more typhoon dangers. Fishing, oyster farming, and other food processing are the city's major industries.

When Japan invaded Korea in 1592, the naval fleet, commanded by Admiral Yi Sun-shin (sometimes spelled Lee Sun-shin), defeated the invading navy. The following year, King Sunjo appointed Admiral Yi as chief commander of the naval forces of the three provinces (a position created just for him). Naval forces were moved soon afterward in 1604. In mid-August of every year, there is a **Hansandae Festival (Battle of Hansan Festival)** ★★★, in honor of Admiral Yi's victory. As well as the re-creation of the battle, many other smaller festivals and events happen simultaneously and it's well worth a visit.

In the spring or fall, the city comes alive with the **Tongyeong International Music Festival** (www.timf.org), a classical music event created in honor of native son and composer Yun Isang. The dates aren't consistent every year, so check the schedule before making a special trip.

Exploring Tongyeong's best sites, the outlying islands, requires at least an overnight stay to catch the early-morning ferries out and back.

Essentials

GETTING THERE If you wish to travel by air, the nearest airport is Jinju's **Sacheon Airport** (see the Jinju section earlier for information). From the airport, catch a limousine bus to Tongyeong.

There are no direct trains to Tongyeong. The closest train stations are at Jinju, Haman, or Masan, and you'll have to take a bus from there.

The most convenient way to get to Tongyeong is by rental car; the least expensive way is by bus. Buses travel regularly from both **Seoul's Nambu Terminal** at Seocho (11 times daily) and the **express bus terminal** at Gangnam (14 times daily). The ride takes about 4½ hours. There are 8 express buses and 14 regular buses a day from Daejeon and about 18 buses from Daegu's Seobu Terminal. Buses from **Busan's Seobu Terminal** run daily from 6:30am to 10:30pm about every 20 minutes. From **Masan's Nambu Terminal,** there are daily buses from 5:10am to 9:15pm every 10 minutes. Buses from Jinju run about 63 times a day from 6am to 9pm.

Driving from Seoul, take the Gyeongbu Expressway to the Tongyeong-Daejeon Expressway, heading toward Tongyeong to the Tongyeong IC. From anywhere in the Gyeongsang-do area, take the Jungbu Expressway to the Namhae Expressway to the Tongyeong-Daejeon Expressway, heading toward Tongyeong. From Jeolla-do, take the Honam Expressway to the Namhae Expressway to the Tongyeong-Daejeon Expressway, heading toward Tongyeong.

GETTING AROUND There are local buses available to get you where you want to go, but Tongyeong's major attractions are all within walking distance of each other.

You can catch a ferry to an outlying island or an excursion tour around the area. The best thing to do is to get one early in the morning so that you'll have plenty of time to explore. Island destinations from **Tongyeong's Ferry Terminal** (✆ 055/644-0364) include Dumi-do, Maemul-do, Mireuk-do, Bijin-do, Yeondae-do, Yeonhwa-do, Yokji-do, Chu-do, and Chubong-do. Tour boats usually leave from the **Excursion Boat Terminal** in Donam-dong, while long-distance boats dock at **Ganguan Port.** Explanations for specific island destinations are below, in the "Outlying Islands" section.

VISITOR INFORMATION There is a **tourist information office** (✆ 055/650-4584) outside the bus terminal and it's open Tuesday to Sunday from 9am to 8pm (closed on national holidays and the day after). The staff's English isn't great, but they do have maps in English. There is also a tourist information booth at the excursion boat terminal at Donam-dong (✆ 055/644-7200), at the Mireuk-san cable car entrance (✆ 055/649-3804), and at the Hakseom Resort (✆ 055/640-5245). The city's official site is at http://eng.tongyeong.go.kr.

Exploring Tongyeong

Cheongyeolsa ★ TEMPLE This temple shrine was built in 1606 by General Commander Yi Un-Ryong to memorialize Admiral Yi Sun-shin's distinguished service to the country. The temple site currently has 17 buildings, including five gates, an exhibition hall, shrines, and a pavilion. It also has on-site the Eight Gifts from the Ming Dynasty and several other cultural assets.

213 Myeongjeong-dong, Tongyeong-si. (℃) **055/862-2840.** Located up the hill from Sebyeong-gwan (see directions below). Alternatively, from the bus terminal, take bus no. 12, 22, or 32 to Cheongyeolsa.

Nammangsan Park ★★ PARK   At Mt. Nammang, there is a park from which you can enjoy a view of the city, located right next to Ganguan Port. On top of the hill are Suhyangjeong Pavilion and a bronze statue of Joseon-era naval hero General Yi Sun-shin. Under the pavilion is an outdoor sculpture garden with 15 works by sculptors who participated in the Tongyeong International Sculpture Symposium.

62-1 Dongho-dong, Tongyeong-si. (℃) **055/640-5371** (Korean). Free admission. Daily 24 hr. From the bus terminal, take bus no. 10, 15, 18, 20, 26, 30, 35, 38, 38-1, 39, 39-1, 40, 45, or 46 and get off at Jung-ang Shijang (Central Market) and walk 5 min.

Sebyeong-gwan ★ HISTORIC SITE   Sebyeong-gwan served as the naval command center for the southern provinces from 1597 to 1896. One of the oldest and largest wooden structures left in the country, it was built in 1604 by General Yi Gyeong-jun, commander of the naval forces during the Joseon period. It was last renovated in 1973, but there are plans to restore it to its former glory.

62-1 Manhwa-dong, Tongyeong-si. (℃) **055/650-5365** (Korean only). Free admission. Mar–Oct Tues–Sun 10am–6pm; Nov–Feb Tues–Sun 10am–5pm. Closed holidays. From bus terminal, take bus no. 10, 15, 18, 20, 26, 30, 35, 38, 38-1, 39, 39-1, 40, 45, or 46 and get off at Jung-ang Shijang. It's a 5-min. walk from there.

MIREUK-DO

Mireuk-do, an island just off the coast of Tongyeong, creates a natural barrier of protection for Tongyeong. A small mountain on the island, **Mireuksan ★★★**, shields the mainland from the ocean winds. Mireuksan is known as the home base of the Mireuk Buddhists. It is connected to the mainland via an undersea tunnel (Pandalegul), and by the Chungmu and Tongyeong bridges. It's a fantastic place to look down at Tongyeong and the outlying islands that disappear far into the surrounding sea.

On the north side of the island is the temple **Yonghwasa,** which was built in 632. When the temple was rebuilt after a fire in 1628, its name was changed. The current buildings are reconstructions made in the 19th century. Instead of the usual deva gate guards, this temple is guarded by four figures from Emperor Jing's tomb in Xian China.

From Yonghwasa, a trail goes up to the top of the mountain, and along the way you'll pass the hermitage **Gwaneum-am.** This meditation center is dedicated to the goddess of mercy, Gwaneum. Just beyond and above it is the older **Doseol-am,** from where you can get a wonderful view of the island and Geoje-do. A hike past the temple and hermitages and to the top should take about 2 hours round-trip.

Those not wanting to make the trek up on foot (pretty much everyone) can take the **cable car ★★★** at San 63-26, Donam-dong ((℃) **055/649-3804** or -3805) for just ₩9,000 round-trip (₩6,000 for youth). The cable car runs 9:30am to 5pm October through February, until 6pm March and September, and until 7pm April through August. The last ride up is an hour before closing.

OUTLYING ISLANDS

To get to any of the nearby islands, you'll have to take a boat. We've tried to make it easier for you by listing which terminal you should head for to catch a boat to each island. To get to the **Tongyeong Ferry Terminal,** take a Donam-dong-bound bus from the bus terminal and get off at the Beach Hotel in Seoho-dong. Walk 5 minutes to the ferry terminal, located across the street from the Seoho Shijang (Seoho Market). To get to the **Excursion Boat Terminal,** take a Donam-dong-bound bus from the bus terminal and get off at the ferry terminal.

Hansan-do ★ NATIONAL PARK   Located in the middle of Hallyeo Haesang National Park, Hansan-do is a historically important site. This is where General Yi Sun-shin fought off the Japanese with his turtle ships (p. 13) during the Imjin Waeran (1592–98). In spite of its history, modern tourists are more attracted to the oysters, pearls, and seaweed grown here. The only place that belies its past history is the **Jeseung-dang,** a re-creation of Admiral Yi's command headquarters, which were moved from Yeosu and housed here for 4 years, before being moved again to Sebyeong-gwan in Tongyeong. The island's other tribute to the naval war hero is an unfortunate lighthouse at the harbor in the shape of a turtle ship.

Admission ₩1,000 adults, ₩500 teens, ₩300 children, free for kids 6 and under. Daily 9am–6pm. From the ferry terminal at Seoho-dong, ships run every 90 min. and the ride lasts 25 min. Car ferries are also available from here. From the excursion boat terminal at Donam-dong, boats travel frequently and the ride lasts 15 min.

Somaemul-do ★★★ NATURAL ATTRACTION   This tiny island is on the outer edge of Hallyeo Haesang National Park, but the view is worth the ride. To get to the peak of the island, Mangtae-bong, you'll take a 30-minute stroll through woods filled with 600-year-old camellias. From Somaemul-do you can get to its tiny neighbor Deungdae-seom (sometimes called "Haegeum-do"). This even-tinier island takes only 20 minutes or so to explore, but the scenery is beautiful. The only facility is a small lighthouse built by the Japanese during their colonization of Korea (1910–45). Twice a day, when the tide ebbs, the receding water reveals a gravel road between the two islands—just be careful not to get stuck when the tide comes back in. Somaemul-do is a wonderful place to enjoy the sunrise or sunset, or to visit when the camellias are in bloom late October through early November.

From the ferry terminal at Seoho-dong, there are 2 boats on weekdays at 7am and 2pm. On weekends, there is also an 11am boat. The ride takes 60 min. and costs ₩25,000 for adults, ₩20,000 for teens, ₩16,000 for children. Check the schedule at ✆ **055/645-3717** (Korean only) before leaving. From the excursion boat terminal at Donam-dong, there is an excursion ferry that goes to the island via Haegeumgang, Maemul-do, and Jeseung-dang. The 4-hr. tour runs every hour 9am–6pm in the summer, 10am–3pm during winter. The tour costs ₩19,500 for adults, ₩13,000 for children. Check the schedule at ✆ **055/646-2307** (Korean) before leaving.

Yokji-do ★★ 🏖 BEACH   The largest island in the Yeonhwa archipelago, it is located about 32km (20 miles) from Tongyeong. It used to be called "Nok-do" (Deer Island) because of the large number of deer that roamed the island, but the population was greatly reduced during the 16th century. That's when Japanese sailors began hunting the deer for their antlers, which they sent to the Japanese royal palace. Fish farming is the principal source of income here, and regular farming (especially of sweet potatoes) is also practiced. All the island's beaches are pebbled, the largest being Deokdong Beach, which is full of black stones called *bamjagal* (night pebbles). Outshone by its more famous neighbors, Yokji-do sees few tourists and doesn't even have any taxis. However, you can bring your own rental car over a ferry. There is a very limited bus service, so check with the tourist office for schedules before venturing out to the island.

There are regular ferries (ride lasts 40 min.) 3 to 4 times a day from Tongyeong Harbor to Yokji-do. Car ferries (which take 90 min.) run about 3 times daily. Call to check for schedules at *℃* **055/641-6181**. Car ferries also run from Samdeok Harbor on Mireuk-do 2 to 4 times a day. Check for schedules at *℃* **055/641-3560**.

Shopping

Tongyeong is best known for its *najeon chilgi* (lacquerware). These are wooden boxes inlaid with elaborate mother-of-pearl designs before being lacquered to a shiny finish. The lacquerware became popular during the Shilla period (A.D. 668–935), although the craft dates farther back, to the Naklang period. During the reign of King Munjong of the Goryeo Dynasty, the government ran workshops to make najeon chilgi. The elaborate boxes made from these workshops were given as gifts to foreign kings and envoys. There's even a **Najeon Chilgi Festival** in August (during the Hansandae Festival). These beautiful works of art are small enough to tuck into your suitcase and make nice gifts. Be sure to shop around for the best prices, since antiques and handmade pieces by master craftsmen will be way more expensive than less elaborate imitations.

A bustling traditional market in town is the **Seoho Shijang,** across from the ferry terminal. Here you can find *halmuhni* (grandmas) selling fresh fish and seafood. The large **Tongyeong Traditional Craft Hall,** 642 Beonji, Donam-dong, Tongyeong-si (*℃* **055/645-3266**), is a good place to buy lacquerware as well as other local craft items, like hand fans, wooden trays, and items made from abalone shells. A couple of smaller markets include the **Geobuk Shijang** (Turtle Market) in Taepyeong-dong and the **Jung-ang Live Fish Market** (the name says it all) near Ganguan Port in Dongho-dong.

For more modern shopping options, there's the **Lotte Mart** in Bukshin-dong, not far from the bus terminal and the main post office.

Where to Stay

There are not many tourist-class hotels in Tongyeong, but you'll have no trouble finding cheaper accommodations (many are clustered around the bus terminal). You can also find some love motels near the harbor, most of them with rooms starting at ₩40,000 on off-season weekdays.

A good option is the **Hotel Chungmu ★★,** 1 Donam-dong, Tongyeong-si (**www.hotelchungmu.com**, Korean only; *℃* **055/645-2091**). The pension has oceanview rooms and is set on nice landscaping in a wonderful location. Doubles start at ₩100,000.

The **Tongyeong Tourist Hotel,** 1141, Chongryang-dong, Tongyeong-si (*℃* **055/644-4411**), is a bit more boring but less expensive and conveniently located near the harbor. Built in 1988 and renovated in 1996, the 47-room hotel does have a sauna and a nightclub.

Also near the water is the **Chungmu Beach Hotel,** 177-15, Seoho-dong, Tongyeong-si (*℃* **055/642-8181**), which has 43 rooms, as well as a buffet restaurant, a coffee shop, and sauna facilities.

An affordable option is the **Napoli Motel**, 160-3-beonji, Dongho-dong, Tongyeong-si (http://tynapoli.co.kr, Korean only; *℃* **055/646-0202**), a love motel with rooms starting at ₩40,000.

If you find yourself stranded or wanting to spend the night on one of the outlying islands, they all have low-priced minbak available. On Yokji-do, there is the **Gorae-meori Tourist Farm** (*℃* **055/641-6089**), a South Korean "condo" that's good for families, located near Deokdong Beach. In Somaemul-do, the **Dasol Penthouse** (☎ **017/857-2915**) and the **Hayan Sanjang** (☎ **017/590-2007**) are good options.

Where to Eat

Like most of South Korea's coastal towns, hwae restaurants are omnipresent, but it's especially fresh and tasty here. A restaurant that serves good Japanese-style sushi and *bokeo maeuntang* (spicy hot pot made with swellfish) is **Tongyeong Daeoe Chobap,** 1158-48 Jeongryang-dong (☎ **055/641-5176**).

Another dish not unique to Tongyeong, but equally delicious is the *junbok jook* (abalone porridge). Although not cheap (usually about ₩15,000), a bowl is great to warm you up on a cold winter day. **Namgyeong Hwaet Jib,** 357-5 Misu-dong (☎ **055/643-3030**), serves a hearty bowl of the porridge. Located on the water near the underwater tunnel, they have a nice array of hwae as well.

From Tongyeong's old name, "Chungmu," comes *Chungmu gimbap,* a dish named after the *Chungmu haelmae* (the Chungmu grandma), a legendary fictional figure. This local specialty is rice rolled in seaweed just like any other gimbap, except that there are no fillings and it's served with a side of *kkakdugi* (radish kimchi) and boiled squid seasoned with vinegar and chili paste. A couple of dozen restaurants specializing in the dish line the city's pier. Most places charge about ₩3,000 for this local "fast food," but the restaurant that originated the dish is the **Chungmu Halmae Gimbap,** 129-1 Jung-ang-dong (☎ **055/643-3105**), just about a 5-minute walk from the bus stop. About 70% of their business is takeout and you may want to pack some to go for an island excursion.

The Tongyeong bibimbap is prepared the regular Korean way, but their variation is the accompanying soup, which is made with sea mustard and sea lettuce cooked in the water in which the rice was washed.

There are plenty of other good seafood restaurants in town. A couple of places that specialize in oysters are the **Hyangto Jip** (☎ **055/645-4808**) and the **Tongyeong Gul Madang,** 647 Donam-dong (☎ **055/644-7891**), located on the first floor of the Marina Condo sports center. **Hodong Shikdang** (☎ **055/645-3138**) specializes in swellfish, which is supposed to be a good hangover cure. A place for generally fresh seafood is **Jinmi Shikdang** (☎ **055/643-0240**), behind the Jeokshipja (Red Cross) Hospital.

Those with a sweet tooth can get Korean "donuts" from **Omisa Ggul Bbang,** 498-1 Donam-dong (☎ **055/646-3230;** www.omisa.co.kr), located near the Seong-u apartment complex. Their fried dough balls (made with rice flour and covered in honey) are so popular that they close shop whenever they run out, which can be as early as 11am, only an hour after they open at 10am.

THE REST OF GYEONGSANGNAM-DO

With the country's largest coastal population, the Southern Gyeongsang Province (sometimes shortened to "Gyeongnam") is mostly oriented toward the sea. The largest cities are Busan and Ulsan, each of which has its own separate governments.

Gyeongnam is home to South Korea's most celebrated temple, **Haeinsa,** located on the southern slopes of Gayasan. There are 15 hermitages associated with Haeinsa, located in the valley nearby. The closest to the great temple is **Hongje-am,** where the famous military leader Monk Samyeongdaesa of the Joseon Dynasty retired, after leading a group of Buddhist warrior monks during the Imjin Waeran. The first hermitage built in the area, **Wondong-am** (which is said to have been the staging site for the building of Haeinsa) is nearby. There are other historical sites in the area, including **Baengnyeon-am,** which has the most beautiful scenery; **Hirangdae** (where the Monk Hirang meditated); and **Jijog-am** (a place for prayer).

In the western part of the province is Jirisan National Park (which is covered in the Jeolla-do chapter) and the small town of **Hadong,** which is located on the western edge of the province. This mountain town is known for its wild tea fields and the vendors in its open-air herb market, **Hwagae Jangteo.**

Gyeongnam is also known for its wonderfully rocky coasts, tiny little islands scattering into the sea, and beautiful beaches, like **Sangju Beach** near Geumsan in Namhae. The country's best dinosaur footprints can also be found on the picturesque coast in **Goseong.**

Essentials

GETTING THERE   The most convenient place to fly in is Busan's **Gimhae Airport,** which has international flights from other destinations in Asia, as well as domestic flights from Incheon, Gimpo, Jeju, Gwangju, and Gangneung. The province also has two domestic airports, one in **Sacheon** (near Jinju) and the other at **Ulsan.** Buses from Sacheon Airport go to Goseong (30-min. ride), Chungmu (1-hr. ride), Geoje (about 80 min.), and other outlying towns.

Visitors traveling by rail usually arrive in Busan first (usually using the high-speed KTX line) and then take one of three rail lines to other parts of the province. The **Gyeongbu line** runs north through Miryang toward Daegu and up. The **Donghae Nambu line** goes to Ulsan, Gyeongju, and Yeongcheon. The **Gyeongjeon line** goes west from Samnyang-jin to Jinju, Hadong, and other destinations in Jeollanam-do.

Rather than infrequent trains, buses are a less expensive way to get around the province. You can also take an **express bus** from Seoul to Andong, Sangju, Gimcheon, Gumi, Daegu, Gyeongju, Pohang, Yeongju, and Yeongcheon. Intercity buses travel all over the province, although schedules may be infrequent. If you're driving, major expressways extend to most parts of the province. The main one, the **Gyeongbu Expressway** (road 1), runs between Seoul and Busan. The **Ulsan Expressway** (road 16) connects Ulsan to Eonyang. The **Namhae Expressway** (road 10) joins Gyeongsangnam-do to Jeollanam-do, with a branch line (road 104), going around Gimchae and running into the southern part of Busan. The **Jungbu Naeryuk Expressway** (road 45) connects Masan to Daegu, while the **Jungbu Expressway** (road 35) connects Hamyang to Jinju and Tongyeong. The **88 Olympic Expressway** (road 12) connects Daegu to Gwangju. When the **Donghae Expressway** (road 65) is completed, it will connect Busan to Ulsan and Pohang and run along the coast up to Gangwon-do.

There are boats from Jinhae and Masan to Geoje-do and from Geoje-do to Busan. The most extensive ferry services are available from Tongyeong to the outlying islands, with some ferries from Samcheonpo.

GETTING AROUND   Local buses from smaller cities and towns take you to outlying areas, but some of them run infrequently to remote or less popular places, so check your return bus schedule and plan accordingly.

VISITOR INFORMATION Gyeongsangnam-do's main **Tourist Information Center,** 484-3 Samdeok-li, Hoehwa-myeon (© **055/673-9503**), is located next to the Oksu Service Station in Goseong County. Another information center can be found near the Hamyang service station in Hamyang County, San 40-1 Bosan-li, Jigok-myeon (© **055/964-2710**). Both are open daily from 9am to 6pm March to June and September to October; until 8pm July to August; and until 5pm November to February.

Gayasan National Park

The name "Gaya" comes from the Sanskrit for "cow." **Gayasan** (© **055/930-8000;** http://english.knps.or.kr) is sometimes called "Someurisan" (head of cow mountain) because (why else?) the mountains are shaped like a cow's head. Consisting of a series of high peaks, Gayasan has long been sacred for Buddhists, so its name was changed to Gayasan in honor of the Buddha's preaching in India.

It takes 2 days and 1 night to climb the whole of Gayasan, starting from Sudosan, but most travelers visit the park for just 1 day. The most popular route passes through **Hongnyudongcheon** (stream) to Haeinsa to the peak, **Sangwangbong,** though the last part of the trail to the peak is closed for natural preservation until 2028 and some other trails are closed until 2017.

Admission to the park is ₩1,600 adults, ₩1,200 teens, ₩800 children. The park is open from sunrise to sunset daily.

There are campgrounds in Haeinsa and near Baegun-dong, but these facilities are used less frequently since new roads have been built, making it easier to get in and out of the area. Camping fees range from ₩5,000 to ₩8,000, depending on the size of your tent. Parking costs ₩4,000 to ₩6,000 per day. There is one midsize hotel and several motels and minbak near Haeinsa. In Baegun-dong, there is one small hotel and a couple of motels. Most people make a day trip to the area and choose not to overnight here.

To get to Gayasan from the Daegu Seobu Bus Terminal, take a bus bound for Haeinsa and get off at the last stop. Buses run every 20 minutes and the ride takes about an hour. From the Hapcheon Intercity Bus Terminal, buses run 8 times a day and it takes about an hour.

Driving, take the 88 Olympic Expressway (road 12) to the Haeinsa IC. Then take local road 1084 toward Yacheon-li, then take national road 59, and follow the signs to Haeinsa and Gayasan.

Cheongnyangsa (Cheongyang Temple) TEMPLE Isolated and a bit difficult to reach, this temple is a peaceful place, located on a steep slope. Not a place to find amazing architecture, Cheongnyangsa is a relatively small temple, but enjoys spectacular scenery. From the park entrance, there is a small road that leads up to the temple.

No phone. Free with admission to the park. Daily sunrise to sunset.

Haeinsa (Haein Temple) ★★★ TEMPLE The name "Haein" comes from the expression "haeinsammae, " which is taken from Hwaeomgyeong Buddhist scripture and which means "truly enlightened world of Buddha and our naturally undefiled mind," comparing the wisdom of the Buddha to the calm sea. One of the "Three Jewel" temples of South Korea, Haeinsa was founded by two monks in A.D. 802.

A Temple Stay in Haeinsa

Although you can do an overnight stay in many of the country's temples, an overnight at Haeinsa is truly special. For 2 days and 1 night, you'll get a rare glimpse into monastic life. You'll be provided with a simple grey monk's outfit and be served vegetarian meals to help cleanse your body. You'll get a brief lecture on temple etiquette (how to sit, how to behave at meals, how to drink tea, and how to behave during meditation). At 6pm, the drum and gong are struck for about 10 minutes. At 3am, there is an early-morning service and meditation, with another ringing of the drum and gong for 10 minutes, followed by a service in the Daejeok gwanjeon. The service is followed by a 1-hour meditation in the assembly hall. You can take a morning stroll with the monks, enjoy conversation and a cup of tea with them, view the Tripitaka Koreana, and see the Ingyeong printing tablets. Bring an open mind and be ready to spend a lot of time bowing (108 bows are said to free you from the anguish of your life) and sitting cross-legged on the floor. ₩50,000 to ₩80,000 per person.

A UNESCO World Heritage site, the temple houses the famed **Tripitaka Koreana.** Begun in 1236, during the Goryeo Dynasty, these three holy Buddhist books took 16 years to complete. They were created as a way to win favor from the Buddha and overcome invading Mongols. The word "tripitaka" comes from Sanskrit, meaning "three baskets." The Tripitaka is the Buddhist equivalent of the Christian Bible or the Muslim Koran. The 81,340 blocks include 6,791 volumes. Each wooden block is 68cm (27 in.) wide, 25cm (10 in.) long, and 3cm (1¼ in.) thick with wood fixed at each end to maintain balance and lacquer applied to prevent corrosion. The oldest engraved wooden block characters in the world (over 770 years old), theyt contains a comprehensive collection of the Buddhist Tripitaka.

Not only are the Tripitaka Koreana housed here in the four halls of the Janggyeong Panjeon, but so too are several public and private treasures, including almost 3,000 other wooden printing blocks of Buddhist scriptures, carved during the Goryeo Dynasty (between 1100 and 1350). They are stored in small, locked halls in the courtyard around the Janggyeong Panjeon and you'll have to peer in through small slats to see them.

If you arrive around sundown, wait a bit on the temple grounds and you can see and hear the drums and the gongs played by the monks.

For a complete experience, you can do a temple stay at Haeinsa (see box below).

10 Chiin-li, Gaya-myeon, Hapcheon-gun, Gyeongsangnam-do. (✆) **055/934-3000.** Admission ₩3,000 adults, ₩2,000 teens, ₩1,000 children, free for seniors 65 and over and kids 6 and under. Parking ₩4,000. Daily 8am–6pm. From the Daegu Seobu Bus Terminal, take a bus bound for Haeinsa and get off at the last stop. Buses run every 20 min. and the ride takes an hour.

Changnyeong

Changnyeong is a small town in a county of the same name with a rich history, located between Daegu and Masan.

A few hundred meters to the north of the town center is a group of ancient mounds from the Gaya period, which are similar to those in Goryeong (northwest of here).

Across the road from the tombs is the **Changnyeong Museum** (℡ 055/530-2246), with an entrance fee of ₩560 for adults, ₩270 for children. On-site is a life-size replica of one of the tombs so that you can see what it looks like on the inside.

One of the oldest relics in town is a stone tablet from the 500s, marking the boundary of the town after Shilla King Jinheung defeated the Gaya Kingdom. Although it's not much to look at now, it is one of the oldest written tablets on the peninsula.

Bugok Oncheon (Bugok Hot Springs) ★ NATURAL ATTRACTION One of the best hot springs in the country, the Bugok Oncheon is located at the foot of Deokamsan. The tourist complex includes a handful of hotels, a small zoo, botanical gardens, and a shopping center. One of the few oncheons that contain sulfur, it contains many other minerals that are supposed to have health benefits. The hot springs themselves have an average temperature of about 172°F (78°C), hot enough to boil an egg. In fact, they serve eggs boiled in the hot springs at the Bugok Tourist Hotel. The largest facility is **Bugok Hawaii** (www.bugokhawaii.co.kr). There is a festival to promote the hot springs every year in October.

233 Geomun-li, Bugok-myeon, Changnyeong-gun, Gyeongsangnam-do. ℡ **055/536-6331.** Admission ₩33,000 ages 19 and up, ₩29,000 ages 7–19, ₩25,000 ages 3 to 7. Daily 6am–9pm; water park 8am–11pm. From Seoul's Nambu Express Bus Terminal, take a bus for Bugok, which runs at 9:45am, 2:45pm, 4pm, and 5:05pm and takes 5 hr. The spa is a 5-min. walk from the Bugok Bus Terminal.

Upo Wetlands ★★★ NATURAL ATTRACTION The largest swamp area in South Korea, the wetlands stretch across three counties and 13 villages. This primitive marsh, which is made up of four smaller, connected marshes, was created about 140 million years ago. There are over 1,000 different species of flora and fauna living in the wetlands. It is beautiful in the early morning or early evening when a light fog-like rain descends upon the waters. The late summer months (Aug–Sept) bring out the fireflies and the winter attracts a variety of migrating birds to the area.

Yibang-myeon/Yueu-myeon/Daehap-myeon areas of Changnyeong-gun, Gyeongsangnam-do. ℡ **055/530-2690.** http://upo.or.kr. Admission ₩2,000 adults, ₩1,500 teens, ₩1,000 children. Tues–Sun 9am–5pm (last admission at 5pm), closed Monday and Jan 1. From the Changnyeong Intercity Bus Terminal, take a bus headed for Yibang-myeon and get off at Somoak Jangjae Village (15-min. ride); walk 5 min. toward the sign that reads GREEN UPO'S FRIEND. You can also take a bus from the Yonshin Bus Terminal (a 5-min. walk from the Changnyeong Intercity Bus Terminal) that is bound for Hanteo and Sejin-li. This bus goes directly to the Upo wetlands parking lot (takes 20–30 min.).

Hadong ★★★

The Hadong region and the small village of Agyang are known for the green tea plants that grow wild on the foot of Jirisan. The green tea has been growing here for over 1,300 years, growing naturally along the gentle slopes of the mountains. Known as the King's Tea, the high-quality leaves were grown for royal teacups for centuries. The farmers here still grow the tea naturally, using no fertilizers or pesticides and picking the leaves by hand. The tea fields line the slopes on either side of the Seomjingang (Seomjin river), which flows by Agyang village.

The best time of year is spring, when the cherry blossoms are in full bloom and the newest leaves from tea plants are picked for the best brew. Unfortunately, the secret's out, so you'll have to fight the hordes of Korean tourists who come here by the bus load, especially during the **Hadong Wild Tea Cultural Festival,** which happens here for 5 days each May.

If you decide to visit in the fall, you can sample the Daebong persimmon, a dried persimmon, which has also been grown for royalty, but only since the early Joseon Dynasty.

No matter what time of year, Agyang's **Hwagae Jangteo** ★★★ 🎁 (Hwagae Street Market) will be going on. This open-air market specializes in medicinal herbs and dried goods grown from the region. The small stalls are run by local farmers with ceramic artisan shops and casual restaurants lining the outer edges. Open around sunrise and closing around sunset, the market is a rare glimpse into the older traditions in the area, including one artisan who still makes iron tools by hand.

Ssanggyesa (Ssanggye Temple) ★★ (☎ **055/833-1901,** 208 Unsu-li, Hwagye-myeon, Hadong-gun, www.ssanggyesa.net, Korean only) is also worth a visit (especially since the bus that runs to Ssanggyesa stops in Agyang). Originally constructed in 723, the temple was destroyed like many others during the Imjin Waeran (1592–98), but was rebuilt in 1632. The main building dates back to the mid-Joseon period. To the east of the main building, there's a great Ma-aebul, an image of the Buddha engraved in a hollowed part of a rock. It is said that Monk Jimgam, who studied Buddhist music in China, watched the fish swimming in the Seomjingang and composed the "paleumryul" (eight tones and rhythms) of Korean Buddhist music. It is also said that another man, Kim Daeryeom, brought seeds from China and planted the first tea shrubs here under the order of Shilla King Heungdeok. Admission to the temple costs ₩2,500 for adults, ₩1,000 for teens, and ₩500 for children; free for children 6 and under and seniors 65 and over. Parking costs ₩2,000 to ₩5,000. The temple is open daily 4:30am to 6pm.

There are a few motels in Agyang just up the road from the Hwagae Jangteo, as well as a handful of hotels along the mountain road on either side of the Seomjin River.

Although this is a tea-growing area, the local cuisine never incorporated the green leaves into their dishes, since they were too busy sending their harvests to the kings. Instead, the specialties of the region are tiny freshwater clams and mitten crabs, which are collected from the Seomjingang. A good place to try the local cuisine is **Gangnam Matjib** (☎ **055/884-4791,** which is just a 100m (328-ft.) walk up the river from the Hwagae Street Market.

To get to Agyang from Seoul, take a bus to Hadong from Seoul Nambu Terminal. There are eight buses daily and the 4½-hour ride costs about ₩26,200. From Hadong Bus Terminal, take a bus bound for Ssanggyesa and get off at Agyang. From the Busan Seobu Bus Terminal, there are two buses a day that go to Ssanggyesa. The ride takes about 3 hours.

If you'd rather travel by train, there is only one daily Mugunghwa train that goes to Hadong from Seoul Station. It starts at 9:35am, takes nearly 9 hours, and will cost ₩32,200.

About an hour from Hadong by bus is **Cheonghak-dong** ★★ ("Blue Crane Village"), a once-remote village in Jirisan that didn't have any electricity or even a road leading up to it until the early 1990s. Unfortunately, their neo-Confucian lifestyle has been disturbed by the introduction of television and contact with the outside world. However, they still live in traditional hanok and continue to follow their cultish beliefs.

Just down the road from the village (about a 20-min. walk) is **Samseong-gung ★★★**, the "Palace of the Three Sages," dedicated to the three originators according to Korea's foundation myth—Hwanin, Hwaneung, and Dan-gun. You can't miss the museum building at the entrance, which has a huge blue crane incorporated into the roof. Visitors are supposed to hit the gong three times and wait for a guide. The guide gives a short talk (in Korean only, unfortunately), explaining the rules for visiting. The "palace" shows a glimpse of Korea's cultural history, its Daoist roots, and its ancient shamanistic rituals. If you're lucky enough to be visiting during the third day of the 10th month of the year (usually sometime in early Oct), you can see the **Cheonje Festival** here.

There are five buses daily from Hadong-eup to Cheonghak-dong, 8:30am, 11am, 1pm, 2:30pm, and 7pm. Ask the bus driver when he will be back so that you can time your trip back.

The rest of Jirisan National Park is covered in the Jeolla-do chapter.

Hallyeo Haesang (Maritime National Park)

Hallyeo Maritime National Park (© 055/831-2114) is spread over Sacheon-si, Geojae-si, Tongyeong-si, Hadong-gun, and Namhae-gun of Gyeongsangnam-do and over Yeosu-si of Jeollanam-do. It covers an area (72.3% of which is water) ranging from Geoje-do in Gyeongsangnam-do to Jeollanam-do, including an archipelago, Bijin-do, and the Haegeum River. Although we've included detailed information in the Tongyeong and Yeosu section, here's an overview of the park here.

Designated a national park in 1968, it is South Korea's only maritime national park. It includes parts of the southern coast and many islands including Namhae-do and Geoje-do (see below). The best, but most crowded, time to visit the beaches is from July to mid-August when the waters are warm, but typhoon season hasn't kicked off yet. Spring and fall are also good to enjoy the varying seasons. Winter rarely sees visitors, so it may be nice for solitude, but boat schedules will be greatly reduced and bad weather may keep you from being able to venture out to far-flung islands.

From Tongyeong's bus terminal, you can take a bus to Geoje (runs every hour) and get off at **Haksong** to catch a ferry. There are several ferries that run there, but the one that goes around Haegeum River and Oedo is quite popular. From the **Jang-seungpo Ferry Terminal,** you can see a different part of the park by taking the bus bound for Hongpo that goes through Gujora, Mangchi, Hakdong, and Yeongcha.

The park's website is http://english.knps.or.kr.

NAMHAE ISLAND (NAMHAE-DO) ★★★

Namhae-do is located between Tongyeong and Yeosu, about a 5-hour drive south from Seoul. The island itself is the fourth largest in the country, and Namhae County is composed of 68 smaller islands.

The country's first suspension bridge (built in 1973) connects the island to the mainland (Namhae is the last stop on road 19). The view from the bridge is spectacular, but there are no places to stop and take it in. If you're driving into the area, be sure to take some time to enjoy the view from the coastal highway. The road hugs the edge of the island and has spectacular views of the sea, the surrounding islands, and the terraced rice paddies that wind up the side of the mountain.

Buses from Seoul leave for Namhae eight times a day, 8:30am to 7pm. The 4½-hour ride costs ₩22,200. Since Namhae is still a very rural area, buses here run infrequently. The best way to get around is by car. You can rent a car from Seoul and drive it to Namhae, or rent one upon arrival. There is only one company in Namhae, **Samsung Rent-a-Car** (*☎* **055/864-8300;** 443-4 Bukbyeon-li, Namhae-gun, Gyeongsangnam-do), located near the bus terminal. Rentals start at ₩70,000 and go up with size. You can also hire a taxi (many will be waiting in front of the bus terminal) for about ₩120,000 per day. Be sure to negotiate with your driver before embarking on your tour.

The tallest mountain in Namhae is **Geumsan (Silk Mountain),** which is sometimes called small Geumgang Mountain because of its relatively low height. Still, it is high enough to provide a wonderful view of the surrounding seascape. It was called Bogwangsan by the Buddhist Priest Wonhyo, who built the temple **Bogwangsa** here in the third year of Shilla King Munmu's reign. If you happen to overnight in the area, catch the sunrise from its peak. It's breathtaking.

On Geumsan, perched just below the summit, is the famed hermitage **Bori-am ★★★,** which is one of the three main holy sites in the country and a designated UNESCO World Heritage site. It is also one of the eight special shrines for the Bodhisattva of Compassion (there is a tall statue of her looking out into the water). People believe that if you faithfully pray here, your prayers will be granted. Regardless of your beliefs, the climb up to Bori-am is worth it for the gorgeous view. There is a ₩1,500 entrance fee.

One of Namhae's best destinations is **Sangju Beach ★★★,** a wide, sandy expanse with clean water, surrounded by the pine forest of Geumsan. The beach gets over a million visitors in the summer and is even crowded in the winter with training athletes. The beach has shower rooms, camping facilities, and parking available. You can take a bus from Daegu's Seobu Bus Terminal, with more frequent service in the summer. From Seoul, catch a bus from the **Nambu Bus Terminal** (off of subway line 3). Buses run daily from 8:30am to 7pm and take about 4½ hours. From the Namhae Gongyong Terminal, take a bus headed for Sangju Beach. It takes about 30 minutes. Behind the pine trees on the edge of the sand, there are several yeogwan and minbak available for overnight accommodations. More expensive during the summer, prices can be bargained down, usually ₩30,000 per person, off season.

About 4km (2½ miles) east of Sanju is **Songjeong Beach.** Similar in shape to its neighbor and usually less crowded, it is also an expansive sandy beach with shallow waters and a spectacular view. A more hidden and less crowded beach is **Wulpo Dudok,** which has less sand and more rocks (*mongdol*), tumbled into their round shapes by the waves. It's on the way to Gacheon from Nam-myeon.

Next to Songjeong is the small port town of **Mijo.** Watching the fishermen unload their catch and seeing the cases of freshly caught seafood in the fish market is quite a sight. This is also a great place to have a fresh meal of hwae from one of the small joints that serve it fresh from the nets of fishermen.

A similar but smaller fishing village is **Mulgeon,** which faces the **German Village** ("Dogil Maeul" in Korean; *☎* **010/3343-4537**; www.germanvillage.co.kr), a town built here by and for Koreans returning from working in Germany. Next to the German Village is a new garden, where you can pay to see the well-designed landscapes of private homes for ₩5,000 for adults, ₩3,000 for teens, and ₩2,000 for children. You can even stay at a 2-bedroom pension here, starting at ₩143,000 on a weeknight.

There is a small forest on the shore, down the hill from the Dogil Maeul, planted by the local people 300 years ago to serve as protection from the high winds from the

Hallyeo Maritime National Park

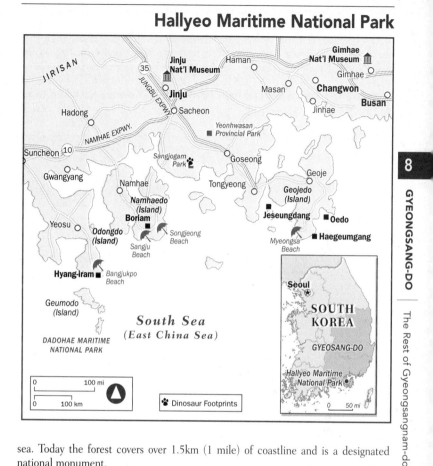

sea. Today the forest covers over 1.5km (1 mile) of coastline and is a designated national monument.

Another tiny fishing port is **Seongnu Village,** along the coastal road. Almost stopped in time, the fishermen of Seongnu continue their old customs and maintain folk traditions long discarded by modern fishermen. The hiking trail from here to Dalaengi Village has the best view of Hallyeo Haesang National Park, but it's not for the faint of heart. **Gacheon Dalaengi Maeul,** 898-5 Gonghyeon-li, Nam-myeon, Namhae-gun (*©* **055/863-3427**), is a more popular tourist site for its terraced rice paddies and the Gacheon Amsu, the town's guardian rock. Be sure to plan your trip for some time between spring and early fall, or you'll miss the green harvest and see only dirt terraces after all the rice and garlic have been farmed. Make your way down to the bottom to get a taste of the local makgeolli.

As far as accommodations are concerned, there are several minbak and yeogwan around popular tourist areas on the island. The one upscale facility is the **Hilton Namhae Golf and Spa Resort ★★** ☺, San 35-5 Deokwok-li, Nam-myeon, Namhae-gun (www.hiltonnamhae.com; *©* **055/860-0100;** fax 055/862-2677), which has an oceanside golf course, spa, restaurants, and cafes. Doubles start from ₩200,000 and suites start at ₩470,000. Some rates include breakfast and dinner.

The local delicacy on Namhae is *galchi hwae* (raw hairtail fish), which is caught in the South Sea, June through November. Sometimes the smaller ones are served bones and all (chew them well). The best hwae restaurants can be found in Mijo, where you can enjoy the catch fresh from the boats. A couple of joints that specialize in galchi hwae are **Gongju Shikdang** (© 055/867-6728) and **Samheon Shikdang** (© 055/867-6498).

GEOJE-DO (GEOJE ISLAND)

Although Geoje-do is connected to Tongyeong by two land bridges, it's a separate city with its own attractions. The second-largest island in South Korea, its largest town is Sinhyeon. With several natural harbors, the second- and third-largest shipyards in the country are both located on the island. Other than the main island, Geoje City encompasses about 60 smaller islands, including **Oedo,** the most popular of the bunch.

The island's most crowded beach is **Hakdong Mongdol Beach,** named for its shape that some say looks like a crane (*hak*). Covered in tiny pebbles, the beach attracts many travelers, especially in the summer as families pitch tents in the nearby campgrounds. You can take an excursion ferry from here to Oedo via Haegeumgang. Other tour boats are available from Jangseungpo, Oehyeon, Gujora, Hakdong, Dojangpo, and Galgot-li.

Haegeumgang, the "diamond" of the south sea, has been designated an official green area of the national park. From this island made of rocks, the best views are at sunset and sunrise from either Ilwoll-bong or Lion Rock. Buses from Tongyeong's Intercity Bus Terminal run about eight times a day and take about 90 minutes. From either the Jangseungpo Ferry Terminal or the Jangseungpo Bus Terminal, take a Hongpo-bound bus and get off at Haegeumgang. Buses run only twice a day, unfortunately.

Although Geoje is a beautiful and peaceful island, the **P.O.W. Camp** (© 055/639-8125; www.geojeimc.or.kr/pow/index.htm) here reminds visitors of its turbulent history. Though a bit cheesy with overdone re-creations of battles and such, it is still a good educational resource for background on the Korean War. The original camp was closed after the 1953 armistice, but a park was created here in 1997. Remnants of the war—tanks, trucks, and the like—are on exhibit here. Open daily from 9am to 6pm, March through October, closing at 5pm November through February; entrance fees are ₩3,000 adults, ₩2,000 teens, ₩1,000 children and seniors, free for kids 6 and under.

About 4km (2½ miles) away from Geojo-do is **Oedo ★★★**, sometimes called "Paradise Island." In 1969, fisherman Lee Chang-ho discovered this small island while seeking refuge from the wind and waves. Since then, he and his wife have been bringing plants here by boatloads, creating the **Oedo Botania ★★★** (© 070/7715-3330; www.oedobotania.com), a beautiful, European-style garden. From the Jangseungpo Ferry terminal, you can catch a ferry to Oedo, which takes about 25 minutes. The ferries, run by a handful of companies, aren't on a regular schedule, but leave daily every 1 to 2 hours depending on the number of passengers. You can also take an excursion ferry (which takes longer, of course), that goes around Haegeumgang to Oedo. The island is open daily, except for Lunar New Year. On top of the ferry charge (which varies by company but runs to about ₩16,000 to ₩19,000 for adults), admission to the gardens is ₩8,000 adults, ₩6,000 children, free for kids 6 and under.

Located between Dojangpo Village and Haegeumgang is the **Sinseondae Observatory,** from where you can get a wonderful view of the surrounding ocean. Found off the coastal highway, a staircase leads up to the lookout point. April and May are the best months to take in the scenery, as the skies are clearer and yellow rape flowers are in bloom then. You can take a ferry to Sinseondae Observatory from Jangseungpo. From the Geoje-do Bus Terminal, it's a 50-minute ride.

Dojangpo Maeul is a quaint fishing village between Hakdong and Hamok beaches. In the springtime, pack a picnic lunch and hike up the hill overlooking the village. From here, you can look out over the ocean, enjoy the ocean breezes, and watch the goats grazing on the grassy hillside.

Goseong ★★★ ☺

Goseong County (✆ **055/673-4101;** http://eng.dinopark.net) is located north of Tongyeong and between Sacheon, Masan, and Jinju. This is the best place in South Korea to see dinosaur footprints. Since the discovery of the sauropod prints in 1982, about 4,300 fossilized footprints of dinosaurs have been found along this 6km (3¾-mile) coastal rock bed, formed about 100 million years ago, during the early and mid-Cretaceous period. Along with sites in Colorado and on the western coast of Argentina, Goseong is one of the world's top three sites for dinosaur prints.

The **Goseong Dinosaur Museum,** 85 beonji, Deokmyeong-li, Hain-myeon, Goseong-gun (✆ **055/832-9021;** http://museum.goseong.go.kr), has exhibits that explain the movements and habits of certain species in the area. It also houses several fossils and skeletons. In front of the building is a giant model of the Mesozoic Era herbivore brachiosaurus, made of steel truss mosaic tiles. The museum is open daily 9am to 6pm March to October, until 5pm November to February.

The real excitement is outside of the museum on the rocky shores nearby. On the coastal area near Sangjog-am are the actual prints from creatures long extinct. The footprints found here can be classified into 12 types. They include ornithopods that walked on two legs, iguanodons and sauropods that walked on four legs, and carnivorous theropods. Dinosaur eggs were also discovered at six sites along the coast of Goseong-eup and Samsan-myeon. The eggs were from three types of dinosaurs, and a nest was discovered, almost intact with very little damage. There is conjecture that Goseong may have been a nesting ground for a variety of dinosaurs.

With Uhang-li and Haenam, Goseong has the highest number of bird footprints found in Korea. These bird prints from the Mesozoic Era led to the discovery of new species, and more research is underway. Not only are the footprints impressive, but the view from **Sangjog-am (Sangjokam) County Park** is also quite spectacular. Be careful when crossing over the wet rocks to the cave, Sangjok-gul, since it can get a bit slippery from the seawater. Although the area is open daily 24 hours year-round, be sure to call the **Korea Travel Phone,** ✆ **1330,** to find out when low tide is so that the dino prints won't be underwater.

There are only three buses daily to Sangjog-am from the Goseong Bus Terminal (8am, 11:10am, and 4:55pm). The schedule is subject to change, so check on that as well before making a special trip. Buses from Sacheon run a bit more frequently to Sangjog-am County Park. Goseong county's official site is http://eng.goseong.go.kr.

On the way in or out of town, stop in for a lunch of *jjajangmyeon* (black-bean noodles) at **Jangbaeksan Suta Sonjjajang ★★★ 🍴☺** (✆ **055/673-8030;** 841-1 beonji, Baedun-li, Hwaehwa-myeon, Goseong-gun). For about ₩6,000 per person, you are treated to a meal and a show as the chef spins and pulls the dough into noodles in just minutes, right before your eyes.

If you want to overnight in the area, there are plenty of motels, pensions, and min-bak in the area. Motels and homestays will run to about ₩30,000 to ₩50,000 per night, but a pension stay will be better for families. A couple of good options in the area are the **Cloud Pension** (www.cloudpension.com; ✆ **055/673-9111;** 865-1 Dongsan-li, Sangni-myeong, Goseong-gun) with rooms in the ₩70,000 to ₩270,000 range and the **Drama In Pension** (www.drama-in.com; ✆ **055/673-8580;** 284-1 Danghang-li, Hoehwa-myeon, Goseong-gun) with rooms in the ₩85,000 to ₩155,000 range. Rooms usually sleep 2 to 4 and up.

BUSAN

South Korea's second-largest city, Busan is filled with towering apartments, crowded streets, and a modern subway system. It's the largest port in the country and the third largest in the world. Located in the Nakdong River Valley, Busan has the ocean on one side, mountains on the other, and hot springs scattered throughout. Called South Korea's summer capital, the thousands of rented umbrellas on Busan's six beaches make it impossible to even see the sand. So it's not the place for a peaceful trip in July or August. Off season winters, however, bring quieter shores and a less hurried atmosphere.

Because Busan grew up along its coastline, the city is unusually long and has more than one city center. The area around Busan's ports bustles with energy as boats arrive daily from all over Asia, and nearby **Nampo-dong** is home to the massive Jagalchi seafood market. The shores of **Haeundae** boast some of the country's finest resort hotels, while the **Seomyeon** neighborhood is a paradise for shoppers. The old city center, **Dongnae,** in the north toward the mountains, is a great place to experience hot springs and Korean-style bathhouses.

Choose a fish for your lunch from the bubbling tanks at **Jagalchi Market.** At night, the cafes along **Gwangalli** Beach fill with people coming to see the lights of the Gwangan Bridge. When you eat, you'll get to enjoy the genuine warmth and hospitality of the Busan people.

ORIENTATION
Arriving & Departing
BY PLANE
The city of Busan is served by **Gimhae International Airport** (**PUS;** ☏ **051/974-3114;** www.airport.co.kr/doc/gimhae_eng), which is located about 35 minutes outside of the city, across the Nakdong River.

Korean Airlines (www.koreanair.com) and **Asiana Airlines** (us.fly asiana.com) are the major national airlines that fly in and out of Gimhae. International flights are available via Japan Airlines, China Eastern Airlines, China Northwest Airlines, Air China, Philippine Airlines, SAT Airlines, and Vladivostok Airlines from cities in Cambodia, China, Japan, Russia, Thailand, the Philippines, and Vietnam. A **standard cab** to the city center costs about ₩30,000 including tolls. **Deluxe cabs,** which are black, cost more (₩45,000), but the drivers all speak English, accept credit cards, and will give a receipt.

Airport buses (☏ **051/972-8653**) cost ₩1,000 to ₩2,000 and run daily every 10 to 40 minutes, depending on which line you take. There is no direct line on the subway to the airport, but you can take bus no. 307 to and from **Deokcheon Station** (line 2, exit 6). **Limousine buses** (© 051/973-9617) start at ₩7,000 and run daily every 30 minutes or so to most parts of the city, including the Lotte Hotel, Haeundae Station, and the Westin Chosun Beach Hotel.

Buses from Incheon Airport can be taken from stop 10C on the first floor about every 2 hours from 8:20am to 10:20pm. The 6-hour journey costs ₩42,400 to ₩46,600.

BY TRAIN

You can take the **KTX express train** from Seoul Station, which takes 2 hours and 50 minutes, or the **Saemaul train,** which takes 4 hours and 10 minutes. The standard KTX fare is ₩55,500, while the first-class fare is ₩77,700 and the standard Saemaul fare is ₩41,100. The **Mugunghwa train** takes just under 5 hours and costs ₩27,700. Kids' fares are half the adult rate. The train station (© 051/440-2497) is located in central Busan. From there, you can hop on the subway, take a bus, or catch a cab to your hotel or any other destination within the city.

To get to the train station from the city center on the subway, take line 1 to stop 13. Follow the signs to exit into the station plaza. The Gyeongbu line travels north to Seoul and the Gyeongjeon line goes west along the southern coast to Mokpo.

BY BUS

There are two main bus stations in Busan. The major one is the **Busan Bus Complex,** which is in the same building as the Busan Dongbu Gyeongnam Intercity Bus Terminal (with buses that travel to the east) at Nopo-dong. From there, you can pick up subway line 1 to get into the city. The other is **Seobu Intercity Bus Terminal** (which has buses to the west), which is on subway line 2, stop 227 (take exit 1). Buses run daily about every 15 minutes to and from major cities throughout South Korea.

Buses from the **Seoul Express Bus Terminal** to the Busan Bus Complex start running at 6am and run daily every 20–30 minutes until 1:30am, with ticket prices ranging from ₩22,000 to ₩36,000. Daily buses departing from **DongSeoul Bus Terminal** to the Busan Bus Complex start running at 6am and run 10 times daily until 11:50pm, costing ₩22,200 to ₩36,100.

BY BOAT

You can take a boat to **Busan Port International Ferry Terminal** from cities in South Korea, China, and Japan (© 1544-1114; http://foreign.busanpa.com/Service. do?id=engmain). The terminal is centrally located, so once you disembark, you'll find it very easy to get to your hotel. You can catch the subway, local buses, or a taxi from the port.

There is also a coastal pier, **Yeonan Ferry Terminal** (for domestic ferries), and an international pier. Both are located in Juang-dong. Ships from the domestic pier daily arrive from and depart to Jeju-do, Changsungpo, Geoje-do, Okpo, Gohyun, Haegeumgang, Hungmu, Tongyeong, and Yeosu. You can also catch a tour boat to explore Jeju and the many islands of the **Hallyeo Maritime National Park**. From the international pier, you can also catch ferries to Fukuoka (Hakata), Izuhara, Osaka, Shitakatsu, and Shimonoseki in Japan and Yodai in China. Keep in mind that whether or not the ships actually sail is completely dependent on the weather, so make sure to confirm your reservations in advance with **Busan Information for Coastal Tours** 16, Jung-ang-dong 5-ga, Jung-gu (© 051/469-0116 or -0117). Japan doesn't

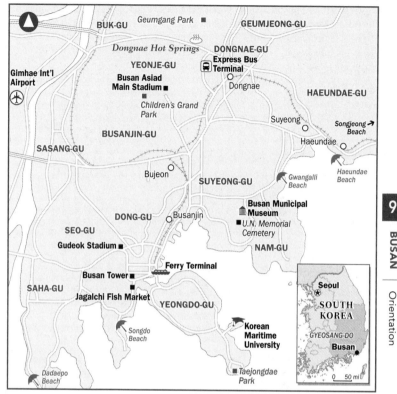

BUK-GU Geumgang Park ■ GEUMJEONG-GU

Dongnae Hot Springs DONGNAE-GU

YEONJE-GU Express Bus Terminal

Gimhae Int'l Airport

Busan Asiad Main Stadium ■ Dongnae

Children's Grand Park HAEUNDAE-GU

BUSANJIN-GU Suyeong Songjeong ➚ Beach

SASANG-GU Haeundae

Bujeon Haeundae Beach

SUYEONG-GU Gwangalli Beach

Busan Municipal 🏛 Museum

DONG-GU Busanjin

SEO-GU U.N. Memorial Cemetery

Gudeok Stadium ■ NAM-GU

Ferry Terminal

Busan Tower ■ Seoul ★

SAHA-GU Jagalchi Fish Market SOUTH KOREA

YEONGDO-GU GYEOSANG-DO

Songdo Beach Korean Maritime University Busan ●

Dadaepo Beach Taejongdae Park 0   50 mi

require visas for short (less than 90 days) visits by citizens of the U.S., U.K., Canada, or Australia. China, however, requires visas even for travelers in transit.

The following ferry companies operate from Busan passenger port: **Dongyang Express Ferry Co.,** Jeju (✆ 051/464-2266); **Gukje Dae-ho Development Co.,** Jeju (✆ 051/464-6601); **Gukje Tong-un Co.,** Jeju (✆ 051/464-2228); **Semo Co.,** Changsungpo, Gohyun, Sungpo, Okpo, Chungmu, Yosu, Saryangdo, Samcheonpo, and Namhae (✆ 051/469-3851); **Shimonoseki Ferry Co.,** Shimonoseki, Japan (✆ 051/463-3161); **Koryo Ferry Co.,** Fukuoka, Japan (✆ 051/466-7799); **Hanguk Express Ferry Co.,** Fukuoka, Japan (✆ 051/465-6114); and **Chinsung Co. Ltd.,** Yunae, China (✆ 051/441-888).

You can get to the boat terminal by taking the subway to Jungang-dong Station (line 1, exit 12). It's one stop from the Busan Train Station. Bus nos. 8, 8-1, 11, 70, 88-1, 97, 101, 109, 139, 190, 240, 302, 309, and 507 all go to the port.

Visitor Information

Good tourist information in English is available at the Gimhae Airport. The office on the first floor of the international terminal is open daily from 9am to 5pm (✆ 051/973-2800). The **Busan Tourist Information Center** office (✆ 051/973-4607;

http://english.busan.go.kr) on the first floor of the domestic terminal is open daily from 9am to 9pm.

There are also several tourist information booths throughout the city. The easiest to find is the one at **Busan Station** (subway line 1, ✆ **051/441-6565**), located next to the ticket counters inside the terminal. Most are open Tuesday to Saturday 9am to 9pm, and Sunday and Monday 9am to 5pm. You'll also find visitor information on the first floor of the **International Ferry Terminal** (✆ **051/465-3471**; daily 8am– 5pm); on the first floor of **Busan City Hall** (✆ **051/888-3527**; daily 9am–6pm); and in **Haeundae Beach,** 629-3 Woo-1(il)-dong, Haeundae-gu (✆ **051/749- 5700**; daily 9am–6pm). Tourist information in English is also available by dialing ✆ **1330** and the foreigner's service center at ✆ **051/441-9685.** The city's official site is at http://english.busan.go.kr.

City Layout

Busan is located in the Nakdong River Valley, and mountains separate some of the city's districts. Mt. Geumjeong looms on the western side, with its hiking trails, views, and the temple, Beomeosa. The city's expansive beaches, the most popular being Haeundae, Gwangalli, and Songjeong, attract visitors year-round, but are positively crawling in the summertime. Its traditional markets and shopping districts are found in Nampo-dong and Seomyeon (the "new downtown").

Busan Neighborhoods in Brief

Songjeong On the far eastern side of the city lies its third-most-popular beach. The northern, rocky part of this shoreline attracts fishermen, but the expansive sandy part draws big beach crowds—though not nearly as big as the crowds that flock to the beaches of Haeundae and Gwangalli. That's because Songjeong is a bit out of the way. Still, it's worth a visit, and early risers should try to catch the sunrise from Haedong Yong-gungsa (p. 311), the temple perched on the rocky cliffs above.

Haeundae Home to the most famous and frequented beach in all of South Korea, Haeundae attracts several hundred thousand visitors annually. Major resort hotels are perched above the sand here, and a few offer the rare experience of soaking in an oceanside hot spring. Though it's a bit far from the shore, this neighborhood offers both budget accommodations and a ton of shopping options.

Gwangalli Near Haeundae, the Gwangalli neighborhood is also a hot beach resort location. Its open-air cafe street draws thousands of visitors with its neon lights and views of the Gwangan Bridge. Popular with the younger crowd, the area has galleries, a cultural center, and plenty of opportunities to shop. The beach's outdoor stage is also the center of rock concerts and various festivals throughout the year.

Nampo-Dong/Gwangbok-Dong/Jung-Gu The city's major markets are here, including the Jagalchi Market, the Dried Seafood Market, and the Herb Market, and there are inexpensive *yeogwan* (inns) within walking distance of them all. The **Busan International Film Festival (BIFF)** is also held every September in (where else?) BIFF Square. Theater lovers will find small, funky productions being put on here, though sadly most are in Korean.

Yeong-do/Taejongdae The island of Yeong-do separates the two halves of Busan harbor. The center of the island is residential, while its harborfront is rather industrial. But the island's southernmost tip belongs to Taejongdae, famous for its views of the Korea Strait—on clear days, you can see all the way to Japan.

Songdo The first of Busan's beaches to be used for recreation, it's less popular (and less dramatic) than the beaches in Haeundae and Gwangalli, so it's best for those looking to avoid huge crowds (though good luck doing that anywhere in July–Aug). Songdo is famous for Amnan Park and its raw fish restaurants; this area is ideal to relax in after a long day of sunbathing.

Eulsuk-do/Dadaepo This island in the middle of the Nakdong River channel is the perfect resting place for migratory birds. A sanctuary for these avian visitors is found on the southeastern part of the island. On the western peninsula nearby is Dadaepo beach, the widest in the city. There is also a cultural center, an outdoor concert hall, a drive-in theater, and an inline skating rink.

Seomyeon The busiest area in Busan, the Seomyeon neighborhood is a sort of second downtown thanks to its open markets, underground shopping arcade, and cheap eateries (especially those in Mokja Golmok [Let's Eat Alley]). It's popular any night of the week with college students and young professionals. This is a good area to stay in if you're interested in shopping and eating more than sunbathing.

Dongnae Located north of Seomyeon, the Dongnae district houses one of the oldest known *oncheon* in the country. This is a great place to experience South Korea's hot spring and spa culture. The area is also home to Busan (Pusan) National University (PNU). Not surprisingly, the PNU area (Busan Daehak-ap) has the city's newer bars, cafes, and nightclubs.

Geumjeong Geumjeong is home to one of the most famous Buddhist temples in South Korea, **Beomeosa** (p. 311). A hike along the walls of the **Geumjeong Fortress** (p. 313) or a visit to the 500 wisteria vines is a great way to get away from the hustle and bustle of the city below. Pack a picnic lunch and don your hiking boots to enjoy a bit of nature and the view.

GETTING AROUND

BY SUBWAY Busan's extensive subway system makes it possible to go just about anywhere within the city. There are three lines and announcements are made in both English and Korean. The trains start running daily at 5:10am and stop at 12:45am. To use the subway, you can buy single tickets at automatic ticket machines. (**Tip:** Single ticket machines accept only ₩1,000 notes or coins, so be sure to carry small notes. They will, however, give you coin change.) One-way fares are ₩1,200 for travel in one "section" (up to a 10km/6¼-mile distance) and ₩1,400 for two sections (distances over 10km/6¼ miles). Fares are reduced for teens and kids. Be sure to hold onto your ticket because you'll need it to exit the subway.

If you plan on taking the subway or bus extensively, you should get either the **Hanaro** (② 051/868-7621) or **Mybi card** (② 1588-8990), which you can purchase for a minimum of ₩5,000 and refill as needed. Cards are sold at bus stops, subway ticket offices, or **Busan Bank** (www.busanbank.co.kr). Fares with either card are ₩1,100 for travel in one section and ₩1,300 for two sections. At the end of your trip, you can get a refund of any unused fares by showing your passport and returning the card at Pusan Bank.

You can also get a **1-day metro ticket** for ₩4,000, good for unlimited rides until the last train of the day. You can also get a ticket that's good for 7 days (up to 20 rides) for ₩19,000 or a 30-day ticket for ₩50,000 good for up to 60 rides on the subway only. The site for the Busan Metro is www.subway.busan.kr/english/main.

BY TAXI Busan has three types of taxis—regular, call, and deluxe taxis. You can flag a **regular taxi** at a taxi stand or along any street. You'll know a taxi is available by the lit sign on top or a red card on the right side of the dashboard. **Call taxis** can be

Busan Subway

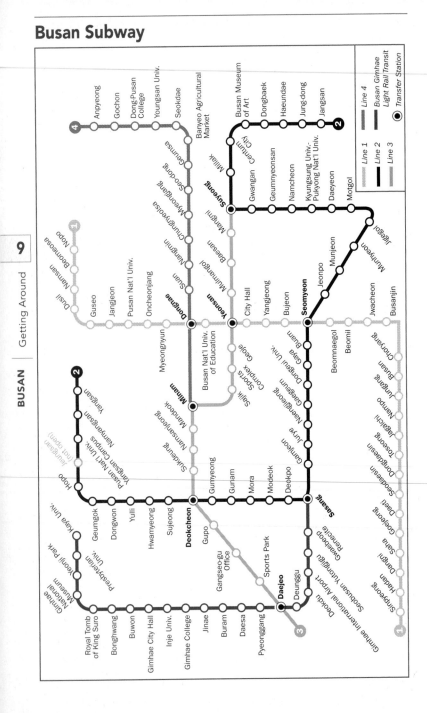

called from hotels or other locations. Some drivers of call taxis speak English, although you shouldn't count on that, as most do not. **Deluxe taxis** are black and charge more than twice the regular fare. Deluxe taxi drivers generally speak English, take credit cards, and provide in-car phones. They can be flagged down anywhere, but can be found more easily at airports, hotels, tourist sites, taxi stands, and transportation terminals. The base fare for regular taxis starts at ₩2,200 and goes up in ₩100 increments, depending on distance and time. There is a 20% increase in fees at night. Deluxe taxis start at ₩4,500 and go up in ₩200 increments. Their fares don't go up at night.

BY BUS   There are three types of local buses in Busan: the regular (which are blue and white and make more stops), the express (which are red and white and make fewer stops), and the late-night bus. Local buses have destinations written in both English and Korean with recorded messages that announce the next stop. Look at the bus route and plan ahead, especially if the buses are crowded. Once you're on the bus, push the button to let the driver know you want to get off and always exit the buses through the back door. Bus drivers generally don't speak English.

Bus fares can be paid with cash (exact change required), tokens, bus passes, or a Hanaro or Mybi card (which can be used on both buses and subways). Cash fare for regular buses is ₩1,200 or ₩1,080 with a Hanaro card, Mybi card, or bus tour pass. For the express bus, fare is ₩1,800 and ₩1,700, respectively. The late-night buses are ₩2,200 cash and ₩2,100 with a card. All buses issue free transfers within 30 minutes. For more info, contact the **Busan Bus Transportation Association** (☎ 051/508-9200; http://bus.busan.go.kr, Korean only).

BY CAR   Busan is easier to navigate by car than Seoul. You will still need an international driver's license, your national driver's license, your passport, and must be over 21. Renting a car in Busan is not cheap, but can be convenient if you plan to travel outside the city to areas where the subway or buses don't go. You can rent a car for as few as 6 hours or for several days. Prices start at ₩45,000 for a small-size car for 6 hours or ₩80,000 per day, with higher rates for larger cars and lower daily rates if you rent for more days. There are dozens of car-rental agencies throughout the city, but only a handful operate from Gimhae Airport. They are **Avis Rent-a-Car** (☎ 051/941-7400); **KT Kumho** (☎ 051/941-8000); **Jeju Rent Car** (☎ 051/972-4777); and **Samsung Rent Car** (☎ 051/973-6611). You can reserve your car online before you arrive, or ask your hotel desk to help you with a rental if you want a car just for a short while during your stay.

ON FOOT   Due to its size, Busan is not a city to explore solely on foot, but there are nice places to walk once you get there by bus or subway. Areas around Gwangalli Beach and Yongdusan are especially nice for strolling. There are also wonderful hiking opportunities in the mountains and parks. See the "Hiking" section on p. 317.

[Fast FACTS] BUSAN

American Express   The American Express office is located on the ninth floor of the Busan Jung-ang Building #51, Daechang-dong 1-ga, Jung-gu (☎ **1588-7000**).

Banks, Foreign Exchange & ATMs   In general, ATMs are located at the airport, the train station, supermarkets, and at banks. Kookmin Bank,

Citibank, Korea Exchange Bank, and Chohung Bank all have international ATMs. Most ATMs provide service in Korean and English, but Citibank ATMs provide information in 11 languages. There are seven Citibank locations throughout Busan (☎ 051/621-0222; www.citibank.co.kr). Most ATMs operate 24 hours.

At banks in Busan, each customer takes a numbered ticket and waits until his or her number is called. If you want to exchange traveler's checks, make sure you have your passport, and if you are exchanging cash, you must visit a bank that is authorized for international exchange. Banks are open Monday to Friday 9:30am to 4:30pm and are closed on weekends and national holidays.

Car Rental See the "By Car" listing in the previous "Getting Around" section.

Cellphones KTF cellphones can be rented at Gimhae Airport and Busan's International Ferry Terminal. See Chapter 12 "Planning Your Trip to South Korea," for details.

Consulates Busan doesn't have an American consulate, but the **U.K.** honorary consulate (☎ (0)51/463-4630 and 070/8862-4100) is at 1401 Yoochang Building, Room 1401, Jungang-daero, Jungu.

Australia has an honorary consulate (☎ 051/647-1762) in room no. 802 of the Samwhan Officetel, 830-295, Bumil 2-dong, Dong-gu.

Canada has an honorary consulate at the Dongsung Chemical Co. Ltd., 472 Shin Pyung-dong, Saha-gu (☎ 051/204-5581). Take bus no. 2, 11, 98, 113, 138-1, 161, or 338 to the Dong-sung Chemical Co. Station.

They're open Monday through Friday 8-11:30am and 1 to 4:30pm.

Currency Exchange
You can change money at most Busan banks on weekdays—just look for the currency exchange desk. The **Korean Exchange Bank,** 89-1, Jung-ang-dong 4-ga, Jung-gu, is the most convenient place to exchange currency downtown. You'll also find currency exchange bureaus at the airport, at the train station, and in large shopping areas. It is more difficult to exchange traveler's checks, but most banks will accept hard currency, like U.S. dollars and British pounds. Be sure to have your passport and keep the receipt to change back any leftover currency you may have at the end of your trip.

Doctors & Dentists
Most of the nicer hotels have medical clinics staffed by registered nurses and have doctors on duty during specified hours or on call 24 hours. Otherwise, your concierge or consulate can refer you to an English-speaking doctor or dentist. In an emergency, dial ☎ 999 or 1339 or call one of the recommendations under "Hospitals," below.

Embassies & Consulates The **Australian Consul** is located at Room 802 Samwhan, Bumil 2-dong, Dong-gu (☎ 051/830-295). The **Australian Embassy** is at 1434-1, U 1-dong, Haeundae-gu (☎ 051/744-2281 or 051/647-1762; www.southkorea.embassy.

gov.au). The **Canadian Consulate** is at the Dongsung Chemical Co., 472 Shin Pyung-dong, Saha-gu or 32-1, 2-ga Daechang-dong, Jung-gu (☎ 051/246-7024 or 051/240-1813). The **U.K. Consulate** is at 25-2 Jung-ang-dong, Jung-gu (☎ 051/463-4630). The **New Zealand Consulate** can be found at 84-10, 4-ga, Jung-ang-dong, Jung-gu (☎ 051/464-5055). There is no American or British embassy in Busan.

Hospitals Several hospitals in Busan have doctors who speak English fluently. If you need medical help, try the **Good Gang-an Hospital,** 40-1 Namcheon-song, Suyeong-gu, easy to find if you take the subway to Geumnyeonsan Station (exit 4; ☎ 051/625-0900); or the **BNU Hospital,** 305 Gudeok-lo, Seogu, Ami-dong (☎ 051/240-7890), which you can get to by taking subway line 1 to Tosung-dong Station. There is a special receptionist for English speakers on the sixth floor.

Internet Access The city of Busan offers free Wi-Fi at 25 tourist locations, including Busan Station; Haeun-dae, Gwangailli, Songdo, and Songjeong beaches; the Geumjeong Sanseong; Yongdusan; and Jagalchi Market. Many of the high-end hotels and love motels in the city provide free Internet access in the rooms. If you don't have your own device, there are also hundreds of **PC** *bahngs* (**computer rooms**) that offer high-speed connections and charge between ₩500 and ₩2,000 per hour. Many are open 24 hours.

Laundry Most of the city's hotels have laundry facilities available. There are a few coin laundries in the city, but it's easier to find dry cleaners scattered around each neighborhood.

Maps Free city maps in English are available at tourist information centers located throughout the city. See "Visitor Information," earlier, for locations.

Newspapers & Magazines English print versions of two Korean newspapers, the **Korean Herald** (www.koreaherald.co.kr) and **The Korea Times** (http://times.hankooki.com) can be found at convenience stores, street stalls, hotels, and bus, train, and subway terminals. A good English-language magazine for what's going on around the city is **Busan Haps** (http://busanhaps.com). News magazines issued abroad can be found in most large hotel bookstores, but for more specialized journals or periodicals, visit the major bookstores. See the "Shopping" section for locations.

Pay Phones Public telephones are difficult to find in Busan. However, some phones take only coins, others accept calling cards, and some take credit cards. Charges start at ₩70 for 30 seconds. Toll and international calls' rates vary. Calling cards may be purchased at newsstands or convenience stores in ₩3,000, ₩5,000, or ₩10,000

denominations. To make an international collect call, dial 00799 for operator assistance.

Pharmacies Simple Western remedies like aspirin are most likely to be found in 24-hour convenience stores and the lobbies of high-end hotels. You can find pharmacies in any neighborhood, but none open 24 hours. Most display a large cross symbol (usually green), but all of them have the Korean word for medicine (약) on their windows.

Police The emergency number for the police is ✆ **112.** There are 14 police stations throughout the city of Busan. The Busan Police are under the jurisdiction of the national government, since all of South Korea is under one national police organization.

Post Offices There are 145 post offices and 80 postal agencies in the city, so it's not difficult to find one, especially since the signs are in English. They're all open 9am to 6pm weekdays, but only a handful are open 9am to 1pm Saturdays.

Restrooms There are free public restrooms available at most subway stations, bus terminals, train stations, and some tourist attractions. However, some restrooms in South Korea do not provide toilet paper or paper towels. It is best to carry a small packet of tissues with you at all times. You can buy them at any corner store or in vending machines outside some restrooms for ₩500. American-style fast-food

restaurants and large department stores have the best public restrooms.

Safety The crime rate is relatively low in all of South Korea. In Busan, you should take the usual precautions as you would in any major city in the world. Watch out for pickpockets and purse snatchers on public transportation, and exercise caution when traveling alone at night, especially around the port areas.

Taxes A value-added tax (VAT) of 10% is usually added to most goods and services. Most stores and restaurants just include it in their prices. In tourist hotels, the VAT is applied to rooms, meals, and services and is included on the bill. A TAX-FREE SHOPPING sign on a store means that you can get a refund on the VAT when you buy at that store. You must get a receipt, and get a stamp from the Customs officer; be prepared to show him or her the purchased item and the receipt. You can get a refund at the Cash Refund Office at the airport. For more info call **Global Refund** at ✆ **02/776-2170.** You must leave South Korea within 3 months from the date of purchase to receive the refund.

Water Drinking tap water in Busan is not advised. Most restaurants will offer water from a self-service water dispenser, which is fine to drink. Otherwise, bottled water is recommended. You can buy bottles at any corner store or tourist attraction for about ₩500.

Weather Located in the temperate monsoon zone and influenced by its seaside location, Busan has four distinct seasons. The city is relatively warm year-round and positively steamy in the summer, reaching up to 90°F (32°C) with high humidity. Its average annual temperature is 57°F (14°C), with average winter temperatures around 39°F (4°C). Weather information can be found on the city's site (http://english.busan.go.kr/main) or by dialing ✆ **131.**

WHERE TO STAY

Accommodations in Busan range from high-end beach resorts and rental condos to small yeogwan and love motels.

Although most of the upscale resorts are in Haeundae, there are a variety of motels and midpriced lodgings throughout the city. Make sure you specify that you want a room with a bed (*chimdae bahng*); otherwise, you'll end up with a Korean-style ondol room where you sleep on the floor on padded blankets (the floors are heated in the winter). Unless otherwise indicated, a 10% VAT will usually be added to prices quoted for high-end hotels. Lower-end motels quote flat fees that you pay upfront when you check in. High season in Busan is from mid-July to August, when the kids are out of school and the water becomes a comfortable temperature for swimming. Be sure to reserve a room in advance if planning a trip during that time. Otherwise, it's not difficult to just walk in and get a room in town.

Other than the accommodations listed below, two of Busan's temples offer overnight stays with an opportunity to meditate and participate in temple life. Spending a night at **Beomeosa** (✆ **051/508-3122**) costs ₩50,000 to ₩80,000 per night, which includes dinner and breakfast. The smaller, less famous **Hongbeopsa** (✆ **051/508-0345**) offers a cheaper stay at ₩20,000 per night. They ask that you make reservations at least 10 days in advance. Additional info about the temples can be found in the "Top Attractions" section, later in this chapter.

Songjeong

SongJung Hotel Located right next to Songjeong Beach, this is one of the larger hotels in the area—which is to say, not that large at all. The hotel doesn't have a lot of amenities, but the rooms are airy, clean, and largely unadorned. They have both oceanview and city-view rooms, but you'll pay extra for the seaside privilege. Even if you opt for a less expensive room, you'll still be within walking distance of the beach. The staff does not speak great English, but they are friendly and helpful.

297-9 Songjeong-dong, Haeundae-gu. www.songjunghotel.co.kr. ✆ **051/702-7766.** 60 units. ₩160,000 single/double, ₩220,000 and up for a suite. MC, V. **Amenities:** Restaurant; cafe; karaoke. *In room:* A/C, TV, minibar, fridge, hair dryer.

Haeundae

EXPENSIVE

Novotel Ambassador Busan ★ Good for both business and luxury travelers, the natural hot spring spa and golf center are a nice touch. With modern facilities, the Ambassador has contemporary dining available on-site. The rooms are spacious and airy with probably the best beds in the city. There is an extra charge for an oceanview room.

1405-16 Jung-dong, Haeundae-gu. www.novotelbusan.com. ✆ **051/743-1234.** Fax 051/743-1250. 327 units. ₩370,000 standard rooms, ₩700,000 suite. AE, DC, MC, V. **Amenities:** 3 restaurants; bar; lounge; cafe; pool; golf center; health club; Jacuzzi; sauna; concierge; babysitting; smoke-free rooms. *In room:* A/C, TV, minibar, hair dryer, Wi-Fi.

Haeundae

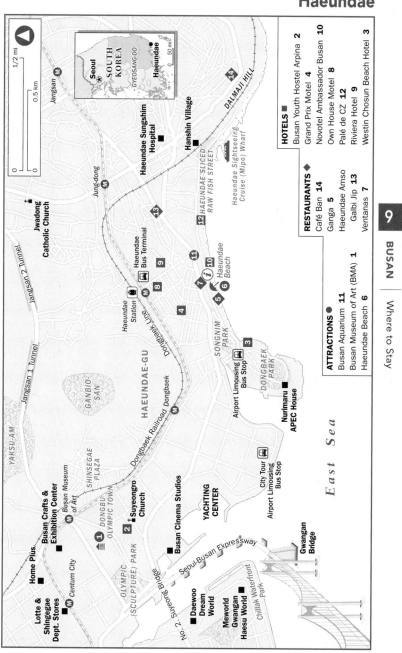

HOTELS ■
Busan Youth Hostel Arpina **2**
Grand Prix Motel **4**
Novotel Ambassador Busan **10**
Own House Motel **8**
Palé de CZ **12**
Riviera Hotel **9**
Westin Chosun Beach Hotel **3**

RESTAURANTS ◆
Café Ban **14**
Ganga **5**
Haeundae Amso
  Galbi Jip **13**
Ventanas **7**

ATTRACTIONS ●
Busan Aquarium **11**
Busan Museum of Art (BMA) **1**
Haeundae Beach **6**

Palé de CZ ★★★   This Korean-style condo stands 17 stories tall, right near the sand. It has a variety of rooms and suites with dining areas, flatscreen televisions and cozy beds with fluffy comforters. Ask for an oceanview to get the most out of the prime location and to see the boardwalk action below. Both beds and ondol rooms available.

1124-2 Jung-dong, Haeundae-gu. ✆ **051/746-1010.** 197 units. ₩200,000 standard room; suites ₩400,000 and up, 10% VAT not included. AE, MC, V. **Amenities:** Restaurant; bar; 2 lounges; cafe; pool; indoor golf; health club. *In room:* A/C, TV, kitchen, fridge.

Riviera Hotel ★ 🏷   Located on top of the Riviera Department store, it isn't the fanciest hotel in the neighborhood, but it is conveniently located, as it's within walking distance to both the subway and the beach. The rooms are basic, but serviceable, and the bathrooms are small, though they offer both a tub and a shower head. The English-speaking staff are exceedingly polite.

1380-14 Jung-1-dong, Haeundae-gu. ✆ **051/466-9101.** Fax 051/462-9101. 77 units. ₩200,000 standard room. AE, MC, V. Parking in the department store below. **Amenities:** Restaurant; room service. *In room:* A/C, TV, fridge, minibar, hair dryer, Wi-Fi.

Westin Chosun Beach Hotel ★★★   Built in 1978, this was Busan's first luxury hotel. With a prime location at the western end of Haeundae Beach, the hotel's rooms all have views of the ocean and Gwangalli Bridge or the forest park. It's worth it to pay a little extra and get the ocean view. The beds aren't as "heavenly" as the hotel claims, but they are comfortable. Most rooms and suites are spacious and Western-style, but they do have ondol rooms, which are also roomy. Staff levels of English vary from very good to passable, but everyone is polite and accommodating.

737 Woo 1-dong, Haeundae-gu 612-600. www.starwoodhotels.com. ✆ **051/749-7000.** Fax 051/742-1313. 290 units. ₩190,000 standard room; ₩460,000 deluxe oceanview suite with king bed. AE, DC, MC, V. Valet and free self-parking. **Amenities:** 3 restaurants; bar; lounge; cafe; pool; driving range; health club; spa; sauna; boat rentals; bikes; concierge; room service; babysitting; smoke-free rooms; Wi-Fi (in lobby). *In room:* A/C, TV, minibar, fridge, hair dryer, Internet (fee).

INEXPENSIVE

Busan Youth Hostel Arpina ★★ 📱☺   This hostel belongs to the Arpina chain (*arpina* is a Korean-made word, short for *areumdapge pieonada,* which translates as "bloom beautifully"), which advertises it as the world's best youth hostel. For the price, the convenient location and facilities can't be beat. Though the rooms are modest, they are modern, some with ocean views of Haeundae Beach and the Gwangalli Bridge. Ideal for families traveling together, ask for one of the twin or triple "business rooms" if you want a Western-style hotel room with a bed. Family rooms are suites (usually with one double bed), complete with dining table and kitchen. They don't take reservations online, but you can e-mail or call to book a room.

1417 Wu-dong, Haeundae-gu. www.arpina.com/english/00.main/main.asp. ✆ **051/731-9800.** Fax 051/740-3225. 469 beds. ₩27,000 bed in dorm room; ₩130,000 standard room. AE, MC, V. On-site parking. **Amenities:** Restaurant; bar; lounge; driving range; health club; pool; sauna; smoke-free rooms. *In room:* A/C, TV, fridge, hair dryer, Internet.

Grand Prix Motel 🏷   Of the many love motels in the area, this one is convenient to both the beach and the subway (about midway between the two), close enough to the main drag, but far enough to be away from most of the noise. In this older building, the rooms are still spacious and comfortable.

644-15 U-dong, Haeundae-gu. ✆ **051/755-5001.** 34 units. ₩40,000 standard room weekdays, ₩55,000 weekends. MC, V. *In room:* TV, A/C, fridge, Internet.

Own House Motel An upscale version of many of the love motels in South Korea, this motel has modern and comfortable rooms. Although a bit on the smaller side, the rooms have understated decor with clean-line and dark wood furnishings. There are only two types of rooms, deluxe and superior, and it's worth paying the ₩10,000 more for the superior.

541-22 U-1-dong, Haeundae-gu. ✆ **051/747-0935**. 34 units. ₩45,000 standard room weekdays, ₩60,000 weekends. MC, V. **Amenities:** Lounge. *In room:* TV/DVD, Internet.

Gwangalli

Hotel Homers ★★ 🛍 This boutique hotel is located near the bridge in Gwangalli. It has state-of-the art facilities, making it one of the most popular places for South Korean tourists. The building is 20 stories tall, with most rooms having seaside views. You can get a much better rate if you book online. Rooms are contemporary yet cozy, with comfortable beds (except in the Korean-style rooms, of course).

193-1 Gwangan-2-dong, Suyeong-gu. www.homershotel.com/english/community/site.php. ✆ **051/750-8000.** Fax 051/750-8001. 104 units. ₩210,000 and up for beachside standard rooms. AE, MC, V. On-site parking. **Amenities:** 2 restaurants; bar; lounge; health club; spa; sauna; smoke-free rooms. *In room:* A/C, TV, hair dryer, Internet.

Jung-gu/Nampo-Dong

Busan Tourist Hotel ★ 🛍 Convenient to both the Gukje and the Jagalchi markets, this hotel is located at the base of Yongdusan (near Busan Tower) so you'll have to walk up a bit of a slope to get to it. Built in 1974, the hotel is a bit dated, but convenient. Rooms are relatively spacious though they are sparsely decorated (ondol rooms are a bit larger than Western-style ones).

12 Donggwang-dong 2-ga, Jung-gu. ✆ **051/241-4301.** Fax 051/244-1153. 275 units. ₩120,000 standard room, ₩160,000 and up suite. MC, V. **Amenities:** 3 restaurants; cafe; health club; sauna; room service; bakery; karaoke lounge. *In room:* A/C, TV, fridge, hair dryer, Internet.

Commodore Hotel ★★ Inspired by palaces from the Joseon Dynasty, this 15-story hotel is hard to miss with its pagoda-like shape and traditional designs incorporated into a high-rise building. Inside, the rooms and amenities are modern. Added bonus: It's centrally located just minutes from the ferry terminals and the Jagalchi Market. If you have extra room in your budget, book a "corner suite" for the best deal in terms of space and amenities.

743-80, Youngju-dong, Jung-gu. www.commodore.co.kr/english/main/main.php. ✆ **051/466-9101.** Fax 051/462-9101. 314 units. ₩150,000 and up standard room, ₩330,000 and up suites. AE, DC, MC, V. On-site parking. **Amenities:** Restaurant; pool; health club; sauna; business center; room service. *In room:* A/C, TV, minibar, fridge, hair dryer, safe, Internet (fee).

Seomyeon

Blue Backpackers Hostel ★★ 🛍 Located inside the Gyeongnam Apartments, this spare but functional hostel is the best value you'll find in the city's center. It's within walking distance to shops, banks, and the subway. The free Internet, laundry, and breakfast (well, toast and coffee) are an added bonus. All beds and rooms have shared bathrooms and the owner speaks English. Be sure to book well in advance during high season in July and August (though the owner will let you sleep on the living room floor or sofa for ₩10,000 if you care less about privacy than about saving money).

Bldg. 106 #1802, Gyeongnam Apt., 944-1 Beomcheon 2-dong Jin-gu. www.busanbackpackers. com. ✆ **051/634-3962.** 14 beds. Cash only. ₩20,000 dorm-room bed; ₩35,000 single; ₩45,000 double. MC, V. **Amenities:** Living room w/TV/VCR; shared kitchen.

Jung-gu/Nampo-Dong

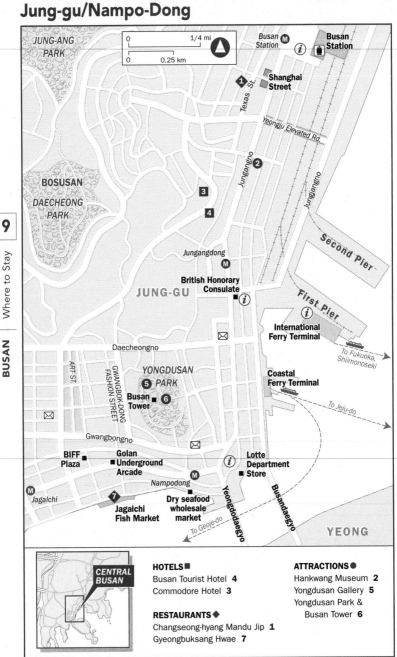

JUNG-ANG
PARK

0   1/4 mi
0   0.25 km

Busan Station

Busan Station

Shanghai Street

Texas St.

1

Yeongiu Elevated Rd.

Jungangno

2

BOSUSAN

DAECHEONG PARK

3

4

Second Pier

Junglangno

Jungangdong

British Honorary Consulate

JUNG-GU

First Pier

International Ferry Terminal

To Fukuoka, Shiimonoseki

Daecheongno

ART ST.

YONGDUSAN PARK

Coastal Ferry Terminal

To Jeju-do

GWANGBOK-DONG FASHION STREET

5

6

Busan Tower

Gwangbongno

BIFF Plaza

Golan Underground Arcade

Lotte Department Store

Jagalchi

Nampodong

Yeongdodaegyo

Busandaegyo

7

Jagalchi Fish Market

Dry seafood wholesale market

To Geoje-do

YEONG

CENTRAL BUSAN

HOTELS ■
Busan Tourist Hotel **4**
Commodore Hotel **3**

RESTAURANTS ◆
Changseong-hyang Mandu Jip **1**
Gyeongbuksang Hwae **7**

ATTRACTIONS ●
Hankwang Museum **2**
Yongdusan Gallery **5**
Yongdusan Park &
  Busan Tower **6**

Busan Lotte Hotel ★★   Built in 1997, this is one of the few luxury hotels convenient for business travelers who have work in the Busanjin area. It's close to shopping, subways, and the financial district. The tropical rainforest lounge is sort of fun and the Lotte department store is conveniently attached. The hotel is 43 stories high; you'll get a magnificent view of the city from any of the higher floors. The rooms aren't huge and the bathrooms are even smaller, especially for the price, but the staff speak English and are very professional.

503-15 Busanjin-gu, Bujin-dong. www.lottehotelbusan.com.✆ **051/810-1000,** LA office 310/540-7010, New York office 201/944-1117. Fax 051/810-5110. 806 units. ₩250,000 standard room; ₩345,000 executive room. AE, DC, MC, V. **Amenities:** 5 restaurants; bar; cafe; pool; golf course; health club; spa; business center; smoke-free rooms; bakery; casino; duty-free shop. *In room:* A/C, TV/ DVD, minibar, fridge, hair dryer.

INEXPENSIVE

Elysee Motel   A love motel conveniently located to Yongdusan Park, BIFF, and the subway, the English-speaking owner will be happy to provide you with a map and local advice. You can't miss the building that looks like a faux Medieval castle made with white logos. Both ondol and beds available.

46-beonji Donggwang-dong, 3(sam)-ga, Jung-gu, www.elyseemotel.com/english/main2.asp. ✆ **011/264-8048** or 051/251-4008. ₩40,000 to₩60,000 standard double. MC, V. On-site parking. *In room:* A/C, TV/DVD, fridge, hair dryer, computer w/Internet.

Dongnae

Hotel Nongshim ★★ 🛏   A midsize building in the hills, the hotel's best attribute is the Heosimcheong (they spell it Hurshimchung) Spa (p. 315), a multilevel bathhouse associated with the hotel. Both Western-style and ondol rooms are available.

137-7 Oncheon-dong, Dongnae-gu. www.hotelnongshim.com/eng/index.asp.✆ **051/550-2100.** 199 rooms. ₩230,000 double/ondol; ₩500,000 and up suite. 10% VAT and 10% service charge not included. AE, MC, V. **Amenities:** 3 restaurants; cafe; health club; spa; sauna; bakery; nightclub. *In room:* A/C, TV, fridge, hair dryer, Internet.

WHERE TO EAT

There is no shortage of places to eat in Busan, with restaurants to fit every budget, and the city is known for its fresh *hwae* (raw fish) and other seafood. Raw-fish restaurants and markets line the shore in Haeundae (on the east of the shore on the other side of the boardwalk away from the Westin Chosun), Gwangalli, and Songdo beaches, and at the Jagalchi Market.

Other specialties of the city include *so galbi* (beef ribs, usually cooked on a tabletop grill at your table), which can be found in eateries throughout the city. Sanseong Village's restaurants specialize in *yeomso gogi* (grilled goat meat) or *heuk yeomso* (black goat), which is usually enjoyed with the local liquor, a type of rice wine. For *dweji galbi* (pork ribs), there is actually a street, Choryang Galbi Street, dedicated solely to restaurants that serve pork.

You can also get your fair share of cheap street food in the ***mokja golmok*** (Let's Eat Alley). There are two of them in town—one in Seomyeon and another in Changseon-dong near the Jagalchi Market. Sit-down joints and street vendors serve everything from flatcakes and noodles to meat and dumplings. There is even a street in the **Nampo-dong** area called the "Original Bossam and Jokbal Alley." *Jokbal* (boiled pig

Dongnae

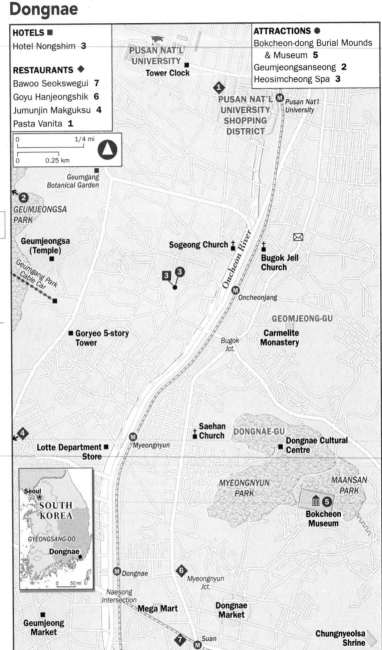

HOTELS ■
Hotel Nongshim **3**

RESTAURANTS ◆
Bawoo Seokswegui **7**
Goyu Hanjeongshik **6**
Jumunjin Makguksu **4**
Pasta Vanita **1**

ATTRACTIONS ●
Bokcheon-dong Burial Mounds
& Museum **5**
Geumjeongsanseong **2**
Heosimcheong Spa **3**

0 ────────── 1/4 mi
0 ────────── 0.25 km

❶ PUSAN NAT'L UNIVERSITY
Tower Clock

PUSAN NAT'L UNIVERSITY SHOPPING DISTRICT

Ⓜ Pusan Nat'l University

Geumgang Botanical Garden

❷
GEUMJEONGSA PARK

Geumjeongsa (Temple) ■

Geumgang Park Cable Car

Sogeong Church ✝

❸ ❸

Oncheon River

Bugok Jeil Church ✝

✉

Ⓜ Oncheonjang

GEOMJEONG-GU

Carmelite Monastery

Goryeo 5-story Tower ■

Bugok Jct.

Saehan Church ✝

DONGNAE-GU

Lotte Department Store ■

Ⓜ Myeongnyun

Dongnae Cultural Centre ■

MYEONGNYUN PARK

MAANSAN PARK

🏛 ❺
Bokcheon Museum

Seoul ⊛
SOUTH KOREA

GYEONGSANG-DO

Dongnae ■

0 ────── 50 mi

Ⓜ Dongnae

❻ Myeongnyun Jct.

Naesong Intersection

Mega Mart

Dongnae Market

Geumjeong Market ■

❼ Ⓜ Suan

Chungnyeolsa Shrine

9

BUSAN | Where to Eat

feet) is actually tender, sliced pork, served with *bossam* (lettuce leaves) to be eaten with rice, *kimchi* (fermented cabbage), and other *banchan* (side dishes).

Open-air cafes are concentrated along the shores of **Gwangalli** looking out onto the view of the bridge and the ocean. Restaurants and cafes are also clustered at Gwangeogol Food Town near **Songjeong Beach.**

Almost all of the larger hotels have their own restaurants, but prices are more expensive, since you're paying for the ambience and the view. Department stores have Korean "fast food" (usually on the basement floor) and restaurants on the top levels. There is no end of street carts selling a variety of snacks and drinks near market streets and at night.

As elsewhere in South Korea, Korean food is usually cheaper than Western cuisine, since most ingredients have to be imported. Even getting a hamburger or pizza won't be cheaper than buying some *ddeokbokgi* (spicy rice cake sticks) or *gimbap* (rice and other stuff rolled in seaweed).

Haeundae

If you saunter along the boardwalk on the beach with the Westin Chosun Hotel at your back, you will come upon a row of hwae restaurants along the shore. Although the seafood here is good and fresh, you're paying a bit more for the location and the view. Haeundae does have its share of upscale restaurants. The fancier ones are located inside the high-end hotels. For less expensive, but equally delicious fare, look for those tucked away in small streets and alleyways away from the waterfront.

EXPENSIVE

Ventanas ★ WESTERN/STEAK AND SEAFOOD   Possibly the best place to get a steak dinner in the city. With the ocean view and the plush chairs, it's a good choice for a romantic dinner or a business lunch. Most meals come with soup, salad, and an appetizer. The best part is the sommelier's selection of imported wines, which are hard to find in Busan.

Inside the Novotel. ℂ **051/746-8481.** Reservations recommended. Entrees ₩48,000 and up. AE, DC, MC, V. Mon–Sat 11:30am–2:30pm and 6–10pm; Sun 11:30am–2:30pm.

MODERATE

Ganga ★★ INDIAN   This Seoul chain has made its way to Busan. Good thing because it's one of the best places to get Indian food in the country. Although prices aren't cheap, no one's complaining since their mouths are too full of chicken masala. Get an extra serving of naan to mop up the sauces, since the rice is the short-grain, Korean style instead of the preferred basmati.

Harbor Town 1F, 627-1 U-1(il)-dong, Haeundae-gu. ℂ **051/740-6670.** www.ganga.co.kr. Curries and tandoori ₩15,000–₩40,000. AE, MC, V. Daily 11:40am–10:15pm (closes between lunch and dinner on weekdays). Parking available.

Haeundae Amso Galbi Jip ★★★ KOREAN BEEF   Known for their *galbi* (beef rib) dishes, they also serve fresh beef for your barbecuing pleasure. For those who aren't in the mood for meat, not to fear—this place serves up excellent noodle dishes, too. Although the sign is only in Korean (large white letters on the brown building), you can't miss the traditional roofed entrance gate to the restaurant (although the building itself is a more modern brick block). While this is not necessarily a cheap place, the beef dishes are still priced fairly reasonably. Near the Paradise Hotel.

1225-1 Jung 1-dong, Haeundae-gu. ℭ **051/746-0033.** Entrees ₩6,000–₩30,000. MC, V. Daily 10am–10pm. Closed Lunar New Year and Chuseok. Bus no. 139, 140, 239, 240, or 302. 2 blocks from the Paradise Hotel.

INEXPENSIVE

Café Ban ★★★ CAFE   In the gallery district of Haeundae, this modern space (with a polished steel, concrete, and wood interior) showcases not only good, strong coffee, but art from famous local artists. The drinks aren't cheap, but you're partly paying for the ambience too. So linger and enjoy a cup of the Brazilian coffee with a simple sandwich on the outdoor patio.

501-15 Jung-dong, Haeundae-gu. ℭ **051/746-8853.** Coffee and sandwiches ₩8,000. MC, V. Sun–Thurs noon–1am; Fri–Sat noon–2am. Parking available.

Gwangalli

For inexpensive and fresh hwae, the **Millak Hwae Town** at the northeast end of Gwangalli Beach is a place to get relatively inexpensive fare. You choose a fish from one of the vendors on the first floor. They run from about ₩20,000 to ₩30,000. For an extra ₩10,000, they'll slice and dice and fix it up for you upstairs. You can't get fresher fish than that! Be sure you bring your appetite because the meal involves several courses, with the hwae as the highlight of the meal, ending with spicy fish stew and rice.

For a different experience, there is a **Kongnamul Haejang Guk (Bean Sprout Seafood Soup) Street** next to Millak Hwae Town where a handful of restaurants specialize in this spicy soup.

If you're not in the mood for fish or soup, head on over to the **Gwangalli Eonyang Bulgogi Street** (on the other side of Gwangalli Beach), which is a street lined with *bulgogi* (marinated sliced rib-eye) restaurants.

Also on the beach side with a view of the Gwangan bridge is **Café Street,** a line of open-air cafes, where you can enjoy the nighttime view of the lights on the water while sipping a coffee with your loved one.

Dongnae-Gu, Geumjeong-Gu & Pnu Area

This neighborhood is famous for its Dongnae *pajeon* (green-onion flatcakes). You can find them being made fresh on the streets or in most of the restaurants in this area. Not a big enough dish to make a meal, it's a great appetizer or snack or can make a good *anju* (drinking snack) with your soju or beer.

MODERATE

Bawoo Seokswegui ★★ KOREAN BEEF   Delicious Korean grilled beef at bargain-basement prices without compromising on taste, with generous portions. The galbi is terrific, and a terrific deal. Just remember, as with dining at any Korean barbecue place, you'll be carrying the scent of your meal long after the flavors have left your tongue, so don't wear anything too fancy.

1-10 Suan-dong, Dongnae-gu. ℭ **051/556-6115.** Entrees ₩7,000–₩25,000. MC, V. Daily 11am–midnight.

Goyu Hanjeongshik ★★ TRADITIONAL KOREAN   This is a great place to try a traditional *hanjeongshik* meal (rice served with side dishes, usually consisting of seasonal vegetables), since that's their specialty. Be sure you bring your appetite, since the dishes will keep coming (they might fool you into thinking you're done just because their service can be slow when they're extra busy). There is a set menu here, but dishes vary depending on the season.

570-16 Myeong-lyun 1-dong, Dongnae-gu. © **051/557-2800.** Set menu ₩15,000–₩30,000. MC, V. Daily 10am–10pm. Closed Lunar New Year and Chuseok. Parking available.

Pasta Vanita ITALIAN   A decent place to get spaghetti in the PNU area. Don't expect authentic Italian fare, but the pastas are passable. You can get good vegetarian pizza and spaghetti with crab, but the biggest draw is the wide selection of imported wines. The restaurant is on the second floor.

420-30 Jangjeon-dong, Geumjeong-gu. © **051/512-9113.** Entrees ₩11,000–₩13,000. MC, V. Daily 11am–midnight. Take subway line 1 to PNU Station; it's a 10-min. walk from there.

INEXPENSIVE

Jumunjin Makguksu ★ KOREAN NOODLES   Located in a nondescript gray building (the name of the place is in Korean in white letters on the side and in front), this crowded joint serves up delicious and inexpensive *makguksu* (buckwheat noodles in broth) and *kalguksu* (handmade "knife" noodles—so called because they're cut from the dough with a knife). Be prepared to wait in line (they'll give you a number). They have only two types of noodles and pork, so it's not difficult to decide what you want. Several locations in town.

In Sajik-dong, across from the Sajik baseball field (at the end of the alley where the Dunkin' Donuts is located). © **051/501-7856.** Entrees ₩5,000–₩15,000. No credit cards. Daily 11am–10pm. Parking available, but difficult to get a spot.

Jung-Gu & Nampo-Dong

Probably the cheapest hwae and seafood can be found at the **Jagalchi Market,** where you buy the fish from vendors on the street level and have them prepare it upstairs for you. They usually offer three meal options, labeled A, B, and C. Even the A course is quite filling with plenty of hwae, an appetizer course of mussels or other seafood, and *maeuntang* (spicy hot pot) to finish up the meal. All of the upstairs restaurants serve similar meals, costing between ₩50,000 and ₩80,000 for two people. Don't be offended by the *ajumma* (married ladies) who grab you by the arm and try to get you to eat at their place. The ones who have tables far away from the view have to use such aggressive tactics to get business during slow days.

For more hwae and other seafood, go to the fish market along the waterfront of Jagalchi shijang. The vendors display their fresh catch as you walk through the narrow walkway. You make your pick and sit at an inside table or outside bench or even watch as the ajumma cooks the food right there in front of you. Choices included a variety of hwae, grilled fish, and other fresh seafood.

If you're not in the mood for seafood, you can try your luck at the **Changsun-dong Mokja, Let's Eat Street,** between Gukje and Jagalchi markets, near the Art Street.

MODERATE

Gyeongbuksang Hwae KOREAN SEAFOOD   One of the many *hwae jip* (raw fish joints) above Jagalchi Market. They don't have the advantage of the table with a view, but they make up for it with their generous portions, so make sure you bring a full appetite for this multicourse meal of seafood. They'll start you out with some snacks and then mussels and other shellfish. Then the large plate of raw fish arrives, and when you think you're too full, they'll bring the rice and a steaming pot of maeuntang with the bones and leftover bits from your hwae. Not a meal to be eaten alone; bring a friend and take your time savoring the fresh seafood.

218-ho, 4-ga, Nampo-dong, Jung-gu. © **051/242-8882.** Set menu for 2 ₩50,000 and up. MC, V. Daily 11am–10pm. On the 2nd floor near the back entrance to Jagalchi shijang.

INEXPENSIVE

Changseong-hyang Mandu Jip ★ KOREAN-STYLE CHINESE Fans of the film *Oldboy* might recognize this dumpling joint. Don't worry that the menu isn't in English, since you can just point at the pictures and order. They have the standard Korean-style Chinese dishes like *jjajangmyeon* (noodles with black-bean sauce) and *tangsuyeok* (sweet and sour pork). But the *mandu* (dumpling) dishes are what the regulars order. The hardest part is trying to decide whether you want them steamed or fried. Look for the name in gold Chinese letters on a brick facade.

609-1 Choryang 1-dong, Dong-gu. © **051/467-4496.** Mandu and noodles ₩3,500–₩7,000. MC, V. Daily 11am–10pm. Take the subway to Busan Station (exit 1) and turn right at the 1st street.

EXPLORING BUSAN

The beaches are the largest draw in Busan, but there are other great things to explore. Whether it's seeing the live fish being sold at Jagalchi Market, watching the sunrise from Yonggungsa, or sitting in a cafe at Gwangalli, there's plenty to do. If you want to see some historical culture but have limited time, at least be sure to visit the famous Beomeosa Temple. Yongdusan Park is a fun place to stop by, especially on weekends when they are usually holding some sort of performance. In the evenings, you can take a cruise around the waters, sit at a cafe, or just watch couples launch bottle rockets off the sandy beaches.

Museums & Galleries

Busan Museum ★★ 🍴 MUSEUM This is the major museum for the art, culture, and history of Busan. Built in 1975, the building was renovated in 2002. With over 4,500 items in its collection, the museum exhibits everything from cultural relics to calligraphic works. Plan on spending a couple of hours here, starting with the prehistoric displays and exhibits spanning the Gaya period to the Joseon Dynasty, through the Korean War to modern-day Busan. Unfortunately, the videos are only in Korean, but artifacts are all displayed with English text.

948-1, Daeyeon 4-dong, Nam-gu. © **051/610-7111.** http://engmuseum.busan.go.kr. Admission free. Tues–Sun 9am–8pm; last entry 1 hr. before closing. English guides at 10:30am, 1:30pm, and 3pm. Closed national holidays. Subway: Take line 2 to Daeyeon, take exit 3, turn around 180 degrees, take the 1st left, and walk 10 min. Bus no. 25, 51, 68, 93, 134, 139, 239, 240, or 302.

Busan Museum of Art (BMA) ★ ART MUSEUM The largest modern art space in South Korea, this is one of the best places in the country to see what contemporary Korean artists are producing. The site of the annual **Busan International Art Festival,** the museum is also responsible for exhibits held at the Yongdusan gallery. Exhibits change every couple of months, so check with the museum to see what's showing before you wish to visit. Plan to spend about an hour here.

1413 Woo-2-dong, Haeundae-gu. © **051/744-2602.** www.busanmoma.org. Admission free, last entry 1 hr. before closing. Tues–Sun 10am–6pm. Closed Jan 1, Lunar New Year, and Chuseok. Subway: Take line 2 to the Busan Museum of Art (BMA) Station, take exit 5. Bus no. 40, 139, 140, 239, 240, 302, or 2003.

Hankwang Museum MUSEUM A museum dedicated to the calligraphy and paintings of Korean, Japanese, and Chinese artists, the Hankwang, it contains more than 500 works that were collected over a 50-year period by the late Han Kwangduk. Although only a fraction of its collection is exhibited at any given moment, it is a wonderful way to glimpse the talents of brush painters and see traditional landscapes of Asia spanning works from the Joseon Dynasty through the present time.

82-1, 4-ga, Jung-ang-dong, Jung-gu (located on the 4th floor of the Hankwang building). © **051/469-4111.** www.asiaart.co.kr. Free admission. Mon–Sat 9am–5pm.

Toam Ceramic Park ★ PARK   Located in Gijang-gun, the most rural of Busan's districts, this park is actually a working center for ceramic artisans. If you time your visit right, you may be able to catch one of the craftsmen at work. Either way, you'll enjoy the over 2,000 ceramic figures created by Seo Tawon, all with smiles and open mouths greeting you from the hillside. You can also just take in the scenery from the lush surrounding garden. The small restaurant on-site is a nice place to get a delicious lunch at reasonable prices: ₩5,000 for a bowl of *pot jook* (red-bean porridge) up to ₩15,000 for *japchae* (sweet-potato noodles).

521-1 Daebyeon-li, Gijang-eup, Gijang-gun. © **051/721-2231.** Free admission. Daily 10am–6pm. Take subway line 2 to Haeundae Station, and then take bus no. 142 or 181.

Yongdusan Gallery MUSEUM   A small exhibition space just north of Yongdu-san park, the gallery usually showcases exhibits from one major artist at a time. Featuring contemporary Korean works, the shows range from painting and sculpture to fashion and ceramics, organized by the Busan Museum of Art.

1-2, 2-ga, Gwangbok-dong, Jung-gu. © **051/244-8228.** Free admission. Daily 10am–6pm. Take the subway to either the Jung-ang-dong or Nampo-dong Station and walk to Yongdusan park. It is the 2-story building just north of the park.

Temples

Beomeosa ★★ TEMPLE   Originally built in 678, Beomeosa (like most of the temples in Korea) was destroyed during the Imjin Waeran in 1592. Renovated in 1713, it is a wonderful example of mid-Joseon temple architecture. The name Beomeosa means "fish of the Buddhist scripture temple." Located at the edge of Geumjeongsan and amid a wisteria grove that blooms each May, it is Busan's most famous temple. A Seon (Zen) temple, hundreds of monks live here and in the 11 adjacent hermitages.

The Beomeosa complex consists of a main hall, which houses the Seokgamoni Buddha and two bodhisattvas; a bell/drum pavilion (with a three-story pagoda and a lantern dating from the Shilla Dynasty); seven royal palace wings; and three gates. The main hall was rebuilt in 1614—look for the dragon's heads carved into its rafters. To the left of the hall is a building that's split into three sections. The first section features murals depicting the eight major scenes from the Buddha's life. Another section is dedicated to the Lonely Arhat, a Buddha saint who attains liberation from the cycle of reincarnation by leading a hermetic lifestyle. The third is filled with statues of Buddha's disciples.

This is a great place to do a temple stay.

546 Cheongryong-dong, Geumjeong-gu. © **051/508-3122.** www.beomeosa.co.kr. Admission free. Wed–Mon 9:30am–5pm; last ticket sold at 4:30pm. Closed Lunar New Year and Chuseok. Subway: Take line 1 to Beomeosa Station, take exit 5 or 7, walk between the 2 exits along the road for 5 min. and you will reach the Samsin bus stop. Take bus no. 90 to temple. Bus no. 37, 47, 48, 49-1, 50, 50-1, 80-1, 147, 148, 247, or 301; get off at the last stop and take bus no. 90.

Haedong Yonggungsa (Haedong Yonggung Temple) ★★ TEMPLE   Initially built in 1376 (during the Goryeo Dynasty), the main sanctuary was reconstructed

A Feast Fit for a Monk

Many of South Korea's temples offer meals to visitors and to those spending the night, and while temple cuisine is likely not the best food you'll encounter on your trip, it does stem from some fascinating traditions. The food served at temples is always vegetarian and usually consists of rice and small banchan made from local and seasonal vegetables. However, the monks will not cook with the five "hot" vegetables, including garlic and ginger, because they believe that these foods lead to obscene thoughts when eaten raw and to anger when consumed cooked.

Indeed, Korean temple food is supposed to cleanse the body and encourage spirituality. Meals are prepared as "medicine" for the mind, body, and spirit and are not supposed to be eaten for pleasure. Still, temple food can be quite tasty, as it's always fresh and subtle in flavor. It's definitely worth skipping a serving of beef ribs to get a taste of South Korea's spiritual heritage.

in 1970. This is one of the few temples found along the coast and it honors the **Haesu Gwaneum Daebul (Seawater Great Goddess Buddha of Mercy),** who is said to live alone in the ocean and to ride on the back of a dragon. Since the temple faces northeast, it offers a spectacular view of the sunrise—many come early on the Lunar New Year to make a wish as the sun rises—and an enormous bronze bell is rung five times at sunset. Special features of the temple include the three-story pagoda with its four lions (symbolizing joy, anger, sadness, and happiness), the Yacksayeorae Healing Buddha, and the Bulbeop Buddhist Sanctum (which is enclosed in a cave). Come see the cherry blossoms in April or the lanterns in May for Buddha's Birthday.

416-3 Sirang-li, Gijang-eup, Gijang-gun. © **051/722-7755.** www.yongkungsa.or.kr/en/. Free admission. Daily 4am–8pm. Take subway line 1 to Dongnae Station, and across from there take bus no. 100 or 100-1 and get off at Songjeong Beach; then transfer to bus no. 181. Or take bus no. 139, 140, 239, 302-1, or 2003, get off at Songjeong Beach, and then transfer to bus no. 181.

Hongbeopsa (Hongbeop Temple) ☺ TEMPLE   Located in the suburbs of Busan, this temple lies in the foothills of Cheolmasan, behind Geumjeongsan. Standing near Sinchang Farm, it aspires to be the center of Saeng-hwal Bulgyo (Buddhism for Everyday Living). There is a river nearby and a pond with about 150 types of waterlilies (they bloom in late summer). If you happen to be here for the celebration of the Buddha's Birthday (usually in May), you can see children who are ordained as monks for the day, in the hopes of planting the seeds of Buddhism in their young minds. (Seeing small boys with shaved heads dressed in the traditional gray robes of the monks is quite a sight!) They have cultural events for foreigners once a month. You can do a temple stay but be sure to book at least 10 days in advance.

1220-1 Dugu-dong, Geumjeong-gu. © **051/508-0345.** www.busanbuddhism.com (Korean only). Free admission. Daily 24 hr. Bus: 1, 2, 2-1, 50-1, or 301. You can also take the subway to the Nopo-dong Station and walk from there.

Samgwangsa (Samgwang Temple) TEMPLE   Built at the foot of the Baekyangsan by the monks of the Chongdae Order, this temple is relatively new. Worth a visit just for the view of the city or the spectacular sunrise, it is a place for praying to Avalokitesvara (the Buddhist Goddess of Mercy). Although the temple's construction is recent, its designs still follow the Buddhist traditions. Other than the main Buddha hall, the guardians' platform, which houses the four treasures of Buddhist ritual (the bell, drum, wooden fish gong, and cloud-patterned gong), is a colorful sight to behold. The nine-level DaeBo Tap (pagoda), built for world peace and the reunification of the two Koreas, with its eight sides carved with 53 Buddhas, is also worth a look.

San 131, Cho-eup Dongjin-gu.(*) **051/808-7111.** Free admission. Daily 24 hr. Bus: 44, 63, 81, 83-1, 103, 112, 133, or 201; get off at Seongyeong Apt.

Seokbulsa (Stone Buddha Temple) ★★ ▮ TEMPLE   Most people don't know about this small temple south of Geumjeong Fortress and north of Mandeok tunnel. Since it's a walk to get here (no buses stop nearby), it's a quiet place even on the busiest of summer weekends. The temple got its name from the statues of the Buddha carved in the rock here (*Seokbul* means "stone Buddha"). The main temple and some of the associated meditation halls are small "caves" carved into the rock. Of course, they have the usual wooden temple structures here, too.

San 2 Mandeok-dong, Buk-gu. Free admission. Daily 24 hr. From the express bus terminal, take bus no. 48, 110, or 111 and get off just after you pass the tunnel. You'll find the start of the trail when you walk toward the right of the upper, older tunnel. Alternatively, take bus no. 33 to the end at Mandeok and walk 40 min. You can also take *maeul* (village) bus no. 9 from Dongnae Station. If you take the Geumgang cable car up, you can walk to the temple via the South Gate (Nam mun).

Historic Sites

Bokcheon-dong Burial Mounds & Museum MUSEUM   At one of the oldest burial sites in the southern part of the country, there were once more than 100 burial mounds dating back to the Gaya Kingdom (6th century). Although part of the mound was destroyed inadvertently by construction in the area in 1969, it has since been designated a historical site. Now over 9,000 relics (including pieces of pottery and ironware) have been excavated from the area. Although many of those finds are no longer here (now part of the Busan Museum's collection)—there is also a museum on-site housing some of the unearthed treasures. A few of the tombs have since been re-created.

50 Bokcheon-dong, Dongnae-gu.(*) **051/554-4263.** Free admission to the site, but the museum is ₩500 adults, ₩300 teens, ₩200 children. Mar–Oct daily 9am–6pm; Nov–Feb daily 9am–5pm. Subway: Take line 1 to Myeongnyun-dong or Dongnae Station, and then take maeul bus no. 6.

Geumjeongsanseong (Mt. Geumjeong Fortress) HIKING TRAIL   High on the peak of Mt. Geumjeong, Geumjeongsanseong was the largest fortress in South Korea. There is only about a 4km (2½-mile) section left from the original today, presumed to be built during the Three Kingdoms period. The present fortress was built in 1703 after the Imjin Waeran to prepare for further invasions from Japan, but none ever came. The hills are great for a half-day of hiking—the small villages nearby are known for their charcoal-grilled goat meat and *makgeolli* (an unfiltered rice wine).

779 Daeyeon 4-dong, Nam-gu.(*) **051/514-5501.** Admission ₩1,000, ₩700 teens 13–18, ₩500 kids 7–12. Subway: to Oncheonjang Station(line 1, exit 3), and then bus no. 203 or Beomeosa Station (line 1, exit 5 or 7), then take bus 90. Alternatively, you can take the cable car from Geumgang Park and walk the trail from the botanical garden.

U.N. Memorial Cemetery & Peace Park MEMORIAL   Located near the Busan Museum, this cemetery honors international soldiers who were killed during the Korean War (1950–53). There are about 2,300 military personnel buried here, from 16 nations. The Korean government gave the 14-hectare (35-acre) property to the United Nations in perpetuity as a tribute to those who gave their lives. Dedicated

in 1951, the majority of the graves are British; 500 Turkish troops and more than 100 Dutch are also interred here. The remains of all American, French, Norwegian, Philippine, Greek, Belgian, Colombian, Ethiopian, and Thai soldiers were sent home for burial.

779 Daeyeon 4-dong, Nam-gu. ℂ 051/625-0625. www.unmck.or.kr. Free admission. Winter daily 9am–4:30pm; summer daily 9am–6pm. Subway: Take line 2 to Daeyeon Station, walk 15 min. toward Gwangalli. Bus: 25, 68, 93, or 134.

Parks

Daeshin Citizen's Park ★ WALKING TRAIL   Located near Dong-A University's main campus on Gubongsan, this small city park is densely populated by older trees on the hillside. A forest retreat in the middle of the city, it's a great place to take a short hike, a leisurely walk, or a run along the jogging trails.

Located in the mountainside above Gudeok Stadium. Free admission. 24 hr. daily. Bus: 2, 11, 13, 15, 16, 40, 42, 58-1, 59, 67, 70, 81, 86, 96, 103, 105, 126, 140, 161, 167, 190, 309, or 310; get off at Gudeok Stadium and walk from there.

Suyeong Park ★ PARK   The site of a naval camp responsible for guarding the seas to the east and to the west during the Joseon Dynasty, the park is located just north of the Suyeong intersection. It includes a couple of military shrines and the **Suyeong Folk Art Center.** In the open theater, they present folk performances here on a regular basis.

Suyeong-dong, Suyeong-gu. ℂ 051/610-4065. Free admission. 24 hr. Subway line 2 or 3 to Suyeong Station (then follow the signs to Suyeong Park, which is about a 300m/984-ft. walk from the station).

Yongdusan Park (Dragon Head Mountain Park) & Busan Tower ★★★
PARK   Yongdusan is so named because the shape of the mountain seems to resemble the head of a dragon that climbs out of the sea. A popular park, it is a small oasis from the cars and skyscrapers of the city. There is a covered escalator from Gwangbok-dong that goes up the incline. This hillside park houses a statue of Admiral Yi Sun-shin, the great naval commander of the Joseon Dynasty.

The most popular attraction here is the **Busan Tower,** which climbs high above the harbor. It's worth paying the admission just to see the view. From the top, you'll be treated to wonderful views of the harbor and nearby Yeong-do. This is also a great place to enjoy the city lights. In addition to the tower, the park has an aquarium, a cafe, and restaurants. Quite often on summer weekends you'll stumble upon free cultural events and performances.

Gwangbok-dong, Jung-gu. ℂ 051/860-7820. Free admission to the park. Admission to the tower ₩4,000 adults, ₩3,500 teens, ₩3,000 ages 3–12. Admission to World Folk Instrument Museum ₩2,500 adults, ₩2,000 teens, ₩1,500 ages 3–12. Park daily 24 hr.; tower and museum Apr–Sept daily 8:30am–10pm, Oct–Mar daily 9am–10pm. Subway: Take line 1 to Nampo-dong (take exit 1) and walk 10 min. From Gimhae Airport, take bus no. 310, get off at the Gumi Cultural Center in Daecheong-dong, and then walk 10 min. The bus takes an hour.

Other Attractions

Busan Aquarium ★ ☺ AQUARIUM   One of the best in the country, this aquarium has three underground levels and an outdoor park, located on the edge of Haeundae Beach. It contains over 35,000 varieties of fish, algae, amphibians, and reptiles. The highlight is on the bottom level, where there is a main tank and tunnel where you can walk through the water, while fish and sharks swim above you. There is an additional ₩4,000 fee to go through the underwater simulation.

1411-4 Jung 1-dong, Haeundae-gu. © **051/740-1700.** www.busanaquarium.com. Admission ₩18,000 adults, ₩16,000 teens, ₩13,000 ages 3–12. Weekdays 10am–7pm; weekends and holidays 9am–9pm (daily 9am–11pm July 16–Aug 24); aquarium stays open an hour after the last admission. Subway: Haeundae Station (line 2, exit 3 or 5) and walk 10 min. toward the beach. Bus: 139, 201, 1001, or 1003. From Gimhae Airport, take bus no. 307 or city coach no. 2002 to Haeundae.

Eulsuk-do Bird Sanctuary/Nakdong Bird Estuary ★★ NATURE RESERVE
The spot where the Nakdong River meets the South Sea has been declared a natural monument since 1966. At the large mouth of the river, there are sand dunes, deltas, and small islands (including Ilung-do). It is now a **bird sanctuary** for migrating species that visit between October and March. There are over 150 species (including many rare birds like white-naped cranes, black-faced spoonbills, and white-tailed eagles) that stop here during their travels. It's difficult to reach by land, so it's best to take a boat from Myeongji-dong harbor. The ideal times to see the birds is early in the day, before it gets too hot.

Nakdong-gang, Nak-dong, Hadan-dong, Saha-gu. http://wetland.busan.go.kr. Free admission to sanctuary; Estuary Eco-center ₩1,000 adults, ₩500 teens, free for children 6 and under and seniors 65 and over. Eco-center daily 9am–6pm. Subway: Hadan Station (line 1, exit 5). From there, take bus no. 58, 58-1, or 300 and get off at Eulsukdo rest stop. *Tip:* It will be a long walk to the bird sanctuary, so be sure to wear comfortable shoes.

Heosimcheong Spa ★ SPA   Claiming to be the largest hot spring spa in Asia, Heosimcheong has multiple levels for your relaxing entertainment. One floor is just *jjimjilbang* (hot saunas), igloo-shaped structures made out of clay where you can steam yourself alive. This floor also has a snack shop and restaurant. On the other floor are the "grand hot springs," a huge atrium full of pools and waterfalls of varying temperatures, ranging from boiling hot to icy cold. Get a scrub, a massage, or just relax at the third floor cafe.

137-7 Oncheon-dong, Dongnae-gu (inside the Nongshim Hotel). © **051/555-1121.** Admission ₩10,000 adults, ₩6,000 children. Daily 5:30am–8pm. Subway: Take line 1 to Oncheonjang Station (exit 1) and walk toward the Dongnae Gweumgangwon. Bus: 51, 51-1, 77, 80, 100, 100-1, 110, 110-1, 121, 131, 131-1, 183, 188, 189, 203, 210, or 301.

YEONGDO

Yeongdo (Yeong Island) separates the two halves of Busan Harbor. The old **Yeongdo Grand Bridge** connects to the rest of Busan to the island's southern road. The scenic drive to Yeong-do leads to a group of hwae restaurants on the coast. The newer **Busan Grand Bridge** runs parallel to the old bridge.

Taejongdae Park ★★ PARK   This place is where Shilla King Taejong (604–661), who united the three Korean kingdoms, loved to practice his archery. There are over 200 pine trees and camellias that line the coast at this gorgeous park. The park overlooks the craggy cliffs and fun-shaped rocks that cascade down into the sea below. Nearby is a 19th-century lighthouse from which you can see Oryuk-do and Japan's Daema-do when the weather is nice. You'll see a statue of a mother with her children called **Mangbuseok (Rock of the Faithful Woman),** after the legend of a woman who waited so long for the return of her husband, who had been captured by the Japanese, that she turned to stone. The statue is located at what used to be called Jasal Bawi (Suicide Rock), where people used to throw themselves into the water. A temple, **Geumyeongsa,** was built here to prevent further suicides and to console the ghosts of the dead.

San 29-1, Dongsam 2-dong, Yeongdo-gu. ✆ **051/405-2004.** Admission ₩1,500 adults, ₩1,000 teens, ₩600 kids, free for kids 4 and under. Daily 4am–midnight. Parking ₩1,000 to ₩3,000. Ticket office Nov–Feb daily 9am–5pm, Mar–Oct daily 9am–6pm. Bus: 8, 13, 30, 88, or 101.

Organized Tours & Cultural Activities

For information and pamphlets on the following tours, stop by one of the tourist info offices or dial the **Korea Travel Phone** at ✆ **1330.** Most larger hotels also have tour desks with staff who can provide guidance.

CITY TOURS For general sightseeing, the **Busan Convention & Visitors Bureau,** 213-A BEXCO, Woo 2-dong, Haeundae-gu (✆ 052/740-3600; http://busancvb.org), offers **city tours buses** (✆ **1688-0098;** www.citytourbusan.com) near Busan Station. There are three day courses plus a nighttime course. The Haeundae Course runs several times a day and goes to Haeundae and Gwangalli beaches, BEXCO, and the Busan Museum. The Taejongdae course also runs several times a day and goes to the Modern History Museum, Taejongdae, Songdo Beach, and Jagalchi Market. Tours run Tuesday through Sunday and cost ₩10,000 adults, ₩5,000 for teens and children. The Haeundae course runs every 40 min., 9:20am to 4:40pm, while the other 2 courses vary, depending on the season. The nighttime course starts at 7pm October to April, at 7:30pm May to September. The bus departs from a stop in front of the Arirag Hotel near Busan Station. Buses 17, 59-1, 61, 67, 81, 85, 103, 167, and 1004 all stop at Busan Station.

BOAT TOURS **Covea Cruise,** 33-1 32-beonji, Dalmiti-gil, Haeundae-gu (✆ **052/742-2525;** www.coveacruise.com), offers a variety of regular and dinnerboat cruises around Busan. They generally last 1½ to 2 hours and range in price from ₩40,000 to ₩90,000.

If you want to try something a little romantic, take the overnight **Panstar Cruise,** offered by **Panstar Line** (✆ **1577-9996**). Tours start at 4pm every Saturday afternoon and go to Jodo, Taejongdae, Molundae, Oryuk Islets, Haeundae, the Gwangan Bridge, and back through Haeundae and the Oryuk Islets, returning around 8:30 to 9am on Sunday morning. Ticket sales start at 2pm and boarding is at 3pm. Regular rates for a standard room (with double bunk beds) start at ₩99,000 and go up to the seaside "Royal Suite" at ₩275,000. Plan to tack on an additional ₩20,000 during high season. Take subway line 1 to Jungang-dong Station.

Outdoor Pursuits

BEACHES

Dadaepo Beach ☺ BEACH This beach is on the western side of Busan where the Nakdong River joins the sea. Perfect for families with small children, the waters are quite shallow and safe. Like all beaches in Busan, Dadaepo is most popular during the summer break time of July and August. The beach becomes one big outdoor concert venue in August when the **Busan International Rock Festival** happens. Take bus no. 2 or 98 to Dadaepo from Busan Station. The beach is open 24 hours with shower booths and a cafeteria.

Gwangalli Beach ★★ BEACH Famous for its fine sand, Gwangalli Beach stretches 1.4km (almost a mile). When Japan colonized Korea in the last century, this beach was used to teach kids how to swim during the summer break. You can rent water skis or jet skis, or even go windsurfing. The beach draws its share of crowds during the summer and sports an outdoor stage where the **Busan Ocean Festival** is held each year. Open 24 hours it's most popular in July and August. Subway: Gwangan Station (line 2, exit 3 or 5) and walk 5–10 min. to the beach. Buses to Gwangalli run frequently (bus no. 42, 139, 140, 239, or 240).

Haeundae Beach ★★ BEACH At Busan's (and perhaps South Korea's) most popular beach, you certainly won't be escaping the crowds if you come during the summer. From June to August this beach is packed, so much so that the rented umbrellas take over the sand. The waters, however, remain warm enough for swimming through September. The sand is rough, as it is made up of eroded rocks washed down by the Chuncheon stream and shells that have been naturally ground down by the wind and sea.

Besides all the other beachside sports you can enjoy, it is one of the few places in the country where you can windsurf. Take a break from your sunbathing and have a little stroll down to **Dongbaek Island.** There are many islands in the South Korean Sea called Dongbaek-do (all named for the *dongbaek* trees that thrive on them). This one in Busan (which is no longer even an island) has a small park and a tall statue of a mermaid. Take subway line 2 to Dongbaek Station or Haeundae Station (exit 3 or 5) or bus no. 139, 140, 240, or 302. For more info, contact the Haeundae Beach Department of Culture and Tourism at ℭ **051/749-5700.**

Songjeong Beach ★ ☺ BEACH On the far eastern side of Busan, Songjeong Beach's shallow waters are also perfect for children. Not as popular as Haeundae or Gwangalli beaches, it still draws a crowd during the summer season. The white sand was created by erosion from the Songjeong River and from crushed seashells. The beach is open from 9am to 6pm. At the entrance to the beach is Jukdo and its thick evergreen groves. At the northeast end are rocky shores, popular for fishing. Take subway line 2 to Haeundae Station (exit 7), and then take bus no. 100, 100-1, 139, or 142. Bus nos. 140, 239, and 302 also go to Songjeong Beach.

HIKING

The mountains in Busan have some good hiking trails. On the west side of town, Geumjeongsan is the most popular place for residents to hike on weekends, so try to visit on a weekday to avoid the crowds. One of the more frequented routes starts from the South Gate (*Nam mun*) of **Geumjeong Fortress.** You can get there by taking a cable car from Geumgang Park (near Myeongnyun-dong Station) or by taking a bus from Oncheonjang Station to **Sanseong Maeul,** a small village hidden in the mountain valley. Walk down to the North Gate (*Buk mun*) and down to Beomeosa. The trail is about 8.8km (5.5 miles) and will take about 3 to 4 hours to complete.

SWIMMING

If you don't mind swimming in chilly waters, you can enter the **Polar Bear Swimming Competition** (ℭ **051/749-4065** or 749-3986), which is one of Busan's many Lunar New Year festivities (a similar event is also held at Jeju-do's Seogwipo City). The dozens of other events include the Haeundae White Sand Races, Haeundae Ocean Swimming Contest, and the Ice Carving Competition (that should give you an idea of how cold the waters are during the winter!). It costs ₩40,000 and only 2,000 people are allowed to compete. So put your hat in the ring early for an icy dip, your free T-shirt, and a surprise souvenir. For more beach information, see p. 316.

All the luxury hotels in town have their own indoor pools, but if you're not lucky enough to stay in one of them, you can still pay a fee to just use their pool and/or spa facilities. The Busan Port Authority is currently building a multiuse megaplex by the port, which will include an indoor pool, a spa, a sauna, and a sports center. If you can't wait until the building is finished in 2020, the **Busan Sports Complex** has an Olympic-size pool, built for the 2002 Asian Games, available for public use. It's open Tuesday through Sunday 6am–9pm. Subway: Sajik Station (line 3, exit 1) or Sports Complex Station (line 3, exit 9). Bus: 10-1, 12, 19, 44, 50, 57, 80-1, 111-2, 131, 189-1 or 1002.

SHOPPING

There is no shortage of shopping to be done in Busan. Be it haggling with old ladies in the open-air markets or browsing the high-end department stores, there are ample opportunities for you to part with your won.

Best Shopping Areas

For bargain hunting and browsing in outdoor markets, the largest *shijang* (traditional market) is Gukje Market, which is also close to the Jagalchi Market. Smaller open-air marketplaces can be found in most neighborhoods in the city.

There are plenty of fashions on display, but most items are made for petite women, so it may be difficult to find larger sizes. If that's what you need, head for the **Choryang Arcade for Foreigners** (usually called Texas Street or Foreigners' Street by locals) in Dong-gu, where you may find a larger variety of sizes.

For more stylish fashions, try the boutiques and stalls in the **PNU Area** of Dongnae, as well as the areas around Kyungsung and Pukyong universities, catering to the college-age crowd. In the college areas are "shopping town" and "beauty town," where you can find the latest clothes, accessories, and cosmetics. A tight group of hip clothing stores is in **Gwangbok-dong.** The cluster of **Nampo-dong** shops and restaurants and the popular night market draws a crowd. There are more shops available in **Seomyeon** as well. The alleys near the cafes on **Gwangalli Beach** also have shops that attract the younger crowd.

For upscale shopping, Busan's department stores are chock-full of everything from designer handbags to housewares. Major stores like **Lotte** and **Shinsegae** can be found in Centum City and Busanjin (in the Seomyeon area). Mega-shopping malls, like **Migliore** and the **Judies Taehwa** in Seomyeon or the **SfunZ** in Haeundae, also have several floors of boutique shops all in one multistoried building or have underground shopping areas. There are some in Nampo-dong and Sasang as well. Duty-free shops can be found near major transportation (at the airport and the ferry terminal) or in luxury hotels, like the **Lotte** in Busanjin or the **Paradise** in Haeundae. Also, **Rodeo Street** in Haeundae is an area dedicated to upscale shops.

Large-scale box marts, like **E-Mart,** can also be found in major sections of town like Haeundae and Busanjin.

In general, you can find vendors who speak English at hotel arcades, department stores, souvenir and duty-free shops, and on Foreigners' Street. Otherwise, be ready to use a lot of sign language and gesturing to get your point across.

Shopping A to Z
BOOKSTORES

Although there are many more smaller bookstores around the city, you'll find a better selection of English-language books and publications at those listed here. **Kyobo Mungo,** 536-3 Bujeon-dongjin-gu (© **051/806-3501**), located on the first floor of the

Kyobo Life Insurance building, also has a selection of stationery and other products. Also in Busanjin are the **Dongbo Bookstore,** 165-5 Bujeon 2-dongjin-gu (✆ 051/803-8000), and the **Yeong-gwang Bookstore,** Bujeon 1-dongjin-gu (✆ 051/816-9500), which has a good selection of English-language magazines and staff who speak pretty good English. In Jung-gu, the **Munwudang,** 3, 4-ga, Nampo-dong, Jung-gu (✆ 051/245-5555), has a small English-language section, and the **Nampo Mungo,** 2-ga, Nampo-dong, Jung-gu (✆ 051/245-8911), on the first two floors of the Horim building, has some English books.

CONTEMPORARY ART & GALLERIES

Although its claim as South Korea's Montmartre is overstated, the **Art Street** inside the Gukje Underground Shopping Center is a good place to get some insight into Busan's art scene. Take subway line 1 to Jagalchi (exit 7) and walk about 5 minutes. There are also a handful of galleries that exhibit and sell works by contemporary Korean artists in Haeundae, Nampo-dong, and Gwangalli.

One of my favorite places, in the Haeundae area, is **Arbazaar,** 1467-2 Jwa-dong, Haeundae-gu (✆ 051/704-0151; located right off the Sangsan subway station), which specializes in art by contemporary South Korean artists.

Also, if you happen to be in the Gwangalli area at night, don't miss the **Gwangalli New Media Art Museum,** 148-15 Namcheon 2(i)-dong (✆ 051/622-4251; http://badavit.suyeong.kr). The outdoor works by such international artists as Jenny Holzer, Jean-Pierre Ratnaud, and Korea's own video artist, Paik Nam-June, span the shores of Gwangalli Beach. Take subway line 3 to Gwang-an Station (exit 5) or Geumnyeonsan Station (exit 5). Buses 20, 38, 51, 51-1, 83, 83-1, 108-1, 131, and 155 stop at the museum.

DEPARTMENT STORES

Like any South Korean city worth its salt, Busan has several multistoried department stores that sell everything from housewares to groceries and high-end fashions. If you need a break from shopping, you can go to the basement or top floors for your choice of upscale or budget food to fuel up.

Your best bet will be to go to **Centum City ★** (subway line 2 to Centum City Station), where the entrance to both the **Lotte** (✆ 051/730-2500) and the 18-floor **Shinsegae** department stores are easily accessible from the subway. They're both open from 10:30am to 10pm daily.

The **Lotte Department Store** (✆ 051/810-2500), attached to the Lotte hotel in Seomyeon, is an 11-story megacomplex with everything from clothes to cosmetics to sporting goods and jewelry. The ninth floor is reserved for restaurants and the top two floors are the Lotte Cinema. Groceries and Korean-style fast food are available on the first basement floor, with a cafe and sports center underneath. Parking is available on basement floors three to five. Take subway line 1 or 2 to Seomyeon (exit 3, 5, or 7). The second basement level of the department store is connected to the subway. They're open daily from 10:30am to 8pm.

Lotte has another location in Dongnae (✆ 051/605-2500). Take subway line 1 to Myeongnyun-dong (exit 1) and walk about 5 minutes.

Slightly smaller (only nine floors) is the **Hyundai Department Store** (✆ 051/667-2233), located right in front of the Beomil-dong subway station, near Busanjin Market. It's arranged more like Western-style department stores, with cosmetics and clothing on the bottom floors and housewares and electronics on the seventh floor. Restaurants are on the eighth floor, with a food court on the second basement floor. The top floor has a health spa, golf center, and swimming pool. Some parking is available on the third basement floor. Open daily 10:30am to 8pm, the store is closed one Monday a month. Take subway line 1 to the Beomil-dong Station (exit 5 or 7). The second basement floor of the store connects to the subway.

DISCOUNT MEGASTORES

Most conspicuous of the large-scale discount stores are the bright yellow and black **E-Marts,** which have several locations in the city. The easiest to get to is the **Haeun-dae E-Mart,** 1767 Gungil 1-dong, Haeundae-gu; take the subway line 2 to Jung-dong Station (exit 7 or 9). They're open daily from 10am to midnight, but closed Lunar New Year and Chuseok.

Home Plus also has several locations in Busan. There is one in Haeundae (© **051/532-2080**), 1406-2 Haeundae-gu 1-dong. Take subway line 2 to Dongbaek Station (exit 1) and walk about 3 minutes. They're open daily from 10am to midnight. The Home Plus in Seomyeon is off subway line 2, Buam Station (exit 4). It's about a 5-minute walk toward Dang-gam-dong and it's open 10am to 11pm daily.

FASHION

There is no shortage of clothing stores in Busan. For high-end designer fashions, you can shop the hotel arcades and departments stores (info above). The best for window shopping are the shopping arcades found in various neighborhoods.

The younger crowds are drawn to the area around **Busan National University (PNU)** in Dongnae, where you'll find a bunch of cute boutiques with the latest fashions, interspersed with restaurants and cafes. A touch smaller, but just as fun and crowded, are the areas around **Kyungsung University** and **Pukyong National University.**

For serious shopping, you can go to the mega-shopping malls, fashioned after Seoul's Dongdaemun Market. These super-sized buildings house dozens of wholesale clothing vendors vying for your business. Some of the complexes even have movie theaters, bookstores, and restaurants. One of the most popular for discovering young designers is **Migliore ★★**, 668-1 Jeunpo 1-dong, Jin-gu (© **051/922-6000**), located in Seomyeon. Open daily 11am to 11:40pm, it's closed the first and third Mondays of the month. Take subway line 1 to Seomyeon Station (exit 5 or 6). Another large shopping complex in the area is **Judies Taehwa** (© **051/667-7000**), also off the Seomyeon Subway Station. Open daily from 11am to 11pm, they're closed the second and fourth Mondays of the month. The street around Judies is a good place to shop for bargains.

Save Zone, 380-14 Jung-dong, Haeundae-gu (© **051/740-9000**), and **SfunZ** (© **051/740-0800**) are both huge malls in the Haeundae area. Take subway line 2 to the Haeundae Station (exit 3 for Save Zone and exit 1 for SfunZ). Save Zone is open daily from 10am to 10pm, while SfunZ opens a half-hour later.

Renicite (© **051/319-5000**) is the huge complex in Sasang-dong. It's open daily 10:30am to midnight (closed on the first Mon of the month). Take subway line 2 to Sasang (exit 3) and walk about 10 minutes.

Hundreds of jewelry wholesalers and vendors are gathered together at **Beomil-dong Gold Theme Street** (a.k.a. Jewelry Street) near the Jayu and Pyeonghwa shijangs. Hours vary, but most are open daily from 10am to 8pm. Take subway line 1 to Beomil-dong (exit 8).

FOOD

Although a bit overpriced, the **Korean Traditional Authentic Food** shop is conveniently located at Gimhae Airport (right next to the airport police station). In this shop, open daily from 8am to 6pm, you can find everything from fermented seafood to ginseng and cookies. For better bargains and variety, try one of the large discount stores in town or the **Maeil Food** shop, 1185-37 Choryang 3-dong, Dong-gu, on the second floor of the Dongbu Goseok (Express) Bus Terminal.

For *insam* (ginseng) specifically, the **Bujeon Insam Wholesale Shopping Center** is your best bet for this dried root. Not only is it the largest ginseng market in the city, but the center has grown to include many other health foods. Expect to see a selection of dried mushrooms and other unidentifiable dried products. It's open daily from 6am to 5:30pm. Take subway line 1 to Bujeon-dong (exit 5).

Worth a look is the **Nampo-dong Dried Fish Market,** located near the Jagalchi Seafood Market. You'll see piles of squid jerky, dried seaweed, and other marine products being sold by dozens of street vendors.

HANDMADE CRAFTS

There is no dedicated area for handmade crafts, artworks, and antiques in Busan. To avoid the mass-produced and overpriced items found in souvenir shops, try the smattering of shops on the streets between Gwangbok-dong and Daecheong-no. You won't discover any fabulous finds here, but they do have a large selection of traditional ceramics and pottery.

Although they're expensive, you can get authentic traditional antiques at the **Korean Antique Gallery Migodang** (✆ 051/731-3444) in Haeundae. Take subway line 2 to Haeundae and walk about 10 minutes. The **Yegwadang Gallery** (✆ **051/752-3016**) in Gwangalli has a nice collection of teapots and teacups made by modern craftsmen. Take bus no. 41 to the Seongshim Hospital or get off at the back entrance to the Sehwa Mart. The **Busan Crafts & Exhibition Center** (✆ **051/740-7588**) on the first basement floor of BEXCO also has a decent selection of wooden crafts, ceramics, and lacquerware. The **Busan Department Store** (second floor), the **Arirang Folk Art Center** (✆ **051/245-6789**), and the **Han-kook Folk Art Center** (✆ **051/555-0092**) also specialize in folk crafts and traditional wares.

SOUVENIRS

Most souvenir shops can be found in the shopping arcades of major hotels, inside department stores, and in the shopping areas of transportation hubs. You'll find items more expensive than those in open-air markets and most of them are mass-produced. However, the items are usually of good quality, the shops take most major credit cards, and the sales staff can speak English.

Of special note is the **Dalwoo Amethyst** shop, 1-2, 2-ga, Gwangbok-dong, Jun-gu (✆ **051/243-8085**), which specializes in all things made of amethyst or jade.

The **Gonglee Art Creation** store (✆ **051/516-6755**), inside the Home Plus building in Yeonje-gu, has a variety of souvenirs made of wood, paper, mother-of-pearl, and metals.

TRADITIONAL & OPEN-AIR MARKETS

The open-air markets of Busan are interesting places to look for hard-to-find items, to browse the crowded stalls, and to haggle with vendors for the best price.

In addition to the major markets listed below, there are a handful of *o-il shijang* (5-day markets) scattered through the city. The **Jwacheon Market** is a village shijang, with a fish and cattle market nearby (open on dates that end in 4 or 9). Near the Gupo and Deokcheon stations is the **Gupo Market,** another traditional shijang (open on dates that end in 3 or 8). The **Gudeok Cultural Market,** open Saturday and Sunday near the Gudeok Stadium, is a great place to buy traditional folk art and handicrafts.

Busanjin Shijang ★ MARKET   Although there is a large cluster of clothing stores in Busan, this one caters to newlyweds. Here you can find everything a new bride needs for her wedding, especially her *hanbok* (Korean traditional outfit). It's also a great place to buy fabric and silks. Open daily from 8am to 8:30pm. Take subway line 1 to Beomil-dong (exit 8) and walk about 5 min.

Gukje Shijang ★★ MARKET   At the largest and oldest market in Busan, the vendors sell a variety of items—everything from food to industrial goods and clothes. Open daily from 9am to 8pm. Take subway line 1 to Jagalchi (exit 7) and walk about 10 min.

Jagalchi Shijang ★★★ MARKET   South Korea's largest seafood market, Jagalchi (roughly translates to "Pebble Village") Market became mostly a fish market after the Korean War. Although you probably won't be buying any fish to take home with you, this is a great place to see a variety of seafood you may have never seen before (most active early morning and late afternoon) and one of the best places to eat fresh raw fish, straight from the tanks. Since most of the vendors are middle-aged women, they are called the *jagalchi ajumma*. The **Jagalchi Festival** is held here every October. Open to wholesalers daily from 2am to midnight; regular retail hours are 7am to 9pm. Take subway line 1 to Nampo-dong Station and walk about 5 min. or to Jagalchi (exit 2) and walk 3 min. You can also take city bus no. 139, which will take you right to the market entrance. There is a paid parking lot that charges by the hour at the end of the street.

Pyeonghwa & Jayu Shingang MARKET   A short walk from the Busanjin Market are the Pyeonghwa (Peace) and Jayu (Freedom) markets. These are great places to get designer shoes, though it's harder to find larger sizes, since they cater to South Korean women's smaller feet. The Jayu shijang, located on the first and second floors of the building, is open 8am to 6pm, while the Pyeonghwa shijang, on the third floor, is open daily from 6am to 6pm. Take subway line 1 to Beomil-dong (exit 8) and it's about a 5-minute walk.

ENTERTAINMENT & NIGHTLIFE

Busan is perhaps a more beautiful city at night than it is during the day. From the glittering neon of the shopping districts to the lights of Gwangalli Bridge, there is no shortage of things to see and do after the sun goes down. In fact, the city's cafe and bar culture doesn't come alive until dark.

Upscale bars and cocktail lounges are located in the city's high-end hotels. Several other nightclubs and bars can be found throughout the city. More informal are the *hofs* (German-style beer bars) and *pojang macha* (neighborhood makgeolli and soju joints) where you can imbibe without breaking the bank. Most places with English-speaking owners can be found in Foreigners' Street and the upscale hotels. A quieter evening can include a cup of coffee from one of Gwangalli's many cafes, a stroll on the boardwalk in Haeundae, or a view of the city lights from Busan Tower.

Performing Arts

Opened in 1977, the **Busan Cultural Center ★★** (Daeyeon 4-dong, Nam-gu) has since added several smaller theaters and performance spaces. It is connected to the Municipal Museum and the main stage can seat 1,600 people. Take subway line 2 to the Daeyeon-dong Station (exit 3 or 5), and then walk 10 minutes toward the U.N. intersection (past the Busan Museum). Take bus no. 51-1 to the center or bus no. 68 or 134 and get off at U.N. Park. Call ✆ **051/625-8130** for info on tickets and dates.

Movie Theaters

Nampo-dong is home to the **Busan International Film Festival** (✆ **1688-3010;** www.biff.kr/structure/eng/default.asp), one of the largest film festivals in Asia. Usually held sometime in October, the BIFF is a showcase for not only domestically produced films, but also movies from international directors. The winners of the festival each year imprint their hands and feet on copper plates (similar to the prints in front of Grauman's Chinese Theater in Hollywood). These copper plates can be seen all across the plaza. Even outside of festival times, the area is crowded with moviegoers of all ages. Unfortunately, South Korean films aren't regularly subtitled (though they are for the festival), but you will be able to watch an English-language film here. Just be sure to make sure they aren't dubbed screenings.

Dance Clubs & Bars

There is no shortage of bars in Busan, but only a few Western-style clubs for dancing, and the action doesn't start until later on in the wee hours. Most dance clubs can be found in the PNU area or in the luxury hotels in Haeundae.

Be aware that if you go to a Korean-style bar or *soju bang* (literally, "soju room"), you're expected to order an overpriced anju with your drinks. Also, they won't let you in if you're dressed down or look like you came straight from the beach. Koreans dress to impress when they go out. The exceptions are the foreigner-friendly bars, mostly near the universities (see below). Also, beware of the "girlie" or "go-go" bars on Texas Street, which will have Western-style or Russian music. Some of the women earn a commission on how many drinks they can get patrons to buy for them. They aren't prostitutes but you can end up with an empty wallet, nevertheless.

Most places close around 2 or 4am, but a few are open well into sunrise. There are bars all over town, but the most popular areas include Nampo-dong, the PNU area, the Kyungsung University area, Haeundae, Gwangalli, and Seomyeon districts.

HAEUNDAE

A popular bar owned by an Englishman is **Starface ★** (✆ **051/742-0600**) in Haeundae; open every night from 7pm to 4am, they have an all-you-can drink deal on Fridays for only ₩20,000. There is a pool table, solid fish and chips, and sometimes live bands in the early evening. Down the hill is **Neo Starface,** known for its weekly salsa lessons on Saturdays (from 8–9pm). They also have a good stage for the occasional live bands that play there.

A casual joint in the area is **U2 Bar** (✆ **070/8924-6811**) a rock-'n'-roll club across the street from the Novotel. Just down the way at the Paradise Hotel is **Club Elune** (✆ **051/802-0555**), which is a stop for international DJs after they've done Seoul. Across from the Paradise Hotel is another Western-style club, **Club Maktum** (✆ **051/742-0770;** www.maktum.co.kr). You can't miss the well-dressed partiers lining up in front of the giant silver phallic entrance.

A foreigner-friendly, late-night option for dancing is the **Fuzzy Navel** (✆ 051/746-6349) (every night 7pm–6am). It's behind the Seacloud Hotel, on the right-hand side on the fourth floor (there are signs on the street level as well). The L-shaped bar has a main dance floor and other subrooms, one with a pool table.

For Western-style options, stop by **Brother's Bar and Grill** (✆ 051/721-5589) on Mipo Street, on the basement level of the DalMaji Hotel. Open noon to 2am daily, the place is run by a PNU English professor who missed his nachos and margaritas.

GWANGALLI

There are a few bars along the narrow beachfront with excellent views of the Gwangan Bridge. The Busan chain that serves good beer and cocktails, **Thursday Party** (✆ 051/758-0822), has a location here. For live jazz with the best view, head over to **LunaBass** (✆ 010/6807-1149; on the 5th floor above Holly's Coffee), which also has DJs spinning and newer acts on Sundays.

SEOMYEON

In the Seomyeon area, many foreigners head over to **O'Brien's Irish Bar and Restaurant** (051/894-6541) for a pint and a burger. (They also have live music on Saturdays.) Take the subway to Gaya Station (exit 2), walk straight ahead, and you'll find the bar on your left-hand side at the basement level.

Another popular nightspot in the neighborhood is **Club Foxy** (✆ 010/7648-1010). You'll see a bunch of Korean hip-hop dancers on the two dance floors, which can be quite entertaining. Cover price is usually half-price for expats and women.

Another happening place is **Guri Bar** (✆ 010/6807-1149), located behind the Lotte Hotel and **Club Fix** (✆ 051/905-5777; www.clubfixkorea.info), with two levels of dancing on the 8th and 9th floors of Judys Tehwa. They're open 24/7, but the real action happens when the guest DJs show up Friday and Saturday nights. Subway line 1 or 2 to Seomyeon Station.

PNU AREA

The younger crowds head out to the bars near the universities. One of the oldest joints in the area is **Soul Trane** (open 8pm–7am) a small, foreigner-friendly bar located underneath **Crossroads,** another bar popular with expats and run by the same owner. They sometimes have open mic night on Thursdays. To get here from the main gate of Busan National U., make the first left and walk about 3 blocks. The bars will be on your left. Around the corner from Soul Trane is what used to be a popular bar, **Moo Monk** (✆ 051/517-5298; 416-1 Jangjeon 3(sam)-dong, Geumjeong-gu) but it has turned quieter as other more popular joints have opened up nearby. Still, the live bands on Saturdays bring in crowds. Across the street is a spacious jazz/blues/folk club, **Interplay** (✆ 011/873-2200). Many of the country's top funk bands play here and it's a good place to get imported beer if you're tired of the weak Korean brews. Take the subway to the PNU Station (exit 3).

BUKYOUNG & KYUNGSUNG UNIVERSITY AREA

Near Kyungsung University is a great place to dance and hear live music, the **Vinyl Underground** (✆ 051/628-0223). International DJs and live bands perform in front of a crowded dance floor on weekends. For a more "meet market" scene, follow the beats to the open terrace of **Ghetto** (✆ 010/4588-4697), where the dance floor is crowded and shots are cheap. A mellower place that also has friendly, English-speaking staff is **Monk** (named after Thelonious Monk, ✆ 051/622-2212; 53-34 Daeyeong 3(sam-dong, Nam-gu). They have regular local jazz bands on Tuesday and

Thursday; live rock/blues/jazz bands on Friday, Saturday, and Sunday; and jams on Monday nights. Take subway line 2 to the Bukyoung/Kyungsung Station. Walk toward Bukyoung U. and turn left at the next-to-the-last street before you reach the entrance to the campus. The Monk Bar will be on your left, and make a left to get to Vinyl Underground (it'll be on your left side).

Another great place to catch live music on weekends is **Ol' 55,** located near Monk and Vinyl. They have an open mic on Wednesdays. Also in the same area is **Thursday Party,** which is a Busan-based chain of bars that serves draft beer and good cocktails. They have several other locations, including Gwangalli, Seomyeon, and one in Haeundae (on the main drag between the subway station and the beach). All of them are popular with foreigners.

Casinos

Like the majority of casinos in the country, the one in Busan is open only to foreigners. So don't forget to bring your passport. They offer free food and drinks, so you won't have to go hungry or thirsty while gambling the night away. The **Paradise Casino,** located inside the Paradise Hotel on Haeundae Beach, is the largest one in Busan (not difficult since it's the only one in the city at the moment) and is open 24 hours a day, 7 days a week. They have blackjack tables, baccarat, roulette, slot machines, and more.

GANGWON-DO

The Taebaek Mountains, sometimes called the backbone of Korea, run the length of Gangwon-do (Gangwon province), dividing the province into two distinct regions.

Traveling in Gangwon-do, you will discover unfettered forests, dramatic rocky coasts, and small towns with their own character.

Nature lovers will find everything from the majestic landscape of **Seoraksan** to the white waters of the region's strong rivers. All seasons bring tourists escaping the insanity of Seoul, but the changing colors of fall (autumn) draw the largest crowds. Winter attracts skiers, sledders, and ice fishermen to **Inje** and other mountain regions. Summer brings campers, and spring attracts hikers to its blooming mountains.

Stop in **Chuncheon** and cook some *dak galbi* (grilled chicken) on your tabletop and finish off your meal with some *mak gooksu* (mixed noodles). Or take a train to **Gangneung** and relax in a cafe there after visiting the gramophone museum. The region is known for their *baechu* (napa cabbage) and *gamja* (potatoes), so don't forget to enjoy some potato flatcakes or have a taste of the *kimchi* (spiced dish) made from cabbages that would have graced the royal table.

10

SEORAKSAN NATIONAL PARK ★★★

As South Korea's most popular national park, Seoraksan (Mt. Seorak) attracts many visitors on the weekends. But when the leaves change color in the fall, traffic basically comes to a standstill. If you want to avoid the crowds, aim to come on a weekday.

Seoraksan, which means "Snow Peak Mountain," was declared a conservation area by UNESCO (the only one in the entire country) in 1982. Since then, the government has tried to protect the 360 sq. km (140 sq. miles) of natural habitat and the unique plants and animals that are found here, while updating the facilities.

In the spring, blooming azaleas, dogwoods, and forsythia carpet the slopes in vibrant yellows, purples, and pinks. The summer brings lush green slopes and full streams and waterfalls as the melted snow makes its way down the rocky slopes. Fall is the most popular, with the brilliant colors of the fall (autumn) foliage in a riot of greens, yellows, reds, and oranges. Even in the winter, the snow blankets the hushed landscape, bringing serenity and a quiet beauty.

Seoraksan is divided into three parts: Outer (Oeseorak), Inner (Naeseorak), and South (Namseorak). Outer Seorak is part of Sokcho city and is the spot where you'll find the best lodging, leisure facilities, beaches,

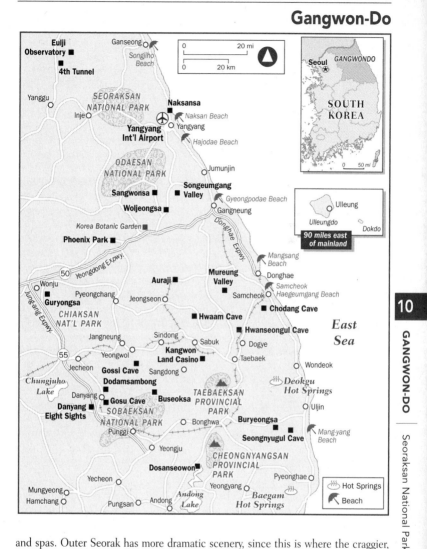

and spas. Outer Seorak has more dramatic scenery, since this is where the craggier, higher peaks can be found. It is closer to the ocean and has steeper slopes.

Less accessible is Inner Seorak, deep within the Taebaek Mountains. The slopes are mellower, but there is thicker vegetation. It has beautiful scenery and famous temples, like **Baekdamsa** (p. 333) and **Bongjeong-am.** There are fewer tourist spots, but more opportunities for hiking. South Seorak is a popular starting point for hikers since it's the most direct route to the Daecheongbong, the main peak where you'll find the **Osaek Hot Springs** (p. 331) and other carbonic acid spas in the area.

The mountains and waterfalls of the region offer spectacular views, not just for serious rock climbers but even for casual hikers. Admission to the park is free but fees apply for individual temples, camping, and other attractions within the park.

Essentials

GETTING THERE   There is a tiny, very underused airport at **Yangyang** (YNY), 281-1, Dongho-li, Sonyang-myeon (☎ **033/670-7317;** www.airport.co.kr/doc/ yangyang_eng); there are infrequent flights from Busan and Jeju-do, as well as charter flights from China, Japan, and Taiwan. Check with China Southern Airlines (www. csair.com), Jeju Air (www.jejuair.net), or Korean Air (www.koreanair.com) for flight info.

There are no rail lines that will take you directly from Seoul or Busan to Seoraksan, but you can take a bus. The closest train station is at Jeongdongjin. From there, you can take a bus to Sokcho. There are local buses from Jeongdongjin to Sokcho seven times a day and buses also go to Samcheok three times a day. Airport limousine buses run three times a day from Yangyang and go to various places, including Naksan, Sokcho, and Tongil Park. Fares range from ₩1,200 to Naksan to ₩6,900 to Tongil Park.

The most popular way to come to Sokcho is to take an express bus from the **Seoul Express Bus Terminal,** 19-3 Banpo-dong, Seocho-gu (☎ **02/535-4151**), or **DongSeoul Bus Terminal,** 546-1 Guui-dong, Seongdong-gu (☎ **02/446-8000**). Buses from Seoul Express Terminal start leaving at 6:30am in 30- to 60-minute intervals and stop running at 11:30pm. Buses from the DongSeoul depart daily every 1½ hours from 7am to 7pm. The trip from the express terminal takes about 2½ hours and costs around ₩17,000. Buses from DongSeoul take nearly 30 minutes longer and cost more, ₩22,000. There is a 20-minute rest stop after about 2 hours. From Sokcho, take bus no. 7 or 7-1 for Seorak-dong and it will take you to Outer Seorak (Oeseorak). The local bus costs about ₩1,200 and takes about 30 minutes.

Driving from Seoul it takes only about 3 hours to get to Seoraksan on the Yeongdong highway (road 50), without traffic of course. If you prefer to take more scenic routes, opt for one of many mountain roads that wind around the terrain of Gangwon-do to Seoraksan. Once inside the national park, you'll have to hoof it.

A South Korean travel agency, **Exodus DMC** (☎ **031/907-8044,** ext. 5; fax 031/907-2393; www.koreabound.com; Mon–Fri 9am to 6pm), offers 3-day/2-night trips from Seoul to Mt. Seorak, which include a stop in Hwajinpo, a coastal town where former North Korean leader Kim Il-Sung and his family used to spend their summer holidays before the two Koreas split.

GETTING AROUND   Since much of Seoraksan is protected natural preserves, there are no buses running through the park. However, buses from nearby towns will bring you to the park's entrance. From there your best bet is to walk or take a taxi to the sections you'd like to see. You may wish to rent a car to give yourself maximum freedom to get around. We recommend renting a car in Seoul and driving here (see chapter 3 for car-rental info). If you wait until you're in the area, you can rent a car at a higher-end hotel or from **Seorak Park Rent-a-Car** (the Gangneung branch, ☎ **033/651-8006**) or KT Rent-a-Car (☎ **033/632-80004266;** 895-2 Gyeo-dong, Sokcho-si).

VISITOR INFORMATION   The official Seoraksan National Park Management Office website is at http://english.knps.or.kr; or call ☎ **033/639-2690** in Sokcho (www.sokchotour.com/english), ☎ **033/672-2883** in Osaek, or ☎ **033/460-2170** in Inje. There is a **tourist information center** (☎ **033/639-2689**) at the Sokcho Express Bus Terminal, which is open daily from 9am to 6pm, but closed in January.

Seoraksan National Park

SEORAKSAN NATIONAL PARK

East Sea

Sokcho

Ulsan Bawi

Yongdae

46

Namgyo

Gyeojoam

Park Front Gate

Geumgang Cave

Seorakdong

Baekdamsa

Gwongeumseong Fortress

Biseondae Cliff

Biryong Falls

Daeseungnyeong

Ansan

Hwachaebong

7

Hangye

44

Jangsudae

Daesung Falls

Gwitegichongbong

Seoraksan

Naksan

Garibong

Sibi Falls

Yongso Falls

Osaek

Seongguksa

44

0   5 mi
0   5 km

RESTAURANTS ◆

Cheogatjip Yangnyeom Tongdak **2**

Haksapyeong Soon Dubu Chon **1**

Jinyang Hwaetjip **3**

ATTRACTIONS ●

Sokcho Beach **4**

Yeongnyang Lake

Dongdae Beach

YEONGNYANG LAKE RESORT

YEONGYANG LAKE GOLF COURSE

Intercity Bus Terminal

Passenger Ferry Terminal

City Hall

CENTRAL MARKET

Sokcho

Seoraksan National Park

Seoul

GANGWONDO

SOUTH KOREA

0   50 mi

Cheongcho Lake

SOKCHO

Expo Tower

Expo Ferry Terminal

[Fast FACTS] SEORAKSAN

The closest "village" to Seoraksan is Seorak-dong, a man-made, hypertouristy enclave of hotels, motels, restaurants, and souvenir shops, but most of the action happens in Sokcho city.

Banks, Foreign Exchange & ATMs Sokcho is the most convenient, though not the most economical, place to get your money exchanged (at the currency exchange desks of banks). You're better off looking for ATMs, which are fairly easy to find.

Post Office The post office (Mon–Fri 9am–4:30pm) is at 46-119 Seorak-dong, Sokcho-si (☏ 033/636-7002).

Exploring Oeseorak (Outer Seoraksan)

There are four different entrances to Seoraksan National Park, and which one you choose will depend on what you'd like to see. The park itself is bordered by four cities and counties—Sokcho, Inje, Goseong, and Yangyang. Outer Seoraksan can be best reached from Sokcho.

Biryong Falls ★ NATURAL ATTRACTION The name, which means "Flying Dragon Falls," came from the idea that the roaring waters tumbling over the rocks evoked the shape of dragons rising from the mist. The hike to these 40m-high (131-ft.) falls is a pleasant one, leading through a bamboo forest and over the Biryong-gyo (Biryong Bridge) in the lower part of the Cheonbuldong (One Thousand Buddhas) Valley. If you walk past the bridge and go about 30 minutes to the left, you will see **Yukdam Falls,** a group of six small waterfalls cascading into a deep pond. A further 20-minute walk will bring you to Biryong Falls.

Cable Car TOUR During high season, there can be up to a 2-hour wait for the cable car, which runs from the park entrance up to Gwongeumseong (see below), so be sure to come early or late, when the crowds have thinned out. The actual ride up takes only 6 minutes and saves an arduous and steep climb that takes over an hour on foot. It doesn't run during strong winds, so check the weather before making a special trip.

₩9,000 for ages 13 and over, ₩6,000 for ages 4–12, free for children 3 and under. Round-trip tickets are good for the date of purchase only. Runs daily every 7 min. 7am–6pm.

Cheoksan Oncheon (Cheoksan Hot Springs) ★ NATURAL ATTRACTION The region's hot spring, which dates back to the Mesozoic era, is known for its slightly blue color. Like many of South Korea's hot springs, the locals claim that the waters are great for people with skin and eye diseases. We don't know how curative the minerals in the water are, but a hot soak is nice after a long day of hiking in Seoraksan. They also have hotel rooms starting at ₩60,000 for a double room on weekdays.

939-7, Nohak-dong, Sokcho-si. ☏ **033/636-4806.** www.chocksanspa.co.kr (Korean only). Admission ₩6,000 adults, ₩3,000 children. Hot springs daily 6am–9pm.

Cheonbuldong (Seorak Valley) ★★★ WALKING TRAIL The main valley in Seoraksan, it got its name because of the many peaks surrounding it, lined up like 1,000 Buddhist saints. There is a river that runs through the narrow valley as the water flows over white boulders. What used to be a difficult path is now overrun with tourists, especially in early October, when the fall colors bring the masses. From Sinheungsa, walk to the **Biseondae (Fairy Rock)** and continue to the valley.

Gwongeumseong (Gwongeum Fortress) RUINS A site of an old castle, it was believed to have been built during the time of the 23rd Goryeo king, Gojong. It is also called Onggeum Castle, Toto Castle, or Gwon-Kim Castle, the latter name derived from a legend that two generals built it to keep peace. Past the Biryong Bridge, there is a path that leads to Gwongeumseong, but it was so steep and rocky that a cable car (see above) was built in 1971. From high on the plateau of the ruin, you can get a wonderful view of the valleys and the rocks below.

Gyejo-am (Gyeojo Hermitage) TEMPLE When starting from the Sokcho entrance to the national park, and climbing up to Ulsan Bawi, this small hermitage temple is a nice place to rest and take in the scenery (especially the view of Cheon-buldong Valley below). Created from a natural stone cave, it was built in A.D. 652, the same year the Hangseongsa and Sinheungsa were built. Near Gyejo-am is **Heundeul Bawi (Teetering Rock),** a massive boulder which sits precariously on a cliff. One person pushing on the boulder can make it rock slightly, but it won't budge from its resting spot regardless of how much force is used to push it. Check out the graffiti that other visitors have left behind, some of which dates back hundreds of years.

Osaek Oncheon (Osaek Hot Springs) NATURAL ATTRACTION Part of Namseorak (South Seorak), the hot springs were supposedly discovered by a Buddhist monk during the Joseon period. Water that is high in iron and carbonic acid flows in rivulets from three base rocks. It's supposed to have many health benefits, including being good for the complexion, and is sometimes called Miin oncheon (Beauty Hot Springs) as well. The area has some easy walks and some very challenging trails, but what draws most visitors are the hot springs and baths available in the area's resort hotels, such as the **Seorak Spa (℃ 033/670-1000).**

Inside Seoraksan, Osaek-li, Seo-myeon, Yangyang-gun. Admission ₩5,000 adults, ₩3,000 youth, free for kids 6 and under. Daily 24 hr.

Seorak Sunrise Park/Naemulchi Park PARK Stretching along the coastal edge of Seoraksan, the park here has become famous for its beautiful sunrise over the East Sea. A Joseon Dynasty scholar, Song Si-yeol, named the place Naemulchi ("a village sunk underwater by heavy rain") on his way to exile on Geoje-do.

Daepo-dong, Sokcho. ℃ **033/625-2003.** Free admission. 24 hr. daily. From the Sokcho Express Bus Terminal, take local bus no. 1, 7, or 9 (takes about 10 min.); from the Sokcho Intercity Bus Terminal, take local bus no. 7-1 or 9-1 (takes about 30 min.).

Seorak Waterpia ★ WATER PARK Located inside the Hanhwa Resort Complex, this water park and oncheon was the first one built in Seoraksan. The pools here are filled with mineral water from Cheoksan. In addition to the usual water park facilities, there is also a theme park with water rafts and body slides. There are plenty of soaking and sauna facilities as well.

24-1 Jangsa-dong, Sokcho-si (inside the Hanhwa Resort Complex). ℃ **033/635-7700.** www. seorakwaterpia.co.kr/irsweb/waterpia/eng/index.asp. Admission ₩34,500 to ₩52,000 adults, ₩24,000 to ₩33,000 children, depending on time of entry. Daily 6am–8:30pm.

Sinheungsa ★ TEMPLE The country's oldest Seon (Zen) temple, it is also the closest to the Sokcho entrance to Seoraksan, only about a 10-minute walk from **Sogong-won** (small park). Built by the Shilla Monk Jajang Yulsa in A.D. 652, it has been destroyed and rebuilt many times. A newer bronze Buddha statue (over 10m/33 ft. high) stands on the path to the temple. Although most of the structures have been rebuilt, the original three-story pagoda, a 1,400-year-old bell, and one of the original stone Buddha statues remain on-site. You may choose to do an overnight temple stay here as well.

170 Seorak-dong, Sokcho-si. (✆) **033/636-7044.** www.sinhungsa.or.kr (Korean only). Admission ~~₩2,500 adults, ₩1,000 teens, ₩600 ages 7–12~~, free for seniors 65 and over and kids 6 and under. Daily 4am–7pm.

Ulsan Bawi (Ulsan Rock) ★ WALKING TRAIL   There is a trail from Gyejo-am that leads straight up the hill to the Ulsan rocks. Made up of six granite peaks, jutting above thick forests, Ulsan Bawi has a view of the surrounding mountains, the East Sea, and the Haksapyeong reservoir that is pretty spectacular. The trail up from Gyejo-am is so steep that a metal staircase was installed to make the climb easier. It is still a steep incline and will take about 45 to 60 minutes to climb to the top from Gyejo-am. From Sinheungsa, it'll take about 2 hours.

HIKING TRAILS

For most visitors to Seoraksan, a half-day or full-day hike is a good way to see the highlights of the park. If you're a serious hiker or backpacker, you can hire a guide for about 3 days to explore the lesser-seen areas. Contact the **Seoraksan National Park Administration Office** (✆ **033/636-7700**) for more info. The following are hikes (Koreans call them courses) that will take less than half a day to a full day. Regardless of how long you plan to be out, check the weather conditions and road closures before heading out. Be sure to bring a hat, sunblock, water, and snacks or a meal. Due to fire hazards, there is no smoking or cooking allowed in the park. The trails listed below are open year-round, except in inclement weather (such as extreme snow conditions in the winter). **Note:** Regardless of how hot it may get in the summer, swimming is also not allowed. Admission to the park is free, but temples and other locations charge a fee.

Biryong Falls-Sinheungsa Course HIKING TRAIL   Head for the Sinheung Temple. From there, go left, where you will see the Biryong-gyo (bridge). The trail starts right after you cross the bridge and takes you to the waterfall. A pleasant hike near the water, it'll take about 2 hours, with no major uphill climbs.

Biseondae Cliffs-Sinheungsa Course HIKING TRAIL   From Sinheungsa, head straight, toward the Iljumun (gate). After passing the cliffs, you'll see Daecheongbong (Great Green Peak). In the center of the Bonguri (rock) is Geumgang-gul (cave). Climbing up the steps to the cave will take about 30 to 40 minutes. This is one of the most scenic hikes in the park, and it's an easy trek for beginners; plan on it taking about 2 hours.

Gwongeumseong-Sinheungsa Course HIKING TRAIL   From the entrance, walk down the path to the park—from there you can take the cable car up to the top. Once you get off the cable car, it's about a 20- to 30-minute hike up to the Gwongeum Fortress. A relatively easy hike, the entire round-trip will take about 80 minutes.

Seongguksa Course (Osaek Area) WALKING TRAIL   This trail runs through Cheonbuldong and Baekdam valleys, as well as the Seongguksa. From the entrance to the park, follow the trail that leads up to Seongguksa. Continue through **Jujeongol Valley** ★★★ and you will come to a fork in the road. The left leads to Sibi Falls, while the right path leads to Yongso Falls. This easy hike will take about 2 hours.

Ulsan Bawi Course HIKING TRAIL   This course is relatively easy from Heundeul Bawi (Teetering Rock) to Gyejo-am. The difficulty comes in the steep climb up the rocks of Ulsan Bawi from the hermitage below. There are metal stairs to help with the climb, but it's still quite dangerous and slippery, especially in wet weather. Still, the view of the mountains and the ocean from the top is worth all that hard work.

Yangpok Course HIKING TRAIL   Starting from the Sinheungsa area, this trail includes the Yang Falls, located in the Cheonbuldong Valley. This hike is well known for its colorful scenery in the fall (autumn); you'll walk along the valley and see mountain peaks, dense forests, and clear water falling from the mountains. This course takes about 6 hours round-trip, but doesn't have any major uphill climbs.

Exploring Naeseorak (Inner Seorak)

Less convenient to get to, the inner part of Seoraksan is much more tranquil and quiet, but not any less beautiful.

Baekdamsa (Baekdam Temple) ★ TEMPLE   Located inside Naeseorak, the temple has been destroyed several times and rebuilt, even changing locations and names. There is a newer stone bridge over the Bokdam Gyegok leading to the entrance of this humble, understated temple. Of its on-site treasures, the most impressive is the wooden Amitayus Buddha, which was made in 1748, and is considered one of the best statues from that time.

690-beonji, Yongdae-li, Bukmyeon, Inje-gun. ℭ **033/462-2554.** www.baekdamsa.org (Korean only). Admission free. Daily 9am–5pm. From the Inje Terminal, take a bus to Wontong or Jinburyeong and get off at Yongdae-li. From there, walk 15 min. to the next bus stop and take a shuttle/village bus to Baekdamsa. Bus costs ₩2,000 adults, ₩1,000 for children.

Baekdam Valley WALKING TRAIL   The valley got its name thanks to a legend about **Baekdamsa.** The temple was moved to this valley sometime in the 1300s, after it was plagued by mysterious fires in its old location. But the fires continued until one night, a monk dreamed that an elder monk tossed water from the mountain above. The name was changed to Baekam (100 Pools)—fitting since there are dozens of pools in the area—and the fires stopped. Unfortunately, the temple was destroyed during the Korean War and has never been fully rebuilt.

A river runs through the valley in an S-shape, from the Naegappyeong Village to the front of Baekdam Mountain Villa. You can walk up from the ticket booth to **Baekdamsa,** located in the middle of the valley, or take a shuttle bus halfway up. About a 10-minute walk from the temple is the Baekdam Mountain Villa. If you continue up, you'll see the Geumgyo, the first bridge on the right side. After crossing the third bridge (the Gang-gyo), you'll see Eunseon-do. From the fourth road, the rest of the paths are sand.

Baekundong Valley HIKING TRAIL   The valley is located between Deoktaesan and Seongaksan, between the Seven Brothers Stones and the Yongdam Falls, starting from Gwuiddegicheong Peak. On either side, there are sheer cliffs, which are popular with mountain climbers but can be enjoyed by all visitors. The largest waterfall in the valley is Baekun Falls, from which you can get a great view of the mountainous scenery.

Daeseung Falls ★★ NATURAL ATTRACTION   This was the main recreational area for the last Shilla emperor, King Gyeong-Sun. The path to the falls starts on a steep, rocky climb from the left of Jangsudae ticket booth. Go past Sajung Falls and continue up the metal ladder until you reach an observation area, where you can see the falls. Walk along on the right walkway to Daseung-ryong for about 5 minutes, and you'll meet a narrow path leading right up to the waterfall.

Gaya-dong Valley ★★★ NATURAL ATTRACTION Located deep in the heart of Seoraksan, Gaya-dong is a relatively small valley, but has its quiet charms. The trail that leads to the valley starts behind the Suryeomdong shelter. Walk up for 30 minutes and you'll come upon Ose Falls. In front of it are the high cliffs, called the **Cheonwang Gates,** the entryway to Gaya-dong. Shortly past the "gates" is Cheonwang Falls, and then Waryongyeon. Above Waryongyeon is Neoreok Rock. If you walk farther up there is a crossway. The old path to Ose-am is on the left and the path to Bongjeong-am is on the right. Stop to enjoy the scenery at Mangyeongdae on the way to Ose-am. If you keep going up, you'll reach Muneomi Ridge. There the path splits into two again—one leads to Bongyrong Ridgeline and the other to Cheonbuldong Valley. If you want to climb to Daecheong Peak, walk past the Huiungak shelter in the Socheong Peak toward Jungcheong Peak. About 2km (1¼ miles) down from Daecheong Peak is **Bongjeong-am,** which is supposed to be one of the best retreats for Buddhists in the country. The most famous structure in the hermitage is a five-story stone pagoda that's over 1,300 years old. Gaya-dong has convenient paths, still unadulterated by any signs or metal steps.

Hangyeryeong NATURAL ATTRACTION One of the three ridges that make up Seoraksan (the other two are Misiryeong and Jinburyeong). If you go down the Hangyeryeong path, you will reach the **Osaek District,** named such since "o" in Korean means five. Everything in this area is supposed to come in fives. The natural carbonated spring water is said to have five flavors; the original stone pagoda that stands in the Seongguksa temple site is said to have rocks of five colors. There is even a mythical flower that is said to have bloomed in five different colors.

Hwangtaedeok Jang (Alaskan Pollack Market) MARKET In the winter (from the end of Dec to Mar), rows of *hwangtae* (Alaskan pollack) are left out to dry in the winter winds. Alaskan pollack (also known as wall-eye pollack) is a meaty white fish and a member of the cod family. It's also something of a staple of the diet around here. Not only is it fun to see row after row of fish laid out to dry, but the scenery in the Inje Yondae-li area is even more gorgeous under a blanket of white snow.

Jangsudae WALKING TRAIL The least popular part of the park, the area is named after the traditional house built here by Korean soldiers, which they called Jangsudae. Surrounded by the Jangsudae cliffs, the house marks the starting point for the trail that leads to Daeseung Falls and the 12 Seonnyetang.

Misiryeong Valley NATURAL ATTRACTION The Misiryeong Valley extends into Seoraksan past **Dojeok Pokpo (Thief Waterfall)** toward Inje. The waterfall is named after a local legend about a thief who lurked in the valley, robbing unsuspecting travelers, and then drowning them in the waterfall. Despite this area's penchant for dark stories, this unfettered forest is peaceful and cool, even in the summer. The path to the waterfall is a bit steep, but a rope is provided to guide you down.

Naerincheon (Naerin Stream) NATURAL ATTRACTION The only *cheon* (small river) in the country that flows north, it crosses Hongcheon and Inje. Naerincheon Gyegok (valley) starts near Odaesan Valley and Hapgang-gyo (bridge) and continues for about 57km (35 miles). Usually, when people say Naerincheon, they mean the downstream area of Naerincheon. The upper stream of Naerincheon is again divided into Misan Valley and Moraeso Valley. Few people go there because it is difficult to reach. On the upper stream of Bangtaecheon, which joins together with Naerincheon, is Jindong Valley, and to the north of Naerincheon is Jumbongsan, Bangtaesan, Bangdong Springs, and Bangtaesan Recreational Forest. Hwangso and

Seori resorts are in the midsection of Naerincheon, and Piasi Valley is downstream. The Piasi River runs between Hyeon-li and Soyang-ho (lake).

Seongguksa (Seongguk Temple) TEMPLE   The original temple was built during the Shilla Dynasty, but the new temple was built in 1995. All that remains of the original is a three-story stone pagoda. The most impressive element of the current temple is a very large bronze Buddha that towers over the area. There is a reclining Buddha statue and a couple of large gold Buddha statues on-site as well. There are also new shrines with rows of smaller golden Buddhas, each dedicated to a family.

San 1-21, Osaek-li, Seo-myeon Yangyang-gun. Admission free. Enter the park through the Osaek area.

Seonnyetang Tangsugol (Valley of the 12 Angels' Bath) ★★★ NATU-RAL ATTRACTION   Seonnyetang Tangsugol is a valley in Yondae-li where a water-fall connects to a pool. Legend has it that 12 angels came down to bathe here (hence the name), but there are only eight pools. Due to natural erosion, there are steep holes and pools in the valley creating the water baths. Unfortunately, some of the scenery has been ruined by the iron bridges that go over the bathing pools, but the bridges do make for easier access.

HIKING TRAILS

Baekdamsa Course HIKING TRAIL   Enter the park from the Baekdam area of Inje-gun. This trail has two options: the first will take you to the Baekdamsa. The well-paved path is easy, but longer. For those less inclined to walk, you can take a shuttle bus, which will take you halfway up the mountain, leaving the last few kilometers for you to hike up yourself.

Daeseung Falls Course HIKING TRAIL   The Daeseung waterfall is one of the three largest in the country. Enter the park from the Inje area and go up the steep steps. On the way up, you will see a forked path. Take the left one to go to the falls. You'll know you're close by when you hear the sound of cascading waters echoing on the rocks. The steep trail takes about 2 hours.

Suryeomdong Course HIKING TRAIL   Enter the park from the Baekdam area of Inje-gun; this trail includes the Baekdam and Suryeomdong valleys. This is a long but not steep trail and will take about 4 hours. If you're short on time, or feeling less than energetic, you can take a shuttle bus that will take you about 4.5km (2¾ miles) up.

Around Seoraksan

SOKCHO

A small city on the eastern coast, Sokcho is the main gateway to Seoraksan National Park. In and of itself, it is a charming town with a beautiful beach and several attractions of its own. It is also one of the only towns in the area with a semblance of a nightlife.

Since there is no rail service and no city airport, the best way to get here is by bus. There are two bus stations in town—one is an express bus terminal and the other is the regular intercity bus terminal. (See "Getting There," earlier in this chapter.)

Sokcho Beach BEACH   Located just about 500m (1,640 ft.) from the Sokcho Express Bus Terminal, just turn left and you'll hit the beach in about 5 minutes. Summer break (mid-July through Aug) draws all the tourists fleeing the heat of Seoul. It's a pleasant, sandy beach, with a volleyball court, a mini-football (soccer) field, and shower and changing facilities. There is a campground nearby as well.

Joyang-dong, Sokcho-si. Daily 6am–midnight. Free admission. Parking available.

YANGYANG

Yangyang is south of Sokcho and the first town you reach on the coast when you come east from Seoul. You can take a bus for Yangyang from the DongSeoul Bus Terminal. They run daily from 7am to 7:30pm about every hour and the trip takes about 3½ hours. There is a small airport in Yangyang (see "Getting There," earlier in this chapter), but most people take the bus. Buses run to and from Osaek, Jangsu-dae, Seoraksan, and Sokcho.

The town and the county (*gun*) have the same name (making this a bit confusing). Yangyang is well known throughout the country for its *songi beoseot* (pine mushrooms). You'll even see a cartoon mushroom "mascot" statue at the entrance to the town.

Included in Yangyang county is **Naksan Provincial Park,** which has 24km (15 miles) of shoreline that extends through the Seonsa relic area, Dongho Beach, and Hajodae Beach. It is centered on Naksansa and Naksan Beach. Entrance to the park is free.

Hajodae Beach ★ BEACH Located 1km (⅔ mile) north of the 38th parallel, there is a small pavilion, the **Hajodae** (dating back to the Joseon Dynasty), overlooking the sea. The **38th parallel,** (there is a boulder indicating it) is where the division was drawn at the end of World War II, so all points north of here were administered by North Korea. When the ceasefire was signed after the Korean War, territory above this line was traded with almost an equal amount of land north of Seoul, below the 38th parallel. On the left side of the beach is an unmanned lighthouse, which is open daily from 9am to 7pm. You can see some spectacular scenery from there. The most popular times to visit are when the waters are warmer in mid-July through August.

Hagwangjeong-li, Hyeonbuk-myeon, Yangyang-gun. Free admission. Daily 24 hr. From the Yangyang Intercity Bus Terminal, take a bus bound for Gangneung or Jumunjin and get off at Hajodae. Buses run every 20 min. and take 10 min.

Naksan Beach BEACH A popular beach on the east coast, a dense pine forest comes right up to the expansive sand here. Facilities include showers, a wrestling area, a mini-volleyball court, and dressing rooms.

Jeonjin-li/Jucheong-li/Josan-li, Ganghyeon-myeon, Yangyang-gun. Free admission. Daily 24 hr. Parking available. From Yangyang Bus terminal, take bus no. 9 or 9-1 to Naksan Station. It's a 5-min. walk from there.

Naksansa (Naksan Temple) ★ TEMPLE This temple burned down in the spring of 2005, and newer, brighter temple buildings were completed in 2009. It is known as the "Temple of Compassion" (because the Avalokitesvara Bodhisattva, who embodies perfect compassion, is housed there). The beautiful stone statue, overlooking the East Sea, was luckily untouched by the fire. A smaller wooden statue and the building that housed it were also unharmed.

The original temple was founded by Uisang, the ambassador for Shilla King Munmu, in A.D. 671. One of the few older items that remain is the arched gate (built in 1467 during the reign of King Sejo), which is said to be made of 26 stones, one for each of the magistrates governing the 26 towns in the area. The seven-story pagoda was said to be constructed during that time as well. The bronze bell on-site dates back to 1469.

Below the temple on a seaside cliff is the small hermitage, **Hongryeon-am,** which was also spared from the fire. When you enter the sanctuary (as always, be sure to remove your shoes), take note of the small hole in the floor through which you can view the waves crashing below.

Tip: Visit during lunch hour and be treated to a free bowl of *janchi gooksu* ("feast noodles"), a humble dish of broth and somen (noodles).

Jeonjin 1-li, Ganghyeon-myeon, Yangyang-gun. ℂ **033/672-2417.** Admission free. Sunrise–sunset. From either the Yangyang or the Sokcho intercity bus terminals, take bus no. 9 or 9-1 and get off at Naksansa. It takes 10 min. from Yangyang or 40 min. from Sokcho. Driving from Yangyang, take national road 7 to Naksan beach and you'll find signs pointing to the temple.

Uisang-dae (Uisang Pavilion) HISTORIC SITE   Located on a hill overlooking the ocean, this small pavilion is on the way to Hongryeonam's Gwaneum Cave from Naksansa. It is believed to have been built by Ambassador Uisang as a place for him to meditate while he was building Naksansa. Like many other historical places in the country, it was destroyed and later rebuilt. The current structure was built in 1925.

Jeonjin-li, Ganghyeon-myeon, Yangyang-gun. Free admission. Daily sunrise–sunset. Follow the directions to Naksansa (see above).

INJE

A county on the western edge of Seoraksan, Inje (ℂ **033/461-2170;** www.inje. go.kr/home/english/html/main.asp) is a rural county with about 90% of the land covered with forests. Most travelers just pass through it to get from Chuncheon to Seoraksan and the eastern sea. While most of the luxury hotels and condos are on the Sokcho side of Seoraksan, Inje has many of the more affordable and humble *minbak* (homestays). The **Inje Bus Terminal** (ℂ **033/463-2231,** Korean only) has buses to and from DongSeoul Station, Chuncheon, Sokcho, Daejin, Seoraksan, and local destinations.

Although the major tourist attractions here are part of Seoraksan, the main draw is the white-water rafting. The conditions on the **Naerincheon River** are ideal for the sport.

Every winter the **Inje Ice Fishing Festival** (ℂ **033/460-2082**) is held, usually in late January to early February. While the area is frozen over and covered in white snow, there are smelt-fishing contests and other winter fun, like sledding, ice bowling, and snowmobiling.

Where to Stay

Being one of the most visited tourist areas in the country, there are plenty of accommodations to choose from. High season is usually during break time in the summer (mid-July through Aug) and even more so when the leaves change color in the fall (autumn) (early Oct to mid-Nov).

For inexpensive lodgings, love motels in the area start at ₩40,000 for a double. *Yeogwan* and minbak have comparable prices for two. Most low-end accommodations don't take reservations, take cash only (payable at check-in), and are the same price per room regardless of whether you're traveling alone or with a companion. Most lower-end accommodations are family owned, which means the owners generally do not speak English, but most of them are very friendly and helpful. All of these places offer TVs, minifridges, and toiletries (some of the love motels have Internet access in the rooms). You can ask for a toothbrush or razor at the desk if you forgot yours.

Yeogwan and love motels in Yangyang start at ₩35,000.

EXPENSIVE

Hotel Maremons ★   This modern building is located on the coast, so some of the rooms have nice views of the East Sea. Within walking distance to Sokcho Beach, rooms are efficient with clean-line furniture, but not very spacious. The beds are the usual, Korean standard—comfortable, but not plush, and ondol rooms are available. You do get better facilities and beds with the deluxe rooms and suites. The on-site facilities are quite modern and staff are ultrafriendly. Ask about package deals when making a reservation and you may get a good discount on the spa and other facilities.

245-5 Daepo-dong, Sokcho-si. www.hotelmaremons.com (Korean only). ⓒ **033/630-7000.** Fax 033/638-8403. 148 units. ₩120,000 and up standard room. AE, MC, V. **Amenities:** 3 restaurants; bar; cafe; pool; health club; spa; sauna; karaoke. *In room:* A/C, TV, fridge, hair dryer, Internet.

Kensington Stars Hotel ★★   Located near the Sokcho entrance to Seoraksan, this may be one of the best hotels in the area. The rooms are comfortable and nicely furnished, and most of them have mountain views and balconies (be sure to request one with a view when making reservations). Built in 1979, the facilities are constantly being updated and the various themes add a fun touch. Both Western-style and Korean-style ondol rooms are available. The wonderful staff speak excellent English and are very accommodating.

106-1 Seorak-dong, Sokcho-si. www.kensington.co.kr. ⓒ **033/635-4001.** 109 units. ₩190,000 and up standard room. AE, MC, V. **Amenities:** 3 restaurants; bar; 2 cafes; pool; sauna; concierge. *In room:* A/C, TV, minibar, fridge, hair dryer.

MODERATE

Hanhwa Resort ★★ ☺   Located near Seoraksan, just outside of Sokcho city, this large resort complex (it claims to be the largest in South Korea) is perfect for families and groups traveling together. There are only two kinds of rooms—the "family" type, which has two bedrooms and sleeps five people, and the "royal" type, which is twice as large and has three bedrooms. Both have living rooms and kitchens. The best parts of the property are its association with the Seorak Waterpia and the view of the surrounding mountainscape.

San 24-1, Changsa-dong, Sokcho-si. ⓒ **033/630-5500** or 1588-2299. 1,564 units. ₩274,000 and up. MC, V. **Amenities:** Restaurant; cafe; sauna; karaoke; Internet. *In room:* A/C, TV, kitchen, fridge.

Hyundae Sky Resort ★ ☺   Conveniently located in Sokcho, they have both Western-style rooms with beds and Korean ondol-style rooms. All units have kitchen facilities. Like all "condos" in South Korea, this location isn't a great bargain for single travelers, but is a good option for families or groups.

1401 Joyang-dong, Sokcho-si. www.hdskyresort.com. ⓒ **02/587-8811** from Seoul. 93 units. ₩200,000 and up. MC, V. **Amenities:** Restaurant; karaoke. *In room:* A/C, TV, kitchen, hair dryer.

Hotel Sorak Park   One of the original hotels in the region, this 12-story, V-shaped building set back against the hills is a sight you can't miss. All the rooms are dated, but have nice mountain views and balconies. The on-site facilities are geared toward your entertainment, including games rooms, a casino, a nightclub, and barbecue facilities. Just be aware that many of these facilities are closed off season.

74-3, Seorak-dong, Sokcho-si. www.hotelsorakpark.co.kr/eng/company/intro_hotel.asp, ⓒ **033/636-7711.** Fax 033/636-7732. 148 units. ₩193,600 and up standard room. AE, MC, V. **Amenities:** Restaurant; bar; cafe; health club; sauna; karaoke; casino. *In room:* A/C, TV, minibar, hair dryer, Internet.

INEXPENSIVE

Motel Orange ★ Just a block inland from the shore, you can't miss the friendly neon orange on top of the building that distinguishes it from the other motels in the area. Some rooms have computers with free high-speed Internet access, but be sure to ask at the front desk when checking in. They also have a Korean condo-style facility with kitchen on the sixth floor, which is great for traveling families or groups.

62-7 Mulshi-li, Ganghyeon-myeon, Yangyang-gun. ℂ **033/671-0813 or 4.** 36 units. ₩40,000 and up single/double. MC, V. *In room:* A/C, TV, hair dryer.

Seorak Youth Hostel 🏄 The cheapest place to sleep in the area, this hostel is within walking distance of the Seoraksan National Park entrance and only a 15-minute bus ride to Sokcho city. You'll find basic dormitory-style rooms, doubles, and family rooms. Sometimes large groups and school trips book the entire place, so check in advance, especially during high season.

246-77 Seorak-dong, Sokcho-si. ℂ **033/636-7115.** Fax 033/636-7107. 61 rooms (with 840 beds). ₩20,000 and up; family room for 4 ₩60,000 and up. MC, V. **Amenities:** Cafe; shared kitchen; Internet. *In room:* Shared bathrooms.

Where to Eat

Since the province is not a rice-producing region, many of the dishes you'll find here feature potatoes as the starch of choice. *Gamja buchingae* (potato pancakes) are popular as a snack, appetizer, or *anju* (drinking snack) and are even cooked into the rice. Because of the surrounding mountains, wild vegetables and mushrooms from the area find their way into traditional dishes. Be sure to try the *sanchae bibimbap* (wild mountain vegetable mixed rice), which is a delicious and inexpensive treat, or the local specialty, *dotoli mook* (savory gelatin made from acorns). One of the popular seafood dishes of the region is hwangtae—the drying and marketplace is mentioned earlier—and *ojing-uh soondae* (Korean sausage made with squid instead of pork).

Inexpensive Korean restaurants serving local fare are easy to find, but Western-style cuisine and upscale dining can be found only in the resorts or high-end hotels, although you are more likely than not to get overpriced, inauthentic fare. If you get tired of Korean food but don't want to break the bank, there are a handful of fast-food options (like pizza and burgers) in Sokcho.

If you love *soon dubu* (soft tofu hot pot), head over to **Haksapyeong Soon Dubu Chon (Soft Tofu Village),** where dozens of restaurants specialize in the dish. A couple of standouts are **Gim Yeong-Hae Halmuhni Soon Dubu** (ℂ 033/635-9520) and **Jaelaeshik Chodang Soon Dubu** (ℂ 033/635-6612). However, you can't go wrong with any of the restaurants here. All of them have comparable menus (with tofu and Alaskan pollack as main menu items). Soon dubu prices generally range from ₩6,000 to ₩8,000. From the Sokcho Bus Terminal, take bus no. 3-1 and get off in front of the Hwahwa Resort.

MODERATE

Jinyang Hwaetjip ★★ KOREAN SEAFOOD This *hwae* (raw fish) house specializes in the local dish—ojing-uh soondae. There are other fresh raw fish on offer, but it's the soondae that brings in the crowds.

478-35 Jung-ang-dong, Sokcho-si. ℂ **033/635-9999.** Entrees ₩10,000–₩25,000. MC, V. Daily 8:30am–10:30pm. Next to the Sokcho Tourist Hotel, across the water from Abai Village.

INEXPENSIVE

Cheogatjip Yangnyeom Tongdak ★ ☺ KOREAN FRIED CHICKEN Although this is a chain, if you've never had Korean-style seasoned fried chicken, it really is finger-lickin' good (though you won't see many Koreans licking their fingers, since it's considered bad manners).

635 Jangsa-dong, Sokcho-si. ℂ **033/631-9965.** Entrees ₩6,000–₩15,000. No credit cards. Daily 11am–10pm.

Yeongbawi Shikdang (Dragon Rock Restaurant) 🍴 KOREAN For over 30 years, this place has been serving hwangtae and traditional local dishes at the same location. The best time to come is in the winter when the fish are all hung out to dry. The *hwangtae gui jeongshik* (grilled pollack meal), *gamja buchim* (potato flatcake), and *dotoli mook* are all worth a try. Wash it down with some *dongdongju* (homemade rice wine). There isn't any English on the sign, so just look for the place with two stone dragon statues flanking the entrance.

401 Yeongdae-li, Buk-myeon, Inje-gun. ℂ **033/462-4079.** Entrees ₩7,000–₩20,000. Cash only. Daily 7:30am–9pm. Located off of highway 46, not far from the Alps ski resort.

GANGNEUNG

Gangneung is one of the largest coastal cities in Gangwon-do. It is located south of Yangyang and north of Donghae. The Taebaek Mountains, which rise up behind the city, help keep it a bit warmer than coastal cities in the west. And unlike in other parts of the country, the rainy season is in the fall, not the summer. It has no commercial port and not a lot of fishing off its coast. Due to its seaside location and cafe culture, it has become a tourist spot for traveling Seoulites.

Essentials

GETTING THERE The nearest airport is at Yangyang, but most people take the bus into Gangneung, since it is the fastest and most economical way to travel into the city. You can take a bus from the **DongSeoul Bus Terminal** (Seoul subway line 2, exit 4) daily from 6:30am to 11pm. It takes about 3 hours and buses run every 30 to 50 minutes. From **Seoul's Express Bus Terminal** (Seoul subway line 3, exit 1), buses run every 15 to 30 minutes, daily from 6am to 11:30pm. There are two bus stations in town, the newer one (far from the city center) and the older one, which has buses from closer cities.

If you prefer to travel by rail, you can take a train from Seoul's Cheongnyangni Station. There are six trains daily into Gangneung. Early risers can take the night train at 11pm, sleep on the train and arrive at 4:56am, just in time to catch the sunrise over Jeongdongjin Beach. Trains cost from ₩21,200 to ₩24,400 for adults (half-price for children).

GETTING AROUND Local buses will get you pretty much anywhere you need to go. Unfortunately, most signs are not in English and drivers don't speak English. However, if you can say the name of your destination in Korean, you can indicate to your driver to let you know when to get off. Local buses run frequently and start at ₩1,100, so be sure you have plenty of change to get around.

Taxis can be found outside of the bus and train stations, or flagged down on the street. The base rate starts at ₩1,800 with higher surcharges for places farther out. Most drivers don't speak English and take cash only.

VISITOR INFORMATION The **Tourist Guide Office,** 992-3 Hongje-dong, Gangneung-si (✆ **033/640-4531;** daily 8:30am–10pm), is located a couple of minutes from the bus terminal. Other tourist info centers can be found at the train station, Jeongdongjin (✆ **033/644-5062**), and the entrance to Gyeongpo Beach. The city's website is www.gangneung.go.kr/english/main.jsp.

[FastFACTS] GANGNEUNG

Banks, Foreign Exchange & ATMs Most banks in the city are located in the downtown area and are open Monday to Friday 9:30am to 4:30pm. ATMs at Korean Exchange Bank (KEB), Kukmin, Shinan, and Noghyup banks downtown are the most foreigner friendly.

Internet Access If you have your own laptop, there is free wireless Internet access on Gyeongpo Beach. If you didn't bring your own computer, you may be able to find one with Internet access at a local love motel. Also, you can stop in at one of the **PC bahng** in the city. Most of these are open 24 hours.

Post Office There are many post offices in Gangneung, but the one downtown is the most convenient and has Saturday hours (9am–1pm), while the other ones are open Monday to Friday 9am to 4:30pm only.

Exploring Gangneung

Chamsori (True Sound) Gramophone Museum & Edison Science Museum ★★ MUSEUM   A private museum, this place was started by Director Seon Seongmok, who had a strong interest in gramophones. The museum is really two separate museums, one focusing on sounds and the other focusing on the inventions of Thomas Edison. The largest such collection in the world, it houses 450 gramophones and hundreds of portables and music boxes. There are also over 150,000 recordings you can listen to in the music hall. The Edison Invention Hall displays 850 of Mr. Edison's inventions.

36 Jeo-dong, Gangneung-si. ✆ **033/655-1130.** www.edison.kr/english/index.php. Admission ₩7,000 adults, ₩6,000 teens, ₩5,000 children, free for kids 6 and under. Daily 9am–5:30pm (until 6pm on summer weekends). From the Gangneung Train Station, take bus no. 300 or 303 and get off at Gyeongpodorip Park. From the Gangneung Bus Terminal, take bus no. 202 or 302. It takes 10–20 min. from either station.

Daegwallyeong Museum ★ MUSEUM   Built in 1993, this private museum displays the collection of Director Hong Gwiseok. Located at the entrance to the old road to Daegwallyeong, the museum has four exhibit halls, named after the guardian gods of the four directions. There are over 2,000 articles in the collection, from prehistoric artifacts to folkloric items. The museum also has an outdoor exhibit area with interesting stone sculptures and totems.

Eoheul-li, Seongsan-myeon, Gangneung-si. ✆ **033/640-4482** (Korean only). Admission ₩1,000 adults, ₩700 teens, ₩400 children. Free parking. Daily 9am–6pm, until 5pm in winter. Take bus no. 503 bound for Eoheul-li.

Gyeongpo Beach ★ BEACH   This beach is located just a kilometer from Gyeongpodae and is essentially a sandbar formed between Gyeongpo Lake and the ocean. It has fine white sand and is surrounded by pine forests and wild roses. Most come to see the nearby historical sites, but the beach is also well known for its sun- and moonrises.

Various cultural events are held here throughout the year, including the Cherry Blossom Festival in the spring and the Beach Festival in the summer. There are shower and changing facilities available.

San 1 Anhyeon-dong, Gangneung-si. ☎ **033/640-5128.** Free admission. Parking ₩2,000. Daily 24 hr. Take bus no. 202 from the express bus terminal. The bus runs every 30 min. and takes 20 min.

Gyeongpodae (Gyeongpo Pavilion) ★ ARCHITECTURE

This pavilion is famous for the spectacular view of the full moon on the 15th day of the first lunar month. Inside, there is writing by scholar Yulgok from when he was only 10 years old. There is also a poem written by the 15th Goryeo king, Sukjong. There are 12 other pavilions in the area, but this is the most impressive. The best time to visit is between March and October.

94 Jeo-dong, Gangneung-si. ☎ **033/640-4414** (Korean only). Free admission. Free parking. Daily 9am–6pm. From Gangneung, take local bus no. 202 to Gyeongpo Provincial Park.

Jeongdongjin Beach ★ BEACH

A tiny fishing village is located on this beach east of Seoul's Gwanghwamun. There is a large hourglass here, installed in 1999, that has enough sand (about 8 tons) to count time for an entire year. At this beach, known for its great sunrises, you can get a nice view by hiking up Goseongsan. Across from the train station, there is a small alley to the right which leads to a hiking trail up the mountain. The wooden steps lead you up to the top and the view. You can catch a short train ride here from the Gangneung Station.

The train station here (which is incidentally in the *Guinness Book of World Records* for being the train station closest to the ocean anywhere in the world) is located right on the beach. The **train ride** (☎ **033/573-5473**) costs ₩10,000 to ₩15,000 for adults, ₩9,000 to ₩13,500 for children.

Jeongdong-li, Gangdong-myeon, Gangneung-si. ☎ **033/640-4414.** Free admission, but there is a small entrance fee for Hourglass Park. From the Gangneung Bus Terminals, take bus no. 109. From the Gangneung Train Station, walk to the right a couple of minutes and take bus no. 300 or 302. Buses run every 10–15 min.

Jumunjin Beach ☺ BEACH

The northernmost beach in Gangneung, its shallow waters make it ideal for families with small children. Located near Jumunjin Harbor, you can hop on over for a fresh seafood lunch. There are shower and changing rooms available.

Hyangho-li, Jumunjin-eup, Gangneung-si. Free admission. Daily 24 hr. Take bus no. 10 or 11 from either the bus terminals or the train station. It's a 40-min. ride. A taxi takes 20–25 min. from the downtown area. Driving from Gyeongju-si, take road 7 toward Bulguksa, turn left on road 902, and follow the signs to the parking lot.

Ojukheon Municipal Museum & Residence ★★ MUSEUM

The Ojukheon museum was created by merging the city's museum with a historic residence. Ojukheon is one of the oldest houses in the country and is perfectly preserved to show how people lived during the Joseon Dynasty. It was also the birthplace of Yul-Gok, a great scholar, whose real name was Yi I. He was a Neo-Confucian who came into prominence in the 16th century. His mother was a great painter and her influence may be what encouraged him to read and write Chinese characters by the age of 3 and to have finished his Confucian classics by age 7. His writings and theories continued to have a profound influence on Korea for years after his death in 1584. Gyeongpo Beach and Seongyeojang are nearby.

201 Jukheon-dong, Gangneung-si. © **033/640-4457.** Admission ₩2,000 adults, ₩1,000 teens, ₩500 children, free for seniors 65 and over and kids 6 and under. Mar–Oct daily 9am–6pm; Nov–Feb daily 9am–5pm. Closed Jan 1, Lunar New Year, and Chuseok. From the Gangneung Train Station, take bus no. 300 or 303 and get off at Ojukheon. From the Gangneung Bus Terminal, take bus no. 202 or 302. It takes 10–20 min. from either station.

Seongyeojang ★★ HISTORIC HOME   This is the former home of nobleman Yi Naebeon, and 10 generations of his descendents have lived here since. Built over 300 years ago, it is remarkably well preserved and reachable by boat from Gyeongpo Lake. Some additions have been made since its original construction, including the Yeolhwadang's terrace, a gift from Russia, and the Hwallaejeong, a picturesque structure, especially when surrounded by the blooming lotus flowers in August.

431 Unjeong-dong, Gangneung-si. © **033/648-5303** (Korean only). Admission ₩3,000 adults, ₩2,000 teens, ₩1,000 children, free for kids 6 and under. Daily 9am–6pm. Closed Lunar New Year and Chuseok. From the Gangneung Express Bus Terminal, take bus no. 202 (a 15-min. ride). From the Gangneung Train Station, take bus no. 202 (a 30-min. ride).

Unification Park ★★ HISTORIC SITE   In 1996, a North Korean submarine was stranded on the rocks at this spot. The 26-member crew got out of the submarine and tried to return to the north, leading to a deadly manhunt that lasted over a month. All but one crew member was killed and there were 17 South Korean casualties. When you see the sub, which is on display here, you may wonder how they managed to squeeze in that many people. The park also houses a U.S. warship from the Korean War, given by the Americans as a gift in 1972.

Jeongdong-li, Gangdong-myeon, Gangneung-si. © **033/640-4414.** Admission ₩2,000 adults, ₩1,200 teens, ₩600 children, free for kids 6 and under. Daily 9am–6pm. From Jeongdongjin, take bus no. 111, 112, or 113.

OTHER POINTS OF INTEREST

Gyeongpoho (Gyeongpo Lake) ★ NATURE RESERVE   Located in the middle of the city's tourist area, the name means "clear as a mirror." Gyeongpoho was created when the mouth of a nearby bay was naturally closed off by sediment brought in by the sea. It used to be much larger, but the continual increase in deposits of sand and sediment decreases its size every year. A destination for migratory birds, it is now a natural preservation site and fishing is banned. The lake is surrounded by a series of bronze statues that tell the story of Hong Gildong, Korea's real-life Robin Hood.

Chodang (front of Gyeongpodae), Anhyeon, Gunjeong, Jeodong, Gangneung-si. Free admission. Take local bus no. 202 to Gyeongpo Lake (takes 25 min.).

Haslla Art World GARDEN   On over 24 hectares (60 acres) of land overlooking the ocean, this art park has a variety of gardens, galleries, viewing areas, and even study rooms where kids can have a hands-on experience creating their own masterpieces.

33-1, Jeongdongjin-li, Gangdong-myeon, Gangneung-si. © **033/644-9411.** www.haslla.kr/web2010/eng/1_sub1.php?bo_table=1_sub1. Admission ₩5,000 adults, ₩4,000 youth. Mar–Oct daily 7am–10pm; Nov–Feb daily 8am–5pm; opens 2 hr. earlier on weekends, depending on when the sun rises. From Jeongdongjin take bus no. 11, 112, 113, or 114. Free shuttle bus on weekends (call for reservations).

Morae Shigae (Hourglass) Park PARK   Gangneung city and Samsung Electronics built this park in 1999 in celebration of the new millennium. It houses the world's largest hourglass (which is actually circular in shape—it takes an entire year for all the sand to fall). ***Fun fact:*** The Korean word for "hourglass" translates to "sand clock." It is rotated every year at midnight on January 1.

Jeongdong-li, Gangdong-myeon, Gangneung-si. ✆ **033/640-4533.** Admission ₩500 for all ages (includes admission to Jeongdongjin). Daily 24 hr. Next to Jeongdongjin Beach.

Where to Stay

Since Gangneung is a popular tourist destination, there are plenty of choices in accommodations. As in most cities in South Korea, you have a choice of upscale hotels, midpriced hotels, and lower-end yeogwan and love motels. Many sleeping options are available in the downtown area near the bus terminals, as well as in the Namdaecheon district.

EXPENSIVE

Hotel Hyundai Gyeongpodae ★★ 🍴   Possibly the best hotel in town, the Hyundai overlooks the East Sea, amidst a grove of pine trees. The rooms are open and nicely furnished. Even the standard rooms have balconies that overlook either the ocean or the mountains. Both Western-style and ondol rooms are available. An extra ₩30,000 gets you an ocean view.

274-1, Gangmun-dong, Gangneung-si. www.hyundaihotel.com/gyeongpodae/index.jsp. ✆ **033/651-2233.** 96 units. ₩160,000 mountain-view standard room; ₩300,000 suite. AE, MC, V. **Amenities:** 3 restaurants; bar; cafe. *In room:* A/C, TV, fridge, Internet.

MODERATE

Hotel Gangneung ★   Located east of the train station, the Hotel Gangneung offers both ondol and Western-style rooms. Whichever you choose, the rooms are well furnished and relatively spacious for the price (though the ondol rooms are a bit bigger).

1117, Ponam-dong, Gangneung-si. ✆ **033/641-7701.** Fax 033/641-7712. 62 units. ₩40,000 and up standard room. MC, V. **Amenities:** 3 restaurants; bar; cafe. *In room:* A/C, TV, fridge, Internet.

Sun Castle Hotel ★   With both hotel-style and Korean condo-style rooms available, it's convenient for singles, couples, or families traveling together. Both Western-style rooms and ondol rooms are available. Condo facilities with kitchens are available for a ₩10,000 surcharge. Rooms are furnished nicely with a decidedly Korean flair. Rates can vary wildly, so be sure to ask before you make a reservation. It's a convenient hotel for those skiing nearby.

San 84-2, Jumunjin-li, Jumunjin-eup, Gangneung-si. ✆ **033/661-1950.** 53 units. ₩60,000 and up standard room; ₩165,000 and up condo rooms. MC, V. **Amenities:** Restaurant; cafe; pool. *In room:* A/C, TV, hair dryer, Internet.

INEXPENSIVE

In general, it's difficult make reservations at lower-priced yeogwan, minbak, and love motels. You just have to walk in and hope that there are rooms available—which can be a dubious proposition in the high season. During the summer, room rates are usually in the ₩45,000 to ₩55,000 range, but rates go down to ₩35,000 during less crowded months. There are a bunch of low-priced options along Gyeongpodae Beach. Additional inexpensive sleeping quarters are available on the streets around the train station and the bus terminals on the west side of town.

Where to Eat

In the pine forest south of Gyeongpo Beach is the **Chodang Soondubu Village,** known for its soon dubu. The soon dubu from this region is unique in that it's made from water from the East Sea, which gives it a soft, light texture. Usually the soft tofu is served in a big bowl with a side of *yangnyeom ganjang* (seasoned soy sauce) for flavor. There are over a dozen restaurants in the "village" that specialize in the tofu dish.

There are plenty of other restaurants where you can get inexpensive Korean cuisine. Western food is more difficult to find. There are some fast-food, pizza, and fried chicken restaurants, mostly near the city center and some scattered near the beaches.

Since the region isn't well known for its rice, the restaurants here tend to have noodles made of buckwheat, potato pancakes, and foods from other starches. Also, since Gangneung is a seaside town, there is no shortage of hwae restaurants along the coast.

Green Hwaetjib ★ 📷 KOREAN SEAFOOD   Located right across the street from the sandy beach, this hwae place has fresh seafood, right from the water. The owners are generous with the portions, so you'll be stuffed to the gills with fish. The menu offers a variety of hwae to choose from, including the most expensive dish, *jeongbok hwae* (raw abalone), for ₩70,000. Even the smallest hwae meals are enough to serve two, and the larger ones can serve four or more.

266-10 Sacheonjin-li, Sacheon-myeon, Gangneung-si. © **033/644-0366** or 644-0169. *Modeum hwae* (mixed raw fish meal) ₩60,000 for a small order (enough for 2). MC, V. Daily 8am–midnight.

Heulim Sutbul Galbi ★★ KOREAN BEEF   If you're in the mood for meat, look no further than this galbi joint in the middle of the city. The menu offers both beef and pork dishes that you cook on your own tabletop grill. The *saeng galbi* (unmarinated beef rib-eye), *yangnyeom galbi* (marinated beef rib-eye), and *dweji galbi* (spicy pork ribs) are all particularly good here.

1148-21 Ponam-dong, Gangneung-si. © **033/643-9125** (Korean). Entrees ₩7,000–₩15,000. MC, V. Daily noon–10pm.

Samgyeori Dongchimi Makguksu ★★ KOREAN NOODLES   This regional chain restaurant specializes in *maemil gugksu* (buckwheat noodles). The broth is made with *dongchimi*, a type of kimchi made from large cubes of radish, and served chilled. A regular bowl of *mak guksu* (noodles in a broth with some vegetables and seaweed) is only ₩4,500—hard to beat in terms of both price and flavor. The menu is simple, but offers good, chewy noodles and a cold broth that's refreshing.

144-2, Samgyeo-li, Jumunjin-eup, Gangneung-si. © **033/642-3935** or 033/661-5396 (Korean). Entrees ₩4,500–₩15,000. No credit cards. Daily 10am–10pm.

ODAESAN NATIONAL PARK & PYEONGCHANG COUNTY

Located west of Gangneung, Odaesan National Park is nestled amid one of the best known mountain ranges in the country (along with Geumgangsan, Hallasan, and Jirisan), but doesn't draw nearly the same number of visitors. Less rocky and rugged than Seoraksan, its highest peaks still rise over 1,400m (4,593 ft.). Although its slopes are not very dramatic, its softer inclines make for good hiking trails through its thick fir forests. The name "Odaesan" means "Five Plains Mountain," named after the five high plains between its five major peaks. Admission to the park is free, but there is an admission fee for Woljeongsa (see p. 348).

Once an isolated retreat for meditating monks, this is where the practice of Seon (Zen) Buddhism in Korea began. Its two major temples are located in the central valley, and short paths lead from the temples to their associated hermitages. There are hiking trails throughout the park, though you'll find fewer here than in most of South Korea's national parks.

The area is home to 25 species of mammals, including the Korean deer and wild boar. Odaesan also has the largest natural forest in the country with about 860 species of alpine flora, including the nuncheukbaek (*Thuja*) tree and thick groves of fir, some over 600 years old. It is well known for its *sansam*, a wild type of *insam* (ginseng) that grows deep in its forest. This rare root is supposed to have wonderful health benefits and can live to be quite old (some over 100 years old have been found here). The water from the mountain streams is also said to have curative effects.

According to a legend associated with the area, Joseon King Sejo visited Woljeongsa to cure an unusual disease he had. On the way up to the temple, he saw the clean water of the valley and was moved to take a bath. Suddenly, a boy appeared and the king asked him to wash his back. The boy did and the king asked him not to tell anyone that he'd seen the king naked. The boy in return asked the king not to tell anyone he saw the Munsu Bosal (the young Buddha). Surprised, King Sejo turned around but the boy had disappeared. It was at that moment that the king realized that he was cured of his disease. King Sejo ordered a statue of the boy Buddha be built and described how the boy looked in detail. The statue is now in Sangwonsa.

A part of Odaesan is located in Pyeongchang-gun, the third-largest county in the country. In preparation to host the 2018 Winter Olympics, the area has been built up with wonderful ski resorts, sledding, snow trekking, and other winter options. They also hold a Trout Festival in **Odaecheon (Odae Stream)** in the winter (dates vary). The website for Pyeongchang County is http://en.yes-pc.net/index.html.

GETTING THERE   The easiest way to get to the park is to take a bus from the Jinbu Bus Terminal. Buses run about 12 times a day (once an hour). To get to Jinbu, take a bus from the **DongSeoul Bus Terminal** (Seoul subway line 2, Gangbyeon Station). There are 27 buses daily from 6:30am to 10:05pm. The ride takes about 2 hours and 15 minutes and costs ₩12,500.

Exploring Pyeongchang County

Daegwallyeong Yangddae Mokjang (Sheep Farm) ★ ☺ FARM   The only exclusive sheep farm in the area, the main attraction is the couple of hundred sheep that are raised here. You can trade in your admission ticket for a basket of hay to feed the sheep lounging in the barn (the building with the bright orange roof). You can also take a leisurely walk around the sheep's grazing area—plan to spend about an hour walking up- and downhill and taking in the idyllic scenery. The sheep graze from about early April to the end of October.

14-104 beonji, Hoenggye 3(sam)-li, Doam-myeon, Pyeongchang-gun. © **033/335-1966.** www. yangtte.co.kr (Korean only). Admission ₩3,500 adults, ₩3,000 children, free for kids 4 and under. From the Hoenggye Intercity Bus Terminal, take a taxi. It should take 10 min. The farm is located behind the Daegwallyeong Rest Stop, where you can park for free.

Geumdang Valley ADVENTURE TOUR   One of the best sites for rafting is the Geumdang Valley on Pyeongchang-gang (river). The 5km (3-mile) course goes along Geumdangsan and Geomunsan from Deungmaeji Village to Baekam-dong. There are occasional sandbanks where you can take a break, should you wish. The

Pyeongchang-gang is also popular for fishing. It costs about ₩30,000 per person to rent a raft for nine people and you have to be 14 and older. For groups over 30, it's ₩25,000 per person and includes a guide and insurance. You can also rent rooms starting at ₩60,000 on weekdays for two to three people. Those not fond of rafting will still find the hiking trails here pleasant.

1 Yupo 1-li, Bongpyeong-myeon, Pyeongchang-gun. ℂ **033/332-5533.** www.irafting.co.kr (Korean only). Rafting daily 10am–4pm May–Oct. Take a taxi from the Jangpyeong Express Bus Terminal and it'll take 5 min.

Herbnara Farm FARM   The country's first herb farm, it opened in 1994. There are seven themed gardens on-site along with ponds and galleries. The farm's restaurant, **Birch House,** offers meals made from the herbs grown right here. The best time of year to see the farm is between June and August and it takes about an hour to tour.

You can stay in the cozy condo-style accommodations as well. Doubles start at ₩80,000 for weekdays (₩100,000 Fri–Sat). All the facilities include private bathroom and a kitchen. E-mail jiin@herbnara.com for reservations.

303 Heungjeong-li, Bongpyeong-myeon, Pyeongchang-gun. ℂ **033/335-2902.** www.herbnara. com. Admission ₩5,000 adults, ₩3,000 youth, Nov–Apr; ₩7,000 adults, ₩4,000 youth May–Oct. From the Jangpyeong Bus Terminal, the bus runs at 11:40am and 3:10pm. A taxi from the bus terminal takes 30 min. Driving from Seoul, take the Yeongdong Expwy. (road 50) to the Myeonnon IC (take road 6) past Phoenix Park and Heungjeong Valley. Then follow the signs to Herbnara.

Korean Botanical Garden GARDEN   Created in 1999, this botanical garden is home to over 1,300 native plants. The gardens include the Indoor Exhibition Hall, Herb Garden, Cultivation Area, Ecosystem Garden, Singal Mountain Path, and Theme Garden. You'll get a free packet of seeds when you buy your ticket. Open only April 1 through October 31; the best time to visit is June through August, when the majority of flowers are in bloom.

405-2 Byeongnae-li, Doam-myeon, Pyeongchang-gun. ℂ **033/332-7069.** www.kbotanic.co.kr (Korean only). Admission ₩5,000 adults, ₩3,000 teens, ₩2,000 children May–Sep; ₩3,500 adults, ₩2,000 children Apr & Oct; free for seniors 65 and over and kids 6 and under. Apr–Oct daily 9am–6pm. From the Jinbu Intercity Bus Terminal, take a bus bound for Woljeongsa or Sangwonsa and get off at the Odaesan National Park Administrative Office. It's about a 25-min. walk from there. By taxi, it should take 15 min.

Samyang Daegwallyeong Ranch HIKING TRAIL   A large green pasture on one of the plateaus in the area, it has been a meadow for dairy cows for centuries. Since it's pretty high up, you can get a good view of the surrounding area and the sunrise over the East Sea beyond the peaks of Odaesan. It takes about 2 hours by shuttle to tour the entire ranch. The area is too large to explore entirely on foot, but the Daegwallyeong Trail is a nice trek, especially in the winter. You can also ride a bike around the ranch in about 5 to 6 hours. There is lodging for families and groups at the ranch, but you must make reservations in advance.

Hoenggye 2-li, Doam-myeon, Pyeongchang-gun. ℂ **033/335-5044.** www.samyangranch.co.kr (Korean only). Admission ₩7,000 adults, ₩5,000 kids 3–18. May–mid-Nov daily 8am–6pm. From the Hoenggye Intercity Bus Terminal, take a taxi. It should take 15 min. and cost about ₩10,000. They have shuttle buses available for visitors every 20–30 min. on weekdays, 10–15 min on weekends. No private vehicles allowed on the ranch.

Sangwonsa (Sangwon Temple) ★ TEMPLE   The actual origin of this temple, located 8km (5 miles) north of Woljeongsa, is unknown. Legend has it that it was built either in 643 or in the 680s. Whatever the case, it was rebuilt in 705, then a destructive fire burned through the place in 1946. Only the original bell pavilion (and one of only three bells from the Shilla Dynasty) remained—the rest of the temple site was rebuilt in 1947. The oldest parts of the temple left today are the Dongjong (the bell), the Munsu Bosal (the child Buddha figure), and the Jungchang (written by seventh Joseon King Sejo).

Another legend involves King Sejo (again). He was visiting this temple, shortly after his encounter with the child Buddha, when he felt a cat tugging at his clothing. When he glanced down at the cat, he caught sight of a would-be assassin who was on the verge of making an attempt at his life and was able to stop the man. In gratitude, the king ordered a statue of a cat be made for the temple and ordered that no cats in Korea be killed from that point forward.

Dongsan-li, Jinbu-myeon, Pyeongchang-gun. (©)**033/332-6666** (Korean only). Admission ₩2,500 adults, ₩1,000 teens, ₩400 children, free for seniors 65 and over and kids 6 and under. Admission includes both Sangwon and Woljeong temples. Daily sunrise–5pm. From the Wonju Bus Terminal, take bus no. 23 bound for Seongnam-li. The ride will take 70 min. From the Jinbu Intercity Bus Terminal, take a bus bound for Sangwonsa, which runs about every hour (a 40-min. ride). By taxi, it should take 35 min.

Woljeongsa (Woljeong Temple) ★★TEMPLE
A temple complex located in the forest valley east of Odaesan, it is made up of 60 small temples and eight hermitages. Established by Monk Jajang, it was destroyed by fire during the Korean War. The temple's main hall was completely rebuilt in 1969 using wood from local fir trees. The headquarters of the fourth district of the Jogye sect, it leads most of the temples in the province.

The main front gate is on the side of the compound with the usual four gate guards. In front of the main hall is the nine-level octagonal pagoda dating back to the Goryeo Dynasty. Facing the pagoda is a Yakgwang Bodhisattva made of stone. The most recent additions in the early 1990s were the Preaching Buddha hall, a pavilion leading to the main hall, a bell pavilion, and a stone stele.

A **Budo site** and **Sagoji** for historic document storage are nearby. The Budo relic site is about a 15-minute walk from the temple on the way to Sangwonsa, just before crossing the Banya Bridge. There are 22 pagodas that contain the remains of monks who lived here. Sagoji is about an hour on foot from the temple toward Sangwonsa, near Yeonggamsa.

The **Seongbo Museum** (open Apr–Oct 9:30am–6pm, Nov–Mar until 5pm, closed Tues) is located in the temple complex. It houses important Buddhist relics from the Shilla Dynasty. Last entry 30 min. before closing.

63 Dongsan-li, Jinbu-myeon, Pyeongchang-gun. (©)**033/339-6800.** www.woljeongsa.org (Korean only). Admission ₩2,500 adults, ₩1,000 teens, ₩400 children, free for seniors 65 and over and kids 6 and under. Admission includes both Sangwon and Woljeong temples. Daily 5am–9pm. From the Jinbu Intercity Bus Terminal, take a bus bound for Woljeongsa, which runs 12 times a day (a 15-min. ride). By taxi, it should take 15 min.

Yongpyong Ski Resort NATURAL ATTRACTION
This resort, whose name means the "land of snow," sits at the foot of **Balwangsan.** It is considered one of the best slopes in the country because the mountain has naturally occurring slopes of varying inclines. Having hosted the 1999 Winter Asian Games, it's good for professional skiing, but also has gentler slopes for beginners.

It takes 3 to 4 hours to hike up to the top of Balwangsan on foot, but only 20 minutes to get there via cable car. The peak is so high up that it's almost impossible to see the resort from the top. Once you're at the summit, there is a Korean restaurant, a Western-style restaurant, and a cafe. In the summer, their 45-hole golf course and swimming pool bring in the masses from Seoul. See **Dragon Valley Hotel** (p. 349) for accommodation information.

130 Yongsan-li, Doam-myeon, Pyeongchang-gun. ℰ **033/332-7069.** www.yongpyong.co.kr/eng/index.asp. Lift ticket and golf prices vary. From the DongSeoul Bus Station, take a bus to Hoeng-gye (runs every 40 min. from 6:30am–8:05pm, taking about 2½ hours). There are free shuttles from the Hoenggye post office (next to the bus terminal) from 4:40am to 11:30pm, every 40–60 min.). The resort runs shuttle buses (₩28,000 round-trip) from Seoul during high season, but advance reservations are required.

Where to Stay

There are several hotels and Korean "condos" in the area, and a handful of motels. There are also plenty of minbak and a campsite near Woljeongsa. A larger campsite and more minbak are available at the entrance to Sogeumgang. A better option may be to overnight in Gangneung (only an hour's drive away) and make your way to the mountains in the morning.

Also, the resorts and farms mentioned above offer accommodations (as noted).

Dragon Valley Hotel ★★   Located in the **Yongpyong Ski Resort,** they have a wide range of accommodations to fit your budget. The hotel has both Western-style and ondol rooms available, but the Tower and Villa condominiums have only ondol rooms. The condo facilities have kitchens as well. The youth hostel has both ondol-style rooms and large bunk bed rooms, but it's mainly designed for groups of school-children traveling together and isn't a Western-style "hostel." The accommodations are great for groups and families, but not very economical for single travelers.

130 Yongsan-li, Doam-myeon, Pyeongchang-gun. www.yongpyong.co.kr/eng/index.asp. ℰ **033/335-5757,** or 02/3270-1230 for Seoul office. Fax 033/335-0160 or 02/3270-1234. Hotel 191 units, condo 635 units, youth hostel 60 beds. ₩250,000 and up standard room; ₩500,000 suite; ₩240,000 and up condo for 4; ₩70,000 and up youth hostel for 5. AE, MC, V. **Amenities:** 2 restaurants; bar; cafe; pool; golf course; health club; sauna; karaoke, nightclub; bowling alley; ski resort; Internet. *In room:* A/C, TV, kitchen (condos), fridge, hair dryer. No in-room amenities in youth hostel.

Kensington Flora Hotel (aka Hotel Odaesan)   Located at the entrance to Odaesan, this 17-story hotel has views of the surrounding mountains and natural scenery. With both ondol-style and Western rooms with beds, this is the only upscale hotel in the area. The rooms are nice, with good lighting and comfortable sofas. Ask for a room with a balcony, since not all of them have one. Discounts up to 50% are usual during the off season.

221-1 Ganpyeong-li Jinbu-myeon, Pyeongchang-gun. www.hotelodaesan.co.kr. ℰ **033/330-5000.** Fax 033/330-5123. 306 units. ₩180,000 and up single/double, ₩280,000 and up suite. AE, MC, V. **Amenities:** 3 restaurants; bar; cafe; pool; tennis courts; health club; sauna. *In room:* A/C, TV, fridge, hair dryer.

Phoenix Park ★★ ENTERTAINMENT COMPLEX   A huge resort complex, Phoenix Park is like a small city in and of itself. It has hotels, Korean-style condo-minium facilities, a water park, a ski resort, a golf course, a bank, a pharmacy, a bowling alley, a supermarket, swimming pools, and a huge cafeteria. It is located about 2 hours from Seoul, on the way to Odaesan. Other than the restaurants associated with the hotel and condo complex, there is also a food court with fast-food chains (Holly's Coffee, Domino's Pizza, and the like) and smaller Korean restaurants.

10

GANGWON-DO | Odaesan National Park & Pyeongchang County

The most popular times of the year are the summer and when the mountains are covered in powder, ready for the hordes of skiers enjoying the slopes on winter weekends.

Hotel facilities have both ondol and standard rooms available. Condo facilities have combinations of bed and ondol rooms and kitchen facilities for cooking. Not the most convenient for single travelers, it's great for families or groups traveling together.

1095 Myeonon-li, Bongpyeong-myeon, Pyeongchang-gun. www.phoenixpark.co.kr. (C) **033/330-6000** or 1588-2828. Fax 02/527-9500. 2,490 units. ₩240,000 condo that sleeps 4, but deep discounts are available; ₩300,000 and up standard room (sleeps up to 3); ₩560,000 and up suite. AE, MC, V. **Amenities:** 8 restaurants; cafe; pool; sauna; children's center; karaoke bar; Internet. *In room:* A/C, TV, kitchen, fridge, hair dryer, dining area.

Where to Eat

There are a number of restaurants near the minbak (some of them are a combination of both), about a 40-minute walk from Woljeongsa. One of the better restaurants between the entrance to the park and Jinbu is **Odaesan Gagneun Gil ★★**, 303-7 Ganpyeong-li, Jinbu-myeon, Pyeongchang-gun (C) **033/333-9982**), whose name means "On the Road to Odaesan." The chefs here serve traditional Korean fare in a nice setting. The outside tables are in a flower garden, while the inside is decorated with paintings and Korean kites. You can get a bowl of *kal guksu* (handmade knife noodles) or *sujebi* (dough flake soup) for ₩6,000.

At the entrance to Woljeongsa is a cozy restaurant, **Odaesan Sanchae,** that specializes in wild vegetables grown in the mountains. Like all temple cuisine, the fare is strictly vegetarian and very affordable. Set meals go for ₩12,000 to ₩24,000.

A nice place at the entrance to the Yongyeong Ski Resort is **Gohyang Iyagi,** 348 Hoenggye 9-li, Doam-myeon, Pyeongchang-gun (C) **033/335-5430**), whose name roughly translates to "hometown story." This family-owned restaurant, inside a lodge-like wooden building, is decorated with photos of Seoraksan taken by the owner. One of the specialty dishes is a *dolsot bap* (stone-pot rice bowl) made with special fragrant herbs that grow only in Gangwon-do. The restaurant next door, **Hoenggye,** also specializes in the dish, as well as the *osam bulgogi,* a special marinated sliced beef dish.

Sigol Bapsang, 331-61 Hwinggae-li, Daegwallyeong-myeon, Pyeongchang-gun (C) **033/333-7767**), which translates to something like "country dinner table," is another good choice. The *sigol bapsang jeongshik* (country-style traditional set meal) is ₩30,000, but you can get the local *gondre bap* (a meal with steamed rice made with a local thistle and special seasoning) for just ₩7,000. It's about 10 minutes by taxi (costing about ₩7,000) to the restaurant from the Jinbu Bus Terminal.

CHUNCHEON

The capital of Gangwon-do, the city lies in the northwestern part of the county in a basin formed by the Soyang and Han rivers. Called the "Lake City," Chuncheon serves as the gateway to the northeastern corner of South Korea. An important location even during the Shilla Dynasty, it served as one of the fortress cities protecting Seoul in the 17th century. Like in many of the cities in the area, most of the infrastructure was destroyed during the Korean War, but it has been rebuilt since.

The city serves as the center for the agricultural products grown in surrounding communities. The main products in the area are soybeans and rice, but Chuncheon, itself, is known for its *dak galbi* (a spicy chicken dish cooked with vegetables) and *mak gooksu* (spicy mixed noodles).

The city hosts several festivals throughout the year, including a mime festival, a puppet festival, a makgooksu festival, and the international taekwondo championships.

Although it has grown into a sprawling city in the past couple of decades, it has maintained the sleepiness of a small town. The older downtown section has remained compact, although it has become more modernized. It has seen a huge growth in visitors ever since it was featured in the popular South Korean television drama *Winter Sonata.*

Essentials

GETTING THERE   Chuncheon is located at the end of the Gyeongchun rail line, which connects the city to Cheongnyangni Station in Seoul (Seoul subway, line 1). It costs about ₩6,500 to take the train from Seoul to **Chuncheon Station** (② 033/255-6550), or **Namchuncheon Station** 366 Toegye-dong, Chuncheon-si (② 033/257-7022), which is being renovated until 2013. Trains run about 20 times daily from 5:25am to 10:30pm and take about 1 hour and 50 minutes.

You can also take a bus from the DongSeoul Bus Terminal or the Sangbong Terminal to the Chuncheon Bus Terminal (② 033/254-3676; www.chterminal.co.kr, Korean only). Buses from DongSeoul run every 15 min. from 6am to 9:20pm. There are 40 buses daily from Sangbong, from 5:40am to 9:30pm. Both buses take about 90 minutes. From Incheon Airport, you can catch a bus directly to Chuncheon. Wait for the bus at platform 9C. Buses cost about ₩18,000 and run every 120 to 180 min. There are also buses available from Yangyang and Wonju airports.

Driving to Chuncheon, the city is the northern end of the Jung-ang Expressway (road 55), which runs through Wonju and continues down south to Busan.

GETTING AROUND   There are two train stations in town: Chuncheon Station, which is the end of the Gyeongchun line, and Namchuncheon Station (which is being renovated through 2013), located about 2km (1¼ miles) from the city center. There are no buses that run to the town center from the Namchuncheon Station, so you'll have to take a taxi or walk (30 min.). The express and intercity bus terminals are in the same place near the city center. Most of the city is concentrated around the shoreline of the lake.

VISITOR INFORMATION   There is a **tourist information center** (② 033/250-3896; http://tour.chuncheon.go.kr/eng/main/main.asp) near the bus terminal and at Namchuncheon station (② 033/250-3322). Open daily 9am to 6pm, the English-speaking staff will provide maps and brochures of the city and all of Gangwon-do. There is also free Internet access. Smaller tourist information booths are near Uiam Lake at **Jogak Park** (② 033/252-3600) and in front of **Chaum Beach,** which are also open daily from 9am to 6pm.

[FastFACTS] CHUNCHEON

Banks, Foreign Exchange & ATMs Most of the major banks in the city are located in the downtown area. The **Korea Exchange Bank,** 655, Hyeoja 2-dong, Chuncheon-si (② 033/252-2407), is located a little way from the main post office. Most banks are open Monday to Friday 9:30am to 4:30pm.

Exploring Chuncheon

Cheongpyeongsa ★★★ ■ TEMPLE   Getting to this temple is part of the fun, since the only way to access it is by water. First built in 973, parts of the temple were lost during the Korean War. The "revolving" door, which symbolizes the transmigration of souls, and the Geukrakbojeon remain today. Inside the temple is **Jinrak-gong,** the oldest garden from the Goryeo Dynasty.

There is a legend associated with the temple. A young man, who loved a princess, was killed and reincarnated as a snake, which stuck itself to the princess and would not leave her. The princess came to the temple to pray to make the snake let go. After holding a ceremony, the snake finally left and she had the three-level pagoda built here above the **Guseong Waterfall** before returning to her kingdom. The pagoda, which still stands today, is called the **Gongju Pagoda** (*gongju* means "princess" in Korean).

To get to the temple, you must take a short boat ride (accessible from the top of Soyang Dam). Once you get off the boat, you pay an entrance fee to the island and the small Guseon Waterfall, which is on the scenic path on the way to the temple. Then, you'll have to pay another admission fee at the entrance to the temple.

674 Cheongpyeong-li, Buksan-myeon, Chuncheon-si. ✆ **033/244-1095.** Round-trip boat fare (includes entrance to island) ₩6,000 adults, ₩5,400 teens, ₩2,900 children. The boat runs every 30 min. Admission to the waterfall is ₩2,000; admission to the temple is ₩2,000 adults, ₩1,700 teens, ₩800 children. Mar–Oct daily 9:30am–6pm and Nov–Feb daily 10am–5pm. From Chuncheon Train Station, take bus no. 12-1 or 11; from the Namchuncheon Station or bus terminal take bus no. 12; get off at to Soyang Dam. A taxi from Chuncheon Station takes about 20 min.

Gangwon Provincial Arboretum GARDEN   Created to preserve and display Gangwon-do's local plant life and flowers, the arboretum includes several gardens, ponds, fountains, a small stone bridge, a forest park, a flower museum, a pavilion, and a shop, where you can buy "forest products" from the region.

218-5, Sanon-dong, Chuncheon-si. ✆ **033/243-6012** (Korean only). Mar–Oct daily 10am–6pm; Nov–Feb daily until 5pm. From the Chuncheon Bus Terminal, take bus no. 38 or 39 bound for Yongsan/Chuncheon Dam and get off at the Gangwon Provincial Arboretum stop. Buses run daily from 5:30am to 7:50pm.

Gongjicheon ★ PARK   When you enter the city from Seoul, this is the first place you'll see. The area includes the scenic lake **Uiam-ho** and the outdoor sculpture garden **Jogak Park.** A small bridge, **Dohojugyo,** is made from wooden planks placed on old boats that sway a bit when you cross it. You can rent a bicycle for ₩3,000 per hour, or ₩5,000 for a tandem, and ride along the road surrounded by white fencing.

Near the sculpture park is **Ladena Resort** (✆ **033/240-8000**), where you can rent a boat or enjoy a number of cultural events and performances on the outdoor stage, near the fountain. See p. 353 for accommodation info.

218-5 Sanong-dong, Chuncheon-si. ✆ **033/253-6012.** Free admission. Daily 24 hr. From Namchuncheon station, take bus 12 or 67. You can also take a taxi from any of the stations and it'll take 5–10 min. Parking ₩600 for 30 min. and ₩100 for every 10 min. thereafter.

Jung-do WALKING TRAIL   One of three small islands that were formed when Uiam Dam was constructed, several Iron and Bronze Age relics were unearthed here, near an ancient burial ground and living quarters. Since it's so close to downtown, it is a popular leisure destination for the city's residents. The wide bike and walking path are great for a stroll. You can rent a bicycle for ₩3,000 per hour, or ₩6,000 for a tandem. You can also play badminton on the island's courts for only ₩3,000 per hour.

200 Samcheon-dong, Chuncheon-si. 𝒞 **033/242-4881** (Korean only). Ferry ride to the island (includes admission) ₩4,300 adults, ₩3,700 teens, ₩2,400 children 7–12, ₩1,500 children 5–6, free for kids 4 and under. Open daily, except when the lake freezes over. There are no buses from the bus terminal or the train stations. You can take a taxi from any of the stations and it'll take 5–10 min. From Myeong-dong St., take bus no. 74 or 75 and get off at Jung-do. Buses run at 1-hr. intervals.

Namiseom (Nami Island) ★ MEMORIAL   Famous for being the location where *Winter Sonata* was shot, this islet was formed when the Cheongpyeong Dam was built. A small piece of land in the shape of a half moon, it houses the grave of General Nami, who led a great victory against the rebels in the 13th year of the reign of Joseon King Sejo. Well known for its beautiful tree-lined lanes, it is a popular weekend getaway for the people of Seoul. There are no telephone poles on the island, since all electric wires were run underground to preserve its natural beauty. There is a theme park and sports center in the middle of the island with swimming pools, facilities for watersports, a merry-go-round, a shooting range, and a roller-skating rink. There is also a campsite and resort facilities for overnight visitors. The most beautiful times of the year are May, July, August, and October, which are also the most popular.

198 Bangha-li, Namsan-myeon, Chuncheon-si. 𝒞 **031/580-8114** (Korean only). www.namisum. com. Round-trip boat ride (includes entrance to the island) ₩8,000 adults, ₩5,000 teens and seniors 65 and over, ₩3,500 children, free for kids 4 and under. Ferries run daily to Namiseom 7:40am–8:20pm (every 30–50 min.) and from the island 7:50am–8:30pm at 30 to 60 min. intervals. From the DongSeoul Bus Terminal, take a bus bound for Chuncheon and get off at Gapyeong. From Gapyeong Intercity Bus Terminal, take a bus to Namiseom or a taxi (it's about a 5-min. ride). No private vehicles are allowed on the island. Parking at the ferry dock ₩4,000. There is a direct shuttle bus from Tapgol Park (in the Insadong area of Seoul) to Gapyeong wharf at 9:30am daily, which takes 1 hr. and 40 min. and costs ₩7,500. Call 𝒞 **02/753-1245** for reservations.

Soyang-ho (Soyang Lake) & Soyang Dam ADVENTURE TOUR   Built in 1973, the Soyang Dam is the largest rock-filled dam in Asia. Although it used to be a beautiful area for boating, the lowered water level, recent floods, and erosion have caused the surrounding hills to lose much of their former beauty. The valleys around the lake are well known for smelt fishing in the winter.

205 Cheongpyeong-li, Buksan-myeon, Chuncheon-si. 𝒞 **033/242-2455.** Free admission to the lake, but the ferry costs ₩12,000 adults, ₩6,000 children. Ferries run at 10am on weekdays with an additional 3pm ferry on weekends. From Chuncheon Train Station, take bus no. 12-1 or take bus no. 11 or 12-1 from the Namchuncheon Station. From the Intercity Bus Terminal, take local bus no. 10 or 11 to Soyang Dam. A taxi from Chuncheon Station takes 15 min.

Where to Stay

As a popular weekend getaway spot, the city has plenty of sleeping options to fit all budgets. Lower-priced motels and yeogwan are generally concentrated around the bus terminals. There is also no shortage of higher-end and tourist-class hotels, condos, and resorts.

EXPENSIVE

Ladena Resort   Because this place is generally run on a membership basis, the rates are expensive for nonmembers, but there are very nice, upscale Korean condo-style facilities. The resort complex is located next to the dock leading to Jung-do. The eight-story building has a variety of room options from beds to ondol. The Korean buffet restaurant is open only on weekends and holidays.

792 beonji, Samcheon-dong, Chuncheon-si. www.ladenaresort.com. ℂ033/240-8000. Fax 033/243-9000. 125 units. ₩130,000 and up accommodations for 4; ₩220,000 unit for 6. **Amenities:** Restaurants; bar; cafe; pool; putting green; tennis court; motorboat and water-ski rental; karaoke; outdoor barbecue. *In room:* A/C, TV, kitchen, hair dryer, Internet.

MODERATE

Chuncheon Sejong Hotel ★★ One of the best value accomodations in the city, the oldest hotel in town is set in a picturesque location at the foot of Bonguisan. The hotel has great amenities for the price and even an outside garden area. It is centrally located near both the train and the bus stations. The rooms are spacious and clean with nice views of the surrounding area.

15-3, Bongeui-dong, Chuncheon-si. ℂ 033/252-1191. Fax 033/254-3347. 68 units. ₩115,000 standard room, with discounts of up to 40% on weekdays and July–Aug (20% on weekends). AE, MC, V. **Amenities:** Restaurants; bar; cafe; pool; health club; sauna; room service; babysitting; karaoke. *In room:* A/C, TV, hair dryer, Internet.

Chuncheon Tourist Hotel ★ Centrally located, this hotel is just 5 minutes away from the train station. It has comfortable and clean rooms with delightful rain shower heads. There are highly polished hardwood floors and old-fashioned paper-screen windows in the ondol rooms (regular Western-style beds are also available). Unfortunately, there is no sign in English, but you can find it located behind the Gukmin Bank, not far from Myeong-dong Street and city hall. Just look for the beige four-story building with a sign that reads HOTEL in white letters on a blue background.

30-1, Nakwon-dong, Chuncheon-si. ℂ033/257-1900. Fax 033/255-3372. 56 units. ₩100,000 and up standard room. MC, V. **Amenities:** 2 restaurants; cafe; room service. *In room:* A/C, TV, fridge, hair dryer, Internet.

Elysian Gangchon ★★ This ski resort offers dozens of ski slopes and an associated condominium complex. The easiest way to get here from Seoul is to take a train to nearby Gangchon Station. Free shuttle buses are available outside the train station every 20 minutes. You can also take a bus from the DongSeoul Station or the Sangbong Station. Open all year, the popular ski season is from mid-December to mid-March. Look for ski/sleep package deals.

The regular condos have two bedrooms, which have small, but serviceable, beds. Bathrooms have bathtubs and flexible shower heads but no shower curtains. The kitchens include dining tables and the living rooms have a sofa and TV.

29-1 Baekyang-li, Namsan-myeon, Chuncheon-si. www.elysian.co.kr. ℂ033/260-2000. 222 units. ₩65,000 and up for condo sleeping 4; ₩130,000 and up deluxe room; rates vary depending on season. AE, MC, V. **Amenities:** 3 restaurants; cafeteria; lobby lounge; pool; children's center; sauna; karaoke. *In room:* A/C, TV, kitchen.

INEXPENSIVE

Gangchon Youth Hostel Although it's often booked by school groups on field trips, it is one of the least expensive places to stay in the area. Especially good for solo travelers on a budget, the hostel offers a surprisingly large array of amenities, including a library and sports facilities.

386 Gangchon-li, Chuncheon-si. www.kyh.or.kr (Korean only). ℂ 033/262-1201. Fax 033/262-1204. 34 rooms sleeping up to 254 total. ₩12,000/bed in a group room (usually sleeping 8 or 10);

₩42,000 4-bed private room. MC, V. **Amenities:** Dining room; soccer field; volleyball court; kitchen; music room; library; snow sleigh course; Internet.

Where to Eat

As I've mentioned earlier, Chuncheon is the home of dak galbi, a dish made with chunks of chicken, garlic, vegetables, and rice cake sticks all mixed with a dollop of spicy *gochujang* (chili paste) and cooked on a tabletop griddle. There is even a street behind Chuncheon's Myeong-dong street called **Dakgalbi Golmok** (Dakgalbi Alley) because of all the restaurants there. You can't really go wrong with any of the restaurants in the area, and the prices are all comparable, ranging from ₩16,000 to ₩20,000 for a meal for two.

The other dish that the city is famous for is mak gooksu, which is sometimes cooked with the leftovers from the dak galbi.

EXPENSIVE

St. Petersburg ★ RUSSIAN   The only Russian restaurant in Chuncheon is worth checking out. The interior is decorated in the old Russian style, with a plethora of elaborate paintings, a fireplace, and high ceilings. And, happily, the food is as nice as the ambience. Try the lobster or the galbi steak dinner, and you won't be sorry. On top of that, you'll get wonderful service from the English-speaking staff and forget you're in the middle of South Korea. If you get a window seat, you'll get nice views of the river below.

100-21, Soyang-no 1-ga, Chuncheon-si. ℂ **033/252-4004.** Daily 10am–11pm. Closed Lunar New Year and Chuseok. Entrees ₩16,000–₩60,000. AE, MC, V. A 5-min. taxi ride from Chuncheon Train Station will cost about ₩2,000. Parking available.

MODERATE

Hongcheon Wonjo Hwalogui ★★★ 🔥 KOREAN PORK   Traveling on expressway55 south from Chuncheon is the small town of Hongcheon off of highway 44 and a crop of restaurants specializing in *hwalogui ssamgyupssal* (three-color sliced pork belly), that has been coated in spicy gochujang and cooked on a tabletop grill. This is the restaurant that started it all. Try the house specialty with an order of *mak gooksu* (spicy mixed noodles) to top it all off.

631-7 beonji, Haoan-li, Hongcheon-gun. ℂ **033/435-8613.** www.hcwonjo.co.kr (Korean only). Noodle dishes ₩4,000–₩5,000, meat ₩10,000. MC, V. Daily 9am–10pm. Parking available up front.

Myeong-dong's Number 1 Dakgalbi ★★ KOREAN CHICKEN   Another restaurant known for Chuncheon's two famous dishes, dak galbi and mak guksu. It is one of the many restaurants located in Dakgalbi Alley. Two orders of dak galbi easily feed three people.

131-9 Joyang-dong, Chuncheon-si. ℂ **033/256-6448.** Entrees starting from ₩8,000. MC, V. Daily 10am–10pm.

Tongnamu Dakgalbi ★★★ 🔥 KOREAN CHICKEN   Located on the road to Soyang Dam, this chicken place offers the famous local dak galbi, served with onions, cabbage, and little pieces of sweet potatoes that caramelize in the heat of the pan. Order an ice-cold beer to help cut the spice and the heat. The sign is only in Korean, but it's brown with white letters and on the lefthand side as you go toward the Soyang Dam.

Sinbuk-eup, Chuncheon-si. ℂ **033/241-5999.** ₩5,000–₩10,000. MC, V. Daily 10am–10pm.

INEXPENSIVE

Shigol Makguksu ★ KOREAN NOODLES Located in front of the Soyang Bridge, this restaurant has been serving the local noodle dish for over 30 years. The prize-winning noodles are made from buckwheat flour and are delicious. If you're not in the mood, there are other things on the menu, including the *dubu jeongol* (tofu hot pot meal), which is very good. But what else would you order in a place whose name translates to "country-style rough noodles"? There is even a 10% discount to seniors over 65.

278-3 Yulmu-li, Sinbuk-eup, Chuncheon-si. 🕐 **033/242-6833.** Entrees ₩4,000–₩5,000. MC, V. Daily 10am–10pm, but closed every other Tues. Parking available.

Shopping

The most popular shopping area in Chuncheon is **Myeong-dong Street,** named after Seoul's most popular shopping district. Located downtown, the district is packed with over 300 shops, including boutiques, restaurants, fast-food joints, night-clubs, and movie theaters. Other than the alleyways filled with shops, there is an underground shopping district. The traditional market, **Jung-ang Shijang,** also in the area, dates back to 1962. Unlike the hip fashions in the boutique shops, the open-air market caters more to middle-aged tastes and also has shops that sell *hanbok,* Korean traditional clothes.

To get to the area from the bus terminal, take bus no. 7, 9, 64, or 64-2. From Chuncheon Train Station, take bus no. 63, and from Namchuncheon Station, take bus no. 1, 32, 32-1, 35, or 67.

THE REST OF GANGWON-DO

Gangwon-do and its North Korean counterpart, Kangwon, are together called the Gwandong region. Other than the main cities highlighted earlier, other major cities in the province include Donghae and Wonju, which are discussed below.

Now that the government has removed most of the barbed wire along its coasts, its beaches have lost some of their hard military edge. There has been a strong push for further development in the region, so be sure to visit before the entire province is ruined by the industrial signs of "progress."

Essentials

GETTING THERE Other than the airport at Yangyang, the only airport in the province is **Wonju Airport** (WJU), 366, Toegye-dong, Chuncheon-si (🕐 **033/344-3311**). Located between Wonju and Hoengseong, it has one flight daily to and from Jeju-do and one from Seoul, served by Korean Airlines. City bus no. 62 goes from the airport to the Hoengseong Intercity Bus Terminal, as well as the train station and Wonju Bus Terminal. The bus stop is located to the right after you come out of the airport.

Bus lines to Gangwon-do start from **Seoul's Express Bus Terminal,** 19-3 Banpo-dong, Seocho-gu (🕐 **02/535-4151**), or the **DongSeoul Bus Terminal,** 546-1 Guui-dong, Seongdong-gu (🕐 **02/446-8000**), for locales in the northern part of the province.

The **Jung-ang rail line** cuts across the southwestern corner of the province running through Wonju on its way down to Busan. Two rail lines pass through the Tae-baek Mountains to the coast. The older, more scenic route is the **Yeongdong line** that runs south. It starts in Yeongju (in Gyeongsangbuk-do) and goes via Cheolam to Gangneung. The **Taebaek line** branches off from Jecheon (in Chungcheongbuk-do) and goes through Yeongwol, meeting the Yeongdong line at Baeksan. The short **Gyeongchun line** connects Chuncheon to Seoul's Cheongnyangni Station and the Jung-ang line.

Driving through the province, the two expressways are the 50 that runs from Seoul through Wonju to Gangneung, connecting to the short 65 expressway that goes north to Hyeonnam and south to Donghae. The Jung-ang Expressway (road 55) starts from Chuncheon and runs through Wonju all the way south down to Busan.

GETTING AROUND   Intercity buses connect cities and small towns to each other, but local buses run less frequently through much of the province. If visiting far-flung sites, plan ahead and check the time of your return bus so that you're not stranded in some remote mountain locale at the end of the day. Taxis are available outside of all bus and train stations and airports, but you'll pay a bit more than you would in Seoul or the larger cities, since the drivers know that sometimes you don't have a choice but to use their services. Negotiate your price with the driver before heading off in any direction. If you want the flexibility, your best option is to rent a car from Seoul and drive it around Gangwon-do.

VISITOR INFORMATION   The Gangwon-do Tourist Information Office (*✆* **033/244-0088**) provides booths and information centers in front of most major transportation hubs and main tourist attractions. Most of them are staffed by helpful, English-speaking guides. Be sure to get maps and local bus schedules. You can also dial the **Korea Travel Phone** (*✆* **1330**) anywhere in the country for travel assistance in English.

[Fast FACTS] GANGWON-DO

Banks, Foreign Exchange & ATMs Most banks throughout the province are open 9:30am to 4pm weekdays. Most major banks will be able to change your currency, but ATMs of bigger banks (e.g. Korea Exchange Bank, Kukmin Bank, Shinan Bank, etc.) will be the most foreigner friendly.

Business Hours Government offices are usually open weekdays from 9am to 6pm March through October, and until 5pm November through February, but note that most government-run locations are closed Mondays. Major department stores are open daily 10:30am to 7:30pm, even Sundays. Smaller shops tend to be open from early morning until later in the evening.

Internet Access If you're traveling with a laptop, you may be able to get high-speed Internet access from your hotel, since most upscale hotels (and even lower-priced love motels) provide Internet access. Otherwise, step into any number of **PC bahngs,** usually located in the downtown area of towns, where you can rent a computer with Internet access for a small fee per hour.

Donghae

The city of Donghae was created in 1980 by consolidating the two small port towns of Mukho and Bukpyeong, as well as surrounding residential and industrial areas. It runs along the coast of the East Sea and includes the country's largest beach, **Mangsang Beach,** and serves as a major transportation port for the area. Though it's not the prettiest city, its best feature is its proximity to the ocean.

The **Donghae Station** (✆ 033/521-7788) is located on the Yeongdong rail line and connects the city to Dongdaegu, Yeongju, Cheongnyangni, Busan, and Daejeon. Additional train services are added during the popular summer months from mid-July to August. Express buses run from **Seoul's Express Bus Station** 24 times a day (three additional buses on weekends) from 6:40am to midnight and take about 4 hours. From the **DongSeoul Station,** buses run only about nine times a day from 7:50am to 7:30pm (one extra run on weekends, until 11:20pm) and also take 4 hours. Bus service is also available to and from Chuncheon, Wonju, Sokcho, Busan, Daegu, Taebaek, Gangneung, Samcheok, Ulsan, and Uljin. You can catch a ferry to Ulleung-do from here.

The **tourist information center** (✆ 033/533-3011; daily 9am–6pm) is just in front of the entrance to **Cheon-gok Donggul.** Donghae's official website is http://english.dh.go.kr/english/index.html.

EXPLORING DONGHAE

Cheon-gok Donggul (Cheon-gok Cave) NATURAL ATTRACTION   The
most famous attraction in the city, this cave is unusual in that it is located within walking distance of the downtown area. Discovered in 1991, it is well lit and contains some unusual calcified formations. About 4 to 5 million years old, only about 700m (2,297 ft.) of the cave is open to the public.

1004 Cheongok-dong, Donghae-si. ✆ **033/532-7303.** Admission ₩2,000 adults, ₩1,100 teens, ₩700 children, free for children under 6 and those over 65. Daily 8:30am–6:30pm, 7am–9pm (July 10–Aug 20), closes at 5pm in winter. It's a two-minute walk from Donghae city hall.

Chuam Beach ★ BEACH   Also called **Haegeumgang Beach,** this sandy beach
is surrounded by beautiful scenery created by the rocky cliffs that surround it. The quiet and shallow waters attract traveling families, especially in the summer months.

472-20, Chuam-dong, Donghae-si. ✆ **033/530-2478.** Free admission. Daily 24 hr. From in front of the Donghae Bus Terminal or the Donghae Train Station (or across the street from the Donghae Intercity Bus Terminal), take bus no. 61 and get off at Chuam (a 45-min. ride). The bus runs about 7 times daily.

Mangsang Beach ★ ☺ BEACH   The most popular beach on the eastern coast
of the peninsula, the sands of Mangsang beach spread farther than the eye can see. The clean and shallow waters are ideal for families with children and you'll see plenty of them here, especially during the most popular time of the year, July and August weekends. There are plenty of hwae restaurants, pubs, inns, and a small amusement park. There are shower rooms, volleyball courts, campgrounds, parking facilities, and even a post office nearby.

393-16, Mangsang-dong, Donghae-si. ✆ **033/530-2867** (the Sea Public Service Center). Free admission. Daily 24 hr. From the Donghae Shiwae Bus Terminal, cross the street and catch the bus headed for Mangsang. From the Donghae Train Station, cross the street and take a bus headed for Mangsang Beach. Buses run every 15–20 min., every 5 min. in the summer and cost about ₩1,400.

Mureung Gyegok (Mureung Valley) ★★ NATURAL ATTRACTION   Sur-
rounded by Dutasan and Cheongoksan and located west of the city, legend has it that this lovely valley is where fairies strolled. Given its idyllic beauty, it's easy to see why. A little way from the entrance is **Samhwasa** (aka Mureung Dowon; ✆ **033/534-7676**), the main temple of the area. Surrounded by granite peaks, you can do a temple stay focused on slow living. It was founded by Monk Jajang during the reign

of Shilla Queen Seondeok. A thousand-year-old temple, it was completely destroyed by the Japanese army in 1907. It was rebuilt the following year, but moved to its current location in 1977. The Vairocana Buddha statue and the trilevel pagoda from the Shilla period survived and were moved intact.

8-tong, Samhwa-dong, Donghae-si. ☏ **033/534-7306.** Admission to Samhwasa ₩1,500 adults, ₩1,000 teens, ₩600 children. Daily 9am–6pm, until 8pm in summer. From the Donghae Express Bus Terminal, take bus no. 12-1, 12-2, 12-3, 12-4, or 12-5 and get off at Mureung Gyegok. The buses run every 30 minutes and take about an hour.

Samcheok

Samcheok city and county is the southernmost of Gangwon-do's coastal areas. It is made up of a loose conglomeration of fishing villages, harbor districts, and a business center. The city is known for its fresh seafood. Express buses run from Seoul's Express Bus Terminal 20 times daily from 6:30am to 8:30pm, and take about 3½ hours. Buses from the DongSeoul Terminal run 17 times daily from 7:10am to 8:05pm and take just over 3 hours. Intercity buses run to and from Donghae, Gangneung, Taebaek, and Uljin. The **tourist information booth** (☏ **033/575-1330;** Mar–Oct daily 9am–6pm, Nov–Feb daily 9am–5pm) is located just to the side of the Samcheok Express Bus Terminal (☏ **033/573-9444**). There is also a tourist info center at the **Samcheok Municipal Museum.** The city's website is http://eng. samcheok.go.kr.

The city offers a **tour bus** daily, year-round. It leaves from Samcheok Station at noon daily, stops for lunch at the Samcheok Harbor fish center, then visits Haeshindang Park and Gainam Observatory before returning to Samcheok Station around 3:30pm. It costs ₩6,000 per person (free for children 6 and under), but does not include the price of lunch or admission to the park.

There are some nice beaches in the area, all reachable by local bus. **Samcheok Beach** is the largest swimming beach. It has shallow waters and convenient facilities, and a beachside resort. **Maebang Beach** is more scenic and popular with families due to its shallow, clean waters. Farther south is **Yonghwa Beach** and nearby **Jangho Beach,** which is a good place to get fresh seafood.

EXPLORING SAMCHEOK

Daegeumgul (Daegeum Cave) ★★ NATURAL ATTRACTION   Although believed to be as old as nearby Hwanseon-gul, Daegeumgul wasn't discovered until the late 21st century and not opened to the public until 2007. What is unusual about the cave is the amount of water that flows within it creating waterfalls and an underground lake. A 610m-long (6,000-ft.) monorail takes you into the cave, and then you'll see various stalactites creating pillars, shields, and smaller caverns. Only 40 people are allowed in at a time and the entire tour takes about 90 minutes.

San 25 Daei-li, Singi-myeon, Samcheok-si. ☏ **033/541-9266** (Korean only). Admission ₩12,000 adults, ₩8,500 teens, ₩6,000 children. Entry every 30 min. 8:30am–5pm (18 times daily). Parking ₩1,000 for cars.

Haeshindang Park ★ PARK   Samcheok is home to the only place in the area where the Korean phallic tradition continues. Indeed, large-scale penis sculptures are the big draw here. Originally created to appease the soul of a dead virgin (whose spirit was said to have kept the locals from being able to catch fish), there are over 50 phallic statues in this surprisingly picturesque park, located along the shore. Called the **Sinnam Village of Wondeok-eup,** the park has the Haeshindang shrine and a

pretty extensive **Fishery Village Tradition Exhibition Center.** This folk museum shows some interesting shamanistic rituals observed by traditional fishermen in order to get a good catch. Unfortunately, the displays lack English explanations, but they are still fun to look at nevertheless. About 20km (12 miles) south of Samcheok.

301 Gallam 2(i)-li, Wondeok-eup, Samcheok-si. ✆ **033/570-3568** (Korean only). Admission ₩3,000 adults, ₩2,000 teens, ₩1,500 children. Mar–Oct 9am–6pm; Nov–Feb until 5pm. From the Samcheok Bus Terminal, take bus 20, 90, or 90-1. The ride takes just under an hour.

Hwanseon-gul (Hwaseon Cave) ★★★ NATURAL ATTRACTION   The longest limestone cave in the country, Hwanseon-gul is located in the hills west of town. There are a number of waterfalls and pools within the cave, as well as a variety of rock formations, which have been given names like the "royal seat." It also contains a number of stalactites and stalagmites. It's about a 30-minute, uphill walk from the ticket booth to the cave's entrance and is a lovely place to visit on a hot summer day. It takes about 2 hours round-trip to tour the cave.

San 117 Daei-li, Singi-myeon, Samcheok-si. ✆ **033/541-7600.** Admission ₩4,000 adults, ₩2,800 teens, ₩2,000 children. Additional fees for the monorail. Mar–Oct daily 8am–5:30pm; Nov–Feb daily 8:30am–4:30pm. Parking ₩2,000 for cars. Take a local bus from the Samcheok Bus Terminal and it'll take about 40 min.

Jukseoru Pavilion HISTORIC SITE   Jukseoru, whose name means "bamboo west pavilion," is the most important historical site in the city. Originally constructed in 1266, it served as an entertainment center for scholars and royalty during the Goryeo Dynasty. The pavilion was rebuilt in 1403, and that structure still stands today. Sitting on the edge of a cliff overlooking the stream, Oship-cheon, you get a fantastic view of the sunset. There is a small bamboo forest, a garden, and a tiny folk museum with artifacts (mostly pottery) from the area.

9-3 Seongnae-dong, Samcheok-si. ✆ **033/570-3670.** Free admission. Daily 9am–7pm. From the Samcheok Express Bus Terminal, take a right at the intersection. Walk straight for 2 blocks past the Samcheok Medical Center to the alley next to it. It should take 5–7 min. on foot. Alternatively, a taxi from the bus or train station will take about 5 to 10 min.

WHERE TO STAY

Although most people don't overnight in Samcheok, you can find a handful of motels around the intercity bus terminal. Most accommodations around here are cheap and not fancy, but serviceable. One of them is the **Crown Motel,** 94-8 Namyang-dong, Samcheok-si (✆ **033/573-8831**), which has standard rooms for ₩35,000 to ₩45,000.

WHERE TO EAT

Since Samcheok is a coastal town, it's known for its hwae and *gul* (oysters). There are several places to get good seafood in the area. At **Haedoji Hwaetjib,** 1-beonji, Jeongha-dong, Samcheok-si (✆ **033/574-1575** or 574-7785), you can get your fill of fresh fish, from ₩10,000 for hwae to up to ₩100,000 for a huge platter to share with your friends. Open daily 10am to 10pm, it's located on the bottom floor of the Viking building (look for white Korean letters on a dark blue background).

Another nice place to enjoy the local raw fish is **Bada Hwae,** 41 Jeongha-dong, Samcheon-si (✆ **033/574-3543**), which has mixed fish platters you can share from ₩30,000 to ₩50,000. They're open daily 7:30am to 10pm, except holidays and every second Monday.

For oysters, try the **Gwaneum Gul Shikdang** (whose name means "oyster restaurant"), 2-bang, Daei-li, Singi-myeon, Samcheok-si (☎ **033/541-1624**). They have spicy seafood hot pots for ₩20,000 and even a roasted chicken meal for ₩30,000.

For a more economical oyster meal, head over to **Gulpajib,** 203 Daei-li, Shingi-meon, Samcheok-si, where oyster flatcakes, mixed rice bowls, and potato flatcakes will cost you only ₩4,000 to ₩6,000.

If you're hungry for a big Korean meal, a good option is **Sae-eunhae,** 1-6 Seung-nae-dong, Samcheok-si (☎ **033/573-7969**), which is located right in front of the Samcheok Medical Center. Open daily from 10am to 10pm, the place is popular with Japanese tourists. The best deal is the *yonsama* (which means Japanese royalty) meal for ₩10,000, which includes a generous variety of *banchan* (side dishes). If you're not that hungry but want to cool off in the summer, you can get a bowl of *naengmyeon* (buckwheat noodles in a chilled beef broth) for a mere ₩5,000.

Also, the road up to Hwanseon Cave is lined with casual restaurants, all of which have fresh local offerings with comparable prices.

Wonju

The most populous city in the province, Wonju is located near the border of Gangwon-do and Gyeonggi-do. During the United Shilla period, the city was one of five secondary capitals. It served as the provincial capital from 1394 until the capital was moved to Chuncheon after the Korean War. Still an agricultural center, it has more ties to Seoul than cities in its own province. Home to a large South Korean army base, Wonju also has several universities, including a satellite campus for Yonsei University.

The small **Wonju Airport** (WJU), 106 Gokgyo-li, Hoengseong-eup, Hoengseong-gun (☎ **033/340-3311**), has one to two flights daily from Seoul, served by **Korean Airlines** (☎ **1588-2001** or 033/344-2000; www.koreanair.com). Despite its name, the airport is much closer to Hoengseong than Wonju. City bus no. 62 goes from the airport to the Hoengseong Intercity Bus Terminal, as well as the train station and Wonju Bus Terminal. The bus stop is located to the right after you come out of the airport.

Wonju Station (☎ **1544-7788**) is one of the major stops on the Jung-ang rail line, and several trains arrive and leave the station in both directions. Trains from Seoul's Cheongnyangni Station run 10 times daily, costing ₩6,300 to ₩7,900.

Express bus service runs from Seoul's Express Bus Terminal to **Wonju Express Bus Terminal** (☎ **033/747-4181**) about every 15 to 20 minutes daily from 6am to 11pm. The 90-minute ride costs ₩6,800 to ₩10,000. From the DongSeoul Bus Terminal, daily buses run every hour 8:40am to 5:30pm and cost ₩6,100. From the Sangbong Intercity Bus Station, express buses run 14 times daily 6am to 4:50pm. The almost-3-hour ride costs ₩6,800. Regular nonstop buses (which actually take less time than the express buses that make stops) from Sangbong run 7am to 8pm 14 times daily and cost ₩6,500. Wonju has another bus terminal; the regular **Wonju Bus Terminal** is located toward the northern end of town, just a couple of kilometers from the downtown area. Bus no. 90 goes from the regular bus terminal to the express bus terminal. Fare for local buses is ₩1,200.

The city's old business district is located in the area between the train station and Wonju Gamyeong Sajeok Park. The center of town is where the **Jung-ang Shijang (Central Market)** is located. An underground shopping district also lies below the main intersection. Wonju is best known as the gateway city to **Chiaksan National Park.**

The **tourist information center** is located at the Wonju Express Bus Terminal. Wonju's official site is http://english.wonju.go.kr.

CHIAKSAN NATIONAL PARK

Chiaksan is located in the Charyeong Mountain ranges and is one of its highest peaks. Within a forested nature preserve on its slopes, the remains of mountain fortresses hint at its past as a defensive stronghold. At the height of its Buddhist fervor, there were 76 temples in the area, but only 8 of them remain today. From the top, you can see Taebaeksan to the east and Sobaeksan to the south.

Chiaksan means "Pheasant Peak Mountain," changed from Jeokaksan to Chiaksan because of a myth about a man who saved a pheasant from being eaten by a snake. Later when the man was looking for a place to sleep, a woman let him into her house. In the middle of the night, she turned into a serpent and accused him of having killed her husband. She said that if she heard the bell of Sangwon Temple ring three times before sunrise, she would let him go—otherwise, she would kill him in revenge. By some miracle, the bell did ring three times, and his life was saved. When the man reached the temple, he found the pheasant dead by the bell. It had rung the bell with its head to save his life and sacrificed its own in return.

From in front of Wonju Station, take bus no. 41 bound for Guryongsa (from 5:30am–9pm, every 25 min.), no. 21 bound for Geumdae-li or Seongnam-li (from 5:40am–10pm, every 30 min.), no. 82 headed for Hwang-gol (10 times per day). Get off at the entrance to Chiaksan. Admission to the park is free, but entrance to the Guryong area is ₩3,200 adults, ₩1,300 teens, ₩700 children. Campsite fees are ₩1,600 adults, ₩1,200 youth (slightly higher during high season). The Seonghwang-li area is closed for natural preservation until 2026.

The mountain range has a long ridge that runs from north to south and acts as the main hiking course. Most of the trails start at the main entrance in the Guryong district and follow short routes centered on the highest peak, **Birobong.** It's best to pack a meal and bring water since there are no restaurants inside the park.

Gukhyangsa (Gukhyang Temple) TEMPLE Although it's a small temple, its view of the forests nearby attracts many visitors. The location of the "festival of defense of the fatherland," it was also the place where the second daughter of Joseon King Jeongjong, Princess Huihui, recovered from a seemingly incurable lung disease. At the suggestion of the doctors, she was sent to recover in Chiaksan. The princess began a 100-day prayer, during which she dreamt about an old man with long white hair who told her that he would cure her. She continued to pray and at the end of the days she was cured. As a token of appreciation, the king had the temple built.

99-beonji, Haeng-gu-dong, Wonju-si. ✆ **033/747-1815.** Daily 4am–7pm. From Wonju, take bus no. 81 headed for Wonju Gongo. It runs about every 30 min.

Guryongsa (Guryong Temple) ★ TEMPLE Located on the north side of Birobong, this temple was built by Monk Uisangin the eighth year of the reign of Shilla King Munmu. It got its name, which means "Nine Dragon Temple," because of a legend that nine dragons lived at the pond, Guryong-ho, which used to be where the main building is now. The name was later changed during the Joseon Dynasty to "Turtle Dragon Temple," but the pronunciation is the same. It takes about an hour on foot from the entrance of the park to the temple. Trees from the thick pine forest that surrounds the temple were used to build the royal palace during the Joseon Dynasty. It is one of the oldest temples in the country.

As you climb up past the temple, you'll see Guryong Waterfall, the Guryong Pond, Nymph Bath, and the Seryeom Waterfall.

1029, Hakgok-li, Socho-myeon, Wonju-si. ℂ **033/732-4800** (Korean only). www.guryongsa.or.kr. Daily 4am–7pm. Admission ₩2,900 adults, ₩700 teens, ₩400 children. From Wonju, take bus no. 41 to Guryongsa (about a 40 min. ride).

Ipseoksa (Ipseok Temple) TEMPLE   Ipseoksa is where Monk Uisang dug a cave and came to meditate. It is a small temple, located in a valley on the way to Hwang-gol from Chiaksan. It is home to the **Maae Yeorane Jwasang** (a seated Buddha statue). The pagoda in the temple was built by King Taejong, who had come to the temple looking for his master, but was unable to see him. The king built the pagoda, thinking of his master, Ungok Won Cheonseok. Right underneath Ipseoksa is the **Ipsok-dae,** a large rectangular stone sitting up on a cliff.

Free admission. Daily 24 hr. From Wonju, take bus no. 82 (which runs 10 times daily 6am–8:20pm) to Hwang-gol and Ipseoksa.

Sangwonsa (Sangwon Temple) TEMPLE   Located at the foot of Namdaebong (peak) of Chiaksan (don't confuse it with the one in Odaesan by the same name), it is one of the highest temples in the country. The walls of the temple have a mural depicting the story of a man whose life was saved by a pheasant (for the full story, see this section's introduction, above). Hiking up the mountain from the Seongnam-ni entrance, it would take 2 to 2½ hours to reach it. There are three rare cinnamon trees growing from the rocks in front of the temple.

1061, Seongnam-li, Shillim-myeon, Wonju-si. ℂ **011/377-2926** (Korean only). Free admission. Daily 24 hr. Take the bus to Yeongwonsa (see below) and hike.

Yeongwonsa (Ywongwon Temple) TEMPLE   Originally built by Monk Uisang in the 16th year of Shilla King Munmu, it was closed shortly afterward and remained so until Monk Kim Gyeongjun reopened it in 1964. Unfortunately, no relics from the past remain today.

North of the temple is what remains of the Yeongwonsanseong (Ywongwon mountain fortress), which was built to defend the lands from outside invaders. This was a point of strategic importance during the Imjin Waeran and the Korean War.

1388-beonji, Geumdae-li, Panbu-myeon, Wonju-si. ℂ **033/762-4783.** Daily 24 hr. From Wonju, take bus nos. 21 to 25 bound for Geumdae-li. Buses run about every 30 min. and take about an hour.

WHERE TO STAY

For lower-priced sleeping options, many *yeogwan* and motels are in the area north of the bus terminal. A few nicer and quieter sleeping options are also located around the main post office. There are also some motels near the central market, including the **Wonju Tourist Hotel,** 94-8 Namyang-dong, Samcheok-si (www.wjhotel.co.kr; ℂ **033/743-1241**), which has rooms going for ₩75,000 for doubles or singles. Suites start at ₩100,000. With both Western-style and ondol rooms, the 10% VAT and service charge are included in the price.

There are plenty of inns and minbak around Chiaksan—most are located in the **Guryong district,** but there are a few in the Shillim area as well. The most upscale accommodation in the area is the **Koresco Condominium,** 539-1 Owon-li,

Hoengseong-gun (www.korescocondo.com, Korean only; ☏ **033/343-8733;** fax 033/343-8730).

WHERE TO EAT

Although there are no famous dishes from Wonju, it is a good place to get sanchae bibimbap, since it's so close to Chiaksan. A good place that specializes in the rice dish is **Unchae** in Haenggu-dong (☏ **033/747-1993**).

Spicy-seafood lovers will enjoy the Alaskan pollack at **Hwangtae Haejang-gook ★★ 🏠**, 865, Dangye-dong, Wonju-si (☏ **033/745-7722**), which specializes in all things hwangtae, running to ₩5,000 to ₩30,000 for a meal.

For an unusual experience try the mud roasted duck at the **Hayan Jib Garden (White House Garden),** 556-3 Botong-li, Jijeong-myeon, Wonju-si (☏ **033/732-4882**). Supposedly very healthy for you, the duck is cooked for 2½ hours with medicinal herbs and sweet rice. Be sure to call ahead since it takes them so long to prepare the tender bird. Another place that specializes in duck is **Jandibat,** Maeji-li, Heungeop-myeon, Wonju-si (☏ **033/762-4480**), whose name means "grassy field."

Most of the restaurants around Chiaksan can be found in the Guryongsa district.

Jeongseon

Jeongseon is the name of both a small town and a county, and is famous for the origin of the classic folk song **"Arirang,"** Korea's version of the blues. First sung as a lament for the former king and homeland as the country was moving from the Goryeo Dynasty to the Joseon period, the song became very popular during the Korean War, when families were split up, never to see each other again. Declared an intangible cultural asset in 1971, there are more than 1,500 lyrical variations. The **Jeongseon Arirang Festival** happens annually in the fall, but free performances are held at the **Jeongseon Arirang Performance Hall** from mid-April to late November. If you time it right, visit the **Jeongseon O-il Jang (5-Day Market) ★★★**, which is held on the 2nd, 7th, 12th, 17th, 22nd, and 27th day of every month. What started as just a market has grown into a local event, with folk performers, artisans, and the usual vendors selling dried herbs and products cultivated from the nearby mountains.

Buses run from the **DongSeoul Bus Terminal** 13 times a day, from 7am to 6pm, and take about 3½ hours. Two buses run daily from Chuncheon, 6 from Wonju, and 11 from Gangneung. Located on the **Taebaek rail line,** Mugunghwa trains run from Seoul's Cheongnyangni Station, from Wonju, Jecheon, Yeongwol, and Jeungsan. On the Jeongseon line, you can catch trains from Jeungsan, Pyeryegok, Seonpyeong, Jeongseon, Najin, and Auraji. The website for Jeongseon is http://eng.jeongseon.go.kr.

The Jeongseon area has become famous for white-water rafting, but most of Jeongseon's attractions are concentrated in the **Hwaam Tourist Area,** which includes the pretty river valley of **Sogeumgang (Little Diamond Mountain).** It includes 12 waterfalls, fun-shaped rock formations, and nice scenery.

Nearby in Gurim Bawi forest is the **Hwaam Yaksu (Mineral Spring Water),** which emerges from the rocks there. Full of iron, calcium, fluoride, and other minerals, the waters are supposed to help cure minor ailments like eye infections, stomach aches, and skin problems. The water is naturally carbonated and has a bit of a sour and sweet taste.

One of the most popular sites is **Hwaam Dong-gul (Hwaa Cave)**, a natural limestone cave. The caverns were discovered between 1922 and 1945 during gold-mining operations. The abandoned mine has been redeveloped into exhibits on mining, a history of the cave, and ore and geological processes, explained by animated demons called "dokkagebi." There are artificial lights that highlight the stalactite and stalagmite formations and a cheesy water fountain inside the main cavern. Entrance to the cave, including the monorail up, is ₩5,000 for adults, ₩3,500 teens, ₩2,000 children. Open daily from 9am to 5pm, it's not recommended for those with heart troubles, weak knees, or claustrophobia, since the walk down the long metallic staircase can be difficult.

Located on the road to Taebaek is the temple **Jeongamsa,** about 350m (1,148 ft.) down from the peak of Mahangjae, toward Gohan. The temple was founded by Monk Jajang in A.D. 636. He built the Seoknamwon, the former shrine of Jeongamsa, by building a gold, silver, and Sumano pagoda 9 years later. The most interesting relic is the **Sumano Pagoda,** which stands on the mountainous slope above the temple. It is said that the Monk Jajang brought the stone on a ship from China. Unfortunately, there are no buses that run to Mahangjae. You'll have to take a taxi from Gohan or Jeongseon.

For a different form of transportation, spend the afternoon biking on railroad tracks, specifically the **Jeongseon Auraji Rail Bike** (✆ **033/563-8787,** www. railbike.co.kr, 290-4 Gujeol 1(il)-li, Buk-myeon, Jeongseon-gun). For ₩22,000, you and a friend can pedal a two-person "rail bike" from Auraji to Gujeol-li, an easy 7.2km (4½-mile) ride. You get to rest your legs on the free train ride back. Four-person vehicles cost ₩32,000 and the rail bikes are available five times daily 9am to 6pm, March through October, and 4 times daily, until 3pm, November through February. From the Jeongseon Bus Terminal take a bus to Yeoryang (10 times daily, from 6:10am–5:35pm). From Yeoryang, take a local bus to Gujeol-li, where you'll find the boarding platform (you can't miss the **Grasshopper Dream Cafe**, which is shaped like its namesake bug).

WHERE TO STAY

The most upscale and fun place to sleep in the county is **Kangwonland Casino and Hotel ★★** 😊 265 High1-gil, Jeongseon-gun (www.high1.com/eng/Hhome/main.high1; ✆ **01588-7789;** fax 033/590-7330), which is closer to Taebaek than Jeongseon-si. Opened in 2000, it is the only casino in the whole country open to South Korean natives. The casino hotel has 199 rooms, while the adjacent large Gangwon Land Hotel has 676 rooms. The casino has 960 slot machines and over 100 tables, where you can play blackjack and other games. The hotel is part of the **High 1 Resort Complex** which has condo facilities, as well. The resort has steep slopes for skiing and snowboarding, an 18-hole golf course, and the usual luxury amenities like fitness centers and indoor swimming pools. Standard rooms start at ₩157,300 at the High 1 Hotel and ₩290,400 in the Kangwonland Hotel, ₩544,500 and up for a suite. Discounts of up to 50% are not unusual off season. There is a ₩5,000 admission fee for the casino. The shuttle bus from the Gohan Train Station takes about 10 minutes or you can get a cab from the Gohan Express Bus Terminal, a 10-minute ride that should cost about ₩5,000.

Lower-priced motels and minbak can be found near the Jeongseon Train Station and Hwaam Cave. Standard rooms go for about ₩40,000.

WHERE TO EAT

The specialty of the area is *gondre* rice, which people relied on during times of famine. Today it's a popular local dish, made by boiling rice and gondre (a type of local thistle) with perilla oil, sesame seeds, and a spicy sauce. You can get it at **Jeongwong Wangjang** (℗ **033/378-5100**), in the small town of Yemi, which is on the way to Hambaeksan.

Another good restaurant in the area is **Jeongseon-gol Hwanggibossam,** 359-3, Bongyang 1-li, Jeongseon-eup, Jeongseon-gun (℗ **033/563-8114**), located about 25 minutes from the Jeongseon Terminal (about 5 min. by taxi). The specialty is *hwanggi bossam,* a special sliced pork dish in which the pork is marinated with ginger, and served with cabbage leaves for you to wrap and eat. A small order is ₩15,000 and the larger order ₩20,000. Don't miss the *bossam kimchi* (a special kind of kimchi made with chestnuts, pears, and pine nuts). The place is open daily, but the sign isn't in English. Just look for a white sign with black and red writing.

If you're in the mood for a boiling pot of soon dubu, a good option in the area is **Sugaseong Soondubu ★ ✦**, 313 Gaeun-dong, Wonju-si (℗ **033/761-1540**), where you can get a meal for just ₩7,000.

Yang-gu and the DMZ

The county of Yang-gu encompasses little-known areas of the DMZ. While the majority of DMZ tours take you to Panmunjeom, Imjingak, and other sections of the DMZ that border Gyeonggi-do, very few take you to the quieter, more natural areas in Gangwon-do. It's best to see the area with a rental car from Seoul (it's about a 2-hour drive on the expressway) and don't forget to bring your passport.

Ironically, Yang-gu and the **Punchbowl** (so named by an unknown foreign correspondent describing the geographic uniqueness of the area, surrounded by mountains 1,000 meters high), actually the small village of **Haean,** saw some of the bloodiest battles during the Korean War. Parts of Yang-gu were actually part of North Korea until the line of demarcation was drawn. Yang-gu is again a quiet farmland, but the scars of the war still remain. The most obvious of these is the **4th Infiltration Tunnel** (which was the 4th tunnel to be discovered). Not much to look at, they run a short mono-rail along the first 100m. More interesting is the **Eulji Observatory** (Hyeon 2-li, Haean-myeon, Yang-gu), which is only 1m (1.5km) from the DMZ and the closest you can get to North Korea. On a clear day you can see the five peaks of North Korea's Geumgangsan. You can visit the tunnel, observatory, and the **War Memorial Hall** by making a same day reservation before 4pm at the Yang-gu Unification Hall (℗ **033/480-2674**) and paying a ₩2,500 adults, ₩1,300 child entrance fee. Open Tuesday to Sunday (Mar–Oct) 9am to 6pm, until 5pm November through February. Closed Monday. Note that the 4th Infiltration Tunnel is closed noon to 1:30pm to recharge the batteries on the monorail.

The best place to visit in the area is **Dutayeon ★★★**, a small river that flows down from Geumgangsan and an area that's been closed to civilians for nearly 50 years. Because the area was (and still is) littered with landmines, it has become a nature preserve where mountain goats, deer, elk, and rabbits can roam free, undisturbed by humans. Remnants of rusted helmets, barbed wire, and shell casings lie alongside the pathways. Part of a special military zone, you have to make a reservation at least 3 days in advance with the Yang-gu Tourist Information Office (℗ **033/480-2251;** www.ygtour.kr). They only let one group in per day (min. 4 people), but they do have a couple of English-speaking guides on their staff. ₩2,000 adults, ₩1,000 children. Be sure to arrive after lunch since no food or drinks are allowed in Dutayeon and there are no restaurants or shops near the entrance (just a gallery and a small souvenir shop).

Happy Mize (© **070/8627-8080;** www.happymize.com) can arrange a Yang-gu DMZ tour for you, if you're worried about exploring the area on your own.

JEJU-DO
(JEJU ISLAND)

J eju-do is a different kind of volcanic island, located 85km (53 miles) off the tip of the Korean Peninsula. Locals say that its three resources are wind, rocks, and women and you'll get to enjoy all three during your visit. Waterfalls cascade into aqua waters and lava columns rise from the ocean's depths. Its dramatic landscape is only rivaled by the open friendliness of the island's people. **Jeju-si** (Jeju City), located on the north of the island, is where the airport and its major port is located. On the opposite side on the south, is **Seogwipo,** home to the major resorts and some of the main attractions—both natural and man-made. At the center is South Korea's largest mountain, **Hallsan,** whose volcanic slopes take 8 hours to traverse (up and back).

The rest of the land is dotted with volcanic craters, dramatic caves, green horse pastures, and miles of beaches of all colors and shapes.

Known for its *jeonbok jook* (abalone porridge), some of the fresh seafood is caught by the *haenyeo*, local women, who venture into the depths using nothing but a mask, a wetsuit, and their own natural breathing techniques. A meal of *hwae* (raw fish) or a bubbling hot pot of seafood can be finished off with a handful of local tangerines or a cup of green tea grown on the island.

ORIENTATION

Arriving
BY PLANE
Jeju International Airport (CJU; ℗ 1688-5002; http://jeju.airport. co.kr/doc/jeju_eng) is located about 4km (2½ miles) from Jeju City. The **Jeju-do Tourist Information Center (℗ 064/742-6051)** is on the first floor of the domestic terminal, in front of the arrival gates. There is also a **Korean Tourism Organization (KTO) Information Center (℗ 064/742-0032)** on the first floor of the international terminal, in front of the arrival gates. Both have helpful, English-speaking staff and provide maps, brochures, and hotel information.

Seventeen airlines fly in and out of Jeju-do, and three domestic airlines fly to Jeju from 13 cities, including Seoul's **Incheon (ICN)** and **Gimpo (GMP)** airports, and Busan's **Gimhae Airport (PUS).** Airlines making

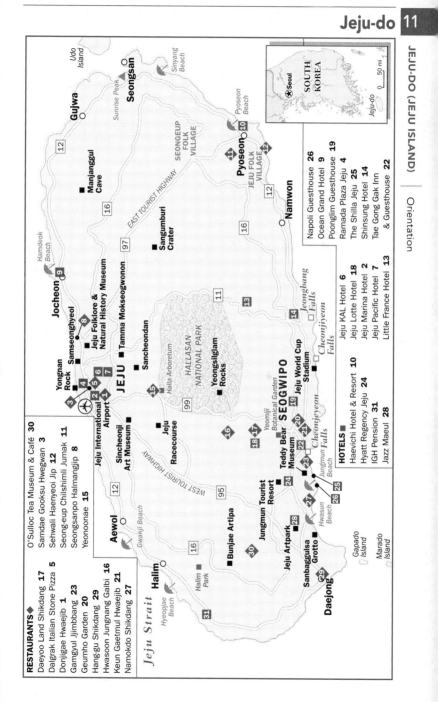

RESTAURANTS◆
Daeyoo Land Shikdang **17**
Dalgrak Italian Stone Pizza **5**
Donjigae Hwaejib **1**
Gamgyul Jjimbbang **23**
Geumho Garden **20**
Hang-gu Shikdang **29**
Hwasoon Jungnang Galbi **16**
Keun Gaetmul Hwaejib **21**
Namokdo Shikdang **27**
O'Sulloc Tea Museum & Café **30**
Samdae Gooksu Hwegwan **3**
Sehwali Haenyeoi Jip **12**
Seong-eup Chilshimli Jumak **11**
Seongsanpo Halmangjip **8**
Yeonoonae **15**

HOTELS ■
Haevichi Hotel & Resort **10**
Hyatt Regency Jeju **24**
IGH Pension **31**
Jazz Maeul **28**
Jeju KAL Hotel **6**
Jeju Lotte Hotel **18**
Jeju Marina Hotel **2**
Jeju Pacific Hotel **7**
Little France Hotel **13**
Napoli Guesthouse **26**
Ocean Grand Hotel **9**
Poonglim Guesthouse **19**
Ramada Plaza Jeju **4**
The Shilla Jeju **25**
Shinsung Hotel **14**
Tae Gong Gak Inn
  & Guesthouse **22**

regular flights to Jeju-do include **Korean Air** (✆ **1588-2001**; www.koreanair.com), **Asiana Airlines,** 2031, Yongdam 2-dong, Jeju-si (✆ **1588-8000**; http://us.flyasiana. com), **Jeju Air** (✆ **1599-1500**; www.jejuair.net), **Jin Air** (✆ **1600-6200**; www.jinair. com), **Air Busan** (✆ **1666-3060**; http://www.airbusan.com/AB/airbusan/english/main. jsp?loc=en), **Eastar Jet** (✆ **1544-0080**; www.eastarjet.com), **China Southern** (www.flychinasouthern.com) **China Eastern** (✆ **02/518-0330**; www.flychina eastern.com), **Japan Airlines** (www.jal.co.jp/en), **ANA** (www.ana.co.jp/asw/wws/ us/e), and **Trans Asia Airways** (www.tna.com.tw/en/index.aspx).

International flights from Japan and China depart less frequently. Each week, there are six flights from Tokyo, four from Osaka, three from Hong Kong, and two from Beijing. Since over 90% of visitors to the island come by air, they are planning a long-term expansion of the airport to be completed in 2020.

BY FERRY

You can travel to and from Jeju-do via passenger ship from various ports in South Korea. The Jeju city harbor is the largest with three terminals; the first two are right next to each other and the third is about a kilometer down the road. Terminal 1 has boats to Busan, Incheon, and Mokpo. Terminal 2 has ferries to Wando and Yeosu, while the International Terminal 3 has services to Wando, Mokpo, and occasional trips to Japan. Although these are domestic boat rides, be sure to bring your passport.

The most popular way to arrive by boat, especially for those bringing their own cars or on organized tours, is from Jeolla-do's **Jangheung Harbor** (✆ **1577-5820**; www. jhferry.com, Korean only). The Orange Ferry leaves daily from Jangheung at 8:30 and 10:30am and returns from Jeju's **Seongsan Harbor** at 12:30 and 5pm. The 2½-hour ride starts at ₩29,500 per person one-way. Be sure to bring cash, since they can't take foreign credit cards.

Overnight ferries from **Busan's Domestic Terminal** leave around 7pm and arrive 11 hours later at 6am. The two different lines depart on alternating days, which means you can sail any day except Sunday. The *Seolbong* (*Orient Star;* ✆ **064/ 751-1901**) is newer and cleaner than the *Cozy Island* (✆ **064/751-0300**), which runs Tuesday, Thursday, and Saturday at 7pm. The *Seolbong,* run by the **Dongyang Express Ferry Co.** (✆ **051/751-1901**), has services Wednesday through Friday at 6:30pm. A second-class room (for three) will set you back around ₩55,000, but it's worth it if you plan on getting a good night's rest. If you want to slum it in third class for ₩39,000, you'll have to sleep in a large room with at least 10 other people (bring your own sleeping bag and mat). On the other hand, if you want to splurge, book a private VIP room for ₩170,000. Call to check current rates and schedules. You can catch the return trip from the Jeju City Terminal 1 at 7pm for another 11 hours back to Busan.

From **Incheon Ferry Terminal,** the *Ohamana* ferry leaves at 5pm and arrives in Jeju-do around 8:30am. Boats run Monday through Saturday, not on Sundays. The return trip to Incheon also starts at 5pm from Jeju-do. Fares start at around ₩63,500 for third class, but you may want to pay the extra fees to upgrade to second or first class.

You can also get a ferry from the **Mokpo Ferry Terminal** (✆ **061/240-6060**). Service is available daily on the *Pink Dolphin* costing ₩49,650 for a 3+ hour trip. It leaves Mokpo at 2pm and departs Jeju-do at 9:30am. The *Queen Mary* costs ₩25,800 to ₩88,800 and leaves Mokpo at 9am daily and arrives in Jeju around

1:20pm. There's no Sunday service for the *Car Ferry Rainbow*, which sails from Mokpo Monday through Saturday at 2:30pm and arrives in Jeju at 7:20pm. The ferry leaves Jeju at 8am and arrives back on Mokpo at 12:50pm. There are no ferries on Sunday or Tuesday.

Service to and from **Wando Ferry Terminal** (✆ 061/554-4207) is available daily (though the car ferry doesn't run Sundays). The ferry from Wando, which starts at 7:30am, costs ₩24,000 for adults, ₩12,000 for children. Most rides last about 3 hours.

Other than destinations listed above, you can also travel to Udo, Sangchujado, and Hachujado from the Jeju Ferry Terminal.

With all of these ferries, you can just buy a ticket the day you leave, but book in advance if you're traveling during the popular summer months or Chuseok. Be sure to bring your passport and plenty of cash, since not all of the services can take foreign credit cards. Schedules are subject to change, especially during inclement weather.

GETTING INTO TOWN   The **Airport Limousine Bus** (✆ 064/713-7000) from Jeju Airport can be found outside gate 1 (turn left). The Limousine Bus no. 600 costs ₩3,500 to Jungmun and ₩5,000 to Seogwipo (half-price for children) and stops at all the major tourist hotels, ending at Seogwipo's KAL Hotel. Service runs 6:20am until 9:50pm, every 15 minutes. Regular buses from the airport include numbers 100, 200, 300, and 500 (to Jeju City Hall) and are cheaper than the limousine bus, starting at ₩1,000.

If you'd like to rent a car (which is the most convenient way to get around the island), all of the rental car agencies have desks right next to each other on the first floor of the airport, right outside of the domestic flight exit. **Avis car rental** (✆ 064/749-3773), **Geumho Rent-a-Car** ✆ 064/743-8107), and Jeju rental car are the largest.

There are two taxi stands at the airport. The short-distance one goes to Jeju-si, Aeweol, Hallim, Jocheon, and Gimnyeong, while the long-distance taxis go to Seogwipo, Jungmun resort, Bukjeju county, Namjeju county, and other areas. On average, a **taxi** from the airport to Seogwipo will cost approximately ₩30,000 and last about an hour. Expect to pay 20% extra after midnight.

Visitor Information

Jeju-do Tourist Association Information Center (✆ 064/742-6051; daily 6:30am–8pm) is located at the airport in front of the arrival gate on the first floor of the domestic terminal, where you can get free Internet access (the airport has Wi-Fi, but you have to pay for it). You can find the **KTO Tourist Info Center** (✆ 064/742-0032; daily 6:30am–8pm) there as well.

There are also tourist information centers, all open daily, at the **Jeju-si Ferry Terminal** (✆ 064/758-7181; 6:30am–8pm), the **Yongduam Rock** (✆ 064/728-3918; 9am–8pm) parking lot, **Jeju-si Intercity Bus Terminal** (✆ 064/753-1153; 9am–8pm), **Jeju-si Underground Mall** (✆ 064/750-7595; 9am–6pm), **Jemu Folk Village** (✆ 064/755-5959; 9am–6pm), **Tap-dong Outdoor Performance Hall** (✆ 064/ 728-3919; 9am–6pm), inside **Jeju City Hall** (✆ 064/735-3544; 9am–6pm), at the **Seogwipo Bus Terminal** (✆ 064/739-1391), in front of **Manjang Cave** (✆ 064/784-2387), **Seongsn Ilchulbong** (✆ 064/784-0959), **Hallim Park** (✆ 064/796-8577), and in **Sanbangsan** (✆ 064/730-1549).

Be sure to get a map of Jeju-do and a current bus schedule, if you're planning to travel by bus; buses run infrequently and on irregular schedules. You can find one on the Jeju-do travel website at http://eng.tour2jeju.net.

GETTING AROUND

Jeju-do isn't as small as you might think. Most people book at least 3 days and 2 nights to get a general overview of the island, since most tourist locations are about an hour from Jeju City. Jeju-do is best explored by car or taxi, if you're not on a strict budget. Driving is relatively easy, since traffic is minimal and roads are easily marked. If you reserve a car in advance online, you can usually get better rates. All the rental car agencies have desks at the airport and provide a free shuttle service. Easier and even cheaper than renting a car is to get a tour taxi for the day.

Buses are available but infrequent, and require the exact fare, making it important to carry a pocketful of ₩1,000 bills wherever you go. There is no rail or subway system on the island.

BY CAR   Renting a car is the easiest and best way to get around Jeju-do. The island's destinations are clearly marked in English and some of the remote places are difficult to access by bus alone. You can take your pick from among the following reputable agencies: **Jeju Rent a Car** (✆ 064/742-3307), **Kumho Rent a Car** (✆ 064/743-8107), **Avis Rent a Car** (✆ 064/749-3773), and **Jeju Rental Car Service Association** (✆ 064/747-4301). There are other rental-car agencies in Jeju-do, but those above are all available at the airport. Advance reservations aren't necessary, but you'll get a better rate and a guarantee of a car, especially during summer high season or national holidays. Rental-car information desks are all next to each other at the airport (on the first floor of the domestic terminal) *Tip:* If you're staying at one of the resort hotels, it's best to rent a car at the hotel's rental office, since they usually offer 50% discounts to guests.

You have to be at least 21, have been driving for at least a year, and have both your International Driving Permit and your passport with you in order to rent a car (see p. 403 of chapter 12). You can get free maps at either the car-rental company or the tourist information desk at the airport. All the rental-car companies have comparable prices (Avis is a little pricier but their employees speak better English), starting at ₩76,000 for a small compact, ₩117,000 for a midsize car, and ₩250,000 for an SUV. The per-day rates get lower the longer you rent and during off-season weekdays.

The maximum speed limit on Jeju highways is 80kmph (50 mph), but most roads are 50kmph to 60kmph (31–37 mph). As on the mainland, the roads have high-tech cameras ready to catch you speeding, so be careful.

BY TAXI   Getting around by taxi is easier in Jeju-do than other parts of the country, since there is comparably little traffic (except a bit in the evenings). Tour taxis are popular among South Korean honeymooners, since they get a driver and tour guide, all in one. It may be a good option for you too if you don't want to drive, but still want access to out-of-the way scenic destinations (although most taxi drivers speak limited English, if at all). The good thing about Jeju-do's taxis are that they are all the same price, with base fares starting at ₩2,900 and going up ₩100 every 213m (⅛ mile). The night fare (midnight–4am) is 20% more. If you decide to use a **tour taxi,** it will cost about ₩100,000 to ₩150,000 per day (plus lunch for the driver). You can negotiate with the taxi driver to try to get a better rate and determine your route before committing.

JEJU trolley TOUR BUS

Don't be fooled by the name, since this tour is neither a trolley nor a limousine (as sometimes referenced), but rather a climate-controlled bus. It's a comfortable way to get an overview of the island, especially if you're on a tight schedule. There are two courses: one that tours the east side of the island and another that goes around the west side of the island, including Seogwipo. Both courses start between 8:30 and 9:30am from the island's major hotels. The eastern course includes Seong-eup Folk Village, Manjang Cave, and Seopjikoji, a scenic peak where many movies have been filmed. The eastern course has an option to see a Mongolian horseback riding show for an additional ₩12,000 (₩9,000 for kids). The western course covers the Psyche World and Crystal Palace (butterfly theme garden), and Cheonjieon Waterfalls, with an option to ride the Seogwipo "Romantic Cruise") for an additional ₩15,000. Both courses end around 6pm at the airport. You must make reservations at least a day in advance by calling ✆ **1544-4118** or http://tbus.co.kr/english/index.php. A 1-day pass costs ₩35,000 adults, ₩28,000 children, and 2-day passes are ₩55,000 adults, ₩44,000 children, including lunch, but not the suggested ₩10,000 tip for the driver. Tours don't run December through March.

BY BUS   The bus system is reliable, but infrequent; the buses do travel to most tourist destinations, but some (like the Manjang Caves) will require an additional bit of walking or hiking on your part. Most bus routes radiate from terminals in Jeju City or Seogwipo, covering most of the island, with services every hour or so. Be sure you get a copy of the current bus schedules at the tourist information center or the bus terminal in Jeju-si. The **Jeju Bus Information System** (✆ **064/710-6278**; http://bus. jeju.go.kr/internet_eng) provides route info, but does not give a detailed schedule.

There are two buses that run on Highway 12, which circumnavigates the island. One bus starts at Jeju-si and goes to Seogwipo via Seongsan (going east), while the other starts at Jeju-si and goes to Seogwipo via Hallim (going west). They both start running at 5:40am and run every hour until 9pm. Regular bus fare is ₩1,000 adults, ₩800 for junior high school students, ₩400 for elementary school kids. You can get additional info on the intercity buses by calling ✆ **064/753-1153** for Jeju-si and ✆ **064/739-1391** for Seogwipo-si.

BY BIKE   Outside of Jeju City and Seogwipo, biking is common. In fact, there is a continuous bike lane on both sides of **Highway 12.** Cycling the entire 182km (113 miles) will take about 3 to 5 days, depending on your skill level. Some shore roads also have bike lanes, but many of them aren't continuous and are inconvenient. Rentals are around ₩6,000 to ₩10,000 per day, most with a minimum 3-day rental, plus an additional ₩3,000 for a helmet. Bikes are available at the airport, the Jeju Ferry Terminal, near the Jeju-si Bus Terminal, **Yongduam** (Dragon Head Rock), Seogwipo, Hyeopje Beach, and other beachfronts. **Hiking Jeju** (✆ **064/721-4802**; www. hikingjejudo.co.kr, Korean only) is a reliable rental company with several locations.

You can also rent a scooter or motorcycle. In Gu-Jeju ("Old" Jeju), there is a motorbike shop where the owner, Mr. Lee, speaks English well, **Keumsung Motorcycle/ Mr. Lee's Bike Shop**, open Monday to Saturday 9am to 8pm (2452 Ora 1(il)-dong, Jeju-si ✆ **064/758-6640**; http://www.jejubike.co.kr/eng/index.html). Scooter rentals start at ₩20,000 per day and motorbikes start at ₩30,000 per day.

Banks, Foreign Exchange & ATMs Normal banking hours are Monday to Friday 9am to 4pm. There are currency exchange bureaus at the airport and inside major hotels. ATMs can be found all over the island, but look for the Global logo, since those are the most foreigner-friendly. ATMs in department stores are usually the most user-friendly.

Business Hours Most businesses open from 9am to 6pm Monday to Friday. Shops are generally open 9am to 10pm Monday through Saturday, while most offices and government buildings are open 9am to 4:40pm on weekdays.

Doctors & Dentists Most first-class hotels can refer you to a doctor or dentist, though very few speak English well. In an emergency, dial ℂ **119** or call one of the recommendations under "Hospitals," below.

Hospitals Those with English-speaking doctors and 24-hour emergency care include **Halla Medical Center,** 1963-2 Yon-dong, Jeju City (ℂ **064/740-5000**); **Cheju National University Hospital,** 690-716, 3-do 2-dong, Jeju City (ℂ **064/717-1114**); and the **Seogwipo Medical Center,** 1530-2 Dongheung-dong, Seogwipo-si (ℂ **064/730-3106**). *Hot Lines* Tourist information is available in English by dialing (ℂ **1330**). For directory assistance in English, dial ℂ **00794.**

Internet Access Most high-end tourist hotels, love motels, and even some hostels have Internet access, but if yours doesn't you can use one of the PC *bahngs* (PC rooms) in Jeju-si or Seogwipo for about ₩1,000 to ₩1,500 per hour.

Newspapers The *Jeju Weekly* (www.jejuweekly.com) is an English-language paper, and two English-language daily newspapers, *Korean Herald* (www.koreaherald.co.kr) and *The Korea Times* (http://times.hankooki.com), are available on the island.

Pharmacies There are no 24-hour drugstores in Jeju-do. However, most pharmacies are located in Jeju-si or Seogwipo, displaying a large green cross symbol or the Korean word for medicine (약). Convenience stores and a few stores in luxury hotel lobbies are open around the clock and carry simple remedies like aspirin.

Police Dial ℂ **112** for the police; although their English will be limited, they will assist you. Police stations are clearly marked in English.

Post Offices There are 40 post offices and 21 postal agencies in Jeju-do, open Monday through Friday 9am to 5pm. The Jeju City post office and the Seogwipo post office are also open Saturday 9am to 1pm. If you have questions, or want to find the nearest post office, call ℂ **064/739-4503.**

Weather Call the Korean Tourism Organization at ℂ **1330** or ℂ **131** for the latest weather (especially useful for planning ferry excursions).

WHERE TO STAY

Jeju-do is popular among honeymooners and Japanese on their holidays, which means that hotel prices are higher here than on the mainland, especially during the summer high season and during Lunar New Year and Chuseok. If you're planning to visit during those times, be sure to make reservations well in advance. Weekend prices are a bit higher, too. Luxury accommodations are centered in Jeju-si and Seogwipo (which is home to the newer, more modern resorts), but there are plenty of lower-end *minbak* (private homestays), motels, and pensions scattered throughout the island. The condo-style pensions can be reserved in advance, but the minbak generally operate on a walk-in basis—again, not a problem except during high season.

Jeju-Si

EXPENSIVE

Jeju KAL Hotel   Rising 18 stories above the center of Jeju City, this hotel is run by Korean Airlines. Although it's not located right on the water, a handful of the rooms have ocean views, so ask for one when booking. The beds are hard and the rooms bare, but they all have down comforters. You can also opt for a traditional ondol room. In addition to courteous service, the hotel has a sky bar on the top floor. Its sister location in Seogwipo is more upscale.

1691-9 Yido 1-dong, Jeju-si. http://english.kalhotel.co.kr. © **064/724-2001.** Fax 064/720-6515. 282 units. ₩280,000 and up standard room. 10% VAT and 10% service charge not included. AE, MC, V. **Amenities:** 3 restaurants; 2 bars; lounge; cafe; indoor pool; health club; spa; sauna; bakery/deli; karaoke; casino; Internet. *In room:* A/C, TV, hair dryer, safe.

Ramada Plaza Jeju ★★ ☺   Located just minutes from the airport, this "floating" hotel is literally right on the water. Built with 100% investment funds from the Korean Teachers Credit Union, the nine-story building's design was inspired by luxury cruise ships. More Western-style rooms are available, but there are also ondol rooms and kids' suites (that have separate rooms with bunk beds, toys, TV, and gaming devices to keep the children occupied). You can choose between mountain- and oceanview rooms (for ₩40,000 more).

1255, Samdo 2-dong, Jeju-si. www.ramadajeju.co.kr. © **064/729-8100.** Fax 064/729-8554. 380 units. ₩280,000 single/double; ₩320,000 and up suite. 10% VAT and 10% service charge not included. AE, MC, V. **Amenities:** 4 restaurants; 2 bars; lounge; cafe; indoor/outdoor pool; fitness center; spa; sauna; concierge; yoga; aerobics; bakery; karaoke; casino; seminar room; Internet. *In room:* A/C, satellite TV, minibar, fridge, hair dryer, safe, Wi-Fi.

MODERATE

Jeju Pacific Hotel   Conveniently located in central Jeju City, this triangular and vaguely Egyptian-themed building offers rooms with ocean and mountain views. The rooms are comfortable and clean, but dated. This older hotel offers both Western-style and ondol rooms, but no specifically non-smoking rooms. Unfortunately, the staff's English is not so great and their sauna is available only to men.

159-1 Young Dam, 1-dong, Jeju-si. www.jejupacific.co.kr. © **064/758-2500.** Fax 064/758-2521. 177 units. ₩100,000 and up single or double; ₩280,000 and up suite. 10% VAT and service charge not included. AE, MC, V. **Amenities:** 3 restaurants; lounge; cafe; health club; sauna (men only); concierge; airport transfers; karaoke; casino. *In room:* A/C, TV, minibar, hair dryer, Internet.

INEXPENSIVE

Jeju Marina Hotel ★ 🛄   Although the staff's English is not so great, they'll make up for it in service and hospitality. The location is not near the coast, but there are some shops and bars within walking distance. You'll find simple and spotless rooms here, along with a nice array of facilities, especially for a hotel in this price range.

300-8, Yen-dong, Jeju-si. www.jejumarinahotel.co.kr. © **064/746-6161.** Fax 064/746-6170. 80 units. ₩80,000–₩120,000 single or double; ₩145,000 suite. AE, MC, V. **Amenities:** 2 restaurants; bar; lounge; cafe; shuttle service; karaoke; Internet. *In room:* A/C, TV, hair dryer.

EXPENSIVE

Haevichi Hotel & Resort ★★ ☺ Luxury accommodations within a stone's throw of the Jeju Folk Village. The English-speaking staff are polite and helpful. Both hotel-style and condo-style rooms are available, so be sure to check which room you're booking. Hotel rooms are more expensive but nicer, while the resort rooms are good for families, since they have kitchenettes and separate rooms for the kids. They provide complimentary shuttles to/from the airport. Ask for an oceanview room, if you want a nice view from your balcony.

40-69 Pyeseon-li, Pyoseon-myeon, Seogwipo. www.haevichi.com/eng. ℂ **064/780-8000.** 288 units. ₩220,000 and up single/double. 10% VAT and 10% service charge not included. DC, MC, V. **Amenities:** Restaurant; bar; deli/cafe; indoor/outdoor pools; golf course; fitness center; spa; Jacuzzi; games room; business center; concierge; massage; babysitting; laundry; bakery; karaoke; convenience store; safe. *In room:* A/C, TV w/DVD player, minibar, tea/coffeemaker, hair dryer, balcony, Wi-Fi.

Hyatt Regency Jeju ★★ This resort hotel is located in an ideal spot, right on Jungmun Beach—it's the closest hotel to the beach in the area. Although it's one of the older ones around, it's still very clean and elegant in an understated way. The outdoor pool is nicer than the indoor one (especially since it includes a swim-up bar), but is usually closed in the off season. Mountain- or oceanview rooms are available, with the ocean views costing a bit more (around ₩50,000) and including very nice balconies. All rooms come with two beds with feather duvets, and they are the typical Korean-style hard mattresses. The service is fantastic, and not at all overwhelming.

3039-1 Saekdal-dong, Seogwipo. http://jeju.regency.hyatt.com. ℂ **800/492-8804** in the U.S. or Canada, or 064/733-1234. Fax 064/732-2039. 224 units. ₩186,000–₩472,000 twin or king room. AE, MC, V. **Amenities:** 4 restaurants; 2 bars; lounge; pool; health club; spa; concierge; babysitting; bakery/deli; casino. *In room:* A/C, TV, minibar, hair dryer, Internet (fee).

Jeju Lotte Hotel ★★★ Lotte's Jeju location is probably the best of the bunch. Supposedly modeled after the Palace of the Lost City resort in South Africa, the grounds are expansive and well manicured. The Las Vegas-type water show draws a crowd, but is a bit cheesy. The restaurants are worthy of the hotel, but still pricey. It's a bit farther from the ocean than the Hyatt, but still within walking distance. Both Western-style beds and ondol rooms are available—ask for one with an ocean view. The rooms are very spacious and comfortable with comfortable bathrooms, complete with warming toilets.

2812-4, Saekdal-dong, Seogwipo. www.lottehotel.com. ℂ **064/731-1000.** Fax 064/738-7305. 500 units. ₩272,000–₩420,000 single or double. 10% VAT not included. AE, MC, V. **Amenities:** 4 restaurants; bar; lounge; pool; tennis court; health club; sauna; concierge; room service; babysitting; smoke-free rooms. *In room:* A/C, TV, hair dryer, Internet.

The Shilla Jeju ★★★ ☺ Inside the Jungmun Resort complex, this high-end hotel is ideal for both business and leisure travelers looking for a peaceful retreat in Jeju-do. Convenient for nearby attraction, the rooms are spacious and comfortable. The grounds are nicely maintained and they even provide tents in the garden for a camping out experience in the summer. The English-speaking staff are beyond polite. Ask for an oceanview room if you want to fall asleep to the sound of the waves below.

3039-3 Saekdal-dong, Seogwipo. www.shilla.net/en/jeju/index.jsp. ℂ **1588-1142.** Fax 064/735-5415. 429 units. ₩290,000 and up single/double. 10% VAT and 10% service charge not included.

MC, V. **Amenities:** Restaurants; bar; lobby lounge; cafe; indoor/outdoor pools; tennis court; fitness center; Jacuzzi; sauna; business center; shopping arcade; concierge; massage; babysitting; laundry/dry cleaning; salon; karaoke; casino. *In room:* A/C, satellite TV, minibar, fridge, tea/coffee-maker, hair dryer, safe, electric kettle, balcony, slippers, bathrobe.

MODERATE

Little France Hotel ★★ ⚑ Don't be fooled by the name, because there's nothing French about this place. The modern-looking building belies the cozy rooms inside. There are four types of rooms (listed from least expensive to most): The modern room, oriental, antique, and the royal classic. All rooms have double beds only and are artfully decorated with decidedly feminine touches. Bathrooms are clean, but have showers only. The amicable owners will even pick you up from the airport, if you make arrangements in advance.

486-1 Seogwi-dong, Seogwipo-si. www.littlefrancehotel.co.kr. ⓒ **064/732-4552** or 732-4662. 30 units. ₩80,000–₩110,000 double during high season (late July to Aug) but cheaper the rest of the year; there is a ₩10,000 discount for single travelers. MC, V. **Amenities:** Restaurant; cafe; tea shop. *In room:* A/C, TV, fridge, hair dryer.

INEXPENSIVE

Shinsung Hotel ★ This is an inexpensive spot with clean rooms and a central location in Seogwipo. Although the rooms on the second floor are the cheapest, you can get a computer and Internet access if you get a room on the third or fourth floors for just ₩10,000 more. Both bed and ondol rooms are available, but it's a bit inconvenient for buses.

637-2 Seogwi-dong, Seogwipo-si. ⓒ **064/732-1415.** Fax 064/732-1417. 34 units. ₩50,000 standard room; ₩130,000 suite. AE, MC, V. **Amenities:** Lobby lounge; driving range. *In room:* A/C, TV, fridge, hair dryer.

Tae Gong Gak Inn & Guesthouse ★★★ ⚑ You'll get to experience the friendliness and hospitality of Jeju folk firsthand through this guesthouse's owners, who are happy to give directions and travel advice. An affordable place to sleep in the Seogwipo area, it's conveniently located near Cheonjiyeon falls. They provide free breakfast and Wi-Fi in the shared kitchen area.

823-1 Seogwi-dong, Seogwipo-si. www.lepotel.kr. ⓒ **064/7762-2623.** Fax 064/762-2625. 50 beds, 15 units. ₩40,000 and up. MC, V. **Amenities:** Shared kitchen; laundry; tangerine orchard; outdoor grills; Internet. *In room:* A/C, TV, minifridge. Take limousine bus #600 from the airport.

Outside the Cities

EXPENSIVE

Ocean Grand Hotel Located near the ocean, overlooking Hamdeok Beach and the mountains nearby, this eight-story building has a modern lobby. The rooms aren't huge but they are clean and have balconies. Both Western-style rooms and ondol rooms are available, with the latter being a bit less expensive, if you don't mind sleeping on the floor.

1252-55 Hamdeok-li, Jocheon-eup, Bukjeju-gun. www.oceangrand.co.kr. ⓒ **064/783-0007** or 02/584-2345 from Seoul. Fax 064/783-7133. 80 units. ₩193,600 standard room; ₩160,000 double ondol room; ₩255,000 and up suite. AE, MC, V. From Jeju International Airport, take intercity bus no. 702. The hotel is located on Hamdeok Beach. The hotel offers free airport pickup, but you must make arrangements in advance. **Amenities:** 2 restaurants; cafe; smoke-free rooms. *In room:* A/C, TV, minibar, hair dryer, Internet.

MODERATE

IGH Pension ★ ☺   Located on the western shore of the island, this pension has condo-style accommodations and two properties. One is especially marketed toward couples on their honeymoon while the other is good for families or groups traveling together. With convenient kitchenettes, the spacious apartment-style accommodations have large windows that face the ocean. Beds are comfortable and set on the usual Korean ondol flooring. Most of the bathrooms have spacious tubs. Not your sandy beach-type resort, the "pension" is on a rocky beach. Located away from the major city, it's a secluded getaway from the touristy parts of the island. The only drawback is you'll need a car and good directions in order to get here.

641 beonji, Geumdong-li, Hangyeong-myeon, Bukjeju-gun. www.igh.co.kr. ✆ **064/772-3340** or 011/9664-3340. 11 units. ₩80,000–₩100,000 standard room; ₩120,000 and up condo-style accommodations. AE, MC, V. **Amenities:** boat rental. *In room:* A/C, TV/DVD, kitchenette, hair dryer.

Jazz Maeul (Jazz Village) ★★★ ☺ 🛍   You might wonder about the name, but you'll understand once you arrive and hear the soft jazz music being piped outside the buildings. This "pension" is located just a few miles outside of Seogwipo and is especially convenient if you plan on renting a car (though the taxi ride is fairly short and inexpensive). Staying here is a lot like renting an apartment—there are two-story spaces complete with kitchenettes, balconies, and loft. They also have hotel-style rooms without kitchens for less. Facilities are great for traveling families and there's even an open-air cinema with movies showing once a week during the summer.

2849 Sangye-dong, Seogwipo. www.jazzvillage.co.kr. ✆ **064/738-9300.** Fax 064/746-6170. 50 units. ₩90,000 standard room, ₩220,000 condo style suite. AE, MC, V. From Seogwipo, take Hwy. 12, and it's on the right side just before you get to the junction to road 95. **Amenities:** 2 pools; badminton courts; bikes; Internet. *In room:* A/C, TV/DVD, kitchenette, hair dryer, dining table.

Napoli Guesthouse ★★ 🛍   Located near the convention center, this pension has apartment-type facilities, but also offers shared beds for a bargain price. Conveniently located near Seogwipo, they even serve you breakfast for free. Check in after 2pm.

2065-beonji, Daepo-dong, Seogwipo. www.jejunapoli.com. ✆ **064/738-4820.** ₩20,000 per bed, or ₩120,000 for a double. MC, V. **Amenities:** Bikes; playground; BBQ grills; Internet. *In room:* A/C, TV/DVD, kitchenette, hair dryer, dining table.

INEXPENSIVE

Poonglim Guesthouse ★   This cozy guesthouse has dorm-style beds in a comfortable setting. Shared bathroom and kitchen. The friendly owner will make you breakfast, if you request it in advance. Make advance reservations since spaces fill up quickly.

2677 Gangjeong-dong, Seogwipo. **jazz064@naver.com**. ✆ **064/739-9001.** 24 units. ₩25,000 per person. No credit cards. Take the limousine bus from the airport. **Amenities:** Shared kitchen. *In room:* A/C, TV.

WHERE TO EAT

Since this is South Korea's largest island, Jeju-do is well known for its *hwae* (raw fish) but adventurous eaters can try the local sea bream or the sea urchin. Other local specialties include *galchi* (hairtail fish) and *jeonbok* (abalone), which used to be so prized it was reserved only for royalty. No more. Now it is made into *jook* (porridge), eaten raw, or added to a variety of other dishes. *Heuk dwaeji* (pork from native black pigs) and pheasant are also local specialties. A holdover from the island's Mongolian days is *bing ddeok* (rice cakes) made with buckwheat and radish instead of rice, which are quite bland. Give it a try, but it may take a couple of tastings before you appreciate its very subtle flavor.

Nearly all of the luxury hotels serve Western cuisine, if you must have an overpriced and not so delicious hamburger. Otherwise, your best bet is to go for the local offerings, which may not be in gourmet settings, but which are generally delicious.

If you're looking for an ocean view and extremely fresh seafood, head for the restaurants along the shores of Jeju-si, which attract crowds of tourists and locals with their straight-out-of-the-water offerings and live performances. The **haenyeoui jip,** which translates to "house of women divers," are seaside restaurants run by the haenyeo themselves. Most of them are found along the coast, near major tourist attractions, and feature abalone jook, octopus, sea cucumbers, and other fresh seafood on their menus. There are locations in Seopjikoji, Jungmun Beach, Seongsan, and Sehwa. You can also see the female divers selling their freshly caught wares at stands in Yongduam or Jungmun Beach.

For less expensive fare, head to **Gogiguksu Golmok** (Pork Noodle Alley) across from the Jeju Culture and Arts Center.

Jeju City

Dalgrak Italian Stone Pizza ★ ITALIAN   On an island where even a good hamburger is hard to find, it's worth visiting this hidden treasure for a slice of thin-sliced goodness, at this friendly joint behind Jeju Jeil High School. The oven takes center stage in this rustic space, where a spicy "house" sauce accompanies the pizza pies.

748-3 Nohyeong-dong, Jeju-si. ✆ **064/713-7483.** Entrees ₩13,000 and up. MC, V. Open Tues–Sun 11:30am–11pm.

Donjigae Hwaejib ★ KOREAN SEAFOOD   Visiting businessmen and tourists alike come here for the fresh offerings, not the stark atmosphere. A great place for fresh hwae, this joint is on the western side of the city. Although their specialty is raw fish, their grilled *godeung-uh* (mackerel) is pretty tasty, too.

2618-11 Dodu 1-dong, Jeju-si. ✆ **064/742-5200.** *Hwae jeongshik* (raw fish meal) ₩25,000 and up. MC, V. Daily 10:30am–10:30pm. Small parking lot.

Samdae Gooksu Hwegwan ★★ KOREAN NOODLES   Located in Gogigooksu Alley, they serve Japanese style noodles swimming in a pork broth, as well as the local delicacy, pig's feet.

1046-12 Ildo-dong, Jeju-si. ✆ **064/759-6644.** Entrees ₩6,000–₩12,000. MC, V. Daily 10am–6am.

Seongsanpo Halmangjip ★ KOREAN SEAFOOD   Specializing in local seafood dishes, like *jeonbok jook* (abalone porridge), *sora muchim* (spicy conch mixed with vegetables), the fresh catch is brought in from the family's women divers.

4090-8 Hwabuk 1(il)-dong, Jeju-si. ✆ **064/725-1525.** Entrees ₩10,000–₩15,000. MC, V. Mon–Sat 10am–8pm.

Yeonoonae KOREAN VEGETARIAN   Known for their vegetarian *bibimbap* (mixed rice bowl), this inviting restaurant has a limited menu, but tasty dishes. Try the *gamja buchim* (potato pancakes) or the *nokcha deulggae sujebi* (dough flake soup with green tea and perilla-seed broth). Perfect for vegetarians or anyone looking for an inexpensive meal in a cozy environment. Both floor and chair seating are available, but no English is spoken.

Across from the entrance to the Halla Arboretum, Yeon-dong, Jeju-si. © **064/712-5646.** Entrees ₩4,000–₩6,000. No credit cards. Daily 9:30am–9pm. From Jeju-si, take the bus bound for Jeju Agriculture High School.

Seogwipo

EXPENSIVE

Keun Gaetmul Hwaejib ★★ JAPANESE SUSHI   In the middle of Daepohang Hwae Town, this sushi restaurant is expensive but worth every last penny. To get the best view of the ocean, ask for a table on the second floor. With probably the freshest fish in town, their hwae comes with more side dishes than you'll be able to finish. Everything comes in several courses with sliced raw fish and spicy hot pot at the end, so make sure you have time for a leisurely meal.

496-8 Daepo-dong, Seogwipo-si. © **064/738-1625.** Reservations not necessary. *Modeum hwae* (raw fish combination) ₩80,000–₩170,000. AE, MC, V. Daily 6pm–2am (last order 10:30pm). Closed Lunar New Year and Chuseok.

Seong-eup Chilshimli Jumak ★★ 📖 KOREAN TRADITIONAL   Near the Seong-eup Folk Village, this restaurant is well known for its barbecued black pig. For many years, this thatched-roof joint has been serving up some of the best local cuisine around. Don't miss the pheasant potato noodles—they boil the pheasant bones for 24 hours. Their homemade *makgeolli* (milky rice wine) in itself is worth a special trip.

496-8 Daepo-dong, Seogwipo-si. © **064/787-0911.** Set menu ₩43,000. MC, V. Daily 9am until the last customer leaves (but usually until 8pm). Closed Lunar New Year and Chuseok. Off Hwy. 16 and road 97. Plenty of parking available.

MODERATE

Daeyoo Land Sikdang ★ KOREAN PHEASANT   Located inside the Jeju-do hunting grounds, this restaurant specializes in all things pheasant. Try the pheasant *shabu shabu* (boiled pheasant, very popular with Japanese tourists), the *naengmyeon* (cold buckwheat noodles), *buchingae* (flatcakes), or even the pheasant dumplings. If you want to splurge, you can go for the multicourse menu, while dining in a distinctly hunting lodge-like environment, complete with wooden paneling and rock walls. The staff speak English and Japanese.

144 Sangye-dong, Seogwipo-si. © **064/738-0500.** www.daeyooland.net (very little English). Entrees ₩7,000–₩13,000; set menus ₩30,000–₩50,000. AE, MC, V. Daily 9am–6pm (until 9pm with reservations). From Seogwipo, take Hwy. 12 to Jungmun Gwangwang Danji, or call for the Daeyoo Land shuttle bus.

Geumho Garden ★ KOREAN BARBECUE   You'll forget the dated decor once you start eating the *heuk dweji* (pork from native black pigs) barbecue at this Jeju standard. You can also have beef to cook on your tabletop grill, or just get the *haemul ddukbaegi* (seafood in a stone pot). The staff speak English and Japanese.

259-4 Gangjeong-dong, Seogwipo-si. © **064/739-3333.** Entrees ₩8,000–₩14,000. MC, V. Daily 10am–10pm. Closed Lunar New Year and Chuseok. Parking available. Close to the World Cup Stadium going toward the Jungmun Resort Complex.

Sehwali Haenyeoi Jip ★★★ KOREAN SEAFOOD   At one of the few joints run directly by the women divers (*haenyeo*), you can taste fresh *jeonbok jook* (abalone porridge), *haemul pajeon* (seafood flatcakes), and other specialties directly from the divers themselves. Not only will you be getting some of the freshest fish on the island, you'll be directly supporting an endangered art.

191 Sehwa-li, Pyoseon-myeon, Seogwipo-si. © **064/787-4917.** www.womandiver.com. Reservations not necessary. Entrees ₩12,000 and up. MC, V. Daily 10am–10pm. On the coast off Hwy. 1132, not too far from the Jeju Folk Museum.

Seong-eup Chilshimli Jumak ★ KOREAN TRADITIONAL   They roast their black pig the slow, old-fashioned way, over a wood fire. They also have your choice of set menus, if you're feeling extra hungry.

580 Seon-eup-li, Pyoseon-myeon, Seogwipo. © **064/787-0911.** Entrees ₩14,000 and up, set menu ₩36,000 and up. MC, V. Daily 9am–8pm.

INEXPENSIVE

Gamgyul Jjimbbang ★★ KOREAN SNACK   At the entrance to Cheonjiyeon falls is this tiny stand where the friendly Mr. Bak serves his brand *jjimbbang* (steamed buns) made from local mandarin oranges ("gamgyul"). Filled with tangerine jam or a combination of the jam and *pot* (sweet red-bean paste), these steamed delights are a nice treat to have on the way to see the falls.

2-3 Namseongjung-ro, Seogwipo-si. © **064/733-2900.** Buns 3 for ₩3,000. No credit cards. Daily 8am–9pm.

Hang-gu Shikdang ★ KOREAN SEAFOOD   Located right across from the water, this hwae joint serves up fresh seafood without breaking the bank. On cold days, you might enjoy the spicy seafood hot pot while watching the fishermen bring in their boats.

Moseulpo, Seogwipo-si. © **064/794-2254.** Entrees ₩9,000 and up. No credit cards. Wed–Mon 9am–9pm.

Hwasoon Jungnang Galbi ★ KOREAN BARBECUE   This *galbi* (short ribs) restaurant specializes in pork barbecue at a bargain price. You can also get naengmyeon or *dwenjang jjigae* (fermented soybean paste hot pot), if you're feeling particularly adventurous.

243-3 Donggwang-li, Andeok-myeon, Seogwipo-si. © **064/794-8954.** Reservations not necessary. Entrees ₩5,000–₩7,000. AE, MC, V. Daily noon–10pm. Located right across the street from the Andeok Junior High School, just east of the Hwasoon Sageoli (4-way).

Outside the Cities

MODERATE

O'Sulloc Tea Museum & Café ★★★ TEAHOUSE   To call O'Sulloc a "museum" is an exaggeration, but the green tea fields, the collection of tea cups, and the associated shop and cafe are worth a visit. The green tea ice cream is so good that visitors order it even in the dead of winter.

1235-3 Seogwang-li, Andeok-myeon, Seogwipo. © **064/794-5312.** www.osulloc.com. ₩5,000 and up. AE, MC, V. Daily 10am–6pm (until 5pm Oct–Mar). From Jeju-si, take road #1135 past the Jeju Horseracing track, when you see the sign for "Donggwang" (about 15 min), turn right and follow the signs.

INEXPENSIVE

Namokdo Shikdang ★ KOREAN TRADITIONAL   For seriously wholesome Korean food, you can't beat the handmade noodles or pork at this unassuming restaurant. You'll wish that your *halmuhni* (grandma) could make dishes half as good as this one, especially for the ridiculously low prices. Unfortunately, the menu is only in

Korean, but it's limited and the dishes I recommend are *soondae gooksu* (Korean sausage noodles), *saeng gogi* (unmarinated meat/pork), and *myulchi gooksu* (noodles in anchovy broth).

1877-6 Gashi-li, Pyeosunmyeon, Nam-jeju-gun. © **064/787-1202.** Entrees ₩5,000–₩7,000. No credit cards. Daily 11am–7pm. From Jeju-si, take Hwy. 97 to Hwy. 16 (toward Pyoseon). When you arrive in Gashi-li, take a left at the 1st 4-way and the restaurant is there behind a large tree.

EXPLORING JEJU-DO

There's no shortage of activities to keep you busy on the island. Be it climbing the tallest mountain in South Korea, exploring a cave, hiking to a waterfall, or just lounging on a sandy beach, you'll find plenty to do.

Hallasan (Mt. Halla)

At 1,950m (6,398 ft.), Hallasan is the highest peak in South Korea. This now-dormant volcano (which erupted during the fourth Cenozoic Era) sits at the center of the island and can be seen from anywhere on Jeju-do—unless, of course, it's hiding behind the clouds, which happens often. Locals say that, like a woman, the mountain is constantly hiding her face. Hallasan also changes with the seasons, putting on bright pink azaleas in the spring and a beautiful white coat of snow in the winter. The crater at the summit is now a lake, Baengnokdam (which is also the old name for Hallasan), and accessible if you take the Eorimok course, which is the most difficult and least scenic. The name Baengnokdam came from the legend that the gods came down from the heavens to ride their white deer *(baengnok)* on the mountain.

There are four trails leading up to the top of the mountain, each varying in difficulty and length. None of them is easy, and you should set aside a whole day if you wish to reach the summit. Although there is natural spring water available on the way up, pack some extra water and a meal to enjoy once you get there. In cooler weather, bring a windbreaker since it will get colder and windier as you climb higher. The **Yeongsil Trail** is the easiest and most scenic, but it still will take just under 4 hours to reach the top (and another 3 down). You can take an intercity bus to the Hallasan National Park management office to pick up the trail head—it starts at the southwestern side of the peak and is 6.5km (4 miles) long. The **Eorimok Trail** is the most beautiful when the azaleas are in bloom, but is also the most difficult. The entrance is 15km (9⅓ miles) from Jeju-si and takes about 40 minutes via intercity bus. It's 7.8km (4.8 miles) long and will take you a little longer than the Yeongsil Trail. If you want a real challenge, take the **Gwaneumsa Trail,** which is steeper than the others. The entrance to the trail is at the Tamna Education Institute, about 11km (6¾ miles) from Jeju-si. From there it's about an hour to Gwaneum Temple, a total of 3 hours to reach the peak and another 2½ down. The **Seongpanak Trail** is an easier climb with several resting spots. Another great trail for enjoying the azaleas in the spring, it takes about 4½ hours to climb and another 4 to return.

Admission to the **Hallasan National Park** (© **064/713-9950;** www.hallasan. go.kr) is ₩1,600 for ages 25 to 64, ₩600 for ages 13 to 24, and ₩300 for children. It's free for seniors 65 and over and kids 6 and under. Open all year-round, the park is closed only for inclement weather. The park is open 5am to 10pm in the summer and 6am to 9pm in the winter. Overnight camping is prohibited. From the Jeju Intercity Bus Terminal, take a bus bound for Seongpanak. Daily buses run from 6am to 9:30pm. The 35-minute ride costs ₩2,000. Alternatively, you can take an Eorimok-bound bus from the terminal, which costs ₩3,000. Those buses run daily from 6am to 4:50pm every 80 minutes.

Jungmun Resort Complex

Located on the seashore in Seogwipo, this is the largest resort area in South Korea. If you're staying nearby, you can explore on foot, but from Jeju-si, take the Jungmun Express Bus (about 50 min.) or the limousine bus #600 from the airport. For additional information, check out www.jungmunresort.com. All the attractions listed below are within the resort complex and are walking distance from Seogwipo.

Cheonjeyeon Waterfalls NATURAL ATTRACTION Cheonjeyeon means the "pond of the Emperor of Heaven" in Korean, since Jeju legend says that seven nymphs helped the Emperor of Heaven descend every night to play and bathe in the waters of the three waterfalls. You can see the seven nymphs carved on the bridge that crosses over the valley (whose lanterns are quite pretty at night). Another legend says that if you swim in the water on the 15th day of the seventh lunar month, you will be cured of whatever diseases you have by the eighth lunar month. But since swimming is prohibited there now, you won't be able to test the myth. The Chilseonyeo (Seven Nymphs) Festival is held here in May of even-numbered years.

ⓒ **064/738-1529.** Admission ₩2,500 adults, ₩1,350 children, free for seniors. Mar–Oct daily 8am–6:30pm; Nov–Feb daily 9am–5:30pm.

Teddy Bear Museum ☺ MUSEUM Teddy bear statues greet you on the grounds of this aptly named "museum." The three halls display teddy bears and other soft creatures from various countries, as well as reinterpretations of the Mona Lisa and Da Vinci's "Last Supper" all in stuffed-bear glory.

ⓒ **064/738-7600.** www.teddybearmuseum.com. Admission ₩7,000 adults, ₩6,000 teens, ₩5,000 children and seniors. Aug 26–July 15 daily 9am–7pm (last tickets at 6pm); July 16–Aug 25 daily 9am–10pm (last tickets at 9pm).

Yeomiji Botanical Garden ★★ GARDEN The largest arboretum in Asia, the Yeomiji gardens house over 2,000 varieties of plants and trees in the greenhouse and over 1,700 semitropical plants in the outside gardens. You can view the traditional landscape styles of Japan, France, Italy, Korea, and, of course, Jeju Island. If you're tired of walking, you can take a tour train around the international gardens.

ⓒ **064/735-1100.** Admission ₩7,000 adults, ₩4,500 teens, ₩4,000 seniors 65 and over, ₩3,500 children 12 and under. Train ₩1,000 adults, ₩500 kids. Daily 9am–6pm. Last ticket sales 1 hr. before closing.

Beaches

Although Jeju-do is called the "Hawaii of Korea," its narrow, rocky beaches are distinctly different from those of the American islands—you won't find as many wide, fine-sand beaches here. However, there are plenty of spots for you to sunbathe or take in the scenery and here are some below.

Gwakji Beach ★ BEACH This wide beach is not as popular as the other beaches on the island, but still offers shallow waters and pristine white sand. There are showers and even an outdoor bathroom at one corner of the beach, where the water is extremely cold. You can even catch clams when the season is right. There is a campsite and minbak nearby.

Gwakji-li, Aewol-eup. Take the Seohwaeseon line from Jeju Bus Terminal.

Hamdeok Beach ★★ BEACH   Perhaps one of the best beaches on the entire island, Hamdeok beach is on the northeastern coast. Since it's big—the sands stretch for about 500m (1,640 ft.)—it's quite popular with the locals. The water is shallow and generally safe (watch for volcanic rocks, though—they can leave nasty cuts). There are parking and camping areas available, as well as dressing rooms, showers, and restrooms. You can also have hwae on the pier or have a drink at the cafe on the water.

Hamdeok-li, Chocheon-eup. ℂ **064/728-7882.** Take an intercity or express bus from Jeju-si Bus Terminal.

Hyeopjae Beach BEACH   Located next to Hallim Park, this cozy beach has white sand and shallow, turquoise waters (1.2m/4 ft. average depth with no sudden drops, making it the perfect spot for families who want to swim), although they've covered the sand with a netting to keep it from blowing away in the harsh winds. Shower and restroom facilities are provided. The beach connects to **Geumreong Beach,** but locals refer to both beaches as "Hyeopjae Beach." Overnight camping is allowed in the adjacent pine forest. The restaurant near the parking lot is quite good and they'll even give you free tangerines when they're in season in the winter.

Hyeopjae-li, Hanrim-eup. From Jeju-si or Seogwipo-si, take the bus to Hallim Park.

Shinyang Beach BEACH   A great place for windsurfing, this beach is on a small peninsula with plenty of sand for sunbathing on both sides. Located on the eastern coast of the island, it's also ideal for sailing (with the best views on clear days in the spring and autumn).

40-1, Pyoseon-li, Pyoseon-myeon, Seogwipo-si. Buses from Jeju Bus Terminal drop you off about 2km (1¼ miles) from the beach. An hourly bus runs to and from the beach. About a 5-minute taxi ride from Seongsan Ichulbong.

Natural Wonders

Because of its volcanic history, Jeju-do has some fascinating basalt rock formations, lovely beaches, stunning waterfalls, and other natural phenomena to explore.

Bijarim Forest NATURAL ATTRACTION   The largest nutmeg forest in the world, it has about 2,800 trees, ranging from 500 to 800 years old. The oldest tree of all of these beauties can be found in the middle of the forest. Looming over 25m (82 ft.) tall with a girth of about 6m (20 ft.), it is called the ancestor of all the *bija* trees and is said to be over 800 years old. There is a nice path provided for a leisurely walk through the forest.

San 25, Pyeongdae-li, Gujwa-eup, Jeju-si. Admission ₩1,500 adults, ₩800 youth. Mar–Oct daily 9am–6pm; Nov–Feb daily 9am–5pm. From Jeju Intercity Bus Terminal, take a bus on the Donghae line (runs every 20 min.) to either Pyeongdae-li or Sehwa-li. From there, take a shuttle bus to Bija-rim Forest (runs every 15 min.).

Cheonjiyeon Waterfall ★★ NATURAL ATTRACTION   Not to be confused with the Cheonjeyeon Waterfall in the Jungmun Resort, the Cheonjiyeon Waterfall is located in a narrow valley in the coastal hills near Seogwipo Port. Its name means "where the sky (*cheon*) meets the land (*ji*)." Especially nice in the evening (when they light the water), the path to the waterfall is through a lush garden of subtropical plants. The pond into which the water falls is home to migrating ducks and the Korean marbled eel, one of many national treasures.

666-1, Seohong-dong, Seogwipo-si. ☎ **064/738-1528.** Admission ₩2,000 adults, ₩1,000 children, free for seniors. Mar–Oct daily 7am–11pm; Nov–Feb daily 7am–10pm.

Jeongbang Waterfall NATURAL ATTRACTION One of the three most famous falls on Jeju-do, the Jeongbang Waterfall is said to be the only one in Asia in which the water falls into the ocean. The water falling from 23m (75 ft.) is a dramatic sight to behold. Be sure to wear shoes with good traction since the only way down is a set of steel steps and the rocks get slippery from the water. If you walk about 300m (984 ft.) east, you'll see a smaller fall, the **Sojeongbang Waterfall,** a cool place to beat the summer heat.

278 Donghong-dong, Seogwipo-si. ☎ **064/733-1530.** Admission ₩2,000 adults, ₩1,000 teens and children, free for seniors. Mar–Oct daily 7am–11pm; Nov–Feb daily 7am–10pm.

Jusangjeolli Cliffs ★★ NATURAL ATTRACTION Thousands of years ago, when Hallasan was an active volcano, the lava flowing down to the ocean created the Jusangjeolli Cliffs, off the Jungmun Daepo Coast. The rocks that make up these cliffs have been sculpted by the elements into a series of hexagonal and cubic pillars. The rock formations look like they've been hand-carved, though they are solely the work of Mother Nature.

Ilwon 2579 Daepo-dong, Seogwipo-si. ☎ **064/746-6616.** Admission ₩2,000 adults, ₩1,000 ages 18 and under. Parking ₩1,000. Mar–Oct daily 8am–7pm; Nov–Feb daily 8am–6pm. From the entrance to the Jungmun Folk Museum (in the resort), walk along the farm road west for 7–8 min.

Manjang-gul (Manjang Cave) ★★★ NATURAL ATTRACTION The world's largest lava cave, Manjang-gul was created centuries ago, when Hallasan was still an active volcano. Only the first kilometer (half mile) of the 13km (8-mile) cave is open to the public, but that's enough to give you a good glimpse of its impressive rock formations and stalactites. The inside temperature is always cool no matter how hot it is outside. Although the cave is well lit, watch your step because the humidity can make the rocks slippery.

7-1 Gimryeong-lisan, Donggimryeong-li, Gujwa-eup, Jeju-si. ☎ **064/783-4818.** Admission ₩2000 adults, ₩1,000 teens and children, free for seniors over 65. Summer daily 9am–7pm; winter daily 9am–5pm. From Jeju-si (30 min.) or Seogwipo (1½ hr.), take the intercity Donghoe line bus to the Manjang-gul parking lot. Take a local bus or taxi to the cave entrance (or walk 20 min.).

Sanbang-gulsa (Sanbang Grotto) NATURAL ATTRACTION Local legend has it that the top of Hallasan was taken off and thrown away, and that piece became Sanbangsan. On the southwestern side of **Sanbangsan** is Sanbang-gul, which used to be called Sanbang Cave, but now is called a grotto since it houses a Buddha statue. This 5m-high (16-ft.) cave is where monk Hye-Il lived during the Goryeo Dynasty. From inside the cave, you can see Marado and **Yongmeoli Haean (Dragon Head Coast)** ★★★, where Sanbangsan stretches into the ocean and looks as if a dragon's head is going underwater. When the tide is low, the walk around Yongmeoli coast is one of the best on the island. The entrance fee includes both Sanbang-gulsa and Yongmeoli Haean.

Andeok-myeon, Sagye-li, Seogwipo-si. ☎ **064/794-2940.** Admission ₩2,500 adults, ₩1,500 youth, free for seniors 65 and over and children 6 and under. Daily 8am–7pm (until 6:30pm Nov–Feb). From Jeju Intercity Bus Terminal, take the bus bound for Sanbangsan, which runs every 30–40 min., 6:40am–9:25pm, a 55-min. ride. From Seogwipo Terminal, take the bus bound for Sagye and get off at Sanbang-gulsa (40-min. ride). It's about a 4-min. walk to the beach.

JEJU-DO'S 10 beauties

Ask any Jeju native and they'll be able to quickly tick off the top 10 natural beauties of the island. Here they are—some visitable, some not:

o **Gosumokma:** *Gosu* means old, primitive forest, and there is some disagreement whether the area adjacent to Hwangsapyeong is the "Gosu." But the name "Gosumokma" refers to the view of horses roaming around the foot of Hallasan.

o **Gyulrimchusaek:** The name comes from the fall (autumn) landscape of mandarin orange orchards around the Ohyeondan Shrine in old Jeju City. There had been some talk about officially designating this orchard, but an ancient document states that "Gyulrimchusaek" refers to mandarin trees on the whole island, not in one particular place.

o **Jeongbang hapok:** On the edge of the ocean, Jeongbang Waterfall is said to have housed a holy

dragon that lived underneath it. People believe that the water contains the dragon's spirit and can cure diseases and bring rain during a drought. The small waterfall nearby is said to look like a servant waiting on a dignified lord.

o **Nokdam mansel:** The snow on Baekrokdam, the crater lake on top of Hallasan, doesn't melt until late spring/early summer. Legend has it that immortal beings drank the water underneath the snow and it is considered a sacred place.

o **Sabong nakjo:** The sunset viewed from the city of Sarabong (or Sara Peak) is called *sabong nakjo*. The Jeju people say it is like the sun and the sky are burning themselves together.

o **Sanbang-gulsa:** Inside the cave, water drops from the ceiling and the natives say it is the tears of the goddess Sanbangdeok, who guards the mountain. Legend has it that the beautiful daughter of

Sangumburi (Sangum Crater) WALKING TRAIL   One of three major craters on the island, Sangumburi crater was, like the rest, a result of volcanic activity. But unlike Hallasan, this one exploded quickly, spewed relatively little lava, and left barely a trace of cone behind. In other words, if you want to see an extinct volcano, but don't feel like climbing, this is the one to visit. There is a well-paved path from the parking lot to the crater's rim. You can walk around part of the rim, but the rest of it and the crater itself are off-limits. Around the grounds are several traditional Jeju-style grave sites as well. Unfortunately, none of the buses from Seogwipo stops here, so you'll have to take a taxi.

Gyorae-li, Jocheon-eup, Jeju-si. Ⓒ **064/783-9900.** www.sangumburi.net (Korean only). Admission ₩3,000 adults, ₩1,500 teens and children, free for seniors 65 and over and children 6 and under. Mar 1–July 14 and Sept 1–Oct 31 daily 8am–6pm; July 15–Aug 31 daily 8am–7pm; Nov 1–Feb 28 daily 8:30am–7pm. From Jeju City, take the bus bound for Pyoseon or take a taxi (30 min.). Driving from Jeju-si, take national road 11 to local road 1112 at Gyorae.

Sarabong (Sara Peak) ★★ NATURAL ATTRACTION   This mountain rises above nearby Jeju port with a lighthouse that sits on the shore at its foot. A small temple **Sarasa** is also nestled on its hillside. You'll find the area dotted with young couples coming to watch the sunset or Hallyu fans visiting the church left here after

Sanbangsan was in love with a youth, Goseong. An official in town had a crush on her and confiscated Goseong's property and sent him into exile. In despair, Sanbangdeok returned to the cave and turned herself into a rock. You can hear her teardrops falling as you look at the ocean from inside the grotto.

o **Sanpojo-eo:** *Sanpojo-eo* refers to the view of the coastal scenery while one is leisurely fishing (the water, other fishing boats, seagulls, white herons). Some say the word should be changed to reflect the fishermen's hard work, but that's the last thing you'll be thinking about as you see the reflected lights of hundreds of fishermen lighting their lamps at night in Jeju harbor.

o **Seongsan ilchu:** Seongsan, which means "holy mountain," got its name because the 99 rocks around its crater form a castle or crown.

The view of it at sunrise is one of the sights not to be missed.

o **Yeong-gu chunhwa:** *Yeong-gu* means "a hill where an immortal being lives" and is in the Pang-seonmun area of Odeung-dong. *Chunhwa* means "spring flowers," specifically referring to the azaleas that bloom there every spring. Looking at hillside flowers, the Jeju ancestors supposedly got a feeling of being close to the immortal beings.

o **Yeongsil Giam:** In a remote part of the Yeongsil trail up to Hallasan, there are about 500 oddly shaped rock pillars. They are said to be the 500 sons of a mother who drowned in the soup pot while making dinner for said 500 sons. Or 500 *arhats* (great monks who have reached nirvana). Or 500 generals guarding the island against enemies. Whatever they are, they are quite a sight to behold.

shooting the drama, "All In." But the show doesn't end when the sun goes down; stay a bit longer to watch the lights go up on Tap-dong and the lights of the fishing boats dotting the nearby waters. On the southeastern (inland) side of the mountain is the shrine **Mochungsa,** built in commemoration of those who fought against the Japanese occupation of Korea during the early part of the last century.

From Jeju Airport take bus 200 or 300 and get off at Dongmun Rotary. From there, take a local bus (nos. 1, 2, 3, or 10) to Jeju Port or Jeju National Museum and it's about a 10-minute walk from there. If driving, take circular road no. 12.

Seongsan Ilchulbong ("Sunrise" Peak) ★★★ HIKING TRAIL
This parasitic volcano rose from the sea about 100,000 years ago. The southeastern and northern side of the crater are cliffs, but the northwestern side is a grassy hillside that connects to **Seongsanpo** (Seongsan Village). The ridge is good for a nice walk or a horseback ride. Bright yellow with rapeseed flowers in the springtime, it's worth an early-morning climb to see the spectacular sunrise from the peak. There are plenty of minbak places to overnight nearby for an early morning hike.

114 Seongsan-li, Seongsan-eup, Seogwipo-si. © **064/784-0959.** Admission ₩2,000 ages 24–64, ₩1,000 ages 7–23, free for seniors over 65 and children 6 and under. Winter daily 5am–9pm; summer daily 4am–10pm. Closed during bad weather. From either Jeju-si or Seogwipo-si, take the

intercity bus to Seongsan Ilchulbong Peak. Buses run every 20 min. and take 1½ hr. from either of the city's bus terminals.

Historical Sites

The island has an isolated history sometimes akin to and at other times different from that of the rest of Korea. Buildings and structures have characteristics unique to Jeju-do and the people have interesting folklore and superstitions associated with almost all rock formations and natural phenomena that occur on the island.

Jeju Folk Village ★★ HISTORIC SITE   Created to preserve the island's historical culture, the village is actually a collection of historically re-created buildings that was designed with consultations from historians and preservationists. In addition to these modern re-creations, several structures, ranging in age from 100 to 300 years old, were relocated here, intact, for visitors to enjoy. You'll get to explore life-size models of mountain villages, fishing villages, and shaman villages. Various artifacts are on display, and there are also folk performances and traditional craftsmen who still practice their art and sell their wares. Although it's a bit touristy, it's a lot of fun to try on traditional wedding outfits or ride the native ponies.

40-1, Pyoseon-li, Pyoseon-myeon, Seogwipo-si. ℂ **064/787-4501.** www.jejufolk.com. Admission ₩6,000 adults, ₩4,000 teens, ₩2,000 seniors 65 and over and kids 12 and under. Oct–Mar daily 8:30am–5pm; Apr–July 20 and Sept daily 8:30am–6pm; July 21–Aug daily 8:30am–6:30pm. From Jeju Intercity Bus Terminal take the bus bound for Jeju Folk Village, which runs every 30 min.

Samseonghyeol Shrine GARDEN   This garden contains three holes in the ground that, according to legend, are the origin of Jeju-do's inhabitants. The story goes that three demigods emerged from these holes and became the ancestors to the three clans of the island—the Goh, Bu, and Yang families. One day the clans found a box sealed in purple clay floating in the ocean. When they opened it, a messenger in purple appeared and said that he was sent by a king from the Byeoklang state. The king wanted his three daughters to marry the three demigods living on a western seashore of Jeju-do, and to create a new kingdom. Then, the messenger flew away. Inside the box was another box in blue. When they opened it three princesses in blue dresses emerged, along with a calf, a pony, and five kinds of seeds. The three demigods married each of the three princesses and divided the island into thirds (who got which third was determined by where arrows shot by each of the three gods fell). The stone marker, known as the **Samsaseok,** where this archery supposedly took place, is near the Jeju Folklore Museum, just a few kilometers east of the Samseonghyeol.

Legend has it that the descendants of these three couples populated the island and ruled it as an independent kingdom called Tamna-guk until A.D. 937, when the people from the Goryeo Kingdom invaded and took control.

Every year, on the 10th day of the 4th and 10th lunar months, members of these three original families gather here to perform the *jesa* (ancestral honoring ceremony). On the 10th day of the 12th lunar month, they have a public ceremony, the **Samseonghyeol-je,** to celebrate the history of the island's founders.

1313 Ido 1-dong, Jeju-si. ℂ **064/722-3315.** Admission ₩2,500 adults, ₩1,700 teens, ₩1,000 children and seniors 65 and over, free for children 6 and under. Mar–Oct daily 8am–7pm; Nov–Feb daily 8am–5pm. It's a 3-min. walk from the Jeju KAL Hotel.

Sancheondan MONUMENT   Located in a grove of trees just 8km (5 miles) from Jeju-si, this former altar site sits along the first trans-island road leading to Seogwipo-si. This is the spot where the winter rites for the Mountain Spirit are performed every year. This ceremony used to be held on top of Mt. Halla, but it was moved here during the Goryeo Dynasty because so many people froze to death during the long ceremonies. Today, rituals are held during the first lunar month. It's worth a stop to check out the eight 600-year-old "bear" pine trees, so-named because their bark is the same dark brown as bear's fur, surrounding the place.

Ara 1-dong, Jeju-si. © **064/710-3312.** Free admission. Daily 24 hr., but best to visit in the daytime. From Jeju Intercity Bus Terminal take a bus to the Jeju College of Technology stop (takes 20 min.).

Seong-eup Folk Village HISTORIC SITE   Located at the foot of Mt. Halla, this preserved (as opposed to re-created) folk village shows how traditional people of Jeju-do have lived for centuries. There are about 3,000 original thatch-roofed houses here, with lava stone and clay walls, and villagers still live in them, although some have added modern comforts. Still, like an outdoor museum, this simple mountain village is a testament to the people of the island. You can see stone statues, which are prevalent throughout the island, as well as old Confucian government buildings and traditional tombs. Most of the signage is in Korean only, but the displays are not difficult to decipher.

Pyoseon-li, Pyoseon-myeon, Seogwipo-si. © **064/787-4501.** Free admission. Daily 24 hr., but best to visit in the daytime. From Jeju Intercity Bus Terminal take the bus bound for Dongbug-wangong Rd. and get off at Seong-eup 1-li (daily 6:10am–9:30pm). The buses run every 20 min. and take an hour. From Seogwipo Intercity Bus Terminal take the bus that runs on Il-ju Rd. to the east and get off at Seong-eup 1(il)-li (daily 6:30am–8:30pm). The buses run every 20 min. and take 50 min.

Museums

Jeju-do has very few traditional museums per se, but several unusual places that call themselves museums. Most of them, like the Chocolate Museum, the African Museum, and the aforementioned **Teddy Bear Museum** (see the Jungmun Resort Complex section), seem to be designed solely to amuse tourists, rather than particularly enlighten them. But just because you won't learn all that much doesn't mean they're not worth visiting—after all, there's nothing wrong with a little amusement when you're on a trip.

Jeju Folklore & Natural History Museum MUSEUM   Just as the name suggests, this museum displays both the folk history and the natural history of the people and animals who have lived on the island. Its displays include shellfish fossils, bird footprints, cave miniatures, and a variety of plants and animals found (or once found) on Jeju-do. Two halls are dedicated to the folklore of the Jeju peoples, and feature dioramas of how people used to live and work.

996-1 Ido, 2-dong, Jeju-si. © **064/710-7708.** http://museum.jeju.go.kr. Admission ₩1,100 adults, ₩500 youth. Mar–Oct daily 8:30am–6:30pm; Nov–Feb daily 8:30am–5:30pm. Closed national holidays and May 24. Take bus no. 100 or 500 and get off at the Jeju KAL Hotel. The museum is about a 5-min. walk about a block down from the hotel (on the opposite side of the street). Or 5 min. via taxi from the center of Jeju-si, about a block from the Jeju KAL Hotel, near city hall.

Jeju Folk Museum ★ MUSEUM   All of the items are actual objects used by the island's people. Some of the more interesting items in the collection include tools used by Jeju-do's women divers, a raincoat made of straw, and a portable sundial.

Outside on the museum grounds are 143 Mushin statues. The Mushin are gods whom natives believed would bring them happiness if they prayed to them with all their hearts. The local people sometimes still hold sacrificial ceremonies in their honor.

2505 Samyang 3(sam)-dong, Jeju-si. 🕐 **064/755-1976** (Korean only). Admission ₩1,000. Daily 9am–6pm (last admission 1 hr before closing). From the Jeju Airport take bus no. 705 bound for Hamdeok. From the Jeju Bus Terminal, take a regular bus headed for Jocheon and get off at the Hwabuk Jugong Apt. stop. It's a 5-min. walk from there.

Jeju Haenyeo Museum MUSEUM   The haenyeo are the women divers who dive deep underwater without any sort of gear to collect shellfish and seaweed. Particular to the island, they are slowly becoming a dying breed. This museum was created to honor the divers and educate visitors about these specially trained women.

3204-1 Hado-li, Gujwa-eup, Jeju-si. 🕐 **064/782-9898.** Admission ₩1,100 adults, ₩500 teens, free for children 11 and under. Mar–Oct daily 9am–7pm; Nov–Feb daily 9am–5pm. At the Jeju Bus Terminal, take a bus bound for Sehwa and Seongsan and get off at the Jeju Haenyeo Japan Resistance Movement Memorial Park in Hado-li, Gujwa-eup.

Jeju Museum of Art MUSEUM   The building itself is a work of art, surrounded by a shallow pool of water, giving the illusion that it's floating. Inside, there are two small floors of exhibition space displaying a variety of contemporary works (mostly sculptures and paintings by both Korean and international artists), with a rotating exhibition space highlighting everything from photographers to potters. Don't miss the rooftop garden, where you can enjoy the scenic view.

401 Shinbiro, Jeju-si. 🕐 **064/710-4300.** http://jmoa.jeju.go.kr. Admission ₩1,000 adults, ₩500 teens, ₩300 children. Tues–Sun 9am to 6pm (until 8pm July–Sept); last admission 30 min. before closing. Closed Jan 1, Chuseok, and Lunar New Year. Take bus no. 46 or 1100 and get off at Jeju Museum of Art.

Jeju National Museum MUSEUM   This museum focuses on the archaeology and history of the island, but the exhibits, displaying mostly objects and relics from excavations from various points throughout Jeju-do, are a bit cramped and oddly organized. Still, it offers a good introduction to the history and culture of the island, including Jeju's time as the "Kingdom of Tamna" before it was absorbed by the Joseon Dynasty (in 1404). The collection includes the usual pottery, tools, and other artifacts, but they also have some interesting costumes, old maps, and displays explaining the origin myth and other legends of Jeju. The modern building has a traditional-looking house in its front yard surrounded by various stone statues. Excavated relics range from prehistoric finds to those from the Joseon Dynasty.

387 Ara 1-dong, Jeju-si. 🕐 **064/720-8000.** http://jeju.museum.go.kr/en. Admission ₩1,000 adults, ₩500 youth, free for seniors 65 and over and children 6 and under. Tues–Fri 9am–6pm; Sat 9am–9pm; Sun 9am–7pm (last tickets sold 1 hr. before closing). Closed Jan 1. Take city bus no. 1, 2, 3, 10, 14, 24, 25, 27, 28, or 38 and get off at Kounimoru (it takes 10 min. from the Dongmun Rotary). Cross the street and walk 5 min. If you're driving from Jeju International Airport, drive to the Seomun Rotary, then to the Dongmun Rotary, and then to the Sarabong 5-way (O-geoli). The museum is on local circular road 12 (about 6km/3¾ miles east of the airport).

Museum of Sex & Health MUSEUM   Since Jeju-do didn't have enough sex museums (Loveland and the Museum of Erotica notwithstanding), they decided to build another one. This one, however, is more of an educational institute than a place of amusement. The displays are tastefully presented for the most part, but do watch where you sit in the periodical room, or else you might be unpleasantly surprised by the wooden seats' appendages.

1736 beonji, Gamsan-li, Andeok-myeon, Seogwipo-si. 🕐 **064/792-5700.** www.sexmuseum.or.kr. Admission ₩9,000 adults, ₩7,000 seniors. Daily 10am–8pm (until 10pm July–Aug).

Trick Art Museum ☺ MUSEUM   This "museum" was designed to showcase the visual tricks and optical illusions created by its various works of art. Although the price is a bit inflated and the place isn't great fun for single travelers, it is a fun photo op for the whole family. So don't forget to bring your camera.

2381 beonji, Seong-eup-li, Pyoseon-myeon, Seogwipo-si. ℂ **064/787-8774.** www.trickart.co.kr. Admission ₩8,000 adults, ₩7,000 teens, ₩6,000 children, free for children 3 and under. Daily 9am–7pm; last admission 1 hr. before closing. About a 40-min. drive from Jeju-si off Hwy. 97.

World Automobile Jeju Museum MUSEUM   Housing 59 classic cars from all over the world, this collection, started by a businessman with a vision, includes a 1928 Hillman Straight 8 (the automobile of choice for the British royal family), a Model T, and the first diesel-powered car from 1886.

2065-4 beonji, Sangchang-li, Andeok-myeon, Seogwipo-si. ℂ **064/792-3000.** www.koreaauto museum.com. Admission ₩8,000 adults, ₩6,000 teens, ₩5,000 children. Free parking. Daily 9am–6pm; last admission at 5pm. From Jeju airport, take limousine bus no. 600.

Temples

Gwaneumsa ★ TEMPLE   This small temple is located on the north side of Hallasan. One of many smaller temples on the island, the current building was erected in 1969 in an attempt to revive Buddhism, which was abolished on the island during the Joseon Dynasty, in the 15th century. The major temple on the island went into a steady decline and closed down for good in 1653, leaving only a handful of hermitages. The original temple, which was destroyed in a fire, was built in 1909. The temple is about a kilometer (0.62-mile) walk from the park's north entrance.

680-26, Yeon-dong, Jeju-si. ℂ **064/724-6830.** Admission to the park ₩1,600 ages 25–64, ₩600 ages 13–24, ₩300 children 7–12, free for seniors 65 and over and kids 6 and under. Summer daily 5am–10pm; winter daily 6am–9pm. Closed only during inclement weather. Overnight camping is prohibited. From the Jeju Intercity Bus Terminal, take a bus bound for Seongpanak. Buses run 6am–9:30pm. The 35-min. ride costs ₩2,000.

Theme Parks

Jeju-do has become an island of many "lands," as unusual theme parks and attractions have popped up in hopes of attracting the thousands of tourists who visit every year. Most of them, like "Elephant Land" or "MiniMiniLand" are tourist traps, but some give a bit of insight into Korean culture, while others are just plain fun.

Jeju Loveland PARK   In a country where you rarely see couples holding hands or even kissing on television, this sex "theme park" may seem terribly out of place. Started by 20 art school graduates from Seoul's Hongdae (Hong-ik University), it's actually a sculpture garden featuring an unusual, sometimes downright puzzling, display of over 140 works of art. There are also monthly exhibits and a display of sex toys. Definitely not a place to bring the kids.

680-26, Yeon-dong, Jeju-si. ℂ **064/712-6988.** www.jejuloveland.com. Admission ₩7,000. Daily 9am–midnight (last entry 11pm). From Jeju Airport, take road 95 to road 99 at the Nohyung intersection. It's a 10-min. drive from the airport.

Jeju Soingook Theme Park ☺ PARK   The name doesn't really describe what you'll find here—there aren't any rides, for example. It's not so much a theme park as an architectural park, featuring miniaturized replicas of everything from Korea's Bulguksa Temple to the Eiffel Tower and the Leaning Tower of Pisa. You'll find over 100 miniature structures here, perfect for kids to explore.

725, Seogwang-li, Andeok-myeon, Seogwipo-si. © **064/794-5400.** www.soingook.com. Admission ₩9,000 adults, ₩7,000 teens, ₩5,000 seniors 65 and over and kids 12 and under. Summer daily 8:30am–7:30pm; winter daily 9am–5:30pm. Take bus no. 12, 16, 95, or 1116 and get off at Seogwang 4-way (Sageoli). It's near where roads 95 and 16 meet.

Coffee Waterworld ★★ ☺ WATER PARK   A coffee-themed water park, they even have a coffee museum, farm, and roaster. You can even soak in the stuff. They also have a herb sauna, a *jjimjilbang* (Korean sauna), fitness facilities, and outdoor spas. Aromatherapy and massages are available.

914-beonji Beop-hwan-dong, Seogwipo-si. © **064/739-1930.** www.jejuwaterworld.co.kr (Korean only). Admission ₩35,000 ages 13 and over, ₩28,000 kids 2–12. Herb sauna and jjimjilbang ₩9,000. Daily 10am–10pm, with reduced hours off season; herb sauna daily 5:30am–midnight. Take bus no. 7 from Seogwipo-si and get off at the Samju Apt. stop. You'll be able to see the water park from there.

Psyche World Theme Park ☺ AMUSEMENT PARK   Pronounced "Puh-see-keh" in Korean. What started as a place to highlight butterflies has morphed into a general amusement park for kids. Attractions include "Maze Park," a big white outdoor maze; "Parody World," with dozens of dioramas depicting historical and cultural events using preserved insects; and "Live World," where visitors can hold live animals, including bunnies, hamsters, cats, birds, and even stag beetles.

155-101 beonji, Sogil-li, Aewol-eup, Jeju-si. © **064/799-7272.** www.psycheworld.net (Korean only). Admission ₩8,500 adults, ₩7,000 teens, ₩6,000 children and seniors. Daily 9am–9pm, last admission at 7:30pm. Take the Jungmun express bus from the Jeju Bus Terminal and get off at Jeju Race Park. By car it's about a 10-min. drive from Jeju-si off Hwy. 1135.

Outdoor Pursuits

Jeju-do's various beaches and rocky terrain make for a variety of watersport options. You can scuba dive, go wind surfing, paraglide, water-ski, or just enjoy swimming in the ocean. For the less aquatic, there are also ground sports options, like horse riding, golf, pheasant hunting, or badminton. If you're more of a spectator than a participant, check out the **Jeju Racecourse** or see if there's a game on at the **Jeju World Cup Stadium.**

HIKING

There is no shortage of hiking opportunities on Jeju-do. The most challenging is the ascent up the island's (and South Korea's) highest peak, **Hallasan**—a round-trip trail to the peak takes about 8 hours. There are four major trails on the mountain, but only two actually go to the peak. You can get information on trails at the visitor's info booth at the entrance to Hallasan National Park. For easier hikes, there are 368 secondary volcanoes on the island (all of them extinct, of course), including **Wollan Crater, Yongnuni Crater, Sonja Crater, Byando Crater,** and **Tarabi Crater.** There are plenty of coastal trails to choose from as well, including **Seongsan Ilchulbong** (Sunrise Peak) and the **Dragon's Tail** trail.

HORSEBACK RIDING

Jeju Island used to be a breeding and training ground for the ponies used by Mongol invaders. The horses you'll see on the island are the descendants of those ponies, who interbred with the native horses. They're smaller than the horses you may be used to riding at home, but they're quite hardy and can carry loads of up to 104kg (230 lb.).

There are over a dozen horse ranches on the island, most of them on hillsides and mountains. One of the best is the **Chowon Seungmajang Ranch** (✆ **064/738-0344;** 150 Sangye-dong, Seogwipo-si), which is open daily 9am to sunset, except during rainy weather. It'll cost you about ₩35,000 for a 30-minute ride.

PARAGLIDING

Jeju-do is one of the best places in the country for paragliding, regardless of your skill level. Because the island has over 360 *oreum* (parasitic volcanoes), there are suitable sites for launching no matter which way the wind is blowing. The best flying conditions are from September to October, but you can fly year-round (except during late-summer typhoon season), since the island's famous winds will carry you along. Equipment rentals are about ₩30,000 and full training for beginners costs about ₩200,000. Contact the **Jeju-do Paragliding Association** (✆ **070/8900-5559;** 1163-4 Ora 1(il)-dong, Jeju-si) for more info.

PARKS & GARDENS

Hallim Park ★★ PARK   A botanical garden located alongside a beach, this park is divided into 16 areas, categorized by the types of plants grown there. The two most popular sites in the park, though, are the two caves. The **Hyeopjaegul** is one of many lava caves in the park, but is unusual in that it has stalactites and stalagmites. The **Ssangyong-gul ("Twin Dragon" Cave) ★** is the only spot in the world that is actually a cave within a cave, a second cave opens within the first cave's caverns. There is also a children's amusement park, a folk village, and an outdoor resort facility.

Hyeopjae-li 2487, Hallimeup, Jeju-si. ✆ **064/796-0001.** www.hallimpark.co.kr. Admission ₩5,000 adults, ₩4,000 teens, ₩2,500 children and seniors. Mar–Oct daily 8:30am–6pm; Nov–Feb daily 9am–5pm. From the Jeju-si Bus Terminal, take a bus bound for Hallim (takes 50 min.). From Seogwipo-si, take a westbound bus to Hallim and get off at Hallim Park (takes 80 min.).

Halla Sumogwon (Halla Arboretum) GARDEN   This arboretum, located at the foot of Hallasan, was established for the study and preservation of Jeju-do's natural environment. There are over 2,700 endangered rare plants and over 900 native and subtropical plants.

1000 Yeon-dong, Jeju-si. ✆ **064/746-4423.** http://sumokwon.jeju.go.kr (Korean only). Free admission, but the greenhouse is open sporadically. Mar–Oct daily 9am–6pm; Nov–Feb daily 9am–5pm. From Jeju-si take the city bus bound for Jeju Agriculture High School.

Jeju Stone Park PARK   This stone park also has a museum dedicated to the *Seomundae Halmang,* the legendary grandmother, who apparently gave birth to those 500 sons (p. 387).

San 119 Gyorae-li, Jocheon-eup, Jeju-si. ✆ **064/710-7731.** http://jejustonepark.com/eng/. Admission ₩3,500 adults, ₩2,500 teens, free for those over 65 and under 12. Open daily 9am–6pm, last admission 5pm, closed the first Monday of each month.

Spirited Garden ★★ GARDEN   One of the world's largest botanical gardens, it was started over 30 years ago as a labor of love by a dedicated farmer. There are now more than 100 rare tree species on display here, along with 100,000 wildflowers and native Jeju plants. Stroll through and enjoy. Lunch served 11am to 2pm.

1534 Jeoji-li, Hangyeong-myeon, Jeju-si. ✆ **064/772-3701.** www.spiritedgarden.com. Admission ₩9,000 adults, ₩7,000 teens/seniors, ₩5,000 children. Ticket sales Nov–Feb daily 8:30am–5pm; Mar–Oct daily 8:30am–6:20pm; closes at sunset. Located near the Chocolate Museum.

JEJU-DO'S OLLE-GIL (OLLE trails) ★★★

A group of volunteers, who called themselves the "Jeju Olle Exploration Team," led by a retired journalist, have discovered and renovated walking trails throughout the island. *Olle-gil* is the Jeju word for the road that connects your front door to the street. "Olle" loosely translates to "Will you come…?" They're generally scenic small roads that explore little-known parts of the island. The trails lead from one into another, so those with the luxury of time can explore many of the island's coasts and extinct volcanoes on foot. ⓒ **064/ 739-0815**; www.jejuolle.org/eng.

o **Route 1 (Siheung to Gwanchigi Beach):** Starting at Siheung Elementary School, this trail climbs up to the extinct volcanoes Malmi Oreum and Al Oreum, with views of Seongsan Ilchulbong and Udo. Then, it continues along the salt fields of Jongdal-li to Siheung-li (you may want to stop at the **Siheung Haenyeo Jip,** ⓒ **064/ 782-9230,** for a seafood lunch), past Sungsan shijang, Dongamsa, and ends at Gwangchi Beach. 15km (9.3 miles), 5 to 6 hours.

o **Route 2 (Gwanchigi to Onpyeong):** From Gwangchigi Beach, this trail climbs up Siksanbong through Ojo-li Village along the coast and inland to Goseong Village. Then, it climbs up to Daesusanbong past an old cemetery, then around the legendary Honinji ("Wedding" pond) and down to Onpyeong Port. 17km (11 miles), 5 to 6 hours.

o **Route 3 (Onpyeong to Pyoseon):** Beginning at Onpyeong Pogu, this trail goes up to the great views from Tong Oreum and Dokjobong. Then, it leads to Samdal-li, past Kim Young-gap Gallery (an elementary school that's been converted into a gallery for the now-deceased photographer), and down to Bada Mokjang (a beachside livestock farm). The road continues through Sincheon Village and Baegopeun "Hungry" Bridge" to Pyoseon Beach. 22km (14 miles), 6 to 7 hours.

o **Route 4 (Pyoseon to Namwon):** The trail goes down to Gatneup (marsh) to Nubeureum. Get to Gama-li, then continue past Geomunmeoje to Tosan New Village. Then head up to Mang-oreum and pass the Gseoseunsaemi (fresh water springs) to Yeongcheonsa. The trail heads down, passes Samseokgyo (bridge), and goes to Taheung and Namwon Port. 23km (14 miles), 6 to 7 hours.

o **Route 5 (Namwon to Soesoggak):** This is the best route for seaside views. Starting from Namwon, the trail takes you along small villages past the Sea Life Research center, inland through the Camellia plant community, past Jobae Museul Koji to Wimi-hang (harbor). Then, it continues along the shore through Gongcheonpo (a beach known for its black sand) past Mangjang Port, ending at Soesoggak estuary. 15km (9.3 miles), 5 to 6 hours.

o **Route 6 (Soesoggak to Oedolgae Rock):** Starting at Soesoggak, this

SCUBA DIVING

Already well known for its amazing women divers, the underwater scene around Jeju-do is spectacular. Because it gets both cold and warm ocean currents, the biodiversity of the marine life here is hard to beat. There is a wonderful mix of colorful tropical excellent trail takes you through Seogwipo-si, past Bomok and Gudumi Ports, and past Geomeunyeo and the KAL and Paradise hotels. Then, it goes past Jeongbang Falls, Sora Seng, the gallery of painter Lee Joong-seop, and Cheonjiyeon Falls, and curves around to end at Oedolgae. 14km (9 miles), 4½ to 5 hours.

o **Route 7 (Oedolgae to Wolpyeong Pogu):** Another seaside course, this route goes past Beop-hwan Pogu (port) and Poonglim Resort to get to Wolpyeong Pogu. 15km (9.3 miles) route, 4 to 5 hours.

o **Route 8 (Wolpyeong to Daepyeong Pogu):** This coastal trail continues through palm tree forests and garlic fields to Daepo Pogu and Jusangjeolli. This route, which was used only by local divers, ends at Daepyeong Port. 18km (11 miles), 5 to 5½ hours.

o **Route 9 (Daepyeong to Hwasun Beach):** A shorter trail, it's perfect for a half-day hike. It goes from the port up to Molijil and down the coast to Hwanggaecheon (stream), past the Hwasun Prehistoric Sights. From there, you can choose to go up through the valley to Jinmoreu Dongsan around Gasegi Village and down to Dongha-dong (village), or just take the shortcut from Hwasun to Dongha-dong and around to Hwasun Beach. 15km (9.3 miles), 4 to 5 hours.

o **Route 10 (Hwasun to Moseulpo):** This seaside trail follows the edges of the land going past salt fields and dipping into the small peninsula where Songaksan sits, which affords a pretty spectacular view. Then the trail ends at Moseulpo. 15km (9.3 miles), 5 to 6 hours.

o **Route 11 (Moseulpo to Mureung):** An inland-only trail, it leads from Moseulpo past Jeju-do's largest cemetery and various historic sites, to end at the Jeju Culture and Ecology Experience Village in Mureung 2(i)-li. 20km (12 miles), 6 to 7 hours.

o **Route 12 (Mureung to Hangyeong):** This trail goes through fields and along the coast, passing parasitic cones and ending at Jolbuam Rock at Yongsu Pogu (port). 18km (11 miles), 5 to 6 hours.

o **Route 13 (Yongju to Jeoji):** Starting from Yongju Port this road goes up into the forest. 15.3 km (9.5 miles), 4 to 5 hours.

o **Route 14 (Jeoji to Hallim):** Starting from the forest, this route takes you back out to the Hallim coast, where the ocean scenery reveals itself as you walk. 19.3 km (12 miles) 6 to 7 hours.

o **Route 15 (Hallim to Gonae):** This trail takes you along a stone-walled path with the ocean at your side. 19 km (11.8 miles), 5 to 6 hours.

o **Route 16 (Gonae to Gwangryung):** Starting from Gonae Port, this trail also takes you into the green hills. 15.7km (9.8 miles) route, 5 to 6 hours.

coral and temperate species, as well as unusual underwater rock formations from lava flows that quickly cooled when they hit the water. There are great dives all around Jeju and its surrounding islands, but the best known is from **Udo,** off the eastern coast. There is also a group of four small islands off the coast of Seogwipo that are popular with divers. The clearest waters are found off Seogwipo, Udo, Sibling Island, Chagwido, and Gwantaldo.

Water temperatures are generally quite chilly, especially compared to other tropical areas in Asia. The best conditions are from September to November, when there are more fish and visibility is excellent. It is a bit difficult to find English-speaking instructors, but check the diving directory on **Scuba in Korea** (www.scubainkorea.com) for dive trips. You can also contact **Big Blue 33** (✆ **064/733-1733;** www.bigblue33.co.kr), which rents equipment and organizes diving trips with English-speaking guides.

SURFING

Jeju-do is popular with Japanese surfers, since the island's southern coast catches the same Pacific swells that make Okinawa so popular. **Jungmun Beach** is the main surfing area on the island. If you don't want to lug your board, you can rent one there for about ₩20,000 to ₩30,000 per day in the summer. Surfers say that the best waves are on the next beach to the west (at the bottom of the cliffs below the Hyatt Regency). During typhoon season, it's reported to have 3.6m (12-ft.) tubes. Another good location is **Sagye Beach,** at Hwaseon, near Sanbangsan.

WINDSURFING

The **Korean Windsurfing Association Cheju Training Center** (✆ **064/782-7552**) at **Shinyang Beach** is your best bet for reliable information about windsurfing or boardsailing on Jeju-do. Although their main business isn't rentals, they have a pretty good selection of boards to rent. The best time for windsurfing is around mid-September through March, when the strong winds from the northwest create good conditions. Another popular spot is **Hamdeok Beach ★★** on the north coast.

Boat Tours

A fun way of exploring the island is to take a tour around it. Most popular are the underwater submarine tours, but the glass-bottom boats are more economical. Unfortunately, guided tours are generally only in Korean.

Daeguk Submarine Tour ☺ADVENTURE TOUR   This long, white submarine is a cross between a submarine and a boat. The passenger area is fully submerged underwater and you can see the underwater display from round fisheye portals. The top part of the submarine remains above water. The ride lasts about 30 minutes and starts from Seogwipo.

707-5, Seohong-dong, Seogwipo-si. ✆ **064/732-6060.** www.submarine.co.kr (Korean). ₩45,000, ₩39,600 junior high/high-school students, ₩29,700 children. Daily 7:20am–6pm; departs every 45 min., depending on weather conditions.

Jeju Submarine Tour ☺ADVENTURE TOUR   For those of us who don't scuba dive, this is a great way to see the beautiful underwater flora and fauna around the island. If you're lucky, you may even catch a glimpse of one of the famed women divers of Jeju-do. This yellow submarine ride lasts about 80 minutes and goes around Mara-do.

2126 Sagye-li, Andeok-myeon, Nam-gun. ✆ **064/794-0200.** www.jejusubmarine.com (Korean). ₩48,000 adults, ₩39,600 junior high/high-school students, ₩29,700 children. Daily 7:15am–5:45pm; departs every 45 min., depending on weather conditions.

Seogwipo Pleasure Boat ☺ ADVENTURE TOUR   A nice way to enjoy the scenery around Seogwipo and its surrounding waters, these glass-bottom boats are specially equipped to show you not only what's over the water, but also what's under it. You can also enjoy a beer or another drink from the boat's bar while letting the sea breezes whip through your hair during this 80-minute ride. Boats depart 18 times a day during high season, but check schedules since weather is a determining factor. There are two types of tours: the more expensive "Romantic Cruise," which caters to newlyweds, and the "Paradise." Both have similar schedules.

Seohong-dong 707 (dock at Seogwipo Port), Seogwipo-si. ☎ **064/732-1717**. Paradise: ₩15,000 adults, ₩7,500 ages 7–18. Romantic Cruise: ₩21,500 adults, ₩15,000 ages 13–18, ₩9,000 ages 7–12, free for children 6 and under. Boarding 11am, 2:10pm, 3:20pm, 4:30pm. Bus no. 600 from Jeju Airport stops directly at the port.

SHOPPING

Given that Jeju-do is such a major tourist destination, there is no shortage of shops or shopping areas. You can buy local products in specialty shops and traditional markets, or shop for jewelry or high-end fashion at department stores and duty-free shops. If you can time it right, try and visit the *O-il Jang* ("5-day" markets, so-called because they're held every 5 days) at the same location. For more information, see the "Markets" section, below.

Some of Jeju-do's offerings include products inlaid with mother-of-pearl, black coral pipes (and other things made of coral), sculptures and souvenirs made from lava rock, shells, and locally made shawls and sweaters. You can also take home a jar of the famous Jeju honey (made from local mandarin orange or clover flowers).

Best Shopping Areas

One of the major shopping areas in Jeju-si is **Tap-dong,** which is located in the center of the city. There is an underground shopping center there, dedicated mostly to women's fashions. Another shopping area is the **Ildo District** in Jeju-si, where there are some great places to eat too. The oldest shopping area in Jeju-si is the **Chilseong-ro** area, which used to be the center of town under Japanese occupation. There are still many shops here, along with plenty of bars and game rooms.

In Seogwipo-si, the streets of **Jungjeong-ro** are filled with shops great for browsing, including the Dongmyeon Department Store and the Maeil ("Everyday") Market. The area is located between Jungjang-dong and Jeongbang-dong. The department store has more expensive and branded merchandise. The rest of the Maeil Market is bustling with small vendors selling their wares on the street. Most of them specialize in women's clothing.

More diverse and unpredictable are the **O-il Jang ("5-Day" Markets),** which happen every 5 days (of course) in fixed locations throughout the island. There are markets in Jeju city, Seogwipo, Hallim, Jungmoon, Sehwa, Hamdeok, Goseong, Daejeong, Seongsan, and Yeoseon. They sell everything from seafood, agricultural goods (such as Jeju's famous mandarins when they are in season), clothes, and household goods.

For inexpensive and large-scale shopping, try the **Hanaro Mart** in Seogwipo or the **E-Mart** in Tap-dong.

Shopping A to Z
ARTS & CRAFTS
Jeju Folk Arts Complex   Although you'll find souvenirs and tchotchkes (knick-knacks) all over the island, if you want authentic handicrafts made by artisans, this is

the place to shop. Don't be fooled by the name; the building is really just one big gift shop. The island's craftsmen often have a number of workshops and displays showing off their traditional methods and talents. It's open daily from 9am to 6pm. © **064/713-7142.** Take the intracity bus bound for Joseon and get off at the Hwabuk Jugong Apartments. The Jeju Folk Arts Complex is right across the street from the bus stop.

FASHION

Jung-ang Underground Shopping District   Be prepared to bargain at this crowded arcade of shops. The small stores specialize in women's fashions or groceries. The district opens daily at 9am and closes at 10pm, but individual shop hours tend to vary depending on the whims of the owners. Take one of the local buses in Jeju-si and get off at the Gwandeokjeong, Jung-ang-no, or Dongmun Market stops.

MARKETS

These traditional markets are mostly good for looking (how are you going to take 10 pounds of seafood on the plane with you?), but they are still a fun way to experience the flavor of the island. Although there are O-il Jang (5-Day Markets) in Sehwa, Hamdeok, Hallim, Goseong, Daejeong, Seongsan, and Pyoseon, we've listed only the ones in the major areas. Those markets not listed as 5-day open daily.

Dongmun Market   Along with smiling pigs' heads, you'll see piles of chili powder, and rows and rows of glistening fresh fish from the ocean nearby. The market is located in the Jung-ang-no area of Jeju-si, around Sanjicheon, and is open daily from 8am to 6pm.

Jeju O-il Jang (5-Day Market)   The vendors at this market sell mostly home-grown foods and local seafood. You can see dried fish and seaweed piled high as locals bargain for their dinner staples. The market is open on the 2nd, 7th, 12th, 17th, 22nd, and 27th of each month. Vendors' hours are from 8am to 1 hour after sunset.

Jungmun O-il Jang (5-Day Market)   Located in the Jungmun area of Seog-wipo-si, this market specializes in agricultural and marine goods, medicinal herbs, livestock, and other foods. Updated in 2000, the market is now run by the Youth Association of Jungmun. Open on the 3rd, 7th, 13th, 18th, 23rd, and 28th days of each month; vendors' hours are from 8am to 1 hour after sunset.

Seogwipo Daily Market & Arcade   In the middle of the commercial district of Seogwipo city, this traditional market has been modernized and enclosed in a covered arcade. With over 200 stores and almost 150 street vendors, it's still a bustling marketplace where you can find everything from clothes to dried seaweed. Open 5am to 11pm, they even have a children's playground and four stories of free parking (1 hr.).

Seogwipo O-il Jang (5-Day Market)   For over 50 years, this market has been a trading center for local goods. Located in the Jungmun area of Seogwipo-si, this market specializes in locally grown foods, fresh seafood, medicinal herbs, and other local specialties. With almost 1,000 vendors, there's plenty to see. The market is open on the 4th, 9th, 14th, 19th, 24th, and 29th day of each month. Vendors' hours are from sunrise (usually around 6am, but later in the winter) to 1 hour after sunset.

ENTERTAINMENT & NIGHTLIFE

The main tourist district in Jeju-si is Tap-dong-ro (Tap-dong St.), which starts near Jeju port. You can enjoy a late dinner, shop at the night street vendors, or just walk along the boardwalk. Many bars and places in the area stay open until 4am during high tourist season.

Other than that, most of Jeju-si's bars are located in the "old city" near city hall. This is where the college students and Jeju-do's English teachers hang out.

In Seogwipo, the nightlife is centered around the luxury hotels and resorts. The **Jungmun Tourist Complex** has upscale hotel lounges and karaoke bars. Also, many major hotels have casinos.

Performing Arts

Jeju Culture & Arts Center   Located in the middle of Jeju-si, the center was built in 1988. It has a large 902-seat theater for major performances, two smaller theaters, and an exhibition hall. Various exhibits and performances by both local performers and international acts are held throughout the year. 852 Ildo 2-dong, Jeju-si. ℂ **064/710-7632.** From Jeju Airport, take bus 200 or 300 and get off at "munya hwegwan."

Jeju Magic World   This 2,000-seat performance space inside Jeju Art Center features acts by acrobats, stunt riders, magicians, and other performers (including about 40 actors from Shanghai). Performances are at 10am, 2pm, 4pm, and 6pm daily March through September (the last two performances are at 3:30 and 5:20pm Oct–Feb). ℂ **064/746-9005** (Korean only) or call the Korea Travel Phone (ℂ 1330). Tickets ₩20,000 adults, ₩15,000 youth, ₩35,000 for VIP seating.

Casinos

Many of Jeju-do's luxury hotels have casinos, which are open 24/7 to visitors only, so don't forget to take your passport. Hotels in Jeju-si, which have casinos, include the **Hyatt, Jeju KAL,** the **Jeju Oriental, Crowne Plaza,** and the **Paradise.** In Seog-wipo, **The Shilla Jeju** and the **Lotte** are the only hotels with casinos.

Bars

JEJU CITY

Several small pubs line the streets in the "old city" opposite Jeju's City Hall, but most of the better bars and nightlife can be found in Shin-Jeju.

A place to get good beer in Shin Jeju is **Modern Time ★** (ℂ **064/748-4180;** 263-6 Yeong-dong), a microbrewery run by a German-Spaniard and his Korean nephew, which is located on the second floor, about a block from the Jeju Grand Hotel. There's also a second location (ℂ **064/726-4141;** 382-14 Ido 2(i)-dong), in the city hall area. You can't miss their large sign and stainless steel brew tanks, visible from the window. Open daily 11am to 1am daily.

Those with more of a penchant for wine can head over to cozy **Ile de Vin ★★** (ℂ **064/745-1982;** 272-49 Yeong-dong), a wine bar with over 100 vintages from Argentina to New Zealand for about ₩40,000 to ₩150,000 per bottle.

The flashiest club on the island is the **Jeju Aroma Super Dome Nightclub** (ℂ **064/746-740;** 274-25 Yeong-dong, Jeju-si), a four-story extravaganza with Vegas-like performers, DJs, bands, and 100 private "booking" rooms (for those on blind dates set up by "booking" agents). Best to go with a group and get a set drink/*anju* (drinking snacks) menu for about ₩15,000 a person. Open daily 7pm to 2am (the actual dome opens up nightly at 10:30pm and 1:30am, and one extra time on summer nights).

SEOGWIPO CITY

Seogwipo's nightlife is mostly found in the luxury hotels in the Jungmun resort complex. One of the more relaxed is the **Ollae Library Bar** (© 064/735-5587) on the fifth floor of The Shilla Jeju, with jazz music and an upscale atmosphere, or the lobby lounge at the Shilla, which is popular for people-watching. You can belt out a song at the **J3 Karaoke Bar** or have a mixed cocktail in the **Island Lounge** of the Hyatt Regency.

For those missing a hamburger or fish and chips, Seoul's famed bar has a Jeju-do location, **Island Gecko's** (© 064/739-0845; www.geckosterrace.com; 2156-3 beonji, Saekdal-dong, Seogwipo-si), just outside the Jungmun resort complex. Play a round of pool or darts while you enjoy a beer on tap. Open daily 11am to 2am.

OUTLYING ISLANDS

Taking a day trip to an outlying island lets you explore the beauty of the southern seas around Jeju-do and experience life in a remote fishing village. There are hundreds of tiny little islands off the coast, but most of them are uninhabitable or too small to even dock on. Below is ferry information for each island from various ports on Jeju-do.

Udo ★★★

Located off the eastern end of Jeju-do, the largest of Jeju-do's surrounding islands is shaped like a cow—Udo translates to "Cow Island." But don't be fooled by the unglamorous name; Udo (also known as Udo Maritime Park) has a stunning natural landscape and is home to South Korea's only coral-sand beach. The island's 1,800 inhabitants make their living by farming, fishing, and tourism. From the top you can get a view of the entire island of Jeju. And much like its larger neighbor, which can be seen from the top of **Udobong** (Udo Peak, Udo's version of Hallasan), the island has volcanic rock formations, stone statues, excellent fishing, and a famous, though sadly shrinking, group of women divers. If you rent a bike, it will take 2 to 3 hours to circle the island, making Udo an excellent day trip from Jeju-do.

The ferry to Udo costs ₩4,000 round-trip for ages 13 and up, ₩1,400 for kids. It departs hourly, on the hour, from Seongsan Harbor and takes about 15 minutes. Once there, you must also pay a ₩1,500 admission fee (₩1,000 for ages 12 and under) to enter Udo Maritime Park. Car ferries start at ₩8,800 for a compact.

Buses are waiting at the harbor to take passengers around the island. Local bus fare is ₩800 for ages 13 and up, ₩400 for kids 12 and under.

Marado

Marado (also known as Marado Maritime Park) is a mere 4.2km (2⅔ miles) long and 39m (128 ft.) across at its widest point (Koreans say it's shaped like a sweet potato).

You can take the **Samyeongho Ferry** (© 064/794-3500) from Moseulpo Harbor, which runs once or twice a day, depending on the season. The 45-minute ride costs ₩3,000 for adults, ₩1,600 for children. Alternatively, you can take the **Songak Ferry,** managed by Yuyang Maritime Tourism (© 064/794-9079), from Sanisudong Dock at Songaksan. The daily ferry leaves about every hour starting from 10am to 2:30pm and costs ₩15,000 adults, ₩9,800 teens, ₩7,800 children.

You can also enjoy a bowl of *jjajangmyeon* (Chinese-style black-bean noodles) or *jjamppong* (Chinese-style noodles in a spicy seafood broth) at **Wonjo Marado Jja-jangmyeon Jip** (© **064/792-8506;** www.maradopia.co.kr), located down the street from Marado Church. Their bowls of noodles come chock-full of fresh seafood.

Entrance to Marado Maritime Park is ₩1,500 adults, ₩800 for teens and children.

PLANNING YOUR TRIP TO SOUTH KOREA

GETTING THERE
By Plane

Most international flights into South Korea arrive at Seoul's Incheon Airport (ICN), while Seoul's Gimpo Airport (GMP) offers flights to/from other major Asian cities and Jeju-do. The airports in Busan (Gimhae, PUS), Jeju (CJU), Gwangju (LWJ), and Daegu (TAE) have mostly domestic flights with few Asian destinations. South Korea has two national airlines, **Korean Airlines** (www.koreanair.com) and **Asiana Airlines** (us.flyasiana.com), which sometimes provide cheaper fares than their competition abroad, and usually have better service and food.

Tip: Try to book a flight that arrives before 10pm, since Seoul's buses and subways stop running around midnight. Your only choice of transportation into the city will be via taxi, which can cost you ₩60,000 to ₩100,000 plus an additional ₩7,500 toll charge.

FROM NORTH AMERICA Flights from North America to Seoul are usually cheaper from west coast cities such as Vancouver, Seattle, San Francisco, and Los Angeles. North American airlines that fly to Seoul include **Air Canada** (www.aircanada.com), with nonstop flights from Vancouver and Toronto; **Northwest Airlines** (www.nwa.com), with nonstops to Seoul from Seattle and Chicago and several flights from other cities via Tokyo or Osaka; **United Airlines** (www.united.com), from several cities to Seoul and Busan; and **American Airlines** (www.aa.com), usually via Tokyo to Seoul.

Among Asian carriers, only Korean Air and Asiana fly nonstop— **Korean Airlines** flies to Seoul from Vancouver, Toronto, Seattle, San Francisco, Los Angeles, Las Vegas, Dallas/Fort Worth, Chicago, New York, Washington, D.C., Atlanta, and Anchorage, and **Asiana Airlines** has many more indirect and direct flights from North America to Seoul. Several other airlines fly with at least one stopover, including **Cathay Pacific** (www.cathaypacific.com) via Hong Kong, **Singapore Airlines** (www.singaporeairlines.com) via Singapore, and **Japan Airlines** (www.ar.jal.com) via Tokyo.

FROM THE UNITED KINGDOM Flights to South Korea from the U.K. originate in London and fly to Seoul, taking about 11 hours. **KLM Royal Dutch Airlines** (www.klm.com), which sometimes stops in

Amsterdam, **Korean Airlines,** and **Asiana Airlines** fly nonstop. Several other providers fly with at least one stopover, including **British Airways** (www.britishairways.com) via Tokyo or Hong Kong, **Air France** (www.airfrance.com) via Paris, **Cathay Pacific** via Hong Kong, **Singapore Airlines** via Singapore, **Lufthansa** (www.lufthansa.com) via Frankfurt, **China Eastern Airlines** (www.chinaeastern.co.uk) via Shanghai, **Aeroflot Russian Airlines** (www.aeroflot.com) via Moscow, **Emirates** (www.emirates.com) via Dubai, and **Qatar Airways** (www.qatarairways.com) via Doha.

FROM AUSTRALIA & NEW ZEALAND   Malaysia Airlines (www.malaysia airlines.com) and **Singapore Airlines** (www.singaporeair.com) fly from Sydney, Melbourne, Adelaide, and Brisbane; **Air China** (www.airchina.com) from Sydney; **Korean Air** from Brisbane, Sydney, and Auckland to Seoul and Busan; and **Asiana Airlines** from Sydney to Seoul. The flight takes about 10½ hours.

ARRIVING AT THE AIRPORT

More than likely you will be arriving at Seoul's **Incheon International Airport** (✆ 032/1577-2600), which is 52km (32 miles) west of Seoul on Yeongjong Island. Arrivals are on the first floor, where you will find global ATMs; foreign currency exchanges (daily 6am–10pm); the Incheon Tourist Information Center (daily 7am–10pm; ✆ 032/743-0011); the KTO Tourist Information Center (daily 7am–10pm; ✆ 1330); and the Hotel Information Center (daily 9am–10pm; ✆ 032/743-2570), a private company that offers some discounts to midrange and high-end hotels. The second floor has a few domestic flights to and from Jeju-do and Busan, and an Internet cafe lounge (₩3,000 per hour; daily 8am–7:30pm; ✆ 032/743-7427).

GETTING INTO TOWN FROM THE AIRPORT

The easiest way to get into Seoul is via special airport buses (called "limousine buses"), which run daily every 10 to 30 minutes, starting around 5:30am until 10pm (a few of them run late at night). The buses also go to various towns throughout the country. A trip to downtown Seoul takes around 90 minutes (longer during high-traffic times) and costs about ₩10,000, while KAL deluxe limousine buses cost ₩15,000 and stop at 20 of Seoul's major hotels.

Regular taxis charge around ₩40,000 to ₩60,000 (₩100,000 after midnight) to downtown Seoul. Deluxe taxis (they are black) charge ₩63,000 to ₩90,000. Deluxe taxis are especially useful for business travelers, since the drivers can speak basic English, they have free phone service, take credit cards, and will offer a receipt. Taxi fares can be considerably more during high-traffic times, since their fares are based on distance and time. Also, your taxi driver may make you pay the ₩7,500 toll charge for the expressway.

The **Airport Railroad (AREX)** connects Incheon to Seoul Station. From there you can connect to other parts of the city's subway station.

By Car

You can't get into South Korea by car (since it's surrounded on three sides by water and on the top by the DMZ and North Korea). Once you're in the country, however, you can get around easily by car. Although I wouldn't recommend driving in the large cities, like Seoul and Busan, the rest of the country is easily traversed by car. For information on car rentals and gasoline (petrol) in South Korea, see "Getting Around by Car," later in this section.

By Train

It's not possible to get to South Korea by train. However, once inside, the country has an extensive domestic rail system operated by the **Korean National Railroad** (*☎* **1544-7788** or 032/741-7788; www.korail.com). Tickets can be purchased up to a month in advance at many travel agents and up to an hour before departure at train stations. Please see the "Getting Around by Train" section below for additional information.

By Boat

There are ferry connections from South Korea to domestic destinations and cities in Japan and China. At the **Incheon International Ferry Terminal,** 1-2 Hang 7-dong, Jung-gu, Incheon (*☎* **032/888-0116** or 1599-5985 www.icferry.or.kr, Korean only), there are boats to and from Dandong (**Dandong Ferry;** *☎* **02/713-5522;** www.dandongferry.co.kr), Tianjin (**Jincheon Ferry;** *☎* **02/517-8671;** www.dae-atour.co.kr; takes 25 hr.), Qingdao (**Weidong Ferry;** *☎* **02/3271-6753;** www.weidong.com; 18 hr.), Weihai (also Weidong Ferry; 14 hr.), Dalian (**Da-In Ferry;** *☎* **02/3218-6550;** www.dainferry.co.kr; 17 hr.), and Yantai (**Hanjung Ferry;** *☎* **02/360-6900;** www.hanjoongferry.co.kr; 16 hr.) in China. The ships go only two or three times per week to each destination and schedules change, so be sure to confirm actual departure times and days.

From **Busan Port,** 15-3 Jung-ang 4-dong, Jung-gu, Busan (*☎* **051/999-3000;** www.busanferry.com or http://busanpa.com), the most frequent boats travel daily to/from Shimonoseki (**Bugwan Ferry;** *☎* **051/463-3161~4**) and three times a week (usually Mon, Wed, and Fri) to/from Hakata, Japan (**Korea Marine Express;** *☎* **051/442-6115**).

From the **Mokpo Ferry Terminal** (*☎* **061-240-6060,** ext. 1) boats run to/from Shanghai on Mondays and Fridays.

GETTING AROUND

By Plane

There are two large national airlines that operate domestic flights, **Korean Airlines** (*☎* **1588-2001**; www.koreanair.com) and **Asiana Airlines** (*☎* **1588-8000**; http://us.flyasiana.com). The majority of domestic flights are serviced out of Seoul's **Gimpo Airport,** which is reachable by Seoul subway or to and from Incheon Airport via the high-speed AREX train. Other international airports include Busan's Gimhae, Jeju International Airport, Daegu, Gwangju, Cheongju, and Yangyang. Domestic airports include those in Yeosu, Sacheon, Ulsan, Pohang, Gunan, and Wonju.

Budget airlines offer flights to and from Jeju-do and the mainland. **Jeju Air** (*☎* **1599-1500**; www.jejuair.net) provides flights from Gimpo and Busan's Gimhae airports to and from Jeju-do. **Jin Air** (*☎* **1600-6200**; www.jinair.com) has only flights to and from Gimpo and Jeju-do.

By Train

Traveling by train can be the most comfortable way to get between larger cities. If you're planning on extensive rail travel in the country, purchase a voucher for a **KR Pass** (www.korail.com/kr_pass.jsp) online or from travel agents in your home country at least 5 days before you leave, since these passes are not available for purchase in

South Korea. Once you arrive, you'll need to exchange the voucher in Seoul for the actual pass, which is good for unlimited travel on the railways. The KR Passes are good for rides during consecutive days in increments of 1 (₩58,200), 3 (₩84,600), 5 (₩127,000), 7 (₩160,400), and 10 (₩185,100) days. A Saver Pass can be purchased for two to five people traveling together at a 10% discount. Those 13 to 24 in age can get a Youth Pass for 20% less. Children 4 to 12 pay 50% of the adult price, while those 4 and under travel free. Purchase your KR Pass on the **Korean Railroad** website (www.korail.com/kr_pass.jsp), from **STA Travel** (U.S. ℂ 800/777-0112 or 02/733-9494 in Seoul; www.statravelgroup.com) or **US Travel** (www.koreatour.us) in Los Angeles (ℂ 213/383-5511), New York ([212/643-2005) or Hong Kong (852/2152-3133). The actual pass can be picked up at the Railroad Information Center in Incheon (ℂ **032/741-7788**), at Seoul Station (ℂ **02/3149-2530**), or at Busan Station (ℂ **051/440-2506**). In Seoul, STA Pass vouchers can be exchanged for train tickets at **Kises Tour,** located in the YMCA Building, 5th Floor, Jongno 2-ga. Take subway line 1 to Jonggak Station, exit 3 (Mon–Fri 9am–6pm; Sat 9am–3pm).

There are three types of trains—the **KTX** (**Korea Train Express**) bullet train, which runs at speeds up to 300kmph (186 mph); the express **Saemaeul;** and the **Mugunghwa** trains. You can purchase tickets up to 2 months in advance or as close as an hour before departure. Tickets are available online, at most travel agents in Seoul, or at ticket counters and automatic ticket machines at the station.

The Gyeongbu line goes to Busan (Seoul to Busan tickets are ₩44,800) in under 3 hours via Daejeon and the Honam line, which travels through west Daejeon, and ends at Gwangju (₩33,300 from Seoul) or Mokpo (₩37,200 from Seoul). You can also buy individual tickets for the cheaper Saemaeul (first-class) or Mugunghwa (second-class) trains.

You can purchase tickets up to 2 months in advance or as close as an hour before departure. I recommend buying tickets in advance for weekend or holiday travel because fares sell out quickly. Tickets are available online, at most travel agents in Seoul, or at ticket counters and automatic ticket machines at the station.

One of the most popular lines is the Jung-an line, which runs southeast from Seoul's **Cheongnyangni Station** to Busan, stopping at Wonju, Jecheon, Danyang, Pung-gi, Yeongju, Andong, Yeongcheon, Gyeongju, and Ulsan along the way. Another way to get to Busan by train from Seoul is via the Gyeongbuseon (the Gyeongbu line), which has stops in some western cities like Cheonan, Jochiwon, and Daejeon, before curving east toward Gimcheon, Dongdaegu, Samrangjin, and Gupo before terminating at Busan.

From Daejeon, the Honamseon goes all the way to Mokpo, with stops at Seodaejeon, Nonan, Iksan, Jeongup, and Songjeong-li along the way. From Iksan, the Jeollaseon runs to Jeonju, Namwon, Gurye, and Suncheon with a terminus at Yeosu. From Songjeong-li, a line runs east through Gwangju, Suncheon, Jinju, and Masan and ends at Samranjin, which connects to the Gyeongbu line.

From Cheonan, the short Janghang line runs out to Janghang. From Seoul's Cheongnyangni, the even shorter Gyeongchun line provides trains to Chuncheon. An east–west route connects Jochiwon to Taebaek, crossing the Jung-ang line at Jecheon with a stop at Jeungsan. The Taebaek line connects Taebaek to Gimcheon, passing through Mungyeong and Yeongju on the Jungang line. A short rail line connects Dongdaegu and Yeongcheon, as well.

See chapter 4 for details and directions to various train stations in Seoul.

By Bus

Buses are the least expensive way to get around South Korea and even the smallest of towns will have a bus service, albeit infrequent. Express buses to major stations originate from either the **Seoul Express Bus Terminal,** 19-4 Banpo-dong, Seocho-gu, Seoul (℃ **1688-4700;** www.exterminal.co.kr), or the **Central City Terminal,** 19-4 Banpo-dong, Seocho-gu, Seoul (℃ **02/6282-0114;** www.centralcityseoul. co.kr/shopguide/sub_facilities_terminal.php), next door. To get to smaller stations, generally those outside the larger cities, you can change buses or take a direct bus from one of Seoul's smaller bus stations. Contact the **Korean Express Bus Lines Association** (℃ **02/538-6469** or 1588-6900, 24 hr.; www.kobus.co.kr/web/eng) for schedules and other info.

Express buses to the Gyeongnam area (Gyubu line), Chungcheong area (Guma line), and Gangwon-do (Yeongdong line) start from the **Seoul Express Bus Terminal.** Buses on the Honam line that go to Jeolla-do to the south and the Namhaeseon (southern coastal line) start from the **Central City Terminal.**

Buses from the **DongSeoul Bus Terminal,** 546-1 Guui-dong, Gwangjin-gu, Seoul (℃ **1688-5979;** www.ti21.co.kr), go primarily north and east from Seoul. You can catch a bus to Andong, Gangneung, Sokcho, and Wonju from here. Also, buses from this terminal take the scenic (but longer) route to Seoraksan National Park in Gangwon-do.

The **Nambu Bus Terminal,** 1446-1 Seocho-dong, Seocho-gu, Seoul (℃ **02/521-8550;** www.nambuterminal.co.kr), services mostly the southern region. Popular destinations from this station include Osan, Pyongtaek, and Songnisan National Park.

Buses from the **Sangbong Bus Terminal,** 83-1 Sangbong-dong, Jungnang-gu, Seoul (℃ **02/435-2122,** ext. 8; http://tm.jamycar.co.kr), go generally east and north. You can get to Chuncheon and Sokcho from this station.

Most cities and large towns within South Korea have their own bus terminals in the center of town. **Goseok buses** travel long distances and make few, if any, stops between cities. **Shiwe buses** operate between shorter distances and make more frequent stops.

Even the smallest of towns will have some sort of neighborhood bus service operated by the local government. Bus drivers generally don't speak English, so it's best to know the Korean name of your destination. Fares vary, but usually range from ₩900 to ₩1,100 per trip, so be sure to carry small bills and change for frequent bus trips. Larger cities have passes that are also good for subways or trains. See detailed information in each chapter's transportation sections.

By Car

Driving in South Korean cities can be a hair-raising experience and is not recommended. However, driving in the rest of South Korea is easier, although not the most economical way to get around. The one place that may be most convenient to have a rental car is on Jeju Island. Car rentals start at around ₩70,000 per day. Prices are cheaper offseason and if you rent multiple days. You have to be at least 21 years old to rent a compact car, and at least 26 years old to rent a 4WD or an SUV. You'll also need an International Driving Permit (IDP), which you can get in your home country before you leave. Most rental agencies will ask that you show your regular driver's permit as well. In the U.S. only two authorized organizations provide IDPs—the **American Automobile Association** (www.aaa.com) and **American Automotive Touring**

Alliance (through the National Automobile Club) (© 800/622-7070; www. thenac.com). The AAA charges $15 for an IDP, which you can get at any of their offices or by mail. From the U.K., IDPs are available from the **Automobile Association Limited** (© 0800/085-2721; www.theaa.com) by mail. It'll take at least 10 working days for the IDP to be processed by post, so be sure to apply in advance.

You can rent a car in person at an airport, a KTX station or express bus station. Check prices at South Korea's largest car-rental company, **KT Kumho** (© 1588-1280 or 02/155-1230; www.ktkumhorent.com), or **Avis** (© 1544-1600 or 02/862-2847; www.ajrentacar.co.kr).

A safer option for Seoul is to rent both a car and a driver, which cost about ₩75,000 for 3 hours and ₩142,000 for 10 hours. Your hotel concierge should be able to help you. Some high-end hotels also have their own limousine service.

Unfortunately, there are no detailed driving maps in English, though the KTO will provide a country map showing major highways and roads. Luckily, most highways and major cities have street signs in both Korean and English.

South Korean cities are connected via an extensive network of toll expressways run by the Korea Expressway Corporation. There are very few exits (which means, if you missed an exit for your town, you may have to wait for the next town to get off the highway). If you plan on doing extensive driving around the country, we recommend getting a **Hi-pass,** an electronic toll pay system, available at highway business offices, major highway rest stops, many gas stations, and some shopping malls. The Hi-pass not only allows you to pass through tollbooths without having to stop, but also provides a 5% to 50% discount depending on where and when you travel. You can load the card with amounts ranging from ₩10,000 to ₩480,000, which can be topped up at any bank. There is an initial ₩5,000 deposit. Make sure you get a rental car with an **OnBoard Unit** (OBU) to be able to use your Hi-pass. OBUs are available where Hi-passes are sold as well as some banks, including Hana Bank, Shinhan Bank, and the Industrial Bank of Korea, but it's not worth the ₩128,000 for one if you're on a short trip.

The speed limit is generally 60kmph (37 mph) on regular roads, 80 to 100kmph (50 to 62 mph) on expressways, and 30kmph (19 mph) near schools and hospitals. Be sure to follow posted speed limits, even though other drivers may not, since Korean police can be harsher to foreigners. Watch your speed especially on expressways, which are littered with speed cameras. Although you won't see any traffic cops, you may get an unfortunate surprise in the mail after your speeding trip.

Painted blue lines (usually on the left side of the road) are bus lanes. Buses are given priority in these lanes during rush hours (weekdays 7am–9pm, 7am–3pm on Sat). Bus lanes on expressways are in effect 9am to 11pm daily.

Always fasten your seatbelt or risk the chance of a ₩30,000 fine. One exception to this rule is that you don't have to wear a seatbelt in the back seat of a taxi (buckle up in the front seat, however). It's illegal to drive while talking on a mobile phone unless it's a hands-free set.

Gas and LPG (diesel) stations are readily available throughout the country, but prices are by the liter and can be expensive for long-distance driving. At the time of writing this book, gas was ₩1,900 to ₩2,100 per liter.

Outside of holiday times, driving to Chuncheon in Gangwon-do takes about 2 to 3 hours from Seoul, Cheongju in Chungcheongbuk-do takes about 3 hours, Daegu takes 2 to 3 hours, Gyeongju takes about 5 hours, and Busan takes about 6 hours.

Travel to Suwon is only about an hour and a half, to Daejeon in Chungcheongnam-do about 2 hours, Jeonju 4 hours, and about 4 hours to Gwangju. Jeju-do can be accessed only by boat or plane. (Although you can take your car to the island by ferry for a ridiculously high fee, it's best to rent a car when you get to the island.)

International visitors should note that insurance and taxes are almost never included in quoted rental car rates. Be sure to ask your rental agency about additional fees for these. They can add a significant cost to your car rental.

By Taxi

Taxis in South Korea are safe, clean, and relatively inexpensive. Most Korean taxi drivers will know a modicum of English, but it's best to know your destination in Korean, or even better to have it written down in Korean (Hangeul). You can flag down a taxi almost anywhere in the country, but it's easiest to grab a taxi in front of major transportation hubs. All taxis are metered with fares determined by distance and time. If you don't see a meter in the taxi, you'll probably want to take a different one. Tipping is not necessary, but most passengers round up and let the driver keep the change. There are two types of taxis in major cities, but most smaller towns will have only regular taxis available.

Regular (Ilban) Taxis are usually silver, blue, or white and have a light-up "taxi" sign on top. The base fare is usually around ₩1,900 and goes up every 2km (1¼ miles), going up ₩100 every 144m (¹⁄₁₀ mile) or 41 seconds.

Deluxe (Mobeum) Taxis, which are black, cost almost twice as much as the regular taxis, but can be convenient for many reasons. The drivers are trained to serve foreigners and can speak basic English. Especially useful for business travelers, deluxe taxis have free phone service, take credit cards, and will offer a receipt.

By Bicycle

South Korea is not a country easily explored solely on two wheels, but there are some excellent biking opportunities, especially for mountain bikers. Biking on city streets can be extremely dangerous because there are no dedicated bicycle lanes and bus, taxi drivers, and truck drivers regard traffic rules more as suggestions than laws. In Seoul, however, the mayor has introduced a bike program in which they created a citywide bike-rental system and expanded trails, starting from those in Han River Park and expanding to Namsan and the city center. The pilot program started in Yeouido and Sangam Digital Media City. Bike rentals along the Han River, which has miles and miles of trails on both sides, cost ₩3,000 per hour (₩6,000 for tandems). Unmanned bike-rental kiosks, run by such companies as Victek and Initus, allow people to rent bicycles using a credit card. Cities like Daejeon and Busan are following Seoul's lead.

If you're bringing your bike into the country, collect it from the oversized luggage pickup at the airport. Taking your bike is much easier on buses than on the train, since trains have no storage capability for bicycles.

Since about 60% of South Korea's terrain is mountainous, it can make for exciting or exhausting rides. However, Gyeongju and Jeju-do are some of the best places to pedal and enjoy the scenery.

Independent tour guide Victor Ryashencev offers a 5-day eco-tour of hiking and biking on Jeju Island (www.earthfoot.org/kr.htm). He will take groups as small as 2 people and up to 10 and he's flexible for tours of any length. **Ibike** (www.ibike.org/ibike) offers three biking itineraries in South Korea.

By Ship

Traveling on the water can be a fun and interesting way to see lesser-known parts of South Korea. Major ferry terminals are located in Busan (℧ **1688-7677**), Incheon (℧ **1599-5985**), Jeju-do (℧ **1544-1114**), Mokpo (℧ **061/240-6011**), Yeosu (℧ **061/663-0117**), Tongyeong (℧ **055/642-0116**), Geoje (℧ **051/660-0256**), and Pohang (℧ **054/242-5111**). Busan, Incheon, Mokpo, and Donghae ferry terminals offer international travel while the other ferry terminals are dedicated to domestic destinations, usually nearby islands off the coasts.

See the Jeju-do chapter for overnight ferry information to and from Busan, as well as other shorter ferries from Wando and other terminals in the south.

On Foot

South Korea is not a country that can be explored solely on foot, although Simon Winchester, author of *Korea: A Walk Through the Land of Miracles*, attempted it. Even he resorted to some hitchhiking and free rides to cover the territory. However, travelers who love to walk or hike will find no shortage of places to stretch their legs. Be sure to pack comfortable shoes.

If the throngs of Koreans on mountain trails are any indication, hiking is the unofficial sport of South Korea. Weekends are filled with Seoulites walking the trails around the city as well as getting out to far-flung places. So, if you want to avoid the crowds, weekdays are your best bet.

TIPS ON PLACES TO STAY

There is a wide range of places to stay in South Korea, from very inexpensive *minbak* (homestays), guesthouses, and love motels (see below) to luxury hotels, condos, and pensions. Deluxe accommodations can range from ₩200,000 to 400,000 for a double room, while third-class motel rooms start at ₩30,000 and up.

When you're booking a room, make sure to specify that you want a Western-style room, if you want a bed. Korean ondol-style rooms don't have beds, but include blankets for you to sleep on the floor, which is usually heated during cold weather. If you stay in one, make sure you don't leave any electronics or anything plastic on the floor.

For a taste of the traditional lifestyle, you can stay in a *hanok* (traditional house), which can be centuries old. These are refurbished and modernized homes (updated with conveniences like electricity, TVs, and running water), whose owners usually live there. Certain areas, like Seoul's Bukcheon Hanok Village or the traditional village in Andong, have groupings of them. The best way to book a room in a traditional house is to contact the Korean Tourism Organization (KTO, ℧ **02/1330,** http://english. visitkorea.or.kr). We've also included some hanok info in each of the regional and city sections.

Outside of high-end hotels and some motels, most places to stay require you to take off your shoes at the front-entry area before entering the room. Bathrooms in lower-priced places to stay usually don't have shower curtains—water flows down a drain in the floor—and Korean bath towels are tiny, usually the size of hand towels.

Temple Stays

Many of South Korea's temples offer temple stay programs. Most of them are overnight programs in which you arrive in the afternoon, have a vegetarian meal, sleep in humble quarters, and wake up for early morning meditation at the crack of dawn,

Motels for Lovers

In back alleys, on side streets, and along country roads lie discreet love motels, aimed primarily at those who are married and having extramarital affairs, and at young couples desperate for some privacy (most Koreans live at home until they get married). Many have obvious names like Hotel Venus, but others can be more obscure. A sure sign of one is the curtains that cover the parking area (to avoid having anyone recognize your car, they'll even give you a placard to cover your license plate) and the dimly lit lobby (usually red, but sometimes with colored lights).

But despite these slightly sleazy trappings, many of these places are just fine for tourists, particularly those on a budget. They are inexpensive, ranging from ₩30,000 to ₩50,000, depending on the day of the week. For a little extra, you can often get an in-room Jacuzzi or sauna. All of them supply toothbrushes, shampoo, lotions, and even condoms. Some of them have round beds with extras like mood lighting, vibrating options, and strategically placed mirrors. And most provide Internet access and in-room movies. If you don't mind the connotations, they're often clean and safe places to stay. It's also an experience you won't soon forget! I've made note of a few I can safely recommend throughout the book.

before a tea ceremony, and other activities. Different temples have different themes and a bit of variation in the program. Some temples also offer longer programs. In general an overnight stay costs ₩50,000 to ₩80,000 per night and it's a wonderful way to get a glimpse into the Buddhist monastic lifestyle. Temples that offer overnight stays have been outlined in each chapter, but you can also contact the **Templestay Information Center** (𝄞 **02/2031-2000;** http://eng.templestay.com; 71 Gyeongji-dong, Jongno-gu), located just across the street from Jogyesa (p. 87) in Seoul. The five-story building incidentally has a fabulous Buddhist restaurant **Balwoo Gong-yang** (p. 87) on its top floor.

Youth Hostels

South Korea has an extensive hostel network (about 52 locations throughout the country). Contact the **Korea Youth Hostels Association,** Room 408, Jeokseon, Hyundai Building 80, Jeokseon-dong, Jongro-gu, Seoul 110-756 (𝄞 **02/725-3031;** fax 02/725-3113; www.kyha.or.kr/english; off Gyeongbokgung Station, Seoul subway line 3, exit 6), for additional information. A Hostelling International Card costs around ₩20,000 (₩15,000 for those under 25 years old). Most hostels are open 24 hours and have dormitory-style shared rooms. Prices range from about ₩5,000 to ₩10,000 for a bed to ₩160,000 for a room spacious enough for a large family. Advance reservations are highly recommended, especially during popular summer months and for hostels close to popular destinations.

FAST FACTS

Area Codes   Seoul, Gwacheon, Gwangmyeong (in Gyeonggi-do), 02; Incheon, Bucheon, Siheung (in Gyeonggi-do), 032; the rest of Gyeonggi-do, 031; Daejeon, 042; Chungcheong-nam-do, 041; Chungcheongbuk-do, 043; Jeollanam-do, 061; Jeollabuk-do, 063; Gwangju,

062; Ulsan, 052; Gyeongsangbuk-do, 054; Gyeongsangnam-do, 055; Daegu, 053; Busan, 051; Gangwon-do, 033; Jeju-do, 064. Drop the zero in front of the city/region code when dialing from overseas.

Business Hours   Banks: Monday through Friday 9am to 4pm. Major department stores: Daily 10:30am to 8pm with extended hours on weekends. Smaller shops: Hours vary, but usually early morning to late evening; stores catering to younger people generally open later and close at 10pm; neighborhood convenience stores often stay open until midnight. Restaurants: Most open daily from 10am to 10pm. Government offices (including tourist info): Monday through Friday 9am to 6pm (Nov–Feb close at 5pm), Saturday 9am to 1pm. Many attractions and museums are closed Monday.

Car Rental   See "Getting There by Car," earlier in this chapter.

Cellphones   See "Mobile Phones," later in this section.

Crime   See "Safety," later in this section.

Customs   If you are over 19, you can bring the following goods into South Korea without incurring a custom tax: 200 cigarettes, 50 cigars, or 250 grams of other tobacco products; one bottle (not exceeding 1 liter) of alcohol; 57 grams of perfume; gifts up to the value of ₩300,000. Expensive watches, cameras, jewelry, precious metals, and furs should be declared upon entry or there will be a tax upon departure (₩8,000 per person). There is no restriction on how much currency you can bring into the country.

Prohibited items: Narcotics and drugs; fruit, hay, and seeds; printed material, films, records, or cassettes considered by the authorities to be subversive, obscene, or harmful to national security or public interests; and products originating from communist countries.

Restricted items: Firearms, explosives, and other weapons and ammunition, even for sporting purposes, unless prior police permission is obtained and items are declared on arrival; plants and plant products require a phytosanitary certificate issued by the plant quarantine office of the country of origin. In order to prevent the spread of hoof-and-mouth disease, if you're bringing any beef or pork into South Korea, you must declare it to Customs officials.

Disabled Travelers   South Korea is not the best equipped for accessible travel. However, in Seoul and other major cities, this is changing, albeit slowly. Most subway stations in Seoul now have elevators and public restrooms with wheelchair access and handrails. And there's a plan to have half of Seoul's buses equipped with wheelchair ramps by the end of 2012. Most of the high-end hotels are accessible, but sidewalks and certain attractions are not. Many tourist attractions, especially those run by the government, offer discounts (and sometimes free entry) to people with disabilities. Some even provide a wheelchair (a passport is required) or an assistant. An accessible map of Seoul is available from the KTO offices and more info is available at www.easyaccess.or.kr.

At Busan's Gimhae airport, Braille maps are provided on the first floor of both terminals for visually impaired travelers and all toilets are wheelchair accessible. Lifts are available in both terminals.

Organizations that offer a vast range of resources and assistance to travelers with disabilities include **MossRehab** (𝒸 **800/CALL-MOSS** [225-5667]; www.mossresourcenet.org); the **American Foundation for the Blind (AFB;** 𝒸 **800/232-5463;** www.afb.org); and **SATH (Society for Accessible Travel & Hospitality;** 𝒸 **212/447-7284;** www.sath.org). **Access-Able Travel Source** (𝒸 **303/232-2979;** www.access-able.com) offers a comprehensive database on travel agents with experience in accessible travel. Travel agencies such as **Flying Wheels Travel** (𝒸 **507/451-5005;** www.flyingwheelstravel.com) and **Accessible Journeys** (𝒸 **800/846-4537** or 610/521-0339; www.disabilitytravel.com) offer customized tours and itineraries.

Mobility-Advisor (www.mobility-advisor.com) offers a variety of travel resources to persons with disabilities. **Flying with Disability** (www.flying-with-disability.org) is a comprehensive information source on airplane travel.

British travelers should contact **Holiday Care** (☎ **0845/124-9971** in U.K. only; www.holidaycare.org.uk) to access a wide range of travel information for the elderly and those with disabilities.

Doctors   English-speaking doctors (some who have received their training abroad) can be found at international clinics and even in regular hospitals in Seoul and Busan (please see each chapter for additional information). Your hotel's concierge will also be able to direct you to a doctor. Korean doctors usually give the worst case scenario first and aren't used to patients asking questions or wanting an explanation for their treatment. Still, at the risk of offending the doctor, you should feel free to ask questions and participate actively in your treatment options. Also see "Hospitals," later in this section.

Drinking Laws   The legal drinking age is not strictly enforced in South Korea. Underage drinking is curbed more by the reluctance of bartenders to serve youth than by strict enforcement of the law. Still, the legal drinking age is 20 (or more specifically Jan 1 of the year the person turns 20, since everyone is considered a year older when the year turns). The legal drinking age for U.S. military stationed in South Korea is 21. Bars and nightclubs generally open from 6pm to midnight daily with longer hours (some opening from noon to the early-morning hours) on Friday and Saturday. In some areas of Seoul (like in Itaewon or Hongik) and other large cities, some bars stay open 24 hours. Beer and *soju* (South Korea's infamous vodka-like liquor) are widely available in grocery and convenience stores, while wine is more likely to be found at specialty wine shops and bars. Traditional Korean liquors (like *makgeolli*) can be found in traditional restaurants and some trendy bars. Alcohol is sold in department stores, supermarkets, and convenience stores.

There are no open-container laws in South Korea, so you may see plenty of people enjoying their beverages on the beach, picnicking in the park, or walking out of a bar. However, don't even think about driving while intoxicated.

Driving Rules   See "Getting Around," earlier in this chapter.

Electricity   Most of South Korea is on a 220-volt, 60-cycle system (the plugs with two round prongs), but a few major hotels have 110-volt, 60-cycle systems. Check before plugging in any electronics. It's very difficult to find universal plug adapters, so it's best to buy your own before you arrive.

Embassies & Consulates   The following are in Seoul: **U.S.** (☎ **02/397-4114;** http://seoul.usembassy.gov), **U.K.** (☎ **02/3210-5500;** http://ukinkorea.fco.gov.uk/en), **Canada** (☎ **02/3455-6000;** www.korea.gc.ca), and **Australia** (☎ **02/2003-0100;** www.southkorea.embassy.gov.au). There are Honorary British (☎ **070/7733-1055**), Canadian (☎ **051/246-7024**), and Australian (☎ **051/647-1762**) consulates in Busan. See the Seoul and Busan chapters for addresses and directions.

Emergencies   Dial ☎ **112** anywhere in the country for the police. Dial ☎ **119** for the fire department and medical emergencies, or ☎ **1339** for medical emergencies (although most operators speak only Korean). Hotel staff can also arrange for a doctor or an ambulance.

Family Travel   South Korea can be a great place to travel with family, since many hotels offer family suites and there are plenty of things for kids to do and see.

To locate places to stay, restaurants, and attractions that are particularly kid-friendly, refer to the "Kids" icon throughout this guide. Also, see the recommended itinerary for families in chapter 3.

Recommended family travel websites include **Family Travel Forum** (www.familytravel forum.com), a comprehensive site that offers customized trip planning; **Family Travel Network** (www.familytravelnetwork.com), an online magazine providing travel tips; **TravelWithYourKids.com** (www.travelwithyourkids.com), a comprehensive site written by parents for parents; and **Take the Family** (www.takethefamily.com), a U.K. site with loads of great advice and insights on family travel.

Gasoline   Please see "Getting There By Car," earlier in this chapter.

Health   Modern medical facilities are widely available in South Korea. However, treatment can be expensive for foreigners and English-speaking doctors can be difficult to find outside the major cities. Contact the **International Association for Medical Assistance to Travelers (IAMAT; ☏ 716/754-4883,** or in Canada 416/652-0137; www.iamat.org) for lists of local, English-speaking doctors. Medical facilities usually require an upfront deposit or proof of insurance before providing care.

Although it's easy to find over-the-counter medication in South Korea, it doesn't hurt to pack a small first aid kit, just in case. Also, remember to bring any prescription medications with you, since most doctors and pharmacists outside of Seoul do not speak English. If you do run out of a prescription, don't worry. Most major medications are available in the big cities, and Koreans' knowledge of English is much better in reading and writing than in speaking—if you write down the name of the drug you need, you'll likely get it.

o   **Dietary Red Flags**   Food and water-borne diseases are the most common ailment travelers experience. Take precautions and make sure you bring an anti-diarrhea medicine. Children are at a higher risk of getting dehydrated, so make sure they get plenty of fluids. Drinking tap water in South Korea is not recommended, but all restaurants and even offices and banks offer free filtered or bottled water. You can purchase 500ml bottles of water at convenience stores for about ₩500.

o   **Bugs, Bites & Other Wildlife Concerns**   Although mosquitoes can be fierce in South Korea in the summertime, the risk of contracting malaria is quite low in most of the country. Malaria risk is limited to the areas near the DMZ and rural areas in northern Gyeonggi and Gangwon provinces. Malaria is transmitted by infected mosquitoes, usually between dusk and dawn. Try to remain indoors or in screened-in areas during peak times. If you must be outside, wear a long-sleeved shirt, long pants, and a hat. Be sure to use an insect repellant that contains DEET for any exposed areas of skin. The U.S. Centers for Disease Control and Prevention (CDC) recommends chloroquine as the antimalarial drug in South Korea, but check with your doctor before taking any medication.

o   **Respiratory Illnesses**   Air pollution used to be a severe problem in South Korea, but tighter environmental controls have improved the air somewhat. However, in the larger cities, especially Seoul, air pollution is still a major problem. If you have asthma or respiratory issues, travel by subway and avoid long exposures to automobile exhaust. Sporadically in the springtime, Asian/yellow dust storms from the deserts of Mongolia, northern China, and Kazakhstan kick up dense soil particles that winds carry all the way to South Korea. This wouldn't be such a problem if the dust didn't also carry so much pollution from Chinese industry. If you have a sensitive respiratory system, it's best to stay indoors when these dust storms are severe, since even face masks won't filter out the fine particles.

o   **Sun/Elements/Extreme Weather Exposure**   Summers are hot and humid in South Korea. If you plan on spending any time outdoors, be sure to bring a hat, sunblock, and sunglasses. Summer is also typhoon season. Although most typhoons lose their strength by the time they make it to the peninsula, some have caused deaths in rare cases. Avoid areas along the coast when there are typhoon warnings.

Hospitals There are many hospitals in the larger cities where some English is spoken, but they are harder to find in rural areas. Note that Koreans' idea of privacy differs from Western sensibilities, so don't be surprised if your doctor begins to examine you in front of others. Just ask for a screen or the curtains to be drawn, if this is a problem for you. The following is a list of hospitals in Seoul with international clinics: Samsung Medical Center (✆ **02/3410-0200**), Sinchon Severance (✆ **02/361-6540**), Asan Medical Center (✆ **02/2224-3114**), Kang Buk Samsung Medical Center (✆ **02/723-2911**), Hannam-dong International Medical Center (✆ **02/790-0857**), Seoul Foreign Medical Center (✆ **02/796-1871**), Samsung First Medical Center (✆ **02/2262-7071**), Yeouido Catholic Medical Center (✆ **02/789-1114**), Gangnam Catholic Medical Center (✆ **02/590-1114**), CHA General Hospital (✆ **02/558-1112**), Soonchunhyang Hospital (✆ **02/709-9881**), and Seoul National University Hospital (✆ **02/760-2890**). See individual city and region chapters for additional and detailed hospital listings.

Insurance Although South Korea is a safe place to travel, you may consider purchasing travel insurance, especially if you plan on traveling for an extended period. For information on traveler's insurance, trip cancelation insurance, and medical insurance while traveling, please visit http://www.frommers.com/planning/.

Internet & Wi-Fi South Korea's Internet connectivity is legendary as it leads the world in **Wi-Fi** (wireless fidelity) hot spots. Many high-end hotels, resorts, airports, cafes, and retailers offer high-speed Wi-Fi access for free or for a small fee. Internet service is offered in public places such as airports, train stations, and bus terminals. **PC *bahngs*** (PC rooms), where you can rent an Internet-connected PC, are usually populated by gaming enthusiasts (that is, young, nerdy males), and are easy to find throughout the country (just look for the letters PC often on higher floors of commercial buildings). Many are open 24 hours and provide snacks and instant noodles for game addicts. Love motels in large cities and popular tourist destinations often offer in-room PCs with high-speed Internet.

Language Korean is the official language of South Korea. Although most schoolchildren learn rudimentary English starting from elementary school, your regular Korean on the street will not be able to speak it very well. The government has taken great pains to make sure English signs and announcements are available on subways, city streets, and highways, but bus signs, menus, and other signage are usually only in Korean. You can call the **BBB (Before Babel Brigade) Translation Service** (✆ **1588-5644**) for translation assistance. Also, consider picking up a Korean–English dictionary and/or phrase book, such as the *Lonely Planet Korean Phrase Book*. See chapter 13, "Useful Terms & Phrases."

Legal Aid If you need legal assistance, contact your embassy or consulate immediately. Although they aren't lawyers, they may be able to refer you to an English-speaking attorney. If you're arrested, you're not entitled to a phone call. Although the police are required to contact your embassy, they may do it in writing, which may take up to a week.

LGBT Travelers Although an increasing number of Koreans are coming out of the closet every day, most gays and lesbians keep their orientation a secret from their families and co-workers, even as younger generations become more tolerant than their parents. Gay and lesbian travelers who publicize their orientation should expect some shock and even some hostile reactions.

However, you will see same-sex friends walking around hand-in-hand or arm-in-arm. Public display of physical affection between same-sex friends is actually more common than between heterosexual partners and is not an indication of sexual preference.

Seoul, Busan, and Daegu have gay neighborhoods with clubs, bars, and saunas, but they generally maintain a low profile. Seoul even has a GLBT Film Festival and a **Queer**

Culture Festival (✆ **0505/336-2003;** www.kqcf.org). See the "Gay & Lesbian" sections in the Seoul chapters for recommendations and visit **www.utopia-asia.com** (click on the "Korea" link) for in-depth information and current events.

The International Gay and Lesbian Travel Association (**IGLTA;** ✆ **800/448-8550** or 954/776-2626; www.iglta.org) offers an online directory of gay- and lesbian-friendly travel businesses and tour operators. San Francisco-based **Now, Voyager** (✆ **800/255-6951;** www.nowvoyager.com) offers worldwide trips and cruises.

Gay.com Travel (✆ **800/929-2268** or 415/644-8044; www.gay.com/travel or www.out andabout.com) is an excellent successor to the popular *Out & About* magazine. British travelers should click on the "Travel" link at **www.uk.gay.com** for advice and gay-friendly trip ideas.

Mail Post offices (www.koreapost.go.kr) in South Korea can be easily spotted by their red signs with a white symbol of a stylized swallow on it, and they say POST OFFICE in English. They're open 9am to 6pm Monday through Friday (until 5pm Nov–Feb), some open Saturday 9am to 1pm. International rates are as follows: Postcards ₩400; airmail letter up to 50 grams ₩950; printed matter up to 20 grams ₩400-610; and registered mail ₩1,800. Airmail to North America takes about 5 to 10 days, but delays are not uncommon. For sending packages overseas, **UPS** (✆ **02/1588-6886;** www.ups.com), **Federal Express** (✆ **080/023-8000;** www.fedex.com/kr_english), and **DHL** (✆ **02/716-0001;** www.dhl.co.kr) have branch offices in Seoul and a few other major cities. Within South Korea, a postal code is recommended but mail will be delivered without it.

Medical Requirements No immunizations are required for entry. Also see "Health."

Mobile Phones Although the three letters that define much of the world's wireless capabilities are **GSM** (Global System for Mobile Communications), South Korean mobile phone carriers use a different, highly specialized system, called CDMA, which is not compatible with GSM technology.

If you have a GSM mobile phone, you can rent a "SIM-compatible" handset from KTF and insert your phone's SIM card into the rental phone. KTF will charge you a cheaper rental fee (₩1,300) per day and you'll be billed any roaming charges directly from your home carrier.

Call your wireless operator and ask to get the code to "unlock" your phone and to activate international roaming on your account. Some American and Canadian cellphone companies offer a loan phone that has CDMA technology. Note that international roaming charges can be exorbitant, from $1 to $5 per minute.

Renting a phone is a better option. Three companies rent mobile phones in South Korea. South Korea manufactures some of the best mobile phones in the world and you will be amazed at the clarity of the calls and the availability of service around the country.

SK Telecom has a customer center at Incheon Airport (✆ **032/743-4011;** 24 hr.) on the first floor of the passenger terminal between exits 6 and 7. They also have a location at the Gimpo Airport (✆ **02/1566-2011;** daily 7am–11pm) on the first floor of the international terminal on the opposite side of the arrival gates. Their location at Busan's Gimhae Airport (✆ **1566-2011;** daily 7am–9:30pm) is on the first floor of the international terminal, across from the departure gates. You need to provide a credit card for deposit and your fee will be due when you return the phone, which you can do at any of the SK Telecom's three airport locations.

You can also rent a mobile phone from **Olleh/KT Telecom** (http://roaming.kt.com/eng/index.asp) which has more locations than SK Telecom. At Incheon Airport (✆ **032/743-4019;** 24 hr.), they're on the third floor, between gates E and F. At Busan's Gimhae Airport (✆ **02/2190-1180;** daily 9am–9pm), you can find them on the first floor of the arrival hall, right next to the information desk. They also have a location at Busan International Port

(℅ **1588-0608;** daily 7am–7pm) on the first floor, near the check-in counter. In Jeju City, they have an office at Jeju KTF Members Plaza (on the first floor of Sung Woo B/D, Leedo-2-dong, Jeju City; ℅ **064/711-8016;** weekdays 9am–6pm, closed holidays). Their Gwangju Airport location (℅ **1588-0608;** daily 7am–8pm) is on the second floor, near the departure gates.

S Roaming (℅ **032/743-6467;** www.sroaming.com/eng/main.asp; 24 hr.) has rental centers between gates 6 and 7 and gates 10 and 11 on the first floor of Incheon Airport. They also have a location on the 2nd floor of the International terminal in the Sky City Mall of Gimpo Airport (7am–7pm).

Phones from any company cost around ₩3,000 per day to rent (₩2,000 if you sign up as a T2K member for free at http://english.visitkorea.or.kr), plus the cost of calls. Domestic calls cost ₩100 per 10 seconds and international rates vary. All fees do not include the 10% VAT.

You can also purchase a prepaid SIM card at **GS Books** (℅ **032/753-5654,** 1st floor of Incheon Airport, 7am–9pm daily).

MONEY & COSTS

THE VALUE OF THE WON VS. OTHER POPULAR CURRENCIES

₩	Aus$	Can$	Euro (€)	NZ$	UK£	US$
1,000	A$0.87	C$0.90	€0.65	NZ$1.15	£0.56	$0.88

Frommer's lists exact prices in the local currency. The currency conversions quoted above were correct at press time. However, rates fluctuate, so before departing consult a currency exchange website such as **www.oanda.com/currency/converter** to check up-to-the-minute rates.

Beware of hidden credit-card fees while traveling. Check with your credit or debit card issuer to see what fees, if any, will be charged for overseas transactions. Recent reform legislation in the U.S., for example, has curbed some exploitative lending practices. But many banks have responded by increasing fees in other areas, including fees for customers who use credit and debit cards while out of the country. Fees can amount to 3% or more of the purchase price. Check with your bank before departing to avoid any surprise charges on your statement.

You can call the **Exchange Rate Information** line in Seoul (℅ **02/2275-5455**) for additional information. For help with currency conversions, tip calculations, and more, download Frommer's convenient Travel Tools app for your mobile device. Go to http://www.frommers.com/go/mobile/ and click on the Travel Tools icon.

Multicultural Travelers   South Korea is a homogeneous country. Some Koreans can be xenophobic, but most are usually quite friendly. When traveling in South Korea, you may experience some gawking (staring isn't considered particularly rude) or an occasional student wanting to practice his or her English.

Ever since the Korean War, Koreans have had a love–hate relationship with Americans. There have been reports of harassment of Westerners (and fights, especially in bars) in the Hongdae and Sincheon areas of Seoul. Some nightclubs and certain establishments may not let you in if you are a foreigner, if you're not dressed properly, or if you're considered too old.

Newspapers & Magazines   English versions of two Korean newspapers, the **Korean Herald** (www.koreaherald.co.kr) and **The Korea Times** (www.koreatimes.co.kr), can be

WHAT THINGS COST IN SOUTH KOREA   ₩

Taxi from the airport to downtown Seoul	40,000–90,000
Double room, moderate	90,000
Double room, inexpensive	30,000
Three-course dinner for one without wine, moderate	30,000–40,000
A large bottle of Korean beer (more for imported)	3,500
Cup of regular coffee (much more in a cafe)	1,500
1 liter of premium gas (petrol)	around 2,000
Admission to most museums	2,000–10,000
Admission to most national parks	3,000

found at convenience stores; street stalls; hotels; or bus, train, and subway terminals for about ₩600. News magazines issued abroad can be found in most large hotel bookstores, but for more specialized journals or periodicals, visit the major bookstores in larger cities (see "Shopping," in the Seoul or Busan chapters).

Packing   Comfortable shoes and seasonal appropriate clothing are a must for travel in South Korea. Bring light, but not too revealing clothes for the summer and warm layers for the harsh winter. Don't forget your power converter, deodorant, and toothpaste (most Korean brands don't contain fluoride). If you plan on staying in budget accommodations, bring a large bath towel, if you can't do with the tiny Korean ones. For more helpful information on packing for your trip, download our convenient Travel Tools app for your mobile device. Go to http://www.frommers.com/go/mobile/ and click on the Travel Tools icon.

Passports   Allow plenty of time before your trip to apply for a passport; processing normally takes 3 weeks but can take longer during busy periods (especially spring). Keep in mind that if you need a passport in a hurry, you'll pay a higher processing fee.

Passport Offices

o   **Australia   Australian Passport Information Service** (📞 **131-232,** or visit www. passports.gov.au).

o   **Canada   Passport Office,** Department of Foreign Affairs and International Trade, Ottawa, ON K1A 0G3 (📞 **800/567-6868;** www.ppt.gc.ca).

o   **Ireland   Passport Office,** Setanta Centre, Molesworth Street, Dublin 2 (📞 **01/671-1633;** www.foreignaffairs.gov.ie).

o   **New Zealand   Passport Office,** Department of Internal Affairs, 47 Boulcott Street, Wellington, 6011 (📞 **0800/225-050** in New Zealand or 04/474-8100; www.passports.govt.nz).

o   **United Kingdom**   Visit your nearest passport office, major post office, or travel agency or contact the **Identity and Passport Service (IPS),** 89 Eccleston Square, London, SW1V 1PN (📞 **0300/222-0000;** www.ips.gov.uk).

o   **United States**   To find your regional passport office, check the U.S. State Department website (travel.state.gov/passport) or call the **National Passport Information Center** (📞 **877/487-2778**) for automated information.

Petrol   Please see "Getting Around by Car," earlier in this chapter.

Police   Dial 📞 **112** anywhere in the country for the police. Police stations are clearly marked in English.

Safety   Although the crime rate in South Korea is very low (you'll often see elementary school children walking or taking public transportation alone), petty crime (such as pick-pocketing) exists in big cities such as Seoul and Busan. As in any foreign place, be aware of your surroundings, don't walk alone at night, and use only official public transport and taxis.

Every so often, political and student riots become violent and have been terminated by the release of tear gas by riot police. Demonstrations are usually held in front of universities, near U.S. Army installations, in front of city halls, and at Seoul Station. If you see police in riot gear or groups of protestors, avoid the area.

Possessing illegal drugs is frowned upon in the country—so don't do it. Penalties for possession of, use of, or trafficking in illegal drugs in South Korea are severe. Korean authorities will open suspicious postal packages. If convicted, you can expect long jail sentences, heavy fines, and deportation at the end of the sentence.

Check with the U.S. State Department (© **888/407-4747** or 202/501-4444; http://travel.state.gov), the British Foreign and Commonwealth Office (© **0845/850-2829;** www.fco.gov.uk), the Australian Department of Foreign Affairs and Trade (© **061/2-6261-3305;** www.smartraveller.gov.au) for last-minute travel warnings before departing.

Senior Travel   Seniors are generally well respected in South Korea. People usually offer their seats to older people and help elders with their bags. As Koreans are dealing with a rapidly aging population, the government is offering discounts to seniors (ages 65 and older), such as lower rates on public transportation and discounted (or even free) entry fees to tourist attractions. You'll need to show your passport or other form of identification showing your age.

Smoking   Although South Korea has one of the highest smoking rates in the world, the government has been aggressive in its antismoking campaign in the past several years. Smoking is banned in public buildings, hospitals, schools, subway platforms, bus stops, office hallways, and restrooms. Smoking is also banned in stadiums. You can smoke outside or in designated smoking rooms. Restaurants, cafes, Internet cafes, and similar establishments of certain sizes are required to provide nonsmoking areas. Women smoking used to be taboo. Although more and more females smoke these days, rarely are they seen smoking in the open outside of clubs, bars, and restaurants. If you're caught violating the smoking ban, you may be fined ₩20,000 to ₩30,000.

Student Travel   Students in South Korea receive discounts on everything from subway passes to entry fees to museums. You need to have a valid student ID with a photo to receive most discounts.

The **International Student Travel Confederation**'s International Student Identity Card qualifies students for substantial savings. It also provides students with basic health and life insurance and a 24-hour help line. The card is valid for a maximum of 18 months. You can apply for the card online or in person at **STA Travel** (© **800/781-4040** in North America; www.statravel.com). If you're 25 or under, you can get their **International Youth Travel Card (IYTC),** which entitles you to some discounts. **Travel CUTS** (© **800/592-2887;** www.travelcuts.com) offers similar services for both Canadians and U.S. residents. Irish students may prefer to turn to **USIT** (© **01/602-1904;** www.usit.ie).

Taxes   Value-added tax (VAT) is levied on most goods and services at the standard 10% rate and usually included in the retail price. You can receive a refund on your VAT if you purchase your item at a shop with a TAX-FREE SHOPPING sign. Ask for a Global Refund Cheque payment slip at the time of your purchase. You can get your refund, within 3 months of purchase, at the Cash Refund Office located at Gate 28 of Incheon Airport.

Telephones Although fewer pay phones are available, there are still some in South Korea. There are two kinds of public phones—ones that take coins and credit cards and ones that take phone cards only. (Your T-money card, used for public transportation, can also be used at these phones.) Coin phones will give you change, but only up to ₩100 coins. Telephone cards can be purchased in small shops near phone booths, convenience stores, or banks and can be used for both local and international calls. Valid for up to three years, they come in denominations of ₩3,000, ₩5,000, or ₩10,000. A local call costs ₩70 for 3 minutes, while long distance calls cost ₩70 for 43 seconds 8am to 9pm, and ₩70 per 61 seconds 9pm to 8am. Calls to mobile phones cost ₩70 every 38 seconds.

To call South Korea: Dial the international access code: 011 from the U.S.; 00 from the U.K., Ireland, or New Zealand; or 0011 from Australia. Dial the country code, 82. Dial the city code (2 for Seoul, 51 for Busan) and then the number. For example, if you are calling KTO Tourist Information Center in Seoul from the U.K., you would dial 00-82-2-729-9497. Phone numbers in South Korea are either seven or eight digits long (not including the area code). ARS (toll-free) numbers are 8 digits and start with either 15 or 16. You don't need to dial a city or district code when calling an ARS number.

To make international calls from South Korea: First dial 001, 002, or 008 and then the country code (U.S. or Canada 1, U.K. 44, Ireland 353, Australia 61, New Zealand 64). Next, dial the area code and number. For example, if you wanted to call the British Embassy in Washington, D.C., you would dial 001-1-202-588-7800. The numbers to dial out for mobile phone carriers vary (for example, 00345, 00365, 00388, 00700, 00727, 00766, and 00770). If you're renting a Korean mobile phone, find out the international dialing number from your mobile phone company.

For directory assistance: Dial ☏ 114 if you're looking for a number inside the country (☏ 00794 for an international operator). You can also call the Korea Travel Phone (☏ 1330).

For operator assistance: If you need operator assistance, dial ☏ 00799 if you're trying to make an international call and ☏ 114 if you want to call a number in South Korea.

Toll-free numbers: Numbers beginning with 800 within South Korea are toll-free, but calling a 1-800 number in the States from South Korea is not toll-free. In fact, it costs the same as an overseas call.

Time South Korea is 9 hours ahead of GMT (Greenwich Mean Time). The country does not observe daylight saving time. For help with time translations, and more, download our convenient Travel Tools app for your mobile device. Go to http://www.frommers.com/go/mobile/ and click on the Travel Tools icon.

Tipping Tipping is not customary in South Korea, but feel free to do so if you've received extraordinary service. In most tourist hotels, a 10% service charge is added to your bill (on top of the VAT). In some major restaurants, a 3% to 10% service charge may be added to your bill. When you're riding a taxi, it's not necessary to tip the driver, but do let them keep the change.

Toilets There are free public restrooms available at most subway stations, bus terminals, train stations, and tourist attractions. However, facilities vary from the usual Western-style toilets to the traditional squat toilets on the floor (the worst being the ones in old temples, which are usually just squat pits). Since not all of them provide toilet paper or paper towels, it's best to carry a small packet of tissues with you at all times. You can buy them at any corner store or in vending machines outside some restrooms for about ₩500. American-style fast-food restaurants, large department stores, subway stations, upscale restaurants, and hotels have the best public restrooms.

VAT See "Taxes" earlier in this section.

Visas A visa is not needed for most visitors staying for fewer than 90 days. American, British, Australian, and New Zealand citizens can visit for up to 90 days without a visa. Canadian citizens can visit for up to 6 months without a visa. South African citizens visiting for fewer than 30 days do not require a visa.

Visas are required for trips over 90 days or for nationals of countries that don't have a reciprocal visa agreement with South Korea. Once approved, visas are valid for multiple entries within a 5-year period (or until your passport expires). In order to get the visa, you'll need to file the application (available for download at www.mofat.go.kr), along with a passport-size color photo and fee (US$50 for single entry visa for more than 90 days, US$80 for a multiple entry visa, US$20 for a prolongation of re-entry permit). A multiple entry visa fee is US$45 for U.S. citizens. Business travelers need an additional letter, invoice, or contract showing the nature of their business in South Korea.

Submit visa applications by mail or in person to a South Korean embassy or consulate near you. We've listed many of those offices below.

In the United States

o **Korean Embassy:** 2320 Massachusetts Ave. NW, Washington, D.C. 20008
  (📞 **202/939-5663** or **202/939-5660;** www.koreaembassyusa.org). Monday to Friday 9:30am to noon, 1:30 to 5pm.

o **Consulate General of the Republic of Korea in Atlanta:** 229 Peachtree St., Suite 500, International Tower, Atlanta, GA 30303 (📞 **404/522-1611**).

o **Consulate General of the Republic of Korea in Boston:** One Gateway Center, 2nd Floor, Newton, MA 02458 (📞 **617/641-2830**).

o **Consulate General of the Republic of Korea in Chicago:** NBC Tower, Suite 2700, 455 N. City Front Plaza Dr., Chicago, IL 60611 (📞 **312/822-9485**).

o **Consulate General of the Republic of Korea in Honolulu:** 2756 Pali Hwy., Honolulu, HI 96817 (📞 **808/595-6109**).

o **Consulate General of the Republic of Korea in Houston:** 1990 Post Oak Blvd., #1250, Houston, TX 77056 (📞 **713/961-0186**).

o **Consulate General of the Republic of Korea in Los Angeles:** 3243 Wilshire Blvd., Los Angeles, CA 90010 (📞 **213/385-9300**).

o **Consulate General of the Republic of Korea in New York** (Visa Section): 460 Park Ave. (57th St.), 6th Floor, New York, NY 10022 (📞 **646/674-6000**) or 335 E. 45th Street, 4th Fl., New York, NY 10017 (📞 **646/ 674-6000**).

o **Consulate General of the Republic of Korea in San Francisco:** 3500 Clay St., San Francisco, CA 94118 (📞 **415/921-2251**).

o **Consulate General of the Republic of Korea in Seattle:** 2033 Sixth Ave., #1125, Seattle, WA 98121 (📞 **206/441-1011**).

In Canada

o **Consulate General of the Republic of Korea in Vancouver:** 1090 W. Georgia St., Suite 1600, Vancouver, BC V6E 3V7 (📞 **604/685-4311;** http://can-vancouver.mofat.go.kr).

o **Consulate General of the Republic of Korea in Toronto:** 555 Avenue Rd., Toronto, ON M4V 2J7 (📞 **416/920-3809;** www.koreanconsulate.on.ca).

o **Consulate General of the Republic of Korea in Montreal:** 1250 René-Lévesque Boulevard West, Montreal, Quebec, H3B 4W8 (📞 **514/845-2555;** http://overseas.mofat.go.kr/english/am/can-montreal/main/index.jsp).

In the United Kingdom

o **Korean Embassy:** 60 Buckingham Gate, London, SW1E 6AJ (📞 **44-[0]20-7227-5500;** http://overseas.mofat.go.kr/english/eu/gbr/main/index.jsp).

In Australia

o **Korean Embassy:** 113 Empire Circuit, Yarralumla ACT 2600 (☎ **61-2-6270-4100;** http://aus-act.mofat.go.kr).

o **Consulate General of the Republic of Korea in Sydney:** Level 13, 111 Elisabeth St., Sydney NSW 2000 (☎ **61-2-9210-0200**).

In New Zealand

o **Korean Embassy:** 11th Floor, ASB Bank Tower, 2 Hunter St., Wellington 6011 (☎ **64-4-473-9073;** http://nzl-wellington.mofat.go.kr).

o **Consulate General of the Republic of Korea in Auckland:** 10th Floor, 396 Queen St., Auckland 6011 (☎ **64-9-379-0818**).

Additional visa information can be found on the South Korean Ministry of Foreign Affairs and Trade website at **www.mofat.go.kr** (click on "Visa") or **http://english.tour2 korea.com** (under "Entry Info").

Visitor Information   The **Korea Tourism Organization (KTO)** has an info desk between gates 1 & 2 and 12 & 13 on the arrival floor of the Incheon Airport (☎ **032/743-2600,** ext. 3; daily 9am–10pm).

The main KTO office is located off of Jonggak Station KTO Building (T2 Tower), level B1, 40, Cheonggyecheon-no, Jung-gu, Seoul 100-180 (☎ **02/729-9497,** ext. 499; daily 9am–8pm; http://english.visitkorea.or.kr). It publishes a variety of free brochures and maps, as well as providing transportation reservations and other travelers' assistance.

One of the best services the KTO provides is what they call **Goodwill Guides.** These English-speaking volunteers (usually students wanting to practice their English) will provide free translation and travel assistance to you (although you should foot the bill for your guide as a courtesy for any transportation, entry fees, or food). Visit the KTO website (see above) 10 to 30 days in advance of your trip, click on "Goodwill Guide Application" in the box on the left, and input the dates you are traveling. If you didn't do any advance planning, you can see which guides are available for the upcoming 3 days. You can also e-mail them at goodwillguide@mail.knto.or.kr for additional assistance.

The Tourist Assistance Center can be reached from anywhere in the country by dialing ☎ **1330** (or from a mobile phone, dial the area code of the region plus 1330).

The KTO has offices all over the world, including several in the U.S.: **Chicago,** 737 N. Michigan Ave., Suite 910, Chicago, IL 60611 (☎ **312/981-1717;** chicago@kntoamerica. com); **Hawaii,** 1188 Bishop St. Ph1, Honolulu, HI 96813 (☎ **808/521-8066**); **Los Angeles,** 5509 Wilshire Blvd., Suite 201, Los Angeles, CA 90036 (☎ **323/634-0280;** la@knto america.com); and the **New York metropolitan area,** 2 Executive Dr., Suite 750, Fort Lee, NJ 07024 (☎ **201/585-0909;** ny@kntoamerica.com). There are also offices in **England** (New Zealand House Haymarket, 3rd Floor, London SW1Y 4TE; ☎ **44-20-7321-2535** or 44-20-7925-1717; london@mail.knto.or.kr); **Canada** (700 Bay St., Suite 1903, Toronto, Ontario M5G 1Z6; ☎ **416/348-9056** or -9057; toronto@knto.ca); **Australia** (Australia Square Tower, Level 16, 264 George St., Sydney, N.S.W. 2000; ☎ **61-2-9252-4147** or -4148; visitkorea@knto.org.au); and major cities throughout Asia.

Here are some websites helpful for your travels in South Korea: www.korea.net, www. lifeinkorea.com, and www.koreanculture.org.

Water   Drinking tap water in South Korea is not recommended, although mountain water is considered healthy by Koreans. Filtered or bottled water is always available in restaurants and you can buy a bottle at convenience stores, usually for about ₩500.

Wi-Fi   See "Internet & Wi-Fi," earlier in this section.

Women Travelers   A woman traveling alone in South Korea is as safe as in most major cities in the world. Still, you should avoid walking around alone at night in dark alleys. If you want to avoid unnecessary stares, be sure to dress conservatively, avoiding crop-tops, miniskirts, or flip-flops. You'll want to dress especially conservatively when visiting temples, since you may not be admitted. Also, always ride in the back of a taxi, not in the front seat next to the driver.

USEFUL TERMS & PHRASES

Although the classification of the Korean language is debated, many believe that it belongs to the Altaic language group, which includes Turkish and Finnish. Others describe it as a "language isolate," which is exactly what it sounds like—a language unrelated to any others. The spoken language bears similarities to Mongolian and shares some words with Chinese and Japanese, but the written language is unique.

About 2,000 years ago, there were two distinct dialects on the peninsula, one spoken by the Goguryeo people up north and the other by the Baekje and Shilla residents in the south. When Shilla leaders unified the peninsula, they also produced one homogenized language from which modern Korean originated. Still, due to the difficulty in travel, regional dialects remain even today (about six major ones in all).

Korean grammar, pronunciation, and sentence structures are generally standard with fewer exceptions than the English language. The basic sentence structure is subject-object-verb, with verbs always ending a sentence. Many pronouns are understood and not often used, and there are no articles. Based on its long Confucian history, the language has two basic levels of speech—one to be used with your elders or superiors, and the other with your equals or subordinates. Most often the honorific is added to the verb endings. When in doubt, it's always best to use the polite form.

THE KOREAN ALPHABET & PRONUNCIATION GUIDE

The Korean alphabet (Hangeul) was invented in 1441 by a team of scholars under the reign of the Great King Sejong (Sejong Daewang). It is made up of 24 letters—14 consonants and 10 vowels. It is what is known in linguistic circles as a syllabary, which means that no letter can stand alone. At least one vowel and at least one consonant must be combined to make a syllable, and each syllable is written separately.

There are two problems with Romanizing Korean: (1) there is no standard and (2) some of the sounds in Korean don't exist in English. The Korean government has introduced a better standard for approximating Korean sounds with the English alphabet, but some older towns and institutions still maintain the old spelling. I've generally followed the newer standard in the book, but tried to keep the spelling as close to how an English speaker would pronounce those letters.

The following is a simple guide to help with some pronunciation.

THE CONSONANTS

ㄱ	A cross between "g" and "k," pronounced like in the word "go," now spelled with the letter "g" (old spelling was "k").
ㄲ	A double consonant, the sound of a hard "g" or "k" as in the Spanish "queso," spelled "kk."
ㄴ	Pronounced the same as "n," and spelled with an "n."
ㄷ	A cross between "d" and "t," as in "dark," spelled with a "d" (old spelling: "t").
ㄸ	A double consonant, the sound of a hard "d/t" as in the Spanish word "tío" or the "t" in "study," spelled with "dd."
ㄹ	A cross between "r" and "l," similar to the Spanish "gracias," spelled with an "l" or "r."
ㅁ	Pronounced like the letter "m."
ㅂ	A cross between the letters "b" and "p," as in "Barbara" or the "b" in "boar," now spelled with the letter "b" (old spelling "p").
ㅃ	A double consonant, the sound of a hard "b" or "p" as in the Spanish "Pepe," spelled "bb."
ㅅ	Pronounced like the letter "s."
ㅆ	A double consonant, the sound of a hard "s" as in the word "sour," spelled with "ss."
ㅇ	When used in the beginning of a syllable, it allows the vowel to be sounded without a hard consonant sound. At the end of a syllable, it sounds like "ng," as in the end of the word "song."
ㅈ	Pronounced like the letter "j" in "jazz" (old spelling "ch").
ㅉ	A double consonant, the sound of a hard "j," pronounced similar to the j sound in "genie," spelled in this book with "jj."
ㅊ	Pronounced like "ch" in "choice."
ㅋ	Pronounced like "k."
ㅌ	Pronounced like "t."
ㅍ	Pronounced like "p."
ㅎ	Pronounced like "h."

THE VOWELS

ㅏ	Pronounced like "ah," as in "spa."
ㅑ	Pronounced "ya."
ㅓ	Pronounced "uh," as in "umbrella," spelled "eo."
ㅕ	Pronounced "yuh," as in "yum," spelled "yeo."
ㅗ	Pronounced "oh," as in "rope."
ㅛ	Pronounced "yo."
ㅜ	Pronounced "ooh," as in "stew," often spelled "u" or sometimes "oo."
ㅠ	Pronounced "yu," as in "you," spelled "yu" or "yoo."
ㅡ	Pronounced "eu," as in "good" or "hood."
ㅣ	Pronounced "ee," as in "see."
ㅔ	A combination vowel pronounced "eh."
ㅒ	A combination vowel pronounced "ye," as in "yes."

과	A combination vowel pronounced "wa."
괘	A combination vowel pronounced "whe," as in "sweat."
귀	A combination vowel pronounced "wuh," as in "was."
귀	A combination vowel pronounced "wee."
긔	A combination vowel pronounced "eui" (but said quickly).

Basic Korean Phrases
GREETINGS & INTRODUCTIONS

ENGLISH	PRONUNCIATION	KOREAN
Hello, how are you?	Ahn nyeong hasehyo? (formal)	안녕하세요.
	Ahn nyeong hashim nikka? (informal)	안녕하십니까?
Hello. (on the telephone)	Yuh boh seh yo.	여보세요.
Good-bye.	Ahn nyoong hi geh seh yo.	안녕히계세요.
Hello/good-bye. (informal)	Ahn nyeong.	안녕.
yes	yeh or neh	예 or 네
no	ah niyo	아니오
Thank you.	Gahm sah hamnida. (formal)	감사합니다.
	Goh mab seumnida. (less formal)	고맙습니다.
You're welcome.	Cheonmahneyo.	천만에요.
I'm sorry/Excuse me.	Jeh sohng hamnida. (formal)	죄송합니다.
	Mi an hamnida. (less formal)	미안합니다.
Pleased to meet you.	Mannaseo bahngapseumnida. (formal)	만나서 반갑습니다.
	Mannaseo bangaweoyo. (less formal)	만나서 반가워요.

NUMBERS

Koreans have two ways of counting. One system is based on the Chinese counting method and the other is the traditional Korean way. In general, the Chinese system is used to count objects and money and the Korean system is used to count people.

ENGLISH	PRONUNCIATION	KOREAN
1	il	일
2	ee	이
3	sahm	삼
4	sah	사
5	oh	오
6	yook	육
7	chil	칠
8	pahl	팔
9	gu	구
10	ship	십

ENGLISH	PRONUNCIATION	KOREAN
11	shibil (combine 10 and 1)	십일
12	shibee (and so forth)	십이
20	ee ship (combine 2 and 10)	이십
30	sam ship (combine 3 and 10)	삼십
100	baek	백
200	ee baek (combine 2 and 100)	이백
1,000	chun	천
2,000	ee cheon (combine 2 and 1,000)	이천
10,000	mahn	만
20,000	ee mahn (combine 2 and 10,000)	이만
100,000	shipmahn (combine 10 and 10,000)	십만
200,000	ee shipmahn (combine 20 and 10,000)	이십만
1,000,000	baek mahn (combine 100 and 10,000)	백만
100,000,000	il eok	일억

USEFUL QUESTIONS & PHRASES

ENGLISH	PRONUNCIATION	KOREAN
When is it?	Uhnje imnikka?	언제입니까?
Where is it?	Uhdi imnikka?	어디입니까?
Where are you?	Uhdieh Isseubnikka?	어디에 있습니까?
Who are you?	Noo goo shipnikka?	누구십니까?
What is it?	Moouh shimnikka?	무엇입니까?
What is this?	Ee guh seun moouh shimnikka?	이것은 무엇입니까?
How much is it?	Uhl mah imnikka?	얼마입니까?
Where is the bathroom?	Hwa jang shili uh di imnikka?	화장실이 어디 입니까?
Do you speak English?	Yeong-uh leul halsu isseumnikka?	영어를 할 수있음니까?
What is your name?	Ileumi moouh shimnikka?	이름이 무엇입니까?
My name is . . .	Je ileum eun . . . imnida.	제 이름은 . . . 입니다.
I don't understand.	Iheh leul mot haget seubnida.	이해를 못하겠습니다.
I don't know.	Jal moleu gaesseumnida.	잘 모르겠읍니다.
Please wait a moment.	Jamsi mahn gidalyeo jooseyo.	잠시만 기다려주세요.

TIME

ENGLISH	PRONUNCIATION	KOREAN
time	shigahn	시간
morning	ahchim	아침
a.m.	ohjeon	오전
afternoon/lunch	jeom shim	점심
p.m.	ohhu	오후
evening/dinner	jeonyuk	저녁
night	bahm	밤
minute	boon	분

ENGLISH	PRONUNCIATION	KOREAN
second	cho	초
now	jigeum	지금
today	ohneul	오늘
yesterday	eohjae	어제
tomorrow	naeil	내일
1 hour	han shigan	한 시간
5 hours	dahseot shigan	다섯 시간
Monday	Weolyeo-il	월요일
Tuesday	Hwayeo-il	화요일
Wednesday	Suyeo-il	수요일
Thursday	Mogyeo-il	목요일
Friday	Geumyeo-il	금요일
Saturday	Toyeo-il	토요일
Sunday	Ilyeo-il	일요일
weekday	jujung	주중
weekend	jumal	주말

TRANSPORTATION

ENGLISH	PRONUNCIATION	KOREAN
taxi	tekshi	택시
car	cha	차
parking	jucha	주차
bus	buhseu	버스
express bus	gosok	고속버스
bus terminal	beoseu teominal	버스터미널
city bus	shinae beoseu	시내버스
subway	jihacheol or jeoncheol	지하철/전철
train	gicha	기차
boat	beh	배
airplane	biheng-gi	비행기
airport	biheng-jang/gohng-hahng	비행장/공항
entrance	ipgu	입구
exit	choolgu	출구
ticket	pyo	표
Do you go to . . . ?	. . . ga-seyo?	. . . 가세요?
Is there a bus to . . . ?	. . . ganeun buseu isseumnikka?	. . . 가는 버스 있습니까?
What times does it leave?	Myeotshi-ae chulbal hamnikka?	몇시에 출발합니까?
What times does it arrive?	Myeotshi-ae dochak hamnikka?	몇시에 도착합니까?
How long does it take?	Uhlmahna geollimnikka?	얼마나 걸립니까?
Please take me to . . .	. . . eulo gajooseyo.	. . . 으로 가주세요 . . .
Please let me know when we arrive.	Dochak ha-myeon allyeojooseyo.	도착하면알려주세요.
Please stop here.	Yeogiseo sewojooseyo.	여기서 세워주세요.

NAVIGATION

ENGLISH	PRONUNCIATION	KOREAN
north	book	북
south	nam	남
east	dong	동
west	seo	서
left	wenjjok/jwacheuk	왼쪽/좌측
right	oleunjjok/ucheuk	오른쪽/우측
turn left	jwahwaejeon	좌회전
turn right	oohwaejeon	우회전
go straight	jigjin	직진
four-way	sa-geoli	사거리
here	yeogi	여기
there	geogi	거기
over there	jeogi (indicating something farther)	저기
Is it close by?	Gakkapseumnikka?	가깝습니까?

MONEY

ENGLISH	PRONUNCIATION	KOREAN
₩500	oh baek won	오백원
₩1,000	cheon won	천원
₩10,000	mahn won	만원
change	jahn dohn	잔돈
Do you have change?	Jahn dohn isseumnikka?	잔돈있습니까?

SHOPPING PHRASES

ENGLISH	PRONUNCIATION	KOREAN
What is this?	Ee guh seun moouh shimnikka?	이것은무엇입니까?
How much is it?	Uhl mah imnikka? (formal)	얼마입니까?
	Uhl mah eh yo? (more informal)	얼마에요?
It's too expensive.	Nuhmoo bissayo.	너무비싸요.
Please give me a deal.	Ssage haejooseyo.	싸게해주세요.
May I try it on? (clothes)	Ibeoh bolsu innayo?	입어볼수있나요?
May I try it on? (shoes)	Shinuh bolsu innayo?	신어볼수있나요?
Please give me that/ I'll take this.	Igeoseul jusipsiyo.	이것을 주십시요.
Please give me only one.	Hana-mahn jooseyo.	하나만 주세요.
Do you take credit cards?	Shinyong kadeu bahdseubnikka?	신용카드 받습니까?
I need a receipt.	Yeong-su-jeung pilyeo hamnida.	영수증 필요합니다.
Please wrap it for me.	Pojang-heh jooseyo.	포장해주세요.

ACCOMMODATIONS

ENGLISH	PRONUNCIATION	KOREAN
hotel	hotel	호텔
motel	motel	모텔
guesthouse	yeogwan	여관
homestay	minbak	민박
room	bahng	방
bed	chimdae	침대
reservation	yeyak	예약
laundromat	setakso	세탁소
Where is a cheap hotel?	Ssan hoteli eodi isseumnikka?	싼 호텔이 어디있습니까?
How much for 1 night?	Halu uhlma-imnikka?	하루 얼마입니까?
Please wake me up at	. . . eh ggaewuh jooseyo.	. . . 에 깨워 주세요.

RESTAURANT

ENGLISH	PRONUNCIATION	KOREAN
Please show me the menu.	Menyu jom boyuh jooseyo.	메뉴 좀보여주세요.
What is your best dish?	Ijibeseo jalhaneun eumsigki moouh sijyo?	이집에서 잘하는 음식이 무엇이죠?
Do you have . . . ?	. . . issuhyo?	. . . 있어요?
Please bring some more of this.	Igeot jogum deo jooseyo.	이것, 조금 더 주세요.
More rice please.	Bapdeo jooseyo.	밥 더 주새요.
Don't make it too spicy.	Mepji-ankeh he-jooseyo.	맵지 않게 해주세요.
I'm a vegetarian.	Chaeshik juuija imnida.	채식주의자입니다.
chopsticks	jeotgalak	젓가락
spoon	sutgalak	숟가락
Please bring me the bill.	Gaesan he-jooseyo.	계산해주세요.
I enjoyed the meal/ I ate well.	Jal meogeo seumnida.	잘먹었읍니다.

Popular Korean Menu Items
RICE

ENGLISH	PRONUNCIATION	KOREAN
rice	bap	밥
five-grain rice	ogok bap	오곡밥
"white rice" with side dishes	baekban	백반
traditional meal with side dishes	hanjeongshik	한정식
mixed rice bowl	bibim bap	비빔밥
stone-pot mixed rice bowl	dolsot bibim bap	돌솥비빔밥
fried rice	bokkeum bap	볶음밥
kimchi fried rice	gimchi bokkeum bap	김치볶음밥

ENGLISH	PRONUNCIATION	KOREAN
rice with black-bean sauce	jja jahng bap	짜장밥
rice with sweet-potato noodles	japchae bap	잡채밥
rice topped with sliced beef	boolgogi dup bap	불고기덮밥
mixed rice with raw fish	hwaedup bap	회덮밥
rice topped with spicy squid	ojingeuh dup bap	오징어덮밥
rice wrapped in seaweed	gim bap	김밥

13 NOODLES

ENGLISH	PRONUNCIATION	KOREAN
hand-cut knife noodles	kal gooksu	칼국수
chicken knife noodles	dak kal gooksu	닭칼국수
seafood knife noodles	haemul kal gooksu	해물칼국수
"party" noodles (somen in broth)	janchi gooksu	잔치국수
spicy cold buckwheat noodles	bibim naeng myeon	비빔냉면
buckwheat noodles in a cold broth	mool naeng myeon	물냉면
cold noodles in soybean broth	kohng gooksu	콩국수
spicy thick noodles	jjol myeon	쫄면
noodles with black-bean sauce	jja jang myeon	짜장면
spicy noodle soup w/seafood	jjamppong	짬뽕
ramen	lamyeon	라면
dough flake soup	sujebi	수제비
potato dough flake soup	gamja sujebi	감자수제비
kimchi dough flake soup	gimchi sujebi	김치수제비
stir-fried yam noodles	japchae	잡채

MEAT

ENGLISH	PRONUNCIATION	KOREAN
marinated sliced beef	boolgogi	불고기
spicy sliced pork	dweji boolgogi	돼지불고기
spicy pork and squid	osam boolgogi	오삼불고기
beef short ribs	galbi	갈비
unseasoned short ribs	saeng galbi	생갈비
stewed beef ribs	galbi jjim	갈비찜
spicy pork ribs	dweji galbi	돼지갈비
sliced pork (bacon cut)	samgyeopssal	삼겹살
marinated grilled chicken	dak galbi	닭갈비
seasoned fried chicken	yangnyeom dak	양념닭

SEAFOOD

ENGLISH	PRONUNCIATION	KOREAN
abalone	junbok	전복
anchovy	myeolchi	멸치
baby octopus	jjookkumi	쭈꾸미
crab	gwe	게
eel	jang-uh	장어
hairtail fish	galchi	갈치
laver	gim	김
mackerel	godeung-uh	고등어
mackerel pike	ggongchi	꽁치
mussel	hong-hap	홍합
octopus	nakji	낙지
oyster	gool	굴
raw fish	hwae	회
sea cucumber	haesam	해삼
seaweed	miyuk	미역
shrimp	se-oo	새우
spicy raw crab	gyejang	게장
squid	ojing-uh	오징어
tuna	chamchi	참치

SOUPS & HOT POTS

ENGLISH	PRONUNCIATION	KOREAN
spicy hot beef soup	yookgyejang	육개장
rice-cake soup	dduk gook	떡국
dumpling soup	mandu gook	만두국
fermented soybean paste hot pot	dwenjang jjigae	된장찌개
thick soybean paste hot pot	cheong-guk jang	청국장
kimchi hot pot	gimchi jjigae	김치찌개
soft tofu hot pot	soon dubu jjigae	순두부찌개
spicy seafood hot pot	haemool tahng/jeongol	해물탕/전골
spicy fish hot pot	maeuntang	매운탕
"army" stew/"Spam" stew	budae jjigae	부대찌개

FLATCAKES

ENGLISH	PRONUNCIATION	KOREAN
potato flatcake	gamja buchingae/gamjajeon	감자 부침개/감자전
green onion flatcake	pajeon	파전
seafood flatcake	hameul pajeon	해물파전
mung bean flatcake	bindaeddeok	빈대떡
kimchi flatcake	gimchi buchingae	김치부침개

KIMCHI

ENGLISH	PRONUNCIATION	KOREAN
napa cabbage kimchi	baechu gimchi	배추김치
cubed white radish kimchi	ggakdookgi	깍두기
water kimchi	mool gimchi	물김치
ponytail radish kimchi	yeolmu gimchi	열무김치
cucumber kimchi	oi gimchi	오이김치
green onion kimchi	pa gimchi	파김치
mustard green kimchi	got gimchi	갓김치
white kimchi	baek gimchi	백김치

OTHER FOODS

ENGLISH	PRONUNCIATION	KOREAN
dumplings	mandu	만두
blood sausage	soondeh	순대
seasoned rice cake snack	ddeok bokgi	떡볶이
fish cakes	odeng/uhmook	오뎅/어묵
"goldfish" bread w/red bean	boong-uh bbang	붕어빵
fried dough w/sugar	hodduk	호떡
drinking snacks	anju	안주
side dishes	banchan	반찬
rice cakes	dduk	떡
rice porridge	jook	죽
red-bean porridge	paht jook	팥죽
pumpkin porridge	hobak jook	호박죽
red-bean shaved ice dessert	paht bingsu	팥빙수

BEVERAGES

ENGLISH	PRONUNCIATION	KOREAN
water	mool	물
milk	ooyoo	우유
soda/soft drink	eumnyosu	음료수
beer	mekju	맥주
sweet potato "vodka"	soju	소주
milky rice wine	makgeolli	막걸리
rice wine	cheongju	청주
ginseng wine	insamju	인삼주
grape wine	podoju	포도주
fermented sweet rice drink	shikheh	식혜
coffee	kuhpi	커피
green tea	nokcha	녹차

ENGLISH	PRONUNCIATION	KOREAN
black tea	hongcha	홍차
barley tea	bolicha	보리차
ginger-cinnamon tea	sujeong-gwa	수정과
Job's Tears (grain) tea	yoolmu cha	율무차
citron tea	yooja cha	유자차
plum tea	meshil cha	매실차
ginger tea	saeng gahng cha	생강차

Index